California
HMH SCIENCE DIMENSIONS™

Grade 8

Watch the cover come alive as you explore the solar system.
Download the HMH Science Dimensions AR app available on Android or iOS devices.

This Write-In Book belongs to

_____

Teacher/Room

_____

Houghton Mifflin Harcourt™

Consulting Authors

Michael A. DiSpezio

Global Educator
North Falmouth,
Massachusetts

Michael DiSpezio has authored many HMH instructional programs for Science and Mathematics. He has also authored numerous trade books and multimedia programs on various topics and hosted dozens of studio and location broadcasts for various organizations in the United States and worldwide. Most recently, he has been working with educators to provide strategies for implementing the Next Generation Science Standards, particularly the Science and Engineering Practices, Crosscutting Concepts, and the use of Evidence Notebooks. To all his projects, he brings his extensive background in science, his expertise in classroom teaching at the elementary, middle, and high school levels, and his deep experience in producing interactive and engaging instructional materials.

Marjorie Frank

Science Writer and Content-
Area Reading Specialist
Brooklyn, New York

An educator and linguist by training, a writer and poet by nature, Marjorie Frank has authored and designed a generation of instructional materials in all subject areas, including past HMH Science programs. Her other credits include authoring science issues of an award-winning children's magazine, writing game-based digital assessments, developing blended learning materials for young children, and serving as instructional designer and coauthor of pioneering school-to-work software. In addition, she has served on the adjunct faculty of Hunter, Manhattan, and Brooklyn Colleges, teaching courses in science methods, literacy, and writing. For *California HMH Science Dimensions™*, she has guided the development of our K–2 strands and our approach to making connections between NGSS and Common Core ELA/literacy standards.

Acknowledgments

Cover credits: (telescope) ©HMH; (Mars) ©Stocktrek Images, Inc./Alamy.

Section Header Master Art: (machinations) ©DNY59/E+/Getty Images; (rivers on top of Greenland ice sheet) ©Maria-José Viñas, NASA Earth Science News Team; (human cells, illustration) ©Sebastian Kaulitzki/Science Photo Library/Corbis; (waves) ©Alfred Pasieka/Science Source

Michael R. Heithaus, PhD

Dean, College of Arts, Sciences & Education
Professor, Department of Biological Sciences
Florida International University
Miami, Florida

Mike Heithaus joined the FIU Biology Department in 2003 and has served as Director of the Marine Sciences Program and Executive Director of the School of Environment, Arts, and Society, which brings together the natural and social sciences and humanities to develop solutions to today's environmental challenges. He now serves as Dean of the College of Arts, Sciences & Education. His research focuses on predator-prey interactions and the ecological importance of large marine species. He has helped to guide the development of Life Science content in *California HMH Science Dimensions™*, with a focus on strategies for teaching challenging content as well as the science and engineering practices of analyzing data and using computational thinking.

Bernadine Okoro

Access and Equity Consultant

S.T.E.M. Learning Advocate & Consultant
Washington, DC

Bernadine Okoro is a chemical engineer by training and a playwright, novelist, director, and actress by nature. Okoro went from working with patents and biotechnology to teaching in K–12 classrooms. A 12-year science educator and Albert Einstein Distinguished Fellow, Okoro was one of the original authors of the Next Generation Science Standards. As a member of the Diversity and Equity Team, her focus on Alternative Education and Community Schools and on Integrating Social-Emotional Learning and Brain-Based Learning into NGSS is the vehicle she uses as a pathway to support underserved groups from elementary school to adult education. An article and book reviewer for NSTA and other educational publishing companies, Okoro currently works as a S.T.E.M. Learning Advocate & Consultant.

Cary I. Sneider, PhD

Associate Research Professor
Portland State University
Portland, Oregon

While studying astrophysics at Harvard, Cary Sneider volunteered to teach in an Upward Bound program and discovered his real calling as a science teacher. After teaching middle and high school science in Maine, California, Costa Rica, and Micronesia, he settled for nearly three decades at Lawrence Hall of Science in Berkeley, California, where he developed skills in curriculum development and teacher education. Over his career, Cary directed more than 20 federal, state, and foundation grant projects and was a writing team leader for the Next Generation Science Standards. He has been instrumental in ensuring *California HMH Science Dimensions™* meets the high expectations of the NGSS and provides an effective three-dimensional learning experience for all students.

Program Advisors

Paul D. Asimow, PhD
Eleanor and John R. McMillan Professor of Geology and Geochemistry
California Institute of Technology
Pasadena, California

Joanne Bourgeois
Professor Emerita
Earth & Space Sciences
University of Washington
Seattle, WA

Dr. Eileen Cashman
Professor
Humboldt State University
Arcata, California

Elizabeth A. De Stasio, PhD
Raymond J. Herzog Professor of Science
Lawrence University
Appleton, Wisconsin

Perry Donham, PhD
Lecturer
Boston University
Boston, Massachusetts

Shila Garg, PhD
Emerita Professor of Physics
Former Dean of Faculty & Provost
The College of Wooster
Wooster, Ohio

Tatiana A. Krivosheev, PhD
Professor of Physics
Clayton State University
Morrow, Georgia

Mark B. Moldwin, PhD
Professor of Space Sciences and Engineering
University of Michigan
Ann Arbor, Michigan

Ross H. Nehm
Stony Brook University (SUNY)
Stony Brook, NY

Kelly Y. Neiles, PhD
Assistant Professor of Chemistry
St. Mary's College of Maryland
St. Mary's City, Maryland

John Nielsen-Gammon, PhD
Regents Professor
Department of Atmospheric Sciences
Texas A&M University
College Station, Texas

Dr. Sten Odenwald
Astronomer
NASA Goddard Spaceflight Center
Greenbelt, Maryland

Bruce W. Schafer
Executive Director
Oregon Robotics Tournament & Outreach Program
Beaverton, Oregon

Barry A. Van Deman
President and CEO
Museum of Life and Science
Durham, North Carolina

Kim Withers, PhD
Assistant Professor
Texas A&M University-Corpus Christi
Corpus Christi, Texas

Adam D. Woods, PhD
Professor
California State University, Fullerton
Fullerton, California

English Development Advisors

Mercy D. Momary
Local District Northwest
Los Angeles, California

Michelle Sullivan
Balboa Elementary
San Diego, California

Classroom Reviewers & Hands-On Activities Advisors

Julie Arreola
Sun Valley Magnet School
Los Angeles, California

Pamela Bluestein
Sycamore Canyon School
Newbury Park, California

Andrea Brown
HLPUSD Science & STEAM TOSA
Hacienda Heights, California

Stephanie Greene
Science Department Chair
Sun Valley Magnet School
Sun Valley, California

Rana Mujtaba Khan
Will Rogers High school
Van Nuys, California

Suzanne Kirkhope
Willow Elementary and Round Meadow Elementary
Agoura Hills, California

George Kwong
Schafer Park Elementary
Hayward, California

Imelda Madrid
Bassett St. Elementary School
Lake Balboa, California

Susana Martinez O'Brien
Diocese of San Diego
San Diego, California

Craig Moss
Mt. Gleason Middle School
Sunland, California

Isabel Souto
Schafer Park Elementary
Hayward, California

Emily R.C.G. Williams
South Pasadena Middle School
South Pasadena, California

Contents

UNIT 1 Energy, Forces, and Collisions

1

© Houghton Mifflin Harcourt Publishing Company • Image Credits: ©Earl Roberge/Science Source

At a hydroelectric power plant, forces help convert the energy of falling water into electrical energy.

v

UNIT 2 Noncontact Forces 117

During thunderstorms, electric charges build up within clouds to produce spectacular lightning displays.

© Houghton Mifflin Harcourt Publishing Company • Image Credits: ©DeepDesertPhoto/RooM/Getty Images

UNIT 3 Space Science 211

UNIT 4 Earth through Time 307

© Houghton Mifflin Harcourt Publishing Company • Image Credits: (t) ©NASA EPIC team; (b) ©Maria Stenzel/National Geographic/Getty Images

UNIT 5 Evolution and Biotechnology 391

UNIT 6 Waves 477

© Houghton Mifflin Harcourt Publishing Company • Image Credits: (t) ©Layne Kennedy/Corbis Documentary/Getty Images; (b) ©Willyam Bradberry/Shutterstock

Contents

Ecosystem health and services are related to the biodiversity of the ecosystem.

Claims, Evidence, and Reasoning

Constructing an Argument

Constructing a strong argument is useful in science and engineering and in everyday life. A strong argument has three parts: a claim, evidence, and reasoning. Scientists and engineers use claims-evidence-reasoning arguments to communicate their explanations and solutions to others and to challenge or debate the conclusions of other scientists and engineers. The words *argue* and *argument* do not mean that scientists or engineers are fighting about something. Instead, this is a way to support a claim using evidence. Argumentation is a calm and rational way for people to examine all the facts and come to the best conclusion.

A **claim** is a statement that answers the question "What do you know?" A claim is a statement of your understanding of a phenomenon, answer to a question, or solution to a problem. A claim states what you think is true based on the information you have.

Evidence is any data that are related to your claim and answer the question "How do you know that?" These data may be from your own experiments and observations, reports by scientists or engineers, or other reliable data. Arguments made in science and engineering should be supported by empirical evidence. Empirical evidence is evidence that comes from observation or experiment.

Evidence used to support a claim should also be relevant and sufficient. Relevant evidence is evidence that is about the claim, and not about something else. Evidence is sufficient when there is enough evidence to fully support the claim.

Reasoning is the use of logical, analytical thought to form conclusions or inferences. Reasoning answers the question "Why does your evidence support your claim?" So, reasoning explains the relationship between your evidence and your claim. Reasoning might include a scientific law or principle that helps explain the relationship between the evidence and the claim.

Here is an example of a claims-evidence-reasoning argument.

Claim	Ice melts faster in the sun than it does in the shade.
Evidence	Two ice cubes of the same size were each placed in a plastic dish. One dish was placed on a wooden bench in the sun and one was placed on a different part of the same bench in the shade. The ice cube in the sun melted in 14 minutes and 32 seconds. The ice cube in the shade melted in 18 minutes and 15 seconds.
Reasoning	This experiment was designed so that the only variable that was different in the set-up of the two ice cubes was whether they were in the shade or in the sun. Because the ice cube in the sun melted almost 4 minutes faster than the one in the shade, this is sufficient evidence to say that ice melts faster in the sun than it does in the shade.

To summarize, a strong argument:

• presents a claim that is clear, logical, and well-defended
• supports the claim with empirical evidence that is sufficient and relevant
• includes reasons that make sense and are presented in a logical order

Constructing Your Own Argument

Now construct your own argument by recording a claim, evidence, and reasoning. With your teacher's permission, you can do an investigation to answer a question you have about how the world works. Or you can construct your argument based on observations you have already made about the world.

Claim	
Evidence	
Reasoning	

 For more information on claims, evidence, and reasoning, see the online **English Language Arts Handbook.**

© Houghton Mifflin Harcourt Publishing Company

Whether you are in the lab or in the field, you are responsible for your own safety and the safety of others. To fulfill these responsibilities and avoid accidents, be aware of the safety of your classmates as well as your own safety at all times. Take your lab work and fieldwork seriously, and behave appropriately. Elements of safety to keep in mind are shown below and on the following pages.

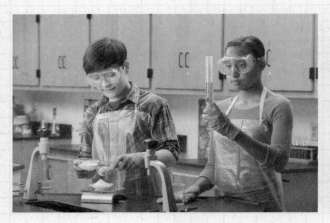

Safety in the Lab

- ☐ Be sure you understand the materials, your procedure, and the safety rules before you start an investigation in the lab.

- ☐ Know where to find and how to use fire extinguishers, eyewash stations, shower stations, and emergency power shutoffs.

- ☐ Use proper safety equipment. Always wear personal protective equipment, such as eye protection and gloves, when setting up labs, during labs, and when cleaning up.

- ☐ Do not begin until your teacher has told you to start. Follow directions.

- ☐ Keep the lab neat and uncluttered. Clean up when you are finished. Report all spills to your teacher immediately. Watch for slip/fall and trip/fall hazards.

- ☐ If you or another student are injured in any way, tell your teacher immediately, even if the injury seems minor.

- ☐ Do not take any food or drink into the lab. Never take any chemicals out of the lab.

Safety in the Field

- ☐ Be sure you understand the goal of your fieldwork and the proper way to carry out the investigation before you begin fieldwork.

- ☐ Use proper safety equipment and personal protective equipment, such as eye protection, that suits the terrain and the weather.

- ☐ Follow directions, including appropriate safety procedures as provided by your teacher.

- ☐ Do not approach or touch wild animals. Do not touch plants unless instructed by your teacher to do so. Leave natural areas as you found them.

- ☐ Stay with your group.

- ☐ Use proper accident procedures, and let your teacher know about a hazard in the environment or an accident immediately, even if the hazard or accident seems minor.

Safety Symbols

To highlight specific types of precautions, the following symbols are used throughout the lab program. Remember that no matter what safety symbols you see within each lab, all safety rules should be followed at all times.

Dress Code

- Wear safety goggles (or safety glasses as appropriate for the activity) at all times in the lab as directed. If chemicals get into your eye, flush your eyes immediately for a minimum of 15 minutes.
- Do not wear contact lenses in the lab.
- Do not look directly at the sun or any intense light source or laser.
- Wear appropriate protective non-latex gloves as directed.
- Wear an apron or lab coat at all times in the lab as directed.
- Tie back long hair, secure loose clothing, and remove loose jewelry. Remove acrylic nails when working with active flames.
- Do not wear open-toed shoes, sandals, or canvas shoes in the lab.

Glassware and Sharp Object Safety

- Do not use chipped or cracked glassware.
- Use heat-resistant glassware for heating or storing hot materials.
- Notify your teacher immediately if a piece of glass breaks.
- Use extreme care when handling any sharp or pointed instruments.
- Do not cut an object while holding the object unsupported in your hands. Place the object on a suitable cutting surface, and always cut in a direction away from your body.

Chemical Safety

- If a chemical gets on your skin, on your clothing, or in your eyes, rinse it immediately for a minimum of 15 minutes (using the shower, faucet, or eyewash station), and alert your teacher.
- Do not clean up spilled chemicals unless your teacher directs you to do so.
- Do not inhale any gas or vapor unless directed to do so by your teacher. If you are instructed to note the odor of a substance, wave the fumes toward your nose with your hand. This is called wafting. Never put your nose close to the source of the odor.
- Handle materials that emit vapors or gases in a well-ventilated area.
- Keep your hands away from your face while you are working on any activity.

Safety Symbols, continued

Electrical Safety

- Do not use equipment with frayed electrical cords or loose plugs.
- Do not use electrical equipment near water or when clothing or hands are wet.
- Hold the plug housing when you plug in or unplug equipment. Do not pull on the cord.
- Use only GFI-protected electrical receptacles.

Heating and Fire Safety

- Be aware of any source of flames, sparks, or heat (such as flames, heating coils, or hot plates) before working with any flammable substances.
- Know the location of the lab's fire extinguisher and fire-safety blankets.
- Know your school's fire-evacuation routes.
- If your clothing catches on fire, walk to the lab shower to put out the fire. Do not run.
- Never leave a hot plate unattended while it is turned on or while it is cooling.
- Use tongs or appropriately insulated holders when handling heated objects.
- Allow all equipment to cool before storing it.

Plant and Animal Safety

- Do not eat any part of a plant.
- Do not pick any wild plant unless your teacher instructs you to do so.
- Handle animals only as your teacher directs.
- Treat animals carefully and respectfully.
- Wash your hands throughly with soap and water after handling any plant or animal.

Cleanup

- Clean all work surfaces and protective equipment as directed by your teacher.
- Dispose of hazardous materials or sharp objects only as directed by your teacher.
- Wash your hands throughly with soap and water before you leave the lab or after any activity.

Student Safety Quiz

Circle the letter of the BEST answer.

1. Before starting an investigation or lab procedure, you should
   A. try an experiment of your own
   B. open all containers and packages
   C. read all directions and make sure you understand them
   D. handle all the equipment to become familiar with it

2. At the end of any activity you should
   A. wash your hands thoroughly with soap and water before leaving the lab
   B. cover your face with your hands
   C. put on your safety goggles
   D. leave hot plates switched on

3. If you get hurt or injured in any way, you should
   A. tell your teacher immediately
   B. find bandages or a first aid kit
   C. go to your principal's office
   D. get help after you finish the lab

4. If your glassware is chipped or broken, you should
   A. use it only for solid materials
   B. give it to your teacher for recycling or disposal
   C. put it back into the storage cabinet
   D. increase the damage so that it is obvious

5. If you have unused chemicals after finishing a procedure, you should
   A. pour them down a sink or drain
   B. mix them all together in a bucket
   C. put them back into their original containers
   D. dispose of them as directed by your teacher

6. If electrical equipment has a frayed cord, you should
   A. unplug the equipment by pulling the cord
   B. let the cord hang over the side of a counter or table
   C. tell your teacher about the problem immediately
   D. wrap tape around the cord to repair it

7. If you need to determine the odor of a chemical or a solution, you should
   A. use your hand to bring fumes from the container to your nose
   B. bring the container under your nose and inhale deeply
   C. tell your teacher immediately
   D. use odor-sensing equipment

8. When working with materials that might fly into the air and hurt someone's eye, you should wear
   A. goggles
   B. an apron
   C. gloves
   D. a hat

9. Before doing experiments involving a heat source, you should know the location of the
   A. door
   B. window
   C. fire extinguisher
   D. overhead lights

10. If you get chemicals in your eye you should
    A. wash your hands immediately
    B. put the lid back on the chemical container
    C. wait to see if your eye becomes irritated
    D. use the eyewash station right away, for a minimum of 15 minutes

Go online to view the Lab Safety Handbook for additional information.

Energy, Forces, and Collisions

How are energy and forces used to describe collisions?

At a hydroelectric power plant, forces help convert the energy of falling water into electrical energy.

You Solve It How Can You Design a Safer Road? Analyze collision simulations for different vehicles to help you make recommendations for improving road safety on a road with a sharp curve.

Go online and complete the You Solve It to explore ways to solve a real-world problem.

Design a Model Roller Coaster

Every roller coaster design is different, but they all have hills, twists, and turns. Some designs have loops and corkscrews. These design features make the roller coasters thrilling to ride.

A. Look at the photo. On a separate sheet of paper, write down as many different questions as you can about the photo.

B. **Discuss** With your class or a partner, share your questions. Record any additional questions generated in your discussion. Then choose the most important questions from the list that are related to designing a model roller coaster. Write them below.

C. Choose some roller coaster features that you want to model. What features are you interested in modeling and what resources could you use for your research?

D. Use the information above to design a model roller coaster.

Discuss the next steps for your Unit Project with your teacher and go online to download the Unit Project Worksheet.

Language Development

Use the lessons in this unit to complete the network and expand your understanding of these key concepts.

© Houghton Mifflin Harcourt Publishing Company

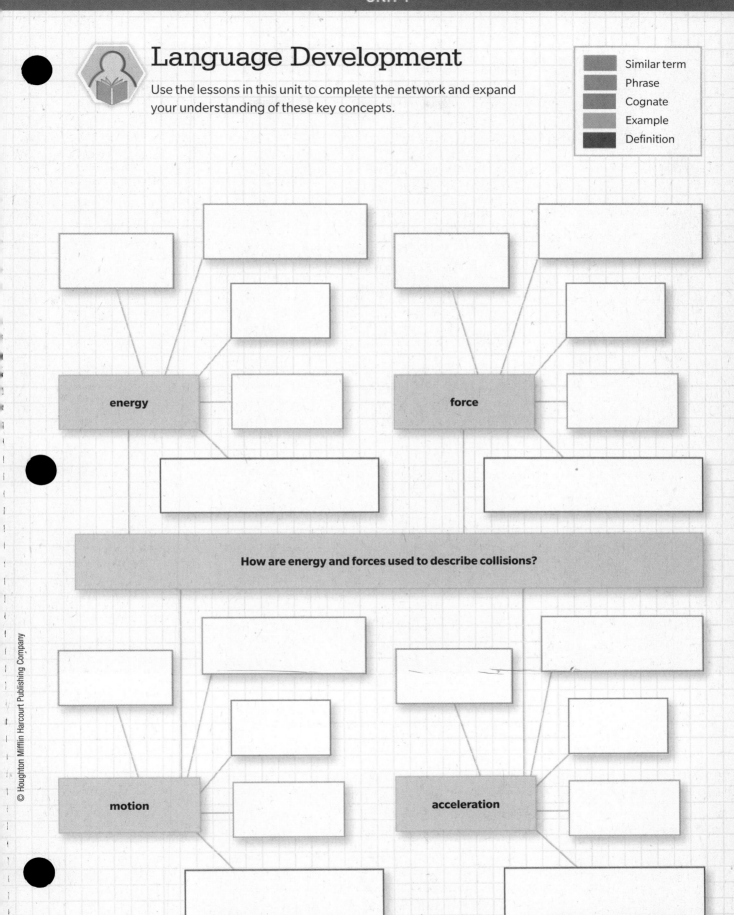

Similar term
Phrase
Cognate
Example
Definition

energy

force

How are energy and forces used to describe collisions?

motion

acceleration

Gathering Evidence about an Ancient Collision

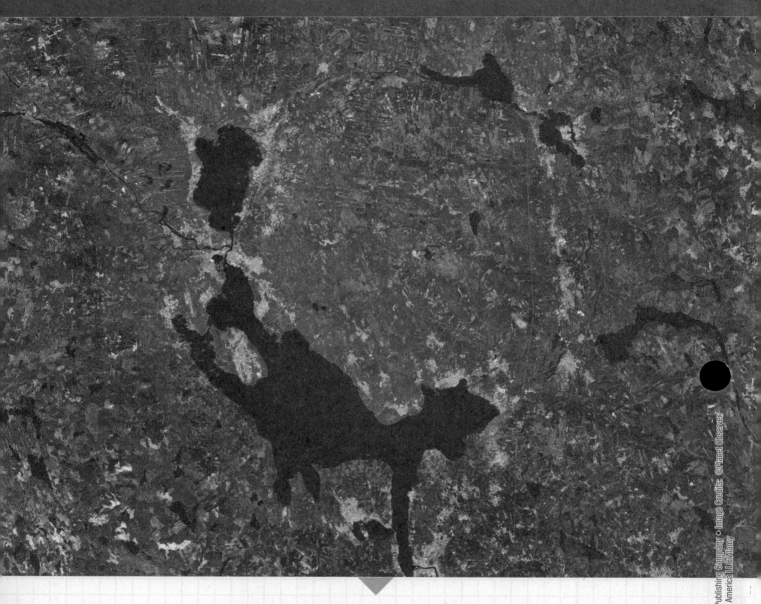

A 52-km-wide circular shape is outlined by lakes in Sweden. The shape is a hint of a collision between a meteorite and Earth that happened 377 million years ago.

Explore First

Identifying Unknowns Work with a partner to make a covered box with a hole large enough for your hand. Place 5 or 6 mystery items in the box for another group to identify by touch only. Take turns investigating each mystery box. What evidence was most useful for correctly identifying each item?

Go online to view the digital version of
the Hands-On Lab for this lesson and to
download additional lab resources.

CAN YOU EXPLAIN IT?

How did scientists solve the mystery of what caused the dinosaurs to become extinct?

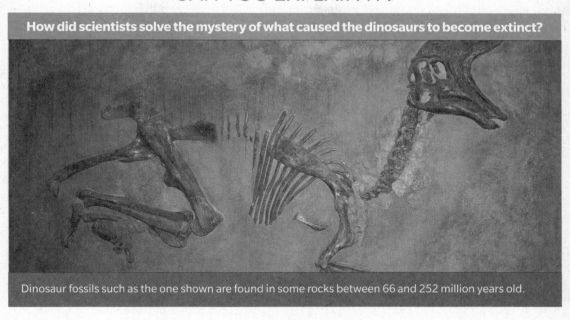

Dinosaur fossils such as the one shown are found in some rocks between 66 and 252 million years old.

1. What evidence could scientists use to show that dinosaurs once lived on Earth but have since died out?

2. How might scientists study something that they cannot observe directly?

 EVIDENCE NOTEBOOK As you explore this lesson, gather evidence to help explain how scientists developed a hypothesis as to what caused the extinction of the dinosaurs.

Identifying Patterns in the Fossil Record

The mass extinction of the dinosaurs 66 million years ago is still a mystery that scientists are trying to solve. But geologists, biologists, engineers, and other researchers are getting closer to an answer. The evidence they are gathering appears to support the theory that an asteroid collided with Earth and ended the reign of the dinosaurs.

3. Think about what you would want to know about dinosaurs to support an explanation for their extinction. Write 3 or 4 questions that you would ask in search of clues.

The Fossil Record

To learn about the past, geologists and other scientists study the fossil record. The **fossil record** is the history of life on Earth based on the traces of living things left in layers of rock. The fossil record is embedded in rock layers all over the planet.

As sediments in air and water settle over time, they form layers that compress and eventually turn to rock. As the layers build up, the more recent layers are on top and the older ones are below. By looking at fossils and other features of the different layers, scientists have reconstructed a geologic timeline of Earth's history. This timeline tells scientists about changes that happened over billions of years, including how things like climate, plants, animals, and even the makeup of the atmosphere have changed.

4. Identify the most likely relative ages of the rock by labeling the image with the terms youngest, oldest, and in between.

© Houghton Mifflin Harcourt Publishing Company • Image Credits: ©joel zatz / Alamy Stock Photo

Extinctions and Mass Extinctions

The fossil record shows the appearance, time span of existence, and the disappearance of different organisms and types of organisms on Earth. By looking at those patterns, scientists have pieced together a picture of the diversity of life and how it has changed over time. The fossil record is constantly updated as scientists make new discoveries. The information scientists have is fairly detailed. Based on what has been found and the use of the latest technologies, scientists know a great deal about the diversity of life and the patterns of change over time.

The death of every member of a species is called **extinction**. A species that has undergone extinction is said to be *extinct*. Sometimes entire groups of similar species— such as genera, families, orders, or clades—can become extinct. The fossil record shows evidence that, at certain points in Earth's history, many species have gone extinct in a short period of time. Episodes when large numbers of species become extinct are called *mass extinctions*.

When scientists identify a mass extinction, it is a mystery that they want to investigate. For example, scientists used patterns in the fossil record to determine that the mass extinction of the dinosaurs happened 66 million years ago. But for a long time, they did not know what caused the dinosaurs to die out.

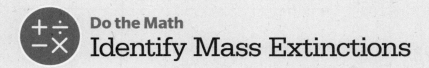

Do the Math
Identify Mass Extinctions

To identify mass extinctions, scientists compare the overall number of genera existing at different times in the fossil record. If a 15 percent or more decrease in genera occurs over a short time period, a mass extinction occurred. Use the graph to answer the questions.

5. At which of the following points in Earth's history did a mass extinction occur? Select all that apply.

   A. 66 million years ago

   B. 75 million years ago

   C. 252 million years ago

   D. 400 million years ago

6. Discuss Analyze the graph with a partner. How many mass extinctions did you identify? How did you determine when they occurred?

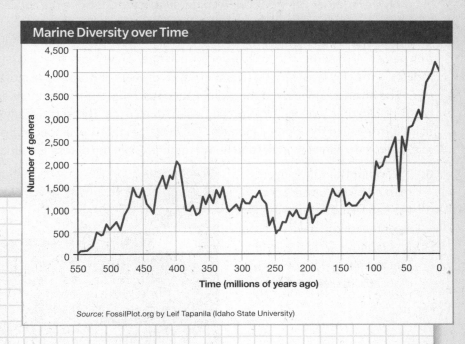

Marine Diversity over Time

Source: FossilPlot.org by Leif Tapanila (Idaho State University)

The Extinction of the Dinosaurs

In the 1980s, geologist Walter Alvarez was studying rock layers in Italy. He noticed something unusual in the fossil record. In one layer of rock, he consistently found fossils of tiny marine organisms. But in a layer above it, he found completely different marine fossils. In between the two layers, he found a thin layer of clay that had no fossils at all. The clay layer was 66 million years old. That meant that the mass extinction of the marine organisms happened at the same time as the mass extinction of the dinosaurs. Further research by Alvarez and other scientists showed that the clay layer was in rock layers all over the world.

Walter Alvarez and his father Luis Alvarez identified a 66-million-year-old layer of clay near Gubbio, Italy, that was deposited at the same time as the extinction of the dinosaurs.

7. Alvarez saw that fossils found below the clay layer were / were not in the layers above. He eventually determined that the layer marked a fossil record / mass extinction.

The Iridium Anomaly

Scientists knew when dinosaurs became extinct but did not know if dinosaurs died out suddenly or slowly. Alvarez realized that he could answer this question if he could find how quickly the clay layer was deposited. If the layer formed over a few years, the dinosaur extinction likely occurred quickly. But if the layer formed over thousands or millions of years, the extinction probably occurred gradually.

Alvarez's father, physicist Luis Alvarez, suggested checking the concentration of iridium in the clay layer. Iridium is an element that is rare on Earth's surface but is more common in space and deep inside Earth. A very small amount of iridium falls to Earth from space all the time. If the clay layer formed over a few years, it would have almost no iridium. If the clay layer formed over thousands of years, it would have more iridium.

The Alvarezes measured the iridium and found that the layer contained 30 times more iridium than would have normally fallen from space. This surprisingly high amount of iridium is called the iridium anomaly. The Alvarezes then developed hypotheses to try to explain the iridium anomaly and how it might explain the dinosaur extinction.

8. The iridium anomaly layer is marked by the upper tip of the hammer. Place a √ in the layer that might have dinosaur fossils and an ✕ in the layer that definitely does not have dinosaur fossils.

© Houghton Mifflin Harcourt Publishing Company • Image Credits: (t) ©Pictorial Press Ltd/Alamy Stock Photo, (b) ©Francois Gohier/Photo Researchers, Inc.

Explaining the Iridium Anomaly

The iridium anomaly sparked several hypotheses. In each case, scientists analyzed the evidence to see which hypothesis was best supported by the evidence.

  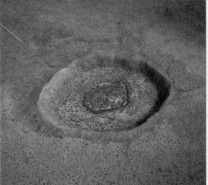

The Supernova Hypothesis A supernova is an exploding star. If a supernova happened near Earth, it could send a large amount of iridium to Earth. Huge doses of radiation might kill most life on the planet. However, a supernova would also send a lot of the element plutonium to Earth, but the clay layer did not contain higher than normal levels of plutonium.

The Volcanism Hypothesis A volcanic eruption can bring iridium from deep inside Earth to the surface. Wide-scale eruptions can cause climate change, which can affect life on Earth. About 66 million years ago, huge volcanic eruptions lasting about 30,000 years covered India with more than 1.5 cubic kilometers of lava. However, that eruption lasted too long to be the source of the thin iridium layer.

The Asteroid Hypothesis Some asteroids contain a lot of iridium. If such an asteroid hit Earth, debris from the impact would send iridium-laced dust into the air. If the asteroid were large enough, the impact would also cause many catastrophic events that could lead to mass extinctions. The dust would then settle over the planet to form a thin, iridium-rich layer. The Alvarezes supported this hypothesis.

9. **Act** Think about the three hypotheses above. With a partner, pretend that a news reporter is interviewing Walter Alvarez. The reporter should ask questions about why one hypothesis might be better supported by the evidence than the others. Alvarez should respond with evidence to support his reasons.

Explain How Extinctions Are Identified

The iridium anomaly layer marked the end of the dinosaurs. But not every species of dinosaur became extinct 66 million years ago. Some species died out well before then.

10. Explain how a scientist can determine when a particular species of dinosaur lived on Earth.

_____

_____

_____

_____

 EVIDENCE NOTEBOOK

11. Investigation of the iridium anomaly layer changed the way researchers looked at the fossil record. How did it lead to new hypotheses about the extinction of the dinosaurs? Record your evidence.

Gathering Evidence about Asteroid Impacts

When an asteroid or meteorite collides with the moon, it leaves behind a circular depression called a crater. The moon is covered with thousands of craters. The craters are evidence of impacts by objects traveling through the solar system.

If the moon has so many craters, why has Earth been spared these impacts? Actually, it has not been spared. Earth's impact craters are hidden or erased by the effects of plate tectonics, volcanic activity, weathering, and erosion. Most impact craters on Earth's surface are underwater, overgrown, or misshapen. They vary in size from small (100 m) to gigantic (200 km). To be evidence of the cause for a mass extinction, an asteroid crater needs to be big. The age of the crater would also need to be just right.

12. Compare and contrast the craters in the two images. Then explain why you think the craters look different from each other.

Craters	Observations and Explanations
 The moon is covered in craters of different sizes.	
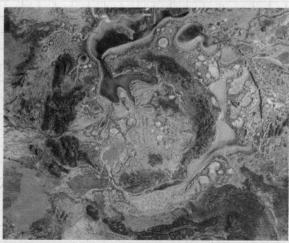 This crater in Australia is one of only a few hundred craters identified on Earth.	

© Houghton Mifflin Harcourt Publishing Company • Image Credits: (t) ©NASA/GSFC/ Arizona State University, (b) ©NASA Johnson Space Center

Discovery of a Crater near the Yucatan Peninsula

The Alvarezes' hypothesis and calculations sent researchers around the world in search of an impact crater at least 200 km in diameter. The crater they were seeking would be difficult, if not impossible, to find. Given that no crater that big had been found, it was likely underwater or severely eroded.

In the late 1970s, geophysicist Glen Penfield made observations about the Yucatan Peninsula near the small town of Chicxulub (CHEEK•shoo•loob), Mexico. By comparing the strength and direction of magnetic fields in the sea floor, he saw a huge semicircle facing south. Then he looked at a study that measured the strength of the gravitational field of the land. He found another semicircle facing north. The two pieces fit together to make a huge circle close to 180 km wide.

Penfield also read a study of samples from the same area that was done 40 years earlier. The samples contained fused rocks and deformed quartz crystals, which are usually formed by violent explosions like volcanic eruptions or asteroid impacts.

Technology Provides Evidence of an Impact Crater

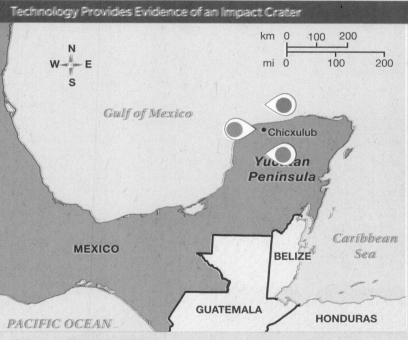

On the Yucatan Peninsula, the town of Chicxulub was identified as "ground zero" for the asteroid impact. Today, the crater is not visible to the unaided eye.

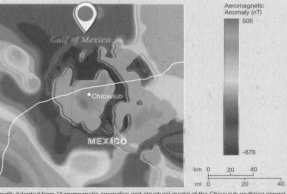

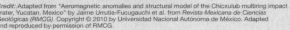

Credit: Adapted from "Aeromagnetic anomalies and structural model of the Chicxulub multiring impact crater, Yucatan, Mexico" by Jaime Urrutia-Fucugauchi et al. from *Revista Mexicana de Ciencias Geológicas (RMCG)*. Copyright © 2010 by Universidad Nacional Autónoma de México. Adapted and reproduced by permission of RMCG.

Magnetic data clearly show an arc underwater pointing toward the land.

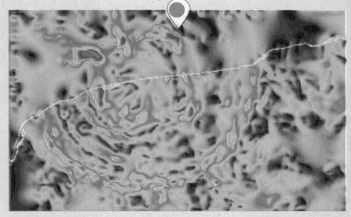

The gravitational field study shows a clear arc on land connecting to the ocean.

© Houghton Mifflin Harcourt Publishing Company • Image Credits: (br) ©Geological Survey of Canada/Science Source, (tr) ©Jacques Descloitres, MODIS Rapid Response Team, NASA/GSFC

Early Evidence of the Chicxulub Impact

Different types of scientists gathered evidence in attempts to solve the mystery of the dinosaur mass extinction. The evidence was compared to the different extinction hypotheses to determine which hypothesis was the best supported. Early evidence supported the idea that an asteroid collided with Earth. The asteroid was so large and fast that it left evidence not only in and around the Gulf of Mexico, but across the planet.

Early Evidence that Supported the Asteroid Hypothesis

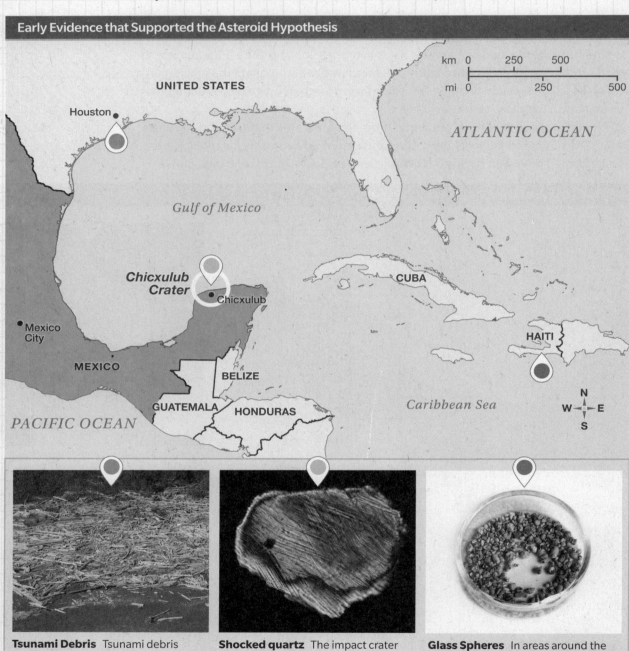

Tsunami Debris Tsunami debris was found in 66-million-year-old rock layers thousands of kilometers away from the impact site. If an asteroid hit off the coast of the Yucatan, it would have caused a huge tsunami that traveled outward from the impact site in all directions.

Shocked quartz The impact crater in the Gulf of Mexico contained a variety of shocked minerals including quartz. The zig-zag pattern in this quartz crystal was caused by extreme pressure changes. Such pressure changes may happen during a powerful explosion or impact.

Glass Spheres In areas around the Caribbean Sea, tiny glass spheres were found in rocks around the same age as the mass extinction. These spheres form when molten rock is thrown into the air during extreme explosions. As droplets of this liquid fly through the air, they cool and form spheres and other rounded shapes.

Evidence Gathered with Advanced Technology

The findings of early scientific research about the Chicxulub impact crater led to the use of advanced technologies to gather more evidence. This evidence has helped scientists to better understand the details of the crater. For example, they learned when it was formed and how it changed over time. When all the evidence had been gathered, it supported the hypothesis that the Chicxulub impact crater was the right age and size to have caused the extinction of the dinosaurs.

Borehole Drilling Large impact craters like the one at Chicxulub form inner "peak" rings as the crust ripples upon impact. Scientists drilled into these rings to collect samples of the layers of rock. The samples helped them to understand how these rings form.

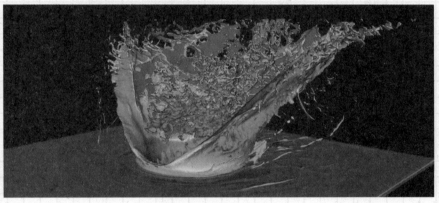

Computer Modeling Scientists use calculations and quantitative data to simulate the moment of impact. This image shows the huge amount of debris, called ejecta, sprayed into the air upon impact. This debris is thought to have clouded the atmosphere for years, contributing to the mass extinctions.

Radar Imaging from Space This radar image was taken by equipment aboard the Space Shuttle *Endeavor*. Computer enhancements brought out the subtle semicircle that forms the southern rim of the crater.

13. **Draw** Look at the radar image. Trace the edge of the impact crater on land. Use a dotted line to complete the outline of the crater in the ocean.

Hands-On Lab
Model Crater Formation

Model the formation of craters and use your data to draw conclusions about how the size and speed of an asteroid relate to the crater it forms upon impact. Finally, make suggestions on how to improve this investigation by using technology.

MATERIALS
- balance
- box or pan at least 10 cm deep
- flour, white
- marbles or other round objects, small, medium, and large
- powdered pudding or drink mix, colored
- ruler, metric
- sifter or sieve
- tape measure

Procedure

STEP 1 Design an experiment that investigates how the size and speed of an asteroid affects the features of its impact crater. Features of an impact crater include diameter, depth, and distance traveled by ejecta. Describe what you want to test and how you plan to test it.

STEP 2 Conduct your experiment and record your data in a data table. A sample table is shown. You may make your own table on a separate sheet of paper and add additional columns or rows as needed.

Marble size	Crater diameter (cm)	Crater depth (cm)	Ejecta distance (cm)

© Houghton Mifflin Harcourt Publishing Company

Analysis

STEP 3 Make a claim about how the size and speed of an asteroid affects the features of its crater. Support your claim with evidence from your investigation.

STEP 4 **Engineer It** Pretend you are an engineer working on this simulation in a computer lab. How might using computer modeling improve this investigation and the evidence gathered?

Crater Size and the Size and Speed of an Asteroid

Looking at crater formation can tell scientists a lot about the object that made the impact. An asteroid in motion has a lot of energy. The bigger and faster the asteroid is, the more energy it will transfer upon impact. This energy creates a crater that is much larger than the impacting object. The diameter of the ejecta spray will be even larger.

Walter Alvarez estimated the size and speed of an asteroid required to cause the mass extinction event. He used complex calculations and comparisons to other, similar known events. When the Chicxulub crater matched his estimate, it was further evidence to support his hypothesis.

14. A large asteroid has a large / small amount of energy and produces a large / small crater. A small crater was likely formed by a large / small asteroid.

© Houghton Mifflin Harcourt Publishing Company

The Age of the Chicxulub Crater

In addition to finding the size and speed of the Chicxulub asteroid, scientists also needed to date the impact. Did it happen before the iridium anomaly layer formed, at the same time, or after? Geologists dated the rock layers of the crater in two ways. They studied radioactive isotope decay in the rocks that melted during the impact to find the *absolute age* of those rock layers. They also compared the *relative ages* of rock layers based on the idea that the layers on top are younger than the layers below. Then they compared the fossils of tiny sea creatures called foraminifera in sea-floor rocks around the crater. They found that the fossils in layers from before and after the impact were very different. Using these methods, scientists determined that the impact happened about 66 million years ago. These results further supported the idea that the impact caused a mass extinction.

Microscopic marine life left fossilized shells in layers of rock. The species of these shells were completely different in layers above and below the impact structure.

 EVIDENCE NOTEBOOK

15. Why are the details about the crater's size, location, and age important to support the asteroid hypothesis about the dinosaur extinction? Which details do you think are most significant? Record your evidence.

Analyze Craters on the Moon

Look at the impact craters in this photo of the moon's surface. Compare them to draw conclusions about the sizes and speeds of the meteoroids or asteroids that caused them.

16. Explain how you can tell which craters are older or younger based on what you see.

_____

_____

_____

_____

Impact craters on the moon vary in size and position.

17. Which craters were formed by more energetic impacts? Explain your reasoning.

_____

_____

_____

_____

_____

Describing the Effects of the Chicxulub Asteroid Collision

When two sets of data follow the same pattern, a *correlation* exists between the variables. However, a correlation does not automatically mean that one thing causes the other. Determining *causation* requires information about how a change in one variable affects the other variable.

18. The graph shows that the number of people flying and the amount of fruits and nuts produced follow / don't follow the same pattern. This means there is a correlation / causation between the number of people flying and the amount of fruits and nuts produced. This does / does not prove that one causes the other.

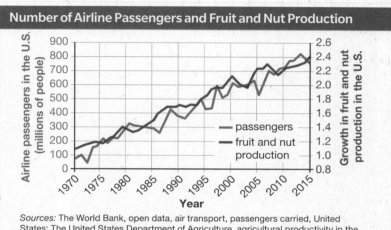

Number of Airline Passengers and Fruit and Nut Production

Sources: The World Bank, open data, air transport, passengers carried, United States; The United States Department of Agriculture, agricultural productivity in the U.S., National Tables, 1948–2015

Correlation and Causation

A correlation can be positive or negative. A positive correlation is one in which the changes in the variables are both increasing or both decreasing. The correlation between the number of airline passengers and fruit and nut production is a positive correlation.

A negative correlation is one in which the change in one variable is opposite to the change in the other variable. For example, the correlation between amount of pesticide residue and eagle population is a negative correlation.

Some correlations are coincidences. No evidence suggests that producing more fruits and nuts encourages people to fly or vice versa.

A correlation may indicate an underlying cause that affects both variables. For example, an increase in car sales may be correlated with a decrease in car accidents. Both variables could be caused by increasing gas prices. Higher gas prices may encourage people to buy new, fuel-efficient cars. Higher gas prices may also cause people to drive less, which would lead to fewer accidents.

Sometimes however, a correlation can have a causal link. To establish causation, a convincing explanation for why a change in one variable would cause a change in the other is needed. For example, scientists investigated the relationship between pesticides and bird populations. They found that the pesticides caused the birds to lay eggs with thinner shells. So, fewer birds hatched.

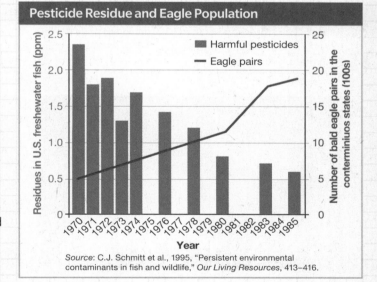

Pesticide Residue and Eagle Population

Source: C.J. Schmitt et al., 1995, "Persistent environmental contaminants in fish and wildlife," *Our Living Resources*, 413–416.

Effects of an Asteroid Collision on Earth's Systems

Using evidence gathered about the Chicxulub impact and the iridium anomaly layer, scientists were able to establish a correlation in time between the impact and the mass extinction of the dinosaurs. They knew that the two events happened at the same time. However, to establish causation, scientists had to determine how the asteroid collision could have caused such a large extinction event. So, they looked at ways that an asteroid collision might affect Earth and life systems.

Wildfires The impact had so much energy that it created intense heat. Also, the ejecta included hot debris that rained down all over the planet, starting fires far away from the impact site. Large wildfires could have damaged or destroyed exposed ecosystems, leading to the death of organisms that lived there.

Ejecta The impact turned rocks and other matter into gases. Ejecta that was not vaporized included ocean water, sediment, and dust. All these ejecta and gases entered the atmosphere. The finer materials could have stayed suspended in the air and blocked out the sun. As a result, plants died and so did the animals that depended on them.

Tsunamis A tsunami estimated to be as high as 500 m followed the impact. It traveled across the oceans and flooded large areas of land, where it left behind boulders, tree trunks, and other debris. The floods and debris could have damaged or destroyed ecosystems on land and in the ocean.

Earthquakes The energy from the impact would have rippled through the ground as earthquakes. The tremors could have been violent enough to shift great expanses of land and cause volcanic eruptions all over the planet. These changes could have disrupted habitats for many organisms.

19. Which impact effects could have caused a decrease in photosynthesis rates? Select all that apply.

A. earthquakes

B. ejecta

C. tsunamis

D. wildfires

 EVIDENCE NOTEBOOK

20. Think about how reducing sunlight would affect Earth. What evidence would you look for that supports these effects? Record your evidence.

The Chicxulub Asteroid and the Extinction of Dinosaurs

Scientists from various fields continue to collect evidence about the Chicxulub impact. They are looking to draw conclusions about its relationship to the extinction of the dinosaurs. Some scientists argue that the asteroid impact was not the sole cause of the extinction. Evidence shows that volcanic eruptions in India led up to and continued beyond the extinction event. These eruptions formed the Deccan Traps. The Deccan Traps are thick, widespread layers of rock formed from volcanic lava flows that erupted for thousands of years before and after the Chicxulub impact event. Gases released by these eruptions may have caused global climate change that contributed to the mass extinction. Therefore, scientists hypothesize that the Chicxulub collision may not have been the only cause of the mass extinction.

The Deccan Traps are some of the largest lava deposits on Earth.

 21. Language SmArts Synthesize what you have learned by writing a persuasive article on whether you think there is a causal link between the Chicxulub impact and the extinction of the dinosaurs. Be sure to explain any correlation between the two events and provide evidence to support your claims.

Analyze Correlations

Use the graph to analyze which mass extinctions are correlated with asteroid impacts and which are correlated with volcanic eruptions. In the graph, the size of the volcano icons correlates to magnitude of the volcanic event.

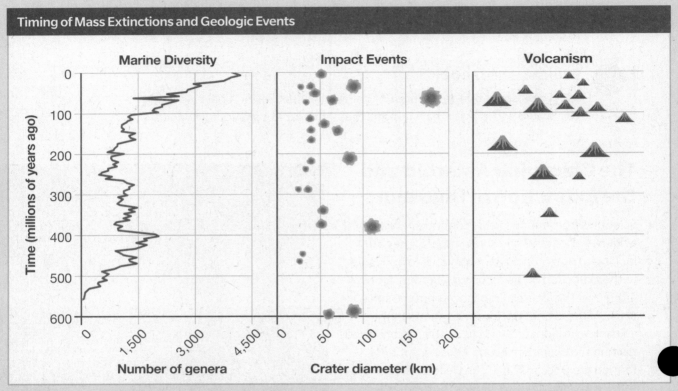

Timing of Mass Extinctions and Geologic Events

Credits: FossilPlot by Leif Tapanila (Idaho State University); Adapted from "The Cretaceous–Tertiary mass extinction" by Gerta Keller from *The End-Cretaceous Mass Extinction and the Chicxulub Impact in Texas*, Special Publication 100. Copyright © 2011 by SEPM, Society for Sedimentary Geology. Adapted and reproduced by permission of SEPM, Society for Sedimentary Geology.

Sources: University of New Brunswick, Planetary and Space Science Centre, Earth Impact Database, diameter and size; A.J. Retzler et al., 2015, "Post-impact depositional environments as a proxy for crater morphology, Late Devonian Alamo impact, Nevada," *Geosphere*, v. 11, no. 1, 123–143.

22. Analyze the graph to determine which event is correlated in time to each mass extinction listed. Write *asteroid impact, volcanic activity,* or *both* in the space provided.

    A. 66 million years ago _____

    B. 250 million years ago _____

    C. 450 million years ago _____

23. What evidence would be useful to establish causation between the mass extinction that happened 250 million years ago and the event that it is correlated with?

_____

_____

_____

_____

_____

Continue Your Exploration

Name: _____   **Date:** _____

Check out the path below or go online to choose one of the other paths shown.

People in Science

- **Cenotes and the Chicxulub Collision**
- **Hands-On Labs** 🖐
- **Propose Your Own Path**

Go online to choose one of these other paths.

Adriana Ocampo

As a planetary geologist at the National Aeronautic and Space Administration, or NASA, Dr. Adriana Ocampo makes connections between what she sees happening in space and what happens on Earth. In 1990, while viewing satellite images taken by NASA, Ocampo noticed a ring of cenotes (su•NO•teez) on the Yucatan Peninsula. A cenote is a water-filled sinkhole. Ocampo realized that the ring outlined the rim of a giant crater formed by an ancient asteroid impact. She determined that this ring of cenotes were further evidence of the Chicxulub impact.

In later research, Ocampo found unusual ejecta debris near the Chicxulub crater. This ejecta looked like it had once flowed like a thick fluid. Fluidized ejecta is not commonly found around craters on Earth. But such ejecta was familiar to Ocampo. She had seen fluidized ejecta surrounding craters on Mars.

Dr. Adriana Ocampo studies the geology of Earth and other planets.

Scientists are not sure how fluidized ejecta form on Mars because they have never seen it form. So, studying the fluidized ejecta that Ocampo found could help scientists understand how craters form on Mars.

1. Why do you think Ocampo uses discoveries on Earth to help with her studies of Mars?

Continue Your Exploration

Crater chains are common features on the moon, Mars, and other rocky bodies in the solar system. Crater chains form when an asteroid or comet breaks apart as it falls toward a planet or moon. The pieces of the asteroid or comet then collide with the planet or moon in a straight line to form a chain of craters.

In 1996, Ocampo used radar imaging to discover a crater chain on Earth. The chain that she found was only the second crater chain identified on Earth. Although crater chains are common on other bodies in the solar system, they are rare on Earth.

2. Why do you think crater chains are rare on Earth?

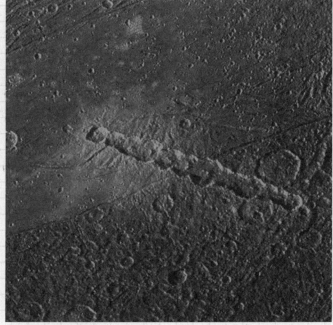

This crater chain is on Ganymede, which is one of Jupiter's moons.

_____

3. Currently, scientists have few opportunities to travel in space. So, Ocampo may never be able to study the geology of other planets in person. Which of the following methods might Ocampo use to study the geology of other planets and moons in the solar system? Select all that apply.

A. satellite images of Earth

B. geologic data gathered on Earth

C. satellite images of planets and moons

D. geologic data gathered by rovers on planets and moons

4. **Collaborate** Work with a partner to find out more about the craters on Mars or another body in the solar system. Find out how scientists study the craters and what they know about how and when they formed.

Can You Explain It?

Name: _____   Date: _____

How did scientists solve the mystery of what caused the dinosaurs to become extinct?

EVIDENCE NOTEBOOK

Refer to the notes in your Evidence Notebook to help you construct an explanation for how scientists developed a hypothesis to explain what caused the mass extinction of the dinosaurs.

1. State your claim. Make sure your claim fully explains how scientists developed a hypothesis for what caused the mass extinction of the dinosaurs.

2. Summarize the evidence you have gathered to support your claim and explain your reasoning.

Checkpoints

Answer the following questions to check your understanding of the lesson.

Use the photo to answer questions 3–4.

3. What feature in the photo identifies the landform as a crater?

   A. the rocks

   B. the water

   C. the circular shape

   D. the gap in the cliff

4. Craters on Earth may be impact craters or craters formed when a volcano erupts. Which questions could you ask to determine what formed this crater? Select all that apply.

   A. Are the sides of the crater eroded?

   B. Is the crater on land or underwater?

   C. Are there layers of hardened lava around the crater?

   D. Are there fragments of meteorites in and around the crater?

Use the diagram to answer questions 5–6.

5. The art shows an imaginary section of rock layers. The shapes represent fossils. What does the fossil record indicate happened between layers B and C?

   A. circles became extinct

   B. squares became extinct

   C. triangles became extinct

   D. crescents became extinct

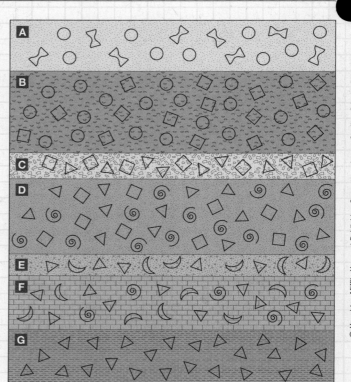

6. Which claims about the spirals can you support with evidence from the rock layers shown? Select all that apply.

   A. They became extinct after layer D formed.

   B. They became extinct before layer E formed.

   C. They came back to life before layer D formed.

   D. They were alive when layer E formed.

Interactive Review

Complete this section to review the main concepts of the lesson.

Studying rock layers and the fossils within them establishes the fossil record. Patterns in the fossil record are used to identify extinctions and mass extinctions.

A. How do scientists identify a mass extinction using the fossil record?

Scientists gathered a variety of evidence to find the location of the asteroid impact that likely caused the extinction of the dinosaurs. Further research, application of scientific principles, and advanced technology helped determine characteristics of the impact.

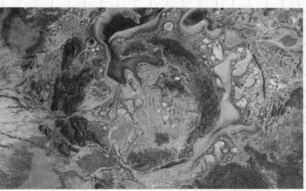

B. How does the speed and size of an asteroid affect the size and shape of the crater it forms when it collides with Earth or the moon?

A correlation exists between variables when the pattern of changes in one variable is related to the pattern of changes in the other. Causation exists between correlated variables if a convincing explanation describes how one variable affects the other.

C. Explain the correlation and causation relationships between the Chicxulub impact and the mass extinction of the dinosaurs.

© Houghton Mifflin Harcourt Publishing Company • Image Credits: (t) ©joel zatz / Alamy Stock Photo; (m) ©NASA Johnson Space Center; (b) ©Frank Krahmer/Corbis/Getty Images

Energy Causes Change

This skier has a mix of kinetic energy and potential energy.

Explore First

Analyzing the Energy of a Ball Drop a rubber ball and watch how it moves. All moving objects have energy. Where does the ball get the energy to move? What happens to its energy? Try to keep the ball bouncing for 10 seconds or more. What did you have to do to keep it bouncing and why did that work?

CAN YOU EXPLAIN IT?

Why doesn't the water balloon hit the student's face?

When the student releases the water balloon, it swings forward. When the water balloon swings back, you can tell that the student expects the water balloon to hit her face. Why does the water balloon not continue on and hit the student's face?

Explore Online

1. Based on what you know about energy, what types of energy does the water balloon have? How could energy explain the water balloon's behavior?

EVIDENCE NOTEBOOK As you explore the lesson, gather evidence to help explain how energy affects the motion of the water balloon.

Analyzing Energy

If you look at the news, you are likely to see a story about energy. Questions about renewable energy, energy conservation, energy cost, and the ways energy is obtained and used are some of the most important issues today. Engineers, scientists, and policymakers are looking for solutions on how to generate, distribute, and store energy.

2. What do you think energy is and how is it important in your life?

Energy

The word energy is used in many contexts, but what does it actually mean? Scientists define **energy** as the ability to cause changes in matter. Changes in matter include changes in the motion of objects, physical changes such as changes of state, and chemical changes such as burning. Changes in matter can be observed in examples as simple as a wind-up toy or as complex as a crane lifting steel beams to construct a skyscraper. In both situations, the objects move because energy is added to them. To operate a wind-up toy, the user turns a key that coils a spring. The energy stored in the spring is released as it unwinds, exerting a force on gears in the toy that cause it to move. The motion of the toy results from an initial input of energy from the user turning the key.

After someone winds up the toy with its key, the toy begins to move.

© Houghton Mifflin Harcourt Publishing Company • Image Credits: ©Lee Rogers/istock/Getty Images Plus/Getty Images

3. Discuss Think about a construction crane moving a steel beam. Where does the energy used to complete the task come from? What evidence do you have that the amount of energy involved in the crane example is different from that in the wind-up toy example?

Energy is present in every situation. Each bird in this photo has energy, and everything else in the photo has energy, too.

Kinetic Energy

All energy can be categorized into two types. One type of energy is **kinetic energy**, which is the energy of motion. As you have observed, every moving object requires energy to set it in motion. Once the object is in motion, it has kinetic energy. For example, every bird in the photo has kinetic energy because it is moving. The more massive the object is or the faster it is traveling, the more kinetic energy it has. Assuming all the birds in the photo have about the same mass, a bird that flies faster than the other birds has more kinetic energy than the others do.

Potential Energy

The other type of energy is potential energy. **Potential energy** is the stored energy an object has based on its position within a system, its condition, or its chemical composition. A roller coaster car at the top of a hill has stored energy that gives it the potential to move down the hill. The birds in the photo have potential energy because of their position above the ground and because of their chemical composition.

4. **Draw** Choose a group of objects that you can see from your seat an draw a diagram of the objects. Label the objects that have kinetic energy or potential energy in your drawing.

Forms of Energy

Energy is not made of matter: it does not have mass or take up volume. So you cannot touch energy or hold it in your hand. However, you observe the effects of energy all the time. How you observe energy depends on the form of energy. Many forms of energy exist, and you can see, feel, and hear various forms of energy. However, keep in mind that all forms of energy are types of kinetic energy and potential energy.

Explore Online

A meteor has several forms of energy as it streaks through the sky, such as kinetic energy, electromagnetic energy, and gravitational potential energy.

Mechanical Energy The mechanical energy of an object is the sum of the object's kinetic energy and potential energy. In other words, mechanical energy is the energy of an object due to its motion and its position. A meteor that flies through the air has mechanical energy because it is moving and is high above Earth's surface.

Thermal Energy Thermal energy is the total kinetic energy of all the *particles* that make up an object. Particles move faster at higher temperatures than at lower temperatures. The faster the particles in an object move, the more thermal energy the object has. Also, the more particles an object has, the more thermal energy it has. Thermal energy is separate from the kinetic energy that contributes to mechanical energy because that energy is the kinetic energy of the object as a whole.

Electromagnetic Energy Electromagnetic energy is the kinetic energy of electromagnetic waves, which include visible light, X-rays, and microwaves. X-rays are high-energy waves used to look at your bones. Microwaves can be used to cook food or to transmit cellphone calls. The light given off by a meteor is electromagnetic energy.

Sound Energy Sound energy is kinetic energy caused by the vibration of particles in a medium, such as steel, water, or air. When you pluck the strings of a guitar, they vibrate, producing sound. These vibrations travel outward from the guitar and transfer energy to air around the strings. As the particles of the air vibrate, they transfer the sound energy to other particles. The vibrating particles strike special structures in your ear, and your brain interprets the vibrations as sound.

© Houghton Mifflin Harcourt Publishing Company • Image Credits: ©Thomas Heaton/ Science Source

Electrical Energy Electrical energy is the kinetic energy of moving electric charges. The electrical energy that powers a toaster oven or a light bulb in a lamp is caused by negatively charged particles moving in a wire. The more electric charges that are moving, the more electrical energy is carried by the wire. Electrical energy can occur in nature in the form of lightning and smaller static electricity shocks.

Gravitational Potential Energy Gravitational potential energy is the potential energy that an object has due to its position relative to Earth. In everyday life, an object's position relative to Earth means how high above the ground an object is. A pencil on a table has gravitational potential energy, but a pencil on a high shelf has more. Gravitational potential energy is important because it constantly affects every object in the universe.

Elastic Energy Elastic energy is the potential energy stored in an object when an elastic material deforms or changes shape. You can observe elastic energy when you stretch a rubber band or squeeze a spring.

Chemical Energy Chemical energy is the potential energy stored in the chemical bonds of substances. The chemical energy in a compound depends on the position and arrangement of the atoms in the compound. Sources of chemical energy include batteries, fuels, and matches. The food you eat also contains chemical energy.

Nuclear Energy Nuclear energy is the potential energy stored in the nucleus of an atom. When an atom's nucleus breaks apart or when the nuclei of two small atoms join together, energy is released. The energy given off by the sun comes from nuclear energy. Light from the sun and other stars come from these reactions. Without nuclear energy from the sun, life would not exist on Earth.

Identify Forms of Energy

Thunderstorms are a spectacular display of energy in nature. The thunder heard during thunderstorms is caused by lightning. Lightning is a giant spark in the atmosphere made of moving electric charges. Lightning rapidly heats the air around it to temperatures as high as 30,000 °C. The increased temperature causes the air to expand quickly, which produces a shock wave. When the shock wave reaches your ears, you hear thunder.

5. Think about everything that you observe during a thunderstorm. Identify the various forms of energy that are displayed during a thunderstorm.

_____

_____

_____

_____

_____

_____

Relating Energy and Work

At the end of a long day, you might say you do not have energy to do your homework, but your body always has energy. You use this energy to do many different things every day. For example, you might use a little energy to push a pencil or you might use a lot of energy to lift a heavy backpack. You might even use energy to play sports like archery.

6. This archer used energy to pull back the string and flex the bow. The flexed bow has potential / kinetic energy. The energy in the bow is due to its motion / condition . When the string is released, it will push / pull the arrow forward / backward .

Energy and Work

When you push a pencil or pick up a backpack, a force applied to an object results in its movement over a distance. The amount of energy required to lift a heavy backpack over a specific distance is much greater than the energy needed to push a pencil over an equivalent distance. This energy can be scientifically measured in terms of work. In science, **work** is defined as the transfer of energy to an object by a force that causes the object to move in the direction of that force. All energy can be used to do work on an object. For example, the kinetic energy of your hand does work on a pencil to move it.

Work (W) can be calculated using the formula $W = Fd$, where F is the force applied to the object and d is the distance the object moved. Force is in units of newtons (N), and distance is in units of meters (m), so work is defined in units of newton-meters (N•m), which is also known as joules (J). Note that if the object does not move, $d = 0$ and no work is done. Just how much is a joule of work? To get an idea, lift an apple (which weighs about 1 N) from your feet to your waist (which is about 1 m).

7. Do the Math Use the equation for work ($W = Fd$) to calculate the work done by each robot, and record the value in the space provided.

Robot 1 applies 20 N of force to lift 2 building blocks 3 m.

Robot 2 applies 30 N of force to lift 3 building blocks 3 m.

Robot 3 applies 10 N of force to lift 1 building block 2 m.

Robot 4 applies 30 N of force to lift 3 building blocks 2 m.

8. Which robot did the greatest amount of work? Which robot did the least work?

In science and engineering, energy and work are related. Energy is the ability to do work, and work requires a transfer of energy. In fact, energy is transferred every time work is done. As the robots move the building blocks, they do work on the blocks by transferring energy from themselves to the blocks. Energy and work are both measured in joules.

Kinetic Energy and Work

Recall that kinetic energy is the energy of motion. Whenever an object is moving, it has the ability to do work. If a swinging baseball bat hits a ball, the ball will move in the direction of the force exerted by the bat. The swinging bat does work on the ball when it hits the ball.

9. The arrow is moving forward. What will happen if the arrow does work on the target?

A. The arrow will stop moving.

B. The arrow will move backward.

C. The target will move forward.

D. The target will move sideways.

A flying arrow can do work if it causes an object to move.

© Houghton Mifflin Harcourt Publishing Company • Image Credits: ©Steve Allen/Stockbyte/Getty Images

Potential Energy and Work

An object does not need to be moving to have the ability to do work. Potential energy can also be used to do work. Recall that potential energy is the energy an object has because of its position, condition, or chemical composition. Imagine a stretched rubber band. You could release that rubber band to shoot it across the room to move another object. The rubber band has the ability to do work because it has been stretched, not because it is moving. The stretched condition of the rubber band gives it the ability to do work when it is released and its potential energy is transformed to kinetic energy. Likewise, a rock on the edge of a cliff has the potential to do work. If it falls, its potential energy is transformed into kinetic energy and the rock can do work on anything that it hits.

This rock perched on a cliff looks like it could fall at any moment.

Engineer It

Design a Safety Barricade

In a soapbox derby race, cars roll downhill and gain speed as their gravitational potential energy is converted into kinetic energy. In your neighborhood, people are setting up a soapbox derby course. As a safety measure, hay bales are set up at the bottom of the hill as a barricade to help stop cars and drivers.

The bales of hay are placed at the bottom of the hill to stop a car and driver.

10. What will happen when the car hits the hay bale? Select all that apply.

   A. The car will do work on the hay bale and push the bale forward.

   B. The car's kinetic energy will transfer to the hay bale.

   C. The hay bale's potential energy will transfer to the car.

   D. The hay bale will do work on the car and stop the car's motion.

11. How would you change the design of the barricade if heavier cars were used? Explain your design changes in terms of energy and work.

_____

_____

_____

_____

_____

_____

_____

Analyzing Kinetic and Potential Energy

Imagine visiting the zoo and seeing animals of all shapes and sizes. You see lumbering elephants, tiny ants building nests, and sleepy sloths hanging from branches. Every animal you see has kinetic energy and potential energy, but the amount of energy they have differs from animal to animal.

This walking turtle has kinetic energy.

This running cheetah also has kinetic energy.

12. Which of these animals do you think has more kinetic energy? Explain your answer.

13. Which animal would be able to do more work? Explain your answer.

Mass, Speed, and Kinetic Energy

Kinetic energy is the energy due to motion. The kinetic energy of an object depends on both the mass and the speed of the object. An object that is moving faster will have more kinetic energy than an identical object moving more slowly. For example, imagine that you are pushing a shopping cart. If you gently push the cart, it will have much less energy and move more slowly than if you pushed it with a lot of force. The faster the cart is moving, the more kinetic energy it has.

Increasing an object's mass will also increase its kinetic energy. Think about a table tennis ball and a golf ball, which are about the same size. If the two balls were moving at the same speed, the golf ball would be able to do more work, because it has more mass.

Do the Math

Graph Kinetic Energy

14. Make a graph using the data in the table. The table shows the kinetic energy of several different balls moving at the same speed. Graph the mass of the balls on the x-axis and the kinetic energy of the balls on the y-axis.

Mass (kg)	Kinetic Energy (J)
1.0	2
2.5	5
3.0	6
5.0	10

Kinetic Energy (J)

Mass (kg)

15. Circle the graph that your plotted points most resemble to identify the relationship between mass and kinetic energy.

    A. $y = x$ **B.** $y = x^2$

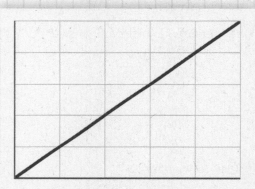 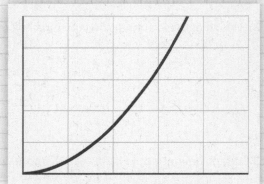

16. Make a graph using the data in the table. The table shows the kinetic energy of one ball moving at various speeds. The same ball was used every time, so the mass is constant. Graph the speed of the ball on the x-axis and the kinetic energy of the ball on the y-axis.

Speed (m/s)	Kinetic Energy (J)
1	1
3	9
4	16
6	36

Kinetic Energy (J)

Speed (m/s)

17. Circle the graph that your plotted points most resemble to identify the relationship between speed and kinetic energy.

       A. $y = x$ **B.** $y = x^2$

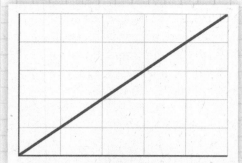 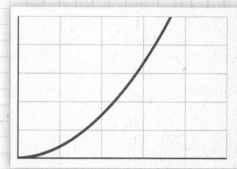

18. Describe the relationship between kinetic energy and mass, and give an example of how changing an object's mass changes its kinetic energy.

19. Describe the relationship between kinetic energy and speed, and give an example of how changing an object's speed would affect its kinetic energy.

The Equation for Kinetic Energy

The kinetic energy of an object depends on both the mass and the speed of the moving object. However, as you have identified, increasing the speed of the object will increase the kinetic energy a lot more than increasing the mass of the object will. The equation used to find the kinetic energy of an object is:

$$\text{kinetic energy} = \tfrac{1}{2}mv^2$$

In this equation, m represents the mass of the object and v represents the speed of the object. Remember that v^2 is the same as $v \times v$. If a 2-kg ball were moving at 3 m/s, you would calculate the kinetic energy like this:

$$\text{kinetic energy} = \tfrac{1}{2}mv^2$$

$$\text{kinetic energy} = \tfrac{1}{2} \times (2\,\text{kg}) \times (3\,\text{m/s})^2$$

$$\text{kinetic energy} = \tfrac{1}{2} \times (2\,\text{kg}) \times (3\,\text{m/s}) \times (3\,\text{m/s})$$

$$\text{kinetic energy} = 9\,\text{kg} \cdot \text{m}^2/\text{s}^2 = 9\,\text{J}$$

Gravitational Potential Energy

The gravitational potential energy of an object depends on the object's height. Think about a rock on a cliff. If a rock is moved to a taller cliff, it will be able to fall farther and has more gravitational potential energy. Gravitational potential energy also depends on the object's mass. If two rocks fall at the same speed, the more massive rock will be able to do more work. Because of this, even when the rocks are stationary, a massive rock will have more potential energy than a less massive rock at the same height. Gravitational potential energy also depends on the strength of gravity. However, gravity is constant on the surface of Earth, so this is not a factor for most objects within the Earth system.

 EVIDENCE NOTEBOOK

20. How does the gravitational potential energy of the water balloon before it was released compare with the gravitational potential energy of the water balloon when it returns almost to its release position? Record your evidence.

 Language SmArts
Argue Using Evidence

Potential Energy vs Height

This graph shows the relationship between the height of an object and the object's gravitational potential energy.

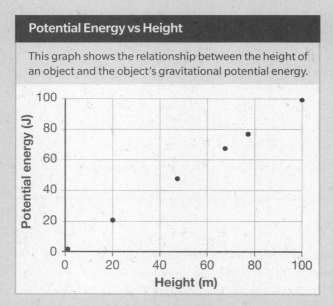

Potential Energy vs Mass

This graph shows the relationship between the mass of an object and the object's gravitational potential energy.

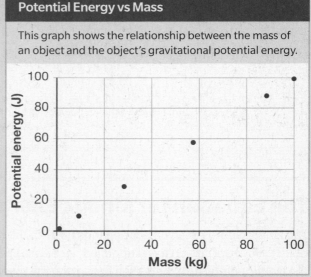

21. Look at the graphs of gravitational potential energy, height, and mass. Based on these graphs, write an argument on whether height or mass has a greater effect on gravitational potential energy.

_____

_____

_____

_____

_____

Analyzing Energy in Systems

Kinetic and Potential Energy of Objects

The energy in an object or system of objects may be either kinetic or potential energy, or both. For example, a falling ball has both kinetic energy and gravitational potential energy. The kinetic energy comes from the ball's motion through the air. The ball is moving, so it has kinetic energy. The ball also has mass and is above the ground, so it has gravitational potential energy. Even though the ball is currently falling, it has the potential to fall even farther. Thus, the ball has a mix of both kinetic and potential energy.

As it flies through the air, the baseball is moving, and it is also above the ground.

22. Compare the energy of the ball in the air with the energy of one of the balls on the ground. Explain why the amount, type, and form of the energy might be different or the same.

Kinetic and Potential Energy in Systems

Energy is not created or destroyed, but it can be transferred between objects and it can be transformed into different types and forms of energy. Because of this, systems are useful for examining energy. How energy moves through a system can be modeled. The systems approach can also be used to track how energy enters a system as an input and how energy leaves a system as an output.

Energy of a Roller Coaster Car

The cars of a roller coaster often have a mix of kinetic energy and potential energy. The amount of each type of energy changes as the cars go up and down.

23. The roller coaster cars move very slowly at the top of the hill, so they have little kinetic energy. The speed of the cars increases as they move down the hill, which increases the cars' kinetic energy. Where does this additional kinetic energy come from?

   A. Kinetic energy was added by the people riding in the cars.

   B. The cars always had kinetic energy.

   C. Potential energy was transformed into kinetic energy.

   D. Kinetic energy was added by a motor pushing the cars.

Energy Transformations

Energy can be transformed from one form into another. For example, if you were to hold a ball above your head, it would have gravitational potential energy. If you drop the ball, it would fall. The farther the ball falls, the less gravitational potential energy it has. However, when the ball is falling, it is also moving and has kinetic energy. The longer the ball falls, the faster it will move. As its speed increases, so will its kinetic energy. The gravitational potential energy is transformed into kinetic energy as the balls drops and moves toward the ground.

Energy Transfers

Energy can also be transferred from one object to another. You know that a rolling ball has kinetic energy because it is moving. If the rolling ball hits another ball at rest, the second ball will start rolling, which means that it now has kinetic energy. Energy was transferred from the first ball to the second ball. When two objects collide, each exerts a force on the other that can cause energy to pass from one to the other. In this example, kinetic energy transferred from one ball to the other. During an energy transfer, the energy may remain in the same form (as it did with the balls), or it may transform into a different form of energy. Transferred energy can stay within a system or be an input or an output of a system.

24. To light a match, you rub the match head on a coarse surface, which causes the match to ignite and burn. Describe the energy transfers and transformations that happen when a match is lit.

Energy Transformations and Transfers During an Asteroid Impact

Many energy transformations and transfers happen as an asteroid falls to Earth. When an asteroid enters Earth's atmosphere, it has a lot of gravitational potential energy because it has a large mass and is very high off the ground. The asteroid also has kinetic energy because it is moving. The speed of the asteroid increases as it falls and its potential energy is transformed into kinetic energy.

As the asteroid falls, it compresses the air in front of it, which increases the air's temperature. In this way, the asteroid's kinetic energy is transferred to the air and is transformed into thermal energy. The hot air surrounding the asteroid increases the temperature of the asteroid itself, and the asteroid glows as thermal energy is transformed into light (electromagnetic) energy.

Even more energy transfers and transformations happen when the asteroid hits Earth. The asteroid strikes the ground with a huge amount of kinetic energy. But the asteroid abruptly stops when it hits, and all of its kinetic energy is transformed or transferred away from the asteroid. Most of the asteroid's energy is transformed into thermal energy and sound energy. The thermal energy melts and vaporizes the rock that makes up the asteroid and the ground where it landed. The thermal energy may also start wildfires as it is transferred to nearby trees and grasses. The rest of the asteroid's kinetic energy is transferred to Earth causing earthquakes and throwing dust, debris, and molten rock into the air. If the asteroid lands in the ocean, its kinetic energy transfers to the water and can produce a tsunami.

The orange-brown streak is rock that melted during an asteroid impact. The liquid rock flowed into cracks in the black rock and solidified when it cooled.

Rocks splashing into water model the energy transfers that happen when an asteroid impact causes matter to be thrown into the air.

25. The kinetic energy of an asteroid depends on its mass and height / speed .
An asteroid that has more kinetic energy will transfer more / less energy to Earth and throw more / less matter into the air.

Conservation of Energy

Like matter, energy is conserved and is not created or destroyed. For this reason, you can track how energy moves through a system. Roller coaster cars can be treated as a system. The cars are lifted up a hill, which gives the system an input of potential energy. This potential energy then transforms into kinetic energy and back again to potential energy as the cars go down and up hills on the track. If no more energy is added to the system during the ride, you know that the cars will never be able to go higher than the peak of the first hill. The cars can go no higher because some energy is transformed into thermal and sound energy due to friction. This thermal and sound energy leaves the system of cars as an output. Although the energy leaves the system, the energy has not disappeared. Instead, it is transferred to objects outside of the system of cars.

Conservation of energy also applies to natural systems. Your body is a system, and you add energy to it when you eat food. Your body converts the food's chemical energy into kinetic and thermal energy so you can live and move. This energy is transferred away from your body, so you have to eat more food to gain more energy to live.

 EVIDENCE NOTEBOOK

26. How does the conservation of energy in a system relate to the water balloon's movement? Record your evidence.

Analyze Energy in Systems

Evaluate different systems to identify how the kinetic energy and gravitational potential energy of objects change over time. Treat each situation as a system and analyze how energy moves through the system.

Procedure and Analysis

STEP 1 Use your materials to set up the system described in the first box of the data table.

STEP 2 Observe the system several times. In the table, describe how the kinetic energy and gravitational potential energy of the object or objects in the system change over time.

STEP 3 Plan out two additional systems using your materials, and record them in the table. Ask your teacher to approve your ideas before moving on.

STEP 4 Repeat Steps 1 and 2 for the two new systems that you have designed.

MATERIALS
- ball, bouncy
- ball, large
- masking tape
- mass set, hanging
- meterstick
- ring stand
- string

System	Observations
A mass hanging from a string, swinging back and forth.	

Analysis

STEP 5 Choose one of the situations that you observed. List any energy inputs or outputs of that system. Consider the different forms of energy, and describe the energy transfers and transformations that took place in that system.

STEP 6 When does the system that you observed have the greatest amount of potential energy?

STEP 7 When does the system that you observed have the greatest amount of kinetic energy?

Describe Energy in a System

27. **Write** Imagine that you are the energy associated with an object. Pick a mechanical system, such as a bike pedaled down a mountainside or a bowling ball rolling down a lane toward bowling pins. Describe how you change from one form of energy to another as the object moves and how you gain or lose energy through inputs or outputs of the system.

_____

_____

_____

_____

_____

_____

_____

_____

_____

Continue Your Exploration

Name: _____   Date: _____

Check out the path below or go online to choose one of the other paths shown.

| Traffic Safety and Energy | • **Energy of a Yo-Yo**
• **Hands-On Labs** 🖐
• **Propose Your Own Path** | *Go online to choose one of these other paths.* |

Coasting downhill on a bicycle or swinging as high as possible on a swing can give you a real sense of the energy of motion. If you are like most people, though, you regularly experience the highest levels of kinetic energy when traveling in a car, truck, or bus. Speed limits, highway construction, and safety features on cars and trucks are all influenced by societal needs and desires to keep people safe when traveling in large vehicles at high speeds.

To meet these needs and desires, automotive safety engineers use technology, such as computer simulations and crash tests, to design and test safety features for all types of vehicles. The larger and faster a vehicle is, the more kinetic energy it has and the more work—and therefore damage—it can do. In an accident, large amounts of energy can be transferred, which can cause a lot of damage. Vehicles are designed to protect people's bodies from the rapid energy transfers and transformations that can occur when large amounts of kinetic energy are involved.

1. What are some factors that affect how much kinetic energy a moving vehicle has? How does the kinetic energy of a car or truck compare to that of a bicycle or a motorcycle?

Crash test dummies are used to test how the energy transfers in automobile accidents affect passengers.

Continue Your Exploration

Safety engineers perform crash tests in laboratory environments under specific, controlled conditions. Out on the road, drivers face a much wider variety of situations. Vehicle safety features protect people from the large changes in energy that occur during accidents and sudden stops. Traffic laws are in place to try to prevent such situations from happening in the first place. You have probably noticed that the speed limit on city streets is different from the speed limit on large highways. In some cases, speed limits also change depending on the time of day and are lower near parks, schools, or other facilities.

2. Some states have different speed limits for cars and large trucks. Why do you think this difference exists? Use what you know about kinetic energy to argue for or against this policy.

3. Cars are designed with safety equipment such as crumple zones and airbags. In a collision, parts of the car surrounding the passengers crumple and deform, and airbags inflate. Describe the energy transfers and transformations that occur during a collision and how these safety features help keep people safe.

4. **Collaborate** With a partner, research the masses of cars, trucks, and buses that drive on local streets. Choose an example of each type of vehicle and record the mass for your chosen model. Then research the speed limits in your area for neighborhood streets, city streets, and highways. Based on your research, develop three recommendations that could make traffic safer. What are some questions you have about how kinetic energy is involved in traffic safety laws and policies?

Can You Explain It?

Name: _____   **Date:** _____

Why doesn't the water balloon hit the student's face?

Explore Online

 EVIDENCE NOTEBOOK
Refer to the notes in your Evidence Notebook to help you construct an explanation for why the swinging water balloon does not hit the student's face.

1. State your claim. Make sure your claim fully explains why the water balloon does not hit the student's face.

2. Summarize the evidence you have gathered to support your claim and explain your reasoning.

© Houghton Mifflin Harcourt Publishing Company • Image Credits: ©HMH

Checkpoints

Answer the following questions to check your understanding of the lesson.

Use the photo to answer Questions 3–4.

3. Suppose the skater is at the highest point in the jump. What are the relative amounts of the skater's kinetic energy and gravitational potential energy at that point?

    A. all kinetic energy, no gravitational potential energy

    B. half kinetic energy, half gravitational potential energy

    C. no kinetic energy, all gravitational potential energy

    D. no kinetic energy, no gravitational potential energy

4. Which of the following statements about the kinetic energy and potential energy of the skater are true? Select all that apply.

    A. As the skater rolls up the side of the half-pipe, the skater gains kinetic energy.

    B. The skater has no gravitational potential energy at the bottom of the half-pipe.

    C. Gravitational potential energy transforms into kinetic energy when the skater rolls down the side of the half-pipe.

    D. The skater transfers gravitational potential energy to the skateboard.

Use the photo to answer Question 5.

5. Eating a healthy breakfast gives your body the energy needed to help you start your day. The girl in the photo is having cereal and orange juice, which have stored thermal / chemical energy, a form of kinetic / potential energy. The girl's body breaks down the components of the food to access the energy stored in them. Later in the day, some of this energy is transformed into the kinetic / potential energy that will allow the girl to study and play sports. Some of the energy is also transformed into thermal /sound energy that keeps her body warm.

6. Two cars are driving down the road. Car A has a mass of 1,100 kg and is moving at 20 m/s. Car B is has a mass of 1,000 kg and is moving at 30 m/s. Which car has more kinetic energy and why?

    A. car A because it has more mass and almost the same speed as car B

    B. car B because it has a greater speed and almost the same mass as car A

    C. car A because it has a lower speed and almost the same mass as car B

    D. car B because it has less mass and almost the same speed as car A

Interactive Review

Complete this section to review the main concepts of the lesson.

Energy is the ability to cause changes in matter. Many forms of energy exist, and each is a form of potential energy or kinetic energy.

A. Identify an object that has kinetic energy and an object that has potential energy and describe how you know the objects have energy.

Work is done when energy is transferred to an object by a force that cause the object to move in the direction of that force.

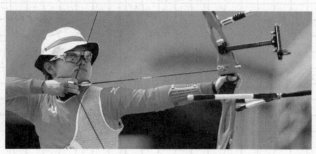

B. Describe how you do work on an object at school or when playing sports.

Kinetic energy depends on the mass and speed of an object. Speed has a much greater effect on kinetic energy than mass does. Gravitational potential energy depends on the mass of an object and its height above Earth's surface.

C. Explain how changing the speed of an object will affect its kinetic energy.

Changes in kinetic energy and potential energy can be modeled by analyzing how energy moves through a system.

D. How do energy transformations, energy transfers, and conservation of energy allow you to track how energy moves through a system?

© Houghton Mifflin Harcourt Publishing Company • Image Credits: (t) ©Thomas Heaton/ Science Source; (tc) ©The Asahi Shimbun/Getty Images; (bc) ©Dirk Freder/iStockPhoto. com; (b) ©Jessica Bethke/Shutterstock

Forces Affect the Motion of Objects

A gymnast moves across the beam with grace and strength. During a handstand, she pushes her hands against the beam.

Explore First

Investigating Speed Set up 25 dominoes in a row and knock them over by pushing only one domino. Set the dominoes up again, this time so that they are very close together before knocking them over. Set them up a third time, so that they are far apart. How did the speed of the dominoes falling compare in your three trials?

CAN YOU EXPLAIN IT?

Which dog will win the tug of war?

These dogs are engaged in a friendly game of tug of war.

1. Look carefully at the two dogs playing tug of war. Each dog is pulling on the rope, but they are pulling in opposite directions. Based on your observations, which dog will win the tug of war? Support your prediction with evidence.

 EVIDENCE NOTEBOOK As you explore the lesson, gather evidence to help explain how forces can help you predict which dog will win the tug of war.

Analyzing How Forces Act on Objects

"The thunderstorm that swept through our town had a lot of force."

"Our team won! It's a force to be reckoned with."

"It took some force, but the janitor finally pried open the stuck locker."

You hear the word *force* in everyday conversations, such as in these examples, but what does it mean in science? In science, a **force** is a push or a pull exerted on an object. A force exerted on a object can change the object's motion or shape.

A strong impact can cause a ball to change shape dramatically. The hard golf club was moving at almost 45 m/s when it made contact with the golf ball.

2. **Write** Look at the ball in the photo. What happened to the ball, and what do you think caused this change? Use action words to describe what you see.

Suppose that you tried to change the shape of a golf ball by using just your hands. You probably could not do it no matter how hard you tried. A very strong force was needed to cause a ball that hard to deform so much. Your choice of action words probably reflected the strength of the force shown in the photo. Forces of different strengths are all around you. A force can cause a change in an object or in its motion, and you can often identify a force acting on an object by observing changes in the object's motion or shape.

Forces

A force is a push or a pull, and all forces have both strength and direction. Every time you see a change in an object's motion, the change in motion was caused by a force. The change in motion could be a change in the speed or the direction of an object's motion. Scientists measure force using a unit called the **newton** (N).

A backhoe moves a pile of rocks.

3. How can you tell that forces are being exerted on the rocks in the photo?

Forces are exerted when objects interact. When an object exerts a force on another object, energy can transfer between the objects. For example, when you pick up a glass of water, you exert a force on it, and the force changes the motion of the glass of water. At the same time, kinetic energy is transferred from your hand to the glass. The force you use to move the water glass is not the only force acting on the glass, though. In most cases, several forces act on an object at once. The combination of various forces acting in different directions determines whether an object's shape or motion will change.

Think about the forces on a chair when a person sits still on it. One force on the chair is the person's weight pushing the chair down toward the floor. A second force is the force of gravity pulling the chair down. Both of these downward forces are balanced by an upward force from the floor. The system is stable because the forces acting on the chair are not changing the motion or the shape of the chair.

The forces acting on this system are balanced.

The forces acting on this system are not balanced.

4. Describe the forces exerted on the seesaw in both diagrams.

Effects of Forces

When a skater pushes off against a wall, she knows she will experience a change in her motion. Before she pushes on the wall, both the skater and the wall are not moving. When she exerts a force on the wall by pushing her hand against it, the wall does not move because the force of her push is balanced by other forces on the wall. But the wall also pushes against the skater's hand. The forces on the skater are unbalanced, which causes her to start moving in the direction of the force.

A change in motion is just one of the many effects forces can have on objects. Forces can also cause objects to change their shape. For example, when you walk on grass, you exert downward forces that bend the blades of grass. Think about other ways in which you can change the shape of objects by exerting forces.

When the skater pushes on the wall, the wall pushes back on her. The force on the skater causes the skater to move in the direction of the force.

 5. **Language SmArts** Think about a time when you experienced or used forces. Write a scientific argument describing the situation and the forces that were applied. Use action words, identify balanced and unbalanced forces, and support your explanations with facts.

6. **Discuss** With a small group, discuss the following scenario: Two birds fly away from the same tree at the same time, and they both fly at 10 km/h for 15 minutes. Why do the birds end up in different places?

Velocity and Acceleration

The speeds of the birds in the example were the same, but their velocities were different. *Speed* is the rate at which a distance is traveled. **Velocity** is the speed of an object *in a particular direction*. The sign of a velocity indicates its direction. For a given situation, a velocity in a certain direction is positive, and a velocity in the opposite direction is negative. An object's velocity changes if either its speed or its direction changes. For example, if a bus speeds up, slows down, or makes a turn, then its velocity changes. Because the bus's velocity changes, the bus accelerates. **Acceleration** is the rate at which velocity changes over time. Forces can change the motion of objects, so both velocity and acceleration are important quantities when describing the effects of forces.

Consider the travelers walking on the moving walkway in the airport. You know the velocity of the walkway relative to the ground and the velocity of the people relative to the walkway. To find the velocity of each person relative to the ground, add the velocities of each person relative to the walkway and the velocity of the walkway relative to the ground. Remember that velocities in opposite directions have opposite signs.

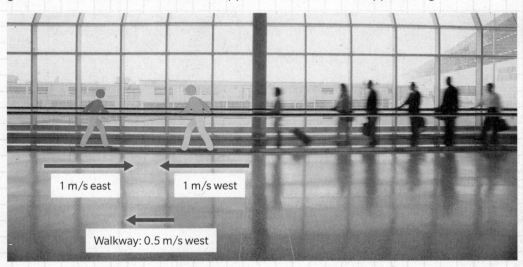

1 m/s east

1 m/s west

Walkway: 0.5 m/s west

The velocity of each figure relative to the moving walkway and the velocity of the walkway relative to the ground are given.

7. These stick figures are each in a hurry to catch a flight. They are both walking at a speed of 1 m/s on a walkway that has a velocity of 0.5 m/s to the west. Explain which stick figure is moving more quickly relative to the ground.

Force Diagrams

What words would you use to describe the forces acting on an object, such as a soccer ball? How would you describe forces of different strengths? Do you think other people will know exactly what you mean? Scientists use *force diagrams* as a way to visually describe the pushes or pulls exerted on an object.

A force diagram is a way to model the forces acting on an object. In a force diagram, both the strength and direction of forces are represented by arrows. The direction that a force arrow points shows the direction of the force, and the length of the arrow models its strength. A force diagram can show all the forces acting on an object or system, or it can show only unbalanced forces or the resultant force on a specific object.

This diagram shows the forces acting on the rocket. The arrow pointing down represents gravity, while the longer upward arrow represents the force pushing the rocket up.

8. Draw Sketch force arrows to make a force diagram for each of the situations shown.

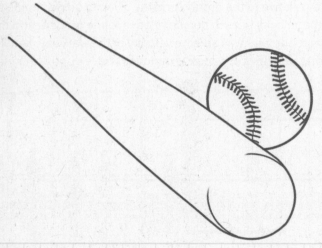

EVIDENCE NOTEBOOK

9. Draw a force diagram of the dogs playing tug of war. Which forces will affect the outcome? Record your evidence.

Analyze Forces at Work

Imagine that you and your friend decide to enjoy a warm, sunny day by going sailboarding. Out on the water, you sail with winds blowing from the east to the west, so you head due west. But then the winds change and blow to the north, so you turn to catch the wind. While you are sailing north, the winds get stronger and push you harder.

Wind blows into the sail of a sailboard, propelling the sailboard and its rider over the water.

10. Describe the forces acting on the sailboard and how they affect your motion. In your description, be sure to include the effects of the forces on your velocity and acceleration.

_____

_____

_____

_____

_____

_____

_____

_____

_____

_____

_____

Investigating Examples of Forces

Many different examples of forces can be observed in the real world. Analyze the forces shown in the scenarios shown in the table.

11. **Collaborate** With a partner, discuss each image and then complete the table. First, describe the activity, identify the effect and the direction of each force, and then diagram the forces. Use a highlighter or another method to indicate any place where you and your partner do not agree.

Description of Activity:	Description of Activity:	Description of Activity:
A bowling ball strikes a set of bowling pins.		A racecar is slowed down by a parachute.
Effect and Direction of Force:	**Effect and Direction of Force:**	**Effect and Direction of Force:**
The forward force of the ball changed the motion of the bowling pins. The pins were still and upright, but then they were knocked down and strewn across the lane.		
Force Diagram:	Force Diagram:	Force Diagram:

Hands-On Lab
Observe Everyday Forces

Investigate different forces, and make and record observations.

    Magnetic forces are forces of attraction and repulsion generated by magnets and other magnetic materials. Frictional forces are forces that oppose motion between two objects that are in contact.

MATERIALS
- bar magnet
- book
- box
- coins
- eraser, pink rubber
- marble
- metal objects
- paper clips
- pencils
- ruler
- safety pins
- toy car
- wood block

Procedure and Analysis

Visit each of the following activity stations, and carry out the procedures described. Answer the questions, and analyze the forces exerted.

- Magnetic Forces Station
- Frictional Forces Station

MAGNETIC FORCES STATION

STEP 1 In the box are several objects, including coins, safety pins, paper clips, and a variety of metal objects. Which objects can be lifted out of the box with a bar magnet? Record your observations.

STEP 2 Make a force diagram to model the forces between the magnet and one of the objects that it attracts.

STEP 3 Use evidence from your observations to explain why a recycling center uses a magnet to sort metals.

© Houghton Mifflin Harcourt Publishing Company

FRICTIONAL FORCES STATION

STEP 4 Lay the book on the table to use as a ramp. Place the wood block on the book at one end, and then slowly raise that end of the book. When the block slides down, measure and record the height of the book using the ruler. This measurement is the ramp height for the block. Lay the book flat again, and repeat the procedure with other objects, such as a coin, a pink rubber eraser, a marble, and a toy car. Record your observations.

STEP 5 How do the ramp heights of the different objects compare? How does the ramp height relate to the strength of the frictional force between the book and the object?

STEP 6 Construct an argument to explain why rubber-soled boots that have deep treads are beneficial for walking on icy sidewalks.

© Houghton Mifflin Harcourt Publishing Company

Contact and Noncontact Forces

Think about the different forces and objects that you investigated. Some types of forces only act between objects that are touching and are called contact forces. Air resistance is a contact force that acts on an object as it moves through the air. Other forces can act at a distance, such as the force between a bar magnet and a metal object. A force that can act at a distance is called a noncontact force.

12. For each of the forces in the table, use a check mark to indicate whether it is a contact force or a noncontact force.

Force	Contact	Noncontact
Magnetic		✓
Gravity		
Air Resistance		
Friction		

Identify Forces

Forces act on all objects whether they are on the ground or in the air.

13. Draw Look at the paper airplane thrown by the boy in the photo. Predict the path of the paper airplane using force diagrams to explain its motion. Then write one scientific question about forces and paper airplanes that you would like answered.

A paper airplane glides through the air. Its path is determined by the forces acting on it.

Determining the Strength of a Force

All forces have strength, but how much force is needed for a given task? What determines the strength of the force?

14. **Discuss** Look carefully at the photo of the woman pushing a lawn mower. With a partner, discuss factors that would affect the strength of force required to push the mower. For example, what effect would the length of the grass have?

Forces Acting on Objects

Forces can change the shape or the motion of an object, and the change in an object's shape or motion allows you to identify the *net force*, which is the sum of all the forces acting on the object. When identifying the net force, you may need to analyze all of the forces acting on an object.

15. Look at the photo of the girl pushing the car and predict what would happen to the car's motion if someone were helping her. Now look at the photo of the man pushing the cart full of plants and predict what would happen to the cart's motion if someone were pushing the cart in the opposite direction.

Combinations of Forces

Usually more than one force acts on an object at a time, and the combination of all of the forces acting on an object is the net force. To determine the net force on an object, you add the forces acting on it. Forces have both strength and direction. Like velocity, a force acting in a certain direction is positive, and a force acting in the opposite direction is negative. The positive direction is arbitrary for a situation, but once chosen, it cannot change. So, if you decide that forces acting from left to right are positive, then forces that act from right to left are negative. If two forces on an object act in opposite directions and are equal in strength, then the net force on the object is 0 N. If the strengths of the forces are different, the net force will be greater than or less than 0 N, and the object will accelerate. The direction of the net force will be the same as the direction of the stronger force acting on the object, and the direction of the net force is indicated by its sign.

Calculate Net Force

Both the smaller person and the bigger person are pushing the box in the same direction: to the right. The forces are both positive, because they are exerted in the positive direction. The net force acting on the box is 50 N to the right.

Net force:
20 N + 30 N = 50 N
to the right

Both people are the same size and are pushing the box with the same amount of force and in the same direction: to the right. The forces are positive, because they are exerted in the positive direction. The net force acting on the box is 60 N to the right.

Net force:
30 N + 30 N = 60 N
to the right

The people are pushing the box in opposite directions. The bigger person is pushing the box in the positive direction, so the larger force is positive. The smaller person is pushing the box in the negative direction, so the smaller force is negative. The net force acting on the box is 10 N to the right, and the box moves to the right, which is the direction of the greater force.

Net force:
30 N + (–20 N) = 10 N
to the right

16. Do the Math Determine the strength and direction of net force on the box. Show your calculations and describe what happens to the box.

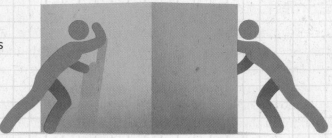

This person is applying 20 N of force to the right.

This person is applying 20 N of force to the left.

EVIDENCE NOTEBOOK

17. Think about the two dogs playing tug of war. What data do you need to be able to calculate the net force on the rope? Record your evidence.

Engineer It
Explain Net Forces

Trains are used around the world to transport goods and people over long distances. Sometimes a train will have two or more locomotives, or engines, pulling it. And, occasionally, a train will have one or more locomotives at the very end.

18. Why would a train need more than one locomotive? Apply what you have learned about forces and net forces to explain what problems might be solved by adding locomotives to a train.

The four locomotives at the front of this train pull the long chain of cars along the tracks.

_____

_____

_____

_____

_____

_____

_____

_____

_____

_____

© Houghton Mifflin Harcourt Publishing Company • Image Credits: ©Mike Danneman/ Moment/Getty Images

Continue Your Exploration

Name: _____   Date: _____

Check out the path below or go online to choose one of the other paths shown.

Roller Coaster Restraints

- • **TV Science Advisors**
- • **Hands-On Labs** ✋
- • **Propose Your Own Path**

Go online to choose one of these other paths.

When you sit in a roller coaster car that is not moving, the force of gravity holds you in your seat, and the seat pushes up on you to balance the force of gravity. Think about what happens when the roller coaster car is moving. You accelerate in many different directions, and the force of gravity may not hold you in your seat. Roller coaster designers have designed different types of restraints to keep you safely in your seat as you accelerate during a ride.

Think of a roller coaster car accelerating down a steep hill. Gravity pulls both you and the car downhill at the same rate. The track keeps the car on a certain path, but what keeps you with the car? Restraints may apply forces to keep you safely in your seat as the car moves.

Look at the different types of restraints in the photos and think about the forces that each restraint exerts on your body. Some restraints allow you to slide around and lift off the seat a little, while others hold you firmly against the seat. Each type of restraint is used because every individual person values staying safe during a thrilling coaster ride.

A T-bar rotates toward a rider and locks in place. This T-bar restraint is combined with an over-the-shoulder restraint.

A lap bar restraint lowers and goes across the lap of a seated rider to prevent the rider from standing up during the ride.

An over-the-shoulder restraint rotates down to fit over the shoulders and sometimes across the chest and waist.

A locking lap bar is similar to a standard lap bar, but more securely locks into place to prevent a rider from falling out.

Continue Your Exploration

1. **Draw** Choose a type of restraint and make a force diagram of the forces acting on a person while sitting in a roller coaster car as it accelerates up a hill.

2. Describe the forces acting on the passenger in your drawing, and explain how these forces affect the motion of the passenger.

3. List the following roller coaster restraints in order from the least restrictive (allows passengers to move in their seats) to the most restrictive (passengers can move very little): over-the-shoulder, T-bar, lap bar, and locking lap bar.

4. **Collaborate** Research and make a recommendation about what types of restraints an engineer should choose when designing a roller coaster. Present your argument about when each type of restraint would be appropriate and what tradeoffs engineers might need to make when choosing restraints for a roller coaster.

Can You Explain It?

Name: _____   **Date:** _____

Which dog will win the tug of war?

EVIDENCE NOTEBOOK

Refer to the notes in your Evidence Notebook to help you determine which dog will win the tug of war.

1. State your claim. Make sure your claim fully explains how you can predict the outcome of the tug of war.

2. Summarize the evidence you have gathered to support your claim and explain your reasoning.

Checkpoints

Answer the following questions to check your understanding of the lesson.

Use the photo to answer Questions 3–4.

3. Which statements are true about the house of cards on the table? Select all that apply.

   A. The force of gravity is acting on the cards and the table.

   B. The forces acting on the house of cards and the table are balanced.

   C. The forces acting on the house of cards and the table are unbalanced.

   D. The house of cards is not stable because too many unbalanced forces are acting on it.

   E. The house of cards is stable because balanced forces are acting on it and the forces are not changing.

   F. The house of cards is stable because there are no forces acting on any of the cards.

4. If you pulled a card from the bottom layer, the house of cards would / would not collapse. The forces would become balanced / unbalanced because friction / gravity would cause the cards to be more flexible / pulled down toward the table.

Use the photo to answer Questions 5–6.

5. The woman is using colorful letters to hold the sheet of paper to the refrigerator. What type of force is pulling the letters toward the refrigerator?

   A. gravitational force

   B. frictional force

   C. air resistance force

   D. magnetic force

6. The force acting between the refrigerator and letters is a contact / noncontact force. The forces acting on the sheet of paper are balanced / unbalanced because there is no change in the force / motion of the paper. The net force on the sheet of paper is 0 N / can't be calculated.

© Houghton Mifflin Harcourt Publishing Company • Image Credits: (t) ©Nigel Noyes/ Photographer's Choice/Getty Images; (b) ©HMH

Interactive Review

Complete this section to review the main concepts of the lesson.

A force is a push or a pull and can change the shape or motion of an object. Forces have strength and direction and are measured in newtons. Balanced forces produce no change in motion, and unbalanced forces produce a change in motion.

A. What do you need to know to analyze the forces in a situation?

People use a variety of forces in everyday activities. Some forces are contact forces, and others are noncontact forces.

B. How does a contact force differ from a noncontact force? Give an everyday example of each.

Objects usually have more than one force acting on them, and the combination of forces on an object is the net force on the object.

C. What model can you use to represent the forces acting on an object? How can it help you determine the net force on the object?

Newton's Laws of Motion Relate Energy, Forces, and Motion

An octopus does not understand Newton's laws of motion, but it demonstrates the laws as it swims around the ocean.

Explore First

Investigating Mass and Motion Place an empty plastic cup on a paper towel. Try to remove the paper towel from under the cup without touching the cup or knocking it over. Fill the cup halfway with water and repeat the task. How did the two tasks compare? Why do you think one task was easier than the other?

CAN YOU EXPLAIN IT?

Why does the golf tee fall into the bottle when the hoop is pulled?

Observe carefully to see how the person gets the golf tee to drop straight into the bottle.

Explore Online

1. What forces act on the golf tee when it is at rest on the hoop? What forces act on the golf tee when it is falling in the bottle?

 EVIDENCE NOTEBOOK As you explore the lesson, gather evidence to help explain the motion of the golf tee.

Describing Motion

Diving into a pool, pedaling a bike, jumping over a puddle, sinking into a comfy chair, and biting into a crisp apple are all types of motion. **Motion** is a change in an object's position over time. Position describes an object's location. Suppose you were diving into a pool. One moment you are standing tall on the edge of the diving board, the next moment you are in the air above the water, and finally, you enter the water. During the dive, you were in motion because your position changed over time.

The motion and the position of an object are related to the object's energy. Any object that is in motion has kinetic energy, and the object's position may determine whether the object has potential energy. An object's energy can be transformed or transferred as the object moves. For example, you have potential energy when you stand on a diving board, and that energy transforms into kinetic energy has you dive toward the water.

A flock of hundreds of starlings fly in formation. They have both kinetic and potential energy when they fly.

2. The starlings flying in formation are / are not in motion. The birds' positions are changing over time. The flock's position can be described as being above / below the clouds and above / below the ground.

3. **Discuss** With a partner, debate whether the couple in the photograph is in motion. Support your claim with evidence.

This couple rides a train to get to their destination.

Motion and Reference Points

How can you tell if something you see is moving? You are actually comparing the object's position to that of another object that appears to stay in place. The object that appears to stay in place is called a **reference point**. You can measure the object's motion as its change in position relative to the reference point, which can be any point you like, as long as you specify what it is. Often it makes sense to choose a set of objects that are all stationary with respect to each other. This set of objects is known as a reference frame. In the train example, you could say that the man and woman are in motion because they are moving relative to the reference frame of the scenery outside the train. However, if you used the train car as your reference frame, you could say that they are not moving.

4. You are in a crowded movie theater waiting for friends and want to describe your location within the theater using reference points. Which descriptions may be unreliable because of the reference point? Select all that apply.

   A. I am sitting near a theater worker, fifth seat from the side.

   B. I am in the fifth row from the back, tenth seat from the right side.

   C. I am in the sixth row from the front, tenth seat from the right side.

   D. I am in the sixth row, to the right of the man in a red shirt.

A radar is used to measure how fast a ball is pitched.

5. The radar device detects the motion of the ball and calculates its speed relative to the pitcher's hand / the swinging bat / the radar device.

Speed, Distance, and Time

If an object's position changes, you know that motion took place but not how quickly the object changed position. The **speed** of an object is a measure of the distance an object moves in a given amount of time. The unit of speed is distance per time, such as meters per second or miles per hour. The choice of what units to use when measuring motion is arbitrary but must be specified so the data can be shared with others. The radar device measures the speed of an object over a very short period of time. The actual speed of an object may vary widely or stay relatively constant. The average speed of an object can be calculated over a longer period of time, such as hours, days, or even longer time periods. For example, the speeds of glaciers are often measured in meters per year.

Average Speed

Knowing that the position of an object has changed tells you that the object moved, but it does not tell you how quickly. The photo shows a dog at three different moments in time. You can see that between each photographed moment, the dog's position has changed. But, this is not enough information to know the speed of the dog. Speed involves two quantities: distance traveled and time traveled. To calculate the speed of the dog, you need to know how much time passed between two photographed moments in time and the distance traveled by the dog during that time. If you know the dog traveled four meters during the two seconds between the first and third moments, you can calculate the speed of the dog as two meters per second. But did the dog travel at exactly two meters per second the entire time? Probably not—it may have slowed down to catch the ball. The speed you calculated is the average speed of the dog during those two seconds. The actual speed of the dog during this time may have varied.

Distance vs. Time

The speed of an object can be determined from a graph of distance traveled over time. The red line shows the distance traveled by a train moving at a constant speed during a four-hour period. The blue line in the graph shows the total distance traveled by a car moving at varying speeds during the same four-hour period.

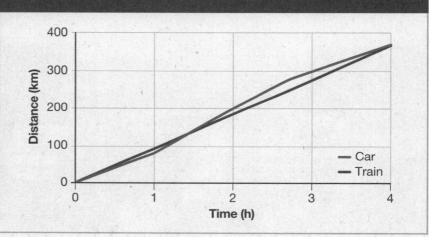

6. Do the Math Use the graph to determine the average speed of the car for the first hour of the trip and for the entire four-hour time period. The total distance traveled for each time period can be read from the blue line on the graph. Estimate the distance traveled to the nearest 10 kilometers.

$$\text{average speed} = \frac{\text{distance traveled}}{\text{travel time}}$$

$$\text{average speed during first hour} = \frac{80 \text{ km}}{1 \text{ h}} = \boxed{80} \text{ km/h}$$

$$\text{average speed for 4 hours} = \frac{\boxed{} \text{ km}}{\boxed{} \text{ h}} = \boxed{} \text{ km/h}$$

Velocity

Sometimes knowing both the speed of an object and which way it is going is important. The velocity of an object is a quantity that describes the speed of the object and its direction of travel. You can think of velocity as the rate of change of an object's position in a reference frame. An object's velocity is constant only if its speed *and* direction do not change. Therefore, constant velocity is always motion along a straight line. If either an object's speed *or* direction changes, its velocity changes. Positive and negative numbers are used to indicate the direction of velocity. If an object moves in the positive direction, a positive number is used to represent the velocity. If an object moves in the opposite direction, the velocity will be negative. Any direction can be positive or negative, but the choice must be consistent. For example, if a ball thrown upwards has a positive velocity when it travels upwards, it must have a negative velocity when it falls.

7. A bus travels north along a straight stretch of road with a constant velocity of 15 m/s. Another bus travels south on the same road at the same speed. What is the velocity of the second bus?

Do the Math
Calculate Resultant Velocity

Suppose that you are riding on a train that is moving in relation to the ground. If you stand up and walk down the aisle while the train is moving, then you are moving relative to the train and to the ground. To find your velocity relative to the ground, add your velocity relative to the train and the train's velocity relative to the ground. Remember that if the velocities are in opposite directions, one velocity will be positive and the other velocity will be negative.

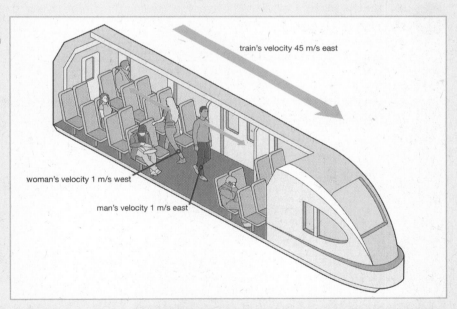

train's velocity 45 m/s east

woman's velocity 1 m/s west

man's velocity 1 m/s east

8. The diagram shows the velocities of a train and two people in the train. If the train is moving in the positive direction, calculate the velocities of the man and woman walking in the train relative to the ground.

Acceleration

The rate at which velocity changes is called acceleration. An object accelerates if its speed, direction, or both change. Velocity is the rate of change of position, and its units are distance per time. If the velocity is measured in meters per second, the acceleration might be measured in meters per second per second, or m/s^2. Like velocity, the direction of acceleration is indicated by using positive and negative numbers. If an object has a positive velocity and its speed increases, it has a positive acceleration. If an object is moving in the positive direction and its speed decreases, it has a negative acceleration. Average acceleration may be calculated in a way similar to average velocity.

Falling objects generally accelerate as they move downward, which means the farther they fall, the faster they travel. As a falling object's velocity increases, its kinetic energy increases, too. The object gains kinetic energy because its gravitational potential energy is converted into kinetic energy as the object moves closer to the ground.

9. **Do the Math** Calculate the average acceleration of the rock in the diagram by using this equation:

$$\text{average acceleration} = \frac{\text{final velocity} - \text{starting velocity}}{\text{time it takes to change velocity}}$$

Use the velocity at 1 second as the starting velocity and the velocity at 4 seconds as the final velocity. Down is the positive direction.

average acceleration = ⬚/⬚ = ⬚/⬚ = ⬚ m/s^2 down

Measure the Motion of a Storm

Suppose that you hear a meteorologist say that a storm is heading east into your area at 40 km/h. What do you know about the motion of the storm?

10. The   speed / velocity   of the storm was given as 40 km/h east. This is the   speed / velocity   because it includes the direction in which the storm is moving in addition to how quickly it is moving. The meteorologist's statement   does / does not   include whether the storm is accelerating.

Analyzing Newton's First Law of Motion

Imagine that you are at bat while playing baseball. The pitch comes in, and—crack—you hit the ball! But instead of the ball flying forward off the bat, the ball just drops straight to the ground. Would that really happen? No! The baseball will move away when you hit it with a bat. You know from experiences like this that the force exerted on an object is related to the motion of the object. In 1686, Isaac Newton explained the relationship between force and motion with three laws of motion.

Newton's First Law of Motion

Newton's first law of motion states that, unless acted on by an unbalanced force, an object at rest stays at rest and an object in motion stays in motion at a constant velocity. In other words, if the forces on an object are balanced, the object will not accelerate. Like velocity and acceleration, forces have direction. A force in one direction will have an opposite sign from a force acting in the opposite direction. To find the net force on an object, add the forces. If the forces on an object are balanced, the net force on the object is 0 N. If the net force is *not* 0 N, the forces are unbalanced and the object will accelerate.

11. A force acting on an object in the upward direction is 3 N. The force that would balance this force could be written as _____. You that know these forces will balance because 3 N + (_____) = _____. The balancing force acts in the _____ direction.

Before the bowling ball hits the pins, the forces on the pins are balanced.
_____

12. Look at the photo of the bowling ball and pins. What do you think will happen next?

Objects at Rest

An object whose position is not changing relative to a reference point is said to be at rest. A golf ball balanced on the tee is an example of an object at rest. The upward force from the tee on the golf ball balances the downward force of gravity on the ball. When the ball is at rest on the tee, no unbalanced forces act on the golf ball. Newton's first law says the golf ball will stay at rest until an unbalanced force acts on the ball. When the moving golf club strikes the ball, it applies an unbalanced force to the golf ball and the ball then moves in the same direction as the unbalanced force.

When an unbalanced force acts on an object, energy is transferred between the object exerting the force to the object that the force acts on. So, when an unbalanced force acts on an object at rest, the object starts to move because energy was transferred to it by the force.

An Object at Rest

The golf ball begins at rest on the tee. When the golf club strikes the ball with an unbalanced force, the ball begins moving in the direction of the force.

Objects in Motion

Newton's first law also says that objects in motion stay in motion with a constant velocity unless they are acted on by an unbalanced force. Recall that if an object moves at a constant velocity, both its speed and direction do not change. Imagine that you are driving a bumper car at an amusement park. Your ride is pleasant—and your velocity is constant—as long as you are driving in an open space. But the name of the game is bumper cars! Eventually, another car hits you head-on, exerting an unbalanced force on your car. As a result, your bumper car stops moving forward. Note that the *car* stops moving, but not you! You continue to move forward in your seat until the unbalanced force from your seat belt stops you.

An Object in Motion

Bumper cars demonstrate how an unbalanced force can change the motion of a moving object.

© Houghton Mifflin Harcourt Publishing Company • Image Credits: (t) ©Image Studios/UpperCut Images/Getty Images; (b) ©Joe McBride/The Image Bank/Getty Images

Friction and Newton's First Law

Imagine a baseball player sliding into second base. The player must run quickly before sliding, and she can slide for only a short distance before stopping. Newton's first law says that an unbalanced force must act on the player to make her stop. The unbalanced force that causes the player to stop sliding is friction. *Friction* is a force that opposes motion between two surfaces that are in contact. To balance the force of friction, a force often needs to be applied to an object to keep the object moving at a constant velocity.

The force of friction causes objects to slow down because of energy transformations and transfers. Friction can cause the kinetic energy of a moving object to be transformed into other forms of energy such as thermal energy or sound energy. Friction can also cause the kinetic energy of a moving object to be transferred to the object that it is rubbing against.

13. Look at the photo of the penguins sliding on the frozen ground. Use Newton's first law of motion to explain the motion of the penguins.

Emperor penguins slide on the frozen ground in Antarctica.

14. **Act** Imagine the penguins in the photo decide to put on a performance on ice. Perform a dance routine or slapstick routine as if you were one of the penguins being sure to include the effects of Newton's first law in your routine.

Inertia and Newton's First Law

Newton's first law of motion is sometimes called the *law of inertia*. **Inertia** is the tendency of objects to resist any change in motion. Because of inertia, an object at rest will remain at rest unless a force makes it move. Similarly, inertia is the reason a moving object stays in motion with the same velocity unless a force changes its speed or direction.

15. Imagine that a passenger sets a phone on the dashboard of a car and that there is little friction between the phone and the dashboard. The car moves at a constant velocity and then turns. What do you expect to happen to the phone when the car turns?

   A. The phone will stay in the same position on the dashboard because inertia will keep it at rest as the car turns.

   B. The phone will slide sideways across the dashboard because inertia will keep it moving in a straight line as the car turns.

   C. The phone will slide forward into the windshield because inertia will keep it moving forward.

   D. The phone will stay in the same position on the dashboard because inertia will cause it to turn with the car.

Mass and Inertia

Objects that have more mass have more inertia than objects that have less mass do. In fact, mass is a measure of inertia. More force is needed to overcome the inertia of a massive object and change its motion than is needed to cause the same change in the motion of a less massive object. A change in motion is an acceleration, which can be an increase in velocity, a decrease in velocity, or a change of direction. Imagine how much force you need to pick up a bucket full of water compared to an empty bucket. You need more force to pick up the full bucket because it has more mass and thus more inertia.

16. A person on a bicycle and a person driving a car are at rest at a stop light. The light turns green and both the cyclist and car begin to move. You would expect the *bicycle / car* to accelerate more quickly because the car has *less / more* mass than the bicycle does, and thus the car has *less / more* inertia.

EVIDENCE NOTEBOOK

17. How does Newton's first law apply to the motion of the golf tee that falls from the hoop into the bottle? Record your evidence.

Engineer It
Design Vehicles for Safety

To improve safety, engineers study impacts that people might experience in a car. Think about a bumper car collision and how it compares to a collision of a real car. Bumper cars have minimal safety equipment, such as simple lap bars or loose shoulder belts. Real cars have more safety features including airbags and locking shoulder and lap belts.

18. How does the airbag in the photo affect the motion of the driver in the car? Would this airbag protect the driver from a sideways collision? Explain your answer.

_____
_____
_____
_____
_____

Analyzing Newton's Second Law of Motion

You know from Newton's first law of motion that when an unbalanced force acts on an object, the object's motion changes. In other words, it accelerates. Newton's second law describes the relationship between the acceleration and mass of an object when an unbalanced force is applied to the object.

The boy pushes a loaded cart down a school hallway.

The same loaded cart is now pushed by two people.

19. How might the motion of the cart change when two people push the cart rather than when the boy pushes the cart by himself?

Newton's Second Law of Motion

Newton's second law of motion says that the acceleration of an object depends on the mass of the object and the amount of force applied. Notice that when talking about an applied force, it refers to the net force on an object because only unbalanced forces will affect the acceleration of an object.

The boy pushes the same cart, but it is now empty.

To understand Newton's second law, consider the amount of force needed to accelerate two different masses. Think about the boy pushing the cart when it is loaded and when it is empty. If he wants the cart to accelerate at the same rate whether it is loaded or empty, he must adjust the amount of force that he uses to push the cart.

20. When the cart is empty, it has less / more mass than when the cart is loaded. The boy must apply less / more force to the loaded cart for its acceleration to be the same as when it is empty.

Hands-On Lab
Investigate Motion

Explore the relationships among force, mass, and acceleration by investigating the motion of a cart that has a constant mass. Increase the force applied to the cart and then measure the resulting acceleration of the cart using an accelerometer.

MATERIALS
- accelerometer
- cart, mass of at least 2 kg
- clamp
- hanger for masses
- masses, slotted or hanging, each 100 g (4)
- pillow
- pulley with string
- video camera (optional)

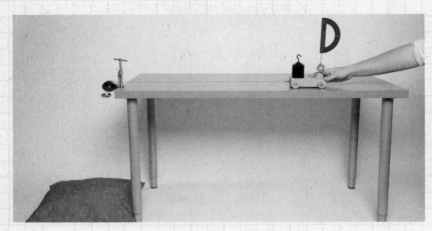

Procedure

STEP 1 Set up the experiment as shown in the photo. The cart is connected to a hanging mass by a string, and the string passes over a pulley mounted at the edge of the table. A pillow will stop the hanging mass at the floor.

STEP 2 You will use the slotted or hanging masses hanging on the string to pull the cart with a constant force. To determine the amount of force for the different masses, multiply the mass, in kilograms, by the acceleration due to gravity, 9.8 m/s². The result will be the force in newtons (N). On a separate sheet of paper, record your answers in a table similar to the one shown.

Mass	Force (N)
100 g = 0.1 kg	0.98

STEP 3 Design a method to measure the acceleration of the cart when it is pulled by different amounts of force. Describe the method you will use.

STEP 4 Carry out your experiment.

STEP 5 Use the following table to convert the angle the string makes on the accelerometer (protractor) to acceleration.

Angle (degrees)	Acceleration (m/s²)
0	0
5	0.86
10	1.7
15	2.6
20	3.5
25	4.6
30	5.7
35	6.9

STEP 6 Repeat Steps 4 and 5 using different amounts of force to pull the cart. On a separate sheet of paper, record the force and acceleration data in a table similar to the one shown.

Force (N)	Acceleration (m/s²)

Analysis

STEP 7 Graph the acceleration and force data by graphing force on the *x*-axis and acceleration on the *y*-axis.

STEP 8 What relationship do you see between the acceleration and force when the mass of the cart is constant?

Do the Math
Express Newton's Second Law Mathematically

The relationship of force (F), mass (m), and acceleration (a) can be expressed mathematically with the equation $F = ma$, where force is in newtons (N), mass is in kilograms (kg), and acceleration is in meters per second squared (m/s^2). The table shows ways that this equation can be rearranged to calculate one of the variables when you know the other two.

Three Forms of Newton's Second Law		
I Want to Know	**I Know**	**Use This Equation**
acceleration (a)	mass (m) and force (F)	$a = F/m$
force (F)	mass (m) and acceleration (a)	$F = ma$
mass (m)	force (F) and acceleration (a)	$m = F/a$

21. Complete the table for the equation $a = F/m$, when $m = 1$ kg. Then graph the points.

Force (N)	Acceleration (m/s²)
0	0
1	
2	
3	

22. How does this graph compare to the data you graphed in the Hands-On Lab? How and why might they differ?

Newton's Second Law of Motion and Friction

As you have seen, the acceleration of an object depends on the applied force. If you have ever pushed cart, you know that you must continually push on the cart to keep it moving at a constant velocity. The cart does not accelerate even though you are pushing it because of friction. In this case, your pushing force is balanced by the force of friction, so the net force on the cart is 0 N, and the cart continues to move at a constant velocity.

The Relationship between Acceleration, Mass, and Force

According to Newton's second law of motion, the relationship between acceleration and force can be represented mathematically by the equation $a = F/m$. By looking at this equation, you can see that when force increases, the acceleration of an object with constant mass also increases. So, the object's acceleration is *directly proportional* to the net force acting on the object.

Imagine that you are helping a library move and have to lift boxes of books onto a cart. Most of the boxes are full of books, so when you lift each box, you use the same amount of force. But one of the boxes was closed with only a few books in it. Not knowing that this box has less mass, you lift this box with the same amount of force as you used to lift the full boxes. How will the acceleration of this box compare to the acceleration of a full box? Newton's second law of motion tells you that if the force remains constant and the mass is decreased, the object will accelerate at a faster rate. Because acceleration increases when mass decreases, acceleration is *inversely proportional* to mass.

The equation for Newton's second law can be rearranged to the form $F = ma$, which shows the force exerted by an object is directly proportional to its mass and its acceleration. Suppose that an asteroid that has a lot of mass has a high acceleration when it strikes a planet. The equation for Newton's second law shows that the asteroid would exert a lot of force when it strikes a planet.

23. Give an example of when you might use the formula for Newton's second law to solve a problem. Explain how the formula would be useful in this situation.

EVIDENCE NOTEBOOK

24. How does Newton's second law apply to the golf tee balanced on the hoop? How does Newton's second law apply to the golf tee when the hoop is pulled away? Record your evidence.

Engineer It
Relate Vehicle Mass to Performance

For a Formula One racecar, the ability to accelerate is critical to the car's performance. Much design effort is spent to develop racecar technology that meets the needs of Formula One drivers. How might the mass of a racecar affect its performance?

25. Engineers want a racecar to have as much / little mass as possible. A car with less mass requires less / more force to accelerate at the same rate as a car with more mass does. So if two cars have the same engine, the car with less mass can accelerate less / more quickly than the car with more mass.

Engineers design racecars to accelerate quickly.

Analyzing Newton's Third Law of Motion

Newton's Third Law of Motion

Newton's third law of motion describes the forces involved when two objects interact. This law states that when one object applies a force to a second object, the second object applies an equal and opposite force to the first object. So when you exert a force to turn a screwdriver, the screwdriver exerts a turning force on you.

26. Astronauts use specially designed screwdrivers in space. Using Newton's third law of motion, explain why it might be difficult to use a normal screwdriver to tighten a screw in space.

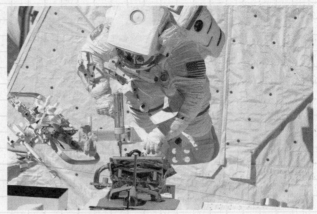

No frictional forces hold astronauts steady when they float in space, so the effects of Newton's third law can be surprising.

Action and Reaction Forces

The pair of forces described by Newton's third law are called action and reaction forces. Such action and reaction force pairs are present whenever two objects interact, even when there is no acceleration. For example, your body exerts a downward action force, your weight, on a chair when you sit on it. The upward reaction force, equal to your weight but in the opposite direction, is the force exerted by the chair on your body.

The action and reaction forces of a pair do not act on the same object. If they did, the net force would always be 0 N and nothing would ever accelerate! In the chair example, you are applying a force to the chair, and the chair is applying a force to you. The object you are analyzing determines which force is the action and which is the reaction. If you are interested in the chair, the upward force is the action force.

When you are identifying force pairs, the action and reaction forces are always the same kind of force. For example, the reaction to a frictional force is a frictional force, and the reaction to a magnetic force is also a magnetic force.

This swimmer's feet push against the wall of the pool, and the wall pushes back against the swimmer's feet.

Language SmArts
Identify Force Pairs

You rely on action and reaction force pairs when you interact with objects every day. When you apply forces to objects, the reaction force on your body gives you information about the interaction.

A child attempts to hit a piñata with a stick.

27. Draw Imagine that the child in the photo is given earplugs, in addition to being blindfolded, so that he cannot see or hear. Draw a force diagram to show how Newton's third law helps him know if he successfully hit the piñata. Include the appropriate force pairs and labels in your drawing.

28. Describe the different action and reaction force pairs involved when the child hits the piñata.

Newton's Second and Third Laws of Motion Combined

Gravity is a force of attraction between objects that is due to their masses. An asteroid will fall to Earth because gravity pulls the asteroid toward Earth. This force is the action force exerted by Earth's gravity on the asteroid. But gravity also pulls Earth toward the asteroid. This force is the reaction force exerted by the asteroid on Earth. The effect of the action force is easy to see—the asteroid falls to Earth. Why do you not notice the effect of the reaction force—Earth being pulled upward?

Newton's third law says that when two objects interact, equal but opposite forces act on them. Newton's second law says that if the two objects have different masses, they will have different accelerations when acted on by the same force. In this example, the force acting on Earth is equal to the force acting on the asteroid, but the mass of Earth is much larger than the mass of the asteroid. Therefore, the acceleration of Earth due to this force is much smaller than the acceleration of the asteroid.

Action and reaction forces also occur when objects collide. Imagine walking around a corner in a hallway and bumping into someone much larger than you. What happens to your motion compared to the other person's motion? Think of other examples in which two objects with different masses collide. How do Newton's laws of motion describe what happens after these collisions?

action force

reaction force

29. A particular bowling ball has a mass of 7 kg, and a standard bowling pin has a mass of 1.5 kg. Use Newton's third law to describe what you expect to happen when the bowling ball collides with the pin. The ball applies an action force to the pin, and the pin applies an equal *action / reaction* force to the ball. The forces in this force pair act in *the same direction / opposite directions* . Using Newton's second law, you know that the pin will accelerate *more / less* than the ball because it has less mass than the ball does.

Apply Newton's Third Law

30. Ouch! Suppose that you bumped your hand against the edge of a table. Use Newton's third law of motion to explain why your hand hurt.

_____

_____

_____

_____

_____

_____

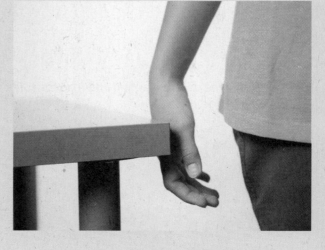

Continue Your Exploration

Name: _____   Date: _____

Check out the path below or go online to choose one of the other paths shown.

Baseball vs. Softball

- Objects in the Space Station
- Hands-On Labs ✋
- Propose Your Own Path

Go online to choose one of these other paths.

Baseball and softball are beloved games played all around the world. They share some similarities, such as being played on a diamond, hitting a ball with a bat, and running around bases. However, compared to a softball, a baseball is lighter and has a smaller circumference, which is the distance measured around the ball. Official game rules allow a narrow range of measurements, as shown in the table.

	Baseball	Softball
Mass	142 to 149 g (5 to $5\frac{1}{4}$ oz)	184 to 198 g ($6\frac{1}{2}$ to 7 oz)
Circumference	229 to 235 mm (9 to $9\frac{1}{4}$ in.)	302 to 311 mm ($11\frac{7}{8}$ to $12\frac{1}{4}$ in.)

When a bat hits a ball, some energy is transferred from the bat to the ball. In addition to this energy transfer, Newton's laws of motion can be used to analyze the motion of both the bat and the ball before, during, and after their collision.

This baseball player is about to hit the ball with a certain amount of force.

If this softball player hits the ball with the same amount of force as the baseball player uses, the ball will not go as far.

Continue Your Exploration

1. Use Newton's laws of motion to explain why it is important that baseballs and softballs each have a small acceptable range of masses.

2. Consider Newton's laws of motion. How would changing the mass of a bat affect a player's ability to swing the bat and adjust the path of the bat to hit a moving baseball or softball?

3. If a player swings a more massive bat with the same acceleration as a less massive bat, which bat would you expect to hit a baseball farther? Explain your reasoning.

4. If a player swings the same bat with the same acceleration to hit a baseball and then a softball, which ball would you expect to go farther? Explain your reasoning using all three of Newton's laws of motion.

5. **Collaborate** Discuss with a partner whether you, as a baseball or softball player, would choose a more or less massive bat. Explain your reasoning.

Can You Explain It?

Name: _____ Date: _____

Why does the golf tee fall into the bottle when the hoop is pulled?

Explore Online

 EVIDENCE NOTEBOOK

Refer to the notes in your Evidence Notebook to help you construct an explanation for the motion of the golf tee.

1. State your claim. Make sure your claim fully explains why the golf tee falls into the bottle when the hoop is pulled.

2. Summarize the evidence you have gathered to support your claim and explain your reasoning.

Checkpoints

Answer the following questions to check your understanding of the lesson.

Use the photo to answer Questions 3–4.

3. This rock, known as Balanced Rock, sits on a thin pedestal of rock in a canyon in Idaho. Balanced Rock exerts *a downward / an upward* force on the pedestal. At the same time, the pedestal exerts *a downward / an upward* force that is equal in size and opposite in direction.

4. Which statement accurately describes the motion of Balanced Rock relative to the chosen reference points?

   A. The rock is moving compared to the sun.

   B. The rock is moving compared to the trees.

   C. The rock is at rest compared to a squirrel running by.

   D. The rock is at rest no matter which reference point is used.

Use the photo to answer Questions 5–6.

5. Imagine that the truck in the photo is acted on by an unbalanced force from the thrust of the air exiting the balloon. From the reference point of the truck, the balloon *is / is not* moving. The balloon *is / is not* moving relative to the reference point of the tape on the floor.

6. As the balloon pushes air backward, Newton's *first / second / third* law of motion states that the air will push the balloon forward. The balloon is attached to the truck, so the force on the balloon is also applied to the truck. Newton's *first / second / third* law of motion states that this *balanced / unbalanced* force on the truck will cause the truck to move forward. Finally, Newton's *first / second / third* law of motion says that the acceleration of the truck will be *directly / inversely* proportional to the unbalanced force on the truck.

7. Given the distance an object travels and the amount of time needed to travel that distance, which of the following can you determine?

   A. The average speed of the object over the given time.

   B. The average velocity of the object over the given time.

   C. The average acceleration of the object over the given time.

Interactive Review

Complete this section to review the main concepts of the lesson.

Motion is a change in position over time relative to a reference point. Speed, velocity, and acceleration are used to describe the motion of objects.

A. How are speed, velocity, and acceleration related to each other?

Newton's first law says that an object at rest stays at rest and an object in motion stays in motion at the same speed and direction unless acted on by an unbalanced force.

B. What is inertia, and how does it relate to Newton's first law?

Newton's second law says that the acceleration of an object depends on the mass of the object and the amount of force applied to the object.

C. What is the relationship between force, mass, and acceleration?

Newton's third law says that whenever one object exerts a force on a second object, the second object exerts an equal and opposite force on the first.

D. Draw a force diagram to model two interacting objects. Show the forces and motion where appropriate.

Collisions between Objects

Percussionists, such as these drummers, use collisions to make music.

Explore First

Analyzing Collisions Roll a toy car so that it collides with an identical toy car and observe what happens. Then collide a toy car with a toy car that has a different mass. Try colliding the cars at different speeds. Compare the results of the collisions. Why do you think the results were different?

Go online to view the digital version of the Hands-On Lab for this lesson and to download additional lab resources.

CAN YOU EXPLAIN IT?

How can Newton's laws be applied to protect a smartphone screen during a collision?

People carry smartphones everywhere. If people are not careful, they can drop or bump their smartphones into other objects. Smartphones may be damaged in a collision.

1. Oh no! Have you ever seen this problem with a smartphone or a tablet? How do you think cases help protect smartphones and tablets from damage?

 EVIDENCE NOTEBOOK As you work through the lesson, record evidence that helps you determine how to protect a smartphone screen during a collision.

Applying Newton's Laws to Collisions

Collisions between objects happen every day. A collision may be as simple as a ball bouncing on the ground, but other collisions, such as car crashes, may involve many objects and multiple impacts. These complex collisions may be more difficult to analyze than simple collisions. The motion of each object in a collision can be described by Newton's laws of motion.

2. **Discuss** Over the years, many asteroids and meteorites have collided with Earth. Many of these collisions occurred long ago, and the craters have changed due to weathering. Look at the shape of Meteor Crater. What information does the crater's shape give you about the collision? What do you think happened to life in the area after the impact?

Meteor Crater in Arizona is a well-preserved impact site on Earth. The crater is about 1.3 kilometers across and 174 meters deep. It formed approximately 50,000 years ago.

Newton's Third Law of Motion and Collisions

When two objects collide, each object pushes the other. When you hit a softball with a bat, the bat collides with the ball and pushes it away. The ball also exerts a force on the bat, which causes a stinging sensation in your hand as the bat vibrates.

Newton's third law states that when one object exerts a force on another, the second object exerts an equal but opposite force on the first object. These forces are sometimes called action and reaction forces or force pairs. These forces act only during the collision itself, which is often a very short period of time.

When the masses of two colliding objects are very different, the effect on the smaller object is greater than the effect on the larger one. When you hit the ball with the bat, the ball flies away, but you and the bat do not. When an asteroid strikes Earth, the force that the asteroid exerts on Earth is the same strength as the force Earth exerts on the asteroid, but the effects are very different. Earth's crust gets a small crater, and the asteroid is destroyed.

Newton's Second Law of Motion and Collisions

The robots are kicking identical balls, and each kick is a collision. The effect of each kick on each ball depends on the force of the kick. The force of the robot's kick causes the ball to accelerate. Remember that a change in the speed or direction of an object is acceleration. The robot is much more massive than the ball is, so the robot accelerates less than the ball does during the collision. This example illustrates Newton's second law of motion—the acceleration of an object depends on the mass of the object and the force applied to it $(F = ma)$.

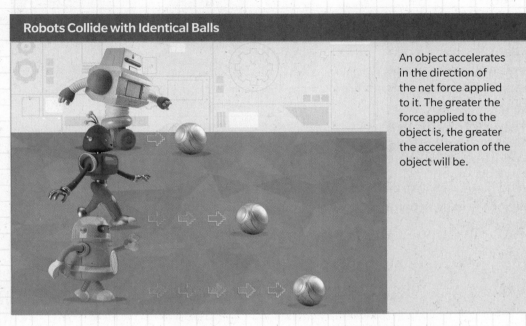

Robots Collide with Identical Balls

An object accelerates in the direction of the net force applied to it. The greater the force applied to the object is, the greater the acceleration of the object will be.

3. If the balls start at rest, the ball kicked with the most force will accelerate faster / slower than the other balls after it is kicked. The ball with the greatest velocity will travel the farthest / shortest distance after it is kicked. The yellow / red / blue robot kicked with the most force. The evidence is the distance the ball traveled / size of the robot.

4. **Draw** Make a sketch of a satellite colliding with debris in space. In your sketch, show the forces involved and indicate their likely effects.

Newton's First Law of Motion and Collisions

Different objects behave differently during collisions. Many objects deform, or change shape, during a collision. Cars are designed to deform in specific ways during a collision. This design is an important safety feature because it reduces the force acting on the passengers in the car. Some of the kinetic energy of the moving car causes the vehicle to deform rather than affecting the passengers.

Recall that Newton's first law of motion describes the inertia of an object, or an object's resistance to a change in motion. How does inertia affect collisions? Look at the car crash shown in the photo. You know that when the car stops, the passengers will continue to move due to inertia. This inertia is why cars have seat belts and airbags to stop passengers during a collision.

Automotive engineers study collisions to protect passengers from harm in collisions such as this one.

5. **Collaborate** With a partner, analyze the collision shown in the photo. Use your knowledge of Newton's laws of motion and collisions to describe the motion of the car throughout the collision.

Simple Collisions

A simple collision can be analyzed using Newton's laws of motion. When analyzing a simple collision, deformations are not considered. Analyzing simple collisions can help engineers and scientists explain more complex collisions, such as car crashes. Examples of simple collisions show how the masses of the objects in a collision affect the objects' motions before, during, and after a collision. As you think about the following examples, consider how each of Newton's laws of motion can be applied to each situation.

Collisions between Objects with Equal Masses

The two marbles shown in the diagram have the same mass. Before the collision, the blue marble is moving from left to right, and the orange marble is at rest. From Newton's first law, you know that the blue marble will continue to move and the orange marble will stay at rest until they collide. When the marbles collide, Newton's third law tells you that the force each exerts on the other is equal in strength and opposite in direction. Because the masses are the same, Newton's second law tells you that the acceleration of the marbles after the collision will also be equal and opposite. The blue marble accelerates in the direction of the force exerted on it. In this example, this acceleration is in the opposite direction of the marble's original velocity, and the blue marble's speed decreases. One possible result of this collision would be that the blue marble stops moving and the orange marble begins moving to the right at the same speed that the blue marble initially had.

During the collision, each marble exerts a force on the other marble. This force pair is shown in the image.

6. Explain how the collision would or would not change if both marbles were moving before the collision, instead of only the blue marble moving. Use Newton's laws of motion to support your reasoning.

Collisions between Objects with Different Masses

Many collisions involve objects that have different masses. The objects in the collision shown will exert equal and opposite forces on one another. From Newton's second law, you know that the acceleration of an object depends on its mass and the applied force. How will that relationship affect a collision between two objects that have different masses?

A glass marble collides with a steel ball. Both have the same dimensions, but the steel ball has a greater mass.

7. Based on Newton's laws of motion, which of the statements are true about the collision of two objects that have different masses? Select all that apply.

A. The objects exert equal and opposite forces on one another.

B. The more massive object will exert a greater force on the less massive object.

C. Each object will accelerate in an opposite direction from the other but at a different rate.

D. The less massive object will accelerate due to the force of the collision, but the more massive object will not.

© Houghton Mifflin Harcourt Publishing Company

Do the Math
Analyze Acceleration During a Collision

When two objects with the same mass collide, Newton's laws tell you that they will accelerate at the same rate, but in opposite directions. The marbles shown in the diagram have the same mass. Before the collision, the marbles move with equal speeds in opposite directions. Recall that force, velocity, and acceleration have both magnitude and direction. Positive and negative signs are used to indicate the direction of each of these quantities.

The force arrows on each marble are equal in magnitude and opposite in direction.

8. Before the collision, the blue marble is moving from left to right, and it has a velocity of 2 m/s. The orange marble is moving at an equal speed, but in the opposite direction. What is the velocity of the orange marble before the collision?

9. During the collision, both marbles accelerate to a stop, or to a velocity of 0 m/s. Use the formula $V_{final} - V_{initial}$ to calculate the change in velocities for the orange and blue marbles.

   Orange marble: 0 m/s – (–2 m/s) = 2 m/s

   Blue marble: 0 m/s – 2 m/s =

10. How do the changes in the velocities of the marbles compare?

11. The velocities of the marbles change, so you know that the marbles accelerate. Acceleration is the rate of change of velocity, which is the change in velocity divided by time. To calculate acceleration during a collision, the time is the duration of the collision, which is the same for both objects in the collision. Compare the accelerations of the blue and orange marbles during this collision.

12. Use Newton's laws of motion to write a description of the motion of both marbles during this collision.

Collisions with Objects in Contact

What happens when an object collides with a second identical object that is touching a third identical object? The object in the middle transfers the force of the collision to the third object. The third object will then move as a result of the collision, but the second object will not move. For example, look at the toy in the photo. When a ball is moving, it has kinetic energy, which is transferred to the other balls during each collision. During each transfer, some energy is lost from the system as it is transformed into other types of energy, such as sound energy. The clicking sound during each collision is evidence of these transformations.

The Newton's cradle is an example of how collisions work when objects are in contact.

 13. **Language SmArts** Based on Newton's laws of motion, you might expect that once the Newton's cradle is set in motion, it will stay in motion forever. Make an argument about whether this is true or not and support your claim with evidence.

 EVIDENCE NOTEBOOK

14. Why might a smartphone be damaged when it falls on a hard surface? Record your evidence.

Analyze a Bocce Shot

In the game of bocce, two teams roll their balls toward a target ball. The goal of the game is to have the ball that is the closest to the small, white target ball after each team throws their balls.

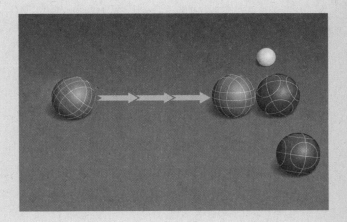

15. The blue team rolls one of their balls toward another of their balls, which is touching an opponent's ball as shown. Explain whether this is a good shot for the blue team.

Engineering a Solution to a Collision Problem

Effects of Collisions

People sometimes use collisions to achieve a goal, such as hammering a nail, bowling, or playing soccer. Unfortunately, not all effects of collisions are desirable; they can be dangerous or damaging. Imagine the hammer hitting your thumb instead of the nail. Ouch! Because damaging collisions sometimes happen, engineers work to develop solutions to reduce the damage caused by collisions.

The airbag will protect the cyclist as he lands.

16. **Draw** The airbag in the photo is designed to slowly bring the stunt cyclist to a rest. Imagine this collision in slow motion and draw a series of three images showing the motion of the cyclist at the beginning, middle, and end of the collision with the airbag.

17. **Discuss** With a partner, discuss how the motion of the stunt cyclist relates to the forces acting on the stunt cyclist during the collision.

The Engineering Design Process

Like all engineers, the engineers who work to reduce collision damage use the engineering design process to develop solutions. The process has several steps, and engineers do not always follow the steps in order. Often, after a problem has been identified and defined, engineers design a solution, test the design, and find a problem with it. They then go back to an earlier step in the process to make a change. The key steps to the engineering design process are listed below.

• **Identifying the Problem or Need** Engineers determine the societal, technological, or scientific problem that must be solved.

• **Defining the Problem** The problem is precisely defined using criteria and constraints.

• **Developing and Testing Solutions** Solutions are proposed, evaluated, and tested.

• **Optimizing Solutions** The best features of various solutions may be combined to build the best solution.

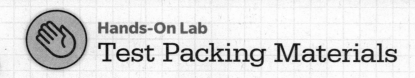

Hands-On Lab
Test Packing Materials

Use the engineering design process to design a testing method and perform tests on different packing materials.

Packaging designers need data about packing materials to choose the best materials to meet their needs. The engineering problem that you will solve is to design a test to collect these data. A successful testing method is repeatable and will give engineers the data they need to choose the best materials for their packing needs.

MATERIALS
- balance
- box, cardboard, about 6 in. on each side
- bubble packing
- cotton balls
- egg, hard-boiled
- meterstick
- rubber bands
- tape or glue

Procedure and Analysis

STEP 1 The engineering design process includes defining the problem. The list below is an incomplete list of criteria and constraints for this engineering design problem. With your group, discuss the problem and add at least one constraint and one criterion to better define the problem.

Criteria	Constraints
Testing method can be used to test a variety of materials.	Testing method can be performed with materials available in the classroom
	Testing can be completed within one class period.

STEP 2 Developing solutions includes brainstorming ideas. Brainstorm ideas for testing methods that can be used to evaluate different packing materials. Record each idea in a notebook, but do not evaluate the ideas yet.

STEP 3 Developing solutions includes evaluating ideas. Choose a method from Step 2 that you will implement. Describe the method, and explain why it is the most promising solution. Show your method and explanation to your teacher.

STEP 4 Implement your chosen testing method, and record the test results for each of the packing materials being tested.

Students examine their egg after a test.

STEP 5 Does your testing method satisfy your criteria and constraints? If you were given a chance to optimize your solution, describe how you would improve your testing method.

STEP 6 Based on your testing, what qualities make a material useful for protecting an item during a collision?

EVIDENCE NOTEBOOK

18. How can the lab results help you design protection for a smartphone screen during a collision? Record your evidence.

Energy and Collisions

Objects and systems may contain different amounts and types of energy. When an object is moving, it has kinetic energy. What happens to this energy during a collision? Some of the energy remains with the object, some of the energy is transferred from one object to the other, and some of the energy is transformed into other forms, such as sound energy or thermal energy. If an object in a collision is made of an elastic material, the energy may temporarily be stored as elastic potential energy as the object deforms. When the object returns to its original shape, this elastic potential energy transforms back into kinetic energy. Whenever energy is transformed into another form, some of the energy is lost from the system as an output. These losses may be desirable depending on the situation. For example, when a percussionist hits a drum, some of the energy is transformed into sound energy and is an output of the system. While Newton's laws of motion can be used to describe the motion of objects during a collision, sometimes other concepts, such as energy, are needed to fully analyze a collision.

19. Language SmArts The image shows a tennis ball during a collision with the ground. Explain in detail why the tennis ball bounces. Use Newton's laws of motion and information from the text to support your reasoning.

A tennis ball deforms as it bounces on the ground.

The Duration of a Collision

When objects collide, the duration of the collision is measured from the time of initial contact to the time when the objects are no longer in contact or when they have stopped accelerating relative to each other. If an object deforms during a collision, the duration of the collision is extended, and the object's acceleration is affected.

20. Do the Math Objects A and B, each with a mass of 20 kg, collide with a much larger object. Both A and B have a velocity of 10 m/s just before the collision and come to a full stop after the collision. The duration of the collision of object A is 0.001 s. The duration of the collision of object B is 0.002 s. Calculate the acceleration of each object using the formula $a = (V_{final} - V_{initial})/t$.

Object A $\dfrac{0\,\text{m/s} - 10\,\text{m/s}}{0.001\,\text{s}} = \dfrac{-10\,\text{m/s}}{0.001\,\text{s}} = -10{,}000\,\text{m/s}^2$

Object B $\dfrac{0\,\text{m/s} - 10\,\text{m/s}}{\boxed{}\,\text{s}} = \dfrac{-10\,\text{m/s}}{\boxed{}\,\text{s}} = \boxed{}\,\text{m/s}^2$

21. Use the accelerations of objects A and B to explain how a collision's duration affects the object's acceleration.

Design Packaging

Products shipped all over the world often need to be protected from collisions that occur during shipping. Shipping packages require various resources, such as material resources used to make the packaging and energy resources consumed during transportation.

22. Explain how you would begin designing a solution to the problem of protecting a fragile item, such as a laptop, during shipping.

_____

_____

_____

_____

_____

A drone delivers a package.

23. Explain how you would modify your technological design solution if the criterion of reducing natural resource use was added to the engineering problem.

_____

_____

_____

Continue Your Exploration

Name: _____ Date: _____

Check out the path below or go online to choose one of the other paths shown.

Careers in Engineering

- **Wrecking Ball Demolitions**
- **Hands-On Labs** 🖑
- **Propose Your Own Path**

Go online to choose one of these other paths.

Crash Test Engineer

You have probably seen videos of crash test dummies in a car collision. Crash test engineers design ways to test the effects of a car collision on a car's passengers and to improve car designs to be safer. Recording devices on crash test dummies measure forces experienced by the dummies during a collision. Engineers then analyze these data and use them to design better safety devices for vehicles. Safety measures include devices such as safety belts and airbags, which apply forces directly to passengers to protect them. Car bodies themselves are engineered to deform in specific places to protect the passengers. A crash test engineer often has a degree in mechanical engineering or industrial engineering. The job requires an understanding of physics, math, and how to use computers to analyze data.

A crash test is performed with a cyclist colliding with the side of a car. Video and sensors on the crash test dummies record data about the acceleration and forces experienced by the dummies.

Continue Your Exploration

1. Based on the description of a crash test engineer's job, which of these engineering tasks might the engineer work on? Select all that apply.

   A. testing prototypes of a new design to determine whether they meet safety criteria

   B. choosing materials used in automobile manufacturing

   C. studying customer preferences to improve marketing

   D. using a computer to analyze large amounts of data

2. Which of the following may affect a passenger's safety during a collision? Select all that apply.

   A. the mass of the automobile in which the passenger rides

   B. the mass of the automobile that collides with the passenger's vehicle

   C. the velocity of the passenger's vehicle

   D. the acceleration of the passenger's vehicle during the collision

3. Automobiles did not always have safety devices such as safety belts, airbags, and roll cages. What societal needs led to the development of these safety measures and the career of crash test engineering?

4. **Collaborate** Working with a partner or a group, consider the engineering design process involved in making cars and trucks. Make a list of other jobs in the automotive industry that could also be filled by mechanical or industrial engineers.

Can You Explain It?

Name: _____ **Date:** _____

How can Newton's laws be applied to protect a smartphone screen during a collision?

EVIDENCE NOTEBOOK

Refer to the notes in your Evidence Notebook to help you construct an explanation for how to protect a smartphone screen during a collision.

1. State your claim. Make sure your claim fully explains how a smartphone can be protected during a collision.

2. Summarize the evidence you have gathered to support your claim and explain your reasoning.

Checkpoints

Answer the following questions to check your understanding of the lesson.

Use the photo to answer Questions 3–4.

3. The mat in the photo helps protect the gymnast by decreasing / increasing the duration of the collision between the gymnast and the floor. Decreasing / Increasing the duration of the collision decreases the acceleration / velocity of the gymnast during the collision.

4. Which of the following criteria are satisfied by the mat in the photo? Select all that apply.

   A. does not interfere with gymnast during a routine on the rings

   B. is easily transported by a single person

   C. protects a gymnast from injury during a dismount from the rings

   D. fits in a small car

Use the photo to answer Question 5.

5. The photo shows evidence of meteorites colliding with the moon. According to Newton's laws, which statement accurately describes these collisions?

   A. During each collision, the moon exerted a greater force on each meteorite than each meteorite exerted on the moon.

   B. The moon and meteorites exerted equal but opposite forces on each other.

   C. The collisions were so small that no forces acted on either the moon or the meteorites during the collisions.

   D. Because the moon has no atmosphere, Newton's laws cannot be applied to the collisions between the moon and meteorites.

6. In a simple collision between two objects, Newton's laws of motion can be used to describe the motion of which of the objects?

   A. both objects

   B. only objects that are moving before the collision

   C. neither object

   D. only objects that are at rest before the collision

Interactive Review

Complete this section to review the main concepts of the lesson.

Newton's laws of motion can be used to describe the motions of objects involved in a collision.

A. How can Newton's laws of motion be used to analyze the collision between two objects?

The engineering design process can be used to develop a solution to an engineering problem, including a problem that involves colliding objects.

B. Collisions may cause unwanted damage to an object. Describe how the engineering design process can be used to design a solution to protect an object during a collision.

Choose one of the activities to explore how this unit connects to other topics.

People in Engineering

Steve Okamoto, Roller Coaster Designer Tall, steep hills and high-speed loops make riding a roller coaster fun and a little scary. But roller coasters are safe to ride thanks to engineers like Steve Okamoto. Okamoto has been fascinated by roller coasters ever since he first rode on one. He studied mechanical engineering and studio art and eventually became a product designer. Designing roller coasters is a complex job, so Okamoto works with teams to design safe and exciting rides.

Research different types of roller coasters and make a poster that explains how energy and forces constrain the design of a particular type of coaster.

Okamoto helped design the Steel Dragon 2000 roller coaster.

Earth Science Connection

Erupting Evidence Earth's crust is broken into large fragments known as tectonic plates. When tectonic plates collide, slide past one another, or separate, earthquakes, tsunamis, volcanoes, or the formation of mountains can occur on Earth's surface.

Research how the movement of tectonic plates affects geology, and explain how scientists measure the forces caused by these movements. Make a multimedia presentation to share what you learn with your class.

Art Connection

Kinetic Sculpture Kinetic art refers to a sculpture or other artwork that moves, often from the forces of wind, a motor, or a person interacting with the object. The American artist Alexander Calder developed the first mobiles, hanging sculptures with individual moving parts that gracefully rotate in a breeze.

Create your own piece of kinetic art and explain how energy and forces affect its motion. Or, select an interesting piece of kinetic art and research the background of its production and the artist who designed it. Make a diagram illustrating the energy and forces that cause movement in the piece of art.

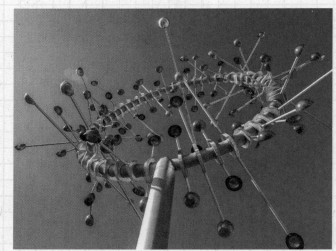

Blowhole is a kinetic sculpture designed by Duncan Stemler for Docklands Park in Melbourne, Australia.

Name: _____   Date: _____

Complete this review to check your understanding of the unit.

Use the photos of the hammers to answer Questions 1–4.

sledgehammer

claw hammer

1. Describe the transfers and transformations of energy involved in using a hammer.

2. Suppose that the two hammers are moving at the same speed. Which hammer has more kinetic energy? Explain your reasoning.

3. Assuming both hammers are moving at the same speed and are the same distance off the ground, which hammer will be able to do more work? Explain your reasoning.

4. Why are different types of hammers used to accomplish different tasks? Why might a sledgehammer or a claw hammer be inappropriate for certain types of tasks? Explain your reasoning.

Name: **Date:**

Use the photo to answer Questions 5–8.

5. Two people wearing inflatable bubble suits collide with one another while playing soccer. Describe the contact and noncontact forces acting on the players.

6. Person A has a mass of 100 kg and Person B has a mass of 50 kg. They are both moving at the same speed toward one another. What will happen when they collide?

7. Use the example of the two soccer players in the ball suits to explain Newton's third law.

8. Explain whether the collision between the two soccer players is a good model for a collision between an asteroid and Earth.

Name: _____   Date: _____

Can you improve the design of a toy hoop?

You work for a toy design company that is trying to update the classic toy hoop. Your boss wants you to explain how a toy hoop stays around a person's waist or arm. Based on your research, she wants you to improve the company's toy hoop design so a person can more easily keep it in motion for a longer period of time. Develop a procedure to accurately test how a change in the mass or size of a toy hoop changes the object's energy and motion. Then prepare a presentation of your findings for your boss.

The steps below will help guide your research to develop your recommendation.

Engineer It

1. **Ask a Question** Develop a statement that clearly defines the problem you have been asked to solve. What questions will you need to answer to explain how a toy hoop stays around a person's waist or arm?

Engineer It

2. **Conduct Research** Research how forces and energy interact to keep a toy hoop around a person's waist or arm. Investigate the average size and mass of a toy hoop.

3. **Plan an Investigation** Plan a procedure to determine how changes in the mass or size of a toy hoop change its energy and motion. Conduct several trials with different design prototypes for comparison.

4. **Develop a Solution** Analyze the data from the trials to find the similarities and differences between the design prototypes. Use these data to identify the best features of each design. Combine the best features into a new design and use evidence to argue why the features you chose to include will result in an optimal design.

5. **Communicate** Prepare a presentation describing your findings for the boss of the toy company. Include evidence from your test results to support your argument.

✓ **Self-Check**

	I asked questions about how toy hoops stay in motion and how changes in mass change an object's motion and energy.
	I researched the forces acting on toy hoops and the average mass and size of a standard toy hoop.
	I planned an investigation to test how changes in the mass or size of a toy hoop affect its motion and energy.
	I prepared a presentation describing my findings and recommended an improved design based on evidence from my test results.

Noncontact Forces

How do noncontact forces behave on Earth and in space?

During thunderstorms, electric charges build up within clouds to produce spectacular lightning displays.

You Solve It How Can You Calibrate a Cathode Ray Tube?

Calibrate the beam in a cathode ray tube by adjusting its electromagnets. See which adjustments aim the beam into the center of the screen using as little electric current as possible.

Go online and complete the You Solve It to explore ways to solve a real-world problem.

Build an Electric Charge Detector

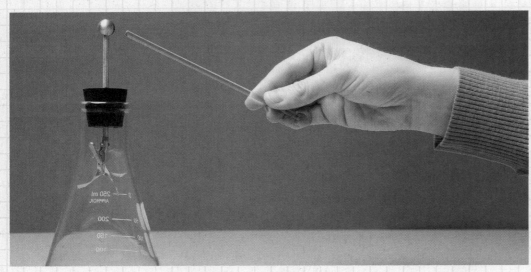

Electroscopes are used to detect the amount of net charge on an object.

A. Look at the photo. On a separate sheet of paper, write down as many different questions as you can about the photo.

B. **Discuss** With your class or a partner, share your questions. Record any additional questions generated in your discussion. Then choose the most important questions from the list that are related to detecting electric charges with an electroscope. Write them below.

C. Identify a topic to research that will better help you to understand how to design an electroscope. Possible topics include:

electroscope uses

electric charges

electric forces

What topic will you research?

D. Use the information above to help in designing and building an electroscope.

Discuss the next steps for your Unit Project with your teacher and go online to download the Unit Project Worksheet.

Language Development

Use the lessons in this unit to complete the network and expand your understanding of these key concepts.

▮	Similar term
▮	Phrase
▮	Cognate
▮	Example
▮	Definition

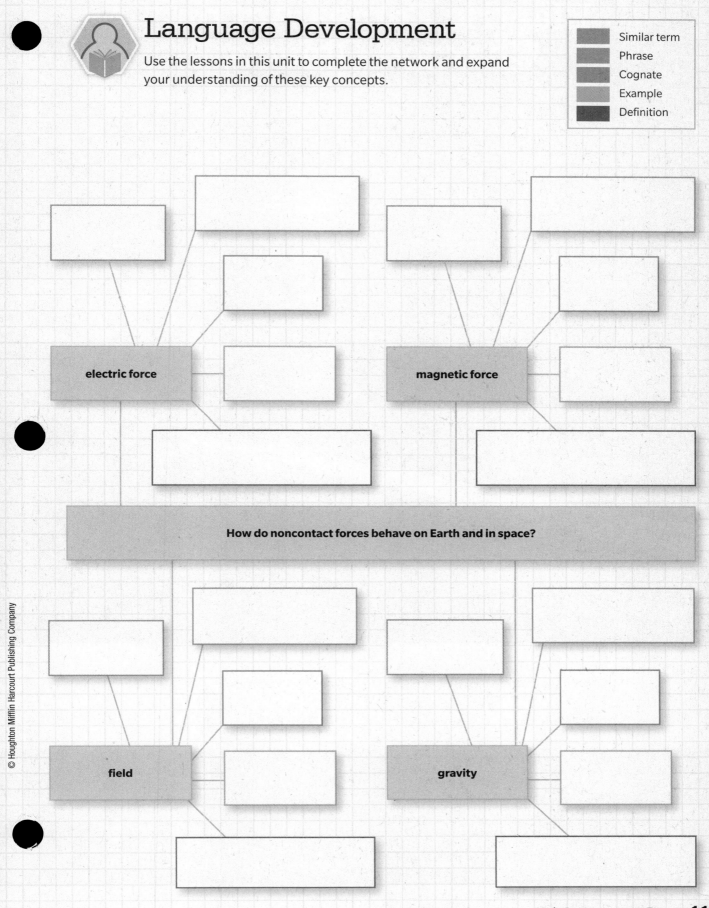

electric force

magnetic force

How do noncontact forces behave on Earth and in space?

field

gravity

Electric Forces Act on Charged Objects

When charges become separated between clouds, lightning can form.

Explore First

Levitating Plates Take a plastic foam plate and rub the bottom of it with a wool cloth. Then lay it face down on the table. Rub the bottom of another plastic foam plate with the same cloth. What happens when you move the second plate over the first plate? What happens when your hand is near either plate? Why do you think this happens?

CAN YOU EXPLAIN IT?

What causes the water droplets to change direction and spiral toward the charged needle?

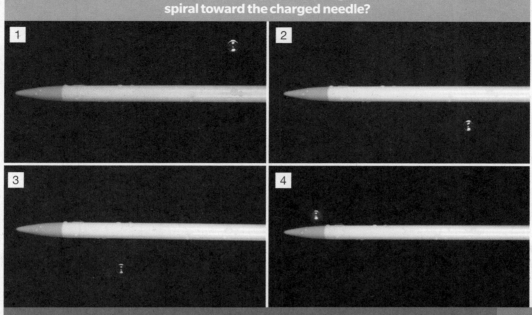

On the International Space Station (ISS), water droplets spiral around this charged knitting needle. Without Earth's gravity pulling objects down, other forces can be observed. Water droplets, like any object, do not change motion unless something pushes or pulls on them.

Explore Online

1. Why might these water droplets move around the charged knitting needle and change direction?

2. What are some other examples of a force acting on an object without touching it?

 EVIDENCE NOTEBOOK As you explore the lesson, gather evidence to help explain the behavior of the water droplets on the ISS.

Analyzing Electric Charge

You might feel a shock when you touch a metal object, such as a doorknob, especially when the weather is dry. If it is dark enough, you may even see a spark. This spark is caused by a property of matter.

3. **Write** Use the space below or write on a piece of paper. What do you think causes these sparks to form? Write about a time that you saw sparks, and try to identify the conditions that caused the sparks.

Electric Charge

Every type of electricity is the result of electric charge. **Electric charge** is a physical property of all matter that leads to electric and magnetic interactions. Electric charges moving through wires are used to power devices such as lamps and computers. Static electricity, which can cause your hair to stick up, is caused by electric charges that are not moving. When you touch a doorknob and are shocked, electric charges that had been on your hand or on the doorknob quickly move between objects, causing a spark.

Electric charges in fabric can cause clothing to stick together. Electrical devices also use electric charge. Electrical devices work because electric charges can move through wires.

Signs of Electric Charges

Electric charges can be positive or negative. Positive charges are represented by a plus sign (+), and negative charges are represented by a negative sign (−). The sign of a charge affects how it interacts with other charges. Objects have many positive and negative charges. Most objects tend to be neutral, meaning they have no net charge. Think about what happens when you add −1 and 1. The result is zero (−1 + 1 = 0). Adding positive and negative charges is the same as adding positive and negative numbers. An object with an equal number of positive and negative charges has a net charge of zero. A positively charged object has more positive charges than negative charges whereas a negatively charged object has more negative charges than positive charges.

4. Static electricity is caused by an imbalance of electric charge. When positive charges build up on an object, the object has a net positive charge. When negative charges build up on an object, the object has a net *positive / negative / neutral* charge. An electric discharge happens when an object loses its extra negative charges. The positive and negative charges in an object are equal after a complete discharge, so the object has a net *positive / negative / neutral* charge.

The Conservation of Charge

The net charge on an object can change. A neutral object can become positively or negatively charged. The amount of net charge on an object can increase or decrease, and charged objects can even become neutral. When the amount of net charge on an object changes, electric charges are never created or destroyed. Instead, negative charges have been transferred between objects.

Forces are needed to separate positive and negative charges because opposite charges are attracted to each other. If possible, opposite charges tend to move toward one another, which leads to many objects having a net neutral charge. Outside forces or energy can be used to separate opposite charges. For instance, friction between two materials can increase the rate at which charges separate. When you drag your feet across the carpet, the carpet can transfer negative charges to you. You become negatively charged because you gained negative charges. The carpet becomes positively charged because it lost its negative charges and kept its positive charges.

When a balloon is rubbed against a person's hair, negative electric charges move from the hair to the balloon. The total number of positive and negative charges does not change when charges move between objects.

5. How is the person in the photos separating the charges in her hair and the balloon?

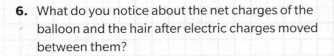

6. What do you notice about the net charges of the balloon and the hair after electric charges moved between them?

Both the balloon and the person's hair are charged. The balloon is negatively charged because it has more negative charges than positive charges. The hair is positively charged because it has more positive charges than negative charges.

7. **Engineer It** Preventing charge from building up on objects is necessary on some job sites. The buildup of charge may be a safety hazard or could damage products. A company wants to design a device to minimize the buildup of charge on an object. Which of the following materials would be the best choice to make such a device out of?

A. aluminum, which transfers charge quickly

B. rubber, which barely transfers charge

C. a new plastic, which transfers charge at a moderate rate

Charges in Neutral Objects

Generally, positive and negative charges are evenly spread out in an object. Opposite charges are attracted to one another, and similar charges are repelled from one another, which typically leads to charges spreading evenly throughout an object. However, charges can move in a neutral object. Wires generally have a neutral charge, but electric charges can move freely through them. Charges are also able to move and separate within an object if exposed to outside forces.

Opposite charges pull on each other, while similar charges push on each other. Though this balloon has a negative charge, it is attracted to a wall that has a net neutral charge.

8. **Discuss** The wall did not seem to have a charge until the negatively-charged balloon was put near it. With a partner, consider the options and determine how the wall could have become charged.

A. The wall transferred electric charges to the balloon.

B. The balloon transferred electric charges to the wall.

C. Negative charges in the wall moved away from the balloon's negative charges, leaving a positively charged area on the wall.

D. The wall gained positive charges to balance the balloon's extra negative charges, producing a positively charged are on the wall.

Movement of Charge within Neutral Objects

A charged object can make the charges in a neutral object move. For example, a negatively charged object pushes negative charges away from it. As a result, the area that the negative charges were moved to becomes negatively charged and the area that the negative charges were moved away from becomes positively charged. When the charged object is moved away, the negative charges in the neutral object are attracted back toward the positive charges and become evenly spread out again.

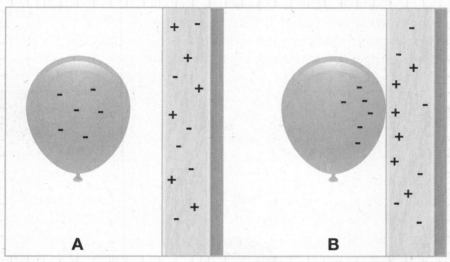

Placing a negatively charged balloon near a neutral wall causes the negative charges in the wall to move away from the balloon. The now positively charged surface of the wall and the negatively charged balloon are attracted to each other.

 EVIDENCE NOTEBOOK

9. Water droplets tend to have a neutral charge. How might they still be affected by the charges of other objects? Record your evidence.

Analyze Charge in a Cloud

All matter, even a cloud, has the property of electric charge. A charge imbalance causes static electricity within the cloud. At times, the charges on a pair of clouds or on a cloud and the ground neutralize through a discharge known as lightning.

10. During thunderstorms, positive and negative charges in clouds become separated. Positive charge builds up on the top of clouds, and negative charge builds up on the bottom of clouds. How might the charged clouds affect the charges in the neutral ground below the clouds? Describe what happens to the charges in the ground.

_____

_____

_____

_____

_____

_____

© Houghton Mifflin Harcourt Publishing Company • Image Credits: (b) ©MvH/iStockPhoto.com

Measuring the Electric Force

The Electric Force

A balloon can stick to a wall due to the electric force. The **electric force** is the force of attraction or repulsion between objects due to their charges. The electric force is a *noncontact force* that can push or pull on objects from a distance. It is similar to other noncontact forces like gravity in that it can act on objects without touching them and that objects affected by an electric force can have potential energy due to their position.

Explore Online

The plastic film would usually fall to the ground, but the balloon keeps it floating in the air. The balloon and the plastic film are both negatively charged.

11. The plastic film and the balloon are able to affect each other's motion because they are charged. How do you think electric charge affects the interaction between these two objects?

EVIDENCE NOTEBOOK

12. Do you think that the water droplets that spiral around the charged needle on the ISS might experience an electric force? Record your evidence.

Hands-On Lab
Explore the Electric Force

Part 1: Variables that Affect the Electric Force

Develop and answer questions to determine the variables that affect the strength and direction of electric forces. When you throw a ball, you are applying a force. How quickly you move your arm is one variable that affects the force's strength. Variables also affect the strength of an electric force.

MATERIALS
- balloons, inflated to about the same size (2)
- cloth, wool
- measuring tape
- paper towels
- thread or fishing line

Procedure and Analysis

STEP 1 Rub the balloons on your hair or on the wool to give the balloons a negative charge and your hair or the wool a positive charge. The more you rub the balloons against your hair or the wool, the greater the magnitude of the negative charge on the balloons.

STEP 2 Experiment to see how the charged objects affect one another. Answer the guiding questions below, and develop at least two additional questions to answer. To remove the net charge from a balloon, wipe it with a damp paper towel and then dry it.

Guiding Questions

- How do the balloons affect each other's motion?
- How do the balloons affect the motion of hair or wool?

STEP 3 On a separate sheet of paper, record your procedure and observations in a table like the one shown below.

Guiding Question	My Procedure	Observations

STEP 4 Compare your observations and determine which factors seem to affect the strength of the electric force. Choose all that apply.

A. distance between objects

B. magnitude of the charges

C. mass of objects

D. sign of the charges

© Houghton Mifflin Harcourt Publishing Company

Sign of the Electric Charge

You observed that the electric force can push balloons with similar charges away from each other. The electric force also pulls oppositely charged objects, such as your hair and the balloon, together. The sign of the electric charges determines whether the electric force pushes or pulls on objects. When objects have like charges, they repel each other. When objects have opposite charges, they attract each other.

The diagram shows how the electric force affects the motion of positive and negative charges. Notice that positive charges repel each other, negative charges repel each other, and positive and negative charges attract each other. The sign of the electric charge does not affect the strength of the electric force. An object with a charge of +1 generates the same strength of electric force as an object with a charge of −1. Neutral objects, which have a charge of zero, do not typically exert an electric force.

Charge Sign and Force Direction

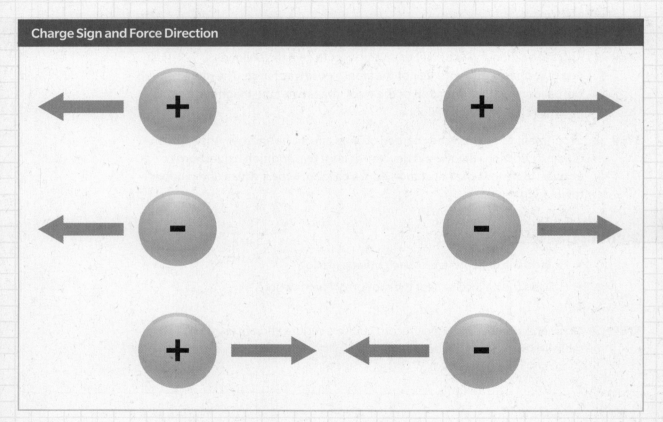

13. Charge two balloons by rubbing them on your hair or with a wool cloth and hold them gently by their knots. Move the balloons near one another. What does your observation tell you about the electric charges of the balloons?

Hands-On Lab
Part 2: Distance between Charged Objects

Record your observations as you explore how distance affects the strength of the electric force. Then use your observations to determine what effect the distance between the two charged balloons has on the electric force.

Guiding Question

How does the distance between two charged objects affect the strength of the electric force between them?

Procedure and Analysis

STEP 1 Use the two balloons from the previous activity. Tie a thread around the knot of one balloon and hang the balloon from a desk, a lab stand, or the ceiling.

STEP 2 Rub both balloons against your hair or the piece of wool ten times to charge them. Be sure to charge all sides of the balloons, not just one spot.

STEP 3 Let the balloon tied to the thread hang freely. Move the other balloon close to the hanging balloon and observe what happens. Experiment with how the distance between the balloons affects the electric force.

STEP 4 **Language SmArts** Record your observations as you explore how distance affects the strength of the electric force. Construct a claim of how distance between charged objects affects the electric force. Support your claim using evidence from your observations.

EVIDENCE NOTEBOOK

14. How might the distance between the needle and the water droplets have affected the movement of the droplets? Record your evidence.

© Houghton Mifflin Harcourt Publishing Company • Image Credits: ©HMH

The hanging balloons will separate when the force between them increases. If the force decreases, the balloons will fall so that they hang straight down.

Part 3: Magnitude of the Electric Charge

Investigate how the magnitude of electric charge on an object affects the electric force. Record your data in the table on the next page.

Both positive and negative electric charges can have different magnitudes. For example, the electric charge on an object with three positive charges on it has a greater magnitude than the electric charge on an object with one positive charge on it. The magnitude of the charge depends on how many extra positive or negative charges build up on the object. The sign of the net charge on an object does not change the magnitude of the charge. For example, a positive charge of +2 and a negative charge of −2 both have a magnitude of 2.

Guiding Question

What effect does increasing the charge on the balloons have on the electric force?

Procedure and Analysis

STEP 1 Place two desks about 50 cm apart. Tie two pieces of thread to the knot of each balloon. Hang the first balloon between the desks by taping the loose end of one thread to the edge of one desk and taping the loose end of the other piece of thread to the edge of the other desk. The balloon should hang loosely between the desks. Hang the second balloon by taping the threads to the same spots as for the first balloon. The two balloons should be touching when they hang freely.

STEP 2 Rub each balloon on your hair/wool once. Make sure to rub each side of the balloons to charge them evenly. Let both balloons hang freely. Record your observations and measure the distance between the two balloons.

STEP 3 Rub each balloon two more times, and repeat your measurements from Step 2.

STEP 4 Repeat Step 3, this time choosing the number of times to rub each balloon between measurements. Repeat this step, giving you four total distances.

© Houghton Mifflin Harcourt Publishing Company • Image Credits: ©HMH

STEP 5 **Do the Math** You can use graphs to identify the relationship between variables. Make a graph of your data to see how the total number of rubs affects the distance between the two balloons.

Total number of rubs on each balloon	Distance between balloons

STEP 6 Look at the relationship between the total number of times you rubbed the balloon and the distance as shown on your graph. What can you determine about how the magnitude of the electric charge affects the electric force between charged objects?

STEP 7 **Discuss** Develop two additional questions to explore using these materials. Using the balloons, try to answer these questions.

© Houghton Mifflin Harcourt Publishing Company

15. Compare the two pairs of charged objects. Which pair of objects, A or B, has a stronger electric force between the two objects? Explain your answer.

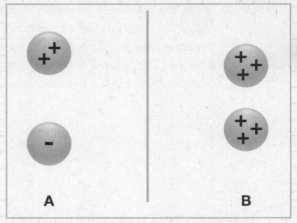

The diagram shows two pairs of charged objects. The number of signs in each object represents the magnitude of the charge.

Analyze the Force on a Stream of Water

Electric force pushes and pulls on objects without touching them. The electric force between objects with like charges pushes the objects apart. The electric force between objects with opposite charges pulls the objects together. The electric force increases as the magnitude of the charge increases and as the distance between objects decreases.

16. Water molecules are neutral. Even though the electric charges are balanced in each molecule, one side of the molecule is slightly positive, and the other side is slightly negative. Why does the stream of water bend toward the negatively charged balloon in the bottom photo?

_____
_____
_____
_____
_____
_____
_____
_____

The balloon has a negative charge and water is neutral. They are far enough apart so that the electric force is very weak.

Moving the charged balloon toward the water causes the stream of water to bend. The water is attracted to the balloon, but it is still pulled down by gravity.

EVIDENCE NOTEBOOK

17. Could the water droplets in the ISS pictures be affected in the same way as this stream of water is being affected? Record your evidence.

© Houghton Mifflin Harcourt Publishing Company • Image Credits: (t, b) ©HMH

Explaining Electric Current

Charge Movement

In many cases, a large number of electric charges move through objects at the same time. When many charges are moving, measuring individual charges becomes difficult and less useful.

18. **Discuss** With a partner, determine a measurement that might be more useful than measuring the movement of an individual charge.

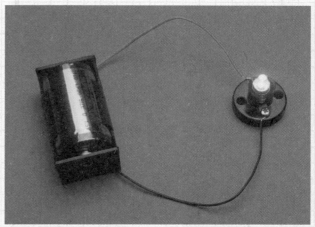

The electric charges flowing through this light bulb cause it to light up.

Current

The movement of electric charges is key to many phenomena. To describe this movement, the term *current* is used. An **electric current** is a continuous flow of electric charges from one region to another. An electric current can be measured by determining the rate at which electric charges move past a certain point.

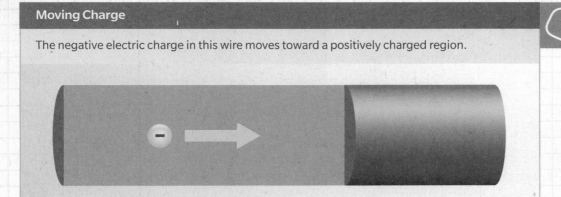

Moving Charge

The negative electric charge in this wire moves toward a positively charged region.

Explore Online

19. **Write** An electric current is a constant flow of electric charges along a path. What are some advantages of using electric current instead of individual charges to discuss the movement of charges? Relate your explanation to another situation where discussing rates of movement would be more useful than discussing the movement of individual items.

20. You cannot see an electric charge move from the hair on your head to a balloon when they are rubbed together, and you cannot see a charge moving through wire. How might you measure the movement of a charge if electric charges are not visible?

A. A physical effect of the charge's movement could be used to measure the charge.

B. Magnification could be used to see the electric charge so its movement can be measured.

C. The electric charge could be measured by the change in mass of the substance that accepts the charge.

D. The time for the electric charge to transfer could be used to measure the movement of the charge.

Ammeters

Ammeters are devices that are used to measure electric current. They measure the rate that electric charges move through a wire. The unit of measure of this rate is called an ampere, or amp. When writing measurements, the symbol *A* is used to represent ampere. The amp is a measure of the amount of electric charge that passes a particular point in a given amount of time. There are several types of ammeters, but all of them use a physical effect of electric current to measure the rate of charge movement.

Ammeters allow people to visualize the effects of electric current in a wire.

Analyze Electric Heaters

When electric charge flows through an object, it can cause the object to become hotter. Many heaters operate using this phenomenon. Electric current is run through wires to warm water in electric kettles, and some portable space heaters also use electric current.

21. What might be some advantages of using an electric current to warm objects instead of other methods, such as burning wood?

_____

_____

_____

_____

_____

_____

_____

© Houghton Mifflin Harcourt Publishing Company • Image Credits: ©GIPhotoStock/Science Source

Continue Your Exploration

Name: _____   Date: _____

Check out the path below or go online to choose one of the other paths shown.

Static Electricity

- **Experimenting with the Charges of Materials**
- **Hands-On Labs**
- **Propose Your Own Path**

Go online to choose one of these other paths.

All animals make some use of electric charges. For example, human brains and nerves use electric signals to communicate with the rest of the body. However, some fish take advantage of electric charges in a variety of other ways. Watery environments are often hard to see in because of salt and sediments. However, those same salt and sediments permit electric charges to move easily through the water, which allows certain fish to make use of electric charges in ways that land animals cannot.

Several types of fish, such as sharks, can detect changes in electric forces and charge. They use this ability to help find prey. Other fish produce small discharges of electricity to communicate and to help them navigate in murky water. A few species of fish that have taken this ability even further and are able to produce strong electric discharges. Electric catfish and electric eels are able to produce electric shocks that are powerful enough to stun prey and predators.

1. Strongly electric fish use electric charges to stun prey. They have to force electric charges to move in order to generate a current. Why do electric fish need to force electric charges to move? What would happen if an electric fish was always negatively charged instead?

Electric catfish use electric charges and currents to locate food. They can also stun prey using an electric discharge.

Continue Your Exploration

Electric eels use electric discharges to stun prey and defend themselves.

2. Some strongly electric fish will stun prey by generating an electric current that runs along the outside of their skin. What must be true about the electric charges on the fish's skin when the fish is stunning its prey?

3. Explain why sharks are able to detect electric charges and electric forces without producing a strong electric force. Relate this phenomena to a way that you were able to cause a charged object and a neutral object to interact.

4. **Collaborate** Together with a partner, research another animal that makes use of electrical phenomena. You could research another species of fish or a completely different animal. Write an explanation of how this animal uses electrical phenomena.

Can You Explain It?

Name: _____   Date: _____

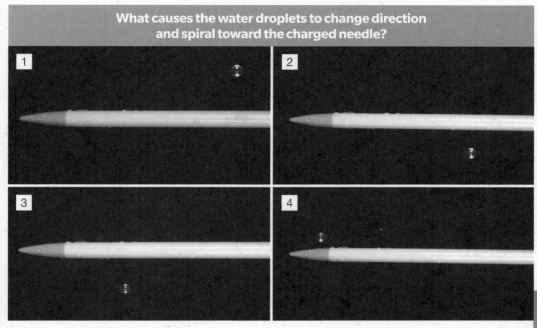

What causes the water droplets to change direction and spiral toward the charged needle?

Explore Online

EVIDENCE NOTEBOOK

Refer to the notes in your Evidence Notebook to help you construct an explanation for why the water drops move around the charged needle.

1. State your claim. Make sure your claim fully explains why the water droplets change direction and spiral toward the charged needle.

2. Summarize the evidence you have gathered to support your claim and explain your reasoning.

Checkpoints

Answer the following questions to check your understanding of the lesson.

Use the diagram to answer Question 3.

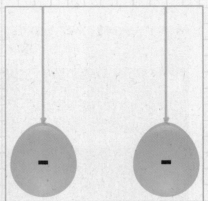

3. Which statements describe how the electric force affects the balloons? Choose all that apply.

   A. The balloons are pulled together by the electric force.

   B. The balloons are pushed apart by the electric force.

   C. The balloons stick together once they are touching because they need to be in contact to be affected by the electric force.

   D. If the balloons move closer together, the electric force acting on them increases.

   E. If one of the balloons becomes positively charged, the electric force increases.

Use the photo to answer Questions 4–5.

4. A student conducts an investigation to find out whether the electric force of a charged object—a comb—is strong enough to pick up very light, neutral objects—foam packing peanuts. To charge the comb, the student rubs the comb with a wool cloth. The cloth becomes positively charged. The student then holds the comb above the foam packing peanuts. The results are shown in the photo. Choose the symbol that represents the charge on the comb and on the packing peanuts:

   A. Charge of the comb: + / − / 0

   B. Charge of the side of a packing peanut that is not touching the comb: + / − / 0

   C. Charge of the side of a packing peanut that is touching the comb: + / − / 0

5. The packing peanuts are removed from the comb and placed on the table. Then the positively charged wool cloth is held close to the packing peanuts. What will happen to the packing peanuts?

   A. They will stick to the wool cloth.

   B. They will be pushed away from the wool cloth.

   C. They will not be affected by the wool cloth.

6. The stationary charges on the surface of a balloon produce a(n) current / electric force . When you are shocked by static electricity, the charges move to produce a current / electric force .

Interactive Review

Complete this section to review the main concepts of the lesson.

Electric charge is a physical property of all matter. Electric charge can be positive or negative, and objects can have overall negative, positive, or neutral charges.

A. When clothes are run through a dryer, they often become charged and stick together. What causes the charges to separate?

Charged objects generate an electric force between them. The direction of the force is determined by the signs of the charges. The strength depends on the magnitude and the distance.

B. Two particles are moving toward one another. Both of the particles have a strong positive charge. As they move toward one another, how will the electric force between the two particles change?

An electric current is a continuous flow of electric charges. An ammeter measures current by measuring the rate that charges move through a wire.

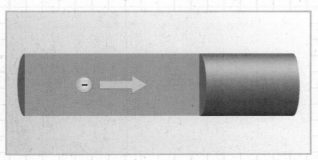

C. An ammeter is used to measure the current in a wire. If an ammeter indicates a current in a wire, what can be said about the charges in the wire?

Magnetic and Electromagnetic Forces Act on Certain Objects

Lodestones are naturally occurring magnets. Slivers of lodestone used to be used to make compasses.

Explore First

Testing a Magnet Using a magnet, determine what types of objects are attracted to the magnet and what types are unaffected. Are paper clips attracted to the magnet? Is aluminum foil? Is cloth? What patterns do you notice in the objects that are and are not attracted to the magnet?

CAN YOU EXPLAIN IT?

How can pieces of metal be picked up and released by this crane?

Cranes such as the one pictured are used to move scrap metal. These cranes do not have any sort of claws or grippers. They pick up metal with large, flat disks. How are these cranes able to lift heavy metal objects, move the objects to another place, and then release them?

Explore Online

1. How might the crane be picking up these pieces of metal?

2. What does the crane's ability to release the pieces of metal indicate about how it is picking up these objects?

EVIDENCE NOTEBOOK As you explore the lesson, gather evidence to help explain how the crane can lift and release metal objects.

Describing Magnets and the Magnetic Force

You use magnets all of the time. Magnets are used in computers, on fridges, and in credit cards. A **magnet** is an object that attracts, or pulls on, materials that contain iron. Other materials, such as cobalt and nickel, are also attracted to magnets. Magnets can attract and repel, or push away, other magnets. All magnets have a north pole and a south pole. These poles affect how magnets interact with each other. Look at the photos and notice how the magnets affect each other, even though they are not touching.

3. Why do you think that these two magnets are able to affect one another's movements even when they are not touching?

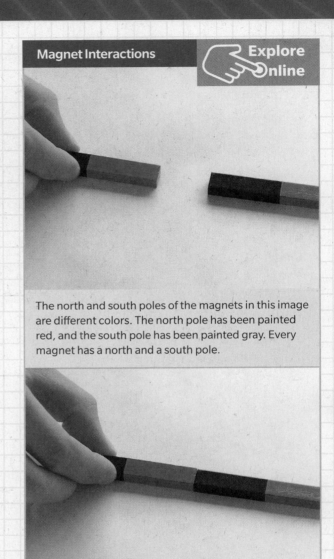

Magnet Interactions

Explore Online

The north and south poles of the magnets in this image are different colors. The north pole has been painted red, and the south pole has been painted gray. Every magnet has a north and a south pole.

When these magnets are brought close enough together, they will jump toward one another. The two magnets affect each other's movement even though they were not originally touching.

The **magnetic force** is the push or pull exerted by magnets. As you can see in the photos, this force acts at a distance. Because of this, the magnetic force is a noncontact force. Like all noncontact forces, objects affected by a magnetic force can have potential energy due to their position. The strength of a magnetic force varies in predictable ways. However, even very strong magnets only attract and/or repel certain materials.

EVIDENCE NOTEBOOK

4. How might the ability of magnets to attract certain metals relate to the crane? Record your evidence.

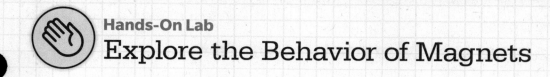

Hands-On Lab
Explore the Behavior of Magnets

Ask questions to investigate the behavior of magnets. Then you will explore how magnets affect a variety of materials and identify the factors that affect the strength of the magnetic force.

MATERIALS
- magnet, bar (2)
- magnet, large (1)
- strip, copper
- strip, iron
- strip, plastic

Procedure

STEP 1 Use your materials to explore how the magnetic force affects various objects. Below are a few questions to consider as you explore the factors that affect the strength of the magnetic force. Explore at least two of these questions. Then develop and explore at least two more of your own questions.

- How do the magnets affect materials that are not magnets?
- How does the force between the two bar magnets compare to the force between the large magnet and a bar magnet?
- How do the poles of the magnets affect the force they exert on each other?

STEP 2 On a separate sheet of paper, record your procedure and observations using a table similar to the one shown.

Question to Explore	Your Procedure	Observations

Analysis

STEP 3 **Discuss** With a partner, compare your observations. Using your combined observations, decide on the factors that affect the strength of the magnetic force. Record your answers below.

STEP 4 The magnetic force is *attractive / repulsive* when two like poles point toward each other. The magnetic force is *attractive / repulsive* when two opposite poles point toward each other. When the like poles of two magnets point toward one another, the strength of the magnetic force is the same as when the opposite poles point toward one another.

Hands-On Lab
Analyze the Magnetic Force

Part 1: Distance and the Magnetic Force

Investigate the relationship between distance and the strength of the magnetic force using a magnet and a compass. The needle of a compass is magnetic and points north due to Earth's magnetic field. If the attractive force between the compass needle and a magnet is strong enough, the compass needle will move toward the magnet.

MATERIALS
• compass
• magnet, bar
• tape
• tape measure or ruler

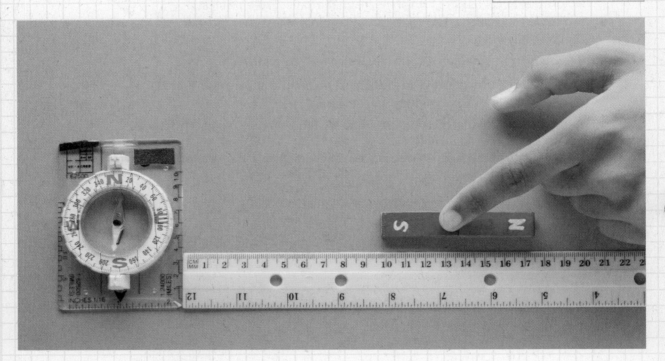

Procedure and Analysis

STEP 1 Using the lab materials, design a procedure to test how the strength of a magnetic force changes due to the distance from the magnet. Make sure that your procedure includes an independent variable, the variable that you are changing, and a dependent variable, the variable that you are measuring. Ask your teacher to approve your plans before continuing.

STEP 2 Follow your procedure and record your observations in an organized manner, such as a data table.

STEP 3 **Do the Math** Make a graph of your data with your independent variable on the *x*-axis and your dependent variable on the *y*-axis. Graphs can help you clearly see the relationship between variables in an experiment.

STEP 4 Look at the trend shown in your graph. Consider how the strength of the magnetic force relates to the needle position. What effect does distance have on the strength of the magnetic force?

Part 2: Magnet Strength and the Magnetic Force

MATERIALS
- magnet, bar
- magnet, large
- paper clips, metal (10)
- mass set, hooked (10 g–1 kg)

Test the strength of the magnetic forces produced by two magnets by comparing the masses that they can hold. If the two magnets hold different masses, you will construct an argument for why the two magnets might have different strengths.

Procedure and Analysis

STEP 1 Design a procedure to test the strength of the magnetic forces generated by different magnets. Write out the steps of your procedure and ask your teacher to approve your plans before continuing.

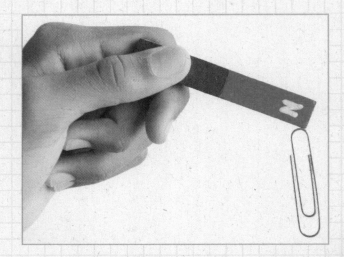

STEP 2 Follow the procedure that you designed to test the strength of the two magnets. Record you observations as you follow your procedure.

STEP 3 **Language SmArts** Write a claim that states how you think the type of magnet affects the strength of a magnetic force. Use evidence from your observations to support your claim, and explain your reasoning. You can also draw on information about the magnetic force that you learned before this investigation.

STEP 4 Based on your observations, what can you infer about individual magnets and the strength of the magnetic forces they produce? Which of the following statements is best supported by your observations?

    A. All magnets produce the same magnitude of magnetic force.

    B. Different magnets produce different magnitudes of magnetic forces.

    C. Bar magnets are the weakest type of magnet.

    D. Paper clips always produce a strong magnetic force.

 EVIDENCE NOTEBOOK

    5. Do distance and the strength of different magnets seem to affect how to the crane lifts metal? Does the crane pick up all of the metal in the photo? Record your evidence.

6. When a magnet is cut in half, what do you think happens? Do you think each half is still magnetic? Would each half have a north and south pole? Explain your reasoning.

The atoms in this material are represented as magnets with north and south poles. Notice that poles point in many different directions. As a result, the tiny magnetic forces average to nearly zero, producing no overall magnetic force.

Atoms and Magnets

The magnetic properties of a material are a result of the magnetic properties of its atoms. Many atoms and molecules generate magnetic forces. These atoms are like tiny magnets, with north and south poles. If this is true, why aren't all objects magnetic? In most materials, the atoms are not aligned to produce a net force. Think about a group of people moving a box. If they all push in one direction, it moves. If they all push in different directions, there is no net force, and the box will not move.

Magnetic Domains

In some materials, such as iron, the north poles of groups of atoms line up in the same direction in areas called **magnetic domains**. Within each domain, the like poles of the atoms point in the same direction, so their magnetic fields are also aligned in the same direction. However, the poles of atoms in one domain may point in a different direction than the poles of atoms in another domain. Materials that form magnetic domains are called ferromagnetic materials. Iron, nickel, and cobalt are examples of ferromagnetic materials.

Magnetic Domain Alignment

Materials that are attracted to magnets, such as iron, can have magnetic domains. However, the domains normally point in random directions. Because the sum of the magnetic forces of the different domains is either zero or very small, iron does not normally exert a magnetic force on other objects.

When a material with magnetic domains is exposed to a magnetic force, the domains align and the material temporarily becomes a magnet. This alignment causes iron to be attracted to magnets. Permanent magnets generate a net magnetic force because their magnetic domains are always aligned.

7. Why are iron nails attracted to magnets, but not attracted to other iron nails?

Engineer It
Solve a Problem Using Magnets

8. Use the engineering design process to identify and define a problem that could be solved with magnets. Then propose a solution to the problem.

9. Draw Make a diagram that shows your design solution and how magnets would be used.

Analyzing Current and the Magnetic Force

Compasses and Electric Current

A compass is an instrument that is used to find north. The needle of a compass is a small magnet that is affected by magnetic fields. Magnetic fields are areas that are affected by magnetic forces. Earth has a large (but relatively weak) magnetic field that surrounds it and attracts the north-seeking side of a compass needle toward the North Pole. However, when another magnet is near a needle, the needle will change direction. The field produced by the closer magnet will often be stronger than Earth's magnetic field.

10. Discuss With a partner, discuss what conclusion you can draw from the differences between the two photos of compasses.

current off

current on

Moving Electric Charge and Magnetic Fields

When an electric current was passed through the wire, the compass needles moved. When an electric charge moves, a magnetic field is generated around the charge. Magnetic fields always exist around permanent magnets, but a temporary magnetic field is generated when a charge moves. A temporary magnetic field is also generated when more than one charge moves. When a current flows through a wire or a charged object moves, a magnetic field will also be generated. These magnetic fields are only produced when the charges are moving. When the charges stop moving, the magnetic field disappears.

Explore Online

Moving Charge

When an electric charge moves, the charge generates a magnetic field in a loop around the moving charge.

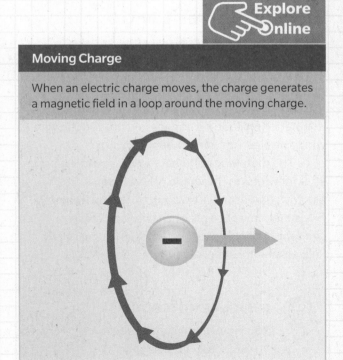

Electromagnetism

The interaction between electricity and magnetism is called **electromagnetism**. When electric charges move, they generate a magnetic field. Likewise, changes in the magnetic field can affect electric charges. Electric and magnetic forces are closely tied together and affect one another.

11. Electric charge and magnetism are related to one another. Magnetic fields are generated by moving / stationary electric charges. When an electric charge is stationary / in motion, there is no magnetic field. Magnetic fields cannot be seen, but its effects can be observed with a light bulb / compass.

12. Electric current is a movement of electric charges. If a wire is connected to an electric power source, such as a battery, electric charges will move through the wire. What will be the effect on the magnetic field around the wire as these charges move through the wire?

When no charge is moving through a wire, a magnetic field is not generated.

Electric Current and the Magnetic Field

Recall what happened when the compasses were placed around the wire. All of the compasses pointed in a circle once there was a current in the wire. A magnetic field loop was generated around the wire while the electric charges were moving.

The magnetic field that forms around a long, straight wire is in the shape of a cylinder. As many electric charges move through a wire, the magnetic fields that they each produce overlap. These overlapping fields produce a cylindrical magnetic field around the wire, along its entire length.

When charges move through the wire, a magnetic field is generated around the wire.

 EVIDENCE NOTEBOOK

13. How might a magnetic force that can be turned on or off be used? Record your evidence.

© Houghton Mifflin Harcourt Publishing Company • Image Credits: ©Houghton Mifflin Harcourt

Solenoids

Current in a wire produces a magnetic field. A wire producing a magnetic field does not have to be completely straight. Changing a straight wire into another shape also changes the shape of the magnetic field. One configuration is a coil of wire. A coil of wire with a current running through it is called a *solenoid*. A solenoid uses loops of wire to concentrate the magnetic field into a smaller area. The loops of wire generate a stronger, smaller magnetic field than a straight wire does. A solenoid also does not have to be a series of empty loops of wire. A solenoid can be wrapped around an object, which is known as the solenoid's core.

14. Why does wrapping wire into a solenoid shape increase the strength of the magnetic field?

Wire Loops

By looping a current-carrying wire on top of itself, the magnetic field can be concentrated in one spot.

straight wire

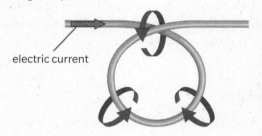

single looped wire

electric current

double looped wire

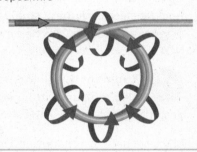

Electromagnets

An **electromagnet** is a coil of wire around an iron core. An electromagnet makes use of the magnetic field generated by an electric current in a wire, just like a solenoid. By placing a piece of iron in the middle, the force is amplified. Iron is a substance that can be made into a magnet under the right conditions. The magnetic field generated by moving charges temporarily aligns the magnetic domains of the iron, making it magnetic. The piece of iron then acts as a magnet as well. This makes an electromagnet much stronger than a solenoid without a core.

By wrapping a solenoid around a material that can become magnetic, the strength of the magnetic field is increased.

Hands-On Lab
Build an Electromagnet

Construct an electromagnet and test its strength. Identify possible ways in which you can improve the strength of your magnet by changing the design. Use your knowledge of electromagnetism to support your exploration.

Electromagnets share many properties with permanent magnets. With permanent magnets, the magnetic force on an object depends on the strength of the magnet and distance between the object and magnet. The force due to an electromagnet depends on the material of the core, but there are other factors that affect the force's strength.

MATERIALS
- batteries, AA (1-3)
- batteries, D (1-3)
- nails, 4, 5, and 6 inch
- paper clips, metal
- ruler
- wire, insulated or coated, cut into assorted lengths

Procedure

STEP 1 Build an electromagnet like the one pictured on the previous page. Wrap a piece of wire around a nail 30 times to build the electromagnet. Make sure you leave enough bare wire at each end of the coil to attach the wire to a battery. Test the electromagnet's strength by measuring the distance at which the magnet will first attract a paper clip. Record the distance in the table. SAFETY NOTE: Do not leave the wires and batteries attached for long periods of time.

STEP 2 **Engineer It** Think about some ways that you could make your electromagnet stronger. In the left column of the table, list your design ideas to increase the strength of the electromagnet.

STEP 3 Make each design change and test it to see at what distance the magnet will attract the paper clip and then record the distance in the table.

STEP 4 Compare your designs using the distances measured for each design.

Electromagnet Designs	Distance
Original electromagnet	

Analysis

STEP 5 With your group, discuss your different designs. What factors affected the strength of the magnetic force generated by an electromagnet? How could the best characteristics of several designs be combined into a new design for an even stronger electromagnet?

Electric Current and the Magnetic Force

Electric current affects the strength of the magnetic force of an electromagnet. Current is a flow of electric charges. The higher the current, the higher the rate of charge movement. Every charge moving through the wire contributes to the magnetic field around the wire. When the current is increased, the electromagnet becomes stronger.

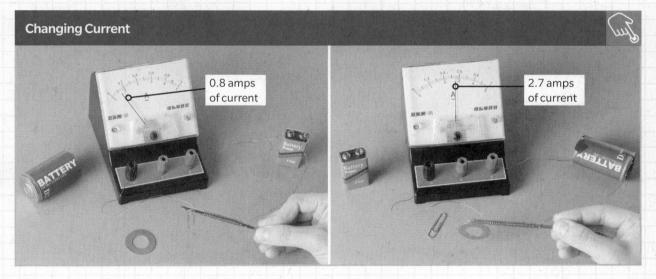

Changing Current

0.8 amps of current

2.7 amps of current

15. The electromagnet with 0.8 amps flowing through it is able to lift *more / less* mass than the electromagnet with 2.7 amps flowing through it.

16. What conclusions can you draw about how changing the electric current in an electromagnet affects the magnetic force generated?

EVIDENCE NOTEBOOK

17. The current in an electromagnet can be controlled. How might the ability to control the strength of an electromagnet relate to the crane's ability to pick up and release metal? Record your evidence.

Number of Loops and the Magnetic Force

The shape of the wire also affects the magnetic force. Recall that a solenoid with current running through it generates a larger magnetic force than a straight wire with a current running through it. Each portion of the wire with charge moving through it generates the same strength of magnetic field. By looping the wire, the magnetic field can be concentrated into a smaller area and become stronger.

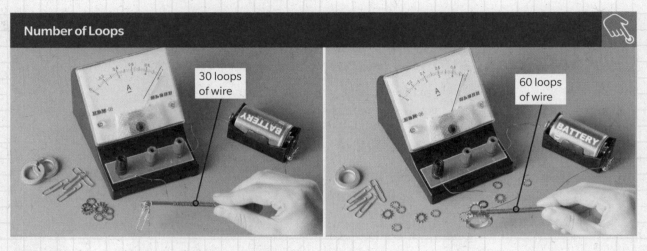

Number of Loops

30 loops of wire

60 loops of wire

18. The electromagnet with 30 loops of wire is able to lift *more / less* mass than the electromagnet with 60 loops of wire.

19. What conclusion can you draw about how changing the number of loops in a wire affects the strength of the magnetic force?

Language SmArts
Explain the Usefulness of Electromagnets

20. Electromagnets are used for many purposes, ranging from cranes to high-end brake systems for cars. What are some reasons that an electromagnet might be more useful than a permanent magnet in many situations? Support your answer with evidence from the text and your own experiences.

_____

_____

_____

_____

EVIDENCE NOTEBOOK

21. Consider how the electromagnets you have seen are used. Are any of them used in similar ways to a crane that picks up scrap metal? Record your evidence.

Measuring the Current Due to a Magnetic Field

Magnetic Field and Current

When electric charges move, they generate a magnetic field. Similarly, a moving magnet or changing magnetic field can have an effect on charges. When a magnet is moved near a wire, the effect on the charges in the wire can be observed by seeing how the current changes.

Explore Online

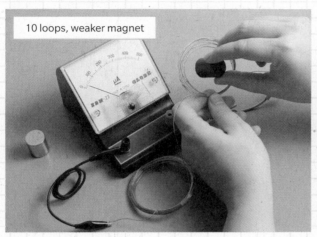

10 loops, weaker magnet

A weaker magnet is moved toward 10 loops of wire, generating a maximum current of 20 microamps in the wire.

30 loops, weaker magnet

A weaker magnet is moved toward 30 loops of wire, generating a maximum current of 40 microamps in the wire.

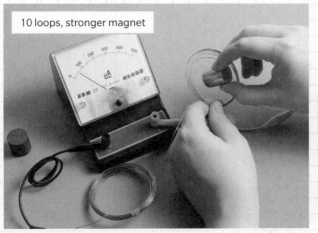

10 loops, stronger magnet

A stronger magnet is moved toward 10 loops of wire, generating a maximum current of 50 microamps in the wire.

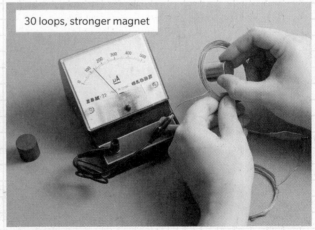

30 loops, stronger magnet

A stronger magnet is moved toward 30 loops of wire, generating a maximum current of 140 microamps in the wire.

22. Using the photos and your knowledge of electromagnetism, select the factors that might affect the amount of current displayed on the ammeter. Choose all that apply.

A. the number of loops in the solenoid

B. the speed of the magnet's movement

C. the magnet used

D. whether the magnet touches the solenoid

Electromagnetic Induction

When a magnetic field changes near electric charges, a force is generated on those charges. This force can cause those charges to move. **Electromagnetic induction** occurs when a current is generated by a changing magnetic field. A current generated in this way is known as an induced current.

Change in a Magnetic Field and Current

The amount of current induced in a wire is directly related to how the magnetic field around the wire changes. When a magnet moves quickly near a wire, the magnetic field around the wire changes by a large amount. When a magnet moves slowly near a wire, the magnetic field around the wire changes slowly and less current is induced.

A magnet's strength can also affect the amount of current induced in the wire. A strong magnet produces a stronger magnetic field. A small movement of a strong magnet can produce a large change in the magnetic field around the wire.

23. Using a stronger magnet will create a smaller / larger change in the magnetic field and cause more / less electric charges to move. Moving the magnet more slowly will create a smaller / larger current.

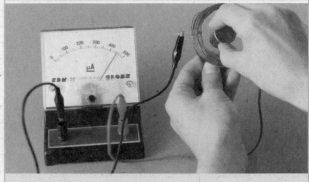

Current and Magnetic Field

When this magnet is moved through this loop of wire, it generates a maximum current of 130 microamps.

A stronger magnet moved through the same loop of wire generates a maximum current of 440 microamps.

Number of Loops and Current

The amount of current induced in a wire also depends on the number of loops in the wire. When the wire is looped, more of the wire is affected by a change in the magnetic field. Increasing the number of loops increases the number of charges in the wire that are affected by a change in the magnetic field. This effect is similar to how a current in a solenoid generates a stronger magnetic field than a current in a straight wire.

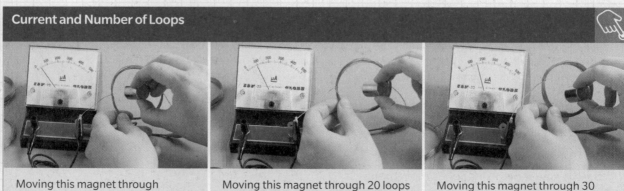

Current and Number of Loops

Moving this magnet through 10 loops of wire generates a maximum current of 40 microamps.

Moving this magnet through 20 loops of wire generates a maximum current of 90 microamps.

Moving this magnet through 30 loops of wire generates a maximum current of 140 microamps.

24. Do the Math Use the photos at the bottom of the previous page to make a graph showing the relationship between the number of loops and the induced electric current. The graph should show the number of loops on the x-axis and the induced current on the y-axis. Because the photos showed three different coils of wire, you should have three data points.

25. From your graph, what conclusion can you draw about how the number of loops in a wire affects the amount of electric current induced?

    A. More loops in the wire increases the electric current induced.

    B. More loops in the wire decreases the electric current induced.

    C. The number of loops in the wire does not affect the electric current induced.

Induced Current

When a magnet or loop of wire moves relative to the other, a current is induced in the loop of wire.

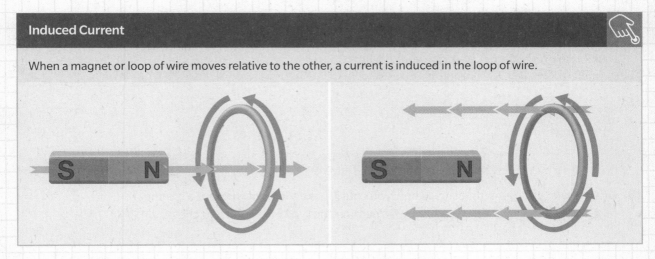

26. Why do you think a current is induced when either the loop of wire or the magnet is moved?

Induction and Reference Frames

A current can be induced in a wire if either the magnet or the wire is moving. The two must be moving in relation to one another. If the magnet is motionless and the wire moves, a current will be induced. If the wire is motionless and the magnet moves, a current will be induced. If both the magnet and the wire move in relation to one another, a current will be induced. However, if both the magnet and the wire have the same velocity, a current will not be induced. If the magnet and wire are moving at the same velocity, they are moving at the same speed in the same direction. The two objects would not be moving in relation to one another, and a current would not be induced.

Engineer It

Design a Generator

The electricity used to run your school, home, and the rest of your community is produced by generators. Generators produce electric energy using electromagnetic induction. Generators move a magnet or loop of wire in a repeating pattern to transform kinetic energy into electric energy. Harnessing different sources of motion requires many different types of generators.

Wind generators use the kinetic energy of wind gusts. The wind turns a large fan, which moves a powerful magnet.

27. What are some possible sources of motion that could be harnessed for a generator?

_____

_____

_____

28. How could you use this motion to repeatedly move a magnet or loop or wire in relation to one another? Describe your design.

_____

_____

_____

_____

29. **Draw** Make a diagram that shows how you could make a loop of wire and a magnet repeatedly move near one another by harnessing the type of motion you chose.

Continue Your Exploration

Name: _____   Date: _____

Check out the path below or go online to choose one of the other paths shown.

Careers in Science

- **Generators and Energy Resources**
- **Hands-On Labs** ✋
- **Propose Your Own Path**

Go online to choose one of these other paths.

MRI Technician

The use of electromagnetism has expanded human capabilities in many areas, including the medical field. One step forward in the medical field was the invention of magnetic resonance imaging (MRI) machines. MRI machines use powerful magnetic fields to generate images of organs. MRI technicians operate these machines and work with patients and doctors to produce accurate images for diagnoses.

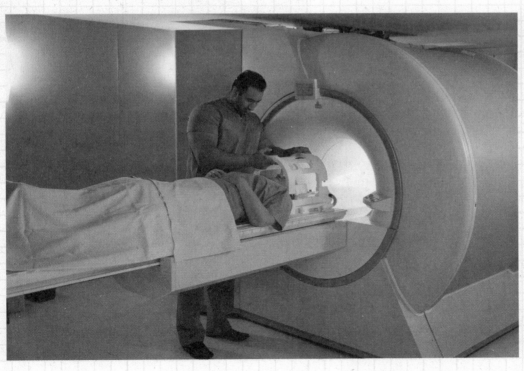

This MRI technician is preparing a patient to go inside an MRI machine, which is the cylindrical device on the right.

1. MRI machines use extremely strong magnetic fields. These fields must be adjustable to produce high-quality images. What might these machines use to generate such a field?

   A. permanent magnets

   B. electromagnets

   C. induced current

Continue Your Exploration

2. Why might the ability to produce three-dimensional images of organs be helpful in diagnosing a patient's ailment?

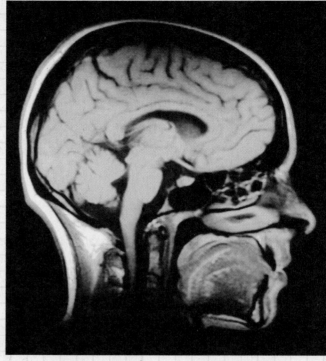

An MRI machine takes images of several cross-sections of a person's body, which can be combined to generate a three-dimensional representation.

3. Due to the connection between electric and magnetic phenomena, the magnetic field generated by an MRI machine can be used to excite the positive charges in hydrogen atoms. These hydrogen atoms emit radio waves that can be used to form an image of their locations. The main source of hydrogen atoms in the human body is water. Which of the following are limitations this method might place on the images that can be generated? Choose all that apply.

   A. Detecting hydrogen atoms allows for certain parts of the body to be imaged better than others.

   B. Hydrogen is not present in the human body.

   C. Areas without large amounts of water are harder to map.

4. When MRI machines are capturing images of a person's body, they produce extremely powerful magnetic fields. What might be some issues that an MRI technician would need to work around due to these magnetic fields?

5. **Collaborate** With a partner, discuss how the ability to generate images of the inside of a person's body may have advanced our understanding of diseases and improved our diagnosis and treatment abilities.

Can You Explain It?

Name: _____   Date: _____

How can these pieces of metal be picked up and then released without the crane grabbing them from their sides or bottom?

Explore
Online

 EVIDENCE NOTEBOOK

Refer to the notes in your Evidence Notebook to help you construct an explanation for how the crane is able to pick up and release the scrap metal.

1. State your claim. Make sure your claim fully explains how electromagnetism is used to make a crane operate.

2. Summarize the evidence you have gathered to support your claim and explain your reasoning.

Checkpoints

Answer the following questions to check your understanding of the lesson.

Use the photo to answer Questions 3–4.

3. If the magnet on the right is flipped so that the south pole is on the left, the magnetic force will be ~~attractive~~ / repulsive. As the two magnets are moved closer together, the magnetic force between them will become stronger / ~~weaker~~.

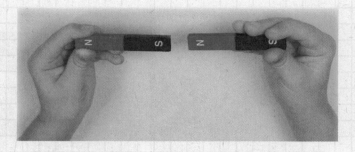

4. If the two magnets were cut in half along the line between the red and blue paint, which statement would describe the four bars that are produced?

   A. Each piece would have one magnetic pole and a nonmagnetic end.

   B. Each piece would have a north pole and a south pole.

   C. Two pieces would only have south poles and the other two pieces would only have north poles.

Use the image to answer Question 5.

5. The permanent magnet and solenoid pictured are equal in strength. How could the force between the two magnets be increased? Choose all that apply.

   A. The magnets could be moved closer together.

   B. The current in the solenoid could be decreased.

   C. The permanent magnet could be turned around.

   D. The number of loops in the solenoid could be increased.

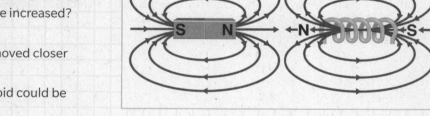

6. A permanent magnet is moved toward a wire. If the permanent magnet is accelerated as it moves toward the wire, what will happen to the induced current in the wire?

   A. The current decreases as the magnet moves faster.

   B. The current increases as the magnet moves faster.

   C. The current in the wire stops.

Interactive Review

Complete this section to review the main concepts of the lesson.

A magnet is a material that attracts iron. The force that a magnet generates depends on the strength of the magnet, the distance in between magnetic objects, and the orientation of those objects.

A. A magnet is passed 10 centimeters above a desk. A paper clip resting on the desk moves as the magnet passes over it. What could be done to increase the effect of the magnet on the paperclip?

An electromagnet is a coil of wire wrapped around an iron core. An electromagnet's strength is affected by the shape of the wire, number of loops, and the current in the wire.

B. How does an increase in the amount of charge flowing through an electromagnet change the current and the magnetic force generated by the current?

Changing magnetic fields causes electric charges to move. These moving charges can be measured as a change in current.

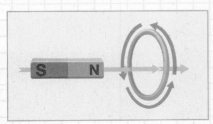

C. Explain how you could increase the amount of current induced in a wire.

Fields Are Areas Where Forces Act at a Distance

This amazing display of swirling colors is called an aurora. The colored lights are the result of charged particles from solar winds interacting with Earth's magnetic field.

Explore First

Testing Noncontact Forces Using charged balloons and magnets, try to determine the farthest distance that you can affect an object using a noncontact force. What other noncontact forces can you think of?

CAN YOU EXPLAIN IT?

How is Earth protected from cosmic radiation?

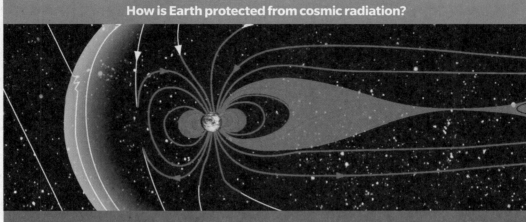

The sun and other stars emit cosmic radiation, which travels through space. However, very little cosmic radiation reaches Earth's surface. Instead, a large amount of cosmic radiation is deflected away from the planet.

1. What might cause cosmic radiation to be deflected around Earth?

EVIDENCE NOTEBOOK As you explore the lesson, gather evidence to help explain why Earth is protected from cosmic radiation.

Analyzing Noncontact Forces

When you push or pull on an object, it is easy to identify where the force on the object comes from. If you pushed your arm forward, you would be applying a force to whatever matter was in front of you. When you pull on an object, you are again applying a force directly to the object. However, noncontact forces do not behave in the exact same way. Noncontact forces are able to affect an object even when the source of the force is not touching the object.

When pushing on an object, you are applying a force in the direction that you are pushing.

2. When you throw a ball, what force or forces act on the ball when it is flying through the air? Is your hand still applying a force on the ball?

3. **Draw** Draw arrows to represent the forces that a paper clip would experience in five different positions around the magnet. Remember to use larger arrows to represent stronger forces.

Noncontact Forces

Electric, magnetic, and gravitational forces are all noncontact forces. A noncontact force can affect an object without the source of the force touching the object. For example, you are always being pulled down by Earth's gravity, whether you are touching the ground or not. Noncontact forces behave differently from contact forces in several ways. Noncontact forces are not exerted in a single direction. The sun exerts a gravitational force on every object in the solar system. All of these objects are constantly moving, but the forces between them are always present. Due to this behavior, noncontact forces are modeled differently than contact forces. You can only push an object that you can touch, but a noncontact force can be applied through objects and in several directions at once.

Fields in Science

What do you think of when you hear the word *field*? Maybe you imagine a large grassy meadow with wildflowers, a baseball diamond, or a profession, such as teaching. These meanings are all correct, but they are not what *field* means in science. In science, a **field** is the area in which a force that acts at a distance can be detected.

Fields can be tricky to study because they do not have mass. However, scientists know fields exist because they can detect noncontact forces near field's source. These forces can be almost undetectable far enough away from a field's source.

Force Arrows vs. Field Lines

Force arrows can be used to model noncontact forces. The force arrows show that while both the leaf and the dog are being pulled toward Earth by gravity, the gravitational force acting on the leaf is smaller than the gravitational force acting on the dog.

The uniformly spaced field lines show that the gravitational field is uniform at the surface of Earth. Everything on the surface of Earth, including the leaf and the dog, are inside Earth's gravitational field.

EVIDENCE NOTEBOOK

4. If cosmic radiation were affected by a field around Earth, how would the amount of radiation that reaches Earth change? Record your evidence.

Language SmArts

Analyze Evidence for Fields

Scientists developed the idea of fields to explain how gravity, electric forces, and magnetic forces can affect objects without touching them. The idea of fields is accepted today because scientists have gathered and carefully analyzed a vast amount of evidence for each of the three forces.

　　Scientists find evidence for gravitational fields as they analyze information about how gravity affects the organization and motion of objects throughout the universe. They have analyzed information about electric fields to explain why all charged objects need to be a certain distance from each other before they are attracted or repelled. Data collected and analyzed about the predictable behavior of magnets provides evidence of magnetic fields.

5. The table below shows evidence for this claim: **Objects are affected by the fields of noncontact forces**. Analyze the evidence and complete the table by filling in the Supports Claim and Reasoning columns. Use the example in the first column to guide your answers.

Evidence	Supports Claim (Yes / No)	Reasoning
Maglev trains hover above the track.	Yes	The magnets in the train and the track exert pushing forces on each other.
If you rub your hair with a balloon, the balloon and your hair attract each other when they are close. They do not attract each other when they are far apart.		
A bike slows down if you do not pedal as its wheels roll over pavement.		
The moons of Jupiter orbit Jupiter because they are pulled toward Jupiter. The moons of Jupiter are too far to be pulled into Earth's orbit.		

Features of Fields

Each noncontact force is modeled using a different type of field. Gravitational fields model gravitational forces, electric fields model electric forces, and magnetic fields model magnetic forces. However, all fields have some similarities. Each only affects certain types of objects. Gravitational fields affect objects with mass. Electric fields affect objects that have a charge. Magnetic fields affect objects containing iron. An object in a relevant field will experience a force and have potential energy. All fields also decrease in strength as the distance from the fields' sources increases. The farther away an object is from a field's source, the less the field affects it, and the weaker the force on the object is.

 6. Do the Math Look at table to see how the force due to a field changes with distance. In the third column, record the change in force between the force at that distance and the previous force. The first two rows have been done for you.

Distance from Magnet (m)	Strength of Magnetic Force (N)	Change in Force (N)
1.00	100	n/a
2.00	25	-75
3.00	11.1	
4.00	6.25	
5.00	4	

7. Describe how the strength of a field changes as distance from the field 's source increases.

 Engineer It
Engineer Solutions Using Fields

Scientists and engineers are investigating how to use ferrofluids to deliver medication directly where it is needed in the body. This procedure could be important for cancer treatments. Doctors use drugs to kill cancer tumors, but these drugs can also kill healthy cells. By delivering the treatment to only cancer cells, doctors hope that some of the side effects of these drugs could be avoided.

Ferrofluids are a mixture of tiny magnetic particles and a liquid. Ferrofluids look and act like other liquids, unless they are in a strong magnetic field. When exposed to a magnetic field, the ferrofluid forms spikes that look and act like solids.

8. When the magnetic field is removed, the ferrofluid becomes liquid / toxic .

9. One potential advantage of using a ferrofluid to deliver medicine is that it can be directed to tumors by a magnetic field / is cheaper than existing treatments .

Modeling Fields

All fields share some common properties. They all model noncontact forces and decrease in strength with distance. They also all only affect objects with the physical property relevant to the field. While all types of fields have similarities, each type of noncontact force has unique characteristics that affect how they are modeled.

Earth and the moon are always attracted to one another, regardless of how they are oriented.

10. What are some of the differences between a gravitational force and a magnetic force?

Different Fields Require Different Models

Gravitational fields, magnetic fields, and electric fields are all slightly different. Though they all are ways to represent noncontact forces in space, each of these forces have different features that must be modeled in different ways. For instance, gravitational forces are always attractive. Electric forces can be attractive or repulsive depending on the electric charges involved while magnetic forces can be attractive or repulsive depending on the orientation of the magnets. If you were to use the exact same method of modeling each field, you would not be able to represent these differences. Long arrows are often used to model fields, but the way that they are oriented and shaped depends on the specific field that they are used to model.

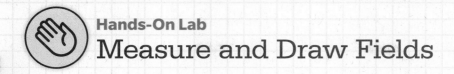

Hands-On Lab
Measure and Draw Fields

Measure the strength of a field at different locations in the field. Then use this information to draw a model of the field. By measuring and modeling the fields you will be better able to predict how noncontact forces behave in different situations.

Fields are commonly represented using arrows. The arrows are most often drawn with the arrowheads representing the direction of the force an object in the field will experience. The density or size of the arrows are generally used to indicate areas where the field is stronger.

MATERIALS
- balloon, non-latex
- cloth, wool
- compass
- magnets
- paper clips, metal
- pencil
- tape
- tinsel
- thread
- wooden stick

Procedure

STEP 1 Charge the balloon by rubbing it on a piece of wool cloth or your hair. Tape a piece of paper to the table and then tape the balloon to one edge of the paper.

STEP 2 Tie a 6 inch piece of thread to the wooden stick. Move the thread around the balloon without allowing the thread to touch the balloon. Draw arrows on the piece of paper to represent how the thread moved in relation to the balloon at different locations.

STEP 3 **Draw** Using the markings that you made, draw the balloon and the field around it. Use arrows to model the field.

STEP 4 Develop a procedure to visualize the magnetic field around a magnet. Describe your procedure.

STEP 5 Use your observations to draw the magnet and the field around it. Use arrows to model the field.

STEP 6 **Draw** Sketch the gravitational field that surrounds Earth. Use your life experiences and your other field models to make your sketch.

STEP 7 What are some differences between your models of the three fields?

EVIDENCE NOTEBOOK

11. Cosmic radiation moves through space, but is repelled around Earth. How would a field explain this behavior? How would the forces on the radiation would change as it neared Earth? Record your evidence.

Gravitational Fields

Because every object has mass, every object exerts a gravitational force and has a gravitational field around it. The **gravitational field** is the area surrounding an object in which another object is pulled toward the object. The entire solar system is in the sun's gravitational field so all objects in the solar system are pulled toward the sun.

Gravitational field lines point toward the object that is exerting the force. The direction of the arrowheads indicate the direction of the forces due to a field. The sun's gravitational field is represented by lines that point toward the center of the sun. The density of the field lines represents the strength of a field. Notice that the sun's gravitational field is strongest at the surface of the sun. The strength of the field decreases as the distance from the sun increases until the field can no longer be detected.

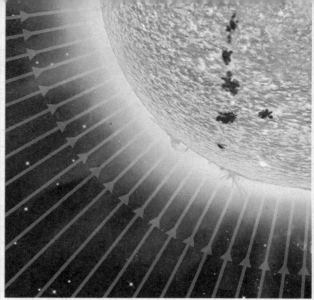

The sun's large gravitational field keeps Earth and every other object in the solar system in orbit around it.

The pattern of field lines can also show how two fields interact. For example, the pattern of field lines around Earth and the moon identify areas where the attractive forces increase the strength of the field and where they cancel each other out. As the moon orbits Earth, the field around the moon moves with it. By studying the field lines in a series of models, a scientist could analyze how the fields change over time.

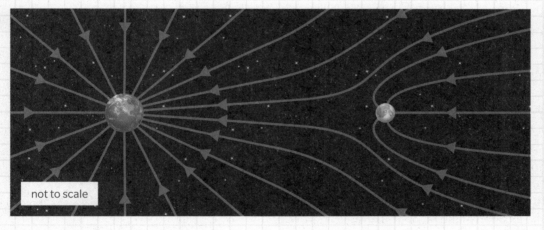

not to scale

The lines around Earth are closer together than the lines around the moon, indicating that Earth's gravitational field is stronger than the moon's. Earth's stronger gravitational field keeps the moon in orbit.

12. Compare the patterns of field lines in each gravitational field model. What can you conclude about the strength of the fields from the models? Choose all that apply.

   A. The strength of the gravitational field is the same at the surface of the sun, Earth, and the moon.

   B. The strength of the sun's gravitational field decreases as the distance from the sun increases.

   C. The gravitational field at Earth's surface is greater than the gravitational field at the moon's surface.

Tiny pieces of iron are pulled toward the magnet by the magnetic field. The iron filings line up to reveal the pattern of the magnetic field. If you wanted to create a model of the field using field lines, the arrows would point away from the north pole and toward the south pole.

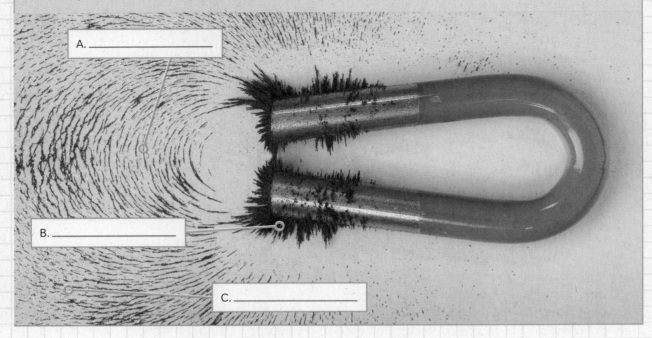

A. _____

B. _____

C. _____

13. The density of the iron filings shows the strength of the magnetic field. Rank the strength of the magnetic field in different spots by labeling where the field is strong, medium, and weak.

Magnetic Fields

Every magnet is surrounded by a **magnetic field**—the area around a magnet in which magnetic forces affect magnetic objects. You can feel the effect of a magnetic field when you hold two magnets near each other. If you put both north poles or both south poles near each other, they will push apart. But if you put a north pole and a south pole near each other, the magnets will pull together.

The strength of a magnetic field depends on the strength of the magnet and the location of the magnet. The field is strongest near each pole of the magnet and decreases as the distance from the pole increases. Field lines represent these characteristics of magnetic fields. They are denser near the poles where the magnetic field is the strongest. The arrows of magnetic field lines point away from the north pole and toward the south pole.

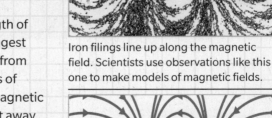

Iron filings line up along the magnetic field. Scientists use observations like this one to make models of magnetic fields.

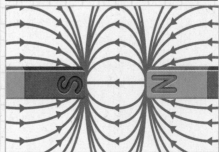

Field lines are used to model the strength, size, and direction of the magnetic field around one or more magnets.

EVIDENCE NOTEBOOK

14. Cosmic radiation is repelled by a field that surrounds Earth. Based on the properties of the fields, is the radiation repelled by a magnetic or gravitational field? Record your evidence.

Electric Fields

Most objects have an equal number of positive and negative charges, so most objects are neutral. However, some objects have more positive charges than negative charges, and the object is positively charged. Other objects have more negative charges, so they are negatively charged. Every charged object is surrounded by an electric field. An **electric field** is the area around a charged object in which another charged object is affected by the electric force. The strength and size of an electric field around a charged object depends on the magnitude of the net charge of the object. The bigger the charge, the stronger and larger its electric field. As with other fields, the electric field decreases as the distance from the charged object increases.

The electric field around a charged object pulls oppositely charged objects toward the charged object and pushes similarly charged objects away. For example, when you rub your foot on a carpet, the carpet will give up negative charges to become positively charged, while your body gains negative charges to become negatively charged. When you touch another object that has a positive charge, the electric fields of your body and the object pull the opposite charges toward each other. The negative charges can suddenly flow to the other object, resulting in an electric discharge. When this sudden flow happens, you feel a shock.

15. Imagine that you ran some jeans through a dryer and they became positively charged. How would you draw field lines around the jeans?

Explore Online

Experiment with Charged Objects in an Electric Field

The student wipes a plastic rod with a wool cloth and then suspends it. When the negatively charged wool cloth enters the positively charged rod's field, the oppositely charged objects are attracted to each other.

The student wipes a second plastic rod with the wool cloth. She then moves the positively charged rod toward the suspended rod. The two positively charged rods repel each other.

Model Electric Fields

Wool fibers are mixed into oil in the diagram. An electric charge from the metal plates is applied to the mixture. When a charge is applied, the fibers line up to reveal the pattern of the electric field. The pattern depends on whether the charges are the same or opposite.

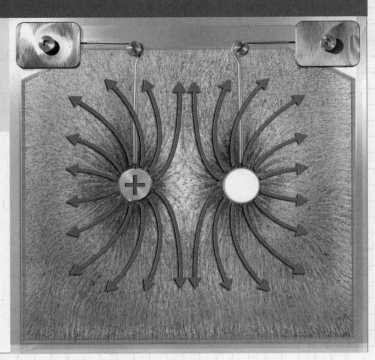

16. Analyze the pattern of the field lines in this model. Do they show that the plates are attracting or repelling each other? Fill in the missing charge to make the model correct.

To model electric fields consistently, field lines always point away from positive charges and toward negative charges. When two charged objects are near each other, the pattern of the field lines shows the overall strength of each field at different locations. For example, when the fields of two opposite or like charges interact, the resulting field between the objects is strong. When two like charges interact, the field lines show that charges push away from each other. And when opposite charges interact, the field lines show that the charges are attracted to each other.

Investigate Earth's Electric Field

In addition to having a gravitational field, Earth also has an electric field. The electric field is the result of positive charges in the upper atmosphere and negative charges at Earth's surface. The field is stronger at higher altitudes and weaker near Earth's surface, which is why you usually do not notice it.

17. **Draw** Look at the model and think about what you learned about electric field lines. Draw arrows to complete the model of Earth's electric field on a sunny day.

Continue Your Exploration

Name: _____   Date: _____

Check out the path below or go online to choose one of the other paths shown.

| Earth's Magnetic Field | • **Can Bumblebees See Electric Fields?**
• **Hands-On Labs** 👋
• **Propose Your Own Path** | *Go online to choose one of these other paths.* |

Earth is like a giant bar magnet and is surrounded by a huge magnetic field. Earth's core is an enormous mass of heavy elements, such as iron and nickel. The magnetic field is generated when the solid inner core and the flowing molten metals in the liquid part of Earth's outer core interact.

Humans and other animals, such as sea turtles, use Earth's magnetic field to navigate around the globe. As scientists and engineers discover new information about Earth's magnetic field, they can develop new ways to use it.

Earth's Poles

The north pole of a compass needle is a magnetic north pole. It is attracted to the geographic North Pole, which is a magnetic south pole. It sounds confusing, but think about it—like all other magnets, Earth has a north pole and a south pole that interact with other magnets. Earth's geographic North Pole attracts the north end of other magnets, so, because opposite poles attract, Earth's geographic North Pole is actually the south pole of Earth's magnetic field. It is called the north magnetic pole because it is in the Northern Hemisphere. It might help to think of Earth's magnetic north pole as the place on Earth that the north pole of magnets point to.

Throughout Earth's history, the north and south magnetic poles have changed places many times in a process known as a magnetic reversal. When the poles change places, the direction of Earth's magnetic field changes. Igneous rock layers contain a record of magnetic reversals. Iron is found in igneous rocks, which form from magma. While the iron is molten, the domains in iron align themselves with Earth's magnetic field like tiny compass needles.

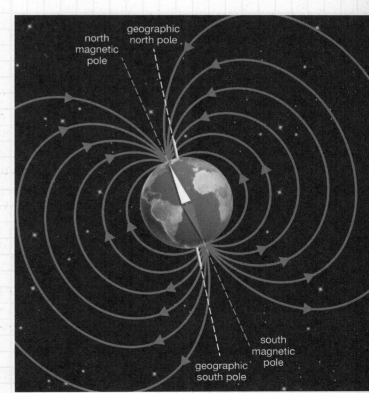

Earth's magnetic field is similar to the magnetic field of a bar magnet that is tilted when compared to Earth's rotational axis.

Continue Your Exploration

1. The current north magnetic pole is near the geographic North Pole, but they are not in exactly the same place. Compasses point toward the north magnetic pole. How does a compass needle help people find the direction that they are going?

2. Most people need a compass to navigate using magnetic fields, but birds, whales, deer, and many other organisms have the ability to detect Earth's magnetic fields without a compass. The mechanism that many organisms use to detect the magnetic field is still not entirely understood. However, the mechanisms of a group of bacteria that align with the magnetic field of Earth are well understood. The bacteria provide scientists with a simple organism that they can study to find out how organisms can naturally detect magnetic fields. What would be a reasonable hypothesis about how these bacteria detect the magnetic field?

    A. The bacteria respond to electric fields.

    B. The bacteria have iron particles in their bodies.

    C. The bacteria can see magnetic fields.

    D. The bacteria can detect gravity.

3. Bacteria that can detect magnetic fields are called magnetotactic bacteria. They contain particles, such as magnetite, that are affected by magnetic fields. These particles form short chains in the bacteria that line up along magnetic fields, similar to the way a compass needle aligns with Earth's magnetic field. Scientists can use fossils of these bacteria to study what Earth's magnetic field was like in the past. Rocks that formed from cooling lava also contain clues about the history of Earth's magnetic field. Which of the following statements are true? Select all that apply.

    A. Rocks that contain iron are affected by Earth's magnetic field.

    B. The magnetic fields of magnetic materials in molten rock align with Earth's magnetic field.

    C. When the poles reverse, the magnetic fields in both fossilized and molten rock reverse.

    D. Rocks contain a record of Earth's changing magnetic field.

4. **Collaborate** Together with a small group, predict possible local and global impacts of a reversal of Earth's magnetic field.

Can You Explain It?

Name: _____   Date: _____

How is Earth protected from cosmic radiation?

 EVIDENCE NOTEBOOK
Refer to the notes in your Evidence Notebook to help you construct an explanation for how Earth is protected from cosmic radiation.

1. State your claim. Make sure your claim fully explains how Earth is protected from cosmic radiation.

2. Summarize the evidence you have gathered to support your claim and explain your reasoning.

Checkpoints

Answer the following questions to check your understanding of the lesson.

Use the photo to answer Questions 3–4.

3. Once a gas's temperature rises above a certain point, its particles start to break apart, and it becomes plasma. Plasma can generate and be affected by electric and magnetic fields. The plasma streams inside the globe are evidence that an electric field *acts throughout the globe / only acts in the center of the globe.* When a person touches the glass globe, he or she affects the pattern of the plasma because of the electric force between their hands and the plasma inside the glass. This is evidence that the electric field acts on objects *that are touching / at a distance.*

4. A student learns that an LED bulb will light up when it is in the electric field of a plasma globe. What steps will help the student map and model the field during an experiment? Select all that apply.

   A. Observe how the plasma moves inside the globe.

   B. Walk around the globe, recording where the LED bulb lights up.

   C. Move the LED bulb closer to the plasma globe until it lights up.

   D. Measure the distance between the glowing LED bulb and the plasma globe.

5. Which of the following are true about gravitational fields? Choose all that apply.

   A. Gravitational fields are always attractive.

   B. All objects with mass are affected by gravitational fields.

   C. Gravitational fields do not vary in strength with distance.

Use the photo to answer Question 6.

6. What does the photo show about the magnetic field around the magnet? Select all that apply.

   A. The magnet can attract iron filings without touching them.

   B. The magnetic field around the magnet is strongest at its poles.

   C. The strength of the magnetic field is the same throughout the liquid.

   D. The magnetic field is three dimensional.

Interactive Review

Complete this section to review the main concepts of the lesson.

The area in which an object experiences a noncontact force is called a field. Examples of fields include electric fields, magnetic fields, and gravitational fields.

A. In your own words, explain what a field is in science. Use examples to support your explanation.

The density of field lines models the strength of a field. Field lines that are close together model a strong field, whereas field lines that are widely spaced model a weak field.

B. Create a checklist of important points to remember when modeling a magnetic field.

© Houghton Mifflin Harcourt Publishing Company • Image Credits: (t) ©HMH; (b) ©Alchemy/Alamy

Gravity Affects All Matter in the Universe

These two spiral galaxies in space are attracted toward one another by gravitational forces.

Explore First

Investigating Gravity Cut a hole near the bottom of a paper cup. Hold the cup over a pan and fill the cup with water while plugging the hole with your finger. What happens when you remove your finger? Fill the cup again and then drop the cup at the same time you unplug the hole. How can you explain what happens to the water in the cup?

Go online to view the digital version of the Hands-On Lab for this lesson and to download additional lab resources.

CAN YOU EXPLAIN IT?

What could explain the motion of these stars near the center of the Milky Way?

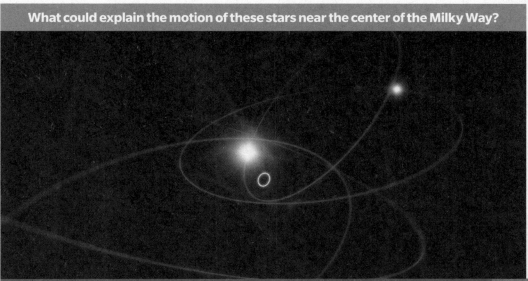

This image shows the paths of stars near the center of the Milky Way galaxy as observed from Earth over several years.

Explore Online

1. Look at the path of one of the stars. How does the star appear to move?

2. Compare the paths of all the stars. How are the paths of the stars similar, and how are they different?

 EVIDENCE NOTEBOOK As you explore the lesson, gather evidence to help explain the movement of stars.

Exploring Gravity

Gravity

For many years, scientists observed the motion of falling objects and the motions of planets. Although they couldn't see gravity, they could see its effects. These observations led scientists to develop models of gravity. **Gravity** is a force of attraction between objects due to their masses. Because gravity exists between objects even when they are not touching, it is called a noncontact force. Gravity is always an attractive force because it always pulls objects toward each other.

A Robot on the Moon

The mass of this robot on the moon is 50 kg, and its weight is about 81 N.

A Robot on Earth

The mass of the same robot on Earth is 50 kg, and its weight is about 490 N.

3. Compare the weight and mass of the robot shown above on Earth and on the moon. Explain the similarities and differences in terms of gravity.

Weight

Mass is the amount of matter in an object. *Weight* is a measure of the pull of gravity on that mass. Weight is a force. Think of it this way: An object is made up of a certain amount of matter, so its mass is constant. The object has a certain weight due to the force of gravity. If the force of gravity decreases, the weight of the object decreases. If the force of gravity increases, the weight of the object increases.

Mass and weight are measured using different units. A common unit for mass in the metric system is the gram (g) or the kilogram (kg). Scientists measure forces with newtons (N), a unit named after Isaac Newton. An apple with a mass of about 102 g weighs one newton (1 N) on Earth. The same apple would weigh 0.16 N on the moon.

4. Do the Math A scientific instrument has a mass of 54 kg, and its weight on Earth is 529 N. Jupiter's gravity is about 2.3 times stronger than Earth's gravity. Use this information to calculate the mass and weight of the instrument if it were on the surface of Jupiter.

Gravity near Earth

The gravitational force Earth exerts on you is equal to the gravitational force you exert on Earth. But because your mass is so much smaller, the effect of that gravitational force is much greater on you.

  The pull of objects toward Earth is not the only gravitational force on Earth. Every object exerts a gravitational force on every other object. Why do you not normally notice the gravitational pull of other objects? Most objects on Earth have too little mass to exert enough force for us to notice the effects. However, the moon and Earth are both large objects with a lot of mass, so the gravitational force between them is large. The tides occur because of gravity and the moon. The force of gravity between Earth and the moon is what holds the moon in orbit around Earth. An **orbit** is the path that a particular object follows as it travels around another body in space such as a star, planet, or moon. Notice that the surface of Earth is not a perfect sphere. What happens to the force of gravity on an object in a canyon or on top of a mountain?

The surface gravity of the moon is one-sixth of Earth's, so an astronaut can jump high despite wearing a large spacesuit.

5. Objects near Earth's surface are attracted toward Earth's center / surface. Because of this, if you dig a hole in Earth's surface and drop an object into the hole, the object will continue to fall until it reaches the original surface level / bottom of the hole.

6. **Collaborate** Working with a partner, imagine that you are able to dig a tunnel through the center of Earth to the opposite surface. Describe how gravity would affect you if you jumped into the tunnel. What would happen as you pass the center of Earth?

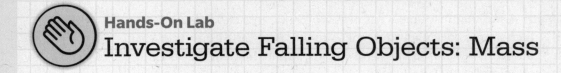

Hands-On Lab
Investigate Falling Objects: Mass

Predict how changing the mass of an object affects how it falls. Test your predictions and record your observations.

MATERIALS
- bottle, plastic, empty, with cap
- funnel (optional)
- marbles or sand
- meterstick
- pillow
- video camera (optional)

Procedure and Analysis

STEP 1 Fill a plastic bottle about one-quarter full with sand or marbles. Make sure to close the lid to contain the sand or marbles. Fill another bottle so that it is completely full of sand or marbles.

STEP 2 Drop the bottles at the same instant from a height of two meters onto the pillow. Repeat this action three more times. Did the bottles land at the same or different times?

STEP 3 Fill the two bottles with two new amounts of sand or marbles and repeat Step 2. Does the mass of the bottle seem to affect the time it takes for the bottle to reach the ground?

STEP 4 Based on your observations, what can you conclude about the relationship between an object's mass and the rate at which it falls?

Mass and Falling Objects

Near Earth's surface, objects will fall toward Earth at the same rate regardless of how much mass they have. Objects near Earth accelerate at the same rate as they are pulled toward the ground. If two objects do not fall at the same rate, it is because other forces are acting on the objects instead of just gravity. For instance, a skydiver can open a parachute, which vastly increases the amount of air he or she has to move through to fall. Pushing through that much air slows the skydiver down. This is the same reason a feather might fall slower than an apple. If there were no air present, the feather and apple would fall at the same rate.

EVIDENCE NOTEBOOK

7. How might these interactions apply to objects in space? Do you think Earth is attracted to the sun in a similar way to the objects you observed in your experiments? Record your evidence.

© Houghton Mifflin Harcourt Publishing Company

The Force of Gravity

When you think about gravity, you probably think about the force that makes objects fall and keeps you from floating off into space. While those effects of gravity are important in everyday life, Newton described gravity as a force that every mass exerts on every other mass. This model also allowed him to mathematically describe the force two objects exert on one another. The strength of the force between two objects depends on the masses of the objects and on the distance between them.

Effect of Mass on Gravity

Imagine a universe that contains only two objects. Newton showed that the gravitational force between them could be calculated using their masses and the distance between them. If both objects have the same mass, it makes sense that the force each exerts on the other is the same strength. If you increase the mass of both objects while keeping the distance the same, the gravitational force increases. The force of gravity on both objects is equal in strength. If you change the mass of only one of the objects, will both experience the same gravitational force? Yes, the force depends on both masses, and both objects always exert the same amount of force on each other. If you increase the mass of one or both objects, the force between them is stronger. If you decrease the mass of one or both objects, the force is weaker.

Effect of Distance on Gravity

For large spherical objects such as stars and planets, the distance between two objects is measured from the center of one to the center of the other. Imagine that you could easily change the distance between two massive objects while keeping their masses the same. If two objects are moved farther apart, the force they exert on each other decreases. If two objects are moved closer together, the force increases. That is why rockets must travel many kilometers above Earth's surface to break free of Earth's gravity.

Stars and planets typically are very far from one another. Though it varies based on the time of year, Earth is typically about 150 million kilometers from the sun. Even though objects such as Earth and the sun are very far apart, they still affect each other's motion because they are so massive. If Earth were closer to the sun, the gravitational force between the two would be even stronger.

Gravitational Forces

8. Draw force arrows to model each scenario correctly. The first scenario has been done for you. Use longer arrows to model stronger forces.

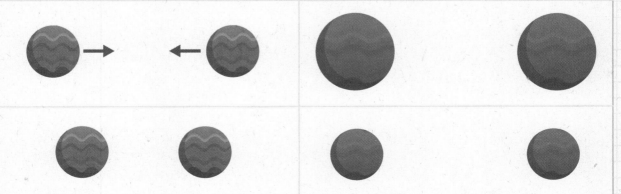

Analyze Gravitational Force

The graphic shows the force of Earth's gravity on a 50 kg object at different distances from Earth. Analyze the information in the image to answer the following questions.

6,400	12,800	19,200	25,600	32,000	38,400	distance in kilometers from Earth's center
486	122	54	30	19	14	gravitational force on a 50 kg object at each location rounded to the nearest newton

9. In the image, the mass of the object remains constant / changes constantly . As the distance from Earth's center increases, the gravitational force on the object increases / decreases.

10. You and your friend are having a discussion about weight. He claims that he weighs less on the 100th floor of a building than he does on the ground floor. Is he correct? Support your answer with evidence.

_____

_____

_____

_____

_____

11. If a 50 kg object is at a location 25,600 km from Earth's center, what is the gravitational force exerted by the object on Earth? In what direction does that force act? Support your answer with evidence.

_____

_____

_____

_____

_____

_____

_____

Modeling Gravity

It is the nature of science to build on previous discoveries. Tycho Brahe was an astronomer who made detailed observations of the motions of the planets, in particular the motion of Mars. After his death, his student Johannes Kepler analyzed Brahe's observations. Kepler wrote three mathematical laws, based on Brahe's data, that described the motions of the planets. While Kepler's laws could be used to predict the motions of the planets, they did not explain why the planets moved the way they did. Isaac Newton was able to use Kepler's laws to help develop a model of gravity that explained the motions of the planets and other bodies in the solar system.

Tycho Brahe 1546–1601

Johannes Kepler 1571–1630

Issac Newton 1643–1727

12. Newton said, "If I have seen further than others, it is by standing upon the shoulders of giants." Explain the meaning of this quotation.

The Law of Universal Gravitation

Newton hypothesized that the same force that causes objects to fall to the ground also causes the motion of the planets. That force is gravity. In 1687, Newton published his work, including the law of universal gravitation.

The law of universal gravitation states that all matter is attracted to all other matter. It describes mathematically the relationship between gravitational force, mass, and distance. The gravitational force is proportional to the mass of each object, and it is inversely proportional to the square of the distance between the centers of the objects. The equation for the law is:

$$F = G\left(\frac{m_1 \times m_2}{d^2}\right)$$

In this equation, F represents the force of gravity, m_1 and m_2 represent the masses of the two objects, and d is the distance between the objects. G is the gravitational constant, and its value depends on the units of mass and distance. The value of the gravitational constant was first measured many years after Newton published his work.

13. Do the Math Which of the following changes will increase the force of gravity between two masses? Use the formula $F = G\left(\dfrac{m_1 \times m_2}{d^2}\right)$. Select all that apply.

A. m_1 increases

B. m_1 decreases

C. m_2 increases

D. m_2 decreases

E. d increases

F. d decreases

The Cavendish Experiment

Almost 100 years after Newton published the law of universal gravitation, Henry Cavendish performed an investigation now known as the Cavendish experiment. It is the first known experiment to measure the force of gravity between objects.

The setup, shown in the diagram, had two small masses hanging from a frame. This frame was supported by a wire so it could rotate. Since even a small breeze would rotate the frame, Cavendish enclosed the entire setup in a shed. Inside the shed, two large lead balls hung on another support. The smaller masses were attracted to the larger masses, causing the frame to rotate until the wire holding the frame would not twist anymore. By carefully measuring the rotation of the frame and knowing the force it took to twist the wire, Cavendish could calculate the force of gravity between the small and large masses.

After this experiment, scientists were able to use Cavendish's measurements and the law of universal gravitation to calculate the gravitational constant and the masses of Earth and other celestial bodies.

14. Discuss With a partner, discuss the design of this experiment. How do you think this experiment could be improved?

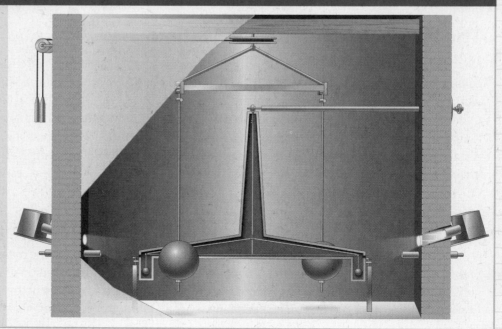

Cavendish Experimental Setup

A frame supporting small masses rotates as the smaller masses are attracted by gravity toward the larger masses. Cavendish used telescopes to observe the rotation of the frame in his shed, so that his own mass would be farther away from the apparatus. If he stood next to the apparatus, his own mass might have interfered with the movement he was trying to observe.

15. The art shows the masses in Cavendish's apparatus from above. In position A, the forces on the smaller masses are balanced. Draw how you expect the orientation of the rod and smaller masses to change when the larger masses are moved to position B.

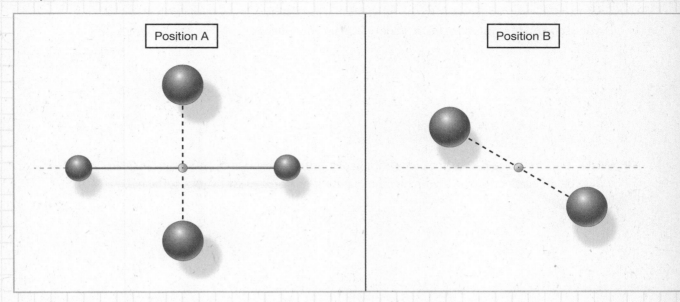

Position A

Position B

Gravity Shapes Celestial Bodies

What do the Earth, moon, sun, and other planets have in common with one another? These bodies and other large celestial bodies all appear to be spherical in shape. Is this just a coincidence? No; gravity has a role in shaping massive celestial bodies. As the mass of an object increases, so does its gravitational field. This gravitational field pulls in all directions with the same strength. Think about what would happen to a lump of clay if you were to press on it equally in all directions at the same time. How would the shape of the clay change?

While gravity is the primary reason large objects in space are spherical, other factors may cause an object to not be exactly spherical. An object's rotation or the material the object is made of may cause deviations in shape. Many planets are not perfectly spherical due to these differences.

This bubble is spherical in shape because the air pressure that shapes the bubble acts evenly in all directions.

16. How does the way that air pressure shapes the bubble relate to the way that gravity shapes massive celestial bodies?

17. Do the Math | Compare the Gravity of Different Planets Remember that the gravitational force between two objects depends on the masses of both objects and the distance between them. Imagine a planet that has the same radius as Earth but only half its mass. How would the gravitational force between you and this planet compare to the gravitational force between you and Earth if you stood on the surface of each planet? Explain your answer.

18. Write Use the space below or a piece of paper to write a short story about how life would be different on a planet with half the gravitational force of Earth at its surface.

Explain Earth's Shape

Satellite data shows that Earth is not exactly a sphere. Earth bulges out near the equator and is slightly flattened near the poles. Newton's first law says that an object in motion will stay in motion, so the points on the surface of a spinning object have a tendency to continue moving at the same speed in the same direction.

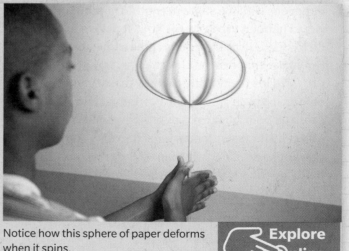

Notice how this sphere of paper deforms when it spins.

Explore Online

19. How does the model shown in the photo relate to the shape of Earth? Select all that apply.

   A. The model shows that a spherical object may deform when it spins.

   B. Places near the equator have a greater tendency to move outward than places near the poles due to their velocity.

   C. The paper sphere is hollow, so this model does not relate to the shape of Earth.

   D. The faster an object spins, the more likely it is to deform.

Exploring Gravity's Role in Earth's Motion

Projectile Motion

An object that is launched or thrown is called a *projectile*. Once a projectile is launched, its motion is controlled by the force of gravity. When you throw an object upward into the air, it goes up for a while and then falls. The gravitational pull between the object and Earth causes it to fall back toward Earth's center. Projectiles may also encounter some air resistance, but their acceleration is mostly due to gravity. An airplane would not be considered a projectile because its motion is not primarily controlled by gravity.

Explore Online

The basketball is a projectile. Notice the path of the ball as it travels toward the hoop.

20. Use the law of universal gravitation to explain how gravity affects the motion of the basketball during a free-throw attempt.

The Effect of Velocity on Projectile Motion

Think about how a ball moves when you throw it in the air. Does it make a difference whether you toss it straight up or at an angle? What about if you throw it faster or slower? The velocity, or speed and direction, of the launch determines what path a projectile follows. When predicting the path of a projectile, it is important to notice in which direction the object will accelerate due to gravity. If acceleration is in the same direction as the velocity of an object, the speed of the object will increase, but its direction will not change. If acceleration is in the opposite direction, its speed will decrease, but the direction will not change. If the acceleration of an object is perpendicular to its velocity, the speed will not change, but the direction will. Acceleration in another direction will cause a change in speed and direction.

Hands-On Lab
Explore the Motion of a Falling Object

Explore how the velocity of a ball rolling on a table affects its path after it rolls off the table and becomes a projectile.

MATERIALS
- paper
- pencils, colored
- steel balls or marbles
- table

Procedure

STEP 1 Based on your knowledge of projectiles and previous observations of motion, predict the path of a ball after it very slowly rolls off the edge of a table. Draw your predicted path on the image in Step 2 using a red colored pencil.

STEP 2 Roll a ball very slowly off the edge of the table. Carefully observe the path that the ball follows as it falls. In the same drawing area as your prediction, draw the actual path that you observed, using a blue colored pencil.

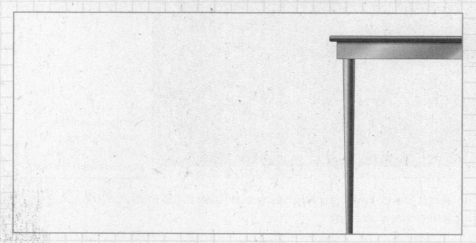

STEP 3 Make a prediction of the path of a ball after it rolls a little more quickly, but still fairly slowly, off the edge of a table. Draw your predicted path in Step 4 in red.

STEP 4 Roll a ball slowly off the edge of a table. Draw the actual path in blue in the same area as your prediction.

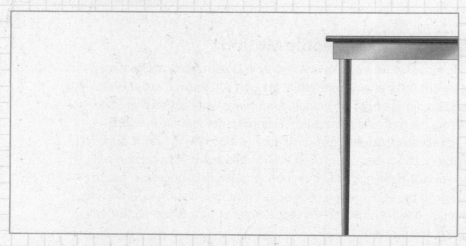

© Houghton Mifflin Harcourt Publishing Company

STEP 5 Make a prediction of the path of a ball after it rolls more quickly off the edge of a table. Draw your predicted path on the image in Step 6 in red.

STEP 6 Roll a ball more quickly off the edge of a table. Draw the actual path in blue in the same area as your prediction.

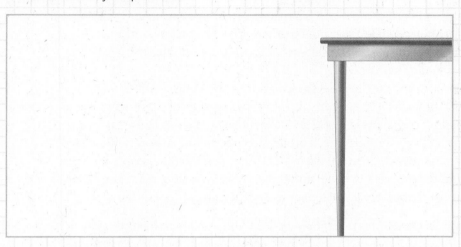

Analysis

STEP 7 How did the results of each step affect your predictions for future steps?

STEP 8 How does the horizontal velocity of the ball on the table affect the path of the ball when it falls off the table?

21. If a cannonball were launched from the surface of Earth, it would eventually fall to the ground. However, if the cannonball was moving fast enough, it would move forward fast enough that it would never fall all the way to the ground, as shown by path 4 in the diagram. If the cannonball in the diagram were launched even faster, what would happen to its motion?

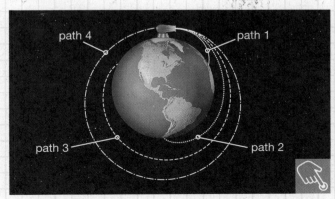

This image shows a thought experiment in which a cannonball is launched at increasing velocities. Path 1 is the slowest, and path 4 is the fastest.

Velocity and Orbits

A *satellite* is an object that orbits a more massive object. An orbit is the path that a particular object follows as it travels around another body in space. A natural satellite forms naturally in space and is attracted by gravity toward a more massive object. Gravity holds the satellite in orbit. The moon is a natural satellite of Earth. Earth is also orbited by about 2,300 human-made satellites and countless bits of debris. These satellites include space telescopes and satellites that provide communications, weather observations, and navigation signals.

Satellites do not all orbit at the same distance from Earth. Some satellites travel in a low Earth orbit (LEO) between 160 km and 2,000 km above sea level. Some satellites travel in a high Earth orbit (HEO) more than 35,786 km above sea level. The distance between an orbiting satellite and the object it orbits is related to the satellite's speed. An object in LEO must travel faster than an object in HEO. An object in LEO also experiences air resistance from the atmosphere. Without additional thrust to maintain its speed, the object will slow down, and gravity will pull it back to Earth's surface.

22. Language SmArts In a geostationary orbit, the satellite remains directly above a specific location on Earth at all times, which is useful for communications and navigation satellites. A satellite in geostationary orbit will complete an orbit every 24 hours. What evidence from the text supports a claim that geostationary satellites must orbit at a specific height above sea level?

Most orbits are not circular, but form an oval-like path called an *ellipse*. Imagine a planet orbiting a star. The planet moves both forward and toward the star. Most of the time, these motions are not perfectly balanced. What if the planet moves forward much faster than it moves toward the star? In that case, it will pass the star. The gravitational force will now pull the planet back toward the star. Eventually, the planet will slow down enough that it curves back and accelerates toward the star. If the two motions of the planet are not perfectly balanced, it will continue to overshoot the star and form an elliptical path.

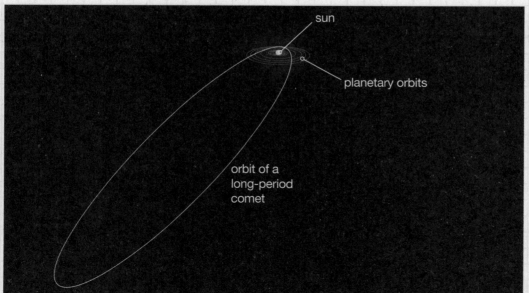

sun

planetary orbits

orbit of a long-period comet

Comets may travel from the outer edges of the solar system in very long, elliptical orbits.

23. At each position of the comet shown, draw an arrow representing the strength and direction of the force of gravity on the comet.

B

C

sun

A

D

not to scale

The blue arrows show the comet's velocity at different points in its orbital path.

24. Discuss With a partner, discuss how the gravitational force between the sun and comet changes the velocity, or speed and direction, of the comet at each position along its orbit.

EVIDENCE NOTEBOOK

25. Would the stars orbiting the center of the Milky Way behave similarly to a planet or comit orbiting a star? Record your evidence.

Engineer It

Choose a Launch Site

26. An object must move very quickly in order to reach orbit. Think about how Earth itself spins. Where is the best place to locate a launch site to get an object into orbit? Explain your answer.

_____

_____

_____

_____

_____

_____

Explaining the Motions of Objects in Space

Matter in the Solar System

Billions of years ago, the matter that currently makes up the solar system was spread out across a vast region of space. Over time, gravitational attractions among the particles of matter caused them to pull together into large clumps of matter. One of these became the sun. The sun contains about 99.8% of the mass in our solar system. Other clumps formed the planets, comets, asteroids, and other bodies. In addition to contributing to the formation of these bodies, gravity holds them in orbit around the sun.

This same process has occurred across the universe, forming other star systems and galaxies. These star systems and galaxies are all held together by gravity. Gravity also keeps star systems, including the solar system, moving within galaxies. Just like planets in a star system orbiting a central mass, the stars in galaxies may also orbit a central mass.

The Solar System

Most of the mass of the solar system is found in the sun. Most of the volume between the planets is empty space.

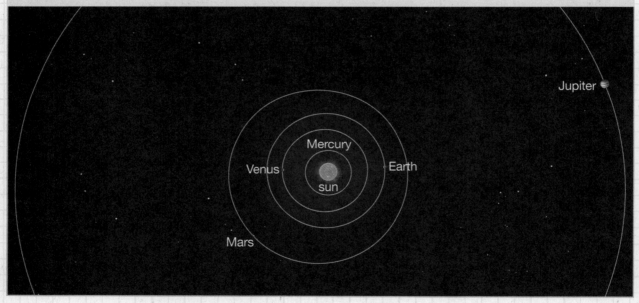

27. Why do the planets and other bodies in the solar system orbit the sun rather than another body in the solar system?

Motion within the Solar System

When the solar system formed, matter was moving in many different directions. Particles near each other were drawn together and formed new, larger masses. The velocity of each new mass depended on the masses and velocities of the particles that collided to form it. Over time, gravity continued to pull masses together, forming larger and larger masses. These larger masses continued moving through space. As these larger masses moved through space, the force of gravity continued to act on them, causing some of them to orbit other, larger masses. Without the force of gravity, masses near each other would continue to move in straight lines, unless they collided with other objects.

28. How does gravity influence the motion of objects in the solar system?

Motion beyond the Solar System

It is easy to see how gravity works in your daily life, but gravity also influences every object in the universe. For example, gravity can be used to model the motion of the solar system through the Milky Way Galaxy. Observations made using large telescopes and other instruments have shown that gravity acts on objects throughout the universe. Scientists have observed planets orbiting stars in other star systems billions of kilometers away as well as the motion of entire galaxies.

When scientists look at the shapes of galaxies and nebulas, they see evidence of circular or elliptical paths of stars, planets, and star systems. Gravity is the force that shapes these paths. Scientists have observed stars and galaxies near each other moving toward one another in ways that strongly suggest the force of gravity is pulling the bodies toward each other.

29. How might the structure of the universe be different if gravity were not acting throughout the universe? What would you observe?

Galaxies have a variety of shapes. This is a spiral galaxy.

Although the object in the center looks like a fuzzy star, it is actually an elliptical galaxy containing several trillion stars.

Gravitational Fields of Massive Objects

The planet Earth has about 10^{23} times more mass than a human (that is a one followed by 23 zeros). The sun has 333,000 times the mass of Earth. There are uncountable stars that are more massive than our sun. There are other objects even more massive than those large stars: black holes. Black holes have masses much larger than that of the sun, but their diameters can be as small as a few kilometers. As a result, the force of gravity at their surface is extremely strong. Even light is not able to escape the gravitational force of these objects, which is why they are called black holes.

Recall that the force of gravity between two objects is proportional to the mass of the two objects and inversely proportional to the square of the distance between them. Because a black hole is so massive, it has the potential to affect the motion of many objects around it, even at a large distance.

30. Imagine two planets of equal mass. Planet A orbits the sun, while Planet B orbits a black hole that has 10,000 times the mass of the sun. The distances from each planet to the bodies they orbit are equal. How does the gravitational force between Planet A and the sun compare with the force between Planet B and the black hole?

EVIDENCE NOTEBOOK

31. Since a black hole cannot be seen, what evidence could be used to locate a black hole? Record your evidence.

Describe Evidence of Gravity in the Universe

From a distance, this galaxy looks like a single object, but it is really made up billions of stars, planets, and other bodies, all orbiting a central point.

Irregular galaxies do not have as organized shapes as spiral or elliptical galaxies do.

32. What evidence in the photos indicates that gravity works throughout the universe in the same way that it works in the solar system?

_____

_____

Continue Your Exploration

Name: _____   Date: _____

Check out the path below or go online to choose one of the other paths shown.

People in Science

- **Building a Space Elevator**
- **Hands-On Labs** 🖐
- **Propose Your Own Path**

Go online to choose one of these other paths.

Nergis Mavalvala, Astrophysicist

Nergis Mavalvala, PhD, is a professor of astrophysics at the Massachusetts Institute of Technology (MIT) and researches gravitational waves. Mavalvala was born and grew up in Pakistan. She attended a school that divided students into either a math and science or a literature track, and was happy to be placed on the math and science track. She eventually moved to the United States to pursue her education and career in physics. Mavalvala embraces being rather unique in her field as a woman in science, a woman of color, and member of the LGBTQ+ community.

Mavalvala researches gravitational waves.

Space-Time

Isaac Newton's universal law of gravitation describes gravity as a force. Newton was troubled by the concept of noncontact forces. If Earth and the sun are attracted, how do they "know" about each other? Albert Einstein answered this question by theorizing that space and time are woven together like fabric and that massive objects curve this fabric. Imagine a bowling ball on a trampoline. The bowling ball causes the trampoline's fabric to dip downward and curve. A marble on the edge of the trampoline will move toward the bowling ball due to the curve in the fabric. Massive objects curve space-time and affect other object's paths. Earth moves around the sun because the sun curves space-time and Earth follows that curvature. While Newton's equations are still used in many situations, Einstein's model of gravity proved more accurate and is now used in sensitive applications, such as GPS systems and astronomy.

1. What would happen if you placed a second bowling ball on a trampoline that already has one bowling ball on it? What kind of situation might this model?

Continue Your Exploration

Gravitational Waves and LIGO

Mavalvala began researching gravitational waves while she was in graduate school at MIT. Gravitational waves are ripples in the fabric of space-time. Einstein predicted that massive objects, such as black holes, could disturb space-time and generate ripples, similar to those made by a rock thrown into a pond.

Although gravitational waves were predicted in 1916, measuring the waves has been a challenge. Mavalvala works on a project built specifically for this task called the Laser Interferometer Gravitational-Wave Observatory (LIGO). The project detects gravitational waves produced by objects millions to billions of light-years from Earth.

The movement of massive objects causes gravitational waves.

LIGO consists of two observation facilities located thousands of kilometers apart that work together to detect gravitational waves. Each facility has two, 4-km arms that are set in an *L* shape. LIGO uses lasers to detect tiny changes in space-time. In 2015, LIGO became the first instrument to detect gravitational waves. The waves that LIGO detected were produced by two black holes that collided 1.3 billion light years away. Mavalvala's lab at MIT continues to develop new ways to improve the sensitivity of LIGO. As the sensitivity of the instrument increases, scientists will be able to detect fainter gravitational waves.

2. Accuracy is how close a measurement is to the true value. Precision is how consistent measurements are to one another. Why is it important to be both accurate and precise when using LIGO to detect extremely small changes to a laser's path?

3. Mavalvala and the rest of the LIGO team have already detected and confirmed the existence of gravitational waves, but they continue to try to improve LIGO. Why is continually improving scientific instrumentation important?

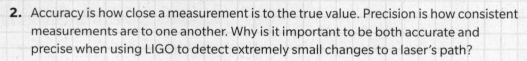

4. **Collaborate** With a small group, develop a way to model space-time and gravitational waves to share with the class. Identify what each part of your model represents and explain the limitations of your model.

Can You Explain It?

Name: _____ Date: _____

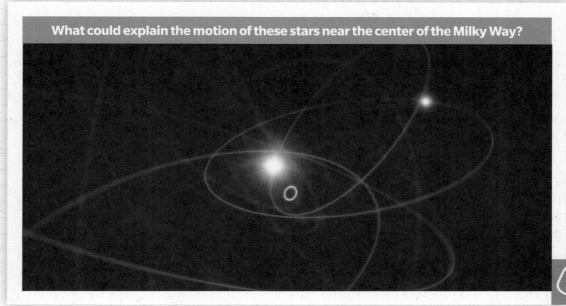

What could explain the motion of these stars near the center of the Milky Way?

EVIDENCE NOTEBOOK

Refer to the notes in your Evidence Notebook to help you construct an explanation for the motion of stars in our galaxy.

1. State your claim. Make sure your claim fully explains the motion of these stars near the center of the Milky Way galaxy.

2. Summarize the evidence you have gathered to support your claim and explain your reasoning.

Checkpoints

Answer the following questions to check your understanding of the lesson.

Use the diagrams to answer Questions 3–4.

3. The diagrams show two planets of different masses with identical orbiting satellites. Which conditions would increase the gravitational force between each pair? Select all that apply.

   A. Move the satellites closer to the planet.

   B. Move the satellites farther from the planet.

   C. Add mass to the satellites.

   D. Remove mass from the satellites.

4. The density of the planets and satellites shown are the same. The gravitational force between the red planet and its satellite is more / less than the gravitational force between the blue planet and its satellite. This is because the combined mass of the red planet and its satellite is greater / less than the combined mass of the blue planet and its satellite, and the distances between each planet and its satellite are different / equal.

Use the image to answer Questions 5–6.

5. Why did the route of Voyager 2 change, without firing its thrusters, as it passed Jupiter?

   A. Gravitational force between Jupiter and Voyager 2 pulled it into a new route.

   B. Solar winds pushed Voyager 2 into a new path.

   C. Jupiter blocked the sun's gravitational pull on Voyager 2.

   D. The gravity of Jupiter caused Voyager 2 to become its satellite.

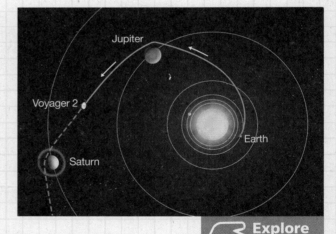

Explore Online

6. Which of the following did scientists and engineers need to know to plan Voyager 2's path through the solar system? Select all that apply.

   A. the positions of the planets

   B. the masses of the planets

   C. the mass of Voyager 2

   D. the law of universal gravitation

7. The law of universal gravitation is a(n) model / experiment of gravity.

Interactive Review

Complete this section to review the main concepts of the lesson.

Gravity is a noncontact force that depends on the masses of objects and the distance between them.

A. Describe two ways you can increase the gravitational force between two objects.

Newton's law of universal gravitation allows scientists to predict the motion of objects in space and on Earth.

B. Why is it useful to model gravity?

Gravity makes the paths of projectiles on Earth curve. Gravity also causes objects in space to orbit one another.

C. How does the speed of an object in an elliptical orbit around the sun change as the object moves around the sun?

The force of gravity in the universe is responsible for the formation of various celestial bodies and for their motion.

D. How do the structures of galaxies give evidence of gravity?

Choose one of the activities to explore how this unit connects to other topics.

☐ People in Science Connection

Sharmila Bhattacharya, Scientist Sharmila Bhattacharya, PhD is a NASA researcher. Her work explores how spaceflight affects biological systems. One of Bhattacharya's studies looked at how the immune systems of fruit flies were affected by altered gravity environments. Her lab has also tested how neurological and cardiovascular systems respond to altered gravity.

Research the known effects of spaceflight on astronauts and discuss why this field of study might become even more important in the future.

☐ Earth Science Connection

Earth's Fireworks Have you ever seen a photograph like this? Perhaps you have seen this phenomenon in person. Auroras, also called northern or southern lights, are beautiful displays of light in the sky caused by electric and magnetic forces in Earth's atmosphere.

Research how electric and magnetic forces create auroras and prepare a digital presentation explaining how scientists can predict when and where they will occur. Include images in your presentation.

☐ Technology Connection

Electromagnets in Technology Cell phones, computers, and electric guitars are all examples of modern technology. Without an understanding of electromagnetism, these devices would not exist. Electromagnets are used in fields ranging from transportation to medicine to scientific research.

Research one example of modern technology that uses electromagnets. Explain how electromagnets make the technology work and the criteria and constraints involved in its design. Present your findings to the class.

Name: _____   **Date:** _____

Complete this review to check your understanding of the unit.

Use the photo to answer Questions 1-4.

1. As a rocket is launched, it burns its fuel and loses mass. Describe how the gravitational forces between the rocket and Earth change as the rocket launches.

2. If this rocket were used to launch a satellite into orbit, describe how the satellite would move after it was in orbit.

3. If this rocket were used to send a lunar lander toward the moon, describe how the gravitational fields surrounding the lander would change as the rocket moved toward the moon.

4. How would the gravitational forces between a lunar lander and the moon compare to the gravitational forces between the rocket-lander assembly and Earth when the rocket is sitting on the launchpad?

Use the diagram to answer Questions 5–8.

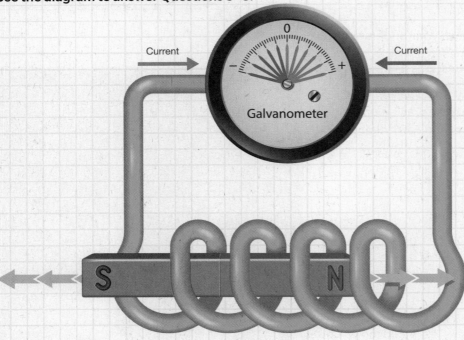

5. What is the effect of moving the magnet back and forth inside the coiled wire?

6. Would moving the coil back and forth instead of the magnet produce the same effect? Explain.

7. Predict what would happen if the entire unit is moving but the magnet and coil are not moving relative to each other.

8. Describe ways to increase the amount of electric current in this setup.

Name: _____ Date: _____

What is the best design for a maglev train?

How would engineers make a train float? Some trains are made to float above a track, which greatly reduces friction from the rails. These trains are known as maglev trains because they float due to magnetic levitation. Magnetic levitation uses attractive and repulsive magnetic forces to suspend and control the speeds and motion of the trains. These trains are able to travel between 400 and 480 kilometers per hour!

Using your knowledge of electromagnets, design a maglev train that can move forward and backward. Follow the steps below to help you through the engineering design process.

The steps below will help guide your research and develop your recommendation.

Engineer It

1. **Define the Problem** Write a statement defining the problem you have been asked to solve. What are the criteria and constraints involved in designing a maglev train?

Engineer It

2. **Conduct Research** To get ideas for your design, research existing maglev trains. Find out how magnets are positioned to balance the force of gravity and achieve back-and-forth motion. Describe how electric and magnetic forces are used in these systems.

3. **Analyze and Evaluate Research** Use ideas from the trains you researched and your knowledge of electric and magnetic forces to create your own design. Your analysis of the research should help you decide where and how the magnets should be positioned to balance the force of gravity and achieve back-and-forth motion.

4. **Create a Model** On a separate sheet of paper, draw a diagram that shows all of the components for your maglev train. Be sure to label the components, including a legend or key if needed. Make certain to indicate how the train can move forward and backward.

5. **Communicate** On a separate sheet of paper, write a brief report to accompany your diagram. In the report, describe how your maglev train works and your reasons for choosing this particular design.

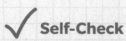 **Self-Check**

	I identified the problem.
	I researched existing maglev systems to get ideas for my design.
	I designed a model using ideas from existing systems and my knowledge of electric and magnetic forces.
	My design was clearly communicated to others.

Space Science

How does gravity explain observations of patterns in space?

This shadow on Earth was cast during a solar eclipse in 2017. During a solar eclipse, the moon moves directly between Earth and the sun, casting a shadow on Earth.

You Solve It When Will an Eclipse Occur? Use a model of the Earth-sun-moon system to analyze patterns of past eclipses and predict when future eclipses would happen.

Go online and complete the You Solve It to explore ways to solve a real-world problem.

Build a Museum Model

The bright band of stars in this image is the Milky Way galaxy, which is home to Earth and our solar system.

A. Look at the photo. On a separate sheet of paper, write down as many different questions as you can about the photo.

B. **Discuss** With your class or a partner, share your questions. Record any additional questions generated in your discussion. Then choose the most important questions from the list that are related to the size and structure of the Milky Way galaxy. Write them below.

C. Choose a feature of the Milky Way galaxy to research. What feature will you research?

D. Use the information above, along with your research, to propose a model of the Milky Way galaxy for a museum or community park. Use the engineering design process to develop a proposal for your installation. Use the model to describe the scale of objects in the universe.

Discuss the next steps for your Unit Project with your teacher and go online to download the Unit Project Worksheet.

Language Development

Use the lessons in this unit to complete the network and expand your understanding of these key science concepts.

	Similar term
	Phrase
	Cognate
	Example
	Definition

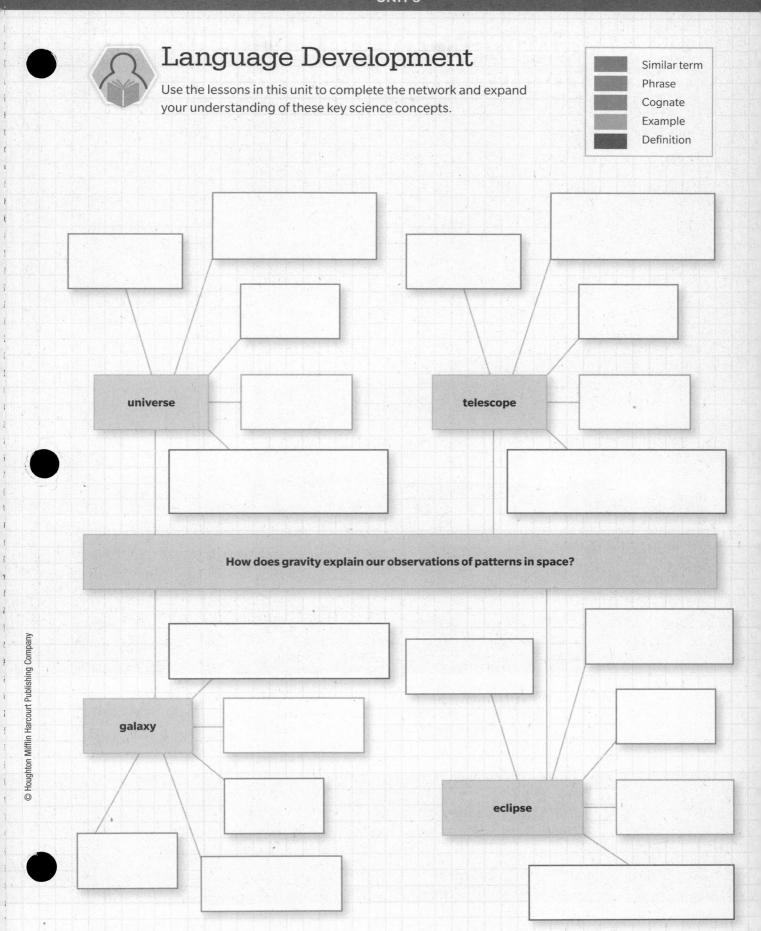

universe

telescope

How does gravity explain our observations of patterns in space?

galaxy

eclipse

Observations Provide Evidence for the Structure of the Solar System

The sun shines through the center gap in Stonehenge in England. This marks the summer solstice, the longest day of the year.

Explore First

Observing Earth's Rotation Place a pencil vertically in the ground where it can cast a shadow from the sun. Mark the spot where the pencil's shadow falls. Mark the shadow again in five minutes. Why has the position of the shadow changed?

CAN YOU EXPLAIN IT?

What are "shooting stars"?

For thousands of years people have watched "shooting stars" streak across the sky. Showers of shooting stars occur at regular times each year. However, shooting stars do not follow the normal movement of stars through the night sky. They appear as a streak of light and disappear moments later.

Explore Online

1. Have you ever seen a shooting star or read about one in a poem or a book? How would you describe a shooting star?

2. What conditions are necessary to see a shooting star?

 EVIDENCE NOTEBOOK As you explore the lesson, gather evidence to help explain why shooting stars behave differently than other stars do.

Analyzing Patterns in the Sky

People have been observing patterns in the movements of the sun, moon, and stars for millenia and have used those observed patterns to develop models of our solar system. During the day, the sun appears to travel across the sky. Stars shine day and night, but you can only see them after the sun sets. Much like the sun during the day, the stars appear to move east to west during the night. The moon always rises along the eastern horizon, appears to travel across the sky, and sets along the western horizon a few hours later. But the moon rises at different times during the month, in a regular pattern.

Although the sun is far away in space, it lights up Earth.

3. **Discuss** Look at the images. What patterns do you see in the apparent motion of objects in the sky. Describe any patterns you observe.

The Daily Path of the Sun, Moon, and stars

In the morning, you can watch the sun rise on the eastern horizon. In the evening, you can look to the west to see the sun set on the western horizon.

east · noon · west · sunrise · sunset · horizon · morning · evening · not to scale

The streaks in this time-lapse photo are made as stars move across the sky during the night.

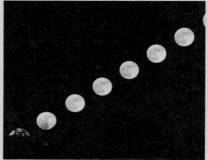

This composite photo shows the moon rising. The sun, stars, and the moon move from east to west across the sky.

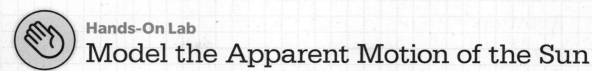

Hands-On Lab
Model the Apparent Motion of the Sun

You will model the Earth-sun system to develop an explanation for night and day and the apparent motion of the sun in the sky.

MATERIALS
- ball, styrene, on a stick
- lamp with removable shade
- markers
- tape

Procedure

STEP 1 **Act** Work with a partner. Choose who will play the part of the sun and who will play Earth. Write *sun* on one piece of paper and *Earth* on another, and tape the labels to each actor. Stand facing each other. Discuss how the motion of the sun or Earth can result in periods of daytime and nighttime on Earth.

STEP 2 **Act** If you are the actor playing Earth, stand facing the sun. Slowly turn in a circle toward your left. Keep your head in line with your body. Your head is representing Earth. Say *night* when you can no longer see the sun and say *day* when you first see the sun again. Take turns being Earth and the sun. NOTE: Turning toward the left models Earth's counterclockwise movement as you are looking down at the North Pole.

STEP 3 Now use the lamp and foam ball to make a model that explains day and night. Write *Earth* on the tape and put the label around the center of the ball. Hold the ball in front of the lamp and turn the stick toward the left.

Analysis

STEP 4 When I was playing Earth and could see the sun, my face represented the part of Earth that was experiencing day / night.

When I could not see the sun, it was day / night.

When I first saw the sun, it was sunrise / sunset.

When I last saw the sun, it was sunrise / sunset.

It was morning / noon / midnight when I was directly facing the sun.

STEP 5 Think about a compass. If you are facing south, your right shoulder is west and your left shoulder is east. In what direction did you first see the sun in the morning? As you turned, in what direction did the sun seem to move throughout the day?

STEP 6 Based on your observations, why does the sun appear to move across the sky?

Earth's Rotation

When you spin around in one place, you are modeling Earth's rotation. You are on Earth, so you do not feel it turning, but you experience the rotation in other ways.

Earth's Rotation Explains the Path of the Sun

The apparent motion of the sun, including daytime and nighttime, is caused by Earth's rotation. A day on Earth is 24 hours because Earth completes one full rotation during that time. As Earth spins, different parts of Earth face the sun. It is daytime when an area faces toward the sun and nighttime when it faces away from the sun.

If you were looking down on Earth from the North Pole, it would rotate counterclockwise. Therefore, on Earth, the eastern horizon turns toward the sun first in the morning. Throughout the day, the sun appears to move from east to west as Earth rotates. The way the sun appears to move always follows the same pattern, rising in the east, moving in an arc across the sky from east to west, and setting in the west.

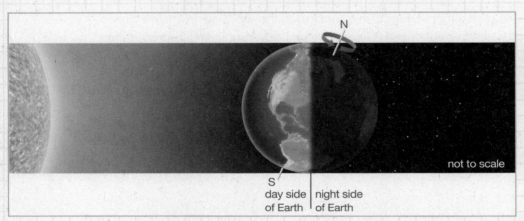

day side of Earth | night side of Earth

not to scale

Stars are visible at night on the side of Earth facing away from the sun.

Earth's Rotation Explains the Path of the Stars

During the daytime, the sun is so bright that you cannot see other stars. Look at the diagram. The area of Earth that is experiencing nighttime faces away from the sun, so you are able to see the stars. As with the sun, the stars appear to move from east to west as Earth rotates. Throughout the night, different stars rise and set. The stars rise and become visible over the horizon as Earth rotates. For example, the constellation Orion comes into view in the eastern night sky around 9 p.m. in late November in the Northern Hemisphere. As Earth spins, Orion appears to move westward. Orion is at its highest point in the sky around midnight. Then Orion continues toward the west, where it sets.

4. How does the daily cycle of daytime and nighttime depend on Earth's rotation?
   A. The sun rises in the west and sets in the east because Earth rotates west to east.
   B. It is morning on the part of Earth that is facing into the sun and evening on the part that is facing away from the sun.
   C. The Northern Hemisphere experiences daytime while the Southern Hemisphere experiences nighttime because Earth rotates around its axis.

 EVIDENCE NOTEBOOK
   5. Do shooting stars match any of the observed patterns in apparent motion of other objects in the sky? Record your evidence.

218 Unit 3 Space Science

© Houghton Mifflin Harcourt Publishing Company

6. Stars appear to move because Earth spins toward the east / west. On the same day, people who live in the eastern United States see the same / different stars in the night sky as those who live in the western United States.

Earth's Rotation Explains the Path of the Moon

The moon also appears to move east to west in the sky as Earth rotates. However, the motion of the moon is a bit different than the motion of the sun and the stars. The moon's orbit causes it to rise slightly later each day, but the timing of the moon's rising and setting is predictable. The moon also appears to slowly move eastward with respect to the background of stars. In addition, the moon is visible sometimes during the day. Although Earth's rotation explains the moon's daily rising and setting pattern, its apparent motion is also affected by other factors.

7. Why are the patterns of movement of the sun, stars, and the moon across Earth's sky similar?

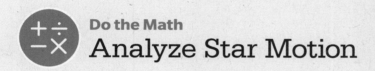

Do the Math
Analyze Star Motion

8. Polaris is also called the *North Star* because Earth's North Pole points toward it. As Earth rotates, other stars seem to spin around Polaris in a counterclockwise direction. In one day, the stars will make one complete circle (360°) around Polaris. Compare the positions of the constellations in the two diagrams. Calculate how many hours have passed between the first and second diagrams.

Polaris

not to scale

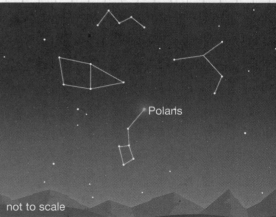

Polaris

not to scale

© Houghton Mifflin Harcourt Publishing Company

Seasonal Star Patterns

Earth's place in its orbit affects which stars can be seen during different seasons. The location of stars in the night sky changes as Earth moves along its orbit. During the year, you will be able to see all the stars visible from one specific place on Earth.

On a given day, you will only be able to see the stars that are in the opposite direction of the sun. The stars seen from the Northern Hemisphere may be different from the stars seen from the Southern Hemisphere. If you are on the North or South Pole, the stars will appear to rotate around a point directly above your head because of Earth's rotation. The sky seen from the North Pole is completely different from the sky seen from the South Pole. As you move from the North Pole toward the South Pole, the sky will change. The sky seen by someone in Florida may have some of the same stars in the sky seen by someone in Brazil, but the whole pattern of stars seen is not the same.

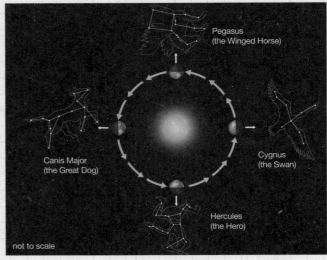

Different stars are seen from Earth at different times of the year. For example, Cygnus is seen in the night sky of the Northern Hemisphere in summer.

Some Stars Are Seen in Different Seasons

These are some of the constellations visible in the night sky of the Northern Hemisphere during **winter**. During the day, the sun blocks summer constellations from sight.

As winter changes to **spring**, Earth faces a different direction during the night and new constellations become visible.

Earth's **summer** position brings new constellations into view. Now the winter constellations are opposite the sun and cannot be seen.

In **fall**, new constellations are visible. Soon, winter constellations will start to be seen once more.

9. **Discuss** If you were an ancient astronomer who observed the seasonal changes in stars, what questions might you ask or what other observations would you want to make before constructing an explanation for this observation?

The Wandering Stars

To ancient astronomers, some stars did not appear to behave like the other stars. They would rise and set along with the rest of the stars. However, when observed over several weeks, they appeared to change their location among the other stars. Greek astronomers called those bodies *astéres planétai*, or "wandering stars." They are the planets we can easily see from Earth: Mercury, Venus, Mars, Jupiter, and Saturn. As planets moved across the sky, they traveled at different speeds. Sometimes, a planet would catch up to and pass another object that appeared to move more slowly. As they moved, planets appeared to pass in front of or behind the sun. Occasionally, they would pass behind, but never in front of the moon. When plotted on a sky chart for days or weeks, some planets' paths through the sky appeared to loop or move backward. This reverse motion puzzled astronomers. They struggled to construct an explanation for this phenomenon.

Language SmArts
Interpret Words and Visuals

Term	Root meanings
retrograde	Latin roots: *retro-* means "backward" and *gradi* means "to walk or step"
transit	Latin root: *transire* means "to cross"

10. Look at the terms and the meanings of their root words. Then create a label for each image by matching the term to the correct image.

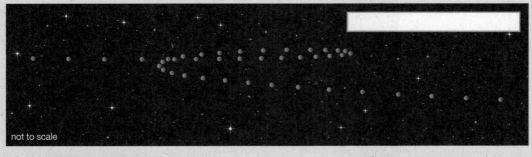

not to scale

Mars appears to move backward or have a looping path as its movement is viewed from Earth over several weeks.

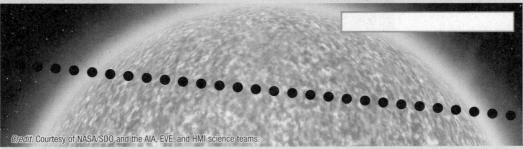

Credit: Courtesy of NASA/SDO and the AIA, EVE, and HMI science teams.

This composite image shows Venus as it passes in front of the sun. The dark circles represent the positions of Venus over several hours.

11. From Earth, the moon is seen to transit in front of both the sun and Venus. Venus transits across the sun but never across the moon. List the three bodies described in order of increasing distance from Earth. Explain your thinking.

_____

_____

_____

_____

Developing Models of the Solar System

Early Models of the Solar System

Early astronomers developed models of the solar system based on what they knew. Because objects in the sky appeared to circle Earth, many astronomers placed Earth at the center of the model. The Greek philosopher Aristotle (384–322 BCE) developed a model that had a fixed, non-moving Earth as the center of the universe. He proposed that all other bodies in the sky—including the moon, the sun, the planets, and the stars—moved around Earth. Aristotle claimed that all objects in the sky moved along regular, perfectly circular paths. This *geocentric*, or Earth-centered model explained why objects in the sky appear to revolve around Earth on regular paths. It explained why Earth appears—to someone on Earth's surface—to be unmoving. It also explained why Venus or Mercury would transit in front of the sun, and why any of the planets would pass behind, but never in front of the moon.

12. Which of the following observations support Aristotle's geocentric model? Select all statements that apply.

A. The sun, moon, and stars appear to follow a circular path through the sky.

B. The sun and moon appear to be the same size and brightness as the stars.

C. The sun, moon, and stars seem to move at the same rate across the sky.

D. For people on Earth, the planet does not feel like it is moving.

E. Some planets appear to cross between the sun and Earth.

F. Some planets appear to pass behind and beyond the sun.

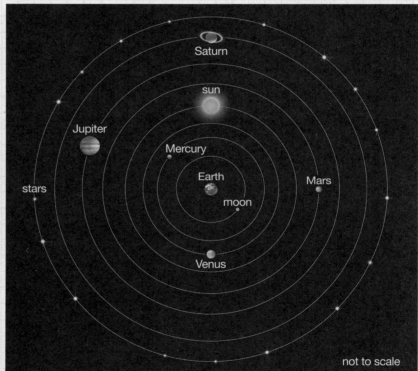

In Aristotle's model of the universe, the planets, sun, moon, and stars all revolved around a fixed, non-moving Earth.

13. What would Aristotle's geocentric model predict about the brightness of the planets when viewed from Earth? What about the stars? Explain your reasoning.

Demonstrating Parallax

Hold your thumb a few inches from your nose. Look at your thumb with one eye closed. Then switch which eye is opened and which eye is closed. Your thumb will appear to shift position.

Parallax and Geocentrism

To understand another argument for the geocentric model, it is important to understand a phenomenon called parallax. **Parallax** is the apparent shift in position of an object when it is viewed from different points. As an example, look at the photos that demonstrate parallax. Parallax can be used to measure the distance to an object based on the size of the apparent shift in position when the object is viewed from two places. The bigger the apparent shift in position is, the closer the object is to the viewer.

The stars and constellations do not appear to change positions relative to each other when viewed from Earth with an unaided eye. Astronomers reasoned that this fact indicated that either the stars are extremely far away or they are all the same distance from Earth. Aristotle's geocentric model proposed that the stars were fixed in position on a sphere that orbited Earth. This explanation fit the evidence, so it was accepted by other astronomers.

Ptolemy Answers the Retrograde Motion Problem

Aristotle's model failed to explain retrograde motion of planets or strange phenomena like shooting stars or comets. About 400 years after Artistotle, Claudius Ptolemy improved Aristotle's model by explaining retrograde motion. He claimed that planets moved in small circles, called *epicycles,* along their orbits around Earth. As the planets moved on these epicycles, they sometimes appeared to move backward. Ptolemy's geocentric model was accepted by most scientists for about 1,000 years.

14. Why would solving retrograde motion "improve" the model over Aristotle's model?

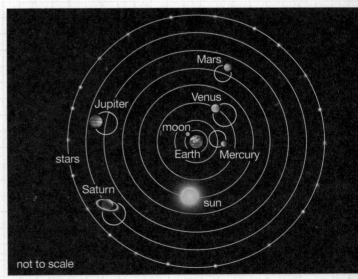

Ptolemy's geocentric model used epicycles to explain retrograde motion.

not to scale

Hands-On Lab
Investigate Parallax

Use parallax to compare the relative distances between objects.

MATERIALS
- markers (4 colors)
- meterstick
- pushpin (at least 10 mm tall)
- sticky notes
- stool or chair
- table
- tape

Procedure

STEP 1 Place the table about 2 m from the wall. Tape the meterstick to the table so that the 100 cm mark is closest to the wall.

STEP 2 Place the pushpin into the meterstick at 100 cm. Sit or kneel on the side of the table farthest from the wall. Place the tip of your nose on the 0 cm end of the meterstick. Make sure you are positioned so that your eyes are evenly spaced on opposite sides of the meterstick.

STEP 3 Without moving your head, close your right eye. Tell your partner where the pin appears against the background. He or she will mark that point on the wall with a labeled sticky note.

STEP 4 Without moving your head, switch your opened and closed eyes. Tell your partner where the pin appears on the grid paper. He or she will mark that point with a labeled sticky note.

STEP 5 Repeat Steps 4–6 with the pushpin at 75 cm, 50 cm, and 25 cm. Make sure your head is in the same position, with the tip of your nose on the 0 cm end, for all four placements of the pushpin.

Analysis

STEP 6 What pattern did you see between the distance between the pin and your nose and the distance between the apparent positions of the pin when viewed with alternating eyes?

STEP 7 Stars do not appear to change position in relation to other stars when viewed from two locations on Earth's surface. How do you think this evidence supported ancient astronomers' belief in early geocentric models?

Analyze Data That Do Not Fit the Model

Aristotle's and Ptolemy's models included stars and planets that moved at a constant rate. The stars did not change their relative positions or brightnesses. These models explained events that fit a pattern. However, ancient astronomers from around the world recorded some events that did not appear to fit the observed patterns of motion of objects in the sky. Resolving these events with existing models of the universe became a challenge for all astronomers.

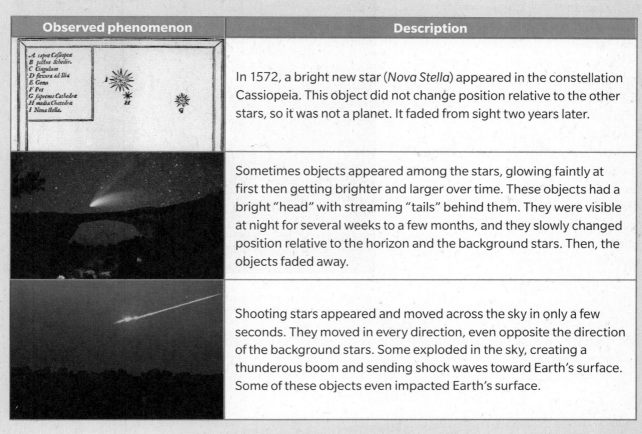

Observed phenomenon	Description
	In 1572, a bright new star (*Nova Stella*) appeared in the constellation Cassiopeia. This object did not change position relative to the other stars, so it was not a planet. It faded from sight two years later.
	Sometimes objects appeared among the stars, glowing faintly at first then getting brighter and larger over time. These objects had a bright "head" with streaming "tails" behind them. They were visible at night for several weeks to a few months, and they slowly changed position relative to the horizon and the background stars. Then, the objects faded away.
	Shooting stars appeared and moved across the sky in only a few seconds. They moved in every direction, even opposite the direction of the background stars. Some exploded in the sky, creating a thunderous boom and sending shock waves toward Earth's surface. Some of these objects even impacted Earth's surface.

15. Explain the similarities and differences between the observations that supported the geocentric models of the solar system and the phenomena described in the table.

_____

_____

16. Imagine that a small, bright object appeared in the sky, moved along with a nearby constellation, and then disappeared a year later. Scientists in China, Persia, Europe, and Central America observed the event. How close to Earth did this phenomenon most likely occur? How do you know?

_____

_____

EVIDENCE NOTEBOOK

17. How close to Earth must shooting stars be, and what does this mean about what causes them? Record your evidence.

Incorporating New Discoveries

Despite the widespread acceptance of the geocentric model, astronomers continued to gather data and refine the model. Many Indian and Arab astronomers made great advances in mathematical models that explained the movements of objects in the solar system. In 1543, a scientist named Nicolaus Copernicus used their calculations to propose a new model of the solar system: one with the sun at the center. Copernicus's *heliocentric*, or sun-centered model explained retrograde motion in a simpler way. It relied on the sun being at the center and the planets arranged around the sun based on how quickly each planet orbits the sun. It takes Earth about 365.25 days, or about one year, to orbit the sun.

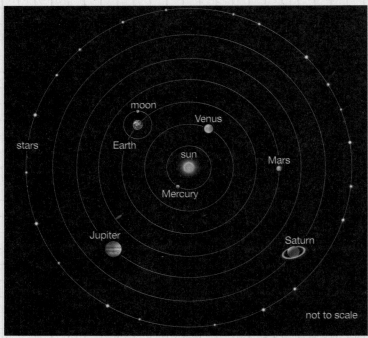

Copernicus's heliocentric model of the solar system put each planet, including Earth, in orbit around the sun. The moon orbited Earth.

18. Using the word bank, complete the Venn diagram by entering the claims made by each scientist.

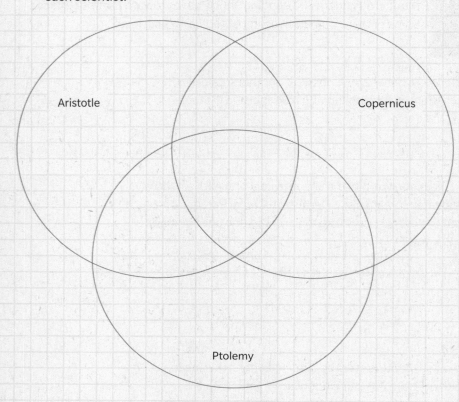

WORD BANK
- sun orbits Earth
- moon orbits Earth
- other planets orbit Earth
- Earth orbits sun
- other planets orbit sun
- sun at center
- Earth at center
- explains retrograde motion
- explains movements of sun and moon

19. Why might scientists favor Copernicus's heliocentric model over Ptolemy's geocentric model?

Revising and Expanding the Model

In the late 1500s, Danish scientist Tycho Brahe built huge instruments that allowed him to take extremely precise measurements of stars and planets. His assistant, Johannes Kepler, used Brahe's data to calculate the shapes of planetary orbits. By suggesting that planets have elliptical, or oval-shaped, orbits rather than circular orbits, Kepler was able to explain complex planetary motions. These new findings helped convince scientists that Earth and the other planets revolve around the sun.

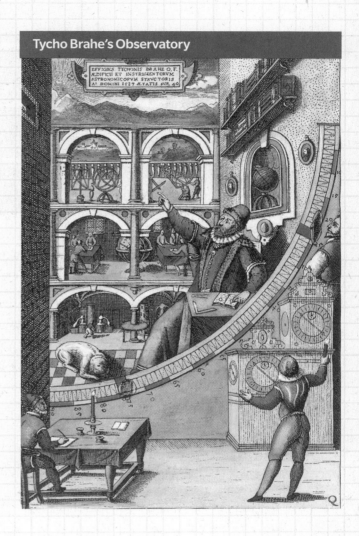

Tycho Brahe's Observatory

20. The immense size of the instruments used by Tycho Brahe allowed him to construct an accurate ~~mathematical / physical~~ model of the solar system. The advantage of such an accurate observations was that it allowed Brahe to make ~~observations / predictions~~ about the future positions of the stars and planets.

New Technology Led to New Discoveries

As Kepler was publishing his work, revolutionary technologies were being developed. In Italy, Galileo Galilei combined two magnifying lenses to make the first telescope in 1609. A **telescope** is an instrument that collects and concentrates light from distant objects to make the objects appear larger or brighter. Early telescopes magnified objects by only three to 30 times. But that small amount had a huge effect on astronomy.

Galileo's observations through his telescopes revealed details of planets and moons that changed centuries of scientific thought. He noticed that the surface of Earth's moon was rugged, not smooth. He observed sunspots on the sun and identified the phases of Venus. He also saw four small objects moving around Jupiter. These moons of Jupiter would finally prove that objects could orbit bodies other than Earth.

Analyze the Movement of Jupiter's Moons

Positions of Jupiter's Moons

Galileo saw what he thought were stars near Jupiter. The "stars" changed positions from night to night. He named these objects Callisto, Europa, Ganymede, and Io. Analyze the location of each object on each night by using the scale on the diagram.

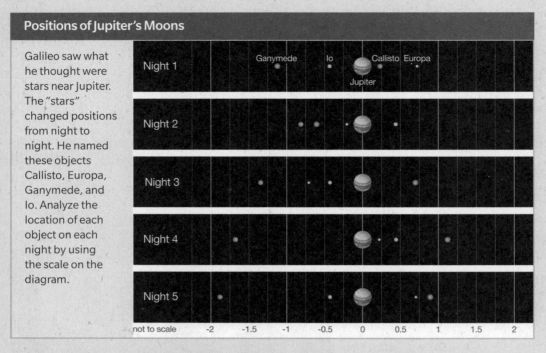

21. Look at the diagram. Which moon appeared to move the fastest? Which moon appeared to move the slowest? Explain your reasoning.

22. Use the scale on the diagram to determine the maximum distance each object travels away from Jupiter. Place that number in the center column of the chart. Then rank the objects in order of increasing distance from Jupiter.

Object	Maximum distance from Jupiter on the scale	Rank by distance from Jupiter (1 = closest and 4 = farthest)
Callisto		
Europa		
Ganymede		
Io		

Exploring the Structure of the Solar System

Astronomers eventually accepted the heliocentric model as the best fit to all the evidence. The development of improved telescopes and space probes has helped astronomers continue to refine our understanding of all the bodies of the solar system.

23. Which of the following lines of evidence support the heliocentric model of the solar system? Select all statements that apply.

  A. The observation that Jupiter has moons that orbit around it.

  B. The discovery that the moon circles around Earth in the same direction that Earth rotates.

  C. The observation that the stars do not appear to change positions relative to each other when viewed from two distant places on Earth.

  D. The discovery that planets move in small circles, called epicycles.

  E. The calculation that planets have elliptical, or oval-shaped, orbits rather than circular orbits.

The planets do not emit light. They reflect light from the sun. Some planets in the solar system are easy to find among the many stars in the night sky. This photo shows Venus, Mars, and Jupiter over Utah.

A Growing Family of Objects

Advancements in telescopes occurred quickly over the 300 to 400 years after Galileo first invented them. Each advancement allowed scientists to see farther or with greater clarity and detail. Scientists collected data and used mathematical modeling to discover and describe new planets, moons, and numerous smaller objects in the solar system. All of these objects are influenced by the sun's gravity, which keeps the objects in motion around the sun.

More Than Planets Orbit the Sun

Mathematical models predicted that planets should exist beyond the orbit of Saturn and between Mars and Jupiter. One model was based on the observation that the radius of each known planet's orbit is roughly proportional. Scientists used telescopes to look for these predicted objects. In 1801, a small, round object was discovered between the orbits of Mars and Jupiter. This object, named Ceres, was not a planet. It was the first object identified in the asteroid belt and is now considered a dwarf planet. The planet Neptune was discovered in 1846, the planet Uranus was discovered in 1871, and the dwarf planet Pluto was discovered in 1930.

24. New technologies, such as astrolabes / telescopes, allowed astronomers to see dim or distant objects in space. The development of new technology is necessary / unnecessary to the advancement of science. Scientists must consider / disregard new evidence as they propose explanations for observed phenomena.

 EVIDENCE NOTEBOOK

25. Use the following information about small bodies in the solar system to record evidence that might help you identify the source of shooting stars.

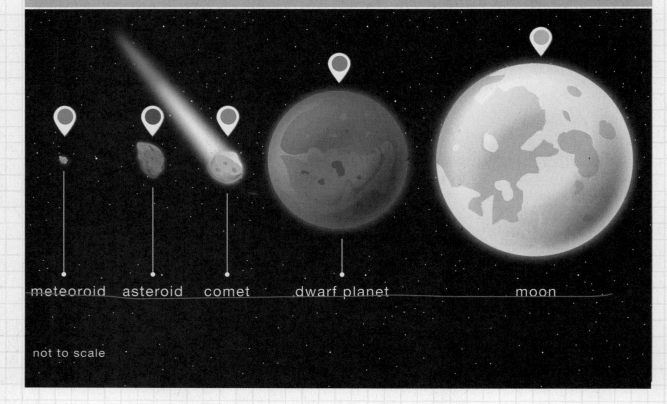

Small Bodies in the Solar System

Sizes of moons and dwarf planets in this illustration are relative and not to scale. The smaller objects, such as meteoroids, would be invisible at that scale, so they are shown in an enlarged view.

meteoroid   asteroid   comet   dwarf planet   moon

not to scale

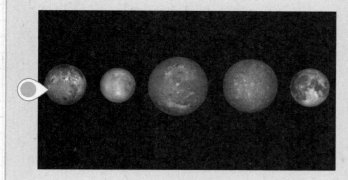

Moons are bodies that orbit larger bodies such as planets, dwarf planets, or asteroids. Moons do not orbit the sun. Some moons are round, such as Earth's moon. Many moons are not round and may be asteroids or other space debris that are captured by the gravity of the larger body they orbit.

Dwarf planets are similar to planets. They orbit the sun, and they are massive enough to be roughly spherical. However, dwarf planets are not large enough to have cleared their orbit of other large objects. Most dwarf planets are in areas that are surrounded by many small and large objects, such as asteroids and other dwarf planets.

Comets are small bodies of ice, rock, and dust. They follow highly elliptical orbits around the sun. As a comet passes close to the sun, gas and dust break off of the comet and form tails. They have not cleared their orbits and may collide with larger objects.

Asteroids are small, irregularly shaped rocky and metallic bodies. They range from the size of a car to several kilometers across. Although most asteroids orbit the sun in the asteroid belt (between the orbits of Mars and Jupiter), some travel through space on elliptical orbits like comets. They cross the orbits of other bodies, including Earth.

Meteoroids are small, rocky or metallic bodies. They may be debris left over from when the solar system formed. They may also break off of comets or asteroids. If a meteoroid enters Earth's atmosphere, it burns up. The short, bright streak of light is called a *meteor*.

© Houghton Mifflin Harcourt Publishing Company • Image Credits: (t, tc) ©Walter Myers/Science Source; (c) ©Science Source; (bc) ©NASA,ESA and A. Feild (STScI); (b) ©Millard H. Sharp/Science Source

Compare and Categorize Solar System Objects

Objects in our solar system are categorized according to their observable characteristics. For example, astronomers use size, shape, and orbit to classify objects. Planets are spherical and are held in orbit around the sun by the suns gravitational pull on them. Moons may be spherical or irregular, and they orbit larger bodies, such as planets, dwarf planets, or asteroids. Knowing the characteristics of space objects helps astronomers classify new objects that are discovered.

Observed Objects in the Solar System				
Body	**Shape**	**Orbits**	**Orbited by**	**Orbit cleared**
Ceres	sphere	sun	––	No
Ida	irregular	sun	Dactyl	No
Mercury	sphere	sun	––	Yes
Neptune	sphere	sun	14 bodies	Yes
Phobos	irregular	Mars	––	––
Pluto	sphere	sun	Charon	No
Titan	sphere	Saturn	––	––
Vesta	irregular	sun	––	No

26. Identify whether each object listed is a planet, dwarf planet, asteroid, or moon. Write the name of each object in the correct column.

WORD BANK
- Ceres
- Ida
- Mercury
- Neptune
- Phobos
- Pluto
- Titan
- Vesta

Planets	Dwarf planets	Moons	Asteroids

27. What information helped you sort the objects into categories?

Continue Your Exploration

Name: _____ Date: _____

Check out the path below or go online to choose one of the other paths shown.

Exploring the Outer Solar System

- **People in Science**
- **Reflecting and Refracting Telescopes**
- **Hands-On Labs** 🖐
- **Propose Your Own Path**

Go online to choose one of these other paths

The sun's gravity holds many objects in orbit. In addition to the planets, smaller objects are found in different parts of the solar system. The asteroid belt between Mars and Jupiter holds hundreds of thousands of objects. These range in size from small specks of dust to the dwarf planet Ceres. Beyond the orbit of the most distant planet, Neptune, is the Kuiper Belt. This ring of rocky and icy bodies is many times larger than the asteroid belt between Mars and Jupiter. The Kuiper Belt includes Pluto and several other icy dwarf planets. Far beyond the Kuiper Belt lies the Oort cloud, a collection of trillions of icy bodies left over from the formation of the solar system.

The *New Horizons* spacecraft was launched in 2006 with the goal of exploring the outer solar system. In July 2015, *New Horizons* flew by the dwarf planet Pluto. The spacecraft is now on a path to fly by objects in the Kuiper Belt.

A number of uncrewed spacecraft have been sent to explore objects in the outer solar system. These space probes carry instruments that can take images and make measurements and send them back to Earth by radio. It would take too much energy to send a spacecraft directly to another solar system object. Instead, spacecraft use the gravitational fields of the sun and the planets to accelerate and change course. These gravitational fields assist maneuvers requiring careful timing to make sure that the spacecraft approaches a planet at just the right time and at the right speed to accurately change course to the next planet it was designed to fly by.

There have been several successful missions to the outer solar system. The spacecraft have returned valuable information that continues to be used by scientists to understand the structure and early formation of the solar system.

1. Why is it useful to send uncrewed spacecraft to explore distant parts of the solar system?

Continue Your Exploration

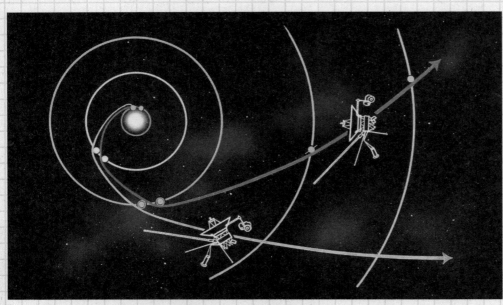

The spacecraft Voyager 1 and Voyager 2 both started from Earth, but their flight paths ended up very differently.

2. What caused the flight paths of Voyager I and Voyager II to differ?

3. Why is it important for the scientists and engineers who plan uncrewed missions to accurately know the masses and the paths of the planets the spacecraft will visit?

4. **Collaborate** Work with a partner to create a poster that describes the mission of another uncrewed space probe. Include information about what the probe was designed to study and how it relayed that information to Earth. Include some kind of labeled diagram on your poster.

Can You Explain It?

Name: _____   Date: _____

What are "shooting stars"?

Explore Online

 EVIDENCE NOTEBOOK
Refer to the notes in your Evidence Notebook to help you construct an explanation for what causes shooting stars.

1. State your claim. Make sure your claim fully explains what causes shooting stars.

2. Summarize the evidence you have gathered to support your claim and explain your reasoning.

Checkpoints

Answer the following questions to check your understanding of the lesson.

Use the photo to answer question 3.

3. The photo shows a *meteoroid / comet*. These objects move in *circular / elliptical* orbits around the sun.

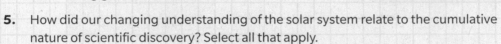

4. Which of the following allows a solar system object to clear its orbit of other large objects?

    A. a highly elliptical orbit

    B. a rocky or metallic body

    C. a spherical shape

    D. a strong gravitational field

5. How did our changing understanding of the solar system relate to the cumulative nature of scientific discovery? Select all that apply.

    A. Scientists favored the simplest model that explained observations.

    B. Scientists adopted new models to account for new observations.

    C. Observations that did not fit a model could be ignored.

    D. Observations improved as new technologies become available.

6. The appearance of different constellations in the night sky during the year provide evidence for which of the following?

    A. that the stars move around Earth

    B. that Earth moves around the sun

    C. that the moon moves around Earth

    D. that the sun moves around Earth

Use the diagram to answer question 7.

7. Which statement is demonstrated by this model?

    A. The same stars are visible all year long.

    B. The sun orbits Earth once every year.

    C. The moon rises and sets at the same time every day.

    D. Earth and the moon rotate in the same direction that they orbit.

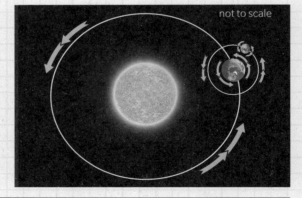

not to scale

8. How can models help us understand the apparent motion of the sun, the moon, and the stars in the sky? Select all that apply.

    A. Models can be used to make predictions.

    B. Models can be used to explain events.

    C. Models can be used to describe events.

    D. Models can be used to make observations.

Interactive Review

Complete this section to review the main concepts of the lesson.

The sun, stars, and moon appear to move across the sky from east to west on a daily basis.

not to scale

A. How did the apparent motions of planets set those objects apart from other stars when observed by ancient astronomers?

Early astronomers developed models of the solar system to explain their observations of the apparent movements of the sun and the planets.

B. Explain why observations of new stars, comets, and shooting stars presented challenges to ancient astronomers using Ptolemy's model to explain the solar system.

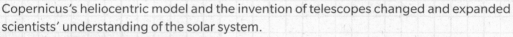

Copernicus's heliocentric model and the invention of telescopes changed and expanded scientists' understanding of the solar system.

not to scale

C. How did the telescope bring about changes in astronomy?

Advances in technology have allowed scientists to understand more about the smaller objects that are found in the solar system.

D. Explain how objects in the solar system are classified.

Case Study: Explaining Eclipses and Lunar Phases

The moon sometimes appears orange as it rises. When the moon is near the horizon, the bending of light in the atmosphere can also distort the moon's shape.

© Houghton Mifflin Harcourt Publishing Company ◦ Image Credit: ©Jonathan Wiggs/The Boston Globe/Getty Images

Explore First

Simulating an Eclipse Hold a ball at arms length. With your other hand, hold a coin between your eyes and the ball. Move the coin back and forth until it blocks your view of the ball. Why are you able to block your view of the ball with the much smaller coin?

CAN YOU EXPLAIN IT?

Why can we see the moon at night and also during the day?

At night, the moon is the biggest, brightest object in the sky. If you look closely, you may also be able to see the moon during the day when the sun is also out. These photographs were taken about 2 weeks apart.

1. How is the moon similar and different in the two photos?

2. Do you think the shape of the moon would appear to be different if photos were taken a few hours later than the photos shown here? Explain your reasoning.

3. Do you think the shape of the moon would appear to be different if photos were taken one week later than the photos shown here? Explain your reasoning.

 EVIDENCE NOTEBOOK As you explore the lesson, gather evidence to help explain why we see the moon at night and also during the day.

© Houghton Mifflin Harcourt Publishing Company • Image Credits: (r) ©Wollertz/Fotolia; (l) ©Marc Moritsch/National Geographic/Getty Images

Go online to view the digital version of the Hands-On Lab for this lesson and to download additional lab resources.

Analyzing Moon Phases

The moon orbits Earth and not the sun because, although the sun has a greater mass, it is much farther away. The gravitational attraction between the moon and Earth is greater than the gravitational attraction between the moon and sun. Because it is so close, the moon is the brightest body in the night sky as seen from Earth. The light we see from the moon is reflected sunlight. The sun always lights half of the moon, and the other half is always dark. From Earth, the moon does not always appear the same. The moon's appearance changes from a totally dark disk to a fully lit disk and back again over the course of a month. These images show a pattern of change in the moon's appearance called the moon's phases. A **phase** is the change in the sunlit area of one celestial body, such as the moon, as seen from another celestial body, such as Earth.

The moon's changing appearance in the sky is shown in these images, taken about four days apart over the period of one month.

4. Does the fraction of the moon that receives sunlight ever change? Explain your reasoning.

The Moon Orbits Earth

Earth rotates on its axis once every 24 hours, which explains the pattern of sunrise and sunset, or day and night. Like the sun, the moon always rises along the eastern horizon and sets along the western horizon. The moon is visible for about twelve hours at a time.

The same side of the moon always faces Earth. This happens because the moon's orbit and the time the moon takes to rotate on its axis are the same—about 27 days. However, the moon takes slightly longer—29.5 days—to complete one cycle of phases. Because Earth is also moving in its orbit around the sun as the moon orbits Earth, after 27 days, Earth and the moon have changed position with respect to the sun. Therefore, the moon must travel a little longer than 27 days before it is directly between the sun and Earth, where the cycle of phases begins again. This pattern can be observed as the moon rises and sets about 50 minutes later each day.

EVIDENCE NOTEBOOK

5. If the moon is lit by the sun, why can you still see it after sunset? Record your evidence.

Model Moon Phases

You will model the Earth-sun-moon system to develop an explanation for the changing appearance of the moon as seen from Earth.

Procedure

STEP 1 Continue working with your partner. The lamp (sun) should be placed at eye level. Use the marker and tape to label the polystyrene ball as *moon*.

STEP 2 **Act** Have the person playing Earth face the sun (the lamp). The other partner stands next to the sun, facing Earth. Earth holds the moon at arm's length so the moon is between Earth and the sun, then raises the moon so that the moon is slightly higher than his or her head. Record your observations of how much of the moon appears to be lit. Each partner records his or her observations in the appropriate column of the table.

STEP 3 **Act** Keeping the moon held in the same position at arm's length, Earth will slowly turn in a circle toward the left, stopping at each quarter turn. At each stop, the partners each record their observations of how much of the moon appears to be lit.

STEP 4 **Act** Switch roles and repeat STEPS 2 and 3, completing the table by recording your observations from the other perspective, from either Earth or next to the sun.

MATERIALS
- ball, styrene, on a stick
- lamp with removable shade
- markers
- tape

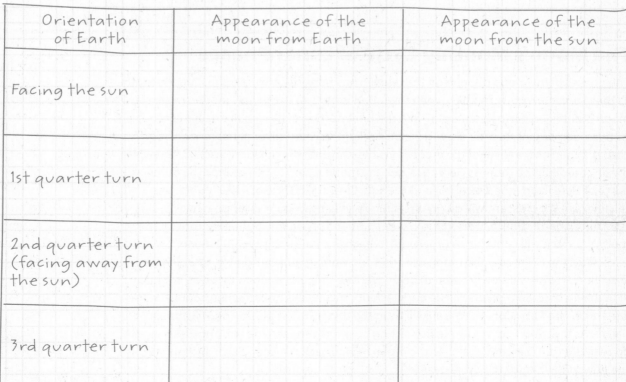

Orientation of Earth	Appearance of the moon from Earth	Appearance of the moon from the sun
Facing the sun		
1st quarter turn		
2nd quarter turn (facing away from the sun)		
3rd quarter turn		

© Houghton Mifflin Harcourt Publishing Company

Analysis

STEP 5 What is being modeled by the ball when the person playing Earth is turning in a circle?

A. Earth's rotation

B. the moon's rotation

C. Earth's orbit around the sun

D. the moon's orbit around Earth

STEP 6 When I was playing Earth, the shape of the fraction of the moon that appeared lit *changed / stayed the same*.

When I was facing the sun, the moon appeared to be completely *dark / lit*. When I was facing away from the sun, the moon appeared to be completely *dark / lit*.

When I was observing the moon from the sun, the fraction of the moon that was lit *changed / was always one half*.

STEP 7 **Language SmArts** Compare the information that you have read so far in the text with what you observed in the experiment. Write an explanation for why the phases of the moon occur. Give examples from the model to support your explanation.

The Moon's Monthly Cycle of Lunar Phases

The phases of the moon depend on the relative positions of Earth, the sun, and the moon as these objects move in space. When the moon is dark, or in the new moon phase, the moon is between Earth and the sun, and the unlit portion of the moon is facing Earth. As the moon begins its orbit around Earth, sunlight makes a sliver of the moon's edge visible. When only a sliver of the moon is visible, the phase is called a crescent, and when the lit portion of the moon is getting larger, the moon is said to be waxing. The outward curve of a crescent moon faces toward the sun. Over the course of a few nights, the thickness of the crescent will grow until after a week, the moon will appear half lit. This is the first quarter phase. During the waxing gibbous phase, the lighted portion of the moon's surface will continue to grow until it reaches a fully lit disk, or full moon.

After the full moon, the moon will enter the waning gibbous phase, in which the size of the lit disk will slowly begin to decrease. The side of the moon that was originally lit in the first crescent phase will be dark. About three weeks after the new moon, or one week after the full moon, the moon will be in the third quarter phase and will appear half lit. As the moon gets closer to its starting position between the sun and Earth, it will appear as a thin crescent again. As the moon moves back between Earth and the sun, the new moon begins the cycle over.

© Houghton Mifflin Harcourt Publishing Company

Phases of the Moon

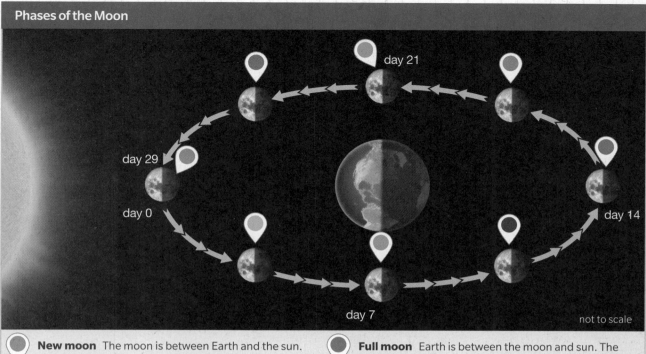

day 21

day 29

day 0

day 14

day 7

not to scale

New moon The moon is between Earth and the sun. From Earth, the moon is completely dark because the side that reflects sunlight is facing away from Earth.

Waxing crescent A thin sliver of the moon becomes visible and continues to grow. *Waxing* means the part of the moon that appears lit is getting larger.

First quarter From Earth's Northern Hemisphere, the right half of the moon appears half lit.

Waxing gibbous The sunlit fraction of the moon that is visible from Earth continues to increase.

Full moon Earth is between the moon and sun. The entire sunlit fraction of the moon is visible from Earth.

Waning gibbous The sunlit fraction of the moon that is visible from Earth decreases. *Waning* means that the part of the moon that appears lit is getting smaller.

Third quarter From Earth's Northern Hemisphere, the left half of the moon appears lit.

Waning crescent The visible fraction of the sunlit moon continues to decrease.

Phases of the Moon Observed from Earth

6. Write the missing labels for the phases of the moon. Some labels may be used more than once.

- full moon
- new moon
- waning
- waxing

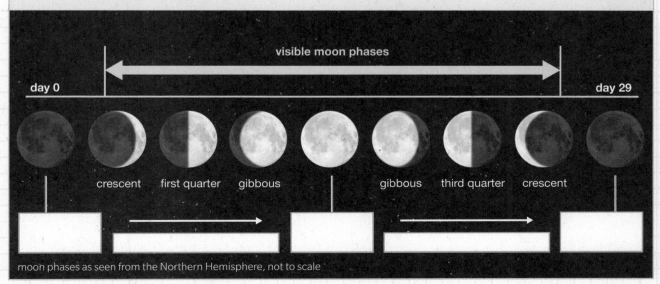

visible moon phases

day 0

day 29

crescent   first quarter   gibbous   gibbous   third quarter   crescent

moon phases as seen from the Northern Hemisphere, not to scale

© Houghton Mifflin Harcourt Publishing Company

7. During a ~~full~~ / new moon, Earth is between the sun and the moon. So, all of the light reflected from the moon is visible from Earth. The moon, Earth, and sun are aligned, with Earth in the middle. The moon's sunlit half, which is its day / ~~night~~ side, faces Earth's day / ~~night~~ side. That is always the case for a full moon.

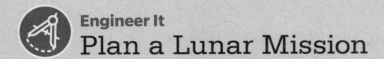

Engineer It
Plan a Lunar Mission

You are planning an expedition to the moon in which astronauts will stay on the moon for four days to collect samples and data. You want them to land on the part of the moon that is lit by the sun so they can see their surroundings. While on the moon, astronauts need to use radio waves to communicate with Earth, and for the radio waves to reach Earth, your transmitter must be pointed toward Earth. Because the same side of the moon always faces toward Earth, and phases of the moon are predictable, you can choose the best location and time for the trip years before launch.

8. During which phase(s) and where on the moon would you want to land? Explain your reasoning and draw a diagram to illustrate and justify your choice.

Exploring Eclipses

You can make shadow puppets, such as the one in the photo, using a flashlight and your hands. You can also use paper cutouts to make shadows. Moving the cutout or your hands makes the shadow move.

9. In the photo, why does the shadow of a dog's head form on the wall behind the hand?

You can make a shadow puppet of a dog's head using your hand and a light source.

Eclipses

Earth and the moon block the light from the sun and form shadows behind them in space. Sometimes, the moon moves into Earth's shadow or Earth moves into the moon's shadow. Both events are called an *eclipse*. An **eclipse** happens when the shadow of one celestial body falls on another. Both solar and lunar eclipses, shown in the photos below, occur in the Earth-sun-moon system. During a *solar eclipse*, the shadow of the moon falls on Earth. During a *lunar eclipse*, the shadow of Earth falls on the moon. Eclipses can be explained by laws that describe the movements of Earth, the moon, and the sun. These laws can be used to make accurate predictions about when future eclipses will occur.

A solar eclipse: from Earth, we can see the moon come between Earth and the sun.

A lunar eclipse: from Earth, we can see the shadow of Earth falling on the moon.

10. Use what you see in the photos to explain how shadows are formed during a solar eclipse and a lunar eclipse. Include the sun, moon, and Earth in your explanations.

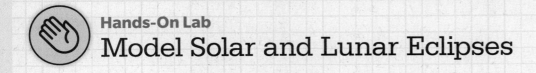

Hands-On Lab
Model Solar and Lunar Eclipses

You will model the Earth-sun-moon system to develop an explanation for solar and lunar eclipses.

MATERIALS
- lamp with removable shade
- moon model from previous activity

Procedure and Analysis

STEP 1 Continue working with your partner. The lamp (sun) should be placed at eye level. One partner plays Earth first, completing STEPS 2–4. Then switch roles and have the other partner play Earth. Each partner records his or her own observations.

STEP 2 **Act** The partner playing Earth faces the sun. Earth holds the moon at arm's length so the moon and the sun are in a straight line with the moon directly between Earth and the sun.

STEP 3 **Act** Earth closes one eye and slowly turns toward the left. As you turn, stop when your view of the moon is completely covered in shadow. Record your observations of the alignment of the Earth-sun-moon system and what you see from Earth.

STEP 4 **Act** Earth continues to turn left. Stop when you notice that the moon blocks your view of the sun. Record your observations.

STEP 5 A solar eclipse happens when the moon casts a shadow on Earth / the sun I modeled a solar eclipse when my head / the ball blocked the light of the sun and cast a shadow on my head / the ball. A lunar eclipse happens when Earth casts a shadow on the moon / sun .I modeled a lunar eclipse when my head / the ball blocked the light of the sun and cast a shadow on my head / the ball .

STEP 6 If time allows, repeat STEPS 2–4, this time holding the moon slightly above your head. What differences do you see?

In the Shadow of the Moon

Solar eclipses occur when the moon moves between the sun and Earth and the moon blocks some sunlight from reaching Earth. The shadow that extends behind the moon has two cone-shaped parts, modeled in the photo. The darker, inner shadow is the *umbra*, and the lighter, larger shadow is the *penumbra*.

At least two solar eclipses occur every year, but, as the diagram shows, the moon's shadow does not completely cover Earth. Only a small area is covered by the shadow, which is why not everyone on Earth can see every solar eclipse. To see a solar eclipse, you must be in the path of the moon's shadow. The dark umbra covers an even smaller area than the larger penumbra. As an area of Earth passes through the umbra, the sun appears to be totally eclipsed. The sun briefly "goes dark," for a few minutes at most, but it may seem like nighttime until that area of Earth moves out of the moon's shadow.

The umbra is the darkest part of a shadow. The penumbra is the lighter part of a shadow.

A Solar Eclipse

The moon casts a shadow on an area of Earth during a solar eclipse. The umbra is the smaller, darker part of the shadow. The umbra is surrounded by the lighter penumbra.

During a solar eclipse, the shadow of the moon falls on Earth.

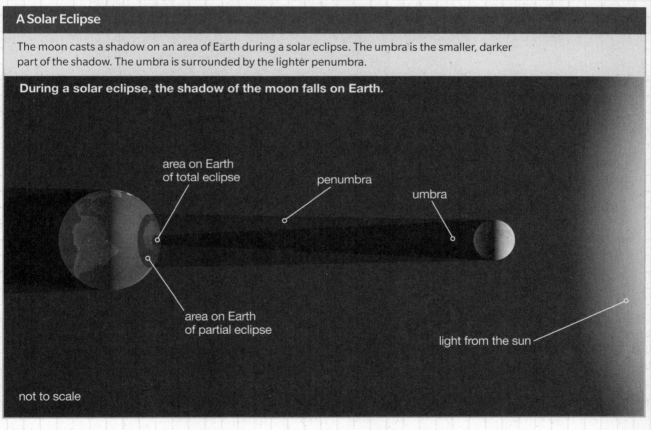

area on Earth of total eclipse

penumbra

umbra

area on Earth of partial eclipse

light from the sun

not to scale

11. Why can solar eclipses be observed only on certain parts of Earth? Circle all that apply.

    A. The moon is smaller than Earth.

    B. Half of Earth is facing away from the sun and cannot see the moon's shadow.

    C. Sunlight in areas outside of the umbra and penumbra is not blocked by the moon.

    D. Solar eclipses occur only once every few years.

Types of Solar Eclipses

There are three types of solar eclipses. A *total solar eclipse* occurs when the sun appears to be completely blocked except for a bright halo of light. A total eclipse happens only when the moon, sun, and Earth are in a straight line, with the moon directly between the sun and Earth. When a total eclipse of the sun occurs, only people who observe from the umbra will see the total eclipse. People who observe from the penumbra will see a *partial solar eclipse*, because from their point of view, the moon only blocks part of the sun's light. An *annular solar eclipse* also occurs when all three bodies are in a straight line. However, the moon is farther away from Earth, because its orbit is elliptical and the umbra shadow does not quite reach Earth. So, the moon does not completely cover the sun. The sun's outer edges can be seen as a ring of light around the darker center during an annular eclipse.

Types of Solar Eclipses	annular solar eclipse	partial solar eclipse
12. Write the correct term from the word bank to label each image.	• annular solar eclipse • ~~uneclipsed sun~~	• partial solar eclipse • total solar eclipse

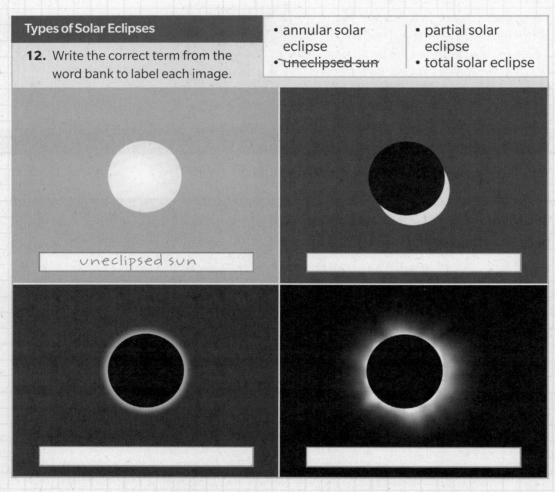

uneclipsed sun

In the Shadow of Earth

During a lunar eclipse, Earth is between the moon and the sun. Because Earth is so much bigger than the moon, Earth's shadow covers the entire moon when they are aligned. As the diagram of a lunar eclipse shows, Earth's shadow also has an umbra and penumbra. Remember, the moon reflects sunlight, so when Earth blocks sunlight from reaching the moon, the moon appears dark. Instead of being totally dark, the moon often appears to be a rusty red color because Earth's atmosphere bends some sunlight into the shadow. Everyone who is on the dark side of Earth can see a lunar eclipse because Earth is casting the shadow.

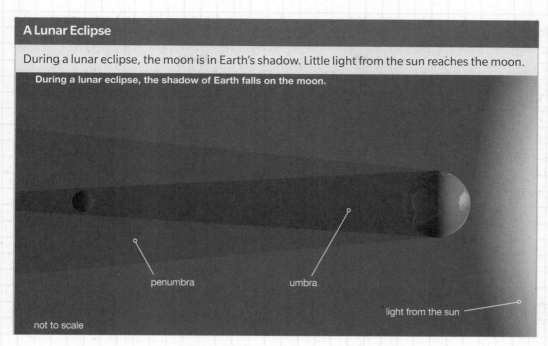

A Lunar Eclipse

During a lunar eclipse, the moon is in Earth's shadow. Little light from the sun reaches the moon.

During a lunar eclipse, the shadow of Earth falls on the moon.

penumbra

umbra

light from the sun

not to scale

13. Analyze the image. The moon will always be new when a lunar / solar eclipse happens. During a lunar eclipse, the moon will be new / full.

Types of Lunar Eclipses

During a lunar eclipse, the moon may appear totally or partially dark depending on where it passes through Earth's shadow. The composite photo shows multiple images of the moon taken over about three and a half hours during a *total lunar eclipse*, which occurs when the whole moon passes through Earth's umbra. During a *partial lunar eclipse*, only part of the moon passes through the umbra. The part of the moon that passes through Earth's shadow becomes dark. There is one more type of lunar eclipse—the *penumbral lunar eclipse*, which occurs when the moon passes through the penumbra. While total and partial eclipses are easy to observe, penumbral eclipses are difficult to see. The penumbra is a lighter shadow, and sunlight still reaches the moon when it passes through this part of Earth's shadow.

As the moon passes through Earth's umbra, more of it becomes dark. It turns a reddish-orange instead of being totally dark because Earth's atmosphere bends sunlight into the shadow.

14. Write total, partial, or penumbral to complete the paragraph.

If the entire moon passes through the part of Earth's shadow called the umbra, a _____ lunar eclipse will occur. If the moon passes only through the penumbra, a _____ lunar eclipse will occur.

Timing of Eclipses

Every time the moon orbits Earth, the moon comes between the sun and Earth, and Earth comes between the moon and the sun. Yet, eclipses do not occur every time the moon orbits Earth. To understand why, you need to think of space in three dimensions. Think of the sun and Earth's nearly circular orbit around the sun in a flat plane. The moon's orbit is not in the same plane, although it may appear that way in many two-dimensional diagrams. The moon's orbit is actually tilted about 5° to the Earth-sun plane as the diagram shows. Because of this tilted orbit, the moon is usually above or below Earth during its orbit instead of being aligned in the same plane as Earth and the sun. So, the moon and Earth usually do not pass through each other's shadows.

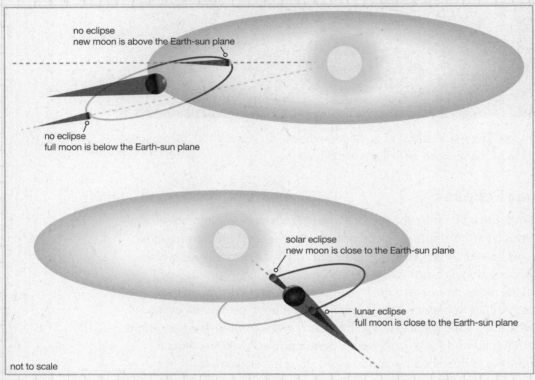

no eclipse
new moon is above the Earth-sun plane

no eclipse
full moon is below the Earth-sun plane

solar eclipse
new moon is close to the Earth-sun plane

lunar eclipse
full moon is close to the Earth-sun plane

not to scale

The moon spends half its time above the Earth-sun plane and half its time below this plane. The moon only passes through Earth's shadow when it is in the same plane as Earth and the sun. Similarly, the moon must be in the same plane as Earth and the sun in order to cause a solar eclipse.

EVIDENCE NOTEBOOK

15. An eclipse season is a period of about a month when a lunar or solar eclipse is likely to occur. Two eclipse seasons occur each year. What is the location of the moon in its orbit during an eclipse season? Record your evidence.

Phases of the Moon During Eclipses

16. Because its orbit is tilted with respect to the Earth-sun plane, the moon spends most of its time either above or below the plane. How many times would the moon cross through the Earth-sun plane each time it orbits Earth? Explain.

© Houghton Mifflin Harcourt Publishing Company

Continue Your Exploration

Name: _____   Date: _____

Check out the path below or go online to choose one of the other paths shown.

| People in Science | • Using Shadows and Shades
• Hands-On Labs 🖐
• Propose Your Own Path | Go online to choose one of these other paths. |

Leon Foucault, Physicist

By 1850, it was widely accepted that Earth rotates on its axis. But a French physicist, Leon Foucault (FOO•koh), was the first person to design an instrument that demonstrated Earth's rotation.

Foucault realized that he could show Earth's rotation using a carefully designed pendulum. A pendulum is a ball that hangs by a wire from a fixed point. Once the ball is released, it swings back and forth. Foucault used a 67-meter-long wire and designed the pendulum so that it could swing in any direction. He hung his first pendulum from the Paris Observatory in 1851. The swinging pendulum appeared to gradually change its direction of swing over the course of a day. This change in direction was evidence that Earth is rotating.

Leon Foucault was a French physicist who designed an experiment to provide evidence that Earth rotates.

© Houghton Mifflin Harcourt Publishing Company • Image Credits: (inset) ©Science Source; (b) ©Cristina Arias/Cover/Getty Images

Explore Online

Foucault's pendulum appears to move as Earth rotates under it. Throughout the day, this pendulum knocks down pegs to show how its swing gradually changes direction.

Continue Your Exploration

1. Why was it necessary for Foucault's pendulum to swing freely in all directions in order for it to demonstrate that Earth rotates?

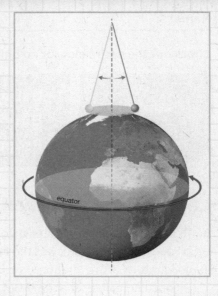

2. How does the explanation for the way Foucault's pendulum appears to move relate to the explanation for why the sun, moon, and stars appear to circle Earth every 24 hours?

3. **Do the Math** Locations other than the North and South Poles move in a circle around Earth's axis as Earth rotates. Because of this motion, Foucault's pendulum does not complete a full circle in one day. For example, it only turns 270° in one day in Paris. How many hours would it take to complete one full circle (360°) in Paris?

   A. 11
   B. 18
   C. 27
   D. 32

4. **Collaborate** With a group, prepare a multimedia presentation to explain how Foucault's pendulum works. Consider including videos or demonstrations.

Can You Explain It?

Name: _____   Date: _____

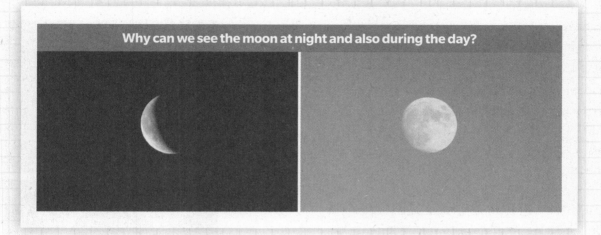

Why can we see the moon at night and also during the day?

EVIDENCE NOTEBOOK

Refer to the notes in your Evidence Notebook to help you construct an explanation for why the moon is visible at night and during the day.

1. State your claim. Make sure your claim fully explains why you can see the moon during the daytime and the nighttime.

2. Summarize the evidence you have gathered to support your claim and explain your reasoning.

Checkpoints

Answer the following questions to check your understanding of the lesson. Use the images to answer Questions 3–4.

3. Why does the annular eclipse in the top image appear to be different from the total eclipse in the bottom image?

   A. In the top image the moon is farther away from Earth.

   B. In the top image the moon is closer to Earth.

   C. In the bottom image the moon does not completely cover the sun.

   D. In the bottom image the moon is not directly between Earth and the sun.

4. In August 2017, a total solar eclipse was visible from the United States. A total solar eclipse happens when   Earth / the moon   moves directly in front of the   moon / sun . A total solar eclipse can be seen from   everywhere / a narrow path   on Earth. The bottom image was seen from the   umbra / penumbra   during the eclipse.

Use the photos to answer Questions 5–6.

5. Why is the moon's appearance different in the two photos? Circle all that apply.

   A. Both photos show phases of the moon.

   B. The top photo shows an eclipse, and the bottom photo shows a phase.

   C. The moon in the bottom photo occurs about once every month.

   D. The moon in the top photo occurs only when the moon is in Earth's shadow.

6. The moon in the bottom photo is in its third quarter. How will the moon look after it moves another quarter of the way through its orbit?

   A. The same as it looks in the photo.

   B. The full circle of the moon will be lit.

   C. The moon will be completely dark.

   D. The quarter moon will be lit on the other side.

Interactive Review

Complete this section to review the main concepts of the lesson.

The moon goes through a pattern of phases over a period of 29.5 days. Phases change as the fraction of the sunlit area of the moon that is visible from Earth changes.

A. About how much time passed between these two images of the moon? Use evidence and reasoning to support your claim.

Eclipses happen when Earth is in the shadow of the moon or the moon is in the shadow of Earth.

B. Explain the difference between a partial solar eclipse and a total solar eclipse.

The Solar System Formed from Colliding Matter

Scientists use technology to understand the events that formed the solar system billions of years ago.

Explore First

Modeling the Formation of Planets Place small pieces of clay on a table top. Roll another larger lump of clay over the smaller pieces until they all stick to the larger lump of clay. What has happened to the size of the larger piece of clay? How do you explain any difference you see?

CAN YOU EXPLAIN IT?

Why do all the planets in the solar system orbit the sun in the same direction?

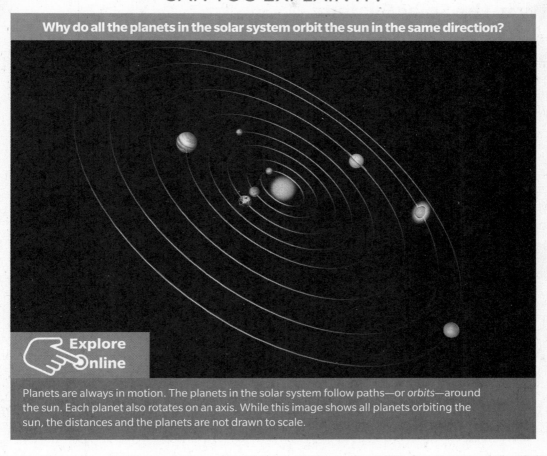

Explore Online

Planets are always in motion. The planets in the solar system follow paths—or *orbits*—around the sun. Each planet also rotates on an axis. While this image shows all planets orbiting the sun, the distances and the planets are not drawn to scale.

1. Why do planets move around the sun?

2. How could the movement of the planets in the solar system be used as evidence for how the solar system formed?

 EVIDENCE NOTEBOOK As you explore the lesson, gather evidence to explain why all planets in the solar system orbit the sun in the same direction.

Exploring Gravity in the Solar System

Gravity in the Solar System

An object's mass determines the strength of its gravitational field. The gravitational fields of stars are very strong and extend far into space. As a result, a star influences the motion of other objects around it. Gravity is always attractive, and the strength of a gravitational field decreases as the distance between objects increases. The law of universal gravitation is written mathematically as:

$$F = \frac{G\,(m_1 \times m_2)}{d^2}$$

In this equation, F is the force of gravity, G is the gravitational constant, m stands for masses of the objects, and d stands for distance between them. The force of gravity between two objects is proportional to the mass of the two objects and inversely proportional to the square of the distance between them.

Planet	Mass (kg)	Mass relative to Earth	Distance from sun (millions of km)	Distance from sun relative to Earth
Sun	1.9×10^{30}	333,000	–	–
Mercury	3.3×10^{23}	0.06	58	0.39
Venus	4.9×10^{24}	0.8	108	0.72
Earth	5.9×10^{24}	1	150	1
Mars	6.4×10^{23}	0.1	228	1.5
Jupiter	11.9×10^{27}	318	778	5.2
Saturn	5.7×10^{26}	95	1,433	9.6
Uranus	8.7×10^{25}	15	2,872	19
Neptune	1.0×10^{26}	17	4,495	30

3. Analyze the data in the table. How does the gravitational force between the sun and Mercury compare to the gravitational force between the sun and Jupiter?

Gravity and the Sun

The sun is an average-sized star, yet it is large enough to contain 1.3 million Earth-sized planets! This large volume is filled with hot, churning hydrogen and helium, as well as trace amounts of many other elements such as oxygen, carbon, and iron. The sun is the largest single object in the solar system. Although it has one-fourth the density of Earth, it is so large that it has 333,000 times more mass. The sun lies at the center of the solar system, exerting a massive gravitational pull in all directions. All of the objects in the solar system are held in orbit by the gravitational pull between themselves and the sun.

4. Look at the photos. What pattern(s) do you see between the mass of an object and its shape? Why do you think this is?

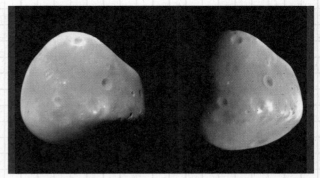
The moon Deimos has a mass of 1.4762×10^{15} kg.

Gravity and the Shape of Objects in the Solar System

Not all of the objects in the solar system have the same shape. Although the planets are all spherical, many of the smaller objects are not. The shape of the objects in the solar system are related to their mass. The more massive an object is, the more spherical shape it has. The shapes of objects in the solar system can provide evidence for how the solar system formed.

When two objects in the solar system interact, each object exerts a gravitational force on the other object. This causes energy to be transferred between the objects. Depending on their relative positions, the objects may contain potential energy. This potential energy will be transferred into kinetic energy if one object collides with another object. Some of the energy transferred changes form to become thermal energy. This thermal energy can cause an object to melt or partially melt.

The moon Phobos has a mass of 10.6×10^{15} kg.

Once an object in space melts or partially melts, the matter becomes more fluid and can change shape. The matter at the center attracts the matter at the outer surface of the body. The matter flows so that it can come as close to the center of the body as possible. The shape that forms when every particle is as close to the center as every other particle is a sphere. Therefore, gravity pulls the material in the object into a more spherical shape. The more massive an object is, the stronger its gravitational field will be, and the more spherical it will become.

The asteroid Vesta has a mass 2.59076×10^{20} kg.

5. Look at the photos. Which of these objects probably had the greatest amount of thermal energy during its formation?

The dwarf planet Ceres has a mass of 9.39×10^{20} kg.

Gravity and the Composition of Planets

The planets are the next largest objects in the solar system, after the sun. The planets can be divided into two groups that relate to their positions and compositions. The inner, or terrestrial, planets—Mercury, Venus, Earth, and Mars—are small, rocky, and dense. These planets have solid surfaces. Below the surfaces of the terrestrial planets are layers of solid and molten rock and metals. At the center of each terrestrial planet is a dense solid core composed of iron and nickel.

The outer planets—gas giants Jupiter and Saturn and ice giants Uranus and Neptune—are larger, icy or gaseous, and less dense. The giant planets do not have solid, rocky surfaces. The outer layers of the these planets are composed of liquids, ices, and gases. These planets do have dense, solid cores, but their cores are composed of rock and ice instead of metal.

The planets are very different from one another but also have some similarities. The layers of each planet increase in density toward the center of the planet. On Earth, the solid iron and nickel core is four times as dense as the rocky surface we are familiar with. The pattern we see in the layers of all the planets is evidence that the planets were all molten at one time in their past.

This layered density pattern found in each planet is similar to the density pattern seen in the solar system as a whole. The denser material is generally found in the planets closer to the sun. The less dense material is generally found in the planets farther from the sun. However, although the inner planets are denser, most of the mass that makes up the planets in the solar system is in the giant outer planets.

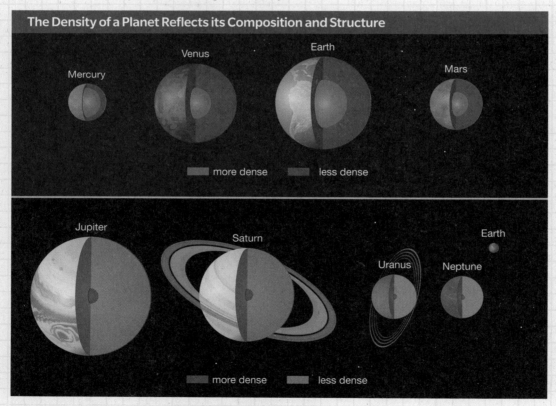

The Density of a Planet Reflects its Composition and Structure

Mercury · Venus · Earth · Mars

more dense · less dense

Jupiter · Saturn · Uranus · Neptune · Earth

more dense · less dense

6. When these terrestrial planets formed, *more dense / less dense* materials stayed near the surface. Within the solar system, a *similar / different* pattern occurred. The inner terrestrial planets are *more dense / less dense*, and the outer gas giant planets are *more dense / less dense*.

Do the Math
Graph the Density of the Planets

7. In the space provided, make a bar graph to compare the densities of the planets.

8. The density of liquid water is 1.0 g/cm³, the density of rock is 2.7 g/cm³, the density of iron is 7.9 g/cm³. Add this information to your graph.

9. Are the densities of the planets roughly proportional to their diameters? Use evidence to support your claim.

_____

_____

_____

_____

_____

Planet	Density (g/cm³)	Diameter (km)
Mercury	5.4	4,879
Venus	5.2	12,104
Earth	5.5	12,756
Mars	3.9	6,792
Jupiter	1.3	142,984
Saturn	0.68	120,536
Uranus	1.3	51,118
Neptune	1.6	49,528

10. How does the graph you made help you visualize the different types of materials that make up the planets?

_____

_____

_____

_____

_____

Building a Hypothesis of How the Solar System Formed

Ancient astronomers used observations of the sky to develop the first models of Earth in space. Similarly, modern astronomers use observations and evidence to model the formation of the solar system.

11. **Discuss** With a partner, make a list of questions about how the solar system formed. What mechanisms or processes would you want to explore in order to develop a hypothesis about the formation of the solar system?

Mercury (Firdousi Crater)

Moon (Goclenius Crater)

Earth (Wolfe Crater)

Mars (Hephaestus Crater)

Mimas (Herschel Crater)

Asteroid Vesta (Licinia Crater)

Collisions as Evidence of the Early Solar System

Impact craters are evidence that collisions have occurred between objects in space. Impact craters on the moons, planets, and asteroids in the solar system vary in size, shape, and age. The sizes and shapes of impact craters differ based on the mass and speed of the bodies that collide. The angle at which an object strikes a surface can affect the shape of a crater. Although the moon and other objects in the solar system show a record of many impacts, there are very few impact craters remaining on Earth's surface. Most impact craters on Earth have been weathered and eroded. However, all impact craters are evidence that matter collided as bodies of different sizes, compositions, and speeds moved through their orbits around the sun.

12. Why are impact craters evident on terrestrial objects but not on outer planets?

Kant's Nebular Hypothesis

In the mid-1700s, Immanuel Kant developed the *nebular hypothesis* of the origin of the solar system. He proposed that matter in the solar system began as separate particles. This cloud of dust and gas from which the planets and sun formed is now known as the **solar nebula.** Kant suggested that attractive forces between the particles caused them to collide and join together, forming larger clumps. As the clumps increased in size, their gravitational fields increased in strength, and they attracted even more particles. The sun formed at the middle of the cloud of particles, where the attractive forces were the greatest. The remaining particles joined with the larger masses until the planets were formed. The large mass of the sun and the gravitational attraction between the planets and the sun kept the planets in orbit around the sun. Kant's hypothesis explained the process in which matter in the solar system went from an unordered state to a structured system with distinct bodies orbiting the sun in a predictable pattern. While Kant's nebular hypothesis described the formation of the solar system, it did not explain several characteristics of the solar system. For example, his hypothesis did not explain why all planets orbit the sun in the same direction or why the planets orbit the sun in roughly the same plane.

13. **Draw** Storyboards can be drawn to illustrate the steps in a sequence. Use the space below to draw a storyboard that explains Kant's nebular hypothesis. Write a caption to support the art you make.

14. **Discuss** According to current criteria, a space object is classified as a planet if it (1) orbits a star, (2) is large enough to have a nearly spherical shape, and (3) has "cleared the neighborhood" around its orbit. The orbital path of a planet is cleared when smaller masses are attracted to and combine with the planet or are pushed to a different orbit. How are Kant's hypothesis and impact craters related to the classification of an object as a planet?

Laplace Refines Kant's Model

About 40 years after Kant's work became known, Pierre-Simon Laplace used mathematics to refine the nebular hypothesis. Laplace suggested that after forming in a collapsing cloud of dust and gas, the sun cooled and became more compact in size. This made the sun rotate more quickly. In the same way, ice skaters spin faster when they draw their arms into their bodies. For both the sun and the ice skater, the rotational speed increases as mass moves toward the center of the object.

Dust and gas were pushed outward while the sun's gravity pulled matter inward toward the sun. The constant push and pull flattened the cloud into a large disk. Scientists refer to these disks of matter as **protoplanetary disks.** The prefix "proto-" means "earliest" in Greek. The disk rotated around the sun, and material in the disk formed concentric rings of debris. Matter collided and fused in the rings, eventually forming the planets.

The ice skater begins to spin with her arms extended and her leg out. As she contracts her mass by bringing her arms and leg inward, she spins faster.

15. Which of the following are explained by Laplace's hypothesis of how the solar system formed? Circle all that apply.

 A. All planets orbit the sun in the same direction.

 B. Planets are dense collections of rock and gas with strong gravitational fields.

 C. Planets spin on their axes at the same rates.

 D. The orbital paths of the planets are in about the same plane.

Laplace's Hypothesis of Solar System Formation

(1) A slowly rotating cloud of dust and gas **(2)** begins to condense, causing it to spin faster. The sun forms at the center of the cloud. **(3)** The cloud flattens into the shape of a disk, and rings of debris form in a plane. **(4)** Materials in each ring collide and clump together due to gravity, **(5)** forming planets and the solar system.

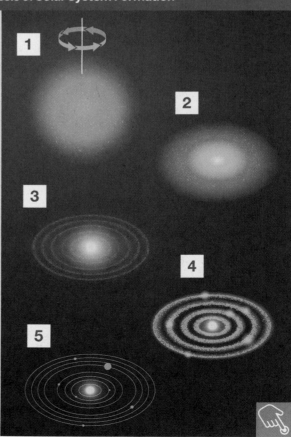

Model Nebular Disk Formation

You will construct a model of nebular disk formation that is consistent with Laplace's hypothesis of solar system formation. Identify similarities and differences between the model and the formation of star systems in space.

MATERIALS
- dowel rod, long and thin
- drawing compass
- glue
- hole punch
- pencil
- ruler
- scissors
- tag board

Procedure

STEP 1 Use the compass to draw three separate circles on the tag board. Make one circle 3 cm in diameter. Make two circles 4 cm in diameter. Cut out the circles carefully using scissors.

STEP 2 Punch a hole in the center of each circle. For the 3 cm circle and one 4 cm circle, the hole should be just big enough to fit snugly over the dowel rod. For the other 4 cm circle, the hole should be slightly larger so that the circle can slide freely over the dowel.

STEP 3 Cut eight strips of tag board that are 1.25 cm wide by 30 cm long.

STEP 4 Glue one end of each strip to the 4 cm circle that fits snugly over the dowel. Pinch and hold in place for 30–60 seconds. Space the strips evenly around the circle. Slide this circle over the dowel and glue it in place about 3 cm from the top of the dowel. Next, slide the 3 cm circle over the bottom of the dowel and glue it in position about 12 cm below the first circle. Give the glue time to dry.

STEP 5 Slide the remaining 4 cm circle over the bottom of the dowel. Glue the loose end of each strip to this circle, making sure the strips are evenly spaced. When the dowel is held upright, this circle should hang below the others and slide freely.

STEP 6 Hold the dowel upright between the palms of your hands. Predict what will happen when you spin the dowel by moving it between your palms. Record your prediction.

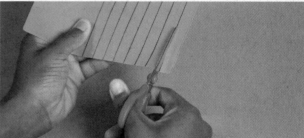
Cut along the lines to form the strips for the sphere.

Glue the strips to the top and bottom tag board circles. Measure distances carefully.

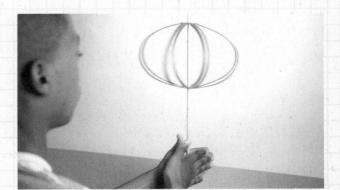
Roll the dowel between both palms to control the spinning. Spin the dowel as fast as you can.

© Houghton Mifflin Harcourt Publishing Company • Image Credits: ©Houghton Mifflin Harcourt

Analysis

STEP 7 Describe what you saw when you spun the dowel.

STEP 8 How does this model relate to the formation of the solar system? Include similarities and differences between the model and the formation of the solar system as described by Pierre-Simon Laplace.

 EVIDENCE NOTEBOOK

16. Imagine the figure skater as the sun and imagine that she was holding a ball in her outstretched hand. How would the motions relate to the orbital direction of the planets? Record your evidence.

 Engineer It
Evaluate the Effect of Gravity

The planets are natural satellites that orbit the sun. The moon is a natural satellite that orbits Earth. Many artificial satellites also orbit Earth. Gravity keeps satellites in orbit around Earth, moons in orbit around planets, and planets and other objects in orbit around the sun. The organization of matter we observe on Earth, in the solar system, and in the universe would not exist without gravity.

17. What would happen to the satellites in orbit around Earth without gravity?

_____

_____

_____

_____

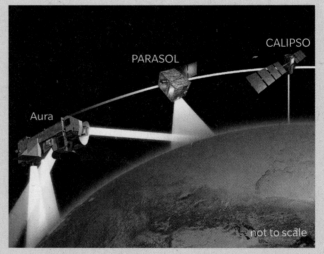

These satellites orbit Earth on a specific path and collect data related to climate change.

18. Brainstorm ways gravity could affect a space probe launched from Earth that is intended to travel to and orbit Jupiter. Why is it necessary to consider gravity when launching a spacecraft or putting a spacecraft into orbit?

_____

_____

_____

Gathering Data on the Formation of Star Systems

In order to understand what is happening in a protoplanetary disk, astronomers develop models based on observations. Gravity plays an important role in the formation of a star system, and the models are based on this. This drawing is based on a model of star system formation. According to this model, the central star is surrounded by a large rotating disk of gas and dust. The central star is pulling in material from the outer disk. The arms of dust and gas form a bridge across the disk. Other material in the disk is forming clumps that will eventually form planets. By developing models like this one, astronomers are able to infer how the star system probably formed.

19. If this star system formed similarly to the solar system, would you expect the star to be stationary or spinning? What about the planets? Use evidence and reasoning to support your claim.

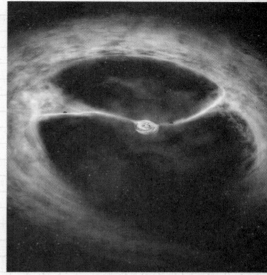

This artist's drawing shows a new star system forming in the disk surrounding a young star.

Evidence of How Star Systems Form

Observations of processes and relationships within our solar system provide evidence for how other star systems may form. Because physical laws are likely the same in other star systems, the way the star and planets in a distant system move can be calculated from how our sun and planets move. These illustrations show the changing positions of sunspots. Sunspots are dark patches that appear temporarily on the sun's surface.

20. What do you know about the sun's motion based on the nebular hypothesis model?

A. The sun and planets both move on the same orbital paths.

B. The sun rotates in the same direction as planets move around the sun.

C. The faster the sun moves, the faster the planets travel in their orbits.

D. There is no relationship between planetary movement and the sun.

21. These images show the position of spots on the surface of the sun over a 1-week period. Based on these images, what conclusion could you draw?

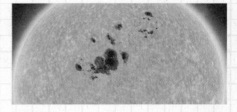

Direct Observation of Star System Formation

The primary source of evidence supporting the hypothesis that the solar system formed from the solar nebula is the observation of similar processes occurring elsewhere in space. By using telescope technology, scientists can observe the formation of stars inside clouds of gas and dust. They can capture images of young stars surrounded by disks of debris. Some telescopes use electromagnetic radiation, such as x-rays, radio waves, gamma rays, and infrared light, to produce images of developing stars and their surroundings.

In recent years, astronomers and engineers have worked together to find evidence for the nebular hypothesis by looking for places elsewhere in the universe where new star systems are forming. Observing these events is expensive. To share the costs and equipment, international science groups worked together to build the Atacama Large Millimeter Array (ALMA). ALMA is a series of 66 radio telescope dishes. The dishes work together to detect clouds of gas and dust like the solar nebula and other signs of star system formation such as protoplanetary disks. One of these disks that has been detected about 450 light-years away is shown in the illustration.

Stars, and perhaps star systems, are forming within the Horsehead Nebula.

This illustration shows a protoplanetary disk. Objects like this can be observed using the Atacama Large Millimeter Array.

22. What stages of the nebular hypothesis do the images above represent? How do you know? Record your claim, evidence, and reasoning.

© Houghton Mifflin Harcourt Publishing Company • Image Credits: (l) ©ESA/STScI/NASA Jet Propulsion Laboratory; (r) ©L. Calcada/Europe an Southern Observatory/Science Source

Computer Modeling and Simulations

Space telescopes do not provide images like those taken with a typical camera. The telescopes collect data, which are translated into an image by a computer. Sometimes artists or a computer program add color to these images. This helps people visualize the object or event being studied. Computers can also model phenomena in space. Models allow scientists to use physical and chemical laws to simulate events that are occurring in space. For example, scientists have modeled the formation of the solar system, the interaction between black holes, and even the collision of a planet and an asteroid.

Explore Online

This computer model shows dense areas of gas as bright areas in the cloud around a forming star.

23. Astronomers use *models /experiments* to represent space events that they cannot see directly or that occur over a long time span. Using *computer models / current data / both models and data* makes it possible to simulate the formation of the solar system. Computers allow scientists to perform investigations in *accelerated / real* time frames. This is important, because modeling the formation of the solar system on a 1:1 time scale would take *billions / millions* of years.

24. **Language SmArts** | **Write an Adventure Story** You may have heard or read fictional stories about people exploring space. Write a story about space travelers exploring a distant solar system that is just beginning to form. You may include an illustration that clarifies important details in your story. Present your story and illustration to a classmate.

Additional Support for the Nebular Hypothesis

Several lines of evidence support the nebular hypothesis. These include the growing number of observations of forming star systems and the observation that the sun rotates in the same direction and plane in which the planets revolve. Other evidence supporting the nebular hypothesis includes computer models that also explain why the inner planets of the solar system are composed of rock and metal, while the outer planets are icy and gaseous. The evidence in support of the nebular hypothesis is so strong that the work of planetary astronomers today is to explain the details of how the solar system went from a cloud of gas and dust to the planets and other bodies seen today.

The Life Cycle of Stars

By observing many stars at different stages, scientists have confirmed that stars follow a predictable life cycle. Stars form in nebulae that are dense and cold. When a nebula collapses, the temperature and pressure increase over time as particles in the nebula collide and clump together. A protostar forms at the center of the nebula, surrounded by gaseous and rocky debris.

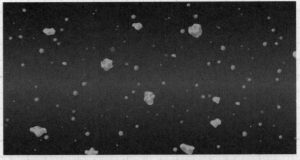

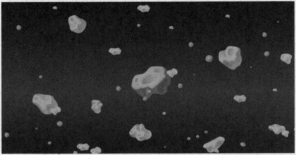

Particles collect into clumps due to the gravitational attraction between masses. The process increases in speed as the clumps get larger and the gravitational attraction increases.

Once the protostar becomes very hot (10 million Kelvin), it becomes a young star. The fusion of hydrogen into helium in the star generates large amounts of thermal energy and light. As the young star warms, the core contracts and begins to spin. At this stage, the debris held by the star's gravity flattens into a protoplanetary disk. The early stages of planet formation occur in the bulging disk of matter surrounding the young star. As the smaller particles are pulled toward the larger clumps, their kinetic energy increases and their potential energy decreases. When the particles collide, the kinetic energy transforms into thermal energy. Gravity pulls the partially molten material into a spherical shape.

Scientists have observed different stages of this process in many places throughout space. The results of computer modeling also support this part of the nebular hypothesis.

25. If you sprinkle magnetic filings in a ring and then drag a magnet through the filings, the magnet will collect a cluster of filings. How is this a model for what happens in a protoplanetary disk?

   A. The magnet moves in an orbit in the same way that planets orbit the sun.

   B. As they move, the magnet and clumps of planetary matter both collect iron because of magnetism.

   C. The magnet collects iron filings as it moves around the ring just as a new planet collects smaller masses due to its strong gravitational pull as it orbits its star.

   D. As they move, the magnet and clumps of planetary matter both collect matter due to their mass and gravity.

26. How does the magnet model differ from what occurs in a protoplanetary disk?

The Composition of the Planets

The temperature near the center of a protoplanetary disk would be very hot. Only elements that are solid at high temperatures would be able to form a solid planet near the center of the disk. This is why the terrestrial planets in the inner solar system consist of elements with high melting points. The outer planets in the solar system consist of elements with lower melting points, such as hydrogen, because those planets formed farther from the center of the disk.

Meteorites collected on Earth also provide evidence of how small bodies formed in the protoplanetary disk. These small, rocky bodies formed at the same time as the planets and are considered "left-over" fragments from the formation of the solar system.

The distance between the planets are not to scale.

The difference in composition between the solar system's terrestrial planets and gas and ice giants provides evidence supporting the nebular hypothesis.

The Orbits of Planets

Humans have directly observed and mapped the movements of planets and other objects in the night sky for thousands of years. These observations show that the planets move across the sky in a narrow band. This suggests that the planets are arranged in a disk shape around the sun. Scientists also observed that all of the planets orbit the sun in the same direction, which is also the same direction in which the sun spins on its axis. These observations support the idea that the planets formed as part of a spinning protoplanetary disk.

 EVIDENCE NOTEBOOK

27. If the planets did not form as part of a protoplanetary disk, how might their path across the sky differ from what is observed? Record your evidence.

The Nebular Theory

Astronomers have gathered enough evidence about the nebular hypothesis to conclude that it is highly likely to be an accurate description of how the solar system must have formed. So it is now widely accepted as a theory that explains how planets form in some detail. According to the nebular theory, gravitational disturbances caused a large cloud of gas and dust in a nebula to collapse into a space the size of the solar system. The particles in the cloud collided and joined to form larger particles with more gravity. As a result of the collisions within the cloud, the nebula became very hot and began to spin. The collapsing and spinning caused the cloud to flatten into a disk shape. The hot, dense center of the cloud became the sun. The rest of the material formed concentric rings around the sun. The rings of material rotated in the same direction that the sun rotated. The observed pattern is that a nebula produces multiple stars, and there seems to be gas and dust that doesn't get incorporated into a new star system but remains in the nebula.

The other seven planets in the solar system will be visible from Earth at the same time on May 6, 2492. This image shows how the planets will be aligned, based on a computer simulation. Notice how the planets are arranged in a narrow band.

Observations, Evidence, and Predictions

28. Imagine you are an astronomer who has discovered a star with a system of planets. Based on the nebular theory, what predictions can you make about the composition and movements of the planets? Use evidence to support your claim.

_____

_____

_____

_____

_____

_____

Continue Your Exploration

Name: _____   Date: _____

Check out the path below or go online to choose one of the other paths shown.

Careers in Science

- **Structure of Other Star Systems**
- **Hands-On Labs** 🖐
- **Propose Your Own Path**

Go online to choose one of these other paths.

Conceptual Space Artist

Imagine using art and science together to inspire people and help them visualize things that we cannot see from Earth. This is what conceptual space artists do every day at the National Aeronautics and Space Administration (NASA). Scientists use various instruments to study objects and events in space. Many of these instruments do not produce normal images. Instead, they collect data in various forms, including series of numbers or simple bands of colored light. Conceptual space artists turn these data into illustrations. This career requires an art background and the ability to use complex computer programs. The drawings and diagrams made by space artists help scientists and laypeople better understand space phenomena.

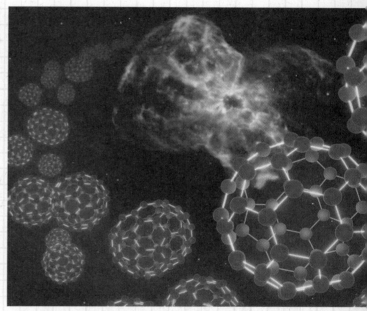

A space artist illustrated carbon spheres exiting a young nebula. Each carbon sphere has 60 carbon atoms arranged in a pattern similar to a soccer ball's.

This space artist's drawing shows what it might look like to watch three suns rising above the horizon from a moon that orbits HD188553 Ab, a large gaseous planet. It is based on data gathered by NASA's Keck telescope.

Continue Your Exploration

1. How is conceptual art different from a photograph?

2. Why are conceptual space artists important for astronomers and the public?

3. What is another example of a profession that translates scientific or professional information for a general audience?

4. **Collaborate** Working in a small group, select one type of space object (a star, nebula, galaxy, supernova, planet, or moon) and create a poster presenting the works of various conceptual space artists. Label each image with the title, artist's name (if available), the distance between the object and Earth, and the technology that provided data for the art.

Can You Explain It?

Name: _____   Date: _____

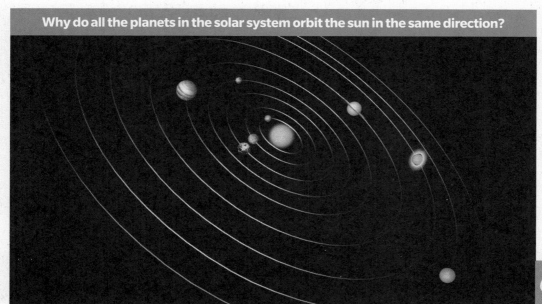

Why do all the planets in the solar system orbit the sun in the same direction?

Explore Online

EVIDENCE NOTEBOOK

Refer to the notes in your Evidence Notebook to help you construct an explanation for why all the planets orbit the sun in the same direction.

1. State your claim. Make sure your claim fully explains why all the planets in the solar system orbit the sun in the same direction.

2. Summarize the evidence you have gathered to support your claim and explain your reasoning.

Checkpoints

Answer the following questions to check your understanding of the lesson.

Use the illustration to answer Questions 3–4.

3. Which of these is most likely the next stage after the one shown in the illustration?

   A. a new star forms

   B. the cloud of dust and gas begins to spin

   C. planets develop with individual orbits

   D. the disk flattens with the star at the center

4. When a new star contracts / expands, it begins to slow down / spin . As a result, the surrounding dust and gases compress into a sphere / disk.

Use the illustration to answer Questions 5–6.

5. Which stages involve the collision and clumping of matter in the nebula? Circle all that apply.

   A. stage 1

   B. stage 2

   C. stage 3

   D. stage 4

6. What evidence supporting the nebular hypothesis is shown?

   A. composition of the planets

   B. composition of the sun

   C. revolving disk of dust and gas

   D. density of the planets

7. Why are there two different types of planets in the solar system?

   A. The amount of material available to form planets was greater in the outer reaches of the protoplanetary disk.

   B. Rocky material could not collect and form planets beyond the asteroid belt.

   C. The nebular cloud from which the solar system formed had very little gas.

   D. The sun's heat allowed only rocky planets to form in the inner portion of the solar system.

Interactive Review

Complete this section to review the main concepts of the lesson.

Gravity played an important role in the shape and composition of the objects in the solar system.

A. Why is the density pattern seen in the layers inside the planets similar to the density pattern seen in the solar system?

The nebular hypothesis of solar system formation explains how the solar system formed from the gas and dust of a nebula and why all planets orbit the sun in the same direction.

B. How was the nebular hypothesis of solar system formation refined to account for the motion of the planets?

Scientists have gathered a variety of evidence to support the nebular hypothesis, including observations of distant star systems and the composition of the planets.

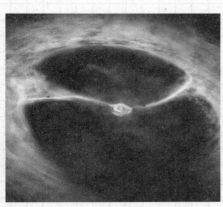

C. What lines of evidence support the nebular theory of solar system formation?

The Solar System and Galaxies Can Be Modeled

This photo shows a star forming near the edge of the Milky Way galaxy. It was taken by the Hubble Space Telescope.

Explore First

Building a Scale Model Use simple materials, such as drinking straws, craft sticks, and tape, to build a simple scale model of your classroom. How many times smaller is your model than your actual classroom? Compare your model to the models built by your classmates. Are they all built to the same scale?

CAN YOU EXPLAIN IT?

How can we make a model of the Milky Way galaxy that shows Earth's location?

Earth is a small planet close to one star, the sun. The sun is one of billions of stars in the Milky Way galaxy. This is an artist's conception of how the Milky Way would look from a distance.

1. If you were standing on a sidewalk, how could you figure out where you are in a city without using a map?

2. How would a map of a galaxy be different from a map of a city?

 EVIDENCE NOTEBOOK As you explore this lesson, gather evidence to explain how scientists determine Earth's location within the Milky Way galaxy.

Modeling the Solar System

Mathematical modeling is important in determining the structure of the solar system. One important part of mathematical modeling is scale. *Scale* is the mathematical relationship between the measurements or distances in a model and the actual measurements or distances of an object or system. It is difficult to imagine distances as large as those in space. Scale provides a way to compare such distances accurately.

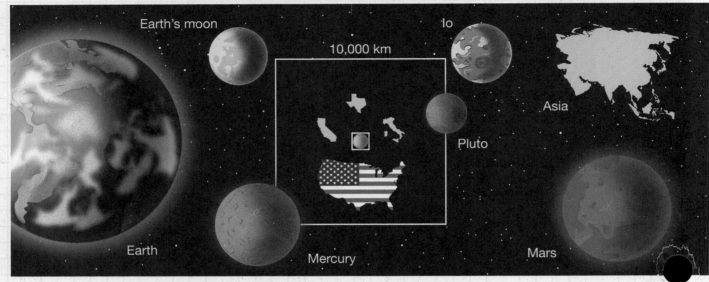

Scale lets us compare familiar objects and distances to astronomical objects and distances. For example, the diameter of Mercury is about the distance across the United States, and the diameter of Mars is about the distance across the continent of Asia.

3. Identify at least three ways scale could help someone understand the solar system.

Size and Distance in the Solar System

Models compare various characteristics of different objects. There are many ways to model the solar system. A physical model or a visual model, such as a drawing or map, could show the structure of the solar system. A mathematical model or a computer model could describe how objects in the solar system move.

Some models are made to scale. Some are not. Both scale and not-to-scale models can be useful. The type of model used depends on what information needs to be shown and how that information is being presented. Some aspects of the solar system are difficult to show with scale models. It is easy to make a scale model of the size of the sun and planets. Adding small asteroids and space dust to that scale model is more challenging. Modeling the huge distances between objects in space is also difficult.

Hands-On Lab
Model the Solar System

Scientists measure distances inside the solar system using kilometers or astronomical units. One **astronomical unit** (AU) is the average distance from the sun to Earth, about 150 million km. Create a scale model of the sun and planets and the distances between them.

Procedure and Analysis (Part 1)

STEP 1 Look at the table called *Solar System Objects*. The table lists the diameter (in km) of the sun and each planet. Use the numbers 1–9 to rank the sun and planets in order from the largest to the smallest.

STEP 2 Look at the objects available for your model. Compare their relative sizes. Predict which objects could be used to represent the sun and each planet in a scale model of the solar system. Write your responses in the table.

STEP 3 Measure and record the diameter of each object.

MATERIALS
- ball, large (20 cm or larger)
- calipers or wire-gauge tool (optional)
- meterstick or measuring tape
- round objects, various sizes

Solar System Objects

Solar system object	Diameter (km)	Relative size (biggest = 1, smallest = 9)	Representative object in model	Diameter of object (cm)
Sun	1,392,000	1		
Mercury	4,879	9		
Venus	12,104			
Earth	12,756			
Mars	6,792			
Jupiter	142,984			
Saturn	120,536			
Uranus	51,118			
Neptune	49,528			

STEP 4 The dwarf planet Ceres has a diameter of 930 km. Analyze the scale properties of the objects in your model to determine which object would best represent Ceres in the model: a pinhead (1 mm), a baseball (75 mm), a grain of salt (0.3 mm), or a table tennis ball (30 mm). Explain your reasoning.

© Houghton Mifflin Harcourt Publishing Company

Procedure and Analysis (Part 2)

STEP 1 To use the same scale for distance in the solar system as you used for size, find the distance of 1 AU at this scale. Remember that the sun is 1,392,000 km in diameter and 1 AU (Earth's distance from the sun) is about 150,000,000 km. Divide the distance of 1 AU in km by the diameter of the sun in km to find out how many solar diameters are in one AU. Then multiply by the diameter of the model sun (in cm) to see how far 1 AU should be in the model.

$$\frac{1 \text{ AU (in km)}}{\text{sun's diameter (in km)}} \times \text{model sun diameter (in cm)} = \text{length of 1 AU in model}$$

STEP 2 Divide the answer in cm by 100 to get the answer in meters. The meter is a convenient unit; one meter is about the length of one very long stride.

STEP 3 Fill in the table below to show how far from the sun each planet should be placed in your model. Round answers to the nearest meter.

Approximate Distances from the Sun to the Planets			
Solar system object	Distance from sun (km)	Distance from sun (AU)	Distance from sun in model (m)
Mercury	58,000,000	0.4	
Venus	108,000,000	0.7	
Earth	150,000,000	1.0	
Mars	228,000,000	1.5	
Jupiter	778,000,000	5.2	
Saturn	1,433,000,000	9.5	
Uranus	2,872,000,000	19	
Neptune	4,495,000,000	30	

STEP 4 Place the model sun in one corner of the room. Place as many planets as you can the correct distance from the sun, using the same scale for distance as for size. How many planets will fit in your classroom?

STEP 5 Some people have said that "There is a huge amount of space in space!" What do you think they mean by that?

STEP 6 **Engineer It** Is it possible for one model to accurately show both the size of the planets and sun and the distance between the planets and sun? On a separate sheet of paper, describe the trade-offs between developing a model that illustrates both accurately and developing a model that illustrates only one of the measurements accurately.

© Houghton Mifflin Harcourt Publishing Company

Do the Math
Calculate Scale as a Ratio

Scale is often expressed as a ratio. A ratio is a way of comparing the relationship of quantity, amount, or size between two numbers. For example, the solar system has eight planets and one star (the sun). Thus, the ratio of planets to stars in the solar system is 8 to 1, or 8:1.

To calculate the scale of a model of the solar system, divide the actual size of a body by the size of the object that represents that same body in the model. The same process can be used to determine the scale for distances. The answer will be a ratio of the actual units to the units in the model. This is commonly expressed as "1" (unit in the model) to "X" (actual units) or "1:X." For example, the miniature town is built on a scale of 1:25. In other words, every 1 m in the model equals 25 m in the real town.

Scale, expressed as a ratio, can be used to make detailed models. The miniature town in this photo was built to scale with the real town. Every streetlight, tree, and building is exactly in proportion with its real-life counterpart.

4. Find the scale ratio that you used to model the solar system. Remember that 1 AU is about 150,000,000 kilometers, which is represented by 22 meters in the model. What is the scale of the model represented by a ratio?

5. How does using ratios or other mathematical comparisons help scientists communicate information?

© Houghton Mifflin Harcourt Publishing Company • Image Credits: ©Lior Patel/Alamy

Modeling the Milky Way

Our galaxy, the Milky Way, is just one out of billions of galaxies. A **galaxy** is a large collection of stars, gas, and dust that is held together by gravity. Most of the Milky Way is not visible when we observe space. Over time, astronomers developed technologies that expanded our ability to observe objects in space. Telescopes and space probes can be used to collect data and give us a much better understanding of our galaxy. These data also expand our understanding of the size of our galaxy compared to the surrounding universe. The **universe** includes space and all of the energy and matter within it.

The Milky Way is easier to see from remote areas. City lights interfere with light from space.

6. **Discuss** How do scientific discovery and technology influence each other?

The Milky Way in the Night Sky

For much of human history, the Milky Way was a mystery. Some civilizations thought it was a flowing river. Others thought it was milk spilled by gods that lived far above Earth. Greek philosophers debated whether it was a band of faint stars or something glowing within Earth's atmosphere. When Persian astronomers observed that larger bodies (planets) would pass in front of the glowing band, they theorized that the Milky Way was a collection of many distant stars. However, without the ability to distinguish individual stars within the band, they could not confirm this hypothesis.

The Milky Way galaxy can be seen only in a very clear and dark sky and appears as a hazy band of clouds.

The Milky Way through a Telescope

When Galileo Galilei first used a telescope to observe the Milky Way in the early 1600s, he described the Milky Way as a collection of "innumerable stars distributed in clusters." Later, astronomers made observations of the Milky Way from different locations on Earth. Over time, it became clear that the Milky Way surrounds Earth and the sun. Our solar system is a part of the Milky Way, not located outside of it.

7. Based on the photos of the Milky Way and the understanding that our solar system is located inside, not outside, the galaxy, what might be the shape of the Milky Way?

   A. sphere

   B. disk

   C. cube

8. What evidence did you use to infer a shape for the Milky Way galaxy?

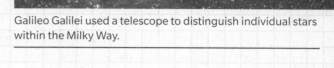

Galileo Galilei used a telescope to distinguish individual stars within the Milky Way.

Explore Online

View of a Bicycle Tire from Different Locations

If you look from the center of a bicycle wheel to the rim, the tire appears to be a line extending across your field of view. This is how we see the Milky Way from Earth.

If you look at a spinning tire from a point outside the wheel, more of the tire may be visible. This is how we would view the Milky Way from outside of the galaxy.

The Shape of the Milky Way

In the late 1700s, astronomer William Herschel and his sister Caroline made a map of the Milky Way galaxy. The Herschels estimated distances to different stars using relative brightness. They reasoned that bright stars are closer to Earth and that dim stars are farther from Earth. The Herschels correctly described the Milky Way galaxy as a giant disk with stars and solar systems orbiting its center. Because dim stars appeared to be equally distant from Earth, William Herschel placed our sun at the galaxy's center. William Herschel's placement of our sun was incorrect because huge clouds of dust in space make it difficult to see the most distant stars.

Determine Your Location within a Field of Objects

You will record observations of a group of objects from a single location, looking in four different directions. You will analyze a set of similar observations to determine the location of the observer.

MATERIALS
- pencil
- sheets of paper to crumple into balls
- sheets of paper for drawing

Procedure

STEP 1 As a class, crumple about 50 sheets of paper into different-sized balls. Scatter the balls of paper inside a large circle on the floor. The balls should be distributed randomly inside the circle and not in an orderly pattern.

STEP 2 Choose an observation point within the circle (there should be balls in all directions around you). Observe the locations of the balls around you, sitting or bending down so that the balls are as close to eye level as possible.

STEP 3 Look toward the front of the class and make a sketch (on a fresh sheet of paper) of how the balls in your field of view are distributed. Make a note of the direction that you are looking. Then turn 90° and make another sketch. Repeat until you have drawings facing four directions. When finished, you should have four separate sketches, each drawn on a separate sheet of paper.

Analysis

STEP 4 Exchange sketches with a partner. Compare your partner's sketches with the balls in the circle. Based on your partner's sketches, try to determine the point from which your partner's observations were made. Explain how you determined from which location the observations were made.

STEP 5 How well could this observation method be used to determine where our solar system is located within the Milky Way galaxy?

Earth's Place in the Milky Way

In the early 1900s, Harlow Shapley used telescopes to view large groups of stars called *globular clusters*. All of the globular clusters that Shapley observed were arranged in a large, spherical shape. This sphere, composed of many globular clusters, seemed to be centered around a point in space far from Earth. Shapley reasoned that these globular clusters were gathered in a spherical shape because they orbit the gravitational center of the Milky Way galaxy. Shapley could view evidence of the galaxy's center through a telescope, so he concluded that our solar system must lie outside the center. Although the Milky Way is indeed a disk, as the Herschels determined, our sun is not at its center. The gravitational forces from the center of the Milky Way attract stars and stellar systems and cause them to orbit around the more massive center of the galaxy. Shapley's data provided strong evidence that our solar system is located far from the galaxy's center.

EVIDENCE NOTEBOOK

9. How might knowing Earth's position relative to the center of the Milky Way help you make a map of the Milky Way? Record your evidence.

Analyze Dark Portions of Space

When you look at the night sky, there are many dark patches, even in portions of the Milky Way.

10. In addition to globular clusters, which can contain as many as 100,000 stars, Shapley saw areas in space that did not seem to have any stars. Given that telescopes had already been used to find stars in areas of the night sky that previously appeared empty, which of the following statements are most likely to be true? Choose all that apply.

A. These dark portions contain no stars.

B. These dark portions contain stars that were too dim for Shapley's telescope to see.

C. There might be matter such as dust blocking the light from stars.

11. What questions do you have about dark portions of the night sky?

_____

_____

_____

_____

Analyzing Other Galaxies

Outer space is filled with many different sources of light. In the daytime, sunlight fills the sky and hides most of the other sources of light. At night, however, you can see the moon, hundreds or thousands of stars, and several planets. If you are lucky, you might even see a comet or a streaking meteor.

The round points of light in this photograph are stars. Some of the stars appear to be much brighter than others. The brighter stars may be closer to Earth, or they may simply be hotter and bigger.

12. As you examine the photo, are there any light sources that stand out in comparison to the others? If so, what makes them different?

Unexplained Light Sources

While observing the night sky, many astronomers noticed light sources that looked very different from stars. These objects often appeared larger than stars and, unlike stars, seemed to have fuzzy edges. Some astronomers thought the unknown objects might be clouds of gas inside the Milky Way galaxy. Others thought they might be very large groups of stars, either inside the Milky Way or beyond it. The blurry patch of light that you can see in the photo is one of these light sources, named Andromeda.

Galaxies beyond the Milky Way

In the years following the observation of fuzzy, unexplained light sources, engineers designed larger telescopes for use in research. Large telescopes capture more light than small telescopes do. Capturing more light allows the telescope to produce more detailed images of distant objects. This is very similar to the way people can see the details of objects more clearly in bright light than they can in dim light.

In 1919, astronomer Edwin Hubble used the largest telescope in the world to photograph a blurry patch of light known as Andromeda. When Hubble examined the new photographs carefully, he identified faint, individual stars. His discovery led to more questions. How many more stars might be a part of Andromeda? Why were so many stars clustered together? Was Andromeda within the Milky Way galaxy? Hubble would continue to gather data and work collaboratively with other scientists to determine the answers to these questions.

Large telescopes built in the 1900s were much more powerful than earlier telescopes. Edwin Hubble took this photograph of Andromeda using one of these more powerful telescopes.

13. Language SmArts What evidence might be needed to determine if a blurry patch of light is located within the Milky Way galaxy or beyond it? Construct a written argument, including claims and reasoning, to present your ideas.

EVIDENCE NOTEBOOK

14. How would the ability to observe other galaxies help in generating models of the Milky Way galaxy? Record your evidence.

Galaxies Are Defined by Their Shape

Edwin Hubble determined that Andromeda was another galaxy outside of the Milky Way. In the 1920s, Hubble began to classify the galaxies that he was discovering based on their shapes. Gravity plays an important role in the shapes of galaxies. There are four types of galaxies.

15. In a spiral galaxy, a larger, central core of stars will exert a strong / weak gravitational pull on stars in the arms of the galaxy. The stars in a spiral / elliptical galaxy orbit in the same plane around the galaxy's center.

Four Types of Galaxies

Elliptical galaxies contain older stars and very little dust and gas. Elliptical galaxies have very bright centers. Some elliptical galaxies look like spheres, while others are more elongated. The stars in these galaxies do not rotate around the galaxy's center in the same plane. Gravity pulls the stars in random directions.

Most galaxies are spiral galaxies. Spiral galaxies contain dust and gas as well as stars. Spiral galaxies have a bulge at the center and very distinct spiral arms. The massive central core of stars exerts a strong gravitational pull on the stars rotating in roughly the same plane around it in the spiral arms.

Barred spiral galaxies are similar in composition to spiral galaxies but have very distinct bars that extend from the center to the spiral arms. The bar shape may be a result of the complex gravitational interactions between stars orbiting the central core. The Milky Way is classified as a barred spiral.

Irregular galaxies are galaxies that don't fit into any other class. Irregular galaxies lack a large center with a strong gravitational pull. The matter in irregular galaxies does not form a defined shape and may contain a relatively large amount of dust and gas.

© Houghton Mifflin Harcourt Publishing Company • Image Credits: (tl) ©NASA, ESA, and the Hubble Heritage (STScI/AURA)-ESA/Hubble Collaboration; (tr) ©NASA,ESA,and The Hubble Heritage Team(STScI/AURA); (bl) ©NASA,ESA,and The Hubble Heritage Team(STScI/ AURA);(br) ©NASA,ESA,A. Aloisi (STScI/ESA),and The Hubble Heritage (STScI/AURA)-ESA/ Hubble Collaboration

Gravity Pulls Galaxies Together

Gravity does not just affect the stars, dust, and gas inside galaxies. Gravity also causes galaxies to interact with one another. Galaxies are massive and so the gravitational pull they have on each other can be large depending on how far apart they are from each other.

Galaxies form clusters that can contain thousands of galaxies held together by gravity. The Milky Way has two small galaxies orbiting it and is one of a cluster of about 20 galaxies called the Local Group. Most galaxy clusters are moving away from each other, but some galaxies within each cluster may collide. As the galaxies become closer, they lose some potential energy but can release enormous amounts of thermal energy.

Galaxy collisions are common in the universe but take millions of years to take place. If one or both of the galaxies is massive enough, they may join together to form a new, larger galaxy. If the galaxies are moving fast enough to overcome the gravitational forces, they may pass through each other.

Galaxy cluster Abell 370 contains hundreds of galaxies held together by gravity.

Explore Online

Colliding galaxies NGC 6050 and IC 1179 are 450 million light years away in the Hercules Galaxy Cluster.

16. How can galaxies exert such a strong gravitational pull on each other when they are millions of light years from each other?

Engineer It
Measure Distances Using Brightness

One way to measure the distance to a star is to use the parallax method. Hold your thumb up in front of your face. Close your right eye. Then close your left eye instead. Your thumb will seem to jump when you switch eyes. The closer your thumb is to your face, the bigger the jump will be. Now, imagine that the distance between your eyes is the diameter of Earth's orbit. You can record the position of a star in the sky and then record the position of the star again when Earth is on the other side of its orbit. The star will appear to be in a different place in the sky. This change in the star's position allows astronomers to calculate the star's distance from Earth. This method becomes less accurate the farther stars are from Earth. Astronomers also tried to use the brightness of stars to determine their distance from Earth, but this method had its own problems.

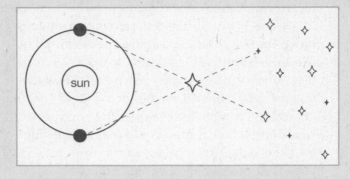

17. Look at the photo of the light bulb. Can you tell how far the light is from the camera? What are some factors that limit your ability to tell how far away objects are?

18. The light on the left is about 30 centimeters from the camera. The light on the right is about 100 centimeters from the camera. You can easily tell that these lights are at different distances because of the table. However, imagine that these lights were two stars that seemed equally bright in the night sky. What else would you need to know to determine which light was farther away?

A Universe Full of Galaxies

Edwin Hubble could not use parallax to measure the distance to the dim stars in Andromeda because they were too far away. However, astronomer Henrietta Leavitt had recently discovered Cepheid variable stars. Over regular time intervals, the brightness of a Cepheid variable star changes. Leavitt measured the distances to close Cepheid variable stars. She discovered that the brightest stars took a longer time to change in brightness, while the brightness of the dimmer stars changed more quickly.

Cepheid variable stars grow brighter and dimmer over time. This behavior gives astronomers a way to calculate how much light the star is producing.

Hubble identified several Cepheid variable stars within Andromeda. He observed these stars over time and determined how quickly each star's brightness changed. Then Hubble was able to use his observations and Leavitt's studies to determine how much light these stars were actually producing. Once Hubble knew how much light each star was producing and how bright each star appeared to him, he was able to determine how far away the stars were. He realized that they were very far away! That discovery provided strong evidence that Andromeda is outside the Milky Way and was, in fact, a galaxy itself.

19. Scientists observe that natural systems display order and consistency. How does this idea relate to Hubble's use of Cepheid variable stars to calculate the distance between Earth and the Andromeda galaxy?

Explain the Value of Measuring Distances between Objects in Space

20. Recall the example of making a map of a city. How could knowing the distance between you and big buildings or other landmarks in the city help you make a map of your city? Would the same strategies work for larger areas such as a state?

_____

_____

_____

21. How does measuring the distances to stars help you figure out where you are in the universe?

_____

_____

Modeling Scales in the Universe

Since Hubble first found evidence that there were other galaxies, our ability to study the universe has greatly improved. Modern telescopes, including some that observe from outside Earth's atmosphere, provide more detail than Hubble's photographs did. Scientists have developed new methods to measure the distance and speed of objects farther away than Andromeda. Our models of the universe have become more accurate over the last hundred years.

22. After astronomers learned techniques for measuring distances to the planets and the sun, our understanding of the solar system grew. What might be some similar ways in which improved measurements and data collection would affect our view of the universe?

The Whirlpool Galaxy is about 23 million light-years away from the Milky Way. There are many galaxies that are even farther away than this.

The Size of the Milky Way

The Milky Way galaxy is so large that it is almost impossible to imagine its size. To describe the size of galaxies, astronomers needed a new unit of measurement. Astronomers often measure distances in *light-years*. A **light-year** is the distance that light travels in a vacuum in one year. Because light travels about 300,000 kilometers every second, a light-year is a very long distance. A light-year is 9.5×10^{12} km. The Milky Way galaxy measures about 100,000 light-years across. So it would take 100,000 years for light to travel from one side of the Milky Way to the other. That means that light from a star on one side of the galaxy could not be seen on the other side until 100,000 years after the light was produced. And there are galaxies even larger than the Milky Way.

EVIDENCE NOTEBOOK

23. How does knowing the distance across the Milky Way help to model the galaxy? Record your evidence.

© Houghton Mifflin Harcourt Publishing Company • Image Credits: ©Science Source

Do the Math
Model the Scale of the Milky Way

The Milky Way galaxy is immense. It is so large that it is hard to describe. Knowing that it measures 100,000 light-years across gives the size a number, but does not really describe the scale. One way to imagine its size is to compare the Milky Way galaxy to our solar system. When numbers of very different sizes are compared, the difference in size can be described using the term *order of magnitude*. If there is a one-order-of-magnitude difference, one measurement is 10 times as large as the other. If there is a two-orders-of-magnitude difference, the larger number is 10 × 10, or 100 times as large.

24. To compare numbers that differ by more than one order of magnitude, it is often easier to use exponents. An exponent tells how many times a number is multiplied by itself. For example, 100 can be represented as 10^2 or as 10 × 10. The number 1,000 can be represented as 10^3 or as 10 × 10 × 10. Each time the exponent is increased, the number is multiplied by itself again.

    _____ can be represented as 10^5 or as 10 × 10 × 10 × 10 × 10.

25. When you read numbers that use exponents, you will notice that a small change in the exponent can indicate a large difference in scale. For example, the thickness of a brick is about 80 millimeters (mm). This number can be written as 8×10^1 mm. The tallest building in the world, the Burj Khalifa, is about 800 meters tall. This height is 800,000, or 8×10^5, mm. How many bricks would there be in a stack of bricks as tall as the Burj Khalifa?

    A. 1,000 (3 orders of magnitude)

    B. 10,000 (4 orders of magnitude)

    C. 100,000 (5 orders of magnitude)

26. The diameter of our solar system is approximately 3×10^{10} km. The diameter of the Milky Way galaxy is about 9×10^{17} km. Based on those measurements, the diameter of the galaxy is 30,000,000 times as big as our solar system's diameter, or about _____ orders of magnitude larger.

Stars and Planets in the Milky Way

It is impossible to count all of the stars in the Milky Way. In some areas, there are so many stars that they cannot be seen individually from Earth. Other stars are blocked by clouds of dust. Some stars are not bright enough to see even with our most powerful telescopes. Based on the stars they can observe, astronomers estimate that there are about one hundred billion, or 10^{11}, stars in the Milky Way. If even a small fraction of those stars have planets orbiting them, there would likely be billions of planets in our galaxy.

27. **Write** The number of stars in the Milky Way is enormous. On a separate sheet of paper, write how you would explain this number to another person. Write about comparisons that you could make to other examples of large numbers.

© Houghton Mifflin Harcourt Publishing Company

28. This photograph, known as the eXtreme Deep Field (XDF), shows the Hubble Space Telescope's observations of a tiny section of space. The section is so small that it is similar to looking at the sky through a drinking straw. Thousands of galaxies were recorded. What does this tell you about the number of galaxies that exist in the universe?

The XDF photo was made using photographs taken over a period of ten years by the Hubble Space Telescope. It shows a tiny section of the distant universe and contains thousands of galaxies.

Moon to scale

XDF

The eXtreme Deep Field (XDF) photo shows a portion of the sky that is much smaller than the area taken up by the moon.

Galaxies

Based on data such as the Hubble eXtreme Deep Field photograph, scientists estimate that there are tens of billions of galaxies in the universe. The closest of these galaxies is the Andromeda galaxy, which is about 3 million light-years from Earth. The most distant galaxies are more than 10 billion light-years away.

Explore Data Collection

29. When astronomers such as Leavitt and Hubble were observing the brightness of stars, they had to manually adjust their telescopes and take images over long periods of time. Modern research telescopes are controlled by computers. What are some ways that being able to control a telescope with a computer might allow us to gather more data about objects in space? Choose all that apply.

A. Computers are able to control the telescopes with more precision than humans.

B. Computers can understand the data better than human observers.

C. Computers can adjust the telescope to take images of an exact location many times.

D. Computers can process data faster than humans.

© Houghton Mifflin Harcourt Publishing Company • Image Credits: (t) ©NASA, ESA, G. Illingworth, D. Magee, and P. Oesch (University of California, Santa Cruz), R. Bouwens (Leiden University), and the HUDF09 Team; (b) ©NASA, ESA, Z. Levay (STScI), T. Rector, I. Dell'Antonio/NOAO/AURA/NSF, G. Illingworth, D. Magee, and P. Oesch (University of California, Santa Cruz), R. Bouwens (Leiden University), and the HUDF09 Team

Continue Your Exploration

Name: _____ **Date:** _____

Check out the path below or go online to choose one of the other paths shown.

> **The Kepler Mission**

- **Contributions of Arab and Indian Astronomers**
- **Other Galaxies**
- **Hands-On Labs** 🖐
- **Propose Your Own Path**

Go online to choose one of these other paths.

The Kepler Mission is NASA's first exploratory data collection mission that is specifically designed to find Earth-sized planets. From its orbit around the sun, the Kepler observatory measures the light coming from distant stars. As it constantly observes more than 100,000 stars for years at a time, the Kepler instruments can detect small changes in a star's brightness. These changes can indicate that a planet is orbiting the star.

1. Astronomers use the Kepler observatory to search the areas around stars for planets that are similar to Earth. As a planet passes in front of its star, the brightness of the starlight reaching the telescope changes. How might the change in the brightness of a star give information about how large a planet is?

The Kepler observatory was launched in 2009 and orbits Earth. It collects data from space and sends it back to Earth.

Continue Your Exploration

2. Which statements describe limitations that could affect the ability of the Kepler observatory to measure the size of a planet? Circle all that apply.

   A. Only planets that move in front of a star can be measured by this method.

   B. Different stars are located at different distances from Earth.

   C. Stars do not all have the same diameter.

   D. Some stars' brightness can vary over time.

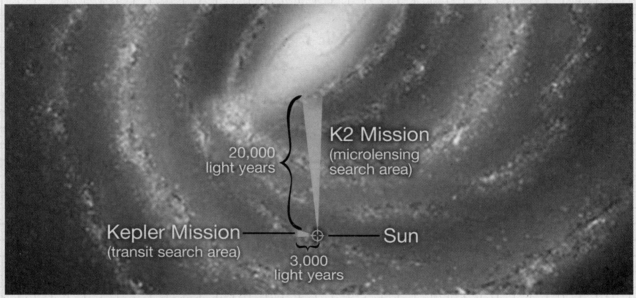

The Kepler observatory was originally used to search for planets that were less than 3,000 light-years from Earth. Under the K2 mission, it was used to search for planets up to 20,000 light-years away.

3. The Kepler observatory observes only a tiny portion of the night sky, as shown in the image. Even so, it has detected thousands of planets. What does this tell you about the number of planets in the Milky Way galaxy?

4. **Collaborate** Research and summarize some of the recent discoveries that have been made using the Kepler observatory. Research and define what the habitable zone is. Explain how the habitable zone relates to the Kepler observatory's mission.

Can You Explain It?

Name: _____   Date: _____

How can we make a model of the Milky Way galaxy that shows Earth's location?

 EVIDENCE NOTEBOOK

Refer to the notes in your Evidence Notebook to help you construct an explanation for how scientists model Earth within the Milky Way galaxy.

1. State your claim. Make sure your claim fully explain how Earth's location in relation to the rest of the Milky Way can be determined.

2. Summarize the evidence you have gathered to support your claim and explain your reasoning.

Checkpoints

Answer the following questions to check your understanding of the lesson.

Use the photo to answer Question 3.

3. If an observer looked out from a planet near the center of this galaxy, what would it look like to that observer?

   A. a broad band of stars forming a ring around the planet

   B. a sphere of stars evenly spread in every direction

   C. a spiral shape with arms reaching out from a center

   D. a band of stars in one direction, with fewer stars in other directions

4. A model solar system is built to a scale of 1: 7.0×10^9. This means that every 1 m in the model / solar system equals 7.0×10^9 m in the model / solar system.

5. Astronomers use parallax / Cepheid variable stars to measure distances between the Milky Way and other galaxies / solar systems.

Use the photo to answer Question 5.

6. Most of the points of light in the photo are likely stars / galaxies. The larger, bright object toward the center of the photo could possibly be a galaxy / universe because of its fuzzier edges. To definitively tell what this object is, you would need to identify stars inside the light and measure how bright / far away those stars are.

7. Two stars on opposite sides of the night sky appear very different. One star is very bright and can be seen before the sky is completely dark. The other can barely be seen on a dark night. Which of the following could be a reason that these two stars have different apparent brightnesses? Select all that apply.

   A. The brighter star emits much more light than the dimmer star does.

   B. A planet orbiting the dimmer star blocks most of its light.

   C. The brighter star is much closer to Earth than the dimmer star is.

   D. Clouds of dust block some of the light from the dimmer star.

Interactive Review

Complete this section to review the main concepts of the lesson.

A scale model can be used to compare the sizes and distances between objects in space.

A. Explain how using scale helps scientists model different sizes or distances in the solar system.

There are many other galaxies beyond the Milky Way. Other galaxies have different shapes due to how they formed.

B. What evidence can be used to show that galaxies other than the Milky Way exist?

Our sun is one of many billions of stars in the Milky Way, which is one of many billions of galaxies in the universe.

C. Explain why using measurements such as the light-year becomes necessary when discussing distances in the universe.

The Milky Way galaxy is a large group of stars that includes our sun.

D. What observations provide evidence for our current understanding of the Milky Way's shape?

Choose one of the activities to explore how this unit connects to other topics.

☐ People in Science

Annie Easley, Computer Scientist Annie Easley grew up in Birmingham, Alabama. In 1955, Easley began to work as a "human computer," solving difficult computations for researchers. Machines eventually replaced human computers, but she adapted to the new technology. Easley became a computer programmer and worked on various NASA programs. In 1977, she graduated from Cleveland State University with a degree in Mathematics.

Research how mathematics and computers are related and create a short presentation on your findings.

☐ Physical Science Connection

Structure of Other Solar Systems Until recently, astronomers expected that other planetary systems would be similar to our solar system. They expected to find small, rocky inner planets and large, gas giant planets farther from the center. However, some distant planetary systems that have been recently discovered include such anomalies as "Super-Jupiters" close to the central sun.

Research current hypotheses about how extrasolar planetary systems form. Describe how these systems inform our understanding of our own solar system and galaxy. Make a multimedia presentation to share what you learned with your class.

☐ Math Connection

Leap Year Archaeological discoveries, such as this ancient Egyptian calendar carved on a stone wall, show that, even thousands of years ago, various cultures tracked time by using calendars.

A leap year is a year that contains one extra calendar day on February 29th. In the Gregorian calendar, most years that are multiples of four are leap years. Research the history behind leap years and determine why we add a day to our calendar every four years. Find out when and how the need for a leap year was first calculated and why the leap year system works. Write a short essay of your findings about leap years and present it to the class.

Name: _____   Date: _____

Complete this review to check your understanding of the unit.

Use the diagram to answer Questions 1–4.

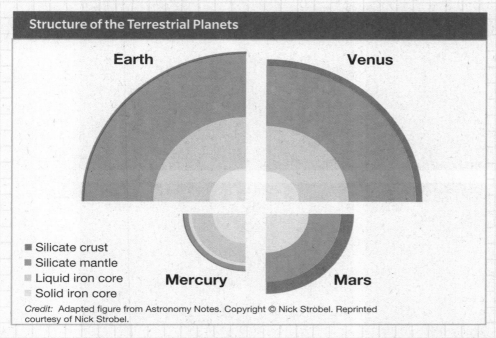

Structure of the Terrestrial Planets

Earth   Venus

■ Silicate crust
■ Silicate mantle
■ Liquid iron core
■ Solid iron core

Mercury   Mars

Credit: Adapted figure from Astronomy Notes. Copyright © Nick Strobel. Reprinted courtesy of Nick Strobel.

1. Compare the internal structures of the terrestrial planets. How do the scales of the internal layers of the planets compare?

2. Compare the diameters of the terrestrial planets. How do the relative sizes of the planets compare?

3. Compare the layers of the terrestrial planets. What role did density play in the structure of the terrestrial planets?

4. Compare the pattern that occurred during the formation of the terrestrial planets with the pattern that occurred during the formation of the solar system. How are these patterns similar?

Use the images to answer Questions 5–8.

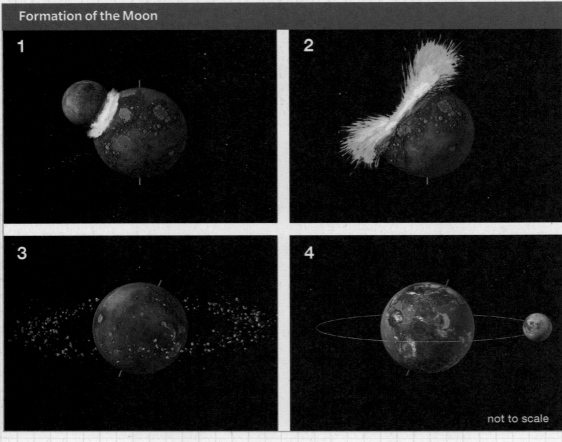

Formation of the Moon

1

2

3

4

not to scale

5. What forces were acting on Earth and on the impacting object before they collided?

6. What role did gravity play in the formation of the moon?

7. How is the formation of the moon around Earth similar to the formation of Earth around the sun? How is it different?

8. Why does the moon orbit Earth in the same direction that Earth orbits the sun?

Name: Date:

What role does gravity play in a lunar landing?

An understanding of gravity has played an important role in the space program and in the lunar landings. You have been invited to participate in the Constellation Program, which aims to have another lunar landing and "sustained human presence" in space in the future. Learn about the space program and how they rely on an understanding of gravity to plan missions and outposts in space. You will focus on how gravity affects sending people and materials into space and landing people and materials safely on other bodies. You will also learn about how changes in gravity affect the human body.

Constellation Mission Diagram

This diagram shows a proposed Constellation mission to land on the moon and includes the outbound and inbound trajectories and landing areas.

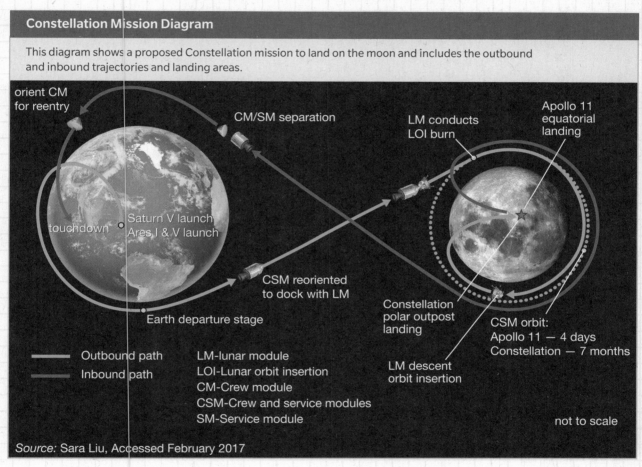

Source: Sara Liu, Accessed February 2017

The steps below will help guide your research and help you write a proposal.

1. **Ask a Question** Develop questions you will need to answer to write a proposal for sending a crewed spacecraft to the moon to develop a colony. Think about how gravity plays a role in what items are brought into space, how people and the spaceships move around, and the structure of the spaceship.

2. **Conduct Research** Research answers to the relevant questions using multiple sources, including NASA and the Constellation Program, as resources. Think about answers to how gravity affects people's bodies, supplies for travel, and spacecraft movement.

3. **Evaluate Data** Analyze your research to identify important variables that you need to consider in your proposal. Include a list of ways that you will address gravity in your plan.

4. **Write a Proposal** Based on your research, construct a written proposal for sending a crewed spacecraft to the moon to develop a colony. Describe how your proposal is supported by evidence.

5. **Communicate** Present your recommendation about a lunar colony to the class.

✓ **Self-Check**

	I identified and accounted for the role gravity plays in sending people into space and landing them back on Earth or another body in space.
	I researched the Constellation Program and how the space program relies on an understanding of gravity in space.
	I constructed a written proposal for sending a crewed spacecraft to the moon to develop a colony.
	My proposal and recommendation were clearly communicated to others.

Earth through Time

How do patterns in the rock record provide evidence for the history of Earth and life on Earth?

© Houghton Mifflin Harcourt Publishing Company • Image Credits: ©Marla Stenzel/ National Geographic/Getty Images

Paleontologists chip away at a rock face in the Republic of Madagascar. They are searching for fossils of organisms that lived during earlier time periods in Earth's history.

You Solve It Is Antibiotic Use Related to Antibiotic Resistance in *E. coli*?

Analyze geographic data on antibiotic prescriptions and antibiotic resistance to see if there is a relationship between the data sets.

Go online and complete the You Solve It to explore ways to solve a real-world problem.

Construct a Family Tree

Sea otters (left) and badgers (right) belong to a family of carnivores called mustelids.

A. Look at the photo. On a separate sheet of paper, write down as many different questions as you can about the photo.

B. Discuss With your class or a partner, share your questions. Record any additional questions generated in your discussion. Then choose the most important questions from the list that are related to the anatomical similarities and differences between these two animals. Write them below.

C. Choose an animal to research in order to construct its "family tree." Here's a list of animal families you can consider:

Mustelids (includes badgers and otters)
Canids (includes dogs and foxes)
Felids (includes tigers and domestic cats)
Hominids (includes humans and gorillas)

D. Use the information above, along with your research, to create a diagram or timeline that shows how your chosen species is related to other animals.

Discuss the next steps for your Unit Project with your teacher and go online to download the Unit Project Worksheet.

Language Development

Use the lessons in this unit to complete the network and expand your understanding of these key concepts.

	Similar term
	Phrase
	Cognate
	Example
	Definition

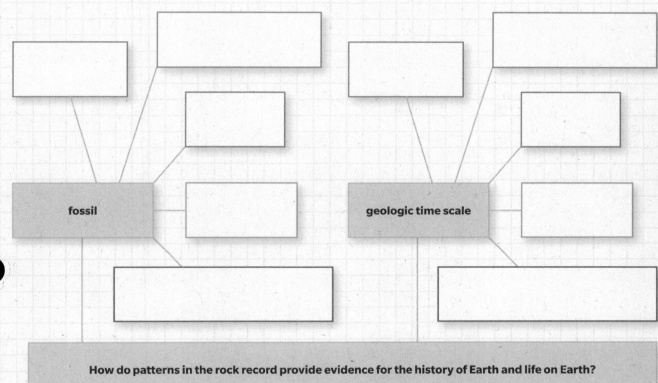

fossil

geologic time scale

How do patterns in the rock record provide evidence for the history of Earth and life on Earth?

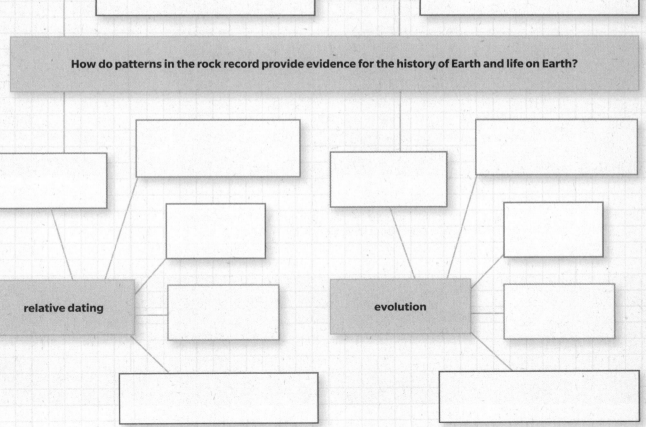

relative dating

evolution

Rocks and Fossils Are Evidence of Earth's History

The colorful rock layers that make up these hills in Oregon contain clues about the history of the area.

Explore First

Inferring Sequence of Events Examine photos of curious situations to determine how they could have come about. In groups, list each step in order that it would have occurred to lead to the situation in the photo.

CAN YOU EXPLAIN IT?

How can scientists determine when these ancient animals lived?

History of Dinosaur Provincial Park

About 76 million years ago, dinosaurs lived alongside turtles, crocodiles, and small mammals. The area consisted of swamps and lush vegetation, as well as many rivers that flowed into a nearby sea.

Around 75 million years ago, the sea rose and covered the area. In the sea lived shelled creatures such as ammonites and large marine reptiles such as this plesiosaur.

Today, sedimentary rock layers are exposed throughout the park. Fossils of the ancient plants and animals that once lived here are found within the sedimentary layers.

1. The rocks and fossils found today in Dinosaur Provincial Park tell us about the area's past environments, plants, and animals. How do you think scientists could determine the age of an ancient item such as a fossil or rock?

 EVIDENCE NOTEBOOK As you explore this lesson, gather evidence to help explain how scientists can determine when these ancient animals lived.

Describing the Formation of Sedimentary Rocks and Fossils

Why would anyone want to study rocks? Rocks can tell us about Earth's past environments and organisms. Some rocks can tell us about events, such as meteorite impacts and volcanic eruptions, that happened in the distant past. It may seem like rocks are permanent, but they form and change over thousands or millions of years through processes such as erosion, deposition, melting, and burial. Different rocks form in different environments. For example, granite forms when magma cools under Earth's surface, while sandstone forms from grains of minerals or other rocks that settle in layers and harden over time.

2. **Discuss** With a classmate, look at the rock layers in the photo. Note any patterns in their ages. Which rock layer formed first?

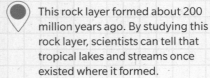
This rock layer began forming about 145 million years ago. Patterns in the rock show that it formed in a desert environment with huge sand dunes, similar to today's Sahara Desert.

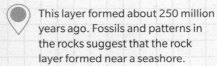
This rock layer formed about 200 million years ago. By studying this rock layer, scientists can tell that tropical lakes and streams once existed where it formed.

This layer formed about 250 million years ago. Fossils and patterns in the rocks suggest that the rock layer formed near a seashore.

Sedimentary Rock Formation

Sandstone is a type of sedimentary rock. Sedimentary rocks are made of tiny bits of material called *sediment*. Sedimentary rock can be made from smaller pieces of rock, or from the remains of plants and animals. For example, limestone can be made of the remains of microscopic organisms.

Sedimentary rock can form when erosion moves sediment to low-lying areas such as valleys and lake bottoms. The sediment settles in layers that become compressed as they are buried under the weight of layers above them. When water containing dissolved substances seeps through the sediment layers, the substances precipitate out of the solution and harden, acting as a cement.

Over time, shells and sediment pile up at the bottom of lakes and oceans and can eventually form sedimentary rock.

As sedimentary layers form, they stack up one by one. If undisturbed by Earth processes, sedimentary rocks stay in horizontal layers. The oldest layer is at the bottom and the youngest layer is at the top.

Fossil Formation

We know a lot about the history of life on Earth from studying fossils. **Fossils** are the remains or traces of once-living organisms. Fossils form when specific conditions occur that preserve an organism's remains. In most cases, an organism's remains are eaten, scattered, dissolved by water, or decomposed before they can be preserved.

The Making of a Fossil

Most fossils found today formed when the remains of dead animals were covered by sediment. Usually only the hard parts of the animal fossilized, but sometimes the soft parts fossilized too.

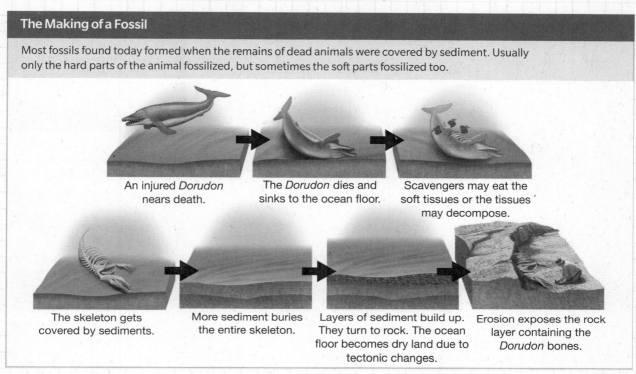

An injured *Dorudon* nears death.

The *Dorudon* dies and sinks to the ocean floor.

Scavengers may eat the soft tissues or the tissues may decompose.

The skeleton gets covered by sediments.

More sediment buries the entire skeleton.

Layers of sediment build up. They turn to rock. The ocean floor becomes dry land due to tectonic changes.

Erosion exposes the rock layer containing the *Dorudon* bones.

It is rare for an organism's remains to form a fossil. A very small percentage of species that have ever lived left behind fossils. Many processes can prevent fossil formation. Fossils form most often when an organism's remains are quickly buried by sediments. That is why most fossils are found in sedimentary rock. Because quick burial by sediments occurs more often in rivers, lakes, and oceans than it does on land, water-dwelling organisms are more likely to be fossilized than land animals.

Fossils may form from bones, teeth, or shells. They may also form from activity, as is the case with fossilized footprints. Fossils of soft-bodied animals such as jellyfish are rare, but they do exist. Proteins and genetic material may also fossilize, and cell structures in fossilized feathers have helped scientists determine the feathers' color.

3. Engineer It You want to explore rock layers in a region to find fossils and clues about the past. There is one problem: there are no exposed cliffs or areas where you can see the rock layers. They are all below the ground. Propose a solution to this problem. Can you think of any helpful tools or technology?

Case Study: The Morrison Formation

The Morrison Formation is a large area of sedimentary rock and is the most concentrated source of fossils in the United States. About 150 million years ago (mya), the area shown on the map was a large floodplain with many rivers. The conditions in this ancient floodplain environment were favorable for the quick burial of organisms that died there.

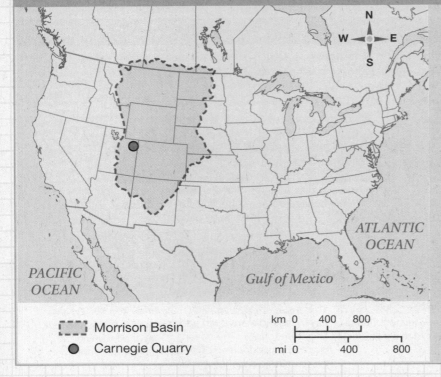

N
W   E
S

ATLANTIC OCEAN

PACIFIC OCEAN

Gulf of Mexico

- - - Morrison Basin
● Carnegie Quarry

km 0   400   800
mi 0   400   800

This is a reproduction of a nearly complete *Stegosaurus* skeleton found in the Morrison Basin.

Fossil remains are often scattered and mixed together, like these from the Carnegie Quarry.

4. Does the high concentration of fossils in the Morrison Formation mean that more organisms lived here 150 mya compared to other parts of the country? Explain your reasoning.

Analyze Fossils to Describe Earth's Past

Fossils provide evidence about past life and environments. For example, a fossilized fern like the one below looks similar to ferns found in tropical areas today.

5. Look at each image. Use the words from the word bank to label each fossil with the name of the environment in which it likely formed.

WORD BANK
- a tropical forest
- a lake
- a grassland

A. _____

B. _____

C. _____

Studying the Ages of Fossils

No one was around millions of years ago to observe fossils forming or to observe other natural processes that occur over very long time spans. Yet we can infer what happed in the past based on what we know about the natural processes that occur today. Scientists assume that the geologic events and phenomena that happen today also happened in the past and that they apply everywhere in nature. This scientific principle is called *uniformitarianism*. We can use these assumptions to interpret fossil data.

sedimentation

This satellite photo shows rivers that carry water and sediment out to sea. Soil and rock particles are eroded from the riverbanks by water, carried down the rivers, and deposited in the sea, which causes sediment to build up.

For example, scientists know that today, sedimentary rock forms when sediments carried by air, ice, water, or gravity are deposited in layers in a new location. Over time, the weight of new sediment layers puts pressure on the layers below, and rock forms. So we can assume that sedimentation and sedimentary rock formation in ancient seas occurred in a similar way.

6. How does knowledge of sedimentary rock formation help us to understand fossils?

Relative Ages of Rock Layers

How can we use rocks to learn about the past? One way is through their relative age. *Relative age* is how old something is compared to something else. You can determine relative age without knowing actual age. For example, you know that an adult is older than a baby, even if you don't know the exact age of either person.

When sedimentary rock forms, the layers on the bottom are deposited first. That means that, unless something happens to disturb the layers, the oldest layer is on the bottom, and the youngest is on the top. This idea is called the *law of superposition*. Scientists use it to find the relative ages of rock layers.

7. The rock layer on the top of the Grand Canyon is the youngest / oldest because it was deposited most recently / in the distant past. Layers in the middle are younger / older than the surface layer. The layer farthest down is the youngest / oldest because it was deposited most recently / the earliest.

Grand Canyon

Hands-On Lab
Model Rock Layers to Determine Relative Age

Build a physical model to help you determine the order in which rocks form and make observations about the rocks' relative ages.

In the real world, rock sequences can span large areas. Often, rocks are not visible because they are beneath Earth's surface, but sometimes they are exposed along cliffs or where a hill was cut through for road construction. A physical model can help you see how a sequence of rocks can form over time.

MATERIALS
- items such as beads or shells to represent fossils
- modeling clay (at least five different colors)
- plastic knife
- tray or container to hold the model

Procedure

STEP 1 **Discuss** Gather your materials. Discuss with a group or partner how you can use your materials to make a model of four sedimentary rock layers.

STEP 2 Choose four rocks from the list. Note the environment in which each type of rock formed. This is also known as a rock's depositional environment.

- **Sandstone with fossils** formed in a sandy ocean bottom (yellow clay with fossil materials)
- **Shale** formed in a deep, muddy lake (brown clay)
- **Siltstone** formed in a river floodplain (red clay)
- **Sandstone** formed in a sandy desert (yellow clay)
- **Coal** formed where a tropical swamp once existed (black clay)
- **Limestone** formed in a shallow sea (white clay)

STEP 3 Build your model. Starting at the bottom of the table, fill in Rows 1–4 with the information listed above for each rock you chose. (Leave Row 5 blank for now.)

Order of Events	Rock type or event	Depositional environment	Material used
5. Fifth			
4. Fourth			
3. Third			
2. Second			
1. First			

STEP 4 Choose one of these events to model in your set of rock layers. Be sure to add the event to the table in the top row. Use the plastic knife or another color of clay to represent the chosen event.

- **Igneous intrusion:** Magma rose and intruded through some of the rock layers. When it cooled it formed a type of rock called *igneous rock*.

- **Lava flow:** Magma intruded through all rock layers making its way to the surface (where it is then called lava). The lava flowed over the top of the existing rock layers and cooled into a new layer of igneous rock.

- **Fault:** Tectonic plate movements can cause rock to break and move along planes called faults. Rock layers can shift up, down, sideways, or at an angle along *faults*.

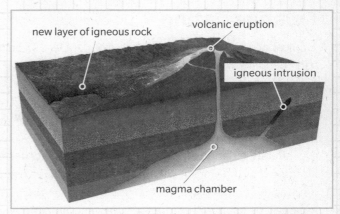

This diagram shows both an igneous intrusion below Earth's surface and a lava flow on Earth's surface.

Analysis

STEP 5 **Language SmArts** Use your table and knowledge of relative age to write a short, informative paragraph that explains how your model represents environmental changes in an area over time.

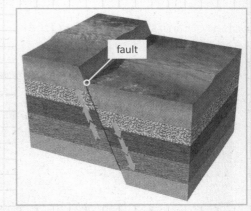

Forces deep within Earth can form a fault where rocks shift up or down.

STEP 6 **Draw** Exchange models with another group. Analyze the other group's model to identify the event and determine the order in which the layers formed. Make a sketch of the model and label it to show the relative ages of the rocks and the event. When you are done, exchange information with the other group to check if you identified the event and sequenced the layers correctly.

Relative Dating

Think about a stack of pancakes on a plate. Even if you don't know exactly what time each pancake was made, you know that the pancake at the bottom of the stack was probably made first, and the pancake on top was probably made last. In other words, you can determine the relative age of each pancake. This is an example of relative dating. **Relative dating** is any method of determining whether something is older or younger than something else.

Relative dating can also be applied to events or processes. In the pancake example, imagine that the stack is sliced in half with a knife. The slicing occurs after the pancakes are stacked on the plate, so it is "younger" than the pancakes themselves. The same logic can be used for sedimentary rock sequences that are disturbed by geologic processes. For example, if a fault or an igneous intrusion cuts across rock layers, scientists assume that the feature is younger than the rocks it cuts across.

Scientists use the relative ages of rocks to compile the rock record. The *rock record* is all of Earth's known rocks and the information they contain. The rock record allows scientists to piece together some of Earth's past environments and events.

igneous intrusion

8. Magma intruded into these sedimentary rocks, cooled, and formed a diagonal band of igneous rock. The intrusion is *older / younger* than the sedimentary rocks it cuts through.

Index Fossils

In most cases, fossils are the same age as the rock in which they are found. An *index fossil* is the remains of an organism that was common and widespread but existed for only about 1 million years (or less). Index fossils can help scientists establish the ages of rocks and other fossils. For example, specific ammonite fossils are found in Dinosaur Provincial Park serve as index fossils. They are about 75 million years old, which means that the rocks in which they are found, and any other fossils in those rocks, are also likely about 75 million years old.

Organizing all of Earth's known fossils from oldest to youngest shows how life on Earth has changed over time. All of Earth's known fossils and the information they provide is known as the *fossil record*. The fossil record grows as more fossils are discovered.

EVIDENCE NOTEBOOK

9. How can undisturbed sedimentary rock layers and index fossils in Dinosaur Provincial Park provide information about the ages of the park's ancient animals? Record your evidence.

10. This type of trilobite is an index fossil that lived about 440 million years ago. Fossils of the trilobite and the brittle star were found in the same rock layer. What can you infer about these two organisms?

A. They likely lived at the same time.

B. They are likely closely related.

C. They likely lived in different habitats.

D. They are likely younger than the rock layer.

Unconformities

Some rock layers are missing, forming gaps in the rock record. Such a gap is called an *unconformity*. These gaps can occur when rock layers are eroded or when sediment is not deposited for a period of time. In this way, rock layers are like pages in a book of Earth's history—only some pages were torn out or never written in the first place!

Explore Online

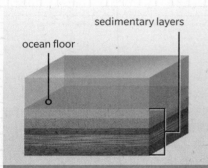

Over millions of years, sediment settles on the sea floor, forming layers.

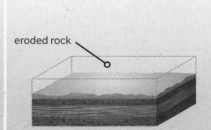

Sea level drops and exposes the sediment. Some layers are eroded.

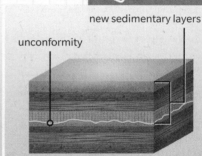

New layers form over the old set of layers—an unconformity now exists.

Determine Relative Age

The positions of rock layers, fossils, faults, and intrusions can be used to determine their relative ages. Scientists use relative dating to piece together Earth's history. Look at the rock layers and features in the diagram.

11. Number the diagram to show the relative ages of the rocks and features. Use the number 1 for the first (oldest) rock layer or feature. Use the number 7 for the most recent (youngest) rock layer or feature.

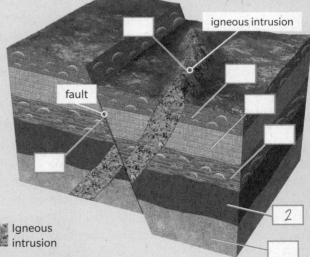

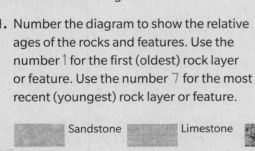

- Sandstone
- Shale with fossils
- Limestone
- Limestone with fossils
- Igneous intrusion
- Andesite

Using Absolute and Relative Age

Relative age is described in terms of whether an object is older or younger than other objects. *Absolute age* identifies how old an object is, expressed in units of time. In other words, absolute age is the actual age of something.

12. Discuss How do you think scientists figured out the absolute age of the zircon crystal in the photo?

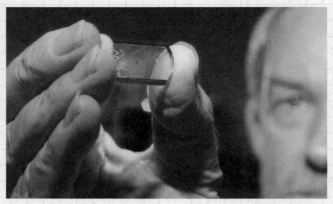

This tiny black speck is a zircon crystal. At about 4.2 billion years old, it is one of the oldest known crystals on Earth. The person holding it is Simon Wilde, who discovered it in Australia in 1984.

13. Write an A next to statements that describe absolute age.
Write an R next to those that describe relative age.

R	I am younger than my cousin.
	I am 14 years old.
	That is the oldest bicycle I've ever seen.

	My cat lived to be 15 years old.
	This coin is the newest in my collection.
	This is the last book in the series.

Absolute Dating

Observing rock layers can tell us about relative age but not absolute age. In the 1950s, technology made it possible to find the absolute ages of some rocks. **Absolute dating** is any method of measuring the actual age of something in years. Absolute dating can be used to find the ages of igneous rocks, which form when molten rock cools and forms crystals. These crystals contain unstable particles that begin to break down, or *decay*, as soon as the crystal forms. Scientists can measure and compare the amounts of unstable and stable particles in the rock, then use the data to calculate when the unstable particles began to decay. This will also tell them when the rock formed.

Rocks contain different types of unstable particles. Each type decays at a specific rate called a *half-life*. For example, unstable potassium decays into argon and has a half-life of 1.3 billion years. This means that it takes 1.3 billion years for half of the potassium to decay into argon. It takes another 1.3 billion years for half of the remaining potassium to decay. This pattern repeats as long as some of the unstable particles remain.

Absolute dating and relative dating are used together to provide a more complete understanding of Earth's history. For example, some of the rock in Dinosaur Provincial Park contains weathered volcanic ash. Absolute dating of the ash indicates that some of the rock layers in the park formed 76 million years ago. Fossils found in the same rock layers must also be 76 million years old.

Geologic Time Scale

Evidence from absolute dating indicates that Earth is nearly 4.6 billion years old. To help make sense of this vast amount of time, scientists use the geologic time scale to organize Earth's history. The geologic time scale divides Earth's history into intervals of time defined by major events or changes on Earth. The largest category of time is the eon, which is further divided into eras, periods, epochs, and ages. Dividing that long period of time into smaller parts makes it easier for scientists to communicate their findings about rocks and fossils.

The Geologic Time Scale

Unlike divisions of time such as days or minutes, the divisions of the geologic time scale are based on events in Earth's geologic history. Some divisions are based on the fossil record.

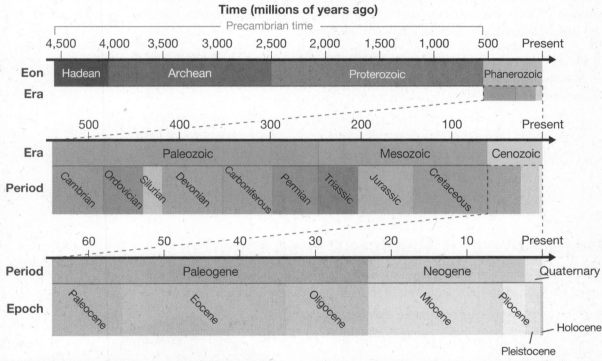

Source: International Commission on Stratigraphy, International Chronostratigraphic Chart, v2016

Do the Math | Using Models Earth formed about 4.6 billion years ago. Use a football field, which is 100 yards long, to model the 4,600,000,000 years since Earth formed.

14. Using these data, how many years of Earth's history would each yard line on the football field represent?

15. The first modern humans appeared on Earth about 200,000 years ago. Would it be possible to represent that time frame by marking feet on a football field? Explain your answer.

© Houghton Mifflin Harcourt Publishing Company

EVIDENCE NOTEBOOK

16. How can absolute dating be used to describe when the fossil organisms in Dinosaur Provincial Park lived? Record your evidence.

The Absolute Age of Earth

Absolute dating can be used to find the age of Earth, but not by using rocks from Earth. This is because the first rocks that formed on Earth had been eroded, melted, or buried under younger rocks long ago. Therefore, most rocks on Earth are younger than Earth itself—with one exception: meteorites.

Meteorites are small, rocky bodies that have traveled through space and fallen to Earth's surface. The absolute ages of meteorites can be determined, because Earth formed at the same time as other bodies in our solar system, meteorites should be the same age as Earth. Absolute dating of meteorites and moon rocks suggests that, like these other bodies, Earth is about 4.6 billion years old.

17. Recall the zircon crystal found in Australia. The zircon formed long before the sandstone it was found in. It was part of an igneous rock before it became part of the sandstone. Complete each statement to make it true.

_____ dating was used to determine the age of the sandstone rock compared to the ages of the rocks around it. _____ dating was used to calculate the actual age of the zircon mineral.

Use Relative and Absolute Dating Together

Scientists use both relative and absolute dating to find the ages of rocks and fossils. A field geologist modeled a sequence of rocks to help determine their ages.

18. What can you conclude based on the absolute ages of the igneous rocks given? Check the statement(s) that are true:

_____ The shale with fossils is 175 million years old.

_____ The limestone is between 200 and 175 million years old.

_____ The sandstone must be less than 200 million years old.

_____ The rocks shifted along the fault less than 175 million years ago.

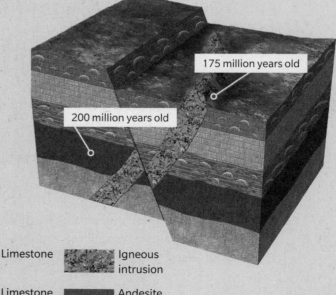

175 million years old

200 million years old

 Sandstone   Limestone   Igneous intrusion

 Shale with fossils   Limestone with fossils   Andesite

Continue Your Exploration

Name: _____   Date: _____

Check out the path below or go online to choose one of the other paths shown.

| Exploring the Ashfall Fossil Beds | • **People in Science**
 • **Exploring Local Geology**
 • **Hands-On Labs**
 • **Propose Your Own Path** | *Go online to choose one of these other paths.* |

Although most fossils are preserved by sedimentary rock, some are preserved by igneous rock. Look at these fossils of ancient animals from the Ashfall Fossil Beds in Nebraska. The animals were killed after a supervolcano erupted nearly 1,000 miles away, in what is now Idaho. Volcanic ash covered the area, and the animals died from inhaling it. As the ash settled into thick layers around the animals, it cooled and hardened into rock, creating detailed three-dimensional fossils.

These rocks contain fossils of rhinos and horses that died in a volcanic ash flow.

 young adult male rhino "Tusker"

 rhino calf

 large three-toed horse "Cormo"

 rhino calves (possibly twins) "T.L." and "R.G.C."

adult female rhino "Sandy" with baby "Justin"

Continue Your Exploration

The following field notes were recorded in the area:

Date: October 9
Location: Ashfall Fossil Beds State Historical Park, Nebraska
Observations and Notes:

- The fossils in the photo were uncovered in the ash layer.
- Layers above and below the ash layer also contain fossils, as shown in the table.
- The ash layer is as thick as 3 meters (9.8 feet) in some places.
- Absolute dating shows that the ash layer formed 12 million years ago.

Rocks and Fossils from the Ashfall Fossil Beds State Historical Park		
Rock Layers	**Fossils Found**	**Position**
loose sand and gravel	zebras, lemmings, giant camels, muskrats, giant beavers	Top
sandstone	barrel-bodied rhinos, giant land tortoises, camels, rodents, horses	Middle
ash layer		
sandstone		
sandy and silty sedimentary rock	alligators, fish, hornless rhinos, giant salamanders	Bottom

Source: The University of Nebraska State Museum and Nebraska Game and Parks Commission, "Geologic Setting of Ashfall Fossil Beds and Vicinity," 2015

1. The ash layer is igneous rock. Absolute dating shows the ash layer is 12 million years old. What can you infer about the animals found in the ash layer?

2. Use the observations and notes to explain what happened in the area over time.

3. Based on the fossils found in each layer, what changes do you think happened in the area before the ash flow that formed the fossil beds?

4. **Collaborate** Many articles about the Ashfall Fossil Beds are available in magazines and on the Internet. Find several articles. In a group discussion, cite specific evidence that could help you identify the article that provides the most accurate and thorough information. Discuss the evidence with the group.

Can You Explain It?

Name: _____   Date: _____

How can scientists determine when these ancient animals lived?

76 million years ago   **75 million years ago**   **Present day**

EVIDENCE NOTEBOOK

Refer to the notes in your Evidence Notebook to help you construct an explanation for how we can determine when these ancient animals lived.

1. State your claim. Make sure your claim fully explains how the ages of the animals shown above were determined.

2. Summarize the evidence you have gathered to support your claim and explain your reasoning.

Checkpoints

Answer the following questions to check your understanding of the lesson.

Use the photo to answer Questions 3 and 4.

3. Which rock layer or feature of the cliff formed most recently?

    A. the thick black rock layer at the top

    B. the fault running through the center

    C. the white rock layer near the bottom

    D. the gray rock layer at the very bottom

4. Which of the following questions could be answered from the information in the photo? Choose all that apply.

    A. Which is the oldest rock layer?

    B. When did the oldest rock layer form?

    C. What are the relative ages of the rocks?

    D. What is the absolute age of the most recent layer?

    E. What year did the fault form?

Use the diagram of undisturbed rock layers and features to answer Questions 5 and 6.

5. Which of the following statements are true? Choose all that apply.

    A. All the fossils are over 175 million years old.

    B. The fault is over 175 million years old.

    C. All the fossils are less than 200 million years old.

    D. The sandstone is over 200 million years old.

    E. The sandstone is 201 million years old.

6. Circle the correct term to complete each statement.

    The igneous intrusion is *younger / older* than the fault.

    The fossils in the shale are from animals that lived *before / after* the animals that formed fossils in the limestone.

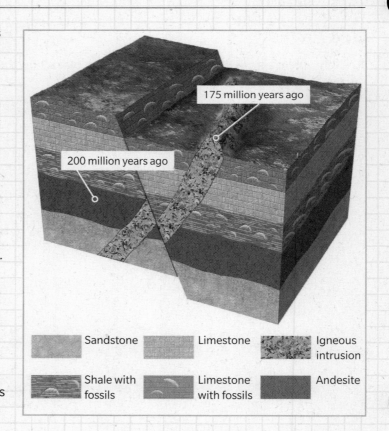

175 million years ago

200 million years ago

Sandstone   Limestone   Igneous intrusion

Shale with fossils   Limestone with fossils   Andesite

Interactive Review

Complete this interactive study guide to review the lesson.

Layers of sedimentary rock and the fossils they contain help us to understand Earth's history.

A. Summarize how sedimentary rock and fossils form.

Geologists use relative dating to compare the ages of different rock layers and the fossils in those layers.

B. A student makes a sandwich with several layers of bread and cheese. Then the student cuts the sandwich and says it models how a fault cut through rock layers after the rock layers formed. Explain how the example of the sandwich relates to relative dating.

The combination of absolute and relative dating allows scientists to determine the ages of rocks and fossils. Absolute dating provides evidence that helps us estimate the age of Earth.

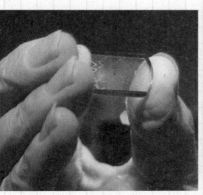

C. How can scientists find the absolute ages of igneous rocks?

The Geologic Time Scale Organizes Earth's History

This fossil of a tyrannosaur skeleton was found buried in a layer of sandstone, a sedimentary rock.

Explore First

Modeling Earth's History Suppose the entire history of Earth is represented by a 12-month calendar. On what date do you think the first modern humans would appear? What about dinosaurs? Discuss your answers with your classmates.

CAN YOU EXPLAIN IT?

What evidence is used to construct this geologic timeline of Earth's history?

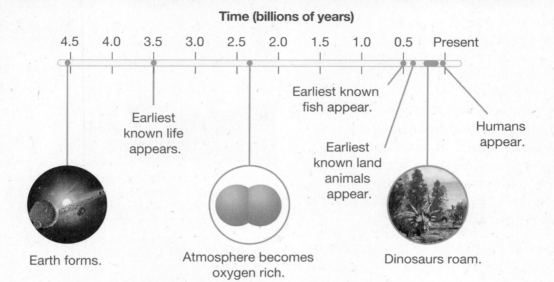

Time (billions of years)

4.5   4.0   3.5   3.0   2.5   2.0   1.5   1.0   0.5   Present

Earliest known fish appear.

Earliest known life appears.

Humans appear.

Earliest known land animals appear.

Earth forms.

Atmosphere becomes oxygen rich.

Dinosaurs roam.

A growing body of evidence shows that the first known life forms appeared at least 3.5 billion years ago. Complex life did not evolve until more than 1 billion years later, and the first humans showed up only 200,000 years ago.

1. Review this geologic timeline of events in Earth's history. What kinds of evidence are used to make timelines like this one?

 EVIDENCE NOTEBOOK As you explore the lesson, gather evidence to help you explain what kinds of evidence are used to construct a geologic timeline.

Describing Geologic Change

You have likely changed a lot since you were born. Just imagine all the changes Earth has been through since it formed about 4.6 billion years ago! Geologic processes such as weathering, erosion, and tectonic plate motion constantly reshape Earth. Many landforms you see today—such as rugged mountains and steep canyons—formed from geologic processes over millions of years.

To learn about changes in Earth's past, we can look to the present. Many geologic processes that shape Earth today also shaped Earth in the past. For example, volcanoes erupted, glaciers carved valleys, and sediment was deposited to form sedimentary rock. These processes will continue to shape Earth in the future as well.

2. **Discuss** Analyze the two photos. How long do you think it took the U-shaped valley to form? Explain.

Glaciers are like slow-moving rivers of ice that scrape over land, picking up and moving rock. This glacier has been inching its way down this valley for thousands of years.

This U-shaped valley was shaped by a glacier that flowed through the area in the past.

The Rate of Geologic Change

Most geologic processes change Earth's surface so slowly that you would not notice a difference in your lifetime. But over thousands to millions of years, geologic processes cause major changes to landscapes. For example, weathering and erosion are wearing down the Appalachian Mountains by about six meters (6 m) every million years. Over time, the rugged peaks have become rolling hills. The movement of tectonic plates is another example—they move at a rate of a few centimeters (cm) each year. Yet over millions of years, this motion builds tall mountain ranges and forms entire ocean basins.

Not all geologic change is slow. Some processes can alter large areas or the whole planet within a short period. An example is the meteorite that struck the Yucatan Peninsula in Mexico about 65 million years ago. It sent debris into the atmosphere that blocked sunlight for years and likely contributed to a mass extinction.

The frequency of meteorite impacts, volcanic eruptions, and glacier coverage have varied during different periods of Earth's history. Scientists take this information into account when they reconstruct Earth's geologic past.

3. Geologic change is shown in each photo. Read each description, and then label the images to tell whether you think the change is relatively fast or slow.

For millions of years, two tectonic plates have been pushing up the Himalayan Mountains. The mountains are still growing today at about 1 cm per year.

The Colorado River has been carving a path through the Grand Canyon for at least 5 million years. In some spots, the canyon is over 1,800 m (1.1 miles) deep and continues to get deeper today.

This landslide happened when rocks and soil suddenly slid down the side of this mountain as a result of the force of gravity.

Do the Math
Describe Scales of Time

How long is 1 million years? It helps to think about this in terms of numbers that are more familiar to us. For example, how many human lifetimes are in 1 million years?

STEP 1 Assume the average human lifetime is 80 years. The question asks how many human lifetimes are in 1 million years, so we need to find out how many times 80 divides into 1,000,000. Let h represent the number of human lifetimes.

STEP 2 $h = \dfrac{1,000,000}{80} = 12,500$. There are 12,500 human lifetimes in 1 million years.

4. The Himalayan Mountains have been growing slowly for about 50 million years. Using the same method, find out how many human lifetimes have passed since the Himalayan Mountains began to grow.

STEP 1 I need to find out how many times _____ divides into _____.

STEP 2 $h =$

Compiling Evidence of Earth's Past

Scientists analyze Earth's rocks and fossils to piece together Earth's past. Rocks and fossils contain clues about how they formed. They also can tell us about the past conditions or environments in which they formed. Comparing rocks from around a region or around the world allows scientists to organize the timing of events in Earth's history.

These layers of volcanic tuff in California formed as volcanic ash settled and cooled. A section of this volcanic tuff came all the way from an eruption that occurred in Wyoming. The eruption was a supervolcano eruption that spread ash over a large part of the United States.

5. If you wanted to know how the supervolcano eruption 640,000 years ago affected living things and the environment, which layers of rock would you look at?

Rocks Give Clues about Earth's Past

Around the world, geologists collaborate and share information about rocks. The *rock record* is a compilation of all of Earth's known rocks. Major geologic events—such as a supervolcano eruption, an asteroid impact, or tectonic plate movements that form or break up continents—are recorded in the rock record. These events can be used as benchmarks to mark the beginning or ending of specific periods of time. Rocks and fossils can be identified as having existed before or after these events occurred. If the event can be given an absolute date, it can provide evidence for the ages of the rocks and fossils that surround it in the rock record.

Long ago, a supervolcano eruption happened in what is now Yellowstone National Park in Wyoming. The cooling ash formed deposits of rock, called volcanic tuff, of varying thicknesses over much of North America. Absolute dating indicates that the tuff is 640,000 years old. The information from all of the known tuff deposits, along with the rocks above and below it, can be compiled to give a big-picture view of what North America was like before, during, and after the eruption.

6. The rocks in the first row of photos give clues about how they formed. The photos in the second row show different environments. Match the rocks in the first row to the type of environment they likely formed in by writing A, B, or C in the correct box.

This dark layer of rock is called *coal*. Coal formation begins in swamp environments, and the entire process takes millions of years.

Rocks are worn down as they are tumbled along river bottoms. Over time, they can be cemented together to form a new rock called *conglomerate*.

This landscape is covered by an igneous rock called *basalt*. The basalt formed as lava flowed over the land and cooled into rock.

Fossils Give Clues about Earth's Past

Like the rocks they are found in, fossils also give clues about Earth's past environments. For example, the teeth of a 10-meter-long shark were found in a rock layer in Kansas and determined to be about 89 million years old. This indicates that a sea covered this part of Kansas about 89 million years ago.

Like major geologic events, fossils can be used to determine relative ages of surrounding rocks and as benchmarks to organize Earth's history. The *fossil record* is a compilation of all of Earth's known fossils and the information they provide about Earth's history. To get an idea of how the fossil record was compiled, imagine a sequence of rock layers, each containing distinctly different fossils. In a different location, researchers find another sequence of fossils that is identical to all or part of the first sequence. As sequences of matching fossils are correlated from around the world, scientists can apply the principles of relative dating to determine how life has changed over time. For example, rock layers that contain only extinct organisms are generally older than rock layers that contain fossils of organisms that still exist today. Appearances of new organisms or disappearances of previously existing organisms in the fossil record can also be related to geologic or environmental changes on Earth.

EVIDENCE NOTEBOOK

7. What types of evidence can major geologic events and changes in organisms provide to help construct a timeline of Earth's history? Record your evidence.

Analysis of Rock Layers

A field geologist conducted a study of an undisturbed sequence of rocks. Explore her sketch, photos, and research notes.

8. Help the geologist complete her analysis to describe the geologic history of this location.

The oldest rock is shale and the youngest is the igneous rock.
Evidence: _____
_____
_____

From 450 to 120 million years ago, no rock was deposited, erosion removed rocks that were deposited, or both.
Evidence: _____
_____

The area was covered by a shallow sea some time between 120 and 50 million years ago.
Evidence: _____
_____

The brittle stars lived long before the sea turtle lived. Evidence: _____
_____
_____

This igneous rock formed as ongoing eruptions covered the area with lava. Absolute dating shows this igneous rock ranges from 50–47 million years old.

This fossilized sea turtle is found in sandstone along with other fossils of organisms that lived in a shallow sea. This fossil shows similarities to some living sea turtles. The oldest known sea turtle fossil is about 120 million years old.

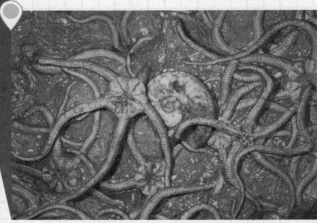

This shale formed in a deep sea and contains fossils of extinct brittle stars. Information from the fossil record indicates that they are between 451 and 443 million years old.

Correlate Rock Sequences

A team of geologists sketched these three different undisturbed rock sequences in a region. They worked together to build this diagram that correlates the fossils from each sequence.

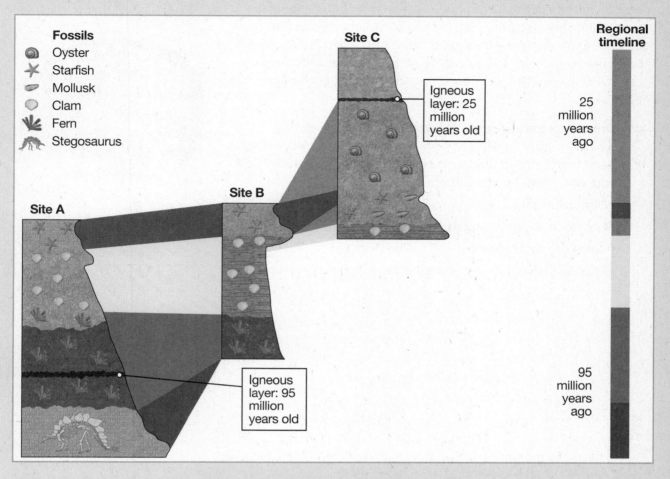

9. Fossils of extinct organisms, such as this *Stegosaurus*, are generally younger / older than fossils that resemble living organisms. Assuming that the fossils formed at the same time as the rocks they are found in, the oyster / Stegosaurus fossils are the oldest fossils shown here. The igneous layer indicates that *Stegosaurus* lived before / after 95 million years ago.

10. Use the information about fossils, igneous layers, and rock types to divide the regional timeline into different sections of your choosing. Make up a name for each section and write it next to the timeline. Use your updated timeline to describe a brief history of life in the area.

_____

_____

_____

_____

_____

Organizing Earth's History

How do the rock and fossil records provide evidence of change over time? Using these records, scientists can construct timelines that describe Earth's history. A geologic timeline can be detailed or general. Some timelines show geologic events, such as ice ages and periods of volcanic activity. Others focus on how life has changed throughout Earth's history.

This insect trapped in 45-million-year-old amber is part of the fossil record.

11. **Draw** A lot has happened on Earth over the course of 4.6 billion years. Create a timeline that shows at least four events or items from Earth's past. Can you make your timeline to scale? Add your own events, or choose from the list.

   • Oldest mineral—4 billion years old

   • First flowering plants appear—145 million years ago

   • Dinosaurs become extinct—65 million years ago

   • Breakup of the super-continent Pangaea—220 million years ago

Earth has existed for about 4.6 billion years. The **geologic time scale** is used to organize Earth's long history into manageable parts. The geologic time scale is continually updated as new rock and fossil evidence is discovered.

   The further we go back in time, the less rock and fossil information we have. This is because Earth's oldest rocks have undergone great changes over the past few billion years. Many of the oldest rocks have either been buried deep below the surface or melted in Earth's hot interior.

Construct a Timeline

Use absolute and relative dating to construct a timeline of different events from your life and the lives of others in a group.

MATERIALS
• markers
• masking tape
• personal items (optional)
• sticky notes

Procedure and Analysis

STEP 1 Gather two objects that represent two events in your life. Label one object with an absolute date. For example, you may have a painting you did when you were younger labeled "Painting of tree, March 2017." Label the second object with a relative date that is based on the absolute date of the first object. For example, your second object might be a book recently given to you, labeled "Book from friend, after March 2017."

STEP 2 In your group, display your labeled objects in a central area. Collaborate with your classmates to try to arrange everything from oldest to most recent. You may want to make a chart to help you organize the events.

STEP 3 Identify any gaps or difficulties you have in your timeline, particularly with events that have relative dates. Ask questions about one another's events and use the answers to finalize the timeline.

STEP 4 What methods did you use to sequence the events? Were you able to arrange all the events in correct chronological order? Why or why not?

STEP 5 How is this activity related to construction of the geologic time scale?

STEP 6 **Engineer It** Think about very slow geologic events that occur over time, such as glacial periods and mountain building. To study these events, scientists need to model them at observable time scales. Explain steps that scientists should take to make a scale model of such an event.

The Geologic Time Scale

Earth's entire history is divided into four major eons, shown in the top row of the diagram. In the second row, the three eras within the Phanerozoic Eon are shown. Within each era are several periods, and within each period are even smaller divisions of time called epochs. Currently, we live in the Holocene Epoch of the Quaternary Period, which is part of the Cenozoic Era and the Phanerozoic Eon.

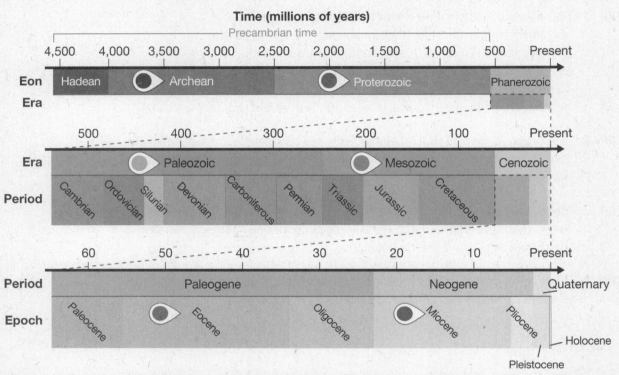

Source: International Commission on Stratigraphy, International Chronostratigraphic Chart, v2016

Over 3 billion years ago, photosynthetic organisms released oxygen into Earth's shallow iron-rich seas. Scientists think that oxygen combined with iron to form the red bands in this rock.

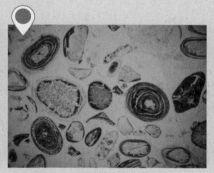

These photosynthetic sea creatures are about 2 billion years old. After all the iron in the seas was used up to form rock, oxygen released by these organisms was added to the air.

Crinoids are animals that flourished during the Paleozoic Era. These creatures lived anchored to the ocean floor. There are some species of crinoids that still exist today.

Divisions in Geologic Time

The geologic time scale is broken up into the following divisions of time: eons, eras, periods, and epochs. Divisions in the geologic time scale are not equal. This is because the divisions are based on major events and changes in Earth's history, such as extinctions.

Look at the clock-shaped diagram of geologic time. If Earth's history were squeezed into 12 hours, Precambrian time would take up most of that time. Precambrian time began around the time Earth formed and lasted for about 4 billion years. That is almost 90 percent of Earth's 4.6-billion-year history!

 12. Language SmArts How do divisions in the geologic time scale differ from the way we organize time using a clock? What are the reasons for these differences?

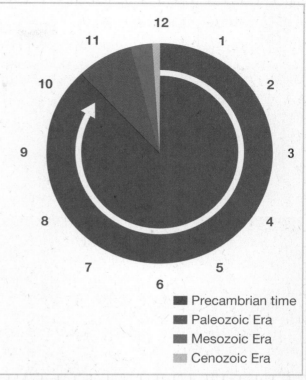

■ Precambrian time
■ Paleozoic Era
■ Mesozoic Era
■ Cenozoic Era

If all of Earth's history were squeezed into one 12-hour period, Precambrian time would end at about 10:30.

Pterodactylus was a flying meat-eating reptile. It lived during the Jurassic Period alongside dinosaurs. The fossil record shows that these animals went extinct at the end of the Cretaceous Period.

This fossil is of a horse-like mammal from the Paleogene Period. During this time, mammals diversified, leading scientists to call this the "Age of Mammals." The first marine mammals also appeared during this time.

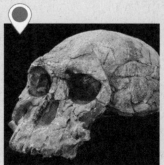

This skull is from one of the earliest members of the genus *Homo*. Modern humans, or *Homo sapiens*, evolved about 200,000 years ago.

13. How can scientists use the rock and fossil records to organize Earth's history into a single timeline? Record your evidence.

Language SmArts

Explain Evidence

Fossils and rocks provide evidence of what Earth was like in the past.

A fossilized trilobite, an organism that once roamed Earth's oceans. Trilobites went extinct about 250 million years ago.

The skull of *Megazostrodon*, one of the first mammals to appear in the fossil record, about 200 million years ago.

Putorana Plateau in Siberia is made up of several layers of igneous rock deposited by volcanic eruptions in the area about 250 million years ago. Scientists think this may have contributed to the extinction of most life on Earth.

14. In your own words, describe how these fossils and rocks could be used as evidence to construct an explanation for an event that changed life on Earth.

_____

_____

_____

_____

_____

_____

Continue Your Exploration

Name: _____   Date: _____

Check out the path below or go online to choose one of the other paths shown.

Careers in Science

- **Exploring the Great Dying**
- **Hands-On Labs** 🖐
- **Propose Your Own Path**

Go online to choose one of these other paths.

Paleoartist

If you have ever seen a reconstruction of a dinosaur skeleton at a museum, you know how impressive these ancient creatures were. From rocks, fossils, and reconstructed skeletons, scientists can tell certain things about an extinct animal's appearance, how it moved, and where it lived. For example, fossil footprints can show how an animal walked. The rock that a fossil is found in gives clues about the past environment.

Paleoart is a profession that combines art and science. Paleoartists help us visualize extinct animals and their environments by creating art, including drawings, three-dimensional models, and digital images. Paleoartists work closely with scientists to make their art as accurate as possible—some paleoartists are even scientists themselves.

This is paleoart of a *Gigantoraptor* on its nest by artist Mohamad Haghani. This dinosaur lived during the Cretaceous Period.

Continue Your Exploration

A scientist exploring in the desert found fossil bones of a sheep-sized dinosaur. The bones were reconstructed as shown in this photo. Analysis of the fossil confirmed that the dinosaur was a land reptile that walked on four legs. The shape of its beak and jaw suggests that it was a plant eater. The fossil was found in a sandstone layer that was deposited along the shoreline of a shallow sea. The same sandstone rock in the area contained fossils of ferns and trees.

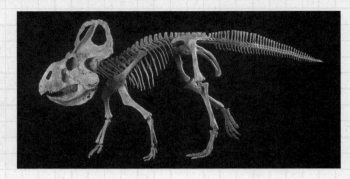

1. What evidence describes this dinosaur and its past environment?

2. **Draw** Use the evidence and the photo to help you draw the dinosaur in its past environment.

3. Fossil evidence does not tell paleoartists everything. For example, the color and skin texture of ancient animals are often unknown. However, paleoartists read scientific papers and study animals alive today to make inferences about these things. What aspects of your drawing are based on inferences (are not based on direct evidence)?

4. **Collaborate** Compare your paleoart with a classmate's. Discuss why there might be differences between your paleoart and your classmate's paleoart.

Can You Explain It?

Name: _____   Date: _____

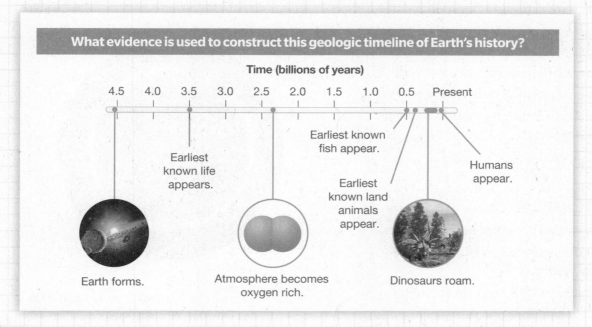

What evidence is used to construct this geologic timeline of Earth's history?

Time (billions of years)

4.5   4.0   3.5   3.0   2.5   2.0   1.5   1.0   0.5   Present

Earliest known
fish appear.

Earliest
known life
appears.

Humans
appear.

Earliest
known land
animals
appear.

Earth forms.

Atmosphere becomes
oxygen rich.

Dinosaurs roam.

EVIDENCE NOTEBOOK
Refer to the notes in your Evidence Notebook to help you explain what kinds of evidence are used to construct a geologic timeline.

1. State your claim. Make sure your claim fully explains what evidence is used to construct timelines of Earth's history.

2. Summarize the evidence you have gathered to support your claim and explain your reasoning.

Checkpoints

Answer the following questions to check your understanding of the lesson.

Use the diagram to answer Question 3.

3. What does this diagram tell you about these different time periods? Choose all that apply.

   A. the actual length of time for each one

   B. the order in which they occurred

   C. the length of time they lasted in relation to each other

4. Which statements correctly describe the geologic time scale? Choose all that apply.

   A. It is divided into equal periods of time.

   B. It is divided based on evidence in the fossil record.

   C. Some events are arranged according to relative dates.

   D. It is divided based on evidence in the rock record.

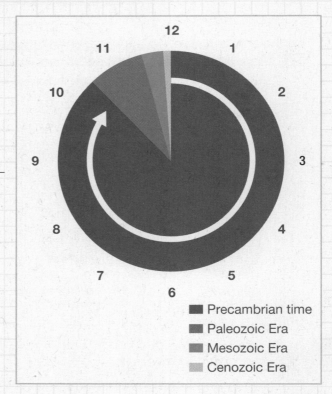

- Precambrian time
- Paleozoic Era
- Mesozoic Era
- Cenozoic Era

Use the photo to answer Questions 5 and 6.

5. The rock layers in this photo were laid down horizontally and are undisturbed. Therefore, you can conclude that the white layer is *older / younger* than the red layer, and that the thick brown layer is the *oldest / youngest* of the layers shown here.

6. An extremely thin layer of volcanic ash is found between the white layer on top and the thin red layer in the middle. Absolute dating showed that the ash is about 43 million years old. What can you conclude based on this information? Choose all that apply.

   A. The top layer is also volcanic.

   B. The middle layer is also about 43 million years old.

   C. The top layer is younger than 43 million years old.

   D. The bottom layer is older than 43 million years old.

Interactive Review

Complete this section to review the main concepts of the lesson.

Scientists study current geologic processes to learn about past processes such as tectonic plate motion, weathering, erosion, and deposition.

A. How is it possible to look at geologic processes that shape Earth today to learn about the past?

Scientists use the rock record and the fossil record as evidence for events and conditions in Earth's past.

B. What can you infer from the rock record and the fossil record? Give two specific examples of evidence and how that evidence helps scientists organize geologic time.

The geologic time scale is used to organize Earth's long history.

C. Why do you think scientists need to organize Earth's history into a time scale?

Fossils Are Evidence of Changes in Life Over Time

Titanis walleri, or Waller's terror bird, was flightless. It could grow up to 1.8 m (5.9 feet) tall, about the same height as an adult human. It lived from about 5 to 2 million years ago.

Explore First

Modeling Fossil Formation Use clay and a few common objects to model fossil formation. Press each item into a thick piece of clay to make a detailed impression. Remove the objects and exchange impressions with another group. What can you learn about the objects by studying their impressions?

Go online to view the digital version of the Hands-On Lab for this lesson and to download additional lab resources.

CAN YOU EXPLAIN IT?

What can explain the presence of a rock layer with no fossils between rock layers with different types of fossils?

fossils found

no fossils found

fossils found

Major changes to populations of organisms and environments happened in the past. Such events are recorded in rock layers as part of the fossil record.

1. What is needed for a fossil to form? Select all that apply.

   A. The organism must first get stuck in rock.

   B. The soft tissue of the dead organism must be eaten by scavengers before the bones can be preserved.

   C. The tracks or burrows of an organism must be filled with sediments before they are disturbed.

   D. The organism's body must be covered by sediment or another substance before its body decays.

2. What are some reasons that fossils may not form?

 EVIDENCE NOTEBOOK As you explore the lesson, gather evidence to help explain why fossils might be absent from one layer but not surrounding layers.

Analyzing Evidence about the History of Life

Only a small percentage of the organisms that ever lived fossilized. Yet, these fossils help scientists learn about how life on Earth changed over time. Fossils show where and when certain extinct organisms lived. They also show patterns in how the body plans of organisms changed over time. Fossils can provide information about past environments. They can even give clues to how extinct species interacted. The fossil record also shows patterns in how species appeared and disappeared throughout Earth's history.

Glyptodonts were about the size of a small car. They ate plants and lived among early humans before the Ice Age.

The insect-eating armadillo shares many features with its extinct relative, the glyptodont. However, it is much smaller.

3. Compare the armadillo to the glyptodont (GLIP•tuh•dahnt). What similarities provide evidence that they might be related?

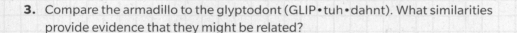

Evidence of Earliest Life Forms

Charles Walcott was an American paleontologist who, in 1909, discovered many well-preserved fossils of ancient sea organisms near Mount Burgess, Canada. The fossils were preserved in layers of shale left by an ancient ocean. The soft tissues of many of the fossilized organisms in the Burgess Shale were preserved in great detail.

Scientists used a method called radiometric dating to find the absolute age of nearby igneous rock layers. These layers contain a type of potassium that changes into argon at a constant rate. Scientists measure how much potassium in the rock has changed to argon. From this measurement, they can determine when the igneous rock formed. After finding the age of the igneous rock, they used relative dating to determine that the Burgess Shale fossils are over 500 million years old. This seems quite old. But, the earliest evidence for life dates back about 3.8 *billion* years! The earliest organisms were single cells, which rarely formed fossils. Evidence of these early cells was found in rock samples with high levels of a type of carbon found only in living things.

Traces of Carbon from Cells

There are different types of carbon atoms, but living organisms use only one of these types. Scientists detected high levels of this type of carbon in ancient rock. Fossilized cells were not found in this rock, but based on this chemical evidence of life, the scientists concluded that there was life on Earth at the time this ancient rock formed, 3.8 billion years ago. The scientists' reasoning is an example of an *inference*, or the use of evidence to draw conclusions when direct observation of a process or event is not possible. These rocks contain the earliest known evidence of life on Earth.

Many types of scientists work together to collect evidence of ancient life. Chemists isolate certain chemicals from rock samples to analyze them. Biologists study how living things use chemicals in their bodies. Geologists determine the age of rocks and what Earth conditions may have caused them to form. Paleontologists find and study fossils.

The ratio of different types of carbon in these 3.8-billion-year-old rocks in Greenland is interpreted as evidence of life on Earth at the time the rocks formed.

Fossil Evidence

The earliest fossilized cells scientists have found are about 3.5 billion years old. The fossils are of a type of *cyanobacteria*, a single-celled life form that makes its own food by photosynthesis. In Greek, *cyano-* means "blue." The bacteria left traces of the blue-green pigment protein that gives them their name. The cyanobacteria also left behind stromatolite formations. *Stromatolites* are layered mounds, columns, or sheets of calcium-rich sedimentary rock. They are made of layers of bacteria and sediment.

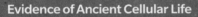

Evidence of Ancient Cellular Life

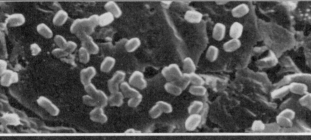

Ancient Cyanobacteria Fossils of bacteria similar to these were found in ancient stromatolites from western Australia. The stromatolites were about 3.5 billion years old. Cyanobacteria are a type of bacteria that capture the energy of sunlight and release oxygen during photosynthesis. They helped create an oxygen-rich atmosphere on ancient Earth.

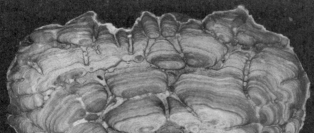

Stromatolite Growth Patterns Notice the light and dark layers of this stromatolite. They are caused by the growth patterns of cyanobacteria that were on Earth when each layer was formed. The bacteria release white-colored calcium compounds that mix with soil or sand deposits. Over time, the layers harden into rock.

Modern Stromatolites These stromatolites line the sea floor of Shark Bay in Western Australia. They are usually columns or domes because the cyanobacteria that form them group together in mat-like sheets. New groups form mats on top of the sediment deposits trapped by older groups.

4. Do the Math Scientists estimate that Earth is about 4.6 billion years old. The fossil record shows the first chemical evidence of life around 3.8 billion years ago. What percentage of Earth's history was without life? Write a formula for the calculation using variables you define. Then use your formula to find the answer.

5. Think about the process of identifying the age of the earliest fossils. How does it show how scientists use evidence and logic to answer scientific questions?

Evidence of Change Over Time

For more than 2 billion years, only single-celled life existed on Earth. That changed about 540 million years ago, during the Cambrian Era. Scientists found a large increase in the number and types of fossils in rock layers that formed during this time. Because of this increase, that time period is often called the *Cambrian explosion*. Cambrian organisms looked very different from living things today. Many Cambrian species, such as *Marrella*, were arthropods. *Arthropods* are a group of invertebrate animals that have segmented bodies. Cambrian arthropods are now extinct, but other arthropods, such as ants and lobsters, exist today.

Marrella is the most common fossil found in Burgess Shale.

Many scientists think the Cambrian explosion happened in part because of an increase in oxygen levels in the air from cyanobacteria and new interactions among organisms. Scientists also infer that a rise of predators on Earth may have led to a greater diversity of life forms. The fossil record shows that many Cambrian animals had hard outer shells or spiny structures, which could protect the animals from predators. Over many generations, populations may have developed these and other characteristics in response to the activity of predators. The fossil record of the Cambrian explosion gives scientists a way to investigate how life changes over time.

6. What evidence from the fossil record supports the observation that life changes over time? Select all that apply.

A. more fossils of the same species found in several rock layers

B. increased numbers of fossils of different species found in younger rock layers

C. several rock layers that do not contain fossils

D. fossils of distant relatives of a modern species found in ancient rock layers

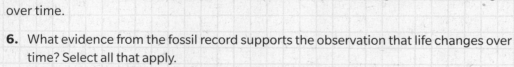

EVIDENCE NOTEBOOK

7. What does a rock layer with very few fossils suggest about conditions in that region when the rock layer formed? Record your evidence.

© Houghton Mifflin Harcourt Publishing Company • Image Credits: ©Chase Studio/Science Source

Increases in the Complexity of Fossils

Scientists find that more recent rock layers contain fossils that have more complex bodies and physical features than earlier fossils. Multicellular organisms first appeared in the fossil record more than 600 million years ago (mya). Jawless fish appeared in the fossil record about 500 mya. Fish with jaws appeared nearly 400 mya. Later rock layers include fossils of amphibians and then reptiles and mammals. Birds appeared more recently. This evidence suggests that new physical features such as feet and lungs enabled organisms to survive in more diverse habitats. Populations in different habitats became more different from each other over many generations.

Fossils from organisms with simpler body plans are found alongside more complex fossils in younger rock layers. This suggests that while life changes over time on Earth, not all populations change in the same ways or at the same rate. For example, modern bacteria do not appear to be more complex than bacteria found in ancient rock layers.

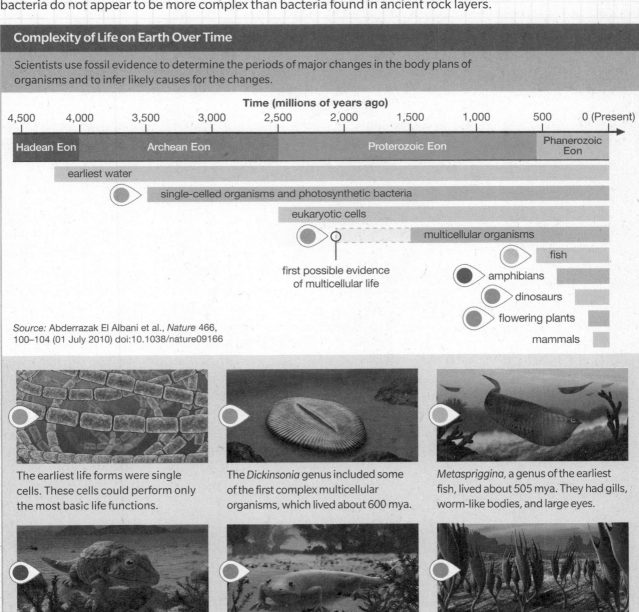

Complexity of Life on Earth Over Time

Scientists use fossil evidence to determine the periods of major changes in the body plans of organisms and to infer likely causes for the changes.

Time (millions of years ago)

4,500   4,000   3,500   3,000   2,500   2,000   1,500   1,000   500   0 (Present)

Hadean Eon   Archean Eon   Proterozoic Eon   Phanerozoic Eon

earliest water

single-celled organisms and photosynthetic bacteria

eukaryotic cells

multicellular organisms

first possible evidence of multicellular life

fish

amphibians

dinosaurs

flowering plants

mammals

Source: Abderrazak El Albani et al., *Nature* 466, 100–104 (01 July 2010) doi:10.1038/nature09166

The earliest life forms were single cells. These cells could perform only the most basic life functions.

The *Dickinsonia* genus included some of the first complex multicellular organisms, which lived about 600 mya.

Metaspriggina, a genus of the earliest fish, lived about 505 mya. They had gills, worm-like bodies, and large eyes.

Members of the *Cacops* genus lived about 280 mya. They evolved from fish with bony fins and lung-like organs.

The *Captorhinus* genus, the first reptiles to live on land, date back to 300 mya. They were similar to lizards.

Seed plants of the *Archaeosperma* genus lived about 375 mya. They gave rise to flowering plants 160 mya.

Transitional Fossils

Based on evidence from the fossil record, scientists conclude that life began in the oceans. Early fish-like organisms gave rise to fish, which gave rise to the ancestor common to amphibians. To determine how changes like these occur in nature, scientists look for *transitional fossils*. These are fossils of organisms that have body structures that are found both in an ancestral species and in its descendants. For example, when scientists investigated the origins of amphibians, they hypothesized that there might have been an organism that had traits of both fish and amphibians. This hypothesis was supported with the discovery of a fossil called *Tiktaalik*. *Tiktaalik* lived in the water. It had bones in its fins that were very similar to the wrist and foot bones of amphibians.

Fossil Evidence of the Transition from Ocean to Land

Tiktaalik is a transitional fossil in the evolutionary progression from fish to amphibians. It has characteristics of both fish and amphibians.

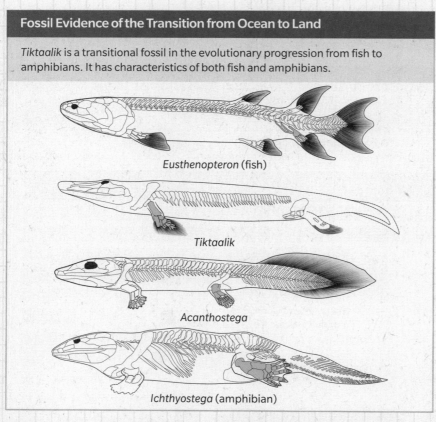

Eusthenopteron (fish)

Tiktaalik

Acanthostega

Ichthyostega (amphibian)

8. Over a period of time in the past, the bones in the fins of a population of fish became larger and longer. The bones became able to support the weight of the organisms when they were out of water. This change happened over many generations. What other changes over time would be needed for fish to live out of the water?

9. The shape (form) of an anatomical structure often enables an organism to perform particular a task (function). What do the forms of the highlighted limbs in the illustration tell you about their functions in each animal?

Infer How Features Changed Over Time

Whales swim and live in the ocean. Yet, they are mammals. They have traits similar to those of mammals that live on land. They give birth to live young, feed their young with milk, and have hair. Evidence from the fossil record supports the theory that the ancestors of whales lived on land before they lived in water. Over time, several body structures, such as the skull, hips, and legs, changed. These changes made the structures better adapted to swimming than walking.

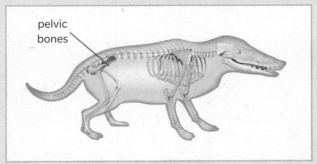

Pakicetus inachus lived around 50 million years ago.

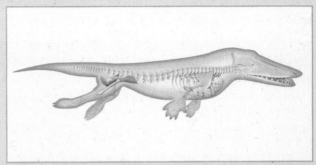

Ambulocetus natans lived 50–45 million years ago.

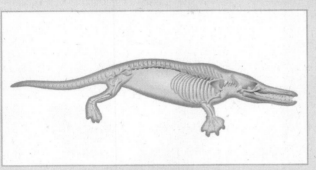

Kutchicetus minimus lived 46–43 million years ago.

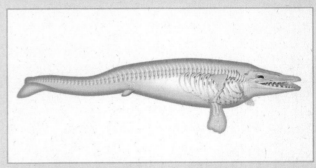

Dorudon atrox lived 40–34 million years ago.

10. Hind legs are connected to pelvic bones, which are important for walking. Modern whales have relatively small pelvic bones. How did the pelvic bones of whales' ancestors change over time?

_____

_____

_____

_____

_____

_____

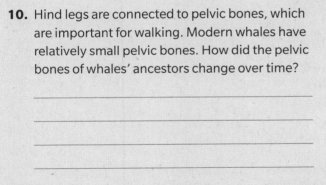

The modern bowhead whale is a living species that has been on Earth for 35 million years.

11. The form of a body structure is related to its function. Given this, how can you tell that Pakicetus inachus most likely lived on land and that Dorudon atrox lived in water?

_____

_____

_____

_____

© Houghton Mifflin Harcourt Publishing Company

Lesson 3 Fossils Are Evidence of Changes in Life Over Time **353**

Analyzing Patterns in the Numbers of Life Forms Over Time

The fossil record shows changes in species over time. It also documents **extinctions**, in which all members of a species die out. When a species becomes extinct, its fossils no longer occur in the fossil record. Scientists observe that the loss of species from the fossil record seems to happen at a regular rate, often called the *background rate* of extinction. But there have been periods in Earth's history when the rate of extinction was very high.

Identifying Extinction Events in the Fossil Record

Geologic time periods are identified by major changes in the fossil record. The side of this cliff in Palo Duro Canyon State Park in Texas includes the Permian-Triassic (P-T) extinction boundary. The P-T mass extinction happened about 248 million years ago.

Coelophysis fossils appear after the P-T extinction. They were a genus of small, meat-eating dinosaurs.

Trilobite fossils are found in the fossil record before the P-T extinction. They are not found afterward.

12. Study the rock and fossil images. What is one inference you can make about when the organisms shown lived? Explain your reasoning.

Extinction

The fossil record shows an extinction when a species is no longer found in sedimentary rock layers. For example, trilobites were once very common marine arthropods. They are not present in the fossil record after the Permian-Triassic extinction, which indicates that trilobites became extinct.

   A *mass extinction* happens when whole groups of related species die out at about the same time. Mass extinctions appear to be caused by large changes to the environment. Some of these changes, such as volcanic eruptions or asteroid impacts with Earth, are natural, while others, such as climate change or habitat destruction, may be related to human activity. After a mass extinction, surviving species have many new opportunities to use ecosystem resources. They then thrive and change over time. The numbers of new species in the fossil record after a mass extinction increase over time.

The Five Mass Extinction Events on Earth

Extinction event	Proposed cause(s)	Organisms affected	A type of animal that went extinct
Ordovician-Silurian, 443 million years ago	Sea-level drop and climate change caused by formation of glaciers after rapid shifts in tectonic plates	Up to 85% of all species; 45%–60% of families of marine organisms died out	*Orthoceras*
Late Devonian, 354 million years ago	Possibly a large comet strike; possible decrease in global temperatures due to dust and debris from comet strike; drop in sea levels	70%–80% of all species; marine life affected more than freshwater and land organisms	*Dunkleosteus*
Permian-Triassic, 248 million years ago	Volcanic eruptions, release of methane from the sea floor; low oxygen levels in oceans; drop in sea levels	Largest extinction; over 95% of marine species and 70% of land species died out, including all trilobites and many insect species	*Dimetrodon*
Triassic-Jurassic, 200 million years ago	Poorly understood; possibly an extreme decrease in sea level and lower oxygen levels in oceans	About 76% of all species disappeared; end of mammal-like reptiles, leaving mainly dinosaurs	*Typothorax*
Cretaceous-Tertiary, 65 million years ago	Volcanic eruptions and climate cooling; drop in sea levels; large asteroid or comet strike	About 70% of all species died, including non-avian dinosaurs; mainly turtles, small reptiles, birds, and mammals survived	*Quetzalcoatlus*

13. Mass extinctions are caused by global / regional environmental changes. During a mass extinction event, biodiversity in the fossil record increases / decreases.

Do the Math
Analyze Extinction Data

Scientists compare rock layers before and after a mass extinction to estimate the number of affected species. They make estimates from several rock layer samples. Then they compare the loss of species to the normal rate of extinction that happens as life changes over time. This allows scientists to estimate the percentage of species on Earth affected by a mass extinction. The number of extinctions over time can be graphed. These graphs show a relatively constant extinction rate, broken up by large changes in the number of families of organisms lost during mass extinction events.

14. Describe the trends you see in each graph. What is the relationship between mass extinctions and biodiversity over time?

Extinction Rate Over Time

The fossil record shows five mass extinctions. During each one, more than half of Earth's species went extinct.

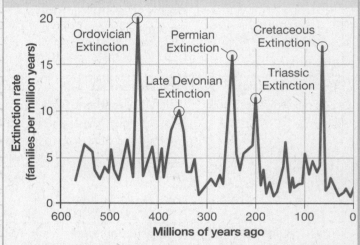

15. Does the top graph provide evidence that extinctions are a normal part of Earth's history? Explain your reasoning.

Diversity of Marine Organisms Over Time

Each mass extinction greatly reduced biodiversity. Yet, the species that remained expanded and diverged over time.

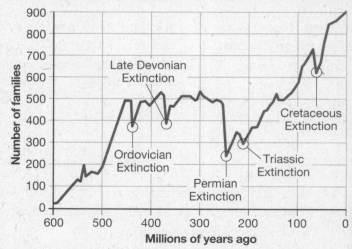

16. Mass extinctions do / do not cause permanent reductions in biodiversity on Earth. After each extinction event, the number of families increases / decreases rapidly over time.

Patterns in Extinction and Biodiversity Data

Scientists want to find the causes of mass extinctions. To do this, they analyze rock layers before, during, and after an extinction event. For example, when studying the Cretaceous-Paleogene, or K-Pg, mass extinction, scientists looked at the rock layers laid down at the beginning of this extinction. They discovered unusual amounts of a metal called *iridium* in one rock layer in many different places of Earth. Iridium is rare on Earth, but it is common in asteroids. They also discovered tiny glass formations that are often found near craters caused by meteorite impacts. The high temperature caused by the impact melts sand. Glass spheres and other shapes form from the melted sand. Scientists used this evidence to infer that a very large meteorite struck Earth and caused large-scale changes to Earth's environment. Large animal species were affected the most. Nearly all dinosaurs disappeared from the fossil record at this time. Fossil evidence shows that small mammals that could burrow to avoid the hot temperatures that resulted from the impact survived. It also shows that surviving species spread and diversified. Mass extinctions such as this are followed by periods of rapid growth in Earth's biodiversity.

The *Alphadon* was a small mammal that survived the K-Pg extinction. It likely did so by burrowing underground to avoid the dangerous conditions.

17. Observe the patterns in plant diversity shown in the graph. How might species of flowering plants have survived the K-Pg extinction?

Plant Diversification Over Time

Mass extinctions also affect plant species. Some plant families decline after extinction events. Other plant families increase in number afterward. Angiosperms, or flowering plants, are a family that diversified over time.

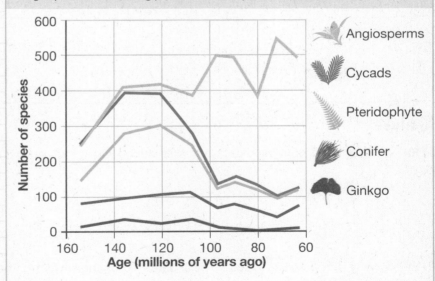

Credit: Adapted from "Quantitative analyses of the early angiosperm radiation" by Scott Lidgard and Peter R. Crane, from *Nature*. Adapted by permission from Macmillan Publishers Ltd. *Nature* (331), 344. Copyright ©1988.

Hands-On Lab
Model Analysis of the Fossil Record

Analyze fossil data to identify evidence of extinction and the appearance of new species over time.

Scientists compare fossil evidence from different places on Earth. They observe certain fossil types in the same rock layers across multiple locations. In some layers, they observe the disappearance of certain fossil types. In some layers, they observe the appearance of new fossil types. By determining the relative age of rock layers that contain fossils, scientists can identify these patterns of appearance and disappearance in the fossil record.

MATERIALS
• colored pencils
• scissors

Procedure

STEP 1 On a separate sheet of paper, copy the *Sedimentary Rock Layers from Four Locations* shown on the next page. Be sure to include the symbols that represent different types of fossils. Cut out the rock sequence from each location. Then line them up so that rock layers with similar compositions are side by side.

STEP 2 Analyze the fossil types found in different layers. Identify the species that appear to have gone extinct based on these fossil data.

STEP 3 Complete the table by drawing the symbols of three different fossils.

Fossil from oldest layer	Fossil from youngest layer	Fossil species that goes extinct

Analysis

STEP 4 What patterns in the rock layer fossils helped you identify an extinction?

STEP 5 Why is it necessary to see a similar pattern of change in fossils from several places in order to conclude that an extinction happened?

STEP 6 Analyze the fossil types found in the youngest rock layer. Which of these fossil species appeared first in the fossil record? Which one appeared more recently? How do you know?

Sedimentary Rock Layers from Four Locations

The different colors represent different types of sedimentary rock. The symbols within the rock layers represent different types of fossils.

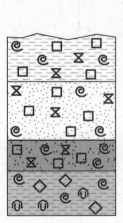

Location 1

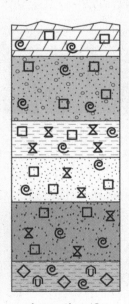

Location 2

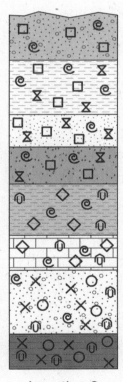

Location 3

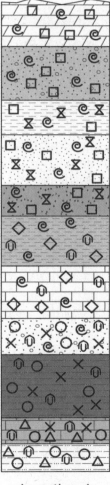

Location 4

EVIDENCE NOTEBOOK

18. Why might different types of fossils be found in rock layers that come before and after a rock layer that contains no fossils? Record your evidence.

© Houghton Mifflin Harcourt Publishing Company

19. Engineer It Computed tomography (CT) scanners are often used by doctors to gather information about the inside of something, such as a person's head, without cutting it. The scanners do this by collecting x-ray images that can be combined to form a 3D virtual model. These virtual models can then be used to make physical 3D models of the object that was scanned. Imagine you are a scientist studying a very delicate skull fossil from an early human ancestor. How could you use a CT scanner to learn more about this fossil without damaging it?

Language SmArts

Explain Inferences from Fossil Record Evidence

Ancient insects grew very large during the Carboniferous Period, about 320 million years ago. Scientists believe this was due in part to air that was high in oxygen. *Meganeura* was an ancestor of dragonflies, but it was more than four times bigger than the dragonflies we see today. It had a wingspan of over 70 centimeters (2 feet)!

Scientists have found thick coal deposits in Carboniferous rocks near *Meganeura* fossils. Coal deposits form from large amounts of decaying plant material. Such large amounts of plant material generally require warm and wet conditions.

Meganeura used its spiny legs to catch and eat other insects living near ponds. Scientists think that these *Meganeura* grew so large because of the high oxygen levels in the air.

20. What modern organisms have an ecological role around ponds today that is similar to the role of *Meganeura* during the Carboniferous Period? Explain your answer.

_____

_____

_____

21. Write a series of logical steps that you could use to infer the type of climate that existed during *Meganeura's* time.

_____

_____

_____

_____

Continue Your Exploration

Name: _____   Date: _____

Check out the path below or go online to choose one of the other paths shown.

Prediction of a Transitional Fossil

- **Reconstruct the Past from Physical Evidence**
- **Hands-On Labs** 🖐
- **Propose Your Own Path**

Go online to choose one of these other paths.

Transitional fossils are an important part of the fossil record. But how do scientists know how to spot a transitional fossil? They make hypotheses about the types of organisms that may have descended from earlier organisms and given rise to more recent organisms.

Scientists studied both ancient fish and amphibian fossils. They then predicted that an organism that shared some features in common with both fish and amphibian families likely lived in the past. They identified certain features that the hypothetical species—a "fishapod"—might have, such as a fish with feet. Their predictions were confirmed when fossils of the "fishapod" *Tiktaalik roseae* were found. The fossils showed that *Tiktaalik* had a skull and ribs like land animals. It also had several fish features, including fins and scales.

Tiktaalik roseae was found in the Canadian Arctic. Scientists found the front end of *Tiktaalik* 10 years before finding the hind end in different rock.

© Houghton Mifflin Harcourt Publishing Company • Image Credits: ©John Weinstein/Field Museum Library/Getty Images

Continue Your Exploration

1. In order for *Tiktaalik* to be considered a transitional fossil, when does it need to have appeared in the fossil record?

    A. before fish and amphibians

    B. after amphibians

    C. at the same time as amphibians

    D. between fish and amphibians

2. It took more than 3 billion years for life to spread from the oceans onto land. All organisms that lived on land evolved during the 550 million years that followed. How might this relatively rapid diversification of land species be explained?

    A. The move to land environments led to more changes in species over time.

    B. The move to land environments led to fewer changes in species over time.

    C. Spreading to land did not affect the amount of change in species over time.

    D. The change in environments resulted in lower biodiversity.

3. Draw a simple sketch of a transitional fossil that might link feathered, tree-climbing reptiles to early birds. Label the features that connect the fossil to the reptile and to the bird.

4. **Collaborate** Work with a small group to research another transitional fossil discovery. What evidence did scientists provide to support the identification of the transitional fossil? Present your findings to the class.

Can You Explain It?

Name: _____ **Date:** _____

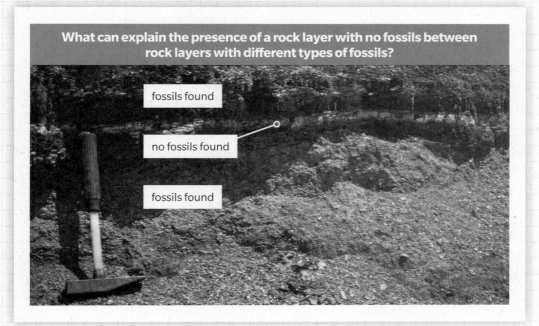

What can explain the presence of a rock layer with no fossils between rock layers with different types of fossils?

fossils found

no fossils found

fossils found

EVIDENCE NOTEBOOK

Refer to the notes in your Evidence Notebook to help you construct an explanation for how a rock layer with no fossils might have formed between rock layers with different types of fossils.

1. State your claim. Make sure your claim fully explains how a rock layer with no fossils might have formed between rock layers with different types of fossils.

2. Summarize the evidence you have gathered to support your claim and explain your reasoning.

Checkpoints

Answer the following questions to check your understanding of the lesson.

Use the diagram to answer Question 3.

3. How are the bones in the fin structure of the *Tiktaalik* evidence of a transition from fish to amphibian? Select all that apply.

   A. It has fins like a fish.

   B. It has limb bones like an amphibian.

   C. It is older than fish fossils.

   D. The limb bones do not look as developed as they do in the amphibian.

---

4. Organisms with more complex body plans are more likely to be found in older / younger rock layers. This prediction is based on observed patterns of increasing / decreasing complexity of physical structures in organisms over time.

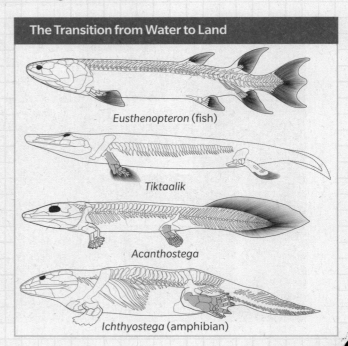

The Transition from Water to Land

Eusthenopteron (fish)

Tiktaalik

Acanthostega

Ichthyostega (amphibian)

Use the graph to answer Question 5.

5. Based on the graph, biodiversity increases / decreases during a mass extinction event and then increases / decreases after the event. In general, biodiversity on Earth increases / stays the same over time.

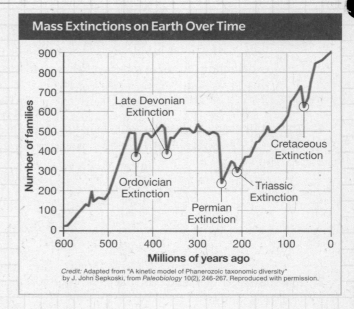

Mass Extinctions on Earth Over Time

Number of families

Late Devonian Extinction

Ordovician Extinction

Permian Extinction

Triassic Extinction

Cretaceous Extinction

Millions of years ago

Credit: Adapted from "A kinetic model of Phanerozoic taxonomic diversity" by J. John Sepkoski, from *Paleobiology* 10(2), 246-267. Reproduced with permission.

---

6. What types of evidence allow scientists to infer that single-celled life likely existed 3.8 billion years ago? Select all that apply.

   A. transitional fossils in ancient rocks

   B. certain forms of carbon in ancient rock

   C. fossil evidence, such as stromatolites

   D. evidence of extinction events

Interactive Review

Complete this page to review the main concepts of the lesson.

Scientists use the fossil record to identify patterns of change in life on Earth. They use evidence to infer possible causes of the changes they observe.

A. What types of changes are recorded in the fossil record?

The fossil record provides evidence of five mass extinctions. Scientists compare fossils found in rock layers to find evidence about how organisms were affected by extinction events.

B. Draw a sketch of rock layers that includes evidence of an extinction. Use symbols to represent species that existed before, during, and after the extinction event.

Fossils and Living Organisms Provide Evidence of Evolution

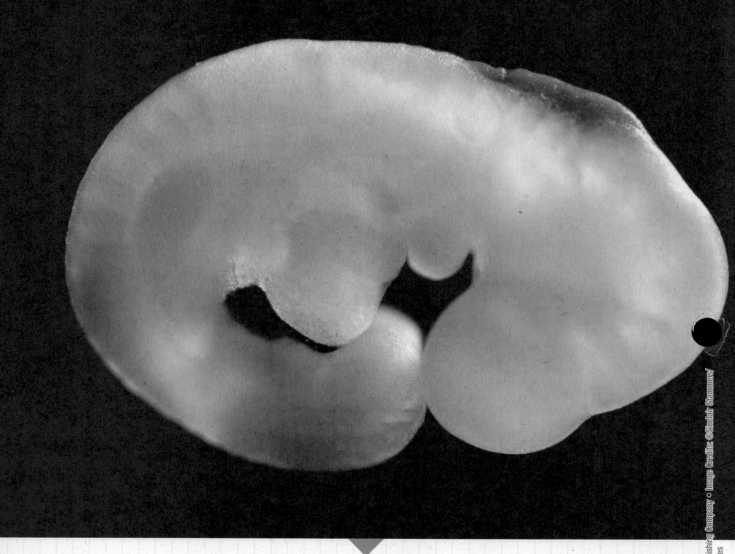

© Houghton Mifflin Harcourt Publishing Company • Image Credits: ©Sinclair Stammers/ Science Photo Library/Getty Images

This is a 9.5-day-old mouse embryo. It has yet to grow organ systems, but it has a head, a tail, and tiny limb buds. Its heart is developing in the larger bulge below its head.

Explore First

Inferring Relationships Sort mixed-up images of organisms at different stages of development. What features helped you match the images? Were you surprised by any mismatches?

CAN YOU EXPLAIN IT?

What evidence supports a relationship between *Confuciusornis* and modern birds?

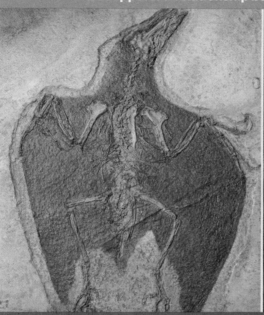

The fossil on the left is of an extinct animal called *Confuciusornis* that lived over 100 million years ago. The x-ray on the right shows the skeleton of a living crow species, *Corvus frugilegus*.

1. What similarities and differences can you observe from these photos?

2. Based on the fossil organism's body structures, how do you think it moved?

 EVIDENCE NOTEBOOK As you explore this lesson, gather evidence to help explain the relationship between *Confuciusornis* and modern birds.

Identifying Similarities among Organisms

What would you think if you planted a sunflower seed and it grew into an oak tree? You would probably be very surprised! Of course, that would never actually happen. You know that sunflower seeds grow into sunflower plants. Oak tree seeds, or acorns, grow into oak trees. This is an example of a consistent and observable pattern in nature: Offspring look similar to their parents. A key assumption of science is that natural systems have consistent, observable, and measurable patterns. These patterns and events happen in the same way today as they did in the past.

Explore Online

The baby elephant has a combination of genes from each parent. This is true of all offspring of living things that reproduce sexually. Because of this genetic recombination, the elephant will not be identical to either of its parents.

3. Would a baby elephant be more likely to look like its parent or to look like one of its great-great-great-grandparents? Explain your reasoning.

Living Organisms Reproduce and Pass on Traits

Organisms reproduce today just as they did in the past. In fact, organisms must reproduce or else life would no longer exist! We know that the offspring of sunflowers look similar to sunflowers, not oak trees. And the offspring of elephants look similar to elephants, not zebras. Offspring look similar to their parents because heritable traits are passed down from generation to generation. These heritable traits are encoded in genetic material called *DNA*. Genetic material is passed from generation to generation through the same processes today as it was in the past.

Evolution is the process of biological change by which populations become different from their ancestors over many generations. Differences develop in populations due to changes in the genetic material of individuals and the genetic make-up of populations. These changes build up over time, so the more recently two species shared a common ancestor, the more closely related those species are. **Common ancestry** is the idea that two or more species evolved from a single ancestor.

Evolution of Populations Over Time

Whales and fish have similar body shapes. However, they are not closely related. Whales, dolphins, and porpoises share a more recent common ancestor with land animals than they do with fish. In fact, these water dwellers' closest living relatives are hippos! Whales are very different from fish. They have lungs, nourish developing young inside the female's body, and produce milk. These characteristics are different from those of fish, but they are shared with mammals such as hippos.

Scientists learn about evolutionary relationships in many ways. They use a variety of evidence, including fossil evidence. They also analyze body structures and genetic evidence. All of these types of evidence support the hypothesis that modern whales evolved from hoofed mammals called *Anthracotheres* that lived on land.

Most Recent Common Ancestor of Whales and Hippopotamuses

Anthracotheres lived around 50–60 million years ago. Over many millions of years, *Anthracotherium* populations evolved and developed into two main groups of organisms.

One group that is descended from anthracotheres lived entirely in water. This group includes all species of whales, dolphins, and porpoises.

The other group lived mostly on land. Today, there are two species of hippos. They are the only remaining members of that group of land animals.

Evolution of Whales

The extinct species shown here are all ancient relatives of whales. The fossils of these extinct species have skeletal features that are similar to whales. Some features, such as the ear structure of the *Pakicetus*, are very similar to modern whales but unlike any other known mammal.

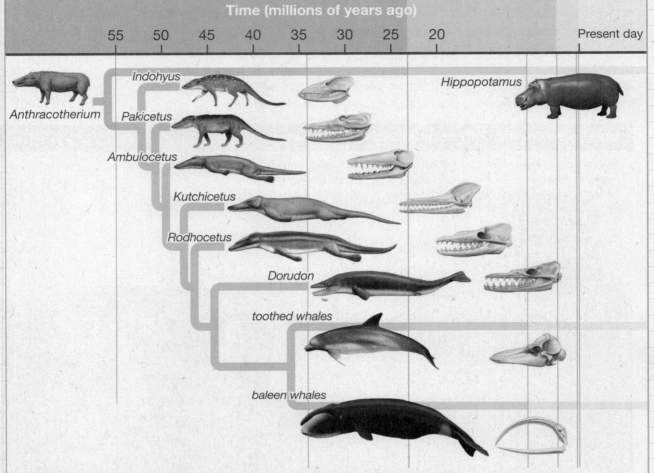

Time (millions of years ago)

55   50   45   40   35   30   25   20   Present day

Anthracotherium
Indohyus
Pakicetus
Ambulocetus
Kutchicetus
Rodhocetus
Dorudon
toothed whales
baleen whales
Hippopotamus

Credit: Adapted from *The Tangled Bank* by Carl Zimmer. Copyright © 2012 by Roberts and Company Publishers. Adapted and reprinted by permission of Macmillan Publishing Company.

4. Genetic information, in the form of DNA / fossils, gets passed from generation to generation. Because of this, offspring look similar to / very unlike their parents. Over time, genetic changes add up. Populations come to look more and more similar to / different from their ancestors. For whales, this explains why Pakicetus / Rodhocetus looks the most different from modern whales. It looks most different because it is a very ancient / recent relative of whales.

5. Which conclusion can be made from the diagram of whale evolution?

   A. All known whale ancestors had four legs.

   B. Whale ancestors transitioned from land to water habitats.

   C. Only skulls show evidence of relationships among whale ancestors.

   D. Whales always existed in their current form, along with many other relatives.

Engineer It

Apply the Use of 3D Printing to Model Fossils

Fossils can be both fragile and tiny, making them very difficult to study. One solution to this problem is using 3D printing technology. People can use 3D printers to make copies of fossils out of sturdy materials such as plastic. They can even make copies that are smaller or larger than the original fossil. Another advantage of 3D printing is that many copies of the fossil can be made.

A 3D printer allows this scientist to create a large model of a tiny 100-million-year-old fossilized ant.

6. Propose at least two ways that 3D printing could help students who are interested in studying fossils but do not have access to actual fossils.

Evidence of Evolutionary Relationships

Evolutionary relationships are inferred based on evidence from the fossil record. They are also inferred from similarities in the bodies of living organisms, similarities between living and fossilized organisms, and similarities among the embryos of different types of organisms. Recently, evolutionary relationships have also been studied at the genetic and molecular level. Scientists infer that the more similar species are at any level, the more closely related they are to each other.

Similarities in Anatomy

The **anatomy** of an organism is its body structure and its structural traits. Related organisms have a similar anatomy. For example, the body structures of insects are more like those of other insects than those of birds. Consider a structural trait such as feathers. It was once accepted that only birds had feathers. Soft, fluffy feathers provide insulation. Longer, sleeker feathers enable flight, but recent fossil discoveries reveal short structures in certain dinosaur fossils that look similar to certain modern bird feathers. Scientists identified these structures as feathers. These feathers provide evidence that dinosaurs and birds are more closely related to each other than was once thought.

7. The front limbs of the bat, dolphin, horse, and cat look different from each other and are used in different ways. But the skeletal structure of the limbs is similar. Use the colors of the leg bones of the bat, dolphin, and horse to color the similar bones of the cat.

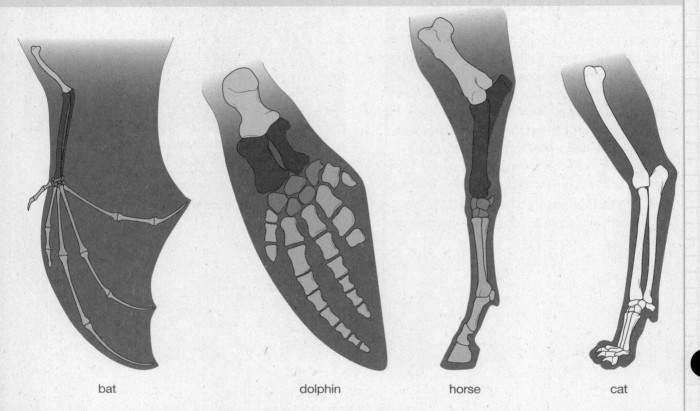

bat   dolphin   horse   cat

8. These limb bones have <u>similar / different</u> overall patterns of bones which can indicate a <u>close / distant</u> evolutionary relationship. However, the limb bones are different sizes and shapes. For example, the "finger" bones, shown in light blue and pink, are different in each animal. The <u>form / color</u> of the bones can help you identify the <u>function / age</u> of the limb.

Many four-legged organisms have similar leg structures that carry out similar functions. Similarities in anatomy can indicate evolutionary relationships. But they are not always the result of a close relationship. Some body structures evolved at different times. Some structures with similar functions also evolved in very different species. Think about the fins of whales and fish. The fins help both animals move in water. But they developed along very different evolutionary paths. So too did the wings in birds, bats, and insects. The presence and function of wings does not indicate a close evolutionary relationship between these groups of organisms because the anatomy of their wings differs so much.

 EVIDENCE NOTEBOOK

9. What anatomical structures do the *Confuciusornis* fossil and the *Corvus* (crow) share? Record your evidence.

Similarities in Embryo Development

The study of the development of organisms from fertilization until they are born or hatch is called **embryology**. Embryos undergo many changes as they grow and develop. Scientists compare the embryo development of different species to look for similar patterns and structures. Based on research and observation, scientists infer that such similarities come from an ancestor that the species have in common. For example, at some time during development, all animals with backbones have a tail. This observation suggests that all animals with a backbone have a common ancestor.

Gill slits are another example of a structure that is present in the early embryos of several animal species. For example, chicken embryos and human embryos both have a stage in which they have "slits" in their necks that are similar to the gill slits of fish. The tissues that make up these gill slits develop further to become parts of the jaw, ears, and neck. Based on this and other evidence, scientists infer that chickens and humans share a common ancestor with fish. Studies of embryo development are not limited to living species. Some fossilized embryos have been found. Scientists use observations from these embryos as evidence to explain the universal process of embryo development.

Early Stages of Embryo Development

A wide range of species go through the same stages of early embryo development. These similarities indicate that these species share a common ancestor.

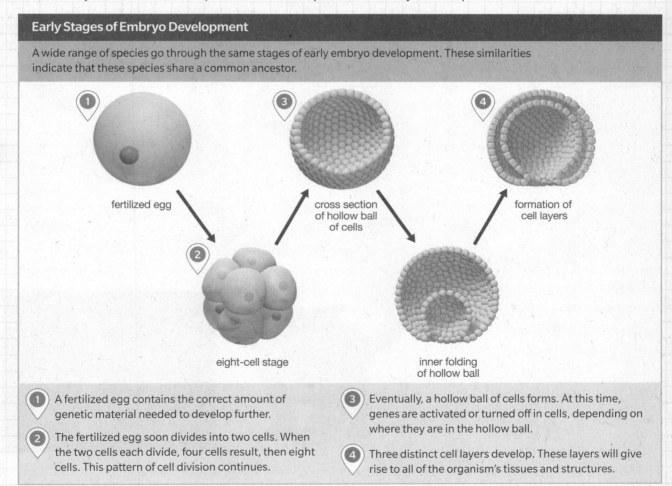

1 fertilized egg

2 eight-cell stage

3 cross section of hollow ball of cells

inner folding of hollow ball

4 formation of cell layers

1 A fertilized egg contains the correct amount of genetic material needed to develop further.

2 The fertilized egg soon divides into two cells. When the two cells each divide, four cells result, then eight cells. This pattern of cell division continues.

3 Eventually, a hollow ball of cells forms. At this time, genes are activated or turned off in cells, depending on where they are in the hollow ball.

4 Three distinct cell layers develop. These layers will give rise to all of the organism's tissues and structures.

10. Why might many different organisms have similar stages of early embryo development even when they have different traits at later stages? Explain your reasoning.

© Houghton Mifflin Harcourt Publishing Company

Embryo Development of Three Species

Different types of animals go through similar stages of embryo development.

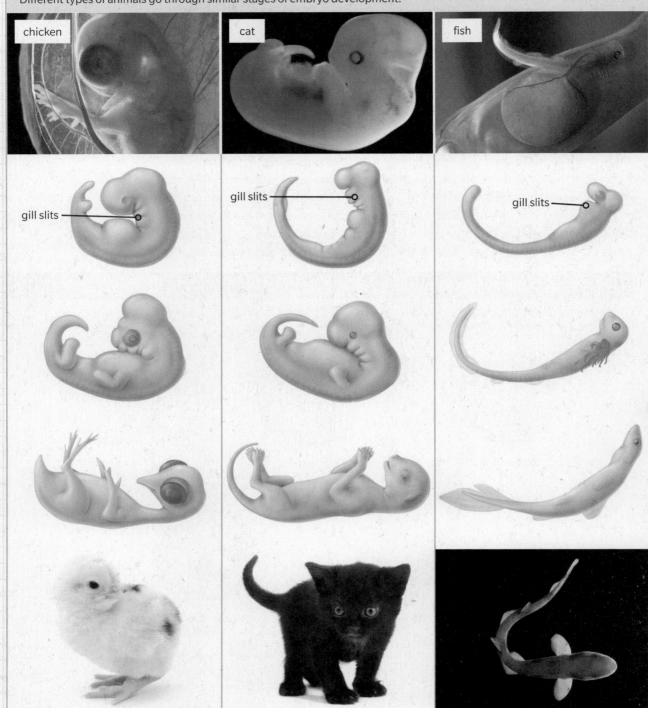

chicken

cat

fish

gill slits

gill slits

gill slits

11. Compare the structures of the cat and chicken embryos in the images above. Which characteristics do the species share as embryos that they do not share when they are fully developed? Select all that apply.

   A. Both animals have gill slits as embryos.

   B. Both animals have feathers as embryos.

   C. Both animals have similar upper limb buds as embryos.

   D. Both animals have tails as embryos.

© Houghton Mifflin Harcourt Publishing Company • Image Credits: (tl) ©J. M. Labat/Visual&Written SL/Alamy; (tc) ©Manfred Kage/Science Source; (tr) ©Paulo Oliveira/Alamy; (bl) ©Anatolii/Fotolia; (bc) ©Maxim Pimenov/Fotolia; (br) ©D.P. Wilson/FLPA/Science Source

EVIDENCE NOTEBOOK

12. What types of similarities would you expect to find in the embryo development of extinct and modern birds? Record your evidence.

Do the Math

Interpret the Geometry of Body Plans

The symmetry of an organism's body is inherited. So similarities and differences in body plans can be used to infer relatedness. Different groups of animals have characteristic body plans. For example, most animals' bodies have *bilateral symmetry*. For these animals, you could draw an imaginary line down the center of their bodies and both sides would be more or less identical to each other. Other animals have *radial symmetry*. These animals have many lines of symmetry. Sponges are an example of an organism with an *asymmetrical* body plan, which means their bodies have no symmetry.

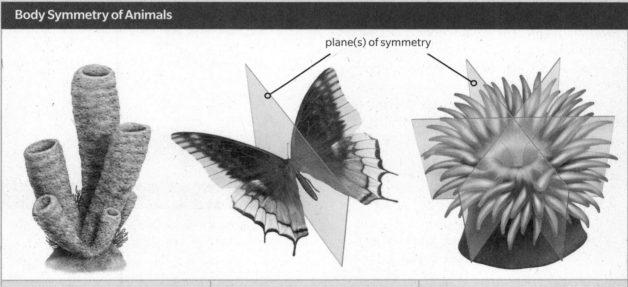

Body Symmetry of Animals

plane(s) of symmetry

| A sponge has no body symmetry. | A butterfly has bilateral symmetry. | A sea anemone has radial symmetry. |

13. The body plan of the sea slug shown in the photo has no / bilateral / radial symmetry.

14. Organisms that have similar body symmetry are considered to be more closely related to each other than to organisms with different body symmetry. Which organism in the diagram do you think this sea slug is more closely related to? Explain your answer.

_____

_____

_____

_____

Inferring Evolutionary Relationships among Organisms

Data from fossils help scientists to make inferences about extinct organisms. For example, data from fossils can be used to infer the sizes of living things, their life spans, what they ate, and how they moved. As new fossils are found, new observations are used to support, modify, or correct earlier ideas. Understanding how living things have changed over time is an ongoing process. New information adds to what scientists understand about evolutionary processes.

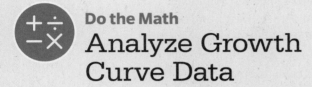

Do the Math

Analyze Growth Curve Data

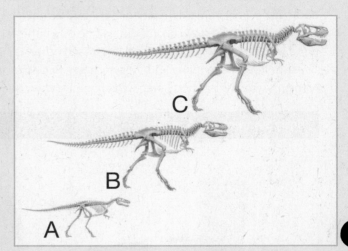

Scientists have found fossils of the various growth stages of many extinct species, including *Tyrannosaurus rex* (*T. rex*). Observations from these fossils are used to infer how the extinct species grew. When the different ages of *T. rex* fossils were first found, it was thought that they were different species because they looked so different. The data used to plot the graph were collected from the fossils of seven *T. rex* individuals.

15. Imagine you are a scientist studying two different *T. rex* fossils.

- Observations from one fossil suggest it is from a *T. rex* with a body mass of about 2,000 kg.

- The other fossil is from a *T. rex* with a body mass of about 3,500 kg.

Based on the growth curve data, what is the age difference between these two fossilized dinosaurs? Why can you assume the larger *T. rex* is more mature, not just bigger? Defend your answer using evidence from the graph.

Growth Curve of *T. rex*

Points A, B, and C represent the sizes of the juvenile, adolescent, and adult *T. rex* shown in the illustration.

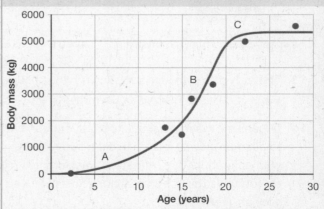

Credit: Adapted from "Gigantism and comparative life-history parameters of tyrannosaurid dinosaurs" by Gregory M. Erickson, et al, from *Nature*. Adapted by permission from Macmillan Publishers Ltd: *Nature* (430), 772–775. Copyright © 2004.

Hands-On Lab
Make Inferences from Evidence

Make inferences based on visual observations, then modify these inferences based on new information and data.

Scientists usually do not have all of the pieces of evidence for the topic they are studying. Instead, they work to understand the natural world by making connections, inferences, and predictions using the information they have.

MATERIALS
• picture, cut into strips

Procedure

STEP 1 Study the strips of an image provided by your teacher. Write down all observations and inferences that you can make about this picture.

STEP 2 Make a prediction about what is shown in the picture. Use your observations to support your prediction.

STEP 3 Record observations, inferences, and a prediction as you receive each remaining strip of "new information" from your teacher.

Analysis

STEP 4 Explain how you modified your prediction about what the picture shows as you gathered more information about the picture.

STEP 5 How is this process similar to how scientists make inferences from fossil evidence? How is it different?

© Houghton Mifflin Harcourt Publishing Company

Lesson 4 Fossils and Living Organisms Provide Evidence of Evolution **377**

Relationships among Fossil Organisms and Living Organisms

Body structures and other features of fossilized organisms may be similar to features present in modern organisms. In general, the more recently the fossilized organism lived, the more similar its body structures are to modern, living organisms.

Similarities and differences in anatomy are used to make inferences about evolutionary relationships among living and extinct organisms. Scientists revise and refine their understanding of evolutionary relationships as new evidence is found.

Case Study: Evolution of Elephants

Modern elephants belong to a group of mammals that includes extinct animals such as the mammoth and the mastodon. Until recently, it was thought that there were only two living elephant species: the African elephant and the Asian elephant. There were two types of African elephant that looked very different from each other. After analyzing DNA, scientists found larger differences between the two types of African elephants than they would expect from the same species. They concluded that there are two African elephant species: savanna elephants and forest elephants.

Scientists have also used anatomical data to make inferences about how modern elephants are related to extinct relatives. For example, scientists use tooth shape to study relatedness among elephants and their ancestors. Modern elephants have flat, ridged teeth to grind up the tough plants they eat. Like elephants, mammoths and mastodons were herbivores. The form of their teeth helped them chew their food.

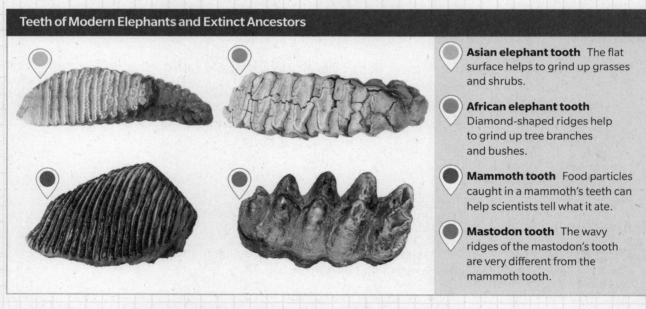

Teeth of Modern Elephants and Extinct Ancestors

Asian elephant tooth The flat surface helps to grind up grasses and shrubs.

African elephant tooth Diamond-shaped ridges help to grind up tree branches and bushes.

Mammoth tooth Food particles caught in a mammoth's teeth can help scientists tell what it ate.

Mastodon tooth The wavy ridges of the mastodon's tooth are very different from the mammoth tooth.

16. Look at the teeth of the four different animals. Based on the structure of the teeth, which extinct animal do you think is most closely related to the Asian elephant? Support your answer with evidence.

Elephant Lineage

The relationships in this diagram were determined by examining the anatomy of modern animals and extinct animal fossils, as well as embryological and genetic data.

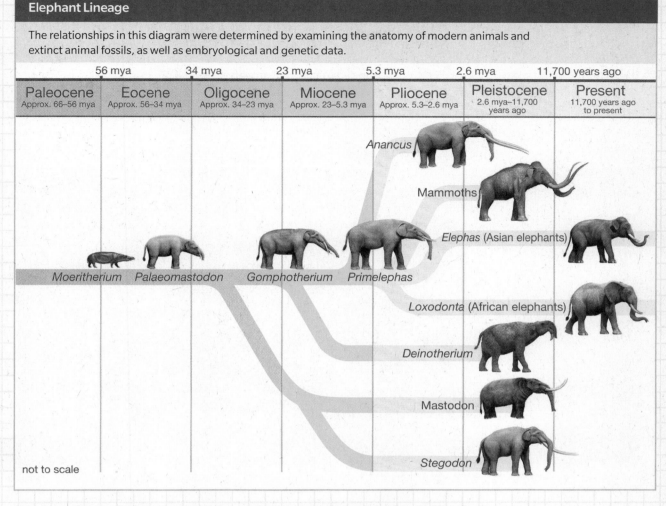

56 mya	34 mya	23 mya	5.3 mya	2.6 mya	11,700 years ago
Paleocene Approx. 66–56 mya	**Eocene** Approx. 56–34 mya	**Oligocene** Approx. 34–23 mya	**Miocene** Approx. 23–5.3 mya	**Pliocene** Approx. 5.3–2.6 mya	**Pleistocene** 2.6 mya–11,700 years ago	**Present** 11,700 years ago to present

Anancus

Mammoths

Elephas (Asian elephants)

Moeritherium   *Palaeomastodon*   *Gomphotherium*   *Primelephas*

Loxodonta (African elephants)

Deinotherium

Mastodon

Stegodon

not to scale

17. Scientists work to understand the evolutionary history of elephants. They look at embryological / anatomical data, such as tooth structure. They infer that Asian / African elephants are most closely related to the mammoth because both animals have very similar / different tooth structures.

18. Based on the diagram, which animal—extinct or alive—would you expect to be most closely related to the mastodon? How long ago did this animal live? Explain your answer.

 EVIDENCE NOTEBOOK

19. What evidence from the *Confuciusornis* fossil could help explain its evolutionary relationship with living birds? Record your evidence.

Defend a Claim with Evidence

The Ashfall Fossil Beds in northeast Nebraska contain many well-preserved fossils of ancient animals. The most common fossilized animal found there is the barrel-bodied rhinoceros (*Teleoceras major*). Fossils of five different species of horses are also found at the beds. About 12 million years ago, these animals all died and were buried in volcanic ash.

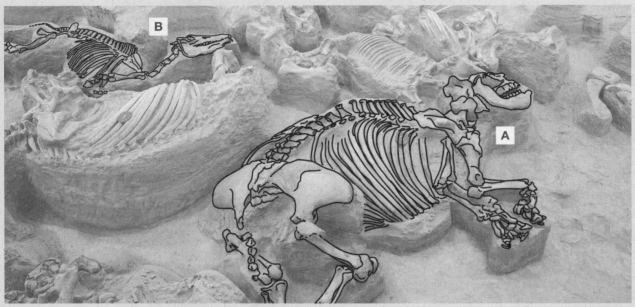

The lines on this photo outline the bone structures of an extinct rhino and a horse that are found in the Ashfall Fossil Beds. It is possible to see some of the anatomical similarities between the fossilized rhino and the living rhino and between the fossilized horse and the living horse.

Black rhinoceros (*Diceros bicornis*)

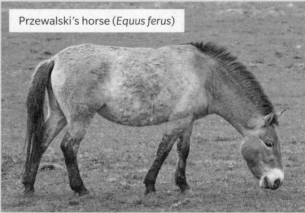

Przewalski's horse (*Equus ferus*)

20. Make a claim about which fossil, A or B, is the rhino and which fossil is the horse. Use anatomical evidence from the photos to defend your claim.

_____

_____

_____

_____

Continue Your Exploration

Name: _____   Date: _____

Check out the path below or go online to choose one of the other paths shown.

Careers in Science

- **People in Science**
- **Classification of Living Things**
- **Hands-On Labs** 🖐
- **Propose Your Own Path**

Go online to choose one of these other paths.

Museum Exhibit Designer

Museum exhibit designers and educators help communicate scientific ideas to the general public through fun exhibits. Exhibit designers use creativity and innovation to share complex ideas in understandable, engaging, and interactive ways. They need a deep understanding of scientific ideas. They also need an understanding of how people learn about science and interact with museum exhibits. A successful exhibit connects with the people who go to the museum. Designers, educators, and others often collaborate to come up with new and exciting ways to share scientific ideas with learners of all ages. Today's science museums often have many opportunities for visitors to actively participate in science.

Interacting with a "living dinosaur" allows students to have fun while learning about the past.

Continue Your Exploration

1. Think of a topic that you would enjoy learning about through a museum exhibit. Describe the topic and why you chose it.

2. Imagine you are an exhibit designer. Using words and drawings, describe how you would set up an exhibit about the topic you chose in order to share it with visitors.

3. What are some limitations you may need to consider while designing your exhibit?

4. **Collaborate** Work with classmates to design an exhibit about a topic from this lesson.
   - Identify the likely visitors to your exhibit (for example, third- to fifth-graders).
   - Propose one or two key messages that you want to communicate in the exhibit.
   - Describe or produce at least one interactive experience for your exhibit.
   - Share your exhibit design with others.

© Houghton Mifflin Harcourt Publishing Company

Can You Explain It?

Name: _____   Date: _____

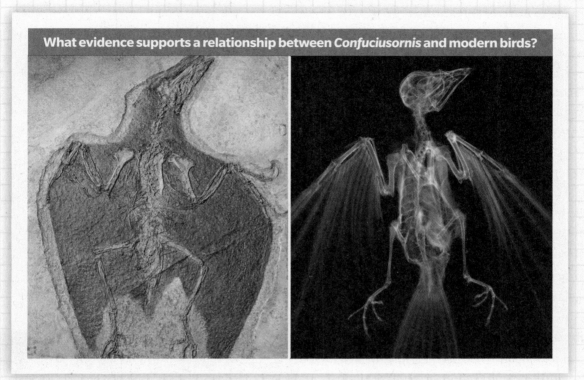

What evidence supports a relationship between *Confuciusornis* and modern birds?

EVIDENCE NOTEBOOK

Refer to the notes in your Evidence Notebook to help you construct an explanation of how evidence indicates that *Confuciusornis* and modern birds are related.

1. State your claim. Make sure your claim fully explains how the extinct and modern organisms might be related.

2. Summarize the evidence you have gathered to support your claim and explain your reasoning.

Checkpoints

Answer the following questions to check your understanding of the lesson.

Use the image to answer Question 3.

3. Gill slits are structural features in cat embryos that *are / are not* found in a fully developed cat. The presence of gill slits is evidence that cats share a common ancestor with chickens and other organisms that have gill slits *as adults/ during embryo development.*

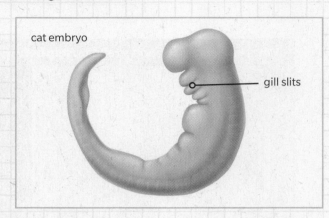

cat embryo

gill slits

4. Which of the following observations provide evidence of evolutionary relatedness among organisms? Select all that apply.

   A. similarities in body structures

   B. similarities in molecular structures

   C. similarities in embryological development

   D. similarities in the foods that organisms eat

Use the photos to answer Question 5.

5. Which statement is the most logical inference that can be made based on observations of the photos?

   A. The two organisms shown are likely related because they have similarities in leaf structure.

   B. The two organisms shown are likely related because the fossilized plant was green like the living plant.

   C. The two organisms shown are NOT likely related because one is a fossil and the other is living.

   D. The two organisms shown are NOT likely related because there is no evidence that they grow and develop in similar ways.

fossil fern

live fern

6. Which description best explains what scientists do if new evidence is found about evolutionary relationships that is different from evidence already gathered?

   A. Scientists discard earlier ideas about the evolutionary relationships.

   B. Scientists revise their understanding about evolutionary relationships.

   C. Scientists rarely change their ideas even if new evidence is found.

   D. Scientists change evidence to fit existing ideas of evolutionary relationships.

Interactive Review

Complete this section to review the main concepts of the lesson.

Offspring look similar to their parents because heritable traits are passed down from parent to offspring. Over time, genetic changes in populations build up.

A. How can anatomy be used to study relationships among different types of organisms?

   A. The more closely related organisms are, the more similar their anatomy is.

   B. Having body structures that look different but have similar functions, such as the wings of insects and birds, indicates a close evolutionary relationship.

   C. The more distantly related organisms are, the more dissimilar their anatomy is.

   D. Developmental stages of embryos can be compared to infer relatedness.

Scientists use fossil, anatomical, embryological, and genetic evidence to make inferences about evolutionary relationships.

B. Explain how inferences about evolutionary relationships can change as new evidence is discovered.

© Houghton Mifflin Harcourt Publishing Company • Image Credits: (t) ©john michael evan potter/Shutterstock; (b) ©Colin Keates/Dorling Kindersley/Natural History Museum, London/Science Source

Choose one of the activities below to explore how this unit connects to other topics.

People in Science

Marie Curie, Chemist and Physicist

Marie Curie was the first woman to win a Nobel prize, and the first person to win two Nobel prizes. The second prize was for her discovery of the elements radium and polonium. Curie found that some forms of these elements break down into different elements by releasing particles. Until her discovery, scientists thought that atoms could not change.

Research social conditions for women during Marie Curie's life. How common was it for women to be scientists? Create a pamphlet from your findings.

Computer Science Connection

Recreating Dinosaurs Using 3D Technology

Advancements in computer animated three-dimensional (3D) technology allow paleontologists to create replicas of dinosaur bones, or fill in missing bones of a partial skeleton fossil. This technology allows scientists to test hypotheses about how dinosaurs and other prehistoric animals moved and lived in their environment.

Using library or Internet resources, research how paleontologists use advancements in 3D scanners and printers to learn more from fossils. Present your findings to the class.

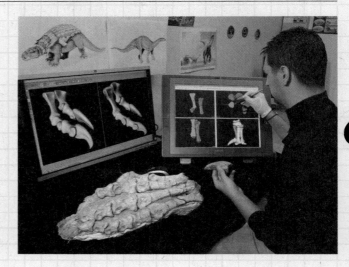

Physical Science Connection

Rock Dating Radioactive isotopes are unstable particles that break down, or *decay*, into more stable particles at a precise rate. Different radioactive isotopes decay at different rates. Scientists compare the amount of a radioactive isotope to the amount of stable particles in a rock sample to find its age.

Research a radioactive isotope that scientists use to estimate the ages of rocks. Identify the *half-life* of this isotope and the stable particles that are formed. Present a graph that shows the decay rate of the isotope over time. Use the graph to help explain what a half-life is and how scientists use the decay rate to estimate the age of the rock sample in which the isotope is found.

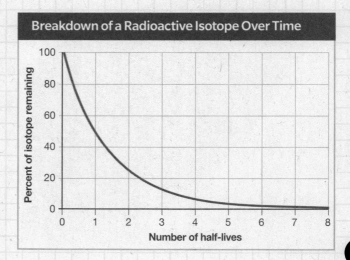

Breakdown of a Radioactive Isotope Over Time

Name: _____ **Date:** _____

Use the images to answer Questions 1–3.

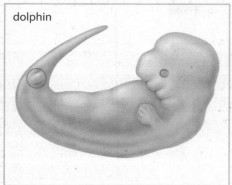 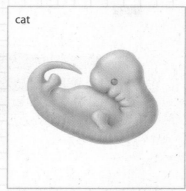 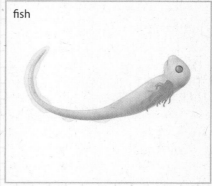

Shown are a dolphin, a cat, and a fish embryo. The red circle on the dolphin embryo indicates the beginning of a hind limb structure.

1. Compare the embryo images above. Describe any similarities you see.

2. Dolphins, whales, and porpoises belong to a group of marine animals that are related to hippos. What evidence of this relationship is present in the images above that is not present in the adult animals? Explain your answer.

3. Based on the images above, which two animals would you expect to have the most recent common ancestor? Explain your answer.

Use the chart to answer Questions 4–7.

4. Which group of organisms represented in this graphic appears earliest in the fossil record? Which group appears most recently?

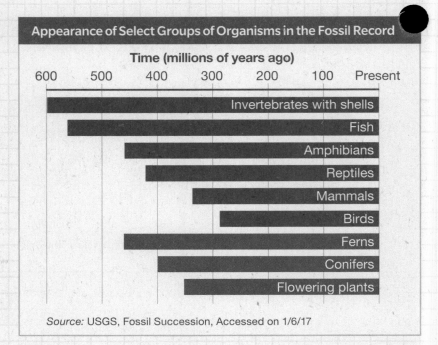

Appearance of Select Groups of Organisms in the Fossil Record

Time (millions of years ago)

600   500   400   300   200   100   Present

Invertebrates with shells
Fish
Amphibians
Reptiles
Mammals
Birds
Ferns
Conifers
Flowering plants

Source: USGS, Fossil Succession, Accessed on 1/6/17

5. Would you expect the earliest mammal fossils to be found in deeper or shallower layers of rock than the earliest fern fossils? Explain your reasoning.

6. Describe how this graphic provides evidence for the general pattern of increasing diversity of life over time.

7. Only multicellular organisms are represented in this graphic. Given that most fossils older than 500 million years are single-celled marine organisms, describe the changes in the level of complexity of organisms in the fossil record over time.

Name: Date:

How did marine fossils end up in the desert?

Imagine that you were hiking at the Grand Canyon in Arizona and you discovered a fossil of a cephalopod embedded within limestone rock. You asked the tour guide about the fossil and learned that a cephalopod was a marine organism that is closely related to a squid. You began to wonder how a marine fossil ended up in this dry, hot desert region. You decided to learn more about the age of this fossil and the environment in which this organism thrived. In order to do this, you need to research the Grand Canyon area and its geologic history. Construct an explanation of how the cephalopod fossil's age was determined and how it ended up in this region.

Cephalopod fossil   The Grand Canyon in Arizona

The steps below will help guide your research and help you construct your explanation.

1. **Define the Problem** Investigate to learn more about cephalopods and other marine fossils found in the Arizona desert. Define the problem you are trying to solve.

2. **Conduct Research** Do research to identify the rock layers in the Grand Canyon and the types of fossils found in each layer.

3. **Analyze Data** What is the name of the rock layer in which cephalopod fossils are commonly found? What type of rock is this layer? Explain your answer.

4. **Interpret Data** Using the data you collected in Steps 1–3, what can you infer about the past environments of this area? Describe any events in Earth's history or geologic processes that may have contributed to the changing environment.

5. **Construct an Explanation** What is the age of the cephalopod fossil you found? What was the environment like in the area at that time? Provide evidence to support your claim.

✓ **Self-Check**

	I identified the rock layer and type of rock in which the fossil was found.
	I researched how geologic processes could have contributed to the Grand Canyon's past environments.
	I analyzed data to estimate an age of the cephalopod fossil.
	I provided evidence to identify the environment of the cephalopod.

Evolution and Biotechnology

How do biological processes explain life's unity and diversity?

© Houghton Mifflin Harcourt Publishing Company • Image Credits: ©Layne Kennedy/ Corbis Documentary/Getty Images

The Galápagos prickly pear cactus is common on the Galápagos Islands, but they do not live anywhere else on Earth. Small finches build their nests between the prickly cactus pads.

You Solve It How Can You Engineer Fluorescent Algae?

Use a bioengineering simulation to produce microalgae that have fluorescent organelles.

Go online and complete the You Solve It to explore ways to solve a real-world problem.

Explore Biotechnology and Crops

The banana trees grown on this banana plantation are all almost genetically identical.

A. Look at the photo. On a separate sheet of paper, write down as many different questions as you can about the photo.

B. Discuss With your class or a partner, share your questions. Record any additional questions generated in your discussion. Then choose the most important questions from the list that are related to food or fiber crops that humans have influenced genetically. Write them below.

C. Choose a food or fiber crop that humans have influenced genetically through artificial selection, genetic modification, or a combination of both. Here's a list of crops you might consider:

bananas	cotton	wheat
corn	soybean	potatoes
jute	tomato	

D. Use the information above, along with your research, to create a timeline that explains the development of a crop over time and how this crop has affected society.

Discuss the next steps for your Unit Project with your teacher and go online to download the Unit Project Worksheet.

Language Development

Use the lessons in this unit to complete the network and expand your understanding of these key concepts.

Similar term
Phrase
Cognate
Example
Definition

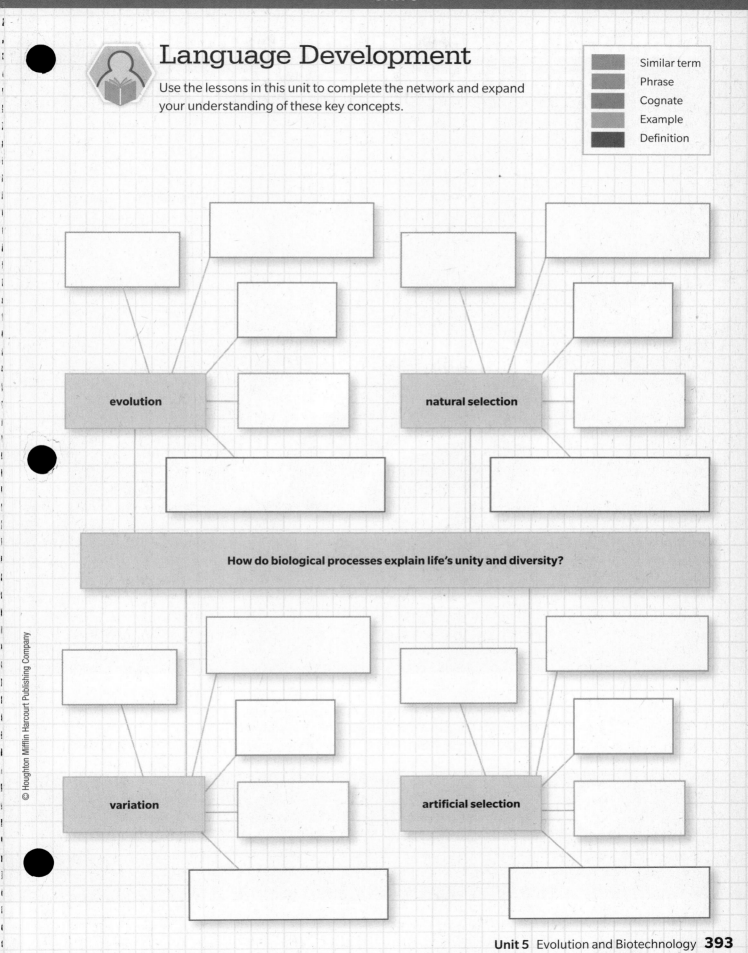

evolution

natural selection

How do biological processes explain life's unity and diversity?

variation

artificial selection

© Houghton Mifflin Harcourt Publishing Company

Natural Selection Explains How Populations Can Change

A manta ray uses long fins on each side of its head to funnel tiny organisms into its mouth. This adaptation helps manta rays gather enough food to support their huge size.

Explore First

Modeling Change Design an activity, model, or experiment that demonstrates how small changes over time can lead to large differences. What examples of change can you find in natural and human-made systems?

Go online to view the digital version of the Hands-On Lab for this lesson and to download additional lab resources.

CAN YOU EXPLAIN IT?

How has the smell of rotting flesh become an adaptation for the rafflesia flower?

Rafflesia flowers smell like rotting flesh. This attracts flies and other insect pollinators.

1. Flowers of many plants produce scents. A flower can smell sweet, fruity, musty, or spicy. How do you think having a specific flower scent benefits a plant?

 EVIDENCE NOTEBOOK As you explore the lesson, gather evidence to help explain how the rotting flesh smell became an adaptation for the rafflesia flower.

Explaining the Diversity of Life

Life on Earth comes in many forms. The diversity of life includes tiny bacteria, giant redwood trees, and everything in between. There are millions of known species on Earth and new ones are discovered every day. Classifying the diversity of life is made easier by using a field of biology called *taxonomy*. This system groups organisms based on similarities and differences between them.

Explore Online

2. **Discuss** Pick three living things. Take turns asking a partner simple questions about his or her living things to help determine how they are similar and how they are different.

Change over Time

Ideas of how life changes over time started to come together in the early 1800's. Naturalists thought about how traits are inherited, or passed from parent to offspring. Acquired traits—traits that an organism develops during its lifetime—are not heritable. However, traits with a genetic basis can be passed from parent to offspring.

Around the same time, geologists were studying how Earth changes gradually over time. The processes that change Earth are the same now as they have been in the past, and will be in the future. If Earth can change slowly over time, maybe populations could also change over time.

Studies of human populations also helped scientists think about change over time. Human populations can grow exponentially, but food and other resources cannot be increased as quickly. This leads to competition over resources that drives changes in human populations.

Incorporating many of these ideas, Alfred Russel Wallace and Charles Darwin separately developed an explanation for how life changes over time. Darwin used evidence from living and fossil organisms to support his ideas. There is competition among organisms to survive. Organisms that are well suited to an environment are more likely to survive and reproduce than organisms that are less suited to the same environment. These organisms pass their traits to their offspring. Over time, beneficial traits may increase in frequency in a population.

These rock layers formed over millions of years.

Evidence of Change

It can be difficult to observe change in a population, especially for organisms that live a long time. However, there are many lines of evidence that support the claim that populations change over time. This evidence includes changes seen in the fossil record, patterns in biogeography (where organisms are located), DNA analysis of degree of relatedness, directed change through selective breeding, and comparative anatomy and embryology that show similarities and differences in how organisms develop.

The Galápagos Islands were visited by Darwin during an international sea voyage. Darwin studied populations and fossils on the islands and found evidence of populations changing over time. When organisms on the islands are compared to related organisms on the mainland, it is possible to determine when some organisms arrived on the islands and how the island populations have changed in response to their new environments.

3. **Collaborate** With a partner or group, select one line of evidence that can be supported by examples from the Galápagos Islands to explain how populations change over time. Combine examples into a class-wide case study about population change on the Galápagos Islands.

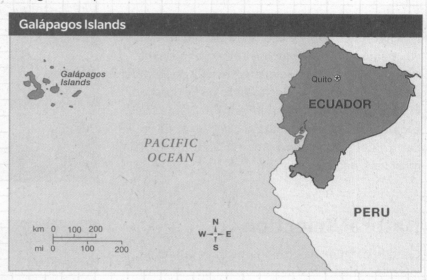

Galápagos Islands

Galápagos Islands

Quito ⊕

ECUADOR

PACIFIC OCEAN

PERU

km 0   100 200

mi 0   100   200

N
W—+—E
S

Linking Change over Time to the Diversity of Life

Populations naturally change over time as beneficial traits become more common in a population. Eventually, a population of organisms may change so much that a new species develops.

4. The beetles on the previous page are all different species. How can change over time account for the diversity of beetles?

_____

_____

_____

_____

_____

_____

_____

_____

_____

_____

Modeling Natural Selection

The three-toed sloth and the nine-banded armadillo look very different from each other, but fossil evidence, DNA analysis, and comparative anatomy indicate that they share a common ancestor that lived millions of years ago. Genetic change over many generations resulted in these two species. Three-toed sloths have strong arms and sharp claws, adaptations that allow them to live in trees. Armor-like plates provide protection for armadillos, which live on the forest floor. How did these adaptations arise? **Evolution** is the change in the inherited traits of a population over many generations. On a small scale, evolution leads to the adaptation of a population to its environment. On a large scale, evolution leads to the amazing diversity of life on Earth. But in order for evolution to occur, a population must have genetic variation.

three-toed sloth

nine-banded armadillo

Natural Selection

Genetic variation determines the traits possible in a population. However, a population's current environment determines if any of those traits provide advantages or disadvantages. For example, the ability for the horned lizard to squirt toxic blood from its eyes helps the lizard avoid becoming a meal for a coyote. However, a coyote with very strong legs might be able to run fast enough to attack the lizard by surprise. **Natural selection** is a process by which a population's environment determines which traits are beneficial and which are not.

Evolution by natural selection occurs in populations, not individuals. Individuals with traits that are advantageous in an environment are better able to survive and reproduce. These traits get passed on more often to the next generation than less helpful traits. While evolution can occur by several different processes, natural selection is the only nonrandom cause of evolution in nature.

Explore Online

This horned lizard has poisonous, foul smelling blood that it squirts out of its eyes as a defense against predators.

© Houghton Mifflin Harcourt Publishing Company • Image Credits: (t) ©Roy Toft/National Geographic/Getty Images; (c) ©sdbower/Fotolia; (b) ©Raymond Mendez/Animals Animals/Earth Scenes

Evolution by Natural Selection

Owls are birds of prey that hunt other animals for food. The great horned owl can be found in many habitats between the Arctic and South America. These owls are named for tufts of feathers on their heads that look like horns. A wide wingspan, powerful talons, and keen eyesight make these owls effective hunters. Evolution by natural selection over many millions of years resulted in these adaptations. In order for natural selection to occur, certain conditions must be present in a population.

Great horned owls can catch large prey, such as other birds. They also eat small rodents, frogs, and scorpions.

Variation in Traits

Through sexual reproduction, offspring get half of their genes from one parent and half from the other parent. There is also variation in which of each parent's genes are passed to each offspring. These owl chicks receive unique genetic combinations that result in genetic variation in the owl population. Random genetic mutations can also add new traits to the owl population. Adaptation is possible when genetic variation provides a variety of traits in the population. Some of these traits may increase a chick's chance of surviving and reproducing.

There are genetic differences between young owls in the same clutch.

5. **Discuss** Brainstorm a list of traits for which there might be genetic variation in this clutch of owls.

Inheritance of Variation

Great horned owl offspring inherit different traits from their parents. For example, some owl chicks may inherit traits that provide advantages in the environment, such as longer talons or sharper eyesight. Others may receive less beneficial traits, such as weaker wing muscles or low birth weight. Animals tend to overproduce, which means they have more offspring than will survive to maturity. The offspring that do survive can pass their traits to their own offspring.

Nearly 30 pounds of force is needed to open the talons of a great horned owl. Captured prey have little chance of escape.

6. Variation in great horned owl body size due to food supply *can / cannot* be acted on by natural selection. Variation in body size due to inherited traits *can / cannot* be acted on by natural selection.

Differential Survival

A population's environment determines which traits allow for a better chance of survival and reproductive success. Over many generations, traits that help an organism survive in the environment tend to add up in a population. Owls with sharper vision can hunt prey better and outcompete owls with poorer vision. These well-fed owls are more likely to survive and pass on their genes to the next generation. Competition is one contributor to natural selection. As the process of natural selection continues through each generation, more and more owls inherit helpful traits.

7. Most birds have feathers that make "whooshing" sounds when they fly. Owls have feathers that result in near-silent flight, allowing them to sneak up on prey. Explain how natural selection led to this adaptation for owls.

Hands-On Lab
Analyze Salamander Species Distribution

Use habitat comparisons and a map to analyze the distribution of a group of closely related California salamanders. Use your analysis to write an explanation about how these different salamanders may have arisen from a common ancestor.

Procedure and Analysis

STEP 1 Read the information about each salamander and its habitat. These salamanders are subspecies of *Ensatina eschscholtzii*. A *subspecies* is a specific group within a species. Make your own salamander card for each subspecies.

STEP 2 On the next page, study the map that shows salamander distribution. Notice that the Central Valley forms a barrier between certain subspecies. Identify which salamanders live on each side of the valley.

STEP 3 Describe any patterns in physical appearance and habitat with the subspecies on each side of the Central Valley.

Habitats of *Ensatina* Salamanders in California

E.e. xanthoptica live in coastal mountain ranges, often hiding under moist logs within coastal forests. The region has a Mediterranean climate.

E.e. platensis live in the inland forests of the Sierra Nevada mountains. Patterned skin helps them hide from predators during the dry summers.

E.e. oregonensis live in coastal mountain ranges and northern forests. They find ample hiding places within the damp forests of the north.

E.e. eschscholtzii live in coastal mountain ranges. They forage for worms and centipedes within the moist soil of coastal forests.

E.e. klauberi live in inland forests of the southern coastal mountain range. Closest to the Mojave Desert, they seek shelter from hawks within lakeside forests.

E.e. croceater live in dry forests of the southern coastal mountain range. With few shrubs for cover, yellow patterning helps them hide on lichen-patched trees.

E.e. picta live in a small range along the Pacific coast in northwest California. Their coloring helps them blend in with logs and leaves they live in on the forest floor.

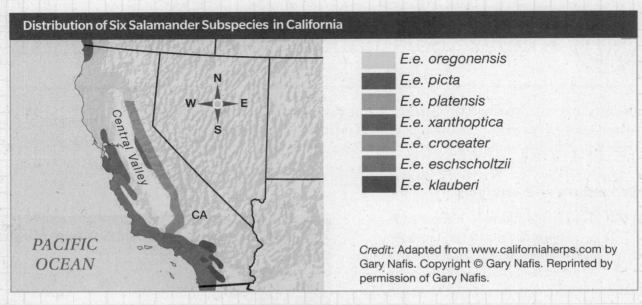

Distribution of Six Salamander Subspecies in California

E.e. oregonensis
E.e. picta
E.e. platensis
E.e. xanthoptica
E.e. croceater
E.e. eschscholtzii
E.e. klauberi

PACIFIC OCEAN

Central Valley

CA

Credit: Adapted from www.californiaherps.com by Gary Nafis. Copyright © Gary Nafis. Reprinted by permission of Gary Nafis.

STEP 4 Use the salamander cards to model how these subspecies may have arisen from a common ancestor as populations spread from the north around California's long Central Valley. Describe your model as a sequence of steps that account for how each subspecies could have formed.

STEP 5 Compare your sequence from Step 4 with the sequence of another classmate or group. Do you have similar evolution stories? Describe any differences.

8. When an environmental change is extreme and rapid, populations may be less / more likely to adapt because the process of natural selection occurs over one / many generation(s). In these cases, populations may be less / more likely to become extinct.

EVIDENCE NOTEBOOK

9. What environmental factors might make a strong odor an advantage for the rafflesia plant? Record your evidence.

Engineer It

Control Selection to Meet Human Needs

Scientists can use their understanding about how the natural world works to engineer solutions to problems. For example, understanding the process of natural selection allows scientists and farmers to work together to produce healthy, plentiful crops for the rapidly growing human population. They can identify beneficial plant traits and control reproduction, making it possible for these traits to be passed on to offspring. This is called *artificial selection* because people, not nature, are selecting desired traits.

10. One source of groundwater pollution is pesticide runoff from crop fields. How could artificial selection be used to address this problem?

   A. Farmers select plants that are most resistant to pests, which reduces the need for pesticides.

   B. Farmers select plants that are least resistant to pests, which increases the need for pesticides.

   C. The environment selects plants that are most resistant to pests, which reduces the need for pesticides.

   D. The environment selects plants that are least resistant to pests, which increases the need for pesticides.

Using artificial selection to improve plant resistance to pests can greatly increase crop yields.

11. What trait would make an individual likely to survive and reproduce in a pest population that feeds on pest-resistant plants? Use your answer to describe a trade-off to using artificial selection to reduce pesticide use.

_____

_____

_____

_____

Relating Genetic Variation to the Distribution of Traits

The distribution of traits in a population can change over time. Sometimes, a sudden change in the environment can affect the distribution of traits in a random way. For example, after a wildfire there might randomly be mostly blue flowers in a lupine population. Other distribution changes are not due to chance and may be predicted using evidence. For example, a newly arrived butterfly population prefers to pollinate white lupine. It is reasonable to predict that lupine color will shift toward white in future generations.

conehead katydid

12. The conehead katydid is an insect that can be either brown or green in color. They are eaten by many predators, including birds, bats, and lizards. What are some random and nonrandom factors that might change how many katydids of each color are found in an area?

Variation in Populations

All organisms of the same species that live in the same geographical area make up a *population*. **Variation** refers to differences between organisms in a population. This variation can be differences in physical features, behaviors, or any other characteristic that is measurable. *Genetic variation* refers to different types of genes in a population for an inherited characteristic, such as flower color or tail length. For evolution to occur, there must be genetic variation in some of the traits present in the population. Genetic variation can be introduced in a population through gene mutations and the movement of individuals between populations. It can also be introduced by new combinations of genes formed during the process of sexual reproduction.

Do the Math
Calculate Allele Frequencies

Different forms of the same gene are called *alleles*. Biologists study how populations evolve by measuring allele frequencies. An **allele frequency** is a measurement of how common a certain allele is in a population. Evolution can occur when an allele frequency changes in a population from one generation to the next.

Mongolian gerbils can be agouti (brown) or black, depending on the combination of alleles they inherit for fur color. The combination of inherited alleles is called a *genotype*. The genotype determines the organism's *phenotype*, or physical characteristics, such as fur color.

13. A population of 200 Mongolian gerbils living near Russia's Lake Baikal includes 80 brown gerbils with the *AA* genotype, 64 brown gerbils with the *Aa* genotype, and 56 black gerbils with the *aa* genotype. Use this information to complete the table.

Genotype	Number of individuals	Number of A alleles	Number of a alleles
AA			
Aa			
aa			
Total number of each allele			
Total number of alleles (A+a)			

The frequency of an allele can be found by first writing a ratio that compares the number of that allele in the population to the total number of alleles in the population. For example:

$$\text{Frequency of the } A \text{ allele} = \frac{\text{number of } A \text{ alleles in population}}{\text{total number of alleles in population}}$$

14. Calculate the frequency of the *a* (brown) allele and the *a* (black) allele.

15. The gerbils are prey for sharp-eyed hawks. How might the frequency of the black fur and brown fur alleles change in the population after a fire blackens the area? Will the frequencies vary proportionally (at the same rate)? Explain your answer.

© Houghton Mifflin Harcourt Publishing Company

Distribution of Traits

Genetic variation causes differences in traits. Some traits may have only one or two possible phenotypes. Other traits may have a wide range of possible phenotypes. For example, wild lupine flowers can be purple, white, blue, violet, or purple-pink. The frequency of each flower color in a lupine population can be shown in a graph. This type of graph shows the *distribution* of different phenotypes for the flower color trait.

lupines

16. Study the distribution graph for wild lupines. Which statement could be defended using data from the graph?

    A. The population has only one allele for flower color.

    B. Conditions in the environment favor purple lupines.

    C. All flower color alleles have an equal chance of appearing in the next lupine generation.

    D. There are fewer pink and white lupines due to drought.

Color Distribution of Lupine Flowers

This graph shows the distribution of flower color for a population of wild lupines. Biologists might compare this graph with one made in the past to study how flower color in the lupine population may be changing.

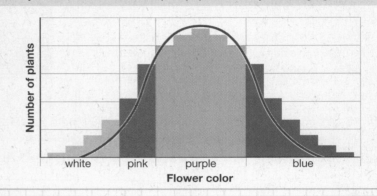

17. Think of odor strength as a range of phenotypes (weak to strong) in the rafflesia population. What might the distribution of traits look like on a graph? Record your evidence.

 EVIDENCE NOTEBOOK

Describe Trait Distribution

Monkey flowers are found in a variety of colors ranging from white to pink to red. Animals, such as bees and hummingbirds, help these plants reproduce by transferring pollen as they travel from flower to flower. Hummingbirds prefer to visit red monkey flowers. Bumblebees prefer to visit pink flowers.

18. Predict what color of monkey flower has the highest likelihood of occurring in a habitat with a large population of bees and few hummingbirds. Graph the distribution of color in monkey flowers in this habitat to support your answer.

Analyzing Patterns of Natural Selection

Hammerhead sharks are predators that can often be found prowling reefs in shallow ocean waters. They eat a variety of prey including fish, octopus, and crabs. Scientists have made hypotheses about the unusual head shape of these sharks. Research suggests that the wide-spaced eyes improve the shark's vision. Improved vision may help the shark better track fast-moving prey. Researchers have also hypothesized that the head shape may help the shark dive and perform movements needed to catch its favorite meal—stingrays. The shark uses its wide, flat head to pin down stingrays that are hiding under the sand on the ocean floor.

Hammerhead sharks are named for their unusual head shape.

19. **Discuss** Choose one of the hypotheses about the function of the shark's head shape. Describe how a scientist might design an experiment to test the hypothesis.

20. **Discuss** Researchers have discovered that the wide-set eyes result in a large blind spot directly in front of the shark's head. How is it possible that this head shape evolved given this disadvantage?

Patterns of Natural Selection

Natural selection is a process that can be observed, measured, and tested. Data have been gathered from the field and the laboratory by thousands of scientists. These data document the evolution of populations in response to changes in their environment. For example, the increase in antibiotic-resistant bacteria, pesticide-resistant insects, and herbicide-resistant plants shows that these populations are changing by the process of natural selection. Scientists have also measured changes in the timing of animal migrations and flowering of plants in response to changes in climate. The patterns observed in these data can help scientists explain how populations may have changed in the past. They can also be used to predict how populations might change in the future.

Case Study: Body Size in Male Salmon

The graph below shows a pattern of selection in male coho salmon. The red-dotted line shows a normal distribution for the trait, where most males have a medium body size. The blue line shows the distribution after selection has occurred.

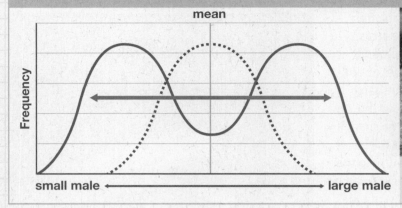

Male salmon, such as this coho salmon, defend territory.

21. Large male salmon defend territory and keep other males away from females. Small males can often sneak into a territory, unseen by the large male. How might this explain the pattern shown in the graph?

Case Study: Coat Color in Polar Bears

Genetic evidence reveals that polar bears are most closely related to a species of brown bear living on Alaska's ABC islands. Brown bears show a range of coat colors from solid brown to brown with light spots. The graph shows the selection pattern for coat color that occurred in polar bears.

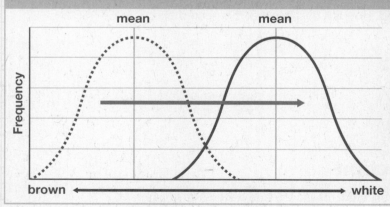

Polar bears spend much of their time on sea ice hunting for seals.

22. Polar bears have coats that help them survive in the cold Arctic where they live. The color of the coat helps them to blend in with their environment. The specialized hair cells that make up the coat keep the bear warm and dry. It is likely that one/more than one environmental factor caused the evolution of one/more than one trait in the polar bear.

Case Study: Spine Number in Cacti

A population of desert cacti shows variation in the number of spines on the cactus surface. Imagine that a new species migrates to the area. This species prefers to eat cacti with fewer spines. There is also a parasite in the area that prefers to lay its eggs on cacti with more spines.

Cactus spines are a limited defense against predators. Predator populations also evolve adaptive traits because of natural selection.

23. Draw Create a distribution graph of the spine-number trait for the cactus population based on the information provided.

Frequency

Number of spines

24. Language SmArts Write an explanation of the selection pattern shown in your graph. Explain how changes in the cacti's environment resulted in changes in the spine number trait.

© Houghton Mifflin Harcourt Publishing Company • Image Credits: ©GoneWithTheWind/Fotolia

EVIDENCE NOTEBOOK

25. How would you expect the distribution of traits for odor strength in rafflesia to change over many generations? How might populations of pollinators be changing at the same time? Record your evidence.

Analyzing Natural Selection in Medium Ground Finches

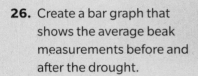

In studies conducted on one of the Galápagos Islands, scientists observed the effect of natural events on the beak shape of a population of medium ground finches. These studies involved measuring the size and shape of the beaks of thousands of finches on the island.

Medium ground finches usually eat small, soft seeds that are plentiful on the island. During a drought in 1977, plants on the island did not produce many seeds. The soft seeds were quickly eaten up. Finches that could eat larger, harder seeds instead of small, soft seeds were able to survive. Finches that could not eat the larger seeds died of starvation. Researchers compared measurements of average beak size before and after the drought.

26. Create a bar graph that shows the average beak measurements before and after the drought.

Average Beak Size in Medium Ground Finches		
	1977 (before drought)	**1978 (after drought)**
beak length (mm)	10.68	11.07
beak depth (mm)	9.42	9.96
beak width (mm)	8.68	9.01

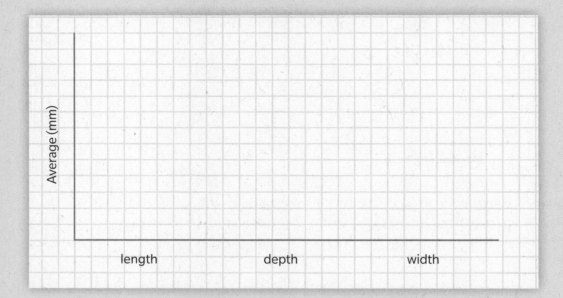

27. Use the graph and the text to summarize how the drought resulted in the selection pattern shown in the ground finches.

_____

_____

_____

_____

_____

Continue Your Exploration

Name: _____ Date: _____

Check out the path below or go online to choose one of the other paths shown.

| People in Science | • **Endangered Species**
 • **Hands-On Labs**
 • **Propose Your Own Path** | Go online to choose one of these other paths. |

Dr. Nancy Knowlton, Marine Biologist

Nancy Knowlton fell in love with marine life while wandering the ocean shore as a child. Her work studying shrimp evolution began in Jamaica, where she learned that the native shrimp population that scientists believed to be a single species actually included four species. Her work with shrimp continued along the Isthmus of Panama—a narrow strip of land that separates the Atlantic and Pacific Oceans. There she studied how the formation of the isthmus contributed to the evolution of several shrimp species.

1. Imagine you were a member of Dr. Knowlton's team conducting research about shrimp species in the waters off Panama. What types of data would you need to collect to determine if the shrimp populations were separate species? What do you think a typical research day would be like?

Dr. Nancy Knowlton spent nearly 14 years studying the diversification of shrimp species along the Isthmus of Panama. She continues to dedicate her life to the conservation of coral reefs.

Continue Your Exploration

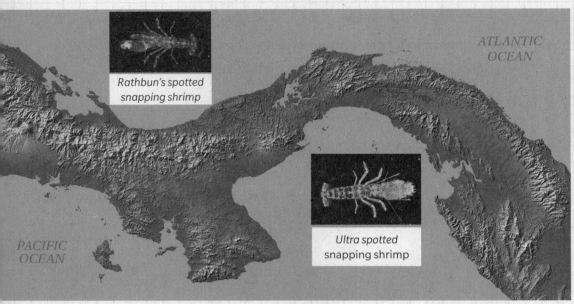

Rathbun's spotted snapping shrimp

Ultra spotted snapping shrimp

ATLANTIC OCEAN

PACIFIC OCEAN

The Isthmus of Panama is a narrow strip of land that connects North and South America and prevents the flow of water between the Atlantic and Pacific Oceans. Two shrimp species separated by the isthmus are shown on the map.

2. The movement of Earth's plates caused the formation of the Isthmus of Panama between 3.5–20 million years ago. Could the formation of the Isthmus of Panama alone cause a shrimp population to diversify into distinct species? Explain your reasoning.

3. To claim that the rise of the Isthmus of Panama contributed to the evolution of different species of shrimp, would Dr. Knowlton need to establish that the east coast and west coast shrimp species diverged before or after the rise of the isthmus? Explain your reasoning.

4. **Collaborate** Rheas, emu, and ostrich are bird species that each live on different continents, but they are more closely related to each other than to nearby bird species. Work with a group to learn about their evolution from a common ancestor. Write a report and present your findings to your classmates. Include photos or drawings of each species in your report.

Can You Explain It?

Name: _____   Date: _____

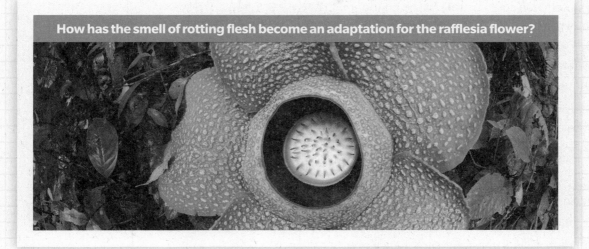

How has the smell of rotting flesh become an adaptation for the rafflesia flower?

EVIDENCE NOTEBOOK

Refer to the notes in your Evidence Notebook to help you construct an explanation for how the adaptations of the rafflesia flower are related to the process of natural selection.

1. State your claim. Make sure your claim fully explains how the smell of rotting flesh became an adaptation for the rafflesia flower.

2. Summarize the evidence you have gathered to support your claim and explain your reasoning.

Checkpoints

Answer the following questions to check your understanding of the lesson.

Use the table to answer Questions 3–4.

3. Which statements could be true based on the data shown in the table? Select all that apply.

   A. The *B* allele does not provide a survival advantage to the population.

   B. This population is evolving.

   C. The *b* allele does not provide a survival advantage to the population.

   D. The population is not evolving.

Generation	Allele Frequency of *B*	Allele Frequency of *b*
1	0.63	0.37
2	0.71	0.29
3	0.78	0.22
4	0.78	0.22
5	0.81	0.19

4. How might the migration of individuals in or out of the habitat affect the frequency of each allele in this population?

   A. Migration will change the frequency of only the *B* allele.

   B. Migration will not change the frequency of either allele.

   C. Migration will change the frequency of both alleles.

   D. Migration will change the frequency of only the *b* allele.

Use the photo to answer Question 5.

5. Which environmental factors might cause a decrease in the size of hooks in the fish hook ant population over time? Select all that apply.

   A. Birds prefer to eat ants with smaller hooks.

   B. Ants with smaller hooks need less food to survive.

   C. Female ants prefer mates with smaller hooks.

   D. Small snakes cannot swallow ants with long hooks.

The fish hook ant has razor-sharp hooks to defend itself from predators.

---

6. Many species produce more offspring than can survive in their environment. How might this contribute to natural selection? Select all that apply.

   A. More offspring results in more competition for resources.

   B. Producing many offspring is a disadvantage.

   C. Helpful traits allow some individuals to outcompete others.

   D. Without competition, advantageous traits may have no effect on survival or reproduction.

Interactive Review

Complete this section to review the main concepts of the lesson.

Life on Earth is diverse because populations change over time through a process that happens now as it has happened in the past.

A. Explain how a single population of organisms can result in multiple different populations after many generations.

Natural selection is a process by which a population's environment determines which traits are beneficial and which are not.

B. Explain how genetic variation and the environment influence the distribution of traits.

Natural selection is a process by which a population's environment determines which traits are beneficial and which are not.

C. Describe the three factors required for natural selection to occur in a population.

Populations become better adapted to their current environments through natural selection.

D. Explain why adaptations are specific to the current environment of a population.

Natural Selection Requires Genetic Variation

The black color of this jaguar is the result of a gene that controls the dark pigment in the jaguar's fur.

© Houghton Mifflin Harcourt Publishing Company • Image Credits: ©stepbennett/iStock/ Getty Images Plus/Getty Images

Explore First

Changing Instructions Write a how-to procedure for an easy task, such as folding a paper airplane. Pair up and perform each other's tasks. Then alter your how-to procedure by adding, removing, or revising a step. Is your partner still able to perform your task? What is the relationship between instructions and a final product?

Go online to view the digital version of the Hands-On Lab for this lesson and to download additional lab resources.

CAN YOU EXPLAIN IT?

How can a change to just one gene cause a lobster to be blue?

Only 1 in about 2 million lobsters is blue. The blue color is the result of a rare genetic mutation.

1. Identify at least three other body features of these lobsters. What do you think determines these traits in the lobsters? How could these traits change?

 EVIDENCE NOTEBOOK As you explore the lesson, gather evidence to help explain how a change to a gene can result in a blue lobster.

Describing the Relationship between Genes and Traits

Observe the students in your classroom. They share many traits, but they do not look identical. Some traits can be inherited, such as eye color and face shape. Inherited traits are passed on from parents to offspring by genetic material. Other traits, such as language and musical taste, are determined by the environment. However, most traits are influenced by both genetic and environmental factors, and every person has a unique combination of many traits.

The differences in eye colors, face shapes, and smiles of these students is due to differences in traits.

DNA Is the Genetic Material Stored in Cells

The genetic material that determines traits in organisms is **DNA**. It is a double-stranded molecule organized into structures called *chromosomes*. In organisms that reproduce sexually, cells have pairs of chromosomes. For each pair, the offspring receives one chromosome from each of the two parents. DNA molecules contain the information that determines the traits that an organism inherits. DNA also contains the instructions for an organism's growth and development.

2. **Discuss** How might an inherited trait, such as height, be influenced by both genetic and environmental factors?

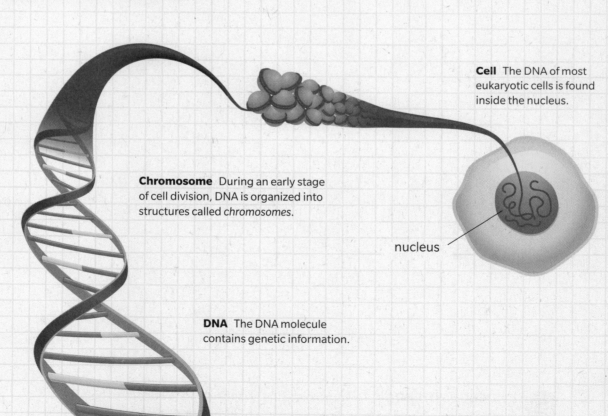

Cell The DNA of most eukaryotic cells is found inside the nucleus.

Chromosome During an early stage of cell division, DNA is organized into structures called *chromosomes*.

nucleus

DNA The DNA molecule contains genetic information.

© Houghton Mifflin Harcourt Publishing Company • Image Credits: ©Christopher Futcher/ iStock/Getty Images Plus/Getty Images

Genes Are Segments of DNA

Each side, or strand, of DNA is a chain of building blocks called *nucleotides*. These repeating chemical units join together to form a DNA molecule. One part of a nucleotide is called the *base*. There are four different nucleotides in DNA, which are identified by their bases: adenine (A), guanine (G), cytosine (C), and thymine (T). Where the two strands connect, A pairs with T and G pairs with C. These paired bases fit together like the pieces of a puzzle.

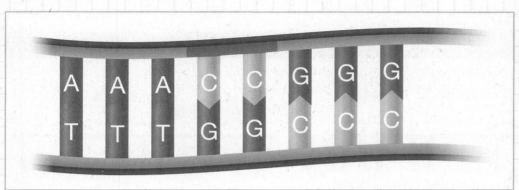

Nucleotides line up so that the DNA backbone is like the handrail of a ladder. The bases—A, T, C, and G—join to make the rungs of the ladder.

Combinations of alphabet letters make meaningful words. Likewise, combinations of DNA base pairs make "genetic words" called *genes*. A **gene** is a specific segment of DNA that provides instructions for an inherited trait. Each gene has a starting point and an ending point. DNA is read in one direction, just as you read words from left to right. Genes are responsible for the inherited traits of an organism. Organisms that reproduce sexually have two versions of the same gene for every trait—one version from each parent.

3. Complete the DNA sequence by adding complementary bases to the DNA strand. You may draw using colors or write letters to represent the nucleotide bases.

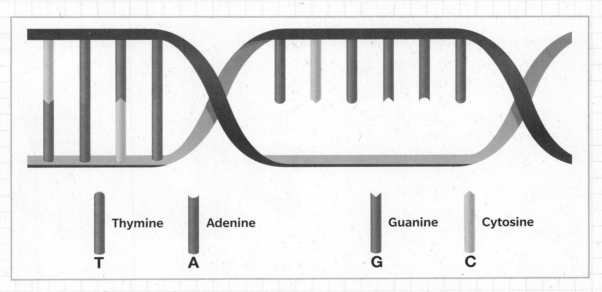

Thymine   Adenine   Guanine   Cytosine
T   A   G   C

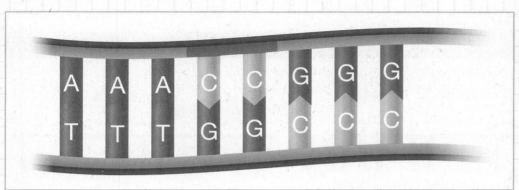

A A A C C G G G
T T T G G C C C

© Houghton Mifflin Harcourt Publishing Company

Genes Code for Proteins

A **protein** is an important molecule that is necessary for building and repairing body structures and controlling processes in the body. Proteins are composed of smaller molecules called *amino acids*. About 20 different types of amino acids combine to make proteins. A specific sequence of three bases on a gene codes for a specific amino acid. These sequences are called *triplets*. The chain of amino acids produced by a gene depends on the order of the triplets. In this way, the genes of a chromosome carry the instructions for the proteins that are produced by cells.

Relate DNA Code to Protein Production

4. The diagram on the left shows the triplet order for six amino acids. Use the diagram to complete the triplets and amino acids on the right.

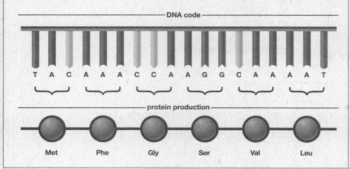

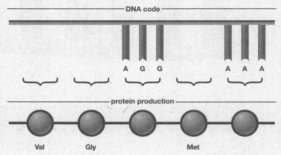

Amino acid chains fold and link together to form the 3D structure of a protein.

Once built, the amino acid chain twists and folds to form the protein's three-dimensional shape. A protein's shape is linked to its function. For example, collagen is a protein that folds into a long, fiber-like chain and strengthens skin. Other proteins, called *hormones*, deliver messages to cells by fitting into specific locations on target cells like a key in a lock.

5. Some triplets code for the same amino acid. Sometimes, a DNA triplet is exchanged for another one that codes for the same amino acid. The function of the resulting protein will / will not be affected. If the DNA triplet codes for a different amino acid, the function of the protein will / will not be affected.

6. *Enzymes* are proteins that help speed up chemical reactions in the body. They often work by binding to target molecules. How do you think the sequence of amino acids in an enzyme relates to its ability to bind to a specific target molecule?

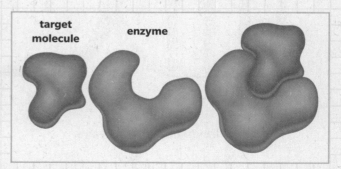

The active site of an enzyme has just the right shape to bind to the target molecule.

Hands-On Lab
Model Protein Folding

You will use paper strips to model protein folding.

Amino acid chains fold or twist when one region of the chain is attracted to, or repelled by, another region. This folding or twisting depends on the chemical structure of each amino acid, as well as how close they are together in the chain.

MATERIALS
- colored pencils, red, blue, green
- paper strips, white, 1 inch wide and 12 inches long (2)
- ruler

Procedure

STEP 1 Consider the amino acid sequence below. On the strip of white paper, draw colored dots indicated by the sequence using corresponding colors—red, blue, or green. Use the ruler to help you leave a 1 cm space between each dot.

Amino acid sequence 1:
His – Lys – Ser – Gly – Ala – Gly – Cys – Pro – Ser – Asp – Val – Leu – Met – Gly – Thr – Pro – Gly – Ala – Cys – Asp – Met

STEP 2 Fold your amino acid chain into a three-dimensional protein by following the guidelines below. Work from one end of the white paper strip to the other. Try to fold halfway between the relevant colored dots when folding.

- Same color next to each other—no fold
- **Red** next to **green**—90° fold down
- **Red** next to **blue**—90° fold up (dotted sides of strip come together)
- **Blue** next to **green**—45° airplane fold (colored dots come together with a diagonal crease)

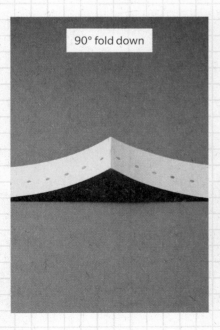
90° fold down

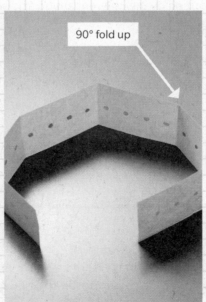
90° fold up

45° airplane fold

© Houghton Mifflin Harcourt Publishing Company • Image Credits: ©HMH

Analysis

STEP 3 Once you have folded your protein, observe its shape. Then set it aside to compare with other proteins you will make.

STEP 4 Now, consider the next amino acid sequence. Following the same procedure as you did for the first sequence, complete the three-dimensional protein.

Amino acid sequence 2:
His – Lys – Ser – Gly – Ala – Gly – Cys – Pro – Ser – Asp – His – Leu – Met –
Gly – Thr – Pro – Gly – Ala – Cys – Asp – Met

STEP 5 Compare the two amino acid sequences. What is the difference between the composition of the two sequences? How does the shape of the proteins differ?

STEP 6 How did the alteration in the amino acid sequence affect protein structure?

STEP 7 Do you think the proteins formed by the different amino acid sequences can still perform the same function?

EVIDENCE NOTEBOOK

7. How might the alteration in the folding pattern of the paper strip proteins relate to the genetic change that causes a lobster to be blue? Record your evidence.

Proteins Affect Traits

Different versions of the same gene can result in proteins with different structures and properties. Proteins perform much of the chemical work inside cells, so they are largely responsible for traits. The variety in proteins results in the variety of traits we observe in organisms. For example, Labrador Retrievers are dogs that exhibit a variety of coat colors. The coat will be brown or black depending on which protein is coded for in the pigment gene. When a different protein inactivates the brown or black coat pigment gene, Labradors have yellow coats.

 Language SmArts

Illustrate the Flow of Genetic Information

Scientists have modified tomato plant genes to produce the same pigments that give blackberries their dark color and health benefits. The result—purple tomatoes!

8. **Draw** Use the terms protein, gene, trait, and amino acids to make a diagram or concept map that shows the flow of genetic information that causes purple tomatoes.

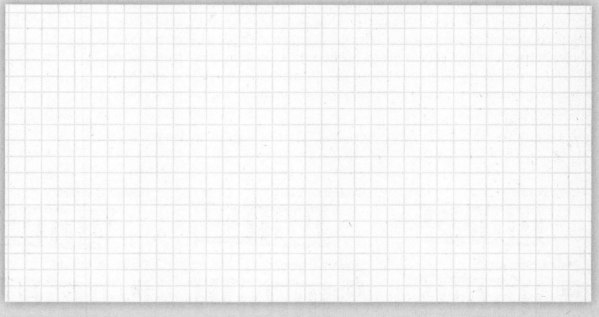

9. Use your completed diagram and evidence from the text to write a summary of the relationship between genes, proteins, and traits.

_____

_____

_____

_____

_____

Exploring the Causes of Genetic Change

Leaf-like scales distinguish the bush viper from its smooth-skinned snake relatives. Keratin proteins shape scales. They arrange in ridges instead of smooth rows to help the viper blend in with leaves. What caused this new trait to appear in bush vipers? The ridged scale pattern in bush vipers is due to genetic changes that result in altered proteins.

10. Which of the following outcomes could result from a change in one of the bush viper's genes? Select all that apply.

   A. no effect on traits

   B. a genetic disease

   C. a new skin color

The African bush viper lives in tropical forests. Its scales help it camouflage within the bright green foliage.

Mutations

A change in the base-pair sequence of a gene is called a **mutation**. Most mutations occur when a cell copies its DNA for cell division. As the DNA is copied, base pairs may be added, deleted, or substituted. These chance mutations may be beneficial, neutral, or harmful to organisms. For example, a mutation that results in longer fangs may be beneficial if it helps the bush viper seize prey. Mutations can also occur when DNA is exposed to *mutagens*, or substances that cause genetic mutations, such as UV radiation and toxic chemicals.

11. Study the DNA base sequences. On the line provided, record whether the mutation is an addition, substitution, or deletion.

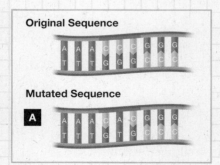

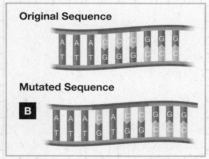

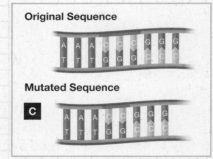

A. _____   B. _____   C. _____

12. **Collaborate** With a partner or group, consider how DNA is used to produce proteins. Which DNA mutation types might have the biggest effect on protein structure? Develop a model to help explain your answer and share your model with your class.

© Houghton Mifflin Harcourt Publishing Company • Image Credits: ©Mark Kostich/iStock/Getty Images Plus/Getty Images

13. Look again at the enzyme diagram and its target molecule. How might a mutation affect the interaction between the enzyme and its target and the function of the enzyme in the organism?

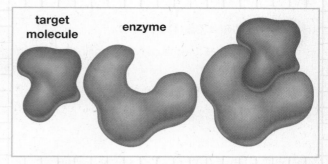

target molecule   enzyme

The target molecule and the enzyme are both proteins. Their 3D shapes are determined by the order of their amino acids.

Body Cells and Reproductive Cells

Mutations can occur in the DNA of body cells or in the DNA of reproductive cells—eggs and sperm. When cells divide, mutations are passed on with the genetic material into the new cell. Only mutations that occur in the DNA of reproductive cells can be passed on from parent to offspring.

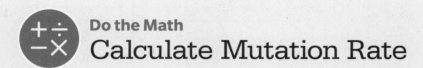

Do the Math
Calculate Mutation Rate

Organisms must copy their DNA to reproduce, and mutations can occur any time DNA is copied. Many of these mutations are corrected by cells, but sometimes a mutation is not corrected and it becomes part of the genetic code of a species.

DNA Mutations Over Time		
Mutations (shown in black) accumulate at a fairly constant rate in the DNA of a particular species.	**Original DNA sequence**	G A A C G T A T T C A G G T C T
	5 million years later	G A A C G T A T T C A G G T C T
	10 million years later	G T A C G T A T T C A G G T C T
	15 million years later	G T A A G T A T T C A C G T C T
	20 million years later	G T A A G T A T T C A C G T C T
	25 million years later	G T A A G A A T T C A C G T C T

14. How many mutations accumulated in this DNA sequence over 25 million years?

15. Based on these data, estimate the mutation rate for this DNA sequence over 100 million years.

EVIDENCE NOTEBOOK

16. What are the connections between mutation, protein structure and function, and the lobster's blue color? Record your evidence.

Sexual Reproduction

Sexual reproduction, like mutation, is a source of genetic change. One or more genes can get reshuffled among chromosomes when the egg and sperm form. Since the shuffling of genes is random, each egg or sperm will carry a different combination of chromosomes. This explains differences among offspring that come from the same parents.

17. When DNA segments switch places during egg or sperm formation, it can affect _only one / several_ gene(s).

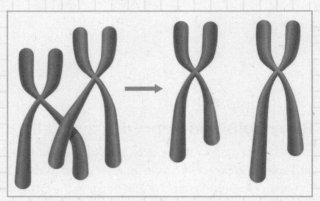

Chromosomes can "cross over" during egg or sperm formation, allowing large segments of DNA to swap locations and providing additional combinations of genes in offspring.

Engineer It
Identify Design Solution Constraints

Earth's atmosphere includes a thin layer of *ozone*, a compound that absorbs UV rays emitted by the sun. UV light can initiate mutations in DNA by causing neighboring thymine bases on the same strand to break their bonds with adenine and bond with each other instead. Human-generated pollutants break down ozone in the atmosphere, putting people at higher risk of sunburn and skin cancer.

18. According to the paragraph, pollution causes the ozone layer to _thin / expand_. As a result, living organisms have a _higher / lower_ risk of UV damage. This represents an engineering problem for which _a solution / an experiment_ can be designed to help reduce ozone depletion.

Earth's ozone layer can be seen from space. It lies within the thin blue band of the outer atmosphere .

19. Which of the following are constraints that should be considered in designing solutions to this problem? Select all that apply.

A. The solution must result in a cure for skin cancer.

B. The solution must not cause harm to living organisms.

C. The solution must prevent thymine-adenine bonds from breaking.

D. The solution must not cause an imbalance of other atmospheric gases.

Explaining the Relationship Between Genetic Change and Natural Selection

The star-nosed mole has a ring of twenty-two finger-like projections around its snout which helps the mole to detect and capture prey in a fraction of a second. Long ago, genetic change that caused nose segments to remain separated was passed from one mole to its offspring. The offspring were able to locate prey better than other moles in the population. These offspring reproduced successfully, passing the mutation to their offspring as well. Over many generations, this segmented structure became more common in the population.

20. Do you think the genetic change that resulted in the segmented nose occurred in the DNA of body cells or the DNA of reproductive cells? Why?

Star-nosed moles mostly eat earthworms and aquatic insects.

Genetic Change and Adaptation

Genetic changes resulting from mutation and sexual reproduction lead to different traits in the individuals of a population. Traits that help organisms survive and reproduce in their current environment are called **adaptations**. An adaptation can be a structure, a function, or a behavior. For example, the structure of the star-nosed mole's nose allows it to locate prey more effectively than a rounded nose. Specialized nervous system function allows the moles to process information from their environment very rapidly. When star-nosed moles search for food, they constantly touch the environment with the star—between 10 and 15 places every second. This behavior helps them to rapidly detect and capture small prey. The adaptations of the star-nosed mole are the result of evolution through natural selection, which requires genetic variation to act on a trait.

EVIDENCE NOTEBOOK

21. Do you think that the mutation that causes the blue color of the lobster is an adaptation? Record your evidence.

© Houghton Mifflin Harcourt Publishing Company • Image Credits: ©Skip Moody/Science Source

Identify Adaptations

22. Read the description of each organism. In the space provided, list one structure, function, or behavior that you think is an adaptation. Then briefly explain how this adaptation benefits the organism.

	The barrel cactus lives in dry, hot deserts. It has a round stem covered with spines. The flowers bloom when temperatures drop and pollinators are plentiful.	
	The scorpion has a tough exoskeleton and poison in its curled tail. It is well armed for life in the desert, and will burrow in the sand to escape the scorching heat.	
	The ocelot hunts a variety of prey, including rodents, iguanas, and monkeys. It has a unique patterned coat, sharp eyesight, and sharp teeth. The ocelot is nocturnal, meaning it is active mostly at night.	

Relate Change to Natural Selection

The mountain goat is well-adapted to its current environment. It has a compact body covered in thick fur, split hooves, strong rear legs, and a narrow snout. It lives on steep, rocky slopes where temperatures can drop well below zero. Plants on these slopes grow only a few inches tall in the shallow, nutrient-poor soil.

23. Draw Suppose climate change affects the mountain goat's environment. Hot summers and more rainfall allow plants to grow tall and cover rocks. What variations in a population might help mountain goats survive these new conditions? Sketch a mountain goat with an adaptation and explain how this trait could increase in the population due to natural selection.

The mountain goat's round, compact body helps it to retain water and heat.

Continue Your Exploration

Name: _____   Date: _____

Check out the path below or go online to choose one of the other paths shown.

| Evolution of Drug-Resistant Bacteria | • **Mutation and Phenotype**
• **Hands-On Labs** 🖐
• **Propose Your Own Path** | *Go online to choose one of these other paths.* |

A bacterial cell may have an allele that results in resistance to an antibiotic medicine. This cell may survive antibiotic treatment and pass the beneficial allele to its offspring, or to other bacterial cells in the medium in which they live. Scientists identified bacterial strains resistant to penicillin within 20 years of the first use of the antibiotic in humans. Bacterial resistance to levofloxacin, an antibiotic used to treat pneumonia and other life-threatening infections, evolved within just one year. Scientists observed two contrasting trends. The number of antibiotic-resistant bacteria was increasing, while the development of new antibiotic medicines was decreasing.

1. What is needed for a population of bacteria to develop resistance to antibiotics? Select all that apply.

   A. the existence of resistance genes in the population

   B. the presence of antibiotics in the bacteria's environment

   C. competition between bacterial species

   D. transfer of alleles from one generation to the next

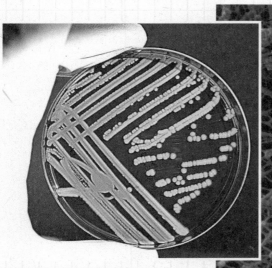

"Superbugs," like *Klebsiella pneumoniae*, the bacteria growing on the petri dish, resist almost all antibiotics. The colored micrograph (right) shows the bacterium trapped by a white blood cell.

Continue Your Exploration

Antibiotic Resistance in *K. pneumoniae*, United States 1998–2010

Klebsiella pneumoniae is a bacteria that causes infections of the respiratory and urinary systems. The graph shows the percentage of *K. pneumoniae* that are resistant to certain antibiotics. Each line represents a different antibiotic.

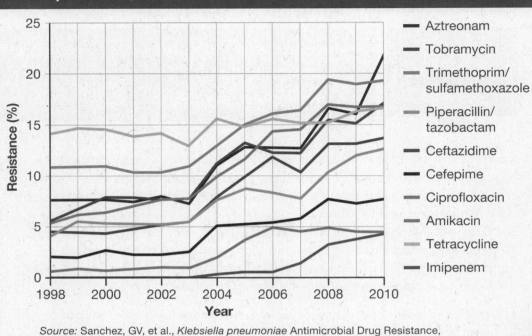

Legend:
- Aztreonam
- Tobramycin
- Trimethoprim/sulfamethoxazole
- Piperacillin/tazobactam
- Ceftazidime
- Cefepime
- Ciprofloxacin
- Amikacin
- Tetracycline
- Imipenem

Source: Sanchez, GV, et al., *Klebsiella pneumoniae* Antimicrobial Drug Resistance, United States, 1998–2010, *Emerging Infectious Diseases,* 2013, 19(1): 133–136

2. Describe the pattern of antibiotic resistance shown in the graph. How many years of data are shown in the graph? What does the percentage of resistance at the beginning of the study tell you about each antibiotic?

3. How do you think the growth and spread of human populations and the use of antibiotics has affected the frequency of the antibiotic resistant allele in populations of *K. pneumoniae*?

4. **Collaborate** Work with a classmate to research other examples of natural selection that have been observed and measured by scientists. Prepare an oral presentation or short play for each example. Identify the variation of traits in the population, describe the environmental change, and explain why certain traits are increasing or decreasing in the population due to natural selection. Be prepared to ask and answer questions at the end of each presentation.

Can You Explain It?

Name: _____   **Date:** _____

How can a change to just one gene cause a lobster to be blue?

EVIDENCE NOTEBOOK

Refer to the notes in your Evidence Notebook to help you construct an explanation for how a change to a single gene can cause a lobster to be blue.

1. State your claim. Make sure your claim fully explains how a change to one gene can cause the blue color in lobsters.

2. Summarize the evidence you have gathered to support your claim and explain your reasoning.

Checkpoints

Answer the following questions to check your understanding of the lesson.

Use the photo of the betta fish to answer Question 3.

3. A gene mutation in the betta fish results in a double-tail. In this example, the mutation results in a change to a ~~physical trait /~~ ~~behavior~~. This change is desirable by fish breeders but does not provide a survival advantage for the fish, so it ~~is~~ / ~~is not~~ considered an adaptation.

4. Which sequence best explains the relationship between DNA and protein structure and function?

   A. DNA → gene → protein → trait

   B. DNA → amino acid triplets → protein → trait

   C. DNA base triplets → amino acid sequence → protein folding pattern → protein shape and function

   D. DNA shape → amino acid sequence → protein shape and function

Use the photo of the bee-eater to answer Questions 5–6.

5. Bee-eaters are birds that eat insects, especially bees and wasps. They grab flying prey from the air with their beaks. Long ago, genetic changes that resulted in ~~shorter /~~ ~~longer~~ beaks were advantageous for the bee-eater.

6. Which statement correctly connects the bee-eater's adaptations with its environment?

   A. The environment determines which bee-eater traits are adaptive.

   B. The bee-eater's traits influence the environment it chooses to live in.

   C. The bee-eater's adaptive traits will not change as the environment changes.

   D. The environment has no relationship to the bee-eater's adaptive traits.

Interactive Review

Complete this section to review the main concepts of the lesson.

Genes in DNA code for proteins that determine an organism's traits.

A. Describe how genes are related to the structure and function of proteins.

Mutations and sexual reproduction are causes of genetic change.

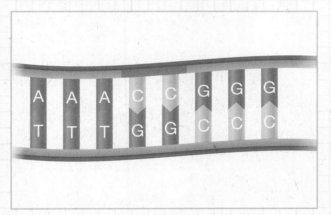

B. Explain how mutations to genes can affect traits in organisms.

Traits that help organisms survive or reproduce in their current environment are called adaptations.

C. Explain the relationship between genetic change and adaptation.

Artificial Selection Influences Traits in Organisms

Dogs have many different traits that humans may find valuable, such as size, shape, or coat color of the dog.

Explore First

Analyzing Dog Breeds In a group, brainstorm as many dog breeds as you can. For each breed, include a list of characteristics. For example, a Dalmatian is a large dog with a spotted coat. What causes differences between the dog breeds?

Go online to view the digital version of the Hands-On Lab for this lesson and to download additional lab resources.

CAN YOU EXPLAIN IT?

How did humans cause alpacas to become different from vicuñas over time?

vicuña

alpaca

Vicuñas are shy, fast animals. They feed on short, tough grasses in the Andes Mountains. Alpacas are their relatives. They are gentle and curious. Alpacas are raised by humans for their warm wool.

1. Compare the way the alpaca and the vicuña look. How are they alike or different?

2. Do you think alpacas or vicuñas are more useful to humans? Explain your answer.

EVIDENCE NOTEBOOK As you explore the lesson, gather evidence to help explain how humans influenced the development of alpaca populations from vicuñas.

Analyzing Human Influence on the Inheritance of Traits

Humans have been influencing the traits of certain plants and animals for thousands of years. For example, people may breed horses to race, or grow fruits that taste a certain way. People grow plants and keep animals for the products or services they provide. They isolate these organisms from their wild populations, which affects the possible traits in the isolated population. Over time, domesticated populations may become very different from their wild relatives.

People at the market may want to buy these tomatoes because of the colors and shapes.

3. **Discuss** What traits make each tomato type unique? Why might farmers want to grow tomatoes with so many different traits?

Traits Are Passed from Parents to Offspring

The Saint Bernard pass lies high in the Alps, a European mountain system. During the 1700s, a single monastery near the pass kept a population of large dogs with thick fur. The dogs helped the monks avoid avalanches and detect people trapped in the snow. The monks depended on the dogs for survival, and they bred only the most gentle and snow-wise dogs. Over time, these traits became common in the population of dogs. Even now, St. Bernard dogs will instinctively help people lying or trapped in the snow.

The monks had little understanding of the biology behind inheritance. Yet, they knew that traits pass from parents to their young. They used this understanding to influence the dogs' traits through *selective breeding*, or the breeding of specific organisms based on preferred traits. More than 100 years later, scientists began to understand the way inheritance works.

Scientific Understanding of Inheritance

Factors That Influence the Frequency of Traits Charles Darwin was an English naturalist who studied the inheritance of traits in living things. He loved raising pigeons. Darwin bred the birds to have certain features. He realized that nature, like humans, might influence the traits of living things. Darwin applied this thinking to data he collected from living and fossil organisms. He observed that traits that provide a benefit in a certain environment become more common in populations over time.

Inheritance Follows Patterns Gregor Mendel was an Austrian monk who studied traits in pea plants. He carefully bred peas and learned that some traits follow a simple pattern when passed from parent to offspring. Dominant traits appear in offspring when present and recessive traits might be present, but masked. Mendel explained that there are two "factors" that can be inherited for each trait—one from each parent. These "factors" are now known as *alleles*. Modern genetics is based on Mendel's work.

Inheritance Patterns Can Be Predicted Reginald Punnett was a geneticist who built on Mendel's work by studying more complex patterns of inheritance. Punnett developed a simple calculation table to predict the likelihood that offspring would inherit certain traits from parents. This table is called a *Punnett square.* Punnett used this table to demonstrate that certain feather colors in chickens are linked to being male.

4. By observing inheritance patterns, Darwin, Mendel, and Punnett developed the foundation for understanding how breeding influences traits in a population. They worked before / after scientists understood the relationship between traits and genetic material. Society can use inheritance patterns to meet various needs because the patterns are unpredictable / predictable.

Hands-On Lab
Analyze Selected Traits in Vegetables

You will compare vegetable plants bred from wild *Brassica oleracea*. You will analyze traits to describe how each vegetable could develop from the wild type by selective breeding.

Procedure and Analysis

STEP 1 Study the diagram of wild *Brassica oleracea*.

MATERIALS
- colored pencils
- samples of fresh vegetables cultivated from wild *Brassica oleracea*, including broccoli, cauliflower, Brussels sprouts, kohlrabi, and kale

Anatomy of Wild *Brassica oleracea*

Many types of vegetables were cultivated from the wild type of this plant, shown below. Some traits were encouraged and other traits were suppressed.

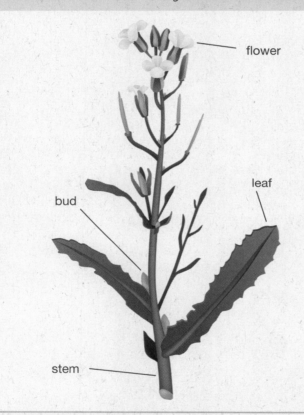

flower

bud

leaf

stem

STEP 2 Choose your first vegetable. Describe it in the table. Sketch the vegetable on a separate sheet of paper.

STEP 3 In your observations, circle specific traits the vegetable has in common with the wild-type plant and note these in the table.

STEP 4 Repeat Steps 2 and 3 for each vegetable.

Vegetable	Observations

STEP 5 Which vegetables are the most and least similar to the wild-type plant? What does this tell you about the selective breeding process for each vegetable?

STEP 6 Choose one of the vegetables from the table. Explain how it might have developed from wild *Brassica oleracea* through selective breeding.

Artificial Selection

The human control of reproduction in order to influence the traits present in offspring is called **artificial selection**. For example, dairy cows are bred for the amount of milk they produce, the milk fat level, and their pregnancy success. Artificial selection can encourage traits in a population that people want. It can also discourage traits that people do not want. Science can help describe the impact of artificial selection on populations. Society must then decide how to apply this knowledge.

The traits present in a population are different when humans are the selective pressure instead of environmental factors. The traits people choose may not improve an organism's chance for survival or reproduction. This is one way artificial selection is very different from natural selection. Yet, natural and artificial selection do follow some of the same rules. Both can only affect traits that are present in a population. Also, both selection types alter the frequency of *phenotypes* (traits) and *genotypes* (gene combinations) in a population.

5. Which of these factors make dairy cows a good choice for artificial selection? Select all that apply.

   A. The cows vary in the amount of milk they make.

   B. The amount of milk cows make is affected by diet.

   C. The amount of milk cows make is an inherited trait.

   D. Many people want to drink milk or cook with milk.

 EVIDENCE NOTEBOOK

   6. What traits might have been selected for in alpacas? Record your evidence.

Predict the Outcome of Artificial Selection

Guppies are a popular fish for home aquariums. They have bright colors, broad tails, and spotted patterns. People who sell fish use selective breeding to emphasize certain traits in offspring. As a result, there are many types of guppies. For example, the half-black yellow guppy has a half-black body and a broad yellow tail. Every part of the albino red guppy is a striking scarlet color, even its eyes.

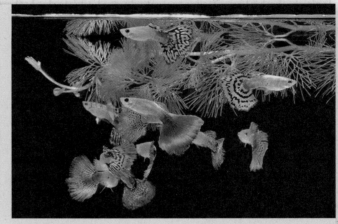

The color, spot pattern, shape, and size of guppies in a population can be influenced through artificial selection.

7. **Draw** Choose one trait of the guppies in the photo. Draw what a guppy might look like if people selected for this trait over ten generations. Include a caption that explains the process.

Modeling the Genetic Basis for Artificial Selection

Humans raised dogs long before they farmed land or raised chickens and sheep. Dogs were the first animals bred by people, beginning between 10,000 and 40,000 years ago. Dogs are different from wolves because of selective breeding. Dogs have smaller skulls, paws, and teeth. Their ears flop forward, they are more friendly than fierce, and dogs can sense some human emotions.

8. How might humans have influenced the inheritance of traits they found desirable in wolves?

Wolves have traits that help them survive in the places they live.

Artificial Selection Acts on Inherited Traits

In the early 1900s, experiments confirmed Mendel's idea that traits are controlled by factors inherited from each parent. Over time, new technologies and discoveries linked traits to DNA. *DNA* is genetic material in cells that is transferred from parent to offspring during reproduction. *Genes* are segments of DNA that produce specific traits. As understanding of inheritance advances, so do the ways humans affect the traits in organisms.

The Shar-Pei on the left has many more wrinkles than the Shar-Pei on the right.

9. A single gene determines if Chinese Shar-Peis will have normal skin or excessively wrinkled skin. Two Shar-Peis that differ in skin type have different genotypes / phenotypes / genotypes and phenotypes . Breeding Shar-Peis so that they are more likely to have wrinkled skin is an example of natural / artificial selection. It requires traits that are / are not inherited from parents.

Dog breeders cannot make new traits, but they can cause traits that dogs already have to become more or less common in a population. They do this by deciding which dogs mate. Puppies are more likely to have desired traits if both of their parents have those traits. Artificial selection directs change in populations that can occur more quickly than with natural selection. Artificial selection outcomes are also more predictable than those of natural selection because people control which individuals reproduce. Reproduction in nature may cause different traits to become more common in the population.

 EVIDENCE NOTEBOOK

10. How do artificial selection and heritable traits relate to the development of alpaca populations from vicuñas? Record your evidence.

© Houghton Mifflin Harcourt Publishing Company • Image Credits: (t) ©Michael Cummings/Getty Images; (b) ©Jean Michel Labat/Pantheon/Superstock

Do the Math
Model Artificial Selection

A *Punnett square* models the transfer of genes from parents to offspring during sexual reproduction. The gene versions (or *alleles*) for an inherited characteristic from one parent are listed above each column as letters. The alleles from the other parent are listed next to each row. Capital letters are used for dominant alleles and lowercase letters are used for recessive alleles.

   To complete the Punnett square, the parent alleles are combined in each cell. In this diagram, the allele for short hair, *H*, is dominant to the allele for long hair, *h*. Having at least one dominant allele will produce short hair, the dominant phenotype. The top parent has an *HH* genotype and the parent to the left has an *hh* genotype. In this example, the predicted ratio of short-haired dogs in a litter of four is 4:4. In other words, you could expect 100% of the dogs to have short hair.

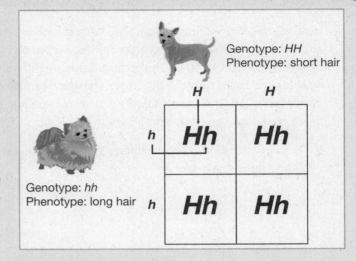

Genotype: *HH*
Phenotype: short hair

Genotype: *hh*
Phenotype: long hair

11. A breeder crosses two *Hh* Chihuahuas. Complete the Punnett square that models this cross.

12. Based on the Punnett square modeling the cross of two *Hh* Chihuahuas, what percentage of Chihuahua puppies should the breeder expect to have long hair?

Short-Haired Chihuahua

Short-Haired Chihuahua

13. What is the predicted ratio of short-haired to long-haired offspring?

14. Which other crosses have a greater probability of producing Chihuahuas with the long-hair trait than the *Hh* x *Hh* cross? Circle all that apply.

   A. *HH* x *Hh*

   B. *hh* x *hh*

   C. *Hh* x *hh*

   D. None of these crosses

Artificial Selection Does Not Modify Genes

Advances in the scientific understanding of genes and inheritance improved selective breeding programs. For example, recessive traits are not always visible in an organism. Understanding inheritance patterns can assist breeders in making recessive traits more or less common in a population, even if the traits cannot be seen in the parents. Humans are still finding new methods to influence desired traits in living things. Biologists now understand how to change genes directly using molecular tools. The process of changing genes directly is called *genetic engineering*. Artificial selection influences how common existing traits are in a population, but it does not alter genes.

Language SmArts

Compare Mechanisms of Change in Species

15. Read the text for each photo to decide if humans or environmental factors are influencing traits. Identify each example as natural selection, artificial selection, or genetic engineering. Use evidence from the lesson to support your choices.

Example		Mechanism and evidence
	Neon-colored zebra fish are produced when DNA from sea anemones, coral, or jellyfish is inserted into the genetic material of wild-type zebra fish.	
	Dutch farmers carefully bred the pineberry, or "reverse strawberry," over several years. Cultivation begins with crossing a nearly extinct white strawberry plant with a red strawberry plant.	
	Farmers want dairy cows to produce as much high-fat milk as possible. The DNA of beef and dairy cows have differences in genes that control milk production.	
	This hummingbird's bill is long and curved. Its food source is nectar, which is found deep in flowers. Some flowers have long tube shapes.	

Applying Artificial Selection to Solve Problems

Artificial Selection as a Biotechnology

Artificial selection is a type of **biotechnology**—the use of biological understanding to solve practical problems. The root word, *technology*, implies that people use creativity to design and implement biological solutions. Using yeast to produce bread and cheese is biotechnology. Other examples are using bacteria to make antibiotics, to break down sewage, or to clean up oil spills. In each case, people use advances in the scientific understanding of a biological process to solve a problem or improve the quality of life.

16. Is natural selection considered a biotechnology? Why or why not?

Case Study: Artificial Selection of Corals

In 2005, the Caribbean lost 50% of its coral reefs due to a rise in the area's ocean temperatures. Warm water causes corals to get rid of the algae living in their tissues. This process is called *bleaching*. The bleached corals become weaker and some corals may die from lack of food without the photosynthetic algae to provide nutrients.

Artificial selection might help corals become more tolerant of warm temperatures. Coral species from Australia have adapted to warmer waters. Breeding corals from Australia with ones found in colder regions introduces warmth-tolerance genes into more coral species. Scientists can continue selective breeding to increase the total number of corals with these genes.

These tanks are full of corals from different world regions. Selectively breeding coral types might help improve a coral species' ability to resist threats in its environment.

Meeting Needs and Desires

When humans use artificial selection to protect corals, they are helping meet a variety of human needs and desires. Coral reefs are beautiful. This makes them a favorite spot for tourists to visit. Companies around reefs, such as ecotourism companies, hotels, restaurants, and local fisheries, provide many jobs. Coral reefs are also areas of high biodiversity. Therefore, there are many species and many individuals present. Ocean algae that live among reef systems provide a large percentage of the oxygen in Earth's air. Some medicines also come from coral reefs. For example, an enzyme used by corals to fight disease is an ingredient in medicines used to treat asthma and arthritis. Protecting reefs through artificial selection will also protect these valuable resources.

Healthy reef systems support nearly 4,000 species of fish. Scientists think there may be over a million undiscovered species that also live among the world's coral reefs.

17. What criteria must be met for artificial selection to be a successful solution to coral bleaching and the long-term success of coral reefs? Select all that apply.

A. Corals must have variation in their ability to survive changing temperatures.

B. The trait being influenced in corals must be beneficial to humans.

C. The offspring of corals must be able to reproduce in nature.

D. The ability to survive changing temperatures must involve heritable traits.

E. The artificial selection process must not harm healthy coral reefs.

 EVIDENCE NOTEBOOK

18. What human needs or desires were met through the development of alpaca populations? Record your evidence.

Engineer It | **Evaluate Uses of Artificial Selection** Ocean water is becoming more acidic. Higher acidity prevents corals from using carbonate to build their skeletons. An effective artificial selection solution will help corals hold on to algae. It will also increase the amount of carbonate corals take up in increasingly warm and acidic ocean water. Two proposed solutions are provided in the table.

Proposed solution	Description
Farming corals in several conditions	Corals are grown in different acidity levels and with different algae in order to detect and breed the healthiest combination.
Exposing lab-raised corals to stress	Scientists think that the DNA of stressed corals changes in a way that makes them better able to withstand the same stress when it occurs again. Corals that can best tolerate stress are chosen for breeding programs.

19. What do the proposed solutions for reducing coral bleaching have in common? Circle all that apply.

   A. They both include identifying variation in traits.

   B. They both include selectively breeding corals for desirable traits.

   C. They both include selectively breeding algae for desirable traits.

   D. They both depend on environmental factors to alter coral DNA.

20. Choose one of the solutions. Explain how it could be improved or expanded to help solve the problem of coral bleaching.

Analyze the Impacts of Artificial Selection on Society

Today's juicy corn is the result of thousands of years of selective breeding. Just five gene locations cause the differences between corn and teosinte, corn's ancestor. Farmers selected plants with more or larger kernels. Now, advances in genetics allow farmers to encourage pest and drought resistance in corn. Corn has become a *super crop*, grown in large amounts to meet many needs.

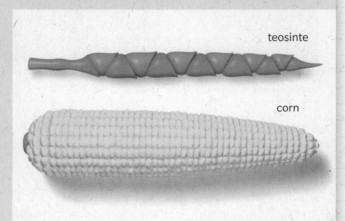

teosinte

corn

21. Describe how important crops that have been highly influenced by selective breeding, such as corn, have affected society.

_____

_____

_____

_____

Continue Your Exploration

Name: _____   Date: _____

Check out the path below or go online to choose one of the other paths shown.

| Breeding Bacteria | • **Accidental Selection**
 • **Hands-On Labs** 🖐
 • **Propose Your Own Path** | *Go online to choose one of these other paths.* |

Plants often depend on bacteria to help them obtain nutrients, fight disease, and resist environmental stress. Humans use plants in many ways, such as for food. Using artificial selection to encourage plant-helping traits in bacteria can help meet human needs. For example, scientists have learned that some bacteria help rice plants survive in locations with high temperatures and acidic soil. Scientists are testing the use of these bacteria to help corals as oceans becomes warmer and more acidic! Using safe bacteria to promote plant health also reduces the need for fertilizers and pesticides that cause pollution.

Bacteria can help plants in many ways. Scientists use the procedures below to identify and choose plant-helping bacteria.

STEP 1 Grow plants in soils treated with different types of plant-helping bacteria.

STEP 2 Compare the plants to determine which bacteria help them the most.

STEP 3 Collect bacteria from the healthiest plants for selective breeding.

STEP 4 Test the offspring bacteria in fresh soil with new plants.

STEP 5 Repeat Steps 1–4 to optimize the effects.

Once this process is complete, the selectively bred plant-helping bacteria can be sold to farmers to improve crop harvests.

These root nodules are the result of a plant-bacteria symbiosis. The bacteria help plants obtain nitrogen and the plants give the bacteria energy-rich sugars.

Continue Your Exploration

1. How might the artificial selection of plant-helping bacteria affect society?
   Select all that apply.

   A. It boosts the economy by increasing farmer profits.

   B. It increases pollution due to pesticide use.

   C. It encourages partnerships between scientists and industry leaders.

   D. It reduces pollution from artificial fertilizers.

2. Is the process used to isolate and increase plant-helping bacteria an engineering
   solution? Use evidence from the passage to support your answer.

3. Scientists use genetic testing to identify specific genes present in organisms,
   including bacteria. How might this technology make it easier to breed plant-helping
   bacteria using artificial selection?

4. **Collaborate** Genetic engineering could also be used to increase plant-helping traits
   in bacteria. What advantages does the use of artificial selection provide compared to
   genetic engineering? Make a list of possible advantages to discuss with your class.

Can You Explain It?

Name: _____   Date: _____

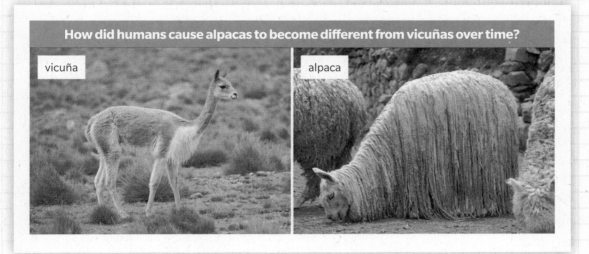

How did humans cause alpacas to become different from vicuñas over time?

vicuña

alpaca

EVIDENCE NOTEBOOK

Refer to the notes in your Evidence Notebook to help you construct an explanation for how humans influenced the development of alpaca populations from vicuñas.

1. State your claim. Make sure your claim fully explains how humans influenced the development of alpaca populations.

2. Summarize the evidence you have gathered to support your claim and explain your reasoning.

Checkpoints

Answer the following questions to check your understanding of the lesson.

Use the Punnett square to answer Questions 3–4.

3. What is the probability that these parents will produce a short-haired Chihuahua?

   A. 0%

   B. 25%

   C. 50%

   D. 100%

4. Which two individuals should be bred to produce the highest probability of having a long-haired Chihuahua?

   A. *HH* and *hh*

   B. *Hh* and *Hh*

   C. *Hh* and *hh*

   D. *HH* and *Hh*

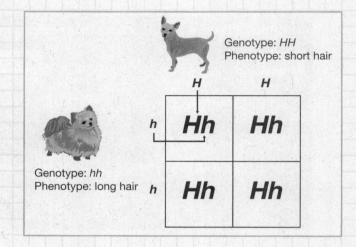

Genotype: *HH*
Phenotype: short hair

Genotype: *hh*
Phenotype: long hair

	H	H
h	*Hh*	*Hh*
h	*Hh*	*Hh*

Use the photograph to answer Question 5.

5. What evidence in the photo suggests that roses have been influenced by artificial selection?

   A. The roses all have very soft petals.

   B. The roses display variety in only one trait.

   C. The roses display traits that appeal to humans.

   D. Some roses have more stripes or flecks than others.

6. How does artificial selection differ from natural selection? Circle all that apply.

   A. During artificial selection, the mating pairs are selected by humans, not the organisms.

   B. The outcomes of artificial selection are predictable.

   C. Artificial selection requires variety in a population.

   D. Artificial selection does not help a population adapt to its environment.

7. How are genetic engineering and artificial selection similar? Circle all that apply.

   A. They influence traits in organisms.

   B. They involve altering DNA sequences.

   C. They attempt to meet human needs or desires.

   D. They expand as scientific understanding of inheritance improves.

Interactive Review

Complete this section to review the main concepts of the lesson.

People have used artificial selection for thousands of years to influence the inheritance of desired traits in living things.

A. What is required for artificial selection? Is an advanced understanding of genes needed?

Artificial selection influences the genotypes and phenotypes of populations.

B. How do Punnett squares help predict the outcomes of artificial selection?

Artificial selection helps meet the needs and desires of humans.

C. Use an example to explain how artificial selection can help solve human problems.

Genetic Engineering Influences Traits in Organisms

This cat is producing proteins that cause it to glow green under certain types of light.

Explore First

Evaluating Genetic Engineering Make a list of the benefits and drawbacks of directly modifying an organism's DNA through genetic engineering. Do you think it's okay for scientists to directly modify the DNA of plants? Of animals? Of humans? Use evidence from your list to support your answer.

Go online to view the digital version of the Hands-On Lab for this lesson and to download additional lab resources.

CAN YOU EXPLAIN IT?

How can goats produce spider silk proteins?

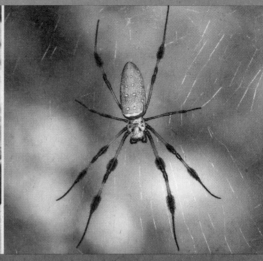

Spiders make silk, a type of protein that is light, strong, and flexible. Scientists have developed goats that produce spider silk proteins in their milk. The spider silk protein can be separated from the milk for human use. Potential uses include protective clothing and wound dressings or sutures.

1. What are the advantages of getting spider silk from goats instead of spiders?

2. Do you think people could breed goats to produce spider silk proteins? Explain your answer.

EVIDENCE NOTEBOOK As you explore the lesson, gather evidence to help explain what can cause goats to produce spider silk proteins.

Exploring Genetic Engineering Techniques

You may have friends with blue, green, or brown eyes. Eye color is an inherited *trait* that is passed from parents to offspring. Traits are controlled by genes. *Genes* are segments of DNA on chromosomes. Genes code for proteins that cause specific traits in an organism, such as eye color. Scientists can change genes to influence traits in organisms.

Inheritance of Eye Color

3. Eye color is a trait influenced by several genes. The *OCA2* and *HERC2* genes determine how much melanin pigment is produced in iris cells. More melanin leads to brown eyes. Less melanin leads to blue eyes. Complete the diagram using terms in the word bank.

WORD BANK
proteins
DNA
traits
genes

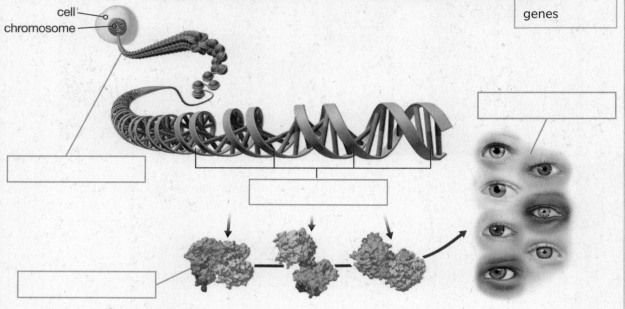

Genetic Engineering as Biotechnology

As scientists improve their understanding of the biological processes that connect genes to traits, they develop technologies to study and influence desired traits in organisms. **Genetic engineering** is the process of modifying DNA for practical purposes. Scientists might modify DNA for use in research, medicine, or agriculture. For example, soybean plants are important for oils and livestock feed. Soybeans are a genetically modified crop. Soybean crop health improved after scientists inserted genes for pest resistance into soybean seeds. Gene insertion is just one biotechnology used by genetic engineers. Other genetic engineering technologies encourage the production of specific proteins, or change genes to modify traits in organisms.

A caterpillar chewed holes in the leaves of this soybean plant. Inserting a pest resistance gene into soybeans can decrease damage due to pests.

Comparing Genetic Engineering and Artificial Selection

Humans have influenced the traits of organisms for thousands of years through artificial selection. *Artificial selection* is the process of breeding organisms to increase the frequency of desired traits in a population. Both artificial selection and genetic engineering influence the traits present in a population. For example, humans can improve pest resistance in soybeans by breeding plants that show increased resistance to pests *or* by inserting a pest-resistance gene. Influencing traits through genetic engineering can be more precise and faster than using artificial selection. In some cases, genetic engineering allows scientists to make changes to the traits of an organism that would not be possible through artificial selection.

Inserting a Gene into a Bacterium

Segments of DNA from one organism may be integrated into the DNA of a different organism. The simple structure of bacterial cells makes them good candidates for genetic engineering.

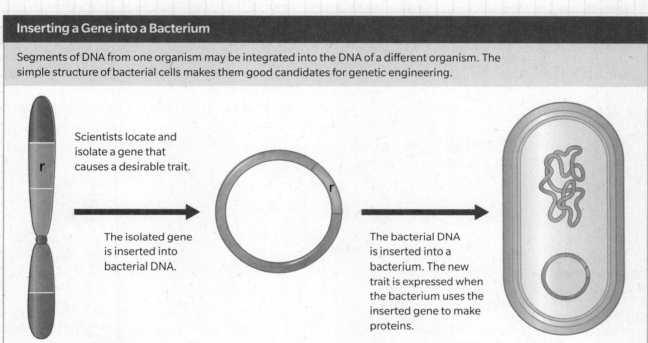

Scientists locate and isolate a gene that causes a desirable trait.

The isolated gene is inserted into bacterial DNA.

The bacterial DNA is inserted into a bacterium. The new trait is expressed when the bacterium uses the inserted gene to make proteins.

4. What is required to insert a new gene into a bacterium and for the bacterium to show the new trait? Select all that apply.

   A. proteins

   B. biotechnology

   C. cellular processes

   D. a breeding program

5. **Discuss** When inserting a new gene into an organism, the gene could come from the same species or it could come from a different species. Generate at least three questions you could research about each of these scenarios.

Milestones in Genetic Engineering

Rapid advancements in genetic engineering began in the early 1970s. Biologists saw that bacteria use special enzymes to repair their DNA. For example, bacteria use enzymes to cut and remove DNA that was inserted by a virus. *Viruses* are small particles that insert viral genetic information into host cells. The discovery about how bacteria use "cut and paste" enzymes inspired scientists to investigate how these enzymes could be used to solve human problems. Developments in genetic engineering reflect scientific progress. Scientists use creativity and existing technology to make new discoveries. This leads to increased understanding and chances for more exploration.

Recombination Technology

When a new gene is inserted into DNA, the DNA is called *recombinant DNA*. Recombinant DNA began by using *plasmids*, or small circles of bacterial DNA.

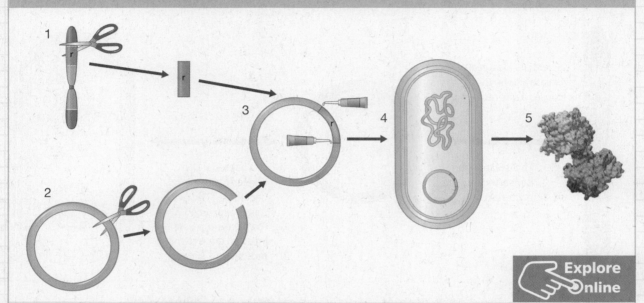

Step 1 The gene that controls a trait is located and cut from the chromosome.

Step 2 The plasmid is opened using "cut" enzymes.

Step 3 The new gene is added to the plasmid using "paste" enzymes.

Step 4 The plasmid with the new gene is inserted into a bacterium.

Step 5 The bacterium produces the new protein.

Explore Online

6. Number the milestones of genetic engineering to show the progression of science.

_____ Foreign DNA is successfully inserted into the DNA of bacteria.

_____ Scientists confirm that the new genes give the bacteria new traits.

_____ "Cut and paste" enzymes are discovered by observing how bacteria use enzymes to destroy the DNA of invading viruses.

_____ Bacteria use inserted genes to make proteins, just as they do with their own genes.

Hands-On Lab
Model the Modification of Bacteria

You will model genetic modification of a bacterium using "cut and paste" enzymes. You will also analyze how genetic modification of bacteria can help humans.

Bacteria are unicellular organisms. Bacteria do not have nuclei. Instead, most of the genes are in a single, circular chromosome in the cytoplasm. The simple structure and rapid reproduction of bacteria make them a good choice for scientific research.

MATERIALS
• colored beads (to fit on pipe cleaner)
• colored pencils
• pipe cleaners
• scissors

Procedure

STEP 1 Locate the circular chromosome and the plasmids in the diagram. Use evidence from the diagram to make a list of traits controlled by the bacterium's DNA.

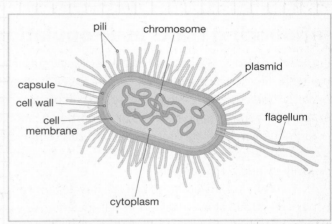

This bacterium has a single large chromosome and several smaller circles of DNA called plasmids. The plasmids contain few genes. They are not essential for the bacterium's survival.

STEP 2 Build a pipe cleaner plasmid to model a circular plasmid in the bacterium. To model DNA bases, use beads similar in color to the letters in the sequence given. Add the correct sequence of DNA "bases" to the pipe cleaner and then twist the free ends together.

DNA sequence: TTGAGCGCATTGCGT

STEP 3 The "cut" enzyme cuts the plasmid between an ATT sequence and a GCG sequence. Cut your plasmid in the correct location. The scissors model the enzyme in this step.

STEP 4 Choose one of the genes from the table to insert into your plasmid. Add the correct sequences of bases. Then "paste" (twist) the free ends together.

Function of protein encoded by gene	DNA sequence of gene
stops the bacterium from building pili that help the bacterium infect cells	TTGAA
causes bacterium to burst	GCGTA
increases production of a protein used in livestock feed	ATTTA

Analysis

STEP 5 Draw the modified bacterium with its new trait.

STEP 6 How might a population of bacteria with this new trait be helpful for people?

Influencing Traits in a Population

Engineers can insert genes that cause desirable traits in an organism. In order to be heritable, the modification must be made to cells passed to offspring. This is easy in bacteria. Bacteria divide in half and pass a complete copy of their DNA to their offspring. In sexually reproducing organisms, genetic modification will only be heritable if it occurs in reproductive cells—egg or sperm—or in early embryos. This makes it more difficult to use genetic engineering to influence traits in a population of organisms that reproduce sexually compared to bacteria.

The cells in early embryos can still develop into any cell type. They pass an identical copy of their DNA to every offspring cell, including any genetic modifications. During the process of *cell differentiation*, cells become specialized for a specific function. Once cells differentiate into various types, such as muscle cells or blood cells, genetic modifications made to the cells will only pass to the offspring cells of that cell type.

Cell Differentiation in Embryos

Early embryo cells differentiate into the different cell types found in an organism. This diagram shows three examples of specialized cell types.

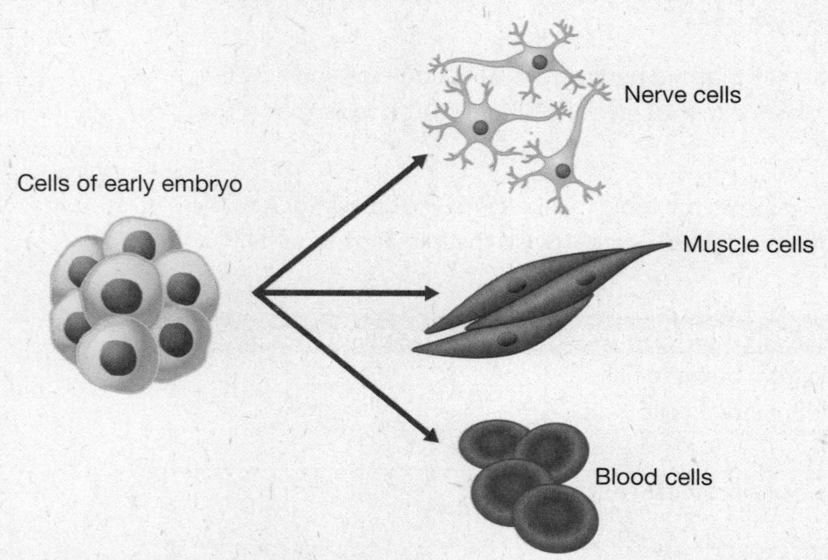

Cells of early embryo

Nerve cells

Muscle cells

Blood cells

7. Do the Math If all of a poisonous frog's eggs are genetically engineered right after fertilization to include a gene that prevents poison production, what is the ratio of poisonous to non-poisonous frogs in the offspring?

A. 1:0

B. 1:2

C. 0:1

D. 1:1

EVIDENCE NOTEBOOK

8. How could genetic engineering cause goats to produce a new protein? Record your evidence.

Genetic Modification of Bacteria

Genetic engineering can be used to help solve human problems. People with diabetes need a dependable supply of insulin. Insulin is a protein that helps regulate blood sugar. Scientists have modified bacteria to produce insulin for human use. Large numbers of the modified bacteria can be farmed to produce large amounts of insulin.

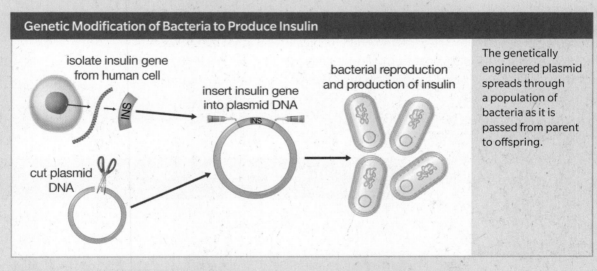

Genetic Modification of Bacteria to Produce Insulin

isolate insulin gene from human cell

insert insulin gene into plasmid DNA

cut plasmid DNA

bacterial reproduction and production of insulin

The genetically engineered plasmid spreads through a population of bacteria as it is passed from parent to offspring.

9. Based on your knowledge of recombinant DNA and the diagram above, explain why is it necessary to genetically engineer the bacteria to produce insulin instead of inserting the insulin gene in humans.

_____

_____

_____

_____

_____

_____

_____

Evaluating Genetic Modification

Genetically engineered crops, especially those not intended for the human food supply, are common in the United States and other industrialized nations. For example, genetically modified soybean plants now make up more than 80% of all soybean crops around the world. Many of these soybeans are used for animal feed. The use of genetically modified crops is increasing. Some modified crops are hardier and more productive than non-modified crops.

10. Why might farmers want to grow cotton plants that have been modified to be resistant to herbicides?

These cotton plants contain genes to resist the herbicides that farmers use to kill weeds.

Genetically Modified Organisms

Inserting foreign DNA into an organism results in a **genetically modified organism**, or GMO. These organisms are often called *transgenic* because genetic modification allows genes to cross the normal barriers between species (*trans* means "across"). GMOs have applications in agriculture, scientific research, medicine, and other industries. For example, genetically modified soybeans provide oils for skin-care products and protein for food products. Many people are cautious about GMOs because they are unsure of potential side effects on humans and other species. This has limited the planting of genetically modified crops in some countries. Some GMO crops allow for reduced use of pesticides. Others require increased pesticide use for a successful harvest.

11. According to the graph, which crop was the first to reach 75% GMO-planted acres?

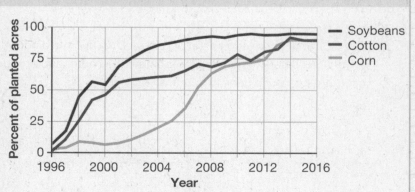

Adoption of Crops Genetically Engineered for Herbicide Tolerance (United States, 1996–2016)

The number of acres planted with genetically modified crops has increased since their introduction in the mid-1990s.

Sources: USDA, Economic Research Service using data from Fernandez-Comejo and McBride (2002) for the years 1996–99 and USDA, National Agricultural Statistics Service, June Agricultural Survey for the years 2000–16.

12. There may be more support for the genetic modification of a crop if it is not used for human food. What pattern in the graph might be explained by this statement?

A. the different adoption rates between cotton and soybeans

B. the different adoption rates between cotton and corn

C. the current adoption level of soybeans, cotton, and corn

© Houghton Mifflin Harcourt Publishing Company • Image Credits: ©STEVEN SIEWERT/ Fairfax Media/Getty Images

Case Study: Glowing Mosquitoes

Malaria and dengue fever are human diseases that are spread by mosquitoes. Scientists can insert a gene that causes mosquitoes to die if they do not receive a specific chemical. Scientists insert a fluorescent gene from jellyfish at the same time to track which mosquitoes have been successfully modified. Researchers release only modified male mosquitoes to the wild because male mosquitoes do not bite humans. When female mosquitoes in the wild mate with the modified males, the offspring inherit the modified gene and die without access to the chemical. This reduces mosquito populations and can slow the spread of some human diseases. However, the release of genetically modified mosquitoes into the wild raises concerns about the impact on birds and bats that may eat the GMOs.

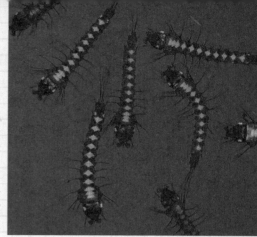
These mosquito larvae glow. Their cells have genes from jellyfish that make fluorescent proteins.

The Impact of Genetically Modified Mosquitoes	
Effect on individuals	Human individuals experience reduced exposure to diseases carried by mosquitoes, including malaria and dengue fever.
Effect on society	Society benefits by saving lives and reducing health care costs associated with malaria and dengue fever. The money saved can be used for other beneficial projects in communities.
Effect on the environment	The release of genetically modified mosquitoes might have negative impacts on birds or bats that feed on mosquitoes.

Case Study: Research Mice

Some research mice are genetically modified for scientific research. *Knockout mice* have a gene in their DNA "knocked out" or disrupted. Scientists then observe the mice to see how their traits change. This helps scientists identify the gene's function. Humans and mice have similar DNA, so research with knockout mice can help scientists learn what human genes do. For example, knockout mice research has provided data about genes involved in cancer and anxiety in humans. However, knockout mice are not a perfect research tool. Knocking out an important gene can cause developmental problems in the mice. Also, data from knockout mice studies cannot always be applied to humans.

A gene has been "knocked out" in the mouse on the left. Scientists use knockout mice to learn what genes do.

13. Identify whether the impacts described in the table relate to individuals, society, or the environment.

The Impact of Genetically Modified Mice	
	Knockout mice stay in a lab to limit the chance of spreading modified genes to wild mice.
	Researchers use information from knockout mice to treat similar diseases in humans.
	Knockout mice might be hurt by changes made through genetic engineering.

© Houghton Mifflin Harcourt Publishing Company • Image Credits: (t) ©Sinclair Stammers/ Science Source; (b) ©Science Source

Case Study: Pharmaceutical Chickens

In 2015, officials in the United States approved the farming of genetically engineered chickens. The chickens produce a special protein in their eggs that can be used to treat a human disorder. The protein is isolated from the eggs and given to people who lack the protein in their bodies. Without this protein, humans cannot break down fat molecules. The condition is fatal to infants and causes heart disease in adults. There is no other effective treatment for the disorder.

Plants, bacteria, and other organisms have been genetically modified for medical purposes. Goats can be modified to produce a chemical in their milk that breaks down blood clots in humans. Using mammals to produce pharmaceutical chemicals in their milk can be effective. Milk production is a natural process, and milking does not harm the animals.

Chickens can be genetically modified to produce a pharmaceutical protein in their eggs.

The Impact of Genetically Modified Chickens	
Effect on individuals	Humans with a protein disorder will experience fewer deaths and reduced illness by receiving replacement protein from the chicken eggs. Laying eggs is a natural process, so the chickens are not harmed.
Effect on society	Some medical chemicals need cellular processes for production. Using GMOs to produce these chemicals provides medicines that cannot be made in a laboratory.
Effect on the environment	The introduction of GMOs into communities can be risky. Scientists try to prevent the transfer of genetically modified DNA by isolating GMOs. Some people worry that modified genes will accidentally spread to wild species.

14. Which of the following are positive impacts that genetically modified chickens have on society? Circle all that apply.

  A. production of pharmaceuticals that cannot be manufactured

  B. improved medical care for humans

  C. increasing numbers of GMOs in communities

  D. production of proteins that cure all diseases

15. Discuss Scientific knowledge can describe the benefits and drawbacks of actions, but society makes decisions about how and when to act. For example, the use of animals in scientific research can help society by providing test subjects that are not humans. However, animals are often harmed during research studies and many people believe that the rights of the animals must be considered. How can you apply the concept of ethics to the subject of animal testing?

16. What evidence suggests that genetic modification is involved in goats that produce spider silk in their milk? Record your evidence.

Engineer It

Evaluate Impacts of Genetically Modified Crops

Corn can be genetically modified to protect the plants from caterpillar damage.

Bacillus thuringiensis (Bt) is a bacterium that makes proteins that kill pests. Scientists isolated the Bt gene and inserted it into the DNA of corn seeds. The result is Bt corn. Bt corn is a GMO that is resistant to leaf-eating caterpillars.

17. Complete the table to explain how genetically modified corn might impact individuals, society, and the environment.

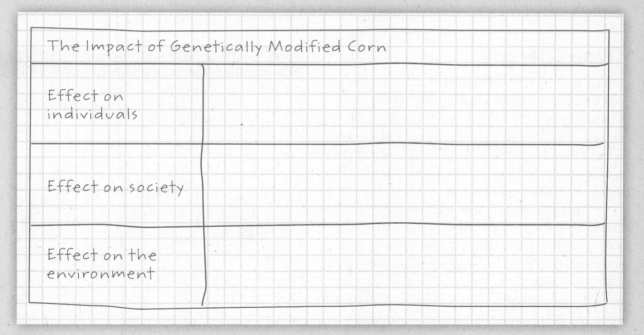

The Impact of Genetically Modified Corn	
Effect on individuals	
Effect on society	
Effect on the environment	

18. Would you grow genetically modified corn if you were a farmer? Provide your reasoning.

_____

_____

_____

_____

_____

Evaluating Gene Therapy

Genetic engineering is not limited to genetic modification using bacteria. Other microbes and molecules can also be used to insert or influence genes in similar ways. For example, viruses are used in genetic engineering. Viruses inject viral genes into a cell. The cell then produces viral proteins that are assembled into new viruses. Scientists can change viruses so that they inject desirable genes into cells instead of viral genes.

19. **Discuss** What might be some advantages and disadvantages of using viruses in genetic engineering to treat human diseases?

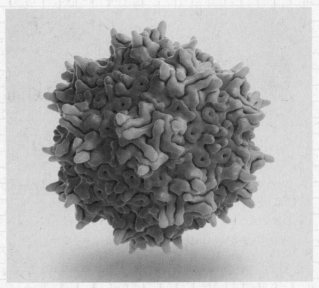

Scientists often choose *adenoviruses* to deliver genes to target cells. These viruses inject their genetic material into a cell's nucleus.

Gene Therapy

Advances in biotechnology allow scientists to treat certain diseases. **Gene therapy** is a technique that uses genes to treat or prevent disease. Gene therapy may be used to insert helpful genes or to remove harmful genes. It may also be used to insert "suicide genes" that cause cell death. This is a promising treatment for cancer.

Most gene therapies are still being tested and studied. To be successfully treated with gene therapy, a disease must have a genetic cause and scientists must know which genes cause the disease. Also, the disease should involve one or only a few genes. Finally, the affected genes must be accessible for treatment for gene therapy to be successful.

A gene therapy success story involves children born with immune cells that do not work. A single gene normally active in bone marrow causes severe combined immunodeficiency disorder. Therapy involves taking bone marrow cells from a patient, inserting the correct gene, and replacing diseased bone marrow cells with modified cells. Without treatment, children born with the disorder must live in germ-free plastic bubbles. Gene therapy allows these children to live healthy lives.

Types of Gene Therapy

Gene therapy can involve adding a functional gene, blocking a malfunctioning gene, or causing a malfunctioning cell to die.

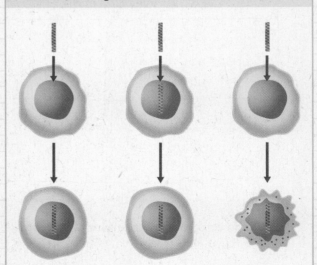

Addition of a therapeutic gene provides normal cell function.

Addition of a therapeutic gene blocks a malfunctioning gene, providing normal cell function.

Addition of a harmful gene produces a lethal substance and the targeted cell dies.

Methods of Gene Delivery

Gene therapy may involve direct or indirect delivery of therapeutic genes. In *direct gene delivery*, a therapeutic gene is inserted into a virus. Then the genetically modified virus is delivered directly to the target site. In *indirect gene delivery*, a therapeutic gene is inserted into a virus. Cells are extracted from the patient. The genetically modified virus is used to introduce the gene to the cells outside of the body. The genetically modified cells are delivered to the target site.

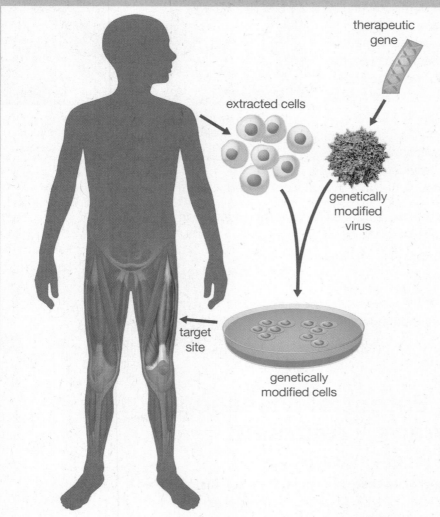

therapeutic gene

extracted cells

genetically modified virus

target site

genetically modified cells

Indirect Gene Delivery

1. **Identify Target Cells** Cells receiving therapeutic genes must be in an isolated area.

2. **Prepare Gene for Delivery** A therapeutic gene is inserted into a virus or other delivery mechanism.

3. **Remove Cells for Modification** Diseased cells are removed from a patient so they can be modified in a lab.

4. **Inject Virus into Extracted Cells** The virus carrying the therapeutic gene is injected into cells removed from the patient's body. Modified cells are grown in the lab.

5. **Deliver Modified Cells** Modified cells are delivered to the patient through injection at a target site.

20. Why might scientists choose indirect delivery instead of direct delivery for a gene therapy?

   A. Indirect delivery methods take less time than direct delivery methods.

   B. Direct gene delivery is only possible if the target area is accessible.

   C. Genetically modified cells are easier to deliver to the target area than genetically modified viruses.

   D. Indirect delivery allows scientists to make sure the cells have been correctly modified and are producing the protein.

21. Why are diseases involving many different genes poor candidates for gene therapy?

Impacts of Gene Therapy

Gene therapy has the potential to treat many diseases. The field of gene therapy is still new. Advances in biotechnology are improving gene delivery methods. While the future of gene therapy looks promising, it faces many challenges. Gene therapy raises many ethical concerns about whether human DNA should be changed. Genetic engineering is also costly. Gene therapy may not be available to poorer populations. Gene therapy can disrupt the function of healthy genes in target cells, and long-term effects are uncertain. New genes often result from natural mutations. Over time, evolutionary forces will minimize genes and traits with negative effects. New genes resulting from genetic engineering do not go through the same evolutionary process.

Cystic fibrosis is a genetic disease that causes persistent lung infections. Treatment includes inhaling medicine through a nebulizer. Gene therapies are being tested for this disease.

22. What are the requirements a disease must meet for gene therapy to be an effective option for treatment? Circle all that apply.

   A. It must have a genetic cause.

   B. It should involve many genes.

   C. Target cells must be accessible.

   D. Target cells must be found throughout the patient's body.

Language SmArts

Identify a Potential Disease for Gene Therapy Treatment

Consider what scientists know about these three diseases:

- The predisposition to have **heart disease** is inherited. The disease is influenced by other factors, including age, diet, high blood pressure, and smoking.

- A single gene causes **hemophilia.** Hemophilia results in a lack of clotting proteins in the blood. Clotting proteins are produced in the liver. The lack of clotting proteins can lead to severe bleeding and joint damage.

- People with **type I diabetes** produce little or no insulin. Insulin is needed to move sugar from the blood into cells. Type I diabetes involves multiple genes. It is triggered by environmental factors.

23. Which disease has the best potential for treatment with gene therapy? Defend your answer using evidence from the text and explain what criteria you used.

_____

_____

_____

_____

Continue Your Exploration

Name: _____   Date: _____

Check out the path below or go online to choose one of the other paths shown.

People in Science

- Careers in Science
- Cockroaches vs. Pandas
- Hands-On Labs
- Propose Your Own Path

Go online to choose one of these other paths.

Dr. Lydia Villa-Komaroff, Molecular Biologist

Dr. Lydia Villa-Komaroff has been a laboratory scientist, a university administrator, a company executive, and an advocate for diversity in STEM during her remarkable career in science. Villa-Komaroff has deep roots in the Southwest. Her mother's family is from the Basque region of Spain and came to America with the conquistadors. Her father's father came from Mexico during the Mexican revolution. She grew up in New Mexico and knew at an early age that she wanted to be a scientist. Education was important to her parents, both the first in their family to go to college.

Dr. Lydia Villa-Komaroff studies the structure, function, and interactions of molecules at the cellular level, a field known as molecular biology.

Villa-Komaroff attended the University of Washington before transferring to Goucher College in Maryland. She had to study harder in college then she did in high school, but she persisted in pursuing science degrees. After studying microbiology and cell biology at MIT, Villa-Komaroff began postdoctoral research at Harvard involving recombinant DNA. Her project at Harvard could not continue when the city of Cambridge banned recombinant DNA research. Villa-Komaroff moved her project using recombinant DNA to study the genome of silk moths to a lab in a different city. Her project was doomed to failure because the tools available were not up to the job of dealing with a large genome; the silk moth genome is almost as large as the human genome. The ban on recombinant DNA research and the unsuccessful project provided valuable lessons about setbacks and learning from failure when working on the cutting edge of science and medicine.

1. How do failures fit into the scientific method or the engineering design process?

Continue Your Exploration

Proinsulin Production in Bacteria

When the research ban was lifted, Dr. Villa-Komaroff returned to Harvard. She was the lead author in a groundbreaking study that explained how to produce proinsulin in bacterial cells by inserting the insulin gene into *E. coli* bacteria. She and her colleagues used rat insulin as a model and these results opened the door for the production of many medically useful proteins. Proinsulin is a precursor of insulin, an important hormone that regulates blood sugar levels. People with diabetes may not produce enough insulin or their bodies may not respond to the insulin that is produced. Eventually, scientists were able to mass produce insulin using bacteria, which decreased the cost and increased the availability of insulin for treating diabetes.

2. Before insulin was available from bacteria, it was taken from animals such as cattle or pigs. Brainstorm potential benefits of using bacteria instead of animals to produce insulin.

Neuroscience and Cell Biology

Dr. Villa-Komaroff also performed neuroscience and cell biology research. For example, Villa-Komaroff collaborated on an experiment that showed beta-amyloid is toxic to neuron cells similar to those found in the brain. The pieces of protein that make up beta-amyloid form plaques in brains affected by Alzheimer's disease. This progressive disease is characterized by dementia and loss of cognitive abilities. It was unclear whether beta-amyloid caused neuron cell death or was a byproduct of the cell death. In the experiment, the gene for the beta-amyloid protein was inserted into neuronal cells. The researchers could turn the gene on and off. When the gene was turned on, the protein was expressed and the cells died, indicating that beta-amyloid was indeed toxic to cells.

3. What aspect of this experiment represents an advancement over the experiment performed to produce proinsulin in bacteria?

   A. cells died

   B. a gene was inserted

   C. a protein was expressed

   D. the gene was turned on or off

4. **Collaborate** Dr. Villa-Komaroff was a co-founding member of the Society for Advancement of Chicanos and Native Americans in Science (SACNAS). Diversity in STEM has been important to Villa-Komaroff throughout her career. Implicit bias and opportunity are two of the major roadblocks to having diverse STEM fields. Select a current, credible research paper that explores one of these topics and summarize the research in a short presentation to the class. Be sure to explain what diversity is and why it is important for STEM.

Can You Explain It?

Name: _____   **Date:** _____

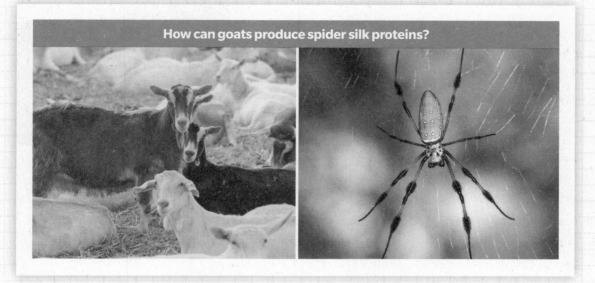

How can goats produce spider silk proteins?

 EVIDENCE NOTEBOOK

Refer to the notes in your Evidence Notebook to help you construct an explanation for what can cause goats to produce spider silk proteins.

1. State your claim. Make sure your claim fully explains how genetic changes allow goats to produce spider silk proteins.

2. Summarize the evidence you have gathered to support your claim and explain your reasoning.

Checkpoints

Answer the following questions to check your understanding of the lesson.

Use the photo of weeds in a cotton field to answer Question 3.

3. This field was sprayed with an herbicide and specific plants survived. What might cause herbicide resistance in the cotton plants or weeds in this field? Select all that apply.

    A. Scientists modified the cotton DNA to resist the herbicide.

    B. Some weeds naturally resist herbicide better than others.

    C. Cotton became herbicide resistant over thousands of years.

    D. Bees transferred herbicide resistance from cotton to weeds.

4. Why are viruses used to deliver therapeutic genes to target cells? Circle all that apply.

    A. scientists can modify viral DNA

    B. viruses carry many beneficial genes

    C. viruses can direct cells to make specific proteins

    D. viruses can be injected directly into cells

5. Some cause-and-effect relationships can only be explained using probability, such as the likelihood that an offspring will inherit a particular trait from one of its parents. Artificial selection *increases / decreases* the likelihood that offspring will inherit a desirable trait. Genetic engineering *can / cannot* bring the likelihood of inheritance of a desirable trait to 100%.

6. What is an advantage of using genetically modified mammals to produce desirable proteins in their milk?

    A. It is easy to genetically modify mammals.

    B. It is difficult to isolate the desirable proteins.

    C. Milk production is a natural process, so there are few negative impacts to the mammals.

    D. Genetic modification of mammals raises few ethical concerns.

Use the eye diagram to answer Question 7.

7. Why is wet macular degeneration a good candidate for gene therapy? Circle all that apply.

    A. The gene therapy is delivered by injection.

    B. The gene therapy makes a single protein that blocks new blood vessels causing the eye disease.

    C. The target cells in the eye are easily accessible.

    D. The modified cell produces new proteins.

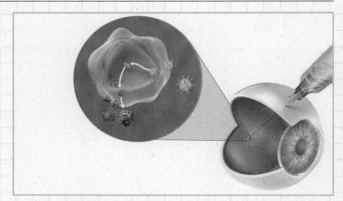

Wet macular degeneration is an eye disease caused by leaking blood vessels. A gene therapy has been made that produces a protein that blocks the production of new blood vessels.

Interactive Review

Complete this section to review the main concepts of the lesson.

Genetic engineering involves the modification of genes for practical purposes.

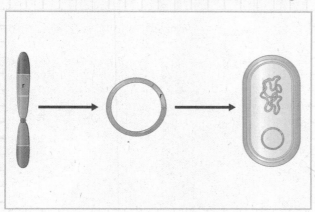

A. Describe the process genetic engineers use to insert genes into a bacterium's DNA so that it produces new proteins.

Inserting a new gene into an organism results in a genetically modified organism (GMO). The introduction of GMOs impacts individuals, society, and the environment.

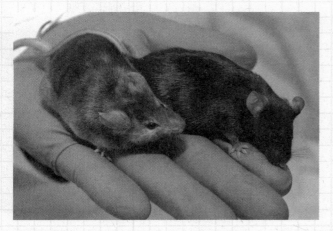

B. What are some impacts of genetically modified organisms on society?

Gene therapy is an experimental technique that uses genes to treat or prevent disease.

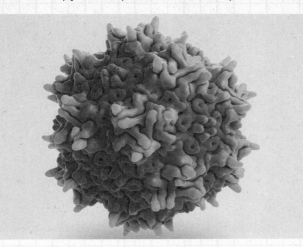

C. Explain the different techniques used to deliver therapeutic genes to target cells.

Choose one of the activities to explore how this unit connects to other topics.

People in Science

Dr. Vanessa Koelling, Evolutionary Biologist

Interest in nature and Earth's history inspired Koelling to become a scientist. Dr. Koelling has Morquio Syndrome, a genetic disease of metabolism that causes physical disability. She has been part of the battle to include people with disabilities in the sciences. Dr. Koelling studies how populations adapt and change, a field known as *population genetics*. She identifies genes involved in adaptations in plant populations.

Research population genetics. Create an infographic that explains this field and highlights five skills or subdisciplines that researchers may use in population genetics, such as mathematical modeling.

Art Connection

Art and Extinction The purpose of extinction art is to raise awareness of endangered species, and species that have already become extinct. This branch of art can also help to relate human impacts on the environment to the risk of losing certain species.

Research an extinct species such as the great auk, shown here, the Wake Island rail, the small Mauritian flying fox, the desert bandicoot, or the Round Island burrowing boa. Find out when and where the species lived and how it went extinct. Create a drawing of your species. Then summarize your research in a short paragraph.

Social Studies Connection

Artificial Selection and Chinese Culture Goldfish were first domesticated in China over 1,000 years ago during the Tang dynasty. People began to breed the gold variety as a sign of wealth. Over the years, more varieties of goldfish have been bred, such as the bubble-eyed goldfish, first bred in 1908. This fish has enlarged fluid-filled sacs beneath its eyes.

Research another example of an animal or plant that has been influenced genetically over time by Chinese culture. Explain the connection between culture and the desired traits. Present your findings in a multimedia presentation.

Name: _____   Date: _____

Complete this review to check your understanding of the unit.

Use the photos to answer Questions 1-4.

This corn has been influenced by artificial selection and genetic modification.

This wheat has been influenced only by artificial selection.

1. Describe the types of traits that can be influenced in these food crops.

2. How are these examples of human influence on traits similar?

3. How are these examples of human influence on traits different?

4. Which is associated with a greater risk for negative impacts on the environment? Use evidence and reasoning to justify your answer.

Name: _____   **Date:** _____

Use the graph to answer Questions 5–8.

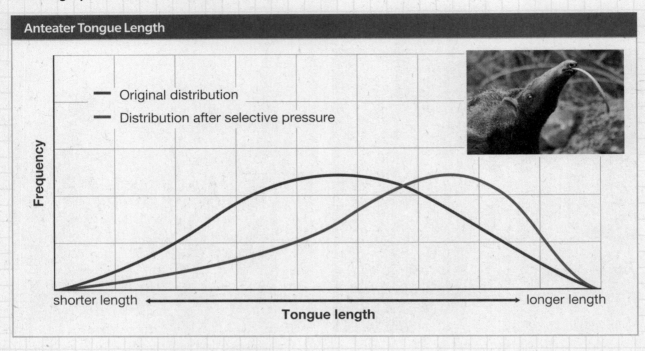

Anteater Tongue Length

— Original distribution
— Distribution after selective pressure

Frequency

shorter length ⟵———————————⟶ longer length

Tongue length

5. What variation of traits is shown in this graph?

6. Explain the connection between genes, proteins, and this variation of traits.

7. Compare and contrast the original distribution of traits prior to selective pressure to the most recent distribution.

8. An anteater's main food source is termites, which live underground. Propose an explanation for how selective pressure could have resulted in the change in traits within the anteater population shown in the graph.

Name: _____   Date: _____

How does the use of insecticides lead to insecticide resistance?

A single genetic mutation causes resistance to the insecticide DDT. This research is key to helping scientists improve malaria-control strategies related to mosquitoes. Research how certain insect species have become resistant to different insecticides over time. What types of variation exist in insect populations that have allowed insect populations to become resistant?

Explain why it is important to minimize the use of harmful insecticides. Create a public education poster using the concept of natural selection to explain the issue of increasing insecticide resistance in insects.

Insecticide Resistance between 1940 and 1990						
Year	Approximate number of species resistant to each insecticide					Total number of resistant insect species
	Cyclodienes	DD1	Organophosphates	Carbamates	Pyrethroids	
1940	<5	<5	<5	<5	<5	<5
1950	25	30	10	<5	<5	45
1960	75	75	40	<5	<5	125
1970	155	125	70	<5	10	235
1980	320	255	215	65	40	435
1990	365	300	305	120	80	505

Source: Metcalfe, R.L., and W.H. Luckmann, eds, *Introduction to Insect Pest Management*, Third Edition, 1994, John Wiley and Sons, N.Y., as quoted by "DDT, Junk Science, Malaria, and insecticide resistance," Bug Gwen, Gwen Pearson, 2007

The steps below will help guide your research and develop your recommendation.

1. **Define the Problem** Write a statement defining the problem you have been asked to solve.

2. **Conduct Research** How have insects become resistant to insecticides over time? During your research, use information from credible and accurate sources, analyze studies for potential bias in methods, and make sure the information you use is supported by evidence.

3. **Analyze the Data** Use the insecticide resistance data to analyze how the resistance to insecticides has changed over time. Then make predictions about how insecticide resistance might change in the future.

4. **Identify and Recommend Solutions** How can the incidence of insecticide resistance be managed? Make a recommendation based on your knowledge of natural selection and your research. Explain your reasoning.

5. **Communicate** Present your findings with a public education poster. Use the concept of natural selection to explain the issue of increasing insecticide resistance, and explain how your solution would help address the problem. Include a graph or other mathematical model to support your conclusions and solution.

✓ **Self-Check**

	I researched how insect species have become resistant to insecticides.
	I analyzed data to describe how resistance to insecticides has changed over time and to predict how it might change in the future.
	I used knowledge of natural selection to make a recommendation about how to manage insecticide resistance.
	My findings and recommendation were clearly communicated to others.

Waves

How are waves and energy related to Earth's seasons?

© Houghton Mifflin Harcourt Publishing Company • Image Credits: ©Wiliyam Bradberry/Shutterstock

Dolphins are at home swimming through waves in the ocean. They communicate with each other using sound waves that travel through water or air. They can even use sound waves to find food.

You Solve It How Can We Harvest Energy from Ocean Waves? Use a model wave power generator to analyze how wave characteristics affect the generation of electrical energy. Choose a location for a wave energy farm.

Go online and complete the You Solve It to explore ways to solve a real-world problem.

Design Wave Interactions

A person wears hearing protection as he inspects an airplane on the tarmac at an airport.

A. Look at the photo. On a separate sheet of paper, write down as many different questions as you can about the photo.

B. Discuss With your class or a partner, share your questions. Record any additional questions generated in your discussion. Then choose the most important questions from the list that are related to minimizing the effect of a wave on humans. Write them below.

C. Make a list of as many different wave types as you can. From the list, identify which types that you or other people interact with and how you interact with the wave. Then choose which interaction you want to research.

D. Use the information above, along with your research, to design a method to minimize the effect of the wave on a person.

Discuss the next steps for your Unit Project with your teacher and go online to download the Unit Project Worksheet.

© Houghton Mifflin Harcourt Publishing Company • Image Credits: ©caia image/Alamy

Language Development

Use the lessons in this unit to complete the network and expand your understanding of these key concepts.

Similar term
Phrase
Cognate
Example
Definition

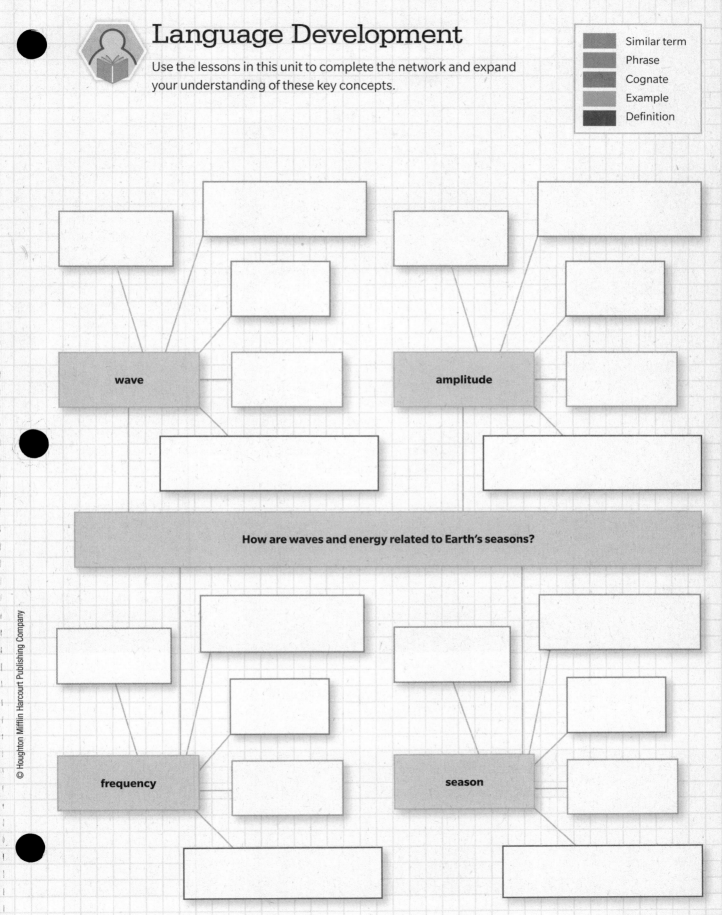

wave

amplitude

How are waves and energy related to Earth's seasons?

frequency

season

Waves Transfer Energy

Ocean waves can be described by the same properties as some other kinds of waves.

© Houghton Mifflin Harcourt Publishing Company • Image Credits: ©Willyam Bradberry/Shutterstock

 Explore First

Exploring Vibrations Tap lightly on one side of an inflated balloon with a stick or unsharpened pencil while a partner places their ear on the other side of the balloon. Trade places and repeat the tapping. What did you notice? Work with your partner to develop an explanation for what you observed.

CAN YOU EXPLAIN IT?

How do falling dominoes compare to a wave?

The person in the picture transfers energy from himself to the first domino, which causes the rest of the dominoes to fall.

Explore Online

1. How does the energy from the person's hand get to the last domino?

EVIDENCE NOTEBOOK As you explore the lesson, gather evidence to help explain how the falling dominoes are similar to and different from a wave.

Exploring Waves

Water crashing onshore, the spotlight on center stage, and a siren blaring may seem unrelated, but they have one thing in common—waves. The world is full of waves, including water waves, light waves, and sound waves.

When a swimmer jumps into a pool, he does not just make a big splash. He also causes waves to spread through the water in the pool.

2. Think about the energy that was needed to form a wave in the pool. Where did the energy come from?

Waves and Energy

A water wave is just one kind of wave. A **wave** is a repeating disturbance that transfers energy from one place to another. A wave transfers energy in the direction that the wave travels. In the diagram of the insect on water, the wave travels to the right, so energy is transferred to the right. How much energy is transferred depends on the size of the disturbance. The greater the disturbance is, the more energy is transferred. However, a wave does not transfer matter. The matter in which a wave travels, called the **medium**, does not move along with it. The plural of medium is media. Waves can be complex, but a lot can be learned by studying simple waves.

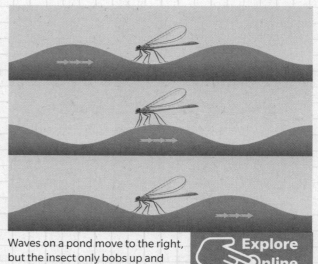

Waves on a pond move to the right, but the insect only bobs up and down due to a small disturbance.

Explore Online

3. Look at the wave traveling through the rope. The left end of the rope is being shaken, so the wave is traveling to the _right / left_ . The energy of the wave travels to the _right / left_ along the rope. As the wave goes by, each piece of the rope moves _up and down / along with the wave_ .

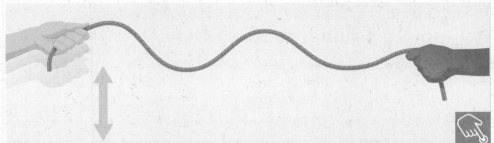

The points on the rope vibrate perpendicularly, or at a right angle, to the direction that the wave moves.

Waves and Wave Pulses

As a wave travels, energy is transferred. If the wave's energy is transferred only one time, then a wave *pulse* is formed. You can see a single pulse as it moves through the medium. If the disturbance transfers energy in a repeating pattern, then a wave is formed and you can see the wave moving continuously.

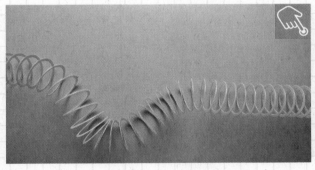

A single wave pulse moves along a coiled spring toy.

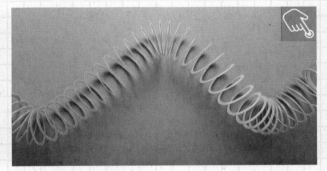

Repeating wave pulses form a wave in a coiled spring toy.

4. **Discuss** Together with a partner, look at the two photos and compare your observations. What wave patterns do you observe? Think about how the wave patterns are similar and how they are different and summarize your conclusions.

5. Which properties of waves discussed so far do the dominoes exhibit? Record your evidence.

Compare a Tsunami to Smaller Water Waves

Waves can be different sizes and shapes, and they can transfer different amounts of energy. A tsunami is a large ocean wave caused by a disturbance in or around the sea, such as an underwater earthquake. A large amount of energy is needed to generate such a large wave, and a tsunami can cause a lot of destruction once it reaches land.

The Formation of a Tsunami

① An underwater fault in the ocean floor releases a massive amount of energy and displaces the water above it. Waves are formed as energy moves outward from the fault.

② Waves build and move as fast as 800 km/h. In deep water, the waves are only 30–60 cm above sea level, but each wave pulse may be hundreds of kilometers long.

③ As the bottom of each wave pulse approaches the shoreline, the wave slows down, increases in height, and the wave pulses come closer together.

④ At the coast, the waves are at their tallest. These giant waves crash onto the shore and can cause massive damage.

6. What does a tsunami have in common with a wave generated by a person jumping into a pool?

_____

_____

_____

_____

_____

_____

_____

_____

Comparing Longitudinal and Transverse Waves

When a wave travels from one end of a rope to the other end, the parts of the rope move up and down. The parts of rope are the "particles" of the medium. In a rope wave, the particles vibrate perpendicularly (up and down) to the direction that the wave travels (to the right), which makes the rope wave an example of a *transverse wave*. In another type of wave, called a *longitudinal wave*, the particles vibrate parallel to the direction that the wave travels. During an earthquake, both types of waves occur.

During an earthquake, the ground can move in dramatic ways. Powerful waves—both longitudinal and transverse waves—travel through Earth's crust.

7. Language SmArts What type of movement do you think is responsible for the damage shown in the photo? Write a paragraph that relates the ground movement during an earthquake to wave type. Create a visual model to clarify how the waves cause damage.

Hands-On Lab
Model Two Types of Waves

Use a coiled spring toy to model two types of waves: a longitudinal wave and a transverse wave.

MATERIALS
• spring toy, coiled

Procedure

STEP 1 Hold a coiled spring toy on the floor between you and a lab partner so that the spring is straight. This is the rest position of the spring. As you do this lab, be sure to keep the spring on the floor as you move it. Another lab partner will document each step.

STEP 2 Move one end of the spring to produce a transverse wave. Describe how you moved the spring and record your observations for Wave 1.

Wave	Observations and Wave Types
Wave 1	
Wave 2	

STEP 3 Allow the spring to return to its rest position.

STEP 4 Move one end of the spring to produce a longitudinal wave. Describe how you moved the spring and record your observations for Wave 2.

Analysis

STEP 5 **Discuss** Together with your partners, compare the waves that you made. How are the waves alike and how are they different? What patterns did you observe? Include examples from your investigation.

Longitudinal and Transverse Waves

Both longitudinal waves and transverse waves transfer energy in the direction that they travel. However, they differ in the way the disturbances move in relation to the direction of wave motion. In a longitudinal wave, the coils move parallel to the direction that the wave travels. An area where the coils are close together is called a compression, and an area where the coils are spread out is called a rarefaction. In a transverse wave, the coils move perpendicularly to the direction that the wave travels. The highest point of the wave is called a crest, and the lowest point is called a trough.

Other types of waves exist, such as surface waves. Surface waves form at the boundary of two media and are a combination of longitudinal waves and transverse waves. Water waves and some seismic waves are examples of surface waves.

8. Label the type and parts of the waves shown in the diagrams.

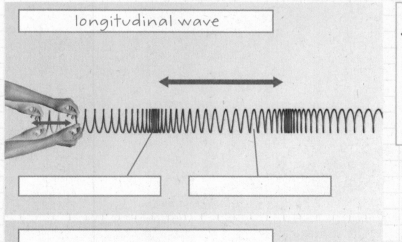

longitudinal wave

WORD BANK
- ~~longitudinal wave~~
- transverse wave
- compression
- rarefaction
- crest
- trough

© Houghton Mifflin Harcourt Publishing Company

9. Describe the movement of the dominoes as energy is transferred through them and then compare the movement of longitudinal waves to the movement of the dominoes. Record your evidence.

Analyze the Types of Waves in Earthquakes

Earthquakes produce both longitudinal waves and transverse waves that travel through Earth's crust. Longitudinal waves and transverse waves often travel at different speeds in a medium. During earthquakes, longitudinal waves are faster, and they arrive first during an earthquake. The transverse waves, which are slower but usually more destructive, arrive seconds later.

10. The arrows in the diagrams show the direction that the seismic waves are traveling. Label the diagrams as either a longitudinal wave or a transverse wave.

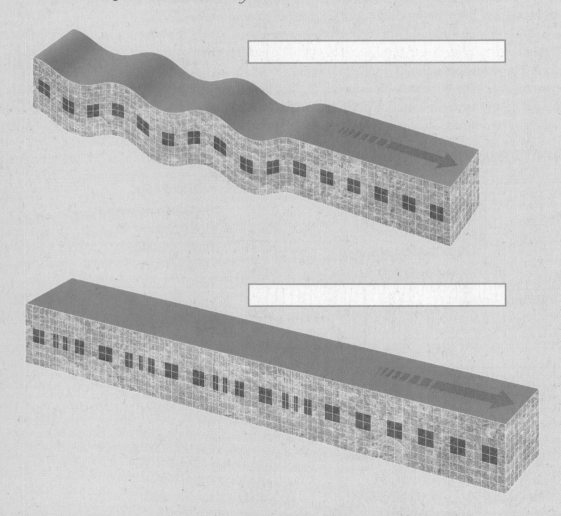

11. If you see the ground moving forward and backward during an earthquake, then you are probably experiencing a longitudinal / transverse wave. If you see the ground moving up and down, then it is likely a longitudinal / transverse wave. In both cases, matter / energy is transferred.

Identifying the Properties of Waves

Picture it: It is a calm day on a quiet street, and a car pulls up to the curb and parks. The driver gets out of the car, pulls down his hat to hide his face, and hurries away. Suddenly, the car explodes!

Fortunately, this violent explosion is part of a scene from a movie. The explosion created a blast wave; a high-pressure wave that radiates out, carrying a lot of energy from the center of the explosion. Special effects experts carefully design and carry out these types of controlled explosions, and set up situations to look like the after effects of an explosion without actually creating a blast wave.

12. A film crew is setting up a scene to show the effects of a blast wave on nearby cars. Why do you think the cars are hanging from cables?

An explosion is a high-energy event that can create a blast wave. A movie's special effects team simulates the effects of a blast wave.

Properties of Waves Can Be Modeled

Waves are described by their properties. A measure of how far a particle in the medium moves away from its normal rest position is the **amplitude**. The amplitude of a transverse wave is half of the difference between the crest and the trough and is equal to the height of the wave above the rest position. The distance from any point on a wave to an identical point on the next wave pulse is the **wavelength**. Wavelength measures the length of one cycle, or repetition, of a wave. A wave can be modeled on a graph.

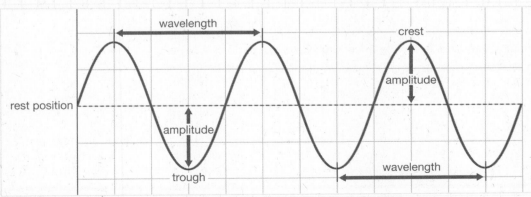

13. **Discuss** In a small group, discuss the wave characteristics shown in the diagram. Explain why the wavelength can be measured as the distance between consecutive peaks or consecutive troughs.

Hands-On Lab
Investigate Waves

Investigate how waves in a water-filled tray affect the medium that they travel through.

MATERIALS
- block, wood, rectangular
- cork
- tray, baking, aluminum, deep
- water

Procedure and Analysis

STEP 1 Fill the tray about halfway with water. Place a cork in the water near the center of the tray.

STEP 2 Choose one group member to move the block up and down in the water at one end of the tray to produce waves. At different times, move the block up and down at different speeds.

STEP 3 Observe the motion of the cork and the water. Sketch and describe your observations.

STEP 4 What is the relationship between the energy of the wave you created in Step 2 and the speed at which the cork moves up and down?

STEP 5 How could you test the following question: Do waves made by a large disturbance carry more energy than waves made by a small disturbance?

14. Collaborate With a partner, develop an informational pamphlet that teaches a student how to graph the properties of a wave. You may use any wave type in your examples.

Frequency and Speed of a Wave

Think about the water waves that you made. The cork bobbed up and down more or less quickly, depending on how quickly you moved the block. The number of wave pulses produced in a set amount of time is the **frequency** of the wave. Frequency is usually expressed in *hertz* (Hz), and for waves, one hertz equals one wave pulse per second (1 Hz = 1/s). The rate at which a wave travels is *wave speed*, which can be calculated by multiplying wavelength and frequency. The equation for wave speed (v) is $v = \lambda \times f$, where wavelength is λ and frequency is f. For example, to determine the wave speed of a wave that has a wavelength of 5 m and a frequency of 4 Hz, substitute the values given for λ and f and solve: $v = 5 \text{ m} \times 4 \text{ Hz} = 20 \text{ m/s}$.

15. Do the Math What is the wave speed of a wave that has a wavelength of 2 m and a frequency of 6 Hz?

16. Engineer It An engineer has been asked to give advice about a wave pool at a local water park. The park guests think that the waves in the pool are too close together. The engineer knows that the wave speed in the pool is constant. Explain why the engineer suggests reducing the frequency of the wave generator.

Energy and Amplitude of a Wave

The amplitude of a wave is dependent on energy. For example, when using a rope to make waves, you have to work harder to produce a wave that has a large amplitude than to produce one that has a small amplitude because it takes more energy to move the rope farther from its rest position. When comparing waves that have the same frequency in the same medium, the wave that has the larger amplitude carries more energy.

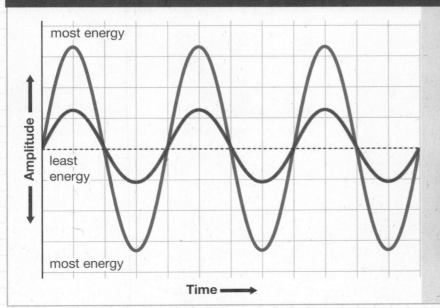

Energy Is Proportional to Amplitude

Lower amplitude waves are perfect for a relaxing day at the beach.

Surfers need higher amplitude waves to catch an exciting ride.

Calculate Amplitude

The relationship between amplitude and wave energy is that energy is proportional to amplitude squared. For example, if the amplitude of the waves at one beach is three times the amplitude of the waves at another beach, you might think that the taller waves have three times as much energy as the shorter waves have. However, the taller waves would actually have nine times as much energy because nine is three squared ($3^2 = 9$).

What if you started knowing energy instead? Suppose that your lab partner told you the energy of a wave increased by a factor of 16, and you want to determine how the amplitude changed. You would find that the amplitude quadrupled because the square root of 16 is equal to 4 ($\sqrt{16} = 4$). You can use the relationship between amplitude and energy to find one variable if you know the other variable.

 17. Do the Math If the energy of a wave increased by a factor of 25, by what factor did the amplitude of the wave increase?

 Language SmArts

Apply Your Knowledge of Wave Energy and Amplitude

Suppose that you are an actor in a movie in which a car explodes. It could be exciting to be next to an exploding car, but it could also be dangerous! An explosion produces a blast wave that radiates out with a lot of energy. Special effects experts have to apply their knowledge of energy and amplitude when designing explosions to keep people on the set safe during such scenes.

18. Special effects experts want the largest explosion that is safe for the people on set. Knowing that the energy of a wave is proportional to its amplitude squared helps them mathematically model the energy of the explosion and the amplitude of the blast wave. How does this knowledge help them determine where to place the actors and crew?

The special effects team is working to modify a vehicle for a special effect that will only last a few seconds.

Continue Your Exploration

Name: Date:

Check out the path below or go online to choose one of the other paths shown.

People in Science

- **Earthquakes and Waves**
- **Hands-On Labs** 🖐
- **Propose Your Own Path**

Go online to choose one of these other paths.

James West, Research Scientist

James West's parents wanted him to be a medical doctor, but he wanted to study physics. His father was sure that West would never find a job in physics, but West wanted to study what he loved. He did study physics, and he did find a job. West worked for Bell Laboratories where he developed a microphone called the electret microphone. Today, versions of West's microphone is in almost all telephones, cell phones, and other equipment that records sound.

West's interest in the microphone started with a question about hearing. A group of scientists wanted to know how close together two sounds could be before the ear would not be able to tell them apart. The scientists needed a very sensitive microphone to produce the sounds for their tests, and at the time, no microphone sensitive enough existed. West and fellow scientist Dr. Gerhard Sessler found that they could make a more sensitive microphone by using materials called electrets. The new microphones were cheaper, more reliable, smaller, and lighter than any microphone before.

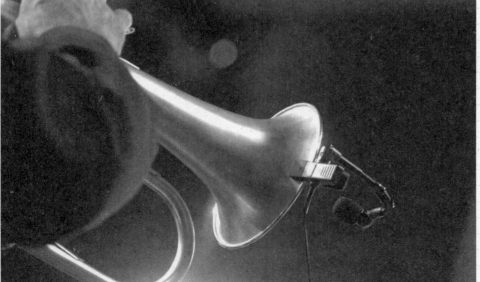

West's research into sound waves and hearing has helped make microphones smaller.

Continue Your Exploration

Microphones convert sound waves into electrical signals. The original design West and his colleagues were researching used a battery to power a material that had no electric charge, but an accident converted the uncharged material to an electret. An electret can be thought of as an electric version of a magnet. It has two oppositely charged poles. West and his colleagues began to study this new material and found that it was not only more sensitive but did not require a battery to maintain its charge. Based on this evidence, the researchers reasoned that this material could be used in more sensitive microphones. At the time, they could not have foreseen the use of this technology in cell phones, so the application was initially purely for research.

1. How does this example show that there is value in research science, even if a practical application for the science does not currently exist?

2. West has always been interested in how things work. When he was younger, he enjoyed taking apart small appliances to see what was inside. Why would curiosity about how things work be useful to a research scientist?

3. Research scientists work in all scientific disciplines. West studied physics and focused his research on sound waves. If you were a research scientist, what discipline would you be most interested in studying and what specific topics would you be interested in researching? Explain why.

4. **Collaborate** Work with a group to find a recent discovery in wave research. As a group, imagine how this discovery may lead to other applications. Share your ideas with the class.

Can You Explain It?

Name: _____ Date: _____

How do falling dominoes compare to a wave?

EVIDENCE NOTEBOOK

Refer to the notes in your Evidence Notebook to help you determine how falling dominoes compare to a wave.

1. State your claim. Make sure your claim fully explains how falling dominoes compare to a wave.

2. Summarize the evidence you have gathered to support your claim and explain your reasoning.

Checkpoints

Answer the following questions to check your understanding of the lesson.

Use the photo to answer Questions 3–4.

3. The upper wave has more / less energy than the bottom wave, because the amplitude / wavelength / frequency of the upper wave is greater than that of the bottom wave.

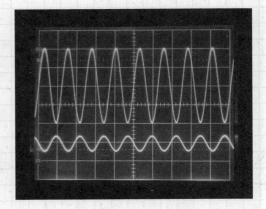

4. Look at the bottom waveform. Approximately how many wavelengths are shown?
   A. 2.5
   B. 4
   C. 8
   D. 16

Use the diagram to answer Questions 5–6.

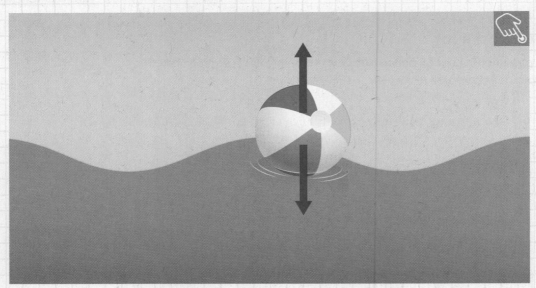

5. Which statements are true about the diagram? Select all that apply.
   A. The ball moves along with the wave as the wave moves.
   B. The ball moves up and down as the wave passes by.
   C. The wave transfers energy as it moves.
   D. The ball transfers energy to the wave.

6. Which medium is the wave traveling through?
   A. air
   B. water
   C. plastic

Interactive Review

Complete this section to review the main concepts of the lesson.

A wave is a disturbance that transfers energy from one place to another and transfers energy in the direction that it travels.

A. Explain how a wave transfers energy from one place to another.

Waves can be classified by comparing the direction of the disturbance and the direction that the wave travels.

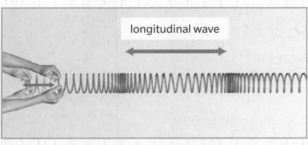
longitudinal wave

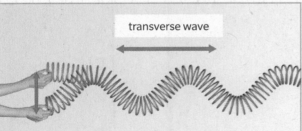
transverse wave

B. Explain the difference between longitudinal waves and transverse waves in terms of particle vibration.

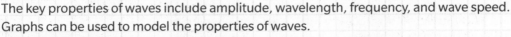

The key properties of waves include amplitude, wavelength, frequency, and wave speed. Graphs can be used to model the properties of waves.

C. Use a model to explain how frequency and wavelength relate to wave speed.

Waves Interact with Matter

When a pool of water is disturbed, a wave spreads out over the surface of the water.

Explore First

Exploring Sound Gently stretch a rubber band. Then pluck the rubber band and listen to the sound that it makes. Stretch the rubber band a little more, and pluck the rubber band again. How does the vibration of the rubber band relate to how high or low the sound is?

Go online to view the digital version of the Hands-On Lab for this lesson and to download additional lab resources.

CAN YOU EXPLAIN IT?

How can features and objects on the sea floor be visualized using mechanical waves?

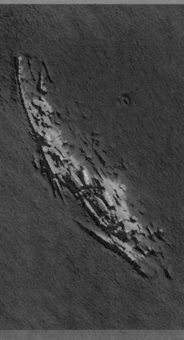

Because waves interact with matter, waves can be used to observe the world. These images were made using sound waves, a type of mechanical wave, interacting with the sea floor and objects on it.

1. What do you think the different colors in the images represent?

2. What do you see in each image?

 EVIDENCE NOTEBOOK As you explore the lesson, gather evidence to help explain how mechanical waves can be used to visualize the sea floor.

Investigating Mechanical Waves

When you shout at your friend across the room, sound waves carry energy through the air. Your friend senses that energy when he or she hears your voice. The air does not move from your vocal cords to your friend's eardrum, though. The sound waves move through the air, causing the air particles to vibrate as the energy passes through them.

3. Tsunamis are often caused by underwater earthquakes. Once a tsunami forms, the wave can travel hundreds of kilometers before reaching land. Explain whether or not the water molecules that touch land are the same ones that the earthquake initially moved.

The waves that can be seen moving through water are similar to sound waves in many ways.

Mechanical Waves

Some waves, such as sound waves, require a medium through which to travel. A medium can be air, water, steel, or any other material. A *vacuum* is a volume that contains no particles of matter, so a vacuum is not a medium. A **mechanical wave** is a wave that travels through a medium due to the motion of matter. When a book is slammed on a table, it creates a disturbance in the air particles around the book. This disturbance creates a mechanical wave that moves out from the book and reaches your ear. The air is the medium that the wave traveled through, and the sound is the mechanical wave.

5. **Language SmArts** Work in small groups and have each group member select a type of wave that they are familiar with. Determine where the initial energy for the wave comes from and what medium the wave travels through, and then sketch the initial energy input and the medium of the wave. Taking turns, present each of your waves to the other members of your group.

Label the Medium

4. Label the medium that each mechanical wave is passing through.

Hands-On Lab
Generate Mechanical Waves

Generate waves in several media and observe how the mechanical waves behave.

Procedure and Analysis

STEP 1 Choose an object to use as a wave medium.

STEP 2 Experiment with ways to generate a mechanical wave in the medium. Note that you may find more than one way to generate waves in a particular medium.

STEP 3 Observe the waves that you generated and record your observations in the data table.

STEP 4 Repeat Steps 1–3 using other media.

MATERIALS
- paper strips, long
- spring toy, coiled
- string or rope
- water, in tub

Medium	Observations

EVIDENCE NOTEBOOK

6. What occurred when a wave moving through the water hit the side of its container? How might this relate to using sound waves in water to visualize the sea floor? Record your evidence.

STEP 5 **Discuss** Choose one of the media that you used to generate mechanical waves and identify how you can observe the amplitude, frequency, and speed of the wave as it travels through the medium.

Waves Interact with Particles of a Medium

The defining characteristic of mechanical waves is the need for a medium. A mechanical wave travels through a substance due to the physical motion of the particles of the medium itself. For example, the waves in the wake of a boat occur when molecules of water move. Similarly, the sound that you hear when a friend shouts occurs when air molecules move, and an earthquake travels through the ground as the particles of rock and soil move up and down, or back and forth. All of these materials are examples of media through which mechanical waves can move.

Types of Mechanical Waves

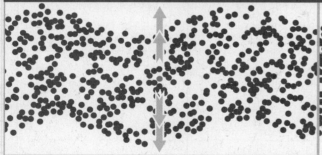

The particles in this transverse wave move up and down as the wave travels to the right. The crests and troughs of the wave are the high and low points in the wave.

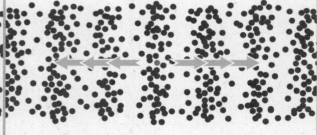

The particles in this longitudinal wave move right and left as the wave travels to the right. The compressions and rarefactions of the wave correspond to high and low concentrations of particles.

7. Which statement best describes how the particles of a medium behave when a mechanical wave moves through the medium?

   A. Particles travel in the direction of the wave, away from the source of the wave.

   B. Particles travel in the direction that is perpendicular to the motion of the wave.

   C. Particles move as the wave passes them but do not move along with the wave.

   D. Particles stay in one place as the wave travels past them.

Sound, Media, and Wave Speed

The arrangement of and type of particles in a medium affect how the particles interact, and the particle interactions affect how waves travel through a medium. Recall that sound waves are a type of longitudinal mechanical wave and that sound waves can travel through gases, liquids, and solids. The speed of sound depends on the density of the medium through which the waves travel. The higher the density of the medium is, the faster sound travels in it. As a result, the speed of sound is lowest in gases and highest in solids. Changing the temperature of a medium may change the particle interactions, which would cause wave speed to vary in the same medium at different temperatures.

Medium	State	Speed (m/s)
Argon	gas	323
Air	gas	343
Neon	gas	435
Ethanol	liquid	1,162
Mercury	liquid	1,450
Water	liquid	1,482
Silver	solid	3,650
Steel	solid	5,200
Aluminum	solid	6,420

8. Do the Math Use the table to calculate the average speed of sound in a gas, a liquid, and a solid, to the nearest m/s. Which of the following statements are true? Select all that apply.

A. The average speed of sound in a liquid is about 3.7 times the average speed of sound in a gas.

B. The average speed of sound in a solid is about 3.7 times the average speed of sound in a liquid.

C. The average speed of sound in a solid is about 0.07 times the average speed of sound in a gas.

D. The average speed of sound in a solid is about 13.9 times the average speed of sound in a gas.

Analyze How a Vacuum Affects Sound Waves

9. Think about how sound travels and decide whether a person outside the boxes would be able to hear the balloon pop. Explain why or why not.

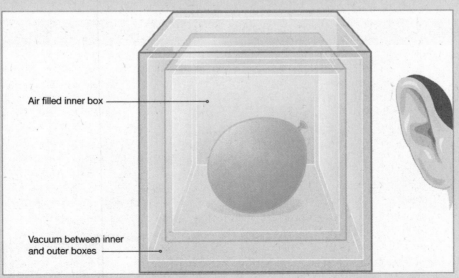

Air filled inner box

Vacuum between inner and outer boxes

The space between the boxes is a vacuum.

Analyzing How Waves Interact with a Medium

Wave Energy and Amplitude

If two waves have identical characteristics, except for their amplitude, the wave that has the greater amplitude carries more energy. Think about what happens to this energy as a wave travels through a medium away from its source.

Large earthquakes can occur as tectonic plates suddenly shift. In the area around this tectonic movement, the waves moving through the ground can be very destructive.

Farther away from the place where the initial disturbance occurred, the waves moving through the ground can still be felt, but are generally much less destructive.

10. Why do you think earthquakes are much more destructive closer to the initial disturbance than they are farther away?

Water Ripples

Ripples that move out from a disturbance in a pool of water are surface waves.

1

2

11. When the drop hits the water's surface, it generates a surface wave in the form of a ripple. What happens to the wave as it expands outward from the initial disturbance?

Explore
Online

Mechanical Waves Spread Out

Mechanical waves spread out through a medium over time, and they spread out in as many directions as they are able. Surface waves on water spread out in a circle around the original disturbance, and sound waves in the air spread out as a sphere around the source of the sound. As a wave spreads out, energy is spread over a larger area. The area over which the energy spreads is related to the diameter of a sphere with the source at the center. As a result, the amplitude of a wave varies with diameter, as shown in the graph. One reason that distant sounds are quiet is that less energy reaches a listener who is farther away than one who is closer.

12. How does the energy of the wave in the graph change with the diameter of a sphere around the wave's source and why might this be occurring?

   A. The energy is decreasing because the amplitude of the wave is decreasing.

   B. The energy is not changing because the amplitude is constant.

   C. The energy is not changing because the frequency is constant.

   D. The energy is decreasing because the frequency of the wave is decreasing.

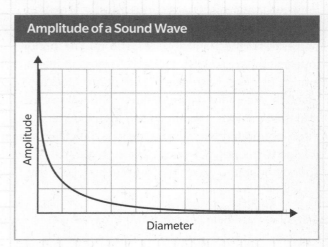

Absorption

Mechanical waves, such as sound waves, cause particles in a medium to move. As a wave passes through a medium, the medium's particles move and bump into one another, which transfers energy. During this movement, some of the wave's energy is converted into thermal energy by friction. **Absorption** is the conversion of a wave's energy into other forms of energy in the medium that the wave is traveling in. When energy is absorbed by a medium, the medium gains energy, and the wave loses that energy.

13. Dolphins locate objects underwater using high-frequency waves that can travel a few hundred meters. Whales communicate using low-frequency sounds that can travel hundreds of kilometers. Why do you think these sounds travel different distances?

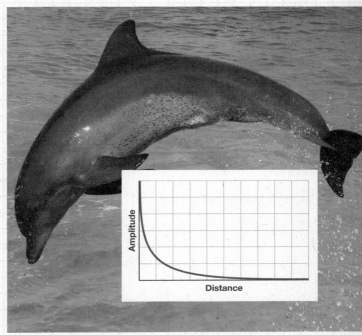

Dolphins and whales make sounds that travel through water. The graph shows how the amplitude of a sound wave changes as it moves farther from the source of the sound.

Absorption and Frequency

Absorption can vary based on the frequency of the wave. Generally, a high-frequency wave will lose more energy to absorption than a low-frequency wave will lose. The more a particle moves, the more energy it loses because of friction. High-frequency waves move a medium's particles more often. The higher the frequency of a wave is, the more energy it will lose to absorption and the more energy is converted into thermal energy. This conversion of energy into thermal energy is similar to what happens when you warm your hands using friction. Rubbing your hands against one another slowly will not generate much thermal energy, but when you rub your hands quickly, the friction between them will generate a lot of thermal energy.

All of the features of sound are related to the properties of mechanical waves. The volume, or how loud something sounds, is directly related to the amplitude of a sound wave. If two sound waves are identical except for their amplitude, the sound wave that has the higher amplitude will sound louder. Pitch, or how high or low a sound is, is directly related to frequency. If you hear a high-pitched sound, the sound waves that are reaching your ear have a high frequency.

14. When you hear sounds through a wall, you can hear lower-pitched sounds more clearly than higher-pitched sounds. Use a model to explain why this phenomenon occurs.

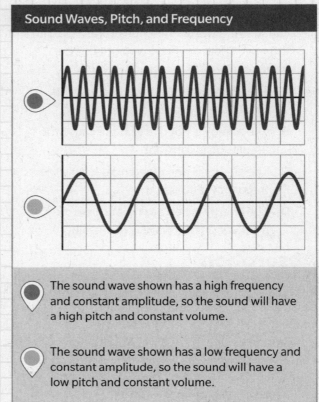

Sound Waves, Pitch, and Frequency

The sound wave shown has a high frequency and constant amplitude, so the sound will have a high pitch and constant volume.

The sound wave shown has a low frequency and constant amplitude, so the sound will have a low pitch and constant volume.

Analyze Sound Volume

15. Headphone earpieces can produce sounds that seem very loud to the listener. However, a person standing a meter away may not even be able to hear those same sounds. Why are these sounds so much quieter a short distance away?

_____

_____

_____

_____

© Houghton Mifflin Harcourt Publishing Company

Explaining the Behavior of Waves at Media Boundaries

Mechanical waves can travel through many different media, but they do not always move easily from one medium to another. Several things can occur when a wave reaches a new medium. For example, when you shout at a distant wall, you may hear an echo a few seconds later. An echo is an example of something that can occur when a mechanical wave contacts a new medium.

Echoes

Explore Online

16. When you yell in a gym and hear an echo, what might be happening to the sound wave?

Transmission

Consider what occurs when you hear sound through a wall. A sound wave traveled through the air, moved through the wall, and then traveled through air again to reach your ear. The sound wave crossed a boundary between two media twice before reaching your ear. A boundary is the surface or edge where two media meet. **Transmission** occurs when a wave travels through a boundary between media. On its path to your ear, the sound wave was first transmitted from the air into the wall. Then the sound wave traveled through the wall and encountered air as it emerged from the wall, and it was again transmitted to a new medium.

Energy absorbed by a medium is not transmitted. For example, loud music may sound faint when heard through a wall because the wall absorbs some of the sound and the person hears only the sound that transmits through the wall. Some waves are neither transmitted nor absorbed when they reach a boundary between media.

Reflection

When a wave encounters a new medium, it is not always transmitted into the new medium.

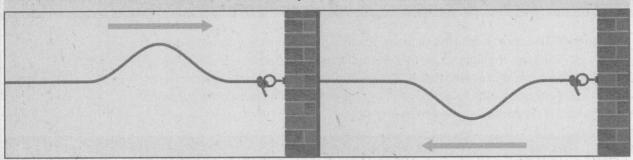

17. What occurs when the wave traveling through the rope encounters a new medium, the wall?

Reflection

When a wave encounters a boundary between two media, it does not always transmit into the new medium. Instead, the wave may bounce off the boundary and travel back through the original medium. When the wave bounces off the boundary, a **reflection** occurs. When you hear sound echo off a wall, you are hearing a reflected sound wave. The sound wave encountered a new medium, the wall, and was reflected.

Amplitude and Energy in Partial Reflection

The frequency of a wave does not change when it encounters a new medium, but the wavelength and amplitude may change.

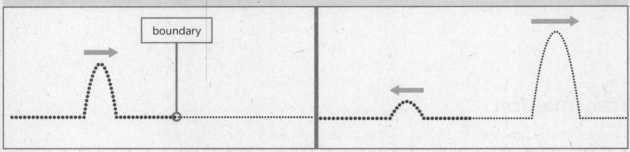

18. How would you best describe the behavior of the wave in the diagrams when it reaches the boundary between the big particles and the small particles?

19. What do you notice about the amplitude of the reflected wave?

Partial Transmission and Reflection

Generally, when a mechanical wave encounters a boundary between two different media, the wave is not entirely reflected or transmitted. Some of the wave can be transmitted into the new medium, and the remaining portion of the wave is reflected back into the original medium. This is why you can hear the sounds of a basketball game from outside a gym, even though there may be echoes inside the gym as well.

When a mechanical wave is partially reflected and partially transmitted, the original wave becomes two waves. The energy from the original wave is split between the transmitted wave and the reflected wave. Because the original wave's energy is split between the two new waves, each of the new waves will have less energy than the original wave had. Amplitude depends on the medium, so the transmitted and reflected waves' amplitudes could be very different.

Refraction

If you push a cart from a smooth floor to a carpeted floor, the carpet will cause the wheels to turn more slowly. If the right wheel hits the carpet first, the right wheel will turn more slowly than the left wheel will, causing the cart to turn to the right. This turning of a cart is an analogy for what happens to a wave when part of the wave changes speed.

The speed of a wave may change when it encounters a different medium. Part of the wave may speed up or slow down before another part of the wave, causing the wave to bend. When the path of a wave bends due to a change in wave speed, **refraction** occurs. The amount of refraction depends on the angle at which the wave encounters the boundary and how much the speed of the wave changes. Refraction can be observed in many types of waves, including seismic waves.

Note that when a wave crosses a boundary, its frequency always stays the same. Wave speed, frequency, and wavelength are related mathematically, so if the speed of a wave changes when it crosses a boundary, its wavelength must also change.

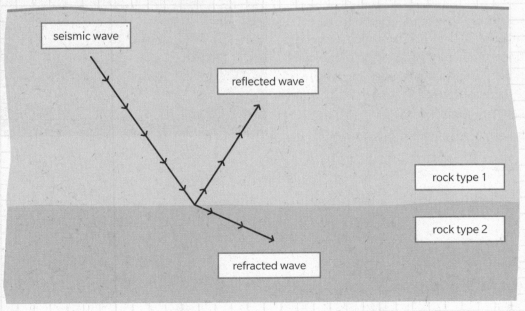

seismic wave

reflected wave

rock type 1

rock type 2

refracted wave

Seismic waves are partially reflected and transmitted at the boundary between different rock types. The transmitted waves refract because the waves travel at different speeds in the two media.

20. **Discuss** With a partner, discuss why a wave might bend when it changes speed. How might refraction look different if a wave speeds up compared to if it slows down when it moves into a new medium?

21. Draw The image shows a mechanical wave as it encounters a boundary between two media. Part of the wave may be reflected, but this is not shown. Draw what will happen to the part of the wave that passes into the new medium and slows down.

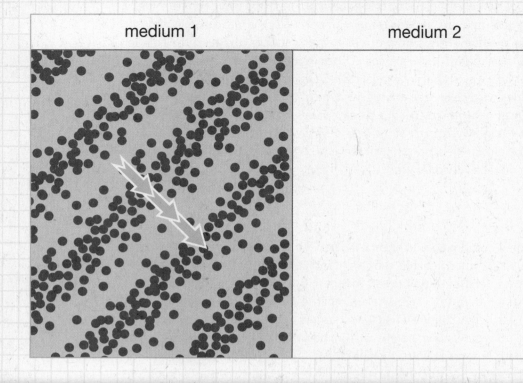

medium 1	medium 2

Engineer It

Explore Mechanical Waves in Medicine

Doctors use ultrasound, or high-frequency sound, to generate images of the inside of a person's body. Waves are sent through the body, bounce off organs, and then return to the imaging device. Ultrasound machines are often used instead of x-ray machines because scientific research has found that x-rays can damage living cells.

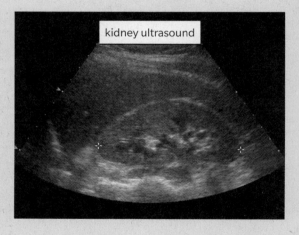

kidney ultrasound

22. What problem do ultrasound machines solve?

_____

_____

_____

_____

EVIDENCE NOTEBOOK

23. Ultrasounds use reflection and transmission to generate an image using sound waves. How might these same principles be used to visualize features and objects on the sea floor? Record your evidence.

© Houghton Mifflin Harcourt Publishing Company Image Credits: ©Zephyr/Science Source

Continue Your Exploration

Name: _____   Date: _____

Check out the path below or go online to choose one of the other paths shown.

> **Designing Soundproof Rooms**

- **Engineering to Prevent Earthquake Damage**
- **Hands-On Labs** 👋
- **Propose Your Own Path**

Go online to choose one of these other paths.

When engineers design recording studios or practice spaces for musicians, they carefully consider ways to make the structures ideal for handling loud sounds. Engineers design the rooms to address several problems. For example, one problem is that echoes inside the room make hearing the desired sound difficult, and another problem is that some sounds are loud enough that they can be heard outside of the room. Engineers take into account the properties of different building materials and how the materials can be shaped and used to solve these problems.

1. Music practice spaces often have very thick walls made of dense materials such as cement. A sound wave moving through one of these walls moves a lot of particles and loses energy. What sound phenomenon are architects making use of with these walls? Explain your reasoning.

Continue Your Exploration

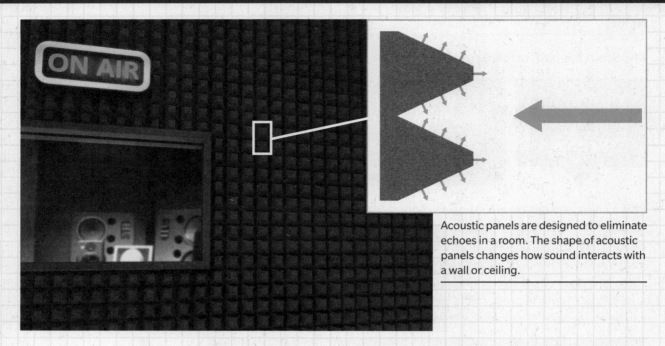

Acoustic panels are designed to eliminate echoes in a room. The shape of acoustic panels changes how sound interacts with a wall or ceiling.

2. Acoustic panels are designed to solve problems mainly related to the

   _____ of sound in a music studio.

   A. absorption

   B. reflection

   C. transmission

3. Compare the structure of the acoustic panels shown in the diagram to a flat wall and explain how the structure reduces echoes.

4. The recording booth shown has a window through which sound may be transmitted. Which of the following window structures would transmit the least amount of sound?

   A. a thin single pane of glass

   B. a thick single pane of glass

   C. double panes of glass with a dense gas between them

   D. double panes of glass with a vacuum between them

5. **Collaborate** With a partner, discuss ways in which the room you are currently in is or is not soundproofed. Consider ways that you could modify the room to better keep sound from escaping out of the room.

Can You Explain It?

Name: _____   Date: _____

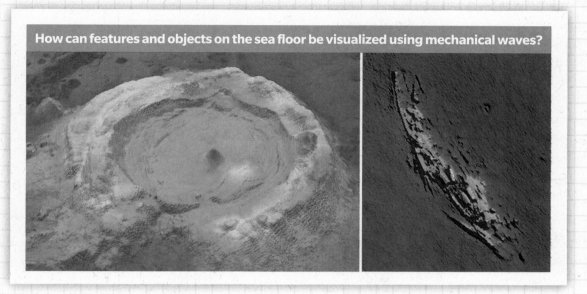

How can features and objects on the sea floor be visualized using mechanical waves?

EVIDENCE NOTEBOOK

Refer to the notes in your Evidence Notebook to help you construct an explanation of how features and objects on the sea floor can be visualized using mechanical waves.

1. State your claim. Make sure your claim fully explains how features and objects on the sea floor can be visualized using mechanical waves.

2. Summarize the evidence you have gathered to support your claim and explain your reasoning.

Checkpoints

Answer the following questions to check your understanding of the lesson.

Use the diagram to answer Question 3.

3. This diagram shows what happened after a wave traveling from the left encountered a boundary between its original medium and another, less dense medium. What happened at the boundary between media? Select all that apply.

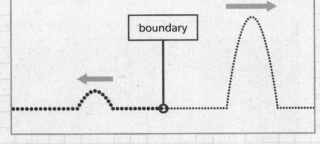

   A. Some of the wave's energy was transmitted to the less dense medium.

   B. Part of the wave was reflected back into the original medium.

   C. Particles were carried from one medium to the other.

4. Sound is made up of transverse / longitudinal mechanical waves. As a sound wave travels through a medium, it permanently / temporarily moves particles in that medium. When the sound wave strikes a boundary between air and water, it will generally be completely / partially reflected.

Use the diagram to answer Question 5.

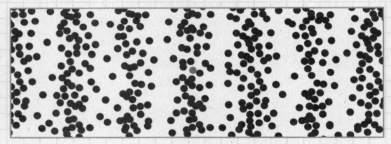

5. This diagram represents a sound wave traveling from left to right. As the wave passes the location of the particle represented by the red dot, how does the particle move?

   A. The particle travels from left to right along with the sound wave.

   B. The particle vibrates horizontally, moving both left and right.

   C. The particle vibrates vertically, moving both up and down.

6. As a sound wave spreads through the air, it moves the air particles smaller and smaller distances. What causes this change in the amplitude of the wave? Select all that apply.

   A. Amplitude decreases as the energy of a wave spreads across a greater amount of the medium.

   B. Amplitude decreases as medium's particles move away from the sound's source.

   C. Amplitude decreases as friction transforms energy from the sound wave.

Interactive Review

Complete this section to review the main concepts of the lesson.

Mechanical waves occur when energy moves through a medium due to the motion of particles.

A. When a mechanical wave travels through a medium, how does the wave affect the medium's particles?

As a mechanical wave travels through a medium, its amplitude can decrease due to the wave being spread across more matter and energy being transformed into other forms.

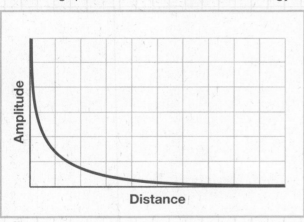

B. Describe why a sound wave's amplitude might decrease as it moves through a medium.

When a mechanical wave reaches a boundary between two media, the wave can be reflected, transmitted, or both. The transmitted wave may refract into the new medium.

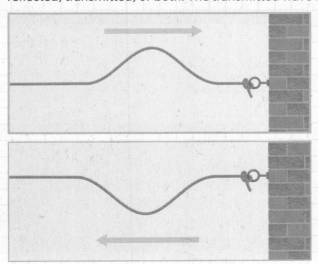

C. Describe how the properties of a wave may change as it is transmitted through a new medium.

Light Can Be Modeled as a Wave

Light streams into this space, and some areas are brightly lit while other areas remain in shadow.

Explore First

Observing Light Using a flashlight or another source of light, investigate how light behaves with one or more of the following devices: a kaleidoscope, a periscope, a mirror, or a prism. Why do you think light behaves the way it does with the devices?

Go online to view the digital version of the Hands-On Lab for this lesson and to download additional lab resources.

CAN YOU EXPLAIN IT?

Why does the same room lit with the same flashlight look different in these photos?

Observe what happens when the flashlight shines on the wall, the mirror, and the rug.

1. In each photo, the boy holds the same light source, a flashlight. Describe the appearance of the light in each photo. Note any similarities and differences.

EVIDENCE NOTEBOOK As you explore the lesson, gather evidence to help explain how the behavior of light affects what we see and how we see it.

Exploring the Nature of Light

A light bulb, a burning log, and a candle are sources of light. Even living things, such as fireflies and some fish, can be sources of light. However, the most important source of light for life on Earth is the sun. Humans detect light using their eyes, and most people rely on their sense of sight in daily life. Think about how you interact with light on a daily basis. What other ways do you interact with light other than seeing with your eyes?

Light from the sun illuminates Earth.

2. Based on what you know about waves and light, do you think that light can be modeled as a wave? Explain why or why not.

The Speed of Light

Recall that mechanical waves, such as sound waves, require a medium through which to travel. Light, however, can travel through a vacuum. Light from the sun travels through space, which is a vacuum, to reach Earth. Light can also travel through different materials. Like mechanical waves, the speed of light varies in different media. Light travels most quickly through a vacuum, where it travels at a speed of about 300,000,000 m/s. Because this number is so large, it is often written using scientific notation as 3×10^8 m/s. Light tends to travel faster in lower-density media than in higher-density media. For example, light travels faster in air than it does in water.

3. **Do the Math** As light travels through a medium, it interacts with the particles of the medium and slows down. Use the graph to determine the ratios of the speeds of light in different media to one another and to the speed of light in a vacuum.

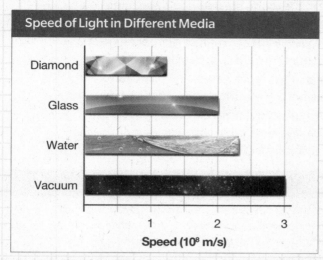

Speed of Light in Different Media

Diamond

Glass

Water

Vacuum

Speed (10^8 m/s)

The ratio of the speed of light through diamond to the speed of light through a vacuum is 5:12 / 3:4 / 12:5 . The ratio of the speed of light through glass to the speed of light through a vacuum is 2:3 / 3:4 / 3:2 . The ratio of the speed of light through diamond to the speed of light through glass is 1:2 / 5:8 / 8:5 .

Light and Energy

You may have noticed that when you leave an object in sunlight, the object gets warmer. Solar water heaters and solar ovens use this property of sunlight to heat water and cook food. Heating water or cooking food is otherwise a process that requires fuel to generate thermal energy. Solar panels use energy from sunlight to generate electrical energy.

Solar water heaters are technology most commonly found in sunny climates. As water moves through the tubes of the heater, it is warmed by sunlight.

4. Waves transfer energy. When energy is
absorbed / reflected / transmitted by matter, it transforms into thermal energy. The fact that sunlight can warm objects indicates that sunlight transfers energy, so it can / cannot be modeled as a wave.

The Electromagnetic Spectrum

When you look around, you see things that reflect light into your eyes. Light that humans readily see is called visible light. If a bee were in the room, the bee would see things differently than you do because bees can see a kind of light—called ultraviolet light—that you cannot see. Both ultraviolet light and visible light are part of a larger range of waves known as the *electromagnetic (EM) spectrum*. The EM spectrum is composed of many different types of EM waves, including x-rays, radio waves, and microwaves. **Electromagnetic waves** are waves made of vibrating electric and magnetic fields. Some of the waves, such as gamma rays, have high frequencies and short wavelengths and are highly energetic. Compared to gamma rays and visible light waves, radio waves have low frequencies and long wavelengths and carry less energy.

The Atmosphere Blocks Some EM Radiation

The sun gives off some radiation in every part of the EM spectrum. The atmosphere absorbs most of the higher-energy radiation, such as x-rays and gamma rays, and they do not reach the ground. Radio waves, visible light, and some ultraviolet light waves do reach the ground.

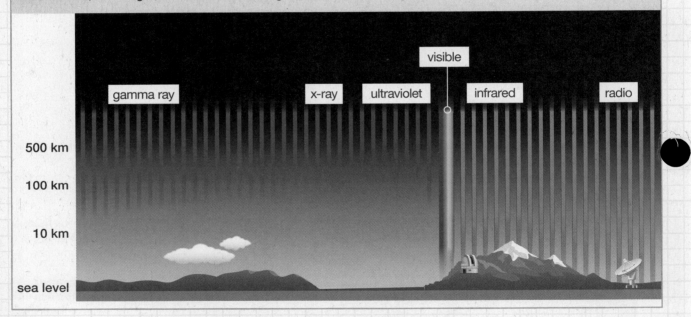

5. Language SmArts Waves that have longer wavelengths are absorbed more slowly by media than waves that have shorter wavelengths. Radio telescopes detect radio waves from space and can be used even on cloudy days. What advantages do radio telescopes on Earth have over visible light telescopes on Earth? Support your claim with evidence, and explain your reasoning.

© Houghton Mifflin Harcourt Publishing Company

Energy and Frequency

The energy of an electromagnetic wave depends on the wave's frequency. High-frequency, short-wavelength EM waves have more energy than low-frequency, long-wavelength EM waves have. The more energy EM waves have, the more dangerous they can be to living tissue. For example, x-rays have very high frequencies and carry a lot of energy. When working with x-rays, people must take special precautions, such as wearing a lead apron to block most of the x-rays. In contrast, radio waves, which have very low frequencies and carry less energy, are much safer. Radio waves are used often in consumer electronics such as radios, walkie-talkies, and baby monitors.

6. **Engineer It** When designing devices, engineers need to understand what makes some EM waves safe and others potentially dangerous. Engineers know that the safety of EM waves has to do with their frequency and the energy that they carry. A higher / lower frequency means more energy and more energy means more / less danger to human cells. Radio waves are safe / not safe for humans because they are high-frequency / low-frequency waves. Ultraviolet light waves, however, have higher / lower frequencies, and they are not at all / can be dangerous to human cells.

Compare Sound Waves and Light Waves

Electromagnetic waves behave similarly to mechanical waves in many ways, but they also have some differences. A vacuum is a space that has no particles of matter. Sound waves and light waves behave differently in a vacuum and in different media.

In this demonstration, tubing is connected to a pump that is removing air from the jar to produce a vacuum. As the air is removed, the buzzing timer sounds quieter and quieter.

7. Mechanical waves need a medium to travel; they cannot travel through a vacuum. Light can / cannot travel through a vacuum; so light waves are / are not mechanical waves. Sound waves are / are not mechanical waves.

8. **Draw** Work with a partner to draw a model that explains the behavior of the sound waves and light waves when the air is completely removed from the container.

Modeling Light Waves

Throughout this lesson you have seen several different representations of light as waves. Think about some of the ways that waves are modeled. Different models help to explain the behavior of light in different situations.

Energy from the Sun

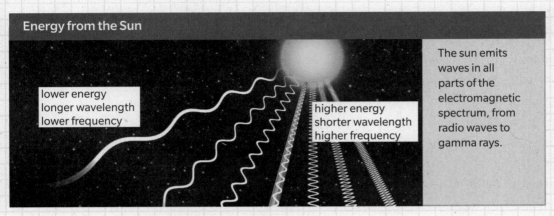

lower energy
longer wavelength
lower frequency

higher energy
shorter wavelength
higher frequency

The sun emits waves in all parts of the electromagnetic spectrum, from radio waves to gamma rays.

9. How is light represented in the diagram above?

Graphs of Light Waves

Graphs can be used to represent the wavelength and amplitude of light waves. Wavelength and amplitude correspond to the color and brightness of a light wave.

Wavelength, Amplitude, Color, and Brightness

Explore Online

Imagine a machine that lets you change the properties of visible light waves to see how they affect the color of light. Examine these images to see some possible results.

10. Do the Math The frequency, wavelength, and amplitude of a light wave can change. As the wavelength changes, so does the light's color / brightness . As the wavelength increases, frequency increases / decreases , which means that wavelength and frequency are directly / inversely proportional. Changing either of these properties changes / does not change the amplitude.

Ray Diagrams

When light travels through a medium that has constant properties, it travels in a straight line. The direction in which light travels can be represented using arrows called rays. Rays are commonly drawn so that they begin at the source of the light and point in the direction in which the light is moving. Because light travels in many different directions from a source, ray diagrams represent only one part of a situation, and the rays are drawn to model a specific behavior of a light wave. For example, when light encounters a boundary with a different medium, the light may change direction. This change in direction is shown by a ray pointing toward the boundary and a second ray pointing away from the boundary. Often the chosen ray points to the eye of an observer to demonstrate what the observer sees.

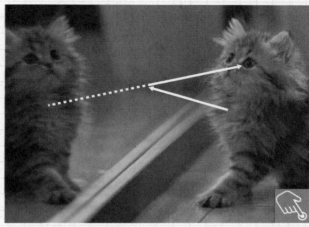

The ray changes direction because it hit a mirror.

11. Draw Sketch a ray diagram that shows how light from a light bulb helps you see a cat in a room.

Use Light Wave Models to Explain Operating Cost

An incandescent light bulb generates light by passing electrical energy through a thin wire called a filament. The filament converts this electrical energy into thermal energy and light energy. The *power* (energy per unit of time) that a light bulb uses is measured in watts. One watt (W) is equal to one joule per second. An incandescent bulb that uses more power is brighter than an incandescent bulb that uses less power. The bulbs generate light with the same wavelengths and frequencies.

12. Based on the information from the text and what you know about amplitude and brightness, draw two waves. One wave should represent a light wave from a red 30 W bulb, and the other should represent a wave from a red 60 W bulb.

13. Use frequency and amplitude to explain how your drawings model the two waves from the different light bulbs.

_____

_____

_____

_____

_____

_____

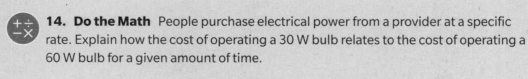

14. **Do the Math** People purchase electrical power from a provider at a specific rate. Explain how the cost of operating a 30 W bulb relates to the cost of operating a 60 W bulb for a given amount of time.

_____

_____

_____

_____

_____

Analyzing Human Perception of Light Waves

You analyzed mechanical waves such as sound waves and water waves and saw that, as the waves get farther from their source, they carry less energy. These energy losses occur because the waves spread out as they move away from the source, spreading their original energy over a greater area. Also, the medium through which the waves travel absorbs some energy, which transforms into other forms of energy and is lost from the wave. You know that the amount of energy carried by a wave is related to the amplitude of the wave. Think about how this behavior of mechanical waves can explain the behavior of light as it moves away from its source.

Brightness Versus Distance

Notice how light from a light source spreads as it moves farther from the source.

candlelight

car headlight

floodlight

15. **Draw** The graph shows how the brightness of car headlights changes as the light moves farther from the source. On this graph, sketch curves to show how the brightness of the light from a candle and from floodlights change with distance.

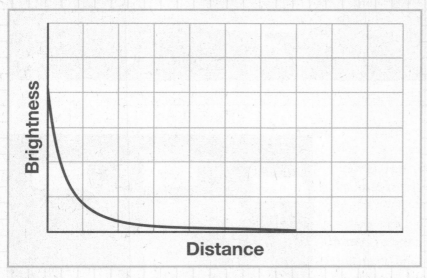

16. **Discuss** Together with a partner, analyze the photos and the graphs. Develop an explanation for why the relationship between brightness and distance is not linear and relate the brightness of the light to the energy of the light waves.

Light Waves and Color

Most waves in the electromagnetic spectrum are invisible to humans because their wavelengths are too short or too long for the human eye to see. However, electromagnetic waves in the visible range appear to humans as a spectrum of colors. Each color corresponds to a certain wavelength of light waves because the human brain interprets these different wavelengths as different colors. For example, blue light has a wavelength of about 475 nanometers, while red light has a wavelength of about 650 nanometers. When your eyes detect all wavelengths of visible light at once in equal proportions, you perceive white light. Sunlight contains all wavelengths of visible light so you see it as white light. Different wavelengths of light interact with matter in different ways, which is why specific colors are reflected when white light strikes an object.

You see many colors in these bubbles because light waves with different wavelengths reach your eyes.

Color Addition

Color addition is the process of combining different colors of light. You may think that you must combine all the colors of visible light to get white light, but that is not the only way. You can also get light that appears white by adding together just three colors of light: red, blue, and green. Red, blue, and green are referred to as the primary colors of light. These three colors of light can be combined in different ratios to produce many different colors. When two primary colors are added in equal amounts, secondary colors (yellow, magenta, and cyan) are formed.

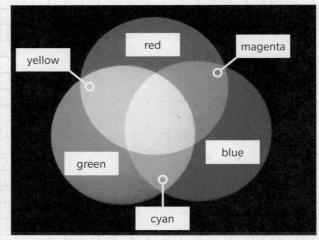

All three primary colors of light combine to produce white light. Red and green form yellow; red and blue form magenta; and blue and green form cyan.

17. When equal amounts of red, green, and blue light waves reach your eyes, the light appears red / green / blue / **white** / black because of a phenomenon called transmission / absorption / **color addition** .

Colors of Objects

Most objects do not generate and emit their own light, so why do these objects appear different colors? When light reaches an object, some of the light is reflected by the object, and some of the light is absorbed. The wavelengths of light that are reflected and reach your eyes determine what color you perceive an object to be.

Light Waves and the Perception of Color

The light rays in the image model various wavelengths of visible light. Compare how the incoming colors of light behave when they encounter the kitten's black fur, its white fur, and the green grass.

18. Draw In the space below, draw a model to illustrate why, in white light, an apple looks red and an orange looks orange.

Filters Affect Light Color

A filter is a medium that transmits certain wavelengths but absorbs others. For example, a red filter transmits the wavelengths corresponding to red light but blocks other visible light wavelengths. Look at the strawberry and the broccoli floret in the top photo. In white light, the strawberry appears mostly red and the broccoli appears mostly green.

If you put a red filter over the light source, as shown in the second photo, the strawberry still appears mostly red, but the broccoli appears mostly black because all colors except red were filtered out. The broccoli normally reflects green light and absorbs red light, but there is no green light to reflect, so the broccoli appears black.

If you replace the red filter with a green filter, your perception changes again. The strawberry now appears mostly black while the broccoli appears mostly green, as shown in the third photo.

19. Draw In white light, a banana appears yellow because it reflects both red and green wavelengths. Would it still appear yellow if you observed it through a blue filter? Draw a diagram to show the effect of a blue filter on your perception of the color of a banana.

Light Color Affects Our Perception of Objects

Explore how filtered light that strikes an object affects the perceived color of the object.

 EVIDENCE NOTEBOOK

20. In what ways might an object or surface change the appearance of white light? Record your evidence.

Relate a Wave Model of Light to Brightness

21. As light moves farther from its source, it becomes less bright. How does a wave model of light explain the change in brightness? Select all that apply.

A. light spreads as it moves away from a source

B. light reflects off boundaries between media

C. energy is absorbed as it travels through different media

D. the amount of energy in an area decreases as light moves away from a source

© Houghton Mifflin Harcourt Publishing Company • Image Credits: ©HMH/Guy Jarvis

Exploring Interactions of Light and Matter

Interactions between light and matter produce many common but spectacular effects, such as rainbows and optical illusions. Light, like other electromagnetic waves, can travel through empty space, but when light encounters a material, it can interact with the material in several ways. These interactions play an important role in how people see light.

The sky appears on the surface of a puddle on the ground.

22. What do you observe in the photo? Why do you think light behaves in this way?

Matter Can Reflect Light

You can see an object only when light from that object enters your eyes. Some objects, such as a flame, give off, or emit, their own light. Most objects do not emit light, but you can see those objects because light from another source bounces off them. The bouncing of light off a surface is called reflection. You can see the ground around the puddle in the photo, because sunlight reflected off the ground and entered your eyes.

Mirrors

A mirror has a very smooth surface that reflects light. Because mirrors are very smooth, they reflect light in a uniform way that results in an image when the reflected light enters your eyes. Other smooth surfaces, such as the surface of the water in the puddle in the photo, also reflect light in a uniform way and can also produce an image.

Light can reflect from surface to surface before it enters your eyes. Light from a lamp, for example, might have reflected off your skin, then reflected off the mirror, and then entered your eyes. When you look at the mirror, you see yourself!

Matter Can Transmit Light

How do the wrapped sandwiches in the photos differ? Why can you not see all three sandwiches beneath the wrappers equally well? The reason is how light interacts with matter. Different amounts of light pass through the different wrappers.

Light and other electromagnetic waves travel from a source in all directions, and they can travel through empty space or through matter. The passing of light waves through matter is called transmission. The medium through which light passes can transmit all, some, or none of the light. As you can see in the photos, the clear plastic wrap transmits almost all of the light, so you can clearly see the sandwich inside. When light travels through the waxed paper, only some of the light is transmitted. That sandwich is visible, but it looks fuzzy. The brown paper transmits none of the light, and as a result, you cannot see the sandwich within it at all.

Transmission and Absorption of Light

The clear plastic wrap around the first sandwich is an example of a transparent material. Light transmits through *transparent* materials, and objects can be seen clearly through them. Clean air, clean water, and smooth glass are also transparent. *Translucent* materials transmit light, but the light is scattered into many different directions. An object appears distorted or fuzzy through a translucent material. Frosted glass, tissue paper, and the waxed paper around the second sandwich are all examples of translucent materials.

Opaque materials do not let any light pass through them. Instead, they reflect light, absorb light, or both. When light enters a material but does not leave it, the light is absorbed. Absorption is the transfer of light energy to matter. Many materials, including wood, brick, and the brown paper around the third sandwich, are opaque.

23. Fill in the blanks to make the statements true.

A. The sandwich wrapped in _____ is easy to see because the medium allows _____ of the light to pass through.

B. The sandwich wrapped in _____ is obscured because the medium allows _____ of the light to pass through.

These sandwiches are wrapped in clear plastic wrap, waxed paper, and brown paper. How do the different wrappers affect what you see?

_____

C. The sandwich wrapped in _____ is not visible. That means the medium allows _____ of the light to pass through.

EVIDENCE NOTEBOOK

24. Think about the ways that matter interacts with light. How do these interactions relate to the flashlight images at the beginning of the lesson? Record your evidence.

© Houghton Mifflin Harcourt Publishing Company • Image Credits: ©Houghton Mifflin Harcourt

Hands-On Lab
Make a Penny Disappear

Observe how viewing an object through different media affects what you see.

MATERIALS
- beaker
- penny
- water

Procedure and Analysis

STEP 1 Place the penny on a flat surface like a lab table or a desk and carefully set the beaker on top of the penny.

STEP 2 Look at the penny from above the beaker and draw a ray diagram that models this situation.

STEP 3 Look at the penny through the side of the beaker and draw a ray diagram that models this situation.

STEP 4 Fill the beaker with water.

STEP 5 Look again at the penny from above the beaker and draw a ray diagram that models this situation.

STEP 6 Look at the penny again through the side of the beaker, from the same location as in Step 3. Draw a diagram to model this situation.

STEP 7 Use your ray diagrams to help explain why you are or are not able to see the penny in Steps 2, 3, 5, and 6.

© Houghton Mifflin Harcourt Publishing Company

Matter Can Refract Light

Light can travel through a vacuum or through a medium. When light of any wavelength travels through a vacuum, it always travels at the same speed. However, light travels slower in a medium. In fact, light of different wavelengths travels at different speeds in a medium. Shorter wavelengths are slowed more than longer wavelengths are. A prism is made of glass or another transparent material, and in a prism, the speed of shorter-wavelength violet light is less than the speed of longer-wavelength red light. These differences in speed cause the different wavelengths of light to separate.

Because light travels at different speeds through different media, the light waves bend when they hit the boundary between media at an angle. This bending of a light wave as it passes from one medium into another is called refraction. The amount and direction of the refraction depends on several factors, including the angle at which the light hits the boundary and the relative speed of light in the two media. Because different wavelengths of light travel at different speeds in a medium, each wavelength refracts at a different angle when white light hits a boundary between two media at an angle.

Light Traveling through a Prism

The top diagram shows that light is refracted when it enters and exits a prism. The bottom photo shows the result of the refraction. Note that the light beam on the bottom left is a reflected beam.

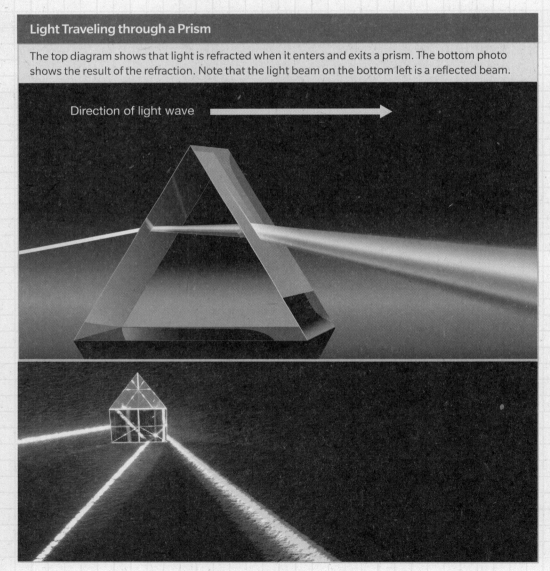

Direction of light wave

25. Act With a small group, act out what can happen when light encounters a new medium.

© Houghton Mifflin Harcourt Publishing Company • Image Credits: ©David Parker/Science Source

Optical Illusions Caused by Refraction

Your mind can play tricks on you because of refraction. The straw in the photo and the coin in the lab are two examples of optical illusions caused by refraction. When you look at an object that is underwater, the light reflecting off the object does not travel in a straight line. Because your brain always interprets light as traveling in a straight line, the images that you perceive do not match reality. For example, the light reflected by the upper part of the straw does, indeed, travel in the air in a straight line to your eye. But the light from the lower part of the straw is refracted as it passes from the water to the glass and refracted again when it passes into the air. The refracted light then travels in a straight line to your eye. Your brain interprets these light rays as coming from different sources, which causes the illusion that the part of the straw in the water is disconnected from the part out of the water.

Refraction explains why the straw appears broken.

Refraction and Media

How much a light wave refracts at the boundary between two media depends on the media, the wavelength of the light, and the angle at which the light hits the boundary.

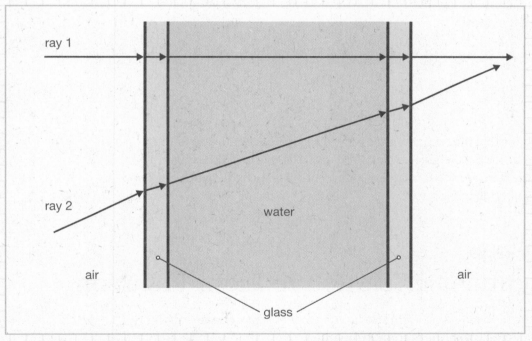

Ray 1 hits the initial boundary, and all other boundaries, at a 90° angle, and it does not refract. On the other hand, Ray 2 is refracted at a different angle at each boundary.

 26. Do the Math The ratio of the speed of light in air to the speed of light in glass is about 1.5. The ratio of the speed of light in water to the speed of light in glass is about 1.14. Explain whether you expect light to refract more when moving from air to glass or from water to glass.

Refraction and Prisms

The shape, material, and size of a prism affect how separated light waves passing through the prism will be. Look at the diagram to see how a prism can also be used to recombine separated light waves.

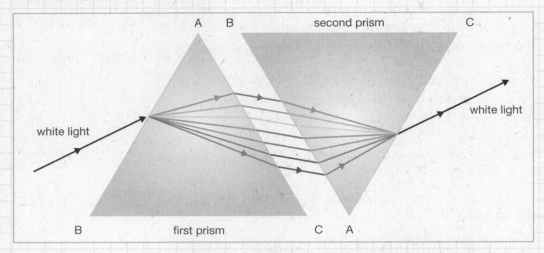

27. Notice how the light waves separate when they hit the first surface of the first prism. How does the shape and size of the prism affect how separated the light waves are when they exit the prism?

28. Discuss Imagine that the two prisms are moved and joined together to form a single block that has parallel sides. Think about this example and discuss with a partner why the light passing through a window appears much the same before and after it passes through the window.

Engineer It

Engineer a Solution to Light Pollution

Light pollution is the term for excess nighttime lighting that obscures the view of the night sky, negatively affects wildlife, and wastes energy.

29. Draw Outdoor lights are one contributor to light pollution. Apply your knowledge of the behavior of light waves to design a parking lot light that reduces excess nighttime light. Use ray diagrams to support your design.

Continue Your Exploration

Name: _____   Date: _____

Check out the path below or go online to choose one of the other paths shown.

| What Color Should the Doghouse Be? | • **What Causes a Rainbow?**
• **Hands-On Labs** 🖑
• **Propose Your Own Path** | *Go online to choose one of these other paths.* |

Light energy that is not reflected by an object is absorbed or transmitted. When light energy is absorbed, it is converted into thermal energy. Combine this information with what you have learned about perceived color to determine which color to paint certain doghouses.

1. What are the needs of a doghouse in a warmer climate? What are the needs of a doghouse in a cooler climate?

2. How might color affect the warmth of a doghouse?

Continue Your Exploration

Light Reflectance Value (LRV) is a measurement that tells you how much light a color reflects. From that value, you can infer how much light the color absorbs. Designers and painters often use LRV in their work. The following table shows the LRV of the paint colors available to paint doghouses.

Available Paint Colors		
Perceived color	Name of color	LRV
	Rosebud	62.26
	Crimson	12.35
	Sky	62.66
	Midnight	4.51
	Mint	74.93
	Forest	8.79

3. How does LRV of a color relate to the amount of light that the color absorbs? Explain.

4. Which colors would you recommend for doghouses built in warmer climates? Use what you know about light and LRV to support your recommendation.

5. Which colors would you recommend for doghouses built in cooler climates? Use what you know about light and LRV to support your recommendation.

6. Collaborate In a small group, list at least eight common car colors and then use a Venn diagram to sort the colors by "good in hot weather" and "good in cold weather." The colors that overlap are good for both hot weather and cold weather. Support your claim and share your results with the class.

Can You Explain It?

Name: _____   Date: _____

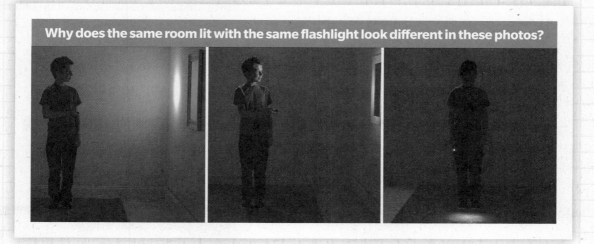

Why does the same room lit with the same flashlight look different in these photos?

 EVIDENCE NOTEBOOK

Refer to the notes in your Evidence Notebook to help you construct an explanation for how a room lit with the same flashlight can look different.

1. State your claim. Make sure your claim explains how the same light source in the same room can produce such different results.

2. Summarize the evidence you have gathered to support your claim and explain your reasoning.

Checkpoints

Answer the following questions to check your understanding of the lesson.

Use the graph to answer Question 3.

3. Which statements are supported by the information in the graph? Select all that apply.

   A. Light travels at the same speed in water, glass, and diamond.

   B. Light travels the fastest in a vacuum compared to the various media.

   C. Light cannot travel through any media at all.

   D. Light travels slower in media than it does in a vacuum.

   E. Light can travel with or without a medium.

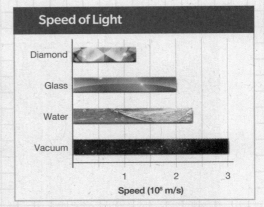

Speed of Light

Diamond · Glass · Water · Vacuum

Speed (10^8 m/s)

Use the photo to answer Questions 4–5.

4. What behavior of light is shown by the sphere?

   A. refraction

   B. absorption

   C. transmission

   D. reflection

5. Light travels in a ~~straight~~ / curved path. The image on the sphere appears curved because the sphere is a ~~prism~~ / mirror. As light hits the sphere's curved surface, light bounces off / ~~bends around~~ it at different angles, causing the image to appear distorted.

6. Some golfers use a blue filter to help see where their ball is in tall grass. The white golf ball will appear white / ~~black~~ / ~~blue~~ when viewed through the filter. Green grass around the ball will appear mostly ~~white~~ / black / ~~blue~~ / ~~red~~ when viewed through the filter, which makes seeing the ball easier.

7. A light wave travels through air toward water. Which statement describes the refraction of the light ray?

   A. The light stops traveling when it reaches the water.

   B. The light's energy transforms into thermal energy.

   C. The light changes direction when it reaches the water.

   D. The light bounces off the water and travels through the air.

8. The brightness of light is related to the light wave's ~~wavelength~~ / amplitude. The color of light is related to the light wave's wavelength / ~~amplitude~~. Changing the amplitude of a light wave ~~will~~ / will not change its wavelength.

Interactive Review

Complete this section to review the main concepts of the lesson.

Light is part of the electromagnetic spectrum. Light transfers energy and can travel through a vacuum.

A. Which behavior of light indicates that light transfers energy? Explain your reasoning.

Modeling light as a wave helps to explain the behavior of light in different situations.

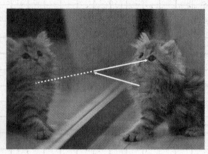

B. Explain why having different models of light waves is useful.

The amplitude and wavelength of a light wave affect the perceived brightness and color of light.

C. Use a wave model of light to explain why white light can be separated to show different colors.

At the boundary between media, light may be reflected, transmitted, refracted, or absorbed.

D. What types of interactions between light and matter can change the direction that light travels?

Energy from Sunlight Causes Earth's Seasons

Fall leaves change color as weather cools and leaves are no longer able to produce food for the tree. This photo of Virginia's Sherando Lake shows an example of this phenomenon.

Explore First

Exploring Solar Heating Place two identical pieces of dark construction paper outside: put one in sunlight and one in shade. After several minutes, touch the pieces of paper and compare their temperatures. What do you observe? With a partner, discuss possible explanations for your observations.

CAN YOU EXPLAIN IT?

Why is winter colder than summer?

This photo shows a cold day in the Tatra Mountains in Zakopane, Poland. Even though the sun is shining, the temperature is cold enough that snow stays on the ground.

Explore Online

1. Look at the photo, which was taken in the middle of the day. What season do you think it is? What evidence do you see to support your answer?

2. One day is defined as an amount of time equal to 24 hours. Why do you think people say winter days are shorter than summer days?

EVIDENCE NOTEBOOK As you explore the lesson, gather evidence to help explain why winter days are colder and shorter than summer days are.

Analyzing Energy from the Sun in the Earth System

Waves from the Sun

The sun emits energy in all directions in the form of electromagnetic waves. When these waves reach Earth, they interact with the atmosphere and Earth's surface in a variety of ways.

3. Think about moving from an area in direct sunlight to an area in the shade. What differences do you notice in the way you feel in these two situations?

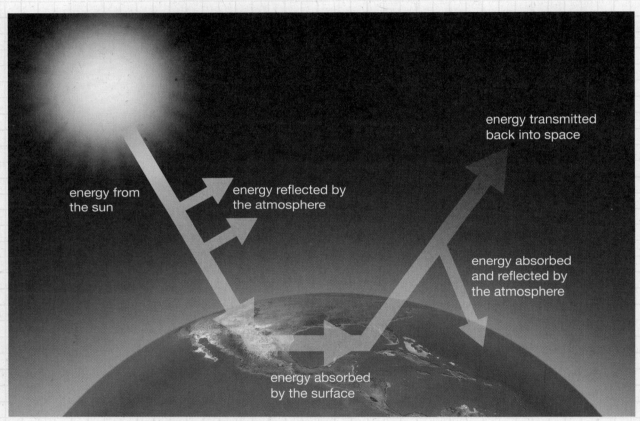

energy transmitted back into space

energy from the sun

energy reflected by the atmosphere

energy absorbed and reflected by the atmosphere

energy absorbed by the surface

The energy from the sun warms the atmosphere and Earth's surface.

4. When waves from the sun reach Earth's atmosphere, the waves behave in different ways depending on their wavelength. Some of the waves are reflected off /refracted by / transmitted through the atmosphere back into space. Some of the waves are absorbed by / transmitted through the atmosphere and reach Earth's surface. Some of the waves are absorbed by the atmosphere and never reach Earth's surface. When waves are reflected / refracted / transmitted / absorbed, the energy transforms into thermal energy.

© Houghton Mifflin Harcourt Publishing Company

Seasons of the Year

A **season** is a division of the year that is associated with particular weather patterns and daylight hours. Weather conditions and daily temperatures at any location on Earth follow a predictable cycle throughout the year. During a year, many places on Earth experience four seasons. Winter may be cold and may bring snow and ice. Spring occurs as winter changes to summer, and the temperatures in the area increase. Summer may be hot. Fall, or autumn, occurs as temperatures decrease and winter returns. The farther from the equator you go, the greater the differences in the seasons. For example, winter and summer at a location near the equator may be very similar to each other.

The Four Seasons of the Year

spring

In the Northern Hemisphere, spring begins in March. The sun moves higher across the sky, the number of daylight hours increases, and temperatures gradually rise.

summer

Summer is the warmest season, beginning in June in the Northern Hemisphere. The sun is in the sky for a greater part of the day.

winter

In December, the Northern Hemisphere begins its coldest season—winter. Freezing temperatures and snowfall are associated with winter months. The sun sets early in the day.

fall

Fall begins in September in the Northern Hemisphere. The number of daylight hours decreases as the sun's path across the sky moves lower, and temperatures gradually cool.

5. Draw Make a diagram that shows the seasonal differences where you live.

Changes across the Seasons

Because of Earth's rotation, you see the sun appear to move across the sky. For people living on the equator, the path of the sun in the sky does not change very much throughout the year. The sun rises on the eastern horizon, goes nearly overhead, and then sets on the western horizon. The sun reaches its highest point in the sky at about noon. Daytime lasts about 12 hours all year long, and the weather is nearly always warm. But as you move north or south away from the equator, the sun's path in the sky changes during the year. For example, in the Northern Hemisphere, the sun rises north of east in the summer and rises south of east in the winter. Sunsets follow a similar pattern. Summer sunsets in the Northern Hemisphere are north of west, while winter sunsets are south of west. As a result, the sun's path changes as seasons change.

The Path of the Sun in Summer and Winter in the Northern Hemisphere

6. Write summer or winter to label each path of the sun.

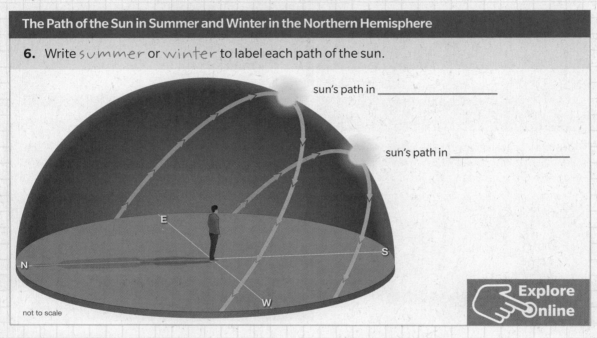

sun's path in _____

sun's path in _____

Explore Online

not to scale

Daylight Hours

During winter, it may be dark outside when you wake up for school and dark again soon after school ends. The sun does not go very high in the sky so its path across the sky is shorter. Because the sun is not up in the sky very long, there is less daylight time during this time of year. As a result, there is less time for sunlight to warm Earth during the daytime and more time for Earth to cool during the longer nighttime hours. The shortest amount of daylight time occurs on December 21 or 22 in the Northern Hemisphere.

During summer, the sun goes higher in the sky and days are longer because more time is needed for the sun to complete its longer path across the sky. Summer is warmer than winter because the sun is up for a longer period of time. There are more hours of daylight to warm Earth during the daytime, and fewer nighttime hours for Earth to cool. The day that has the greatest amount of daylight time is June 20, 21, or 22 in the Northern Hemisphere.

EVIDENCE NOTEBOOK

7. Use the path of the sun across the sky to help to explain why winter has shorter days than summer has. Record your evidence.

Hands-On Lab
Model Sunlight Distribution

Do the Math Explore what happens when light is spread out compared to when it is not spread out.

Procedure

STEP 1 Work with a partner. One partner shines a flashlight straight down on graph paper from a height of 15 cm. Using a protractor, the second partner makes sure the light strikes the paper at a 90° angle. The second partner then traces around the lit area on the paper with a pencil and labels it *90°*.

STEP 2 Switch holding the flashlight between partners. Keep the flashlight at the same height as it was in Step 1 (15 cm). Using the protractor, one partner guides the other to change the position of the flashlight so that the angle of the light striking the paper is 60°. That partner traces the lit area and labels it *60°*.

STEP 3 Next, using the protractor, change the angle so that the light striking the paper is 30°. Trace the lit area and label it *30°*.

STEP 4 Calculate the total area of each lit area using the following method:

    a. Count and record the number of full squares in each area.
       Example: 4 full squares

    b. Count the number of partial squares and divide the number by 2.
       Example: 12 partial squares ÷ 2 = 6

    c. Add the number of full squares to the number calculated for partial squares to find the total area. Example: 4 + 6 = 10

Angle of light	4a. Full squares	4b. Partial squares	4c. Total area
90°			
60°			
30°			

Analysis

STEP 5 Describe the relationship between the angle of light and area lit. How might this relate to sunlight distribution?

Energy from the Sun

There are two reasons why a place on Earth receives different amounts of the sun's energy in summer and winter: changes in the length of the sun's path across the sky and changes in the height of the sun at midday. In the summer, the sun has a longer path across the sky, which means the sun is in the sky for a longer period of time. There are more hours of daylight, so there is more time for Earth to absorb solar energy, and fewer hours of darkness for Earth to cool before the next day.

The height of the sun in the sky determines the angle at which the sunlight strikes Earth. As demonstrated in the activity, when the sun is overhead, the light is less spread out and the energy on each square meter is more intense. The amount of energy striking a small area will result in warmer temperatures than the same amount of energy striking a spread-out area. In summer, when the sun is higher in the sky, solar energy is more concentrated, but in winter, when the sun is lower in the sky, the sun's energy reaches Earth at a lesser angle. The angle at which sunlight strikes Earth influences Earth's temperatures, making it warmer in summer and colder in winter.

In addition to changing the distribution of sunlight over Earth's surface, the height affects the intensity of the energy at Earth's surface. As the electromagnetic waves from the sun pass through the atmosphere, energy is absorbed. Solar energy passes through more atmosphere when it strikes Earth at a lesser angle, making the sun's rays striking Earth less intense.

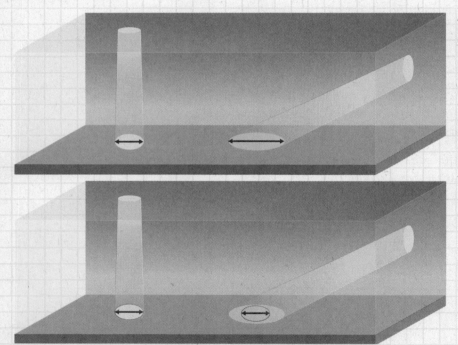

As the sun moves lower in the sky, the energy from sunlight is spread over a larger and larger area. A given amount of ground gets all of the light when the sun is directly overhead but gets only a part of the light when the sun strikes at an angle.

8. **Discuss** Together with a partner, talk about the amount of solar energy that falls on a given area. What happens when light is not spread out, and what happens when the light is more spread out? Relate this idea to the sun's energy and Earth.

 9. **Language SmArts** On a separate sheet of paper, write a short essay to compare what you observed in your investigation to what you saw in the image and what you read about the angles of sunlight striking Earth.

© Houghton Mifflin Harcourt Publishing Company

Patterns of Sunlight and Latitude

Electromagnetic waves from the sun are often referred to as sunlight. The rays of sunlight move in straight lines, and because the sun is so far away, the rays that strike Earth are very nearly parallel. Because of Earth's spherical shape, these parallel rays strike Earth most directly near the equator. As you move from the equator to the poles, the rays strike at lesser angles.

The diagram shows Earth lit by the sun on a day in the spring or fall. The diagram shows that the sun appears overhead as viewed from the equator, which means that people who live on or near the equator feel the intense energy of the sun. On the other hand, people who live at the North Pole or the South Pole would see the sun on this same day as very low in the sky. This diagram helps to illustrate why it is nearly always warm near the equator and cold at the poles.

polar region

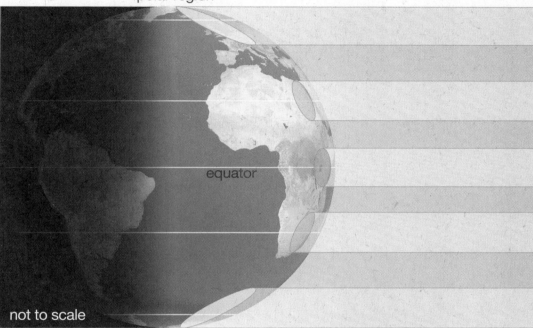

equator

not to scale

polar region

Due to the shape of Earth, sunlight strikes different latitudes on Earth's surface at different angles.

10. Imagine three people pointing toward the sun: a person at the equator, a person at the North Pole, and a person somewhere in between. Describe where in the sky each person is pointing.

© Houghton Mifflin Harcourt Publishing Company

11. Which of these statements describes the differences in sunlight striking Earth at different latitudes? Select all that apply.

   A. The intensity of the sun's energy received at the equator is greater than the intensity of the energy received at the poles.

   B. Sunlight strikes at a greater angle at the equator, which spreads out the sunlight.

   C. As you move away from the equator, the rays of sunlight striking Earth are no longer parallel.

   D. Sunlight passes through less atmosphere at the equator, so more sunlight gets through, which makes locations around the equator hotter.

Analyze How Earth's Shape Affects Patterns of Sunlight

12. The diagram shows an imaginary, cube-shaped planet. Explain how the range of temperatures at noon at different latitudes on a cube-shaped planet would compare to temperatures on the spherical Earth.

_____

_____

_____

_____

_____

13. Draw To the right of the cube, draw a model of the way the sun's rays would strike a cube-shaped planet.

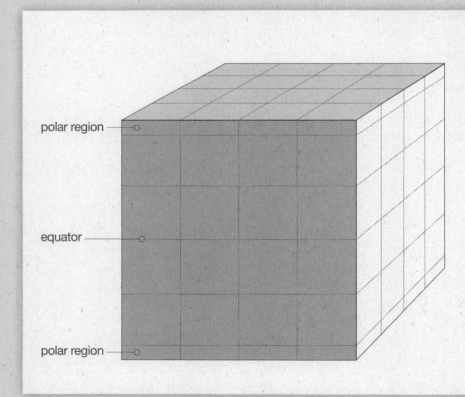

Analyzing an Earth-Sun Model to Explain Seasons

Earth orbits the sun in a predictable pattern. The pattern of Earth's seasons depends on how much sunlight reaches different areas of Earth as the planet moves around the sun. One complete orbit around the sun is called a revolution. One complete revolution takes one year.

Earth-Sun Models

Earth has a nearly circular, elliptical orbit around the sun. Earth also rotates around its north-south axis, which is an imaginary line passing through Earth from pole to pole.

14. What does the model in the first diagram show? Select all that apply.

    A. Every place on the planet gets 12 hours of light and 12 hours of dark each day.

    B. Temperature conditions on the planet change depending on distance from the sun.

    C. There are colder temperatures at the poles and warmer temperatures at the equator but no temperature changes during the year.

15. Does the first model explain the seasons that occur on Earth? Give at least one example to support your answer.

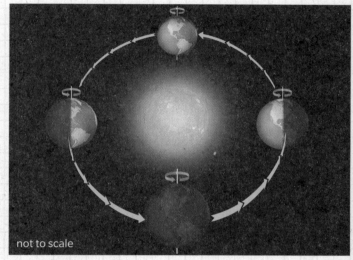

not to scale

Earth has a nearly circular orbit around the sun. This model of a fictional Earth shows an axis that is not tilted.

© Houghton Mifflin Harcourt Publishing Company

Unlike the planet in the first model, Earth's axis is not perpendicular to the plane of Earth's orbit around the sun. Earth's axis is tilted 23.5° from perpendicular to the plane of its orbit. This tilt remains the same throughout Earth's orbit, so Earth's axis is pointed in the same direction no matter where Earth is in its orbit around the sun.

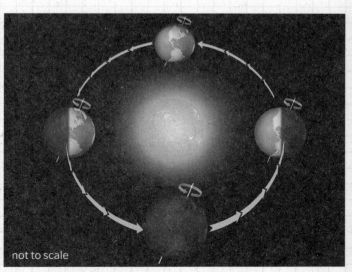

not to scale

This model shows Earth with its axis tilted 23.5°.

Hands-On Lab
Model Patterns of Sunlight throughout Earth's Revolution

Model the tilt of Earth in the Earth-sun system and show the way different areas of Earth receive more or less sunlight throughout the year.

MATERIALS
- ball, foam, 1"
- clay, modeling non-drying
- light source
- marker
- paper, construction
- protractor
- ruler, metric
- toothpick

Procedure

STEP 1 Use the modeling clay to make a base for your foam ball sphere.

STEP 2 With the marker, mark both poles and draw an equator on the sphere. Push the toothpick carefully through the sphere from pole to pole.

STEP 3 Insert the toothpick into the base and use the protractor to set the tilt of the axis at 23.5° from vertical.

STEP 4 Cut the construction paper so that it is a square and then fold it exactly in half. Draw a line along the fold. Use the protractor to mark 90° on both sides of the line and connect those marks. Label the four connected folds beginning with *Spring* and moving counterclockwise to label *Summer*, *Fall*, and *Winter*.

STEP 5 Place the light source on the center of the paper where the lines cross to act as the sun in the model.

STEP 6 Set the sphere directly on *Summer* with the North Pole (the top of the toothpick) tilting toward the light. Observe where the sphere is light and dark. Record your data by drawing and shading to show your *Summer* sphere in the table below.

STEP 7 **Keep the angle and direction that the sphere is pointing the same.** Move the sphere to *Fall*. Observe where the light falls and record your data in the table for *Fall*.

STEP 8 Repeat Step 7, moving the sphere to *Winter* and then *Spring*.

Summer	Fall	Winter	Spring

Analysis

STEP 9 What did you observe about sunlight on Earth in winter? Use your observations to explain why the Northern Hemisphere has lower temperatures in winter.

STEP 10 When the Northern Hemisphere tilts away from the sun, what season would you expect to experience in the Southern Hemisphere? Explain your answer.

The Tilt of Earth

The spherical shape of Earth explains why it gets colder as you get closer to the poles and why the height of the sun appears lower in the sky as you get closer to the poles. But these ideas alone do not completely explain why it is warmer in summer than in winter.

What did you learn as your model Earth moved around the model sun? Because Earth's tilt did not change, the amount of sunlight reaching a specific area of Earth did change. As Earth orbits the sun, the area of Earth that is pointed more toward the sun changes because Earth is always tilted in the same direction. So, the reason that Earth has seasons is because of a combination of Earth's tilt and Earth's revolution.

When the Northern Hemisphere points toward the sun, the Southern Hemisphere points away from the sun. As a result, seasons in the Southern Hemisphere are opposite from those in the Northern Hemisphere. In December, it is winter in Canada and summer in Australia.

16. Do the North Pole and the South Pole always stay in the same position relative to the sun? Explain your reasoning.

Earth's Revolution around the Sun

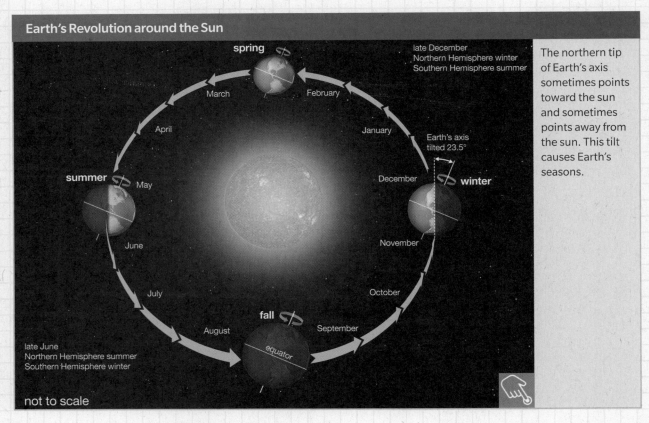

spring

late December
Northern Hemisphere winter
Southern Hemisphere summer

March

February

April

January

Earth's axis
tilted 23.5°

December

summer

May

winter

June

November

July

October

fall

September

August

equator

late June
Northern Hemisphere summer
Southern Hemisphere winter

not to scale

The northern tip of Earth's axis sometimes points toward the sun and sometimes points away from the sun. This tilt causes Earth's seasons.

17. It is summer in the hemisphere tilted ~~away from~~ / toward the sun, and it is winter in the hemisphere tilted away from / ~~toward~~ the sun. The seasons are ~~the same~~ / reversed in the Northern and Southern Hemispheres.

The Effect of Earth's Tilt on Daylight Hours

The number of hours of daylight increases as spring changes to summer because of Earth's tilt. If Earth had no tilt, days and nights would last about 12 hours each day everywhere. Because of the tilt, areas pointed toward the sun have more hours of daylight than those areas pointed away from the sun have.

Hours of Daylight by Latitude

18. Complete the labels to show how much daylight an area at each latitude would have when Earth is in this position.

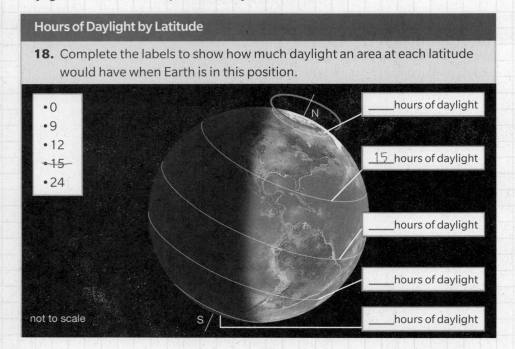

- 0
- 9
- 12
- ~~15~~
- 24

N

_____ hours of daylight

_15_ hours of daylight

_____ hours of daylight

_____ hours of daylight

S

_____ hours of daylight

not to scale

© Houghton Mifflin Harcourt Publishing Company

The Solstices and Equinoxes

Solstices mark the two days of the year when Earth's axis is tilted directly toward or away from the sun. The June solstice, also called the summer solstice, occurs when Earth's north axis is tilted toward the sun, between June 20 and June 22. The June solstice is the day of the year that has the greatest number of daylight hours in the Northern Hemisphere. This longest day of the year in the Northern Hemisphere is at the same time as the shortest day of the year in the Southern Hemisphere.

The December solstice, also called the winter solstice, occurs when Earth's north axis is tilted away from the sun, around December 21. The December solstice is the day with the fewest number of daylight hours in the Northern Hemisphere. In the Southern Hemisphere, the December solstice is the longest day of the year.

The days that begin spring and fall are marked by the equinoxes. Earth's axis does not tilt directly toward or away from the sun. The word *equinox* means "equal night," and on an equinox, there are equal hours of day and night at all locations on Earth.

On the June solstice, there are 24 hours of daylight at the North Pole, 12 hours of daylight at the equator, and 24 hours of darkness at the South Pole.

19. The solstices / equinoxes mark the dates on which Earth's axis is tilted directly toward or away from the sun. The days get shorter / longer as you move from the June solstice to the December solstice in the Northern Hemisphere.

The Tilt of Earth Affects the Energy Received from the Sun

Earth's tilt affects the temperatures at different locations on Earth. Because of Earth's tilt, some parts of Earth receive more solar energy than others. At the North Pole, Earth's tilt means that the sun rises above the horizon in mid-March and continues to shine without completely setting until mid-September. But because the sun shines on the North Pole at a lesser angle instead of striking from directly overhead, less energy is received in a given area at the North Pole than at the equator. When sunlight strikes at a lesser angle, the light spreads out. So, although daylight lasts longer at the North Pole than at the equator, the temperature is not as warm.

The angle at which sunlight strikes a particular location on Earth changes as Earth revolves around the sun. Areas are warmer where sunlight is not as spread out, such as in those areas around the equator.

20. When the South Pole is tilted toward / away from the sun, the Southern Hemisphere experiences winter. The amount of the sun's energy that strikes the area increases / decreases as compared to the sun's energy in the summer. The daylight hours are longer / shorter, and the area temperatures increase / decrease.

Note that Earth's distance from the sun is not what determines the seasons. In fact, Earth is closest to the sun around January 3 and farthest from the sun around July 4. It is Earth's tilt that determines the seasons.

© Houghton Mifflin Harcourt Publishing Company • Image Credits: ©Planet Observer/ Universal Images Group Editorial/Getty Images

21. How can the tilt of Earth be used in an explanation of why winter has cold temperatures and short daylight hours? Record your evidence.

Relate Patterns of Sunlight and Solar Panels

Solar panels capture light from the sun and convert the solar energy into electrical energy. The more sunlight that reaches your solar panels, the more electrical energy you can generate.

How would you position solar panels to receive the maximum amount of light energy from the sun? You know that when the sun's energy is less spread out, the amount of energy reaching that location on Earth is greatest. One way to get maximum light energy to the solar panels is by changing the angle of the panels to directly face the sun. The angle at which the panels capture the most solar energy depends on how close to the equator the panels are located.

22. Engineer It An engineer must decide how to set up a field of solar panels. Which of these should the engineer consider to capture the maximum amount of solar energy? Select all that apply.

A. how far away the location of the solar panel field is from the equator

B. that the panels will be closer to the sun in the summer than in the winter

C. whether the solar panels can be adjusted to a 90° angle to face the incoming light rays

D. whether the panels should face north, south, east, or west

These solar panels are adjusted to the best angle at which to capture solar energy.

23. The photo of these solar panels was taken at noon. Explain whether you think these panels are in an area close to or far from the equator.

_____

_____

_____

_____

_____

Continue Your Exploration

Name: _____   Date: _____

Check out the path below or go online to choose one of the other paths shown.

| **Land of the Midnight Sun** | • **Exploring Ways Organisms Adjust to the Seasons**
 • **Hands-On Labs** 🖐
 • **Propose Your Own Path** | *Go online to choose one of these other paths.* |

The *land of the midnight sun* describes parts of Earth where, for at least some of the year, a part of the sun is visible above the horizon for 24 hours of the day, including at midnight. Midnight sun occurs in the summer months in places north of the Arctic Circle and south of the Antarctic Circle.

Day and night at the poles are not at all like day and night on the rest of Earth. At the poles, there are six months of daylight and then six months of darkness in a year, which means that the poles experience one sunrise and one sunset each year.

Areas inside the Arctic and Antarctic Circles also experience periods during the year in which there is darkness or daylight for more than 24 hours. But as you move farther away from the poles these periods get shorter. Locations between the Arctic Circle and the equator and between the Antarctic Circle and the equator do not have days with a midnight sun.

During summer in the Arctic, the sun travels in a complete circle near the horizon but does not set. This time-lapse photo was taken at ten-minute intervals before and after midnight near Kópasker, Iceland.

1. If the sun is out all day, why is it not warm during an Arctic summer?

Continue Your Exploration

2. When people above the Arctic Circle are experiencing the midnight sun, what are people at the South Pole experiencing?

   A. long nights with only a few hours of sunlight

   B. equal hours of day and night

   C. stars and 24-hour nights

   D. 24-hour days and a midnight sun

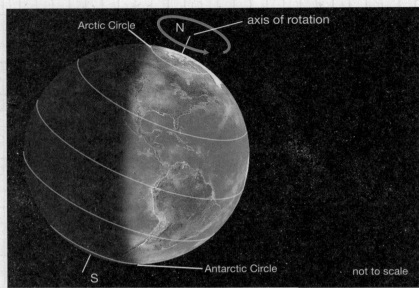

The midnight sun is due to the tilt of Earth's axis. This image shows Earth's orientation to the sun during summer in the Northern Hemisphere.

3. **Draw** Sketch a model of Earth similar to the one above, but instead show Earth when the areas near the South Pole are experiencing midnight sun. Indicate where sunlight falls and where it is dark. Label Earth's axis and indicate the area south of the Antarctic Circle.

4. **Collaborate** Work with a partner to make a poster that explains the midnight sun. Include some kind of labeled diagram on your poster.

Can You Explain It?

Name: _____   **Date:** _____

Why is winter colder than summer?

EVIDENCE NOTEBOOK

Refer to the notes in your Evidence Notebook to help you construct an explanation for why winter is colder than summer.

1. State your claim. Make sure your claim fully explains the differences between winter and summer.

2. Summarize the evidence you have gathered to support your claim and explain your reasoning.

Checkpoints

Answer the following questions to check your understanding of the lesson.

Use the photo to answer Question 3.

3. Which of these statements describe what is shown in the photo?

   A. The Southern Hemisphere is in summer and the Northern Hemisphere is in winter.

   B. Both polar regions are experiencing daytime and nighttime hours of relatively equal length.

   C. The Southern Hemisphere is closer to the sun than the Northern Hemisphere.

Use the diagram to answer Questions 4–5.

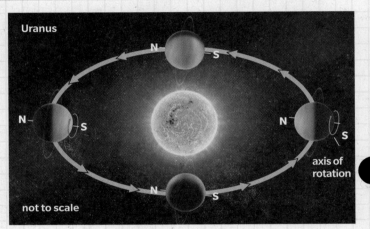

4. How would the seasons on Uranus compare to the seasons on Earth?

   A. The four seasons on Uranus would be different from Earth's because the tilt of Uranus is different.

   B. Seasons on Uranus would be exactly opposite of seasons on Earth.

   C. Uranus rotates on its side, so Uranus would not experience different seasons.

5. Which of these statements describes the seasons on Uranus?

   A. Uranus has two seasons, summer and winter.

   B. Summer and winter each last for about half of Uranus's complete orbit, with very short spring and fall seasons.

   C. When it is summer in the Northern Hemisphere of Uranus, the Southern Hemisphere has no daylight hours.

6. Which of these are affected by Earth's tilt? Select all that apply.

   A. the number of daylight hours in June

   B. changes in yearly temperatures across the seasons

   C. how long each season lasts

7. Electromagnetic waves travel from the sun to Earth through the vacuum of space. Some of the energy from these waves transforms into thermal energy when the waves are absorbed / transmitted / reflected by Earth's atmosphere and surface. The Earth-sun system follows a pattern in which the sun's energy in a particular location on Earth is more intense during the summer / winter.

Interactive Review

Complete this section to review the main concepts of the lesson.

The path of the sun across the sky and energy from the sun can help explain the seasons of the year.

A. How does the path of the sun affect the energy received by Earth at any particular location on Earth?

Earth's tilt and position in its revolution determine the amount of the sun's energy that strikes any particular location on Earth.

B. Explain why Earth's tilt is responsible for the seasons.

Choose one of the activities to explore how this unit connects to other topics.

☐ People in Science

Percy Spencer, Physicist Despite having only an elementary education, Percy Spencer became a productive scientist and inventor. While working at Raytheon during World War II, he helped to develop devices called magnetrons for use in radar equipment. When he and colleagues noticed that the magnetrons quickly heated food, he investigated the phenomenon. This research led to the development of the first commercial microwave oven in 1947.

Research the design of modern microwave ovens. Develop a presentation that explains how the microwave oven can cook food while a user safely stands next to the device.

☐ Music Connection

Sound Waves and Music Music is a mixture of sounds that have different pitches and volumes. Musical instruments are designed to produce a range of pitches. Musicians know how to play instruments to produce the pitch and volume of the sounds they need to make music.

Choose a musical instrument and research how the instrument produces different pitches and volumes. Develop a multimedia presentation to share with the class that explains how the instrument works. Include a simple mathematical model that shows how the properties of the sound waves relate to the frequency and volume.

☐ Social Studies Connection

Mythological Explanations of the Seasons Throughout history, many different cultures have told stories and developed explanations to make sense of the changing of the seasons. The ancient Greeks and Native Americans both used stories, called myths, to explain the changing seasons.

Research one ancient Greek myth and one Native American myth that explain the seasons. Compare and contrast the two myths. Produce a presentation with images showing the similarities and differences between the ways these cultures viewed the changes in seasons.

Name: **Date:**

Complete this review to check your understanding of the unit.

Use the images to answer Questions 1–3.

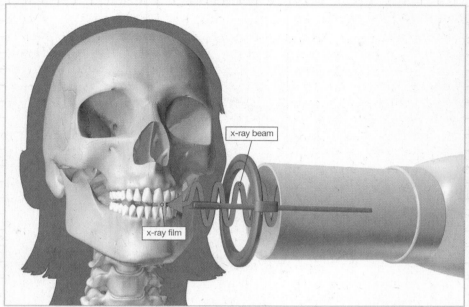

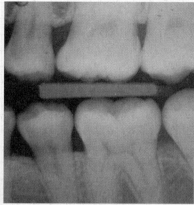

This diagram shows how an x-ray image of teeth is taken at the dentist's office. The lighter areas in the resulting x-ray image of the teeth are like the shadows that you see when you block visible light.

1. Based on the diagram and the x-ray image, what can you conclude about how x-rays interact with your teeth and the tissues in your mouth? Use evidence of the behavior of light waves to support your claim.

2. Recall that ultrasound machines use high-frequency sound waves to form images. How is the process of using ultrasound machines different from the process of taking x-ray images?

3. Ultrasound machines, not x-ray machines, are used to take images of a developing fetus. Sound waves are also used to take images of the sea floor, while x-rays can provide information about the sun and distant bodies in space. How do the properties of sound waves and x-rays affect the ways they are used? Make a claim and use evidence to support it.

© Houghton Mifflin Harcourt Publishing Company • Image Credits: ©DadaDento/istock/Getty Images Plus/Getty Images

Name: Date:

Use the images to answer Questions 4–7.

4. What relationship can you identify between the latitude of a location and the pattern of daylight hours throughout the year?

5. What can you infer about the difference in seasonal temperature changes in Honolulu, Minneapolis, and Fairbanks? Explain your reasoning.

6. Based on these patterns, what could you infer about the pattern of daylight hours over a year and the seasonal temperature changes for a location on the equator?

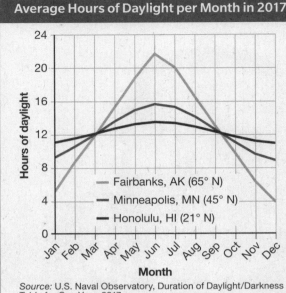

Average Hours of Daylight per Month in 2017

Legend:
Fairbanks, AK (65° N)
Minneapolis, MN (45° N)
Honolulu, HI (21° N)

Source: U.S. Naval Observatory, Duration of Daylight/Darkness Table for One Year, 2017

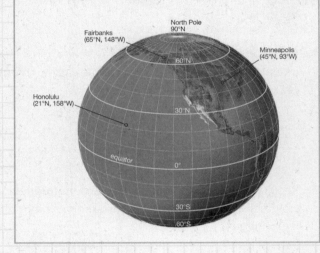

7. Choose a date and location from the graph. Use the data to explain how energy from the sun relates to the number of daylight hours and expected season in the area.

Name: Date:

Will your audience be able to hear you?

Imagine that you are planning to produce a play that is going to be performed outdoors without microphones. There will be 100 tickets for each performance and the audience will sit on the ground or on folding chairs. You need to design the seating area so that everyone in the audience will be able to hear the performers. Develop a proposal for a performance area that will maximize the audience's ability to hear the play.

The steps below will help guide your research and develop your recommendation.

Engineer It

1. **Define the Problem** Write a statement to clearly define the problem you are trying to solve. Identify the criteria and constraints that you need to consider in your design.

Engineer It

2. **Conduct Research** How will distance affect the audience's ability to hear sound? Research theaters without sound systems. How do these theaters use sound wave properties to ensure that all of the actors are heard?

3. **Develop a Model** What types of seating arrangements might work better than others? Apply your research to make a diagram or model of your seating area. Include how you expect the volume to change for audience members.

4. **Optimize a Solution** Compare your solution to the Royal Albert Hall in London, England; the Epidaurus Ancient Theatre in Epidaurus, Greece; or the Vienna Musikverein in Vienna, Austria. How is your theater design different or similar? Based on what you know about sound, how is your solution more or less effective? Is your design the optimal solution? If not, modify your solution.

5. **Communicate** Present your design proposal to the class. Include design specifics, such as seating arrangement and stage location. Explain why your design is the optimal solution. Ensure your presentation includes a thorough explanation of the properties of the sound wave behavior involved.

✓ **Self-Check**

	I identified the criteria and constraints of the problem.
	I described how sound volume changes with distance.
	I drew a diagram to model the seating arrangement that included how sounds would change.
	I provided a thorough explanation of my design proposal in a class presentation.

© Houghton Mifflin Harcourt Publishing Company

Technology and Human Impact on Earth Systems

How do technology and human activity relate to biodiversity?

Ecosystem health and services are related to the biodiversity of the ecosystem.

You Solve It How Can You Compare Digital and Analog Communication Signals?

Compare analog and digital signals by simulating different ways to transmit a photo. Choose the signal type and communication channel, and vary signal and noise levels.

Go online and complete the You Solve It to explore ways to solve a real-world problem.

Monitor Biodiversity

This redwoods forest is high in biodiversity and is a popular tourist destination.

A. Look at the photo. On a separate sheet of paper, write down as many different questions as you can about the photo.

B. **Discuss** With your class or a partner, share your questions. Record any additional questions generated in your discussion. Then choose the most important questions from the list that are related to monitoring biodiversity. Write them below.

C. Choose an ecosystem to research. Here is a list of ecosystems you can consider:

redwood forest   coastal wetlands   grasslands

kelp forest   oak woodland   desert

D. Use the information above, along with your research, to develop a plan for monitoring biodiversity in your chosen ecosystem.

Discuss the next steps for your Unit Project with your teacher and go online to download the Unit Project Worksheet.

566 **Unit 7** Technology and Human Impact on Earth Systems

Language Development

Use the lessons in this unit to complete the network and expand your understanding of these key concepts.

	Similar term
	Phrase
	Cognate
	Example
	Definition

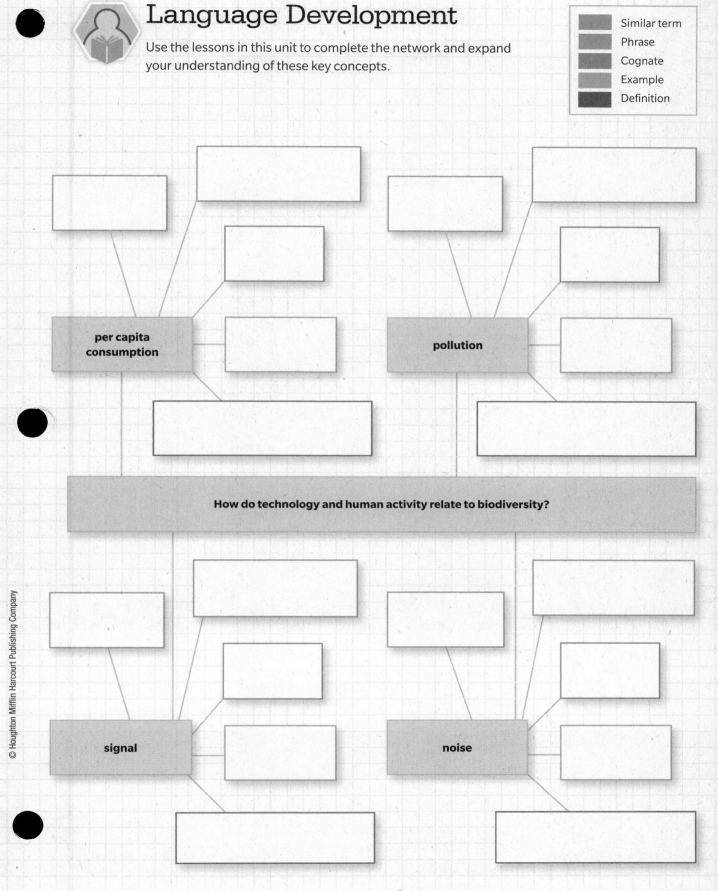

per capita consumption

pollution

How do technology and human activity relate to biodiversity?

signal

noise

Changes in Human Population Affect Resource Use

Many farmers in Bali, Indonesia, use gradual steps, called *terraces*, to grow rice in steep, hilly areas. As the human population grows, demand for rice increases.

Explore First

Modeling Population Change A small town has 100 people. Each year, 10 babies are born for every 100 people in the town, and the death rate is 8 people for every 100 people in the town. Work with a partner to develop a model of what happens to the population of the town over 10 years. What happens to the population? What are the strengths and weaknesses of the model?

CAN YOU EXPLAIN IT?

What might explain the patterns of population density in northern Africa?

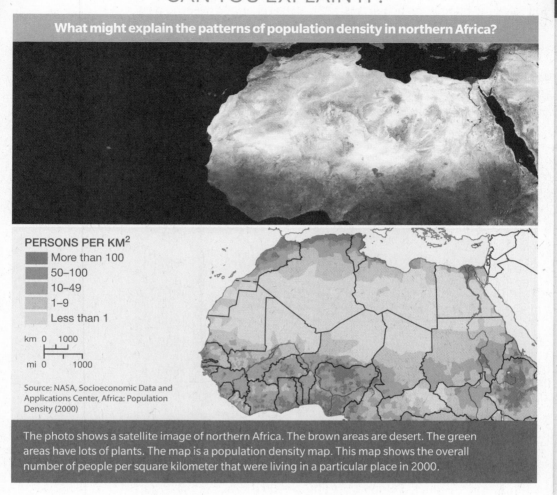

PERSONS PER KM²
- More than 100
- 50–100
- 10–49
- 1–9
- Less than 1

km 0   1000

mi 0   1000

Source: NASA, Socioeconomic Data and Applications Center, Africa: Population Density (2000)

The photo shows a satellite image of northern Africa. The brown areas are desert. The green areas have lots of plants. The map is a population density map. This map shows the overall number of people per square kilometer that were living in a particular place in 2000.

1. Compare the satellite image with the map. What do you notice on the satellite image about the places in northern Africa with the greatest population density?

 EVIDENCE NOTEBOOK As you explore this lesson, gather evidence to help explain what might determine population density in northern Africa.

Analyzing Human Population Data

How do you think the population of humans on Earth has changed over the past 12,000 years? Think about what factors affect whether a population increases or decreases. Consider how these factors may have changed over the past 12,000 years.

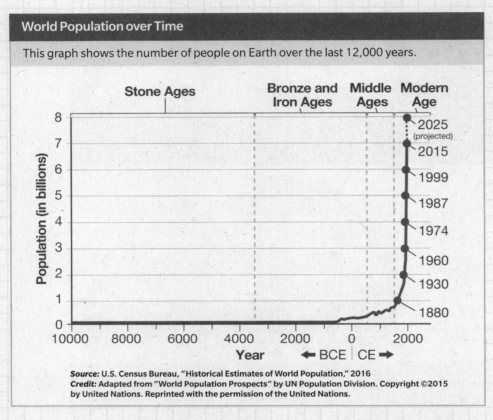

World Population over Time

This graph shows the number of people on Earth over the last 12,000 years.

Source: U.S. Census Bureau, "Historical Estimates of World Population," 2016
Credit: Adapted from "World Population Prospects" by UN Population Division. Copyright ©2015 by United Nations. Reprinted with the permission of the United Nations.

2. Look at the data in the graph. During what time period do you see the largest change in the number of people on Earth? What factors do you think caused this change to happen?

Population

A **population** is a group of individuals of the same species living in the same place at the same time. Every organism on Earth is part of a population. The human population can be analyzed on many different levels. For example, you might think about the population of your school, your state, or the whole Earth.

For most of human history, the human population size was many times smaller than it is today, and it did not change much. However, around 500 BCE the population began to increase. Then, less than 200 years ago, around the beginning of the Modern Age, the human population began to grow rapidly.

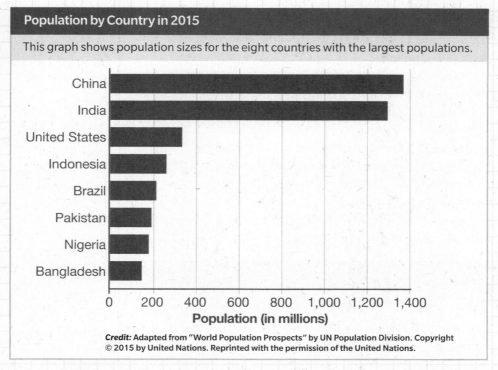

Population by Country in 2015

This graph shows population sizes for the eight countries with the largest populations.

Population (in millions)

Credit: Adapted from "World Population Prospects" by UN Population Division. Copyright © 2015 by United Nations. Reprinted with the permission of the United Nations.

3. According to the graph, how does the population of China compare to the population of the United States?

Data about Populations

Government agencies measure the populations of different areas, and they measure more than just the total number of people. For example, population data can include the distribution of ages and the ratio of males to females within the population. The data gathered are organized in databases that can be searched and sorted, and the data can be analyzed to make inferences about a population.

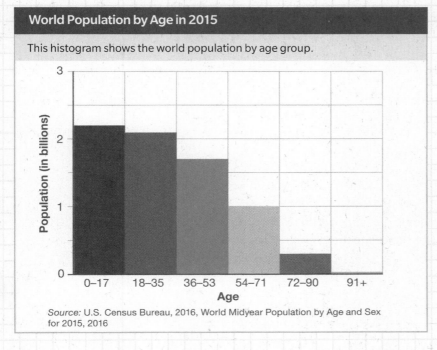

World Population by Age in 2015

This histogram shows the world population by age group.

Source: U.S. Census Bureau, 2016, World Midyear Population by Age and Sex for 2015, 2016

4. What can you conclude from the data shown in the graph?

A. The population is mostly made up of adults over the age of 17.

B. Most of the population that has lived to age 90 will continue to live for many more years.

C. Humans who are ages 54–71 make up about half the population.

D. People are not expected to live much past age 53.

Population Growth Rates

Population data can be used to calculate a growth rate, which indicates whether a population has grown and how fast it has grown. The growth rate of a population depends on the birth rate, the death rate, and the migration of people into or out of a region. Birth rates, death rates, and growth rates are ratios. A ratio compares one amount to another amount, and so a birth rate compares the number of babies born to the total population size. For example, the birth rate in India in 2016 was 19 births per 1,000 people. The death rate for the same year was 7 deaths per 1,000 people. There were more births than deaths per 1,000 people. There was also not a large movement of people out of the country, and as a result, the population grew. Taken all together, the trends in population data can tell a story about a particular region's population. Proportions may be used with the birth rate and death rate and the total population to find the total number of births and deaths for a population.

Birth Rate, Death Rate, and Population Size

Examine this graph to see how birth rate and death rate can affect population size.

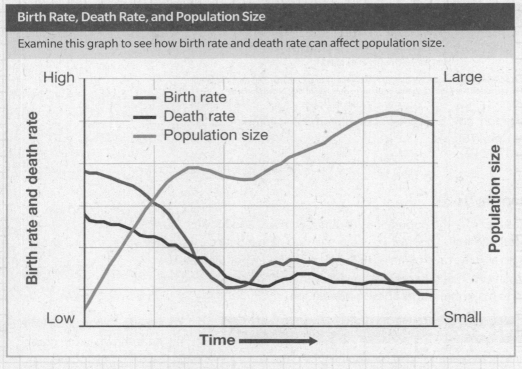

5. Examine the patterns and trends shown in this graph. How are birth rate, death rate, and population size related?

6. **Do the Math** A country has a population of 9,507,000. In a given year, the country's birth rate is 11 births per 1,000 people. The country's death rate that year is 13.5 deaths per 1,000 people. Use proportions to calculate the total births and total deaths for the year. Then calculate the change in population.

Factors Affecting Population Growth

Rates of population change can be used to analyze causes of population change and to predict future changes. Significant changes in population are often related to environmental changes in a region or to events in history.

In the data shown earlier, several key factors influenced the huge increase in the world's population over a short period of time. Improvements in agriculture led to a larger and more reliable food supplies. Technology and innovations led to increases in planting and harvesting crops. Thus, more food was available than when people relied on hunting and gathering. People invented and improved machines that used fossil fuels, and these industrial developments increased the efficiency of agriculture, industry, and transportation. Improvements in sanitation, diet, and medical care led to population growth by increasing survival rates and the average human lifespan.

Factors That Affect Population Growth

Improvements in transportation and agriculture meant more food could be distributed to more places.

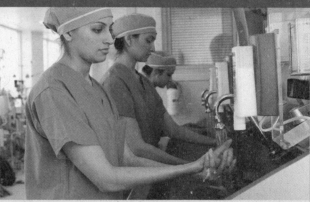

Improvements in sanitation and medicine helped to decrease death rates.

Population by World Region, 1750–2050

Population growth rates differ by region. The last bar shows projected population sizes. These sizes are estimated based on current data.

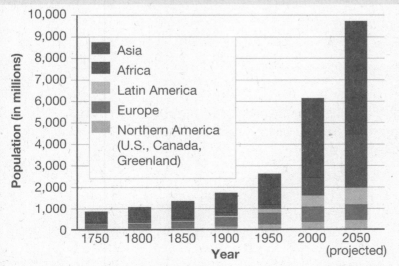

Credit: Adapted from "World Population Prospects" by UN Population Division. Copyright ©2015 by United Nations. Reprinted with the permission of the United Nations. Adapted from "The World at Six Billion" by UN Population Division. Copyright ©1999 by United Nations. Reprinted with the permission of the United Nations.

7. Which of the following likely contributed to increased global population growth between 1950 and 2000? Circle all that apply.

   A. increases in birth rates

   B. improvements in agriculture

   C. increases in death rates in Europe

   D. immigration from Latin America to Africa

Project Population Growth

Population data from a span of time can be used to project future population growth. To project population growth means to predict a future change in population based on current data. The table below shows the world's population size from 1900 to 2000.

Population Data						
Year	1900	1920	1940	1960	1980	2000
Population	1.7 billion	1.9 billion	2.3 billion	3 billion	4.4 billion	6 billion

8. **Draw** In the space provided, graph the data in the table to show global population change from 1900 to 2000. Label the *x*-axis "Years" and the *y*-axis "Population."

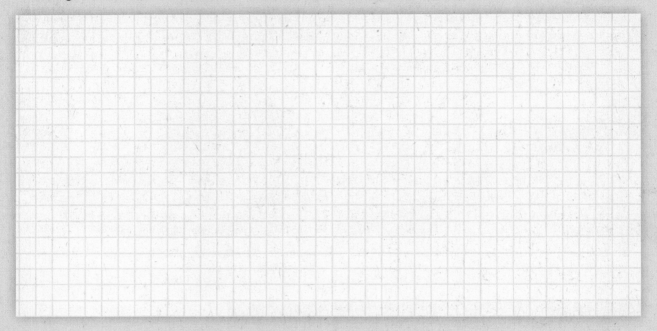

9. Use your graph to predict the world's population in 2040. Include a reason for your prediction.

_____

_____

_____

10. **Write** Describe an event or scenario that would increase or decrease the projected size of the world's population. Make an argument for why the event would affect the population, and support your argument with evidence.

_____

_____

_____

_____

_____

© Houghton Mifflin Harcourt Publishing Company

Investigating Rates of Resource Use

Some of the foods you eat provide your body with energy. Every day, these nutrients fuel your body's processes. All living things need energy, but they obtain energy in different ways. You get energy when your body breaks down the food you eat. Plants use energy from the sun to make their own food, and then they break down this food and use its stored energy. Sunlight is an endless source of energy, but other energy sources can run out.

This oil rig extracts oil from beneath the ocean floor.

11. Identify the natural resources that are shown or represented in the photo.

12. Discuss Together with a partner, discuss whether each resource identified in the photo can run out or whether its supply is unlimited.

Natural Resources

All human activity depends on natural resources. Some natural resources are renewable. They either cannot be used up or can be replaced at about the same rate at which they are used. Sunlight is renewable. Some resources are nonrenewable because they cannot be replaced as quickly as they are used. Coal and petroleum are nonrenewable.

Other resources can be either renewable or nonrenewable, depending on how the resource is used and managed. For example, bamboo and wood can be renewable or nonrenewable, depending on how fast the plants are cut down compared with how fast they are replaced by regrowth. Water is renewable, but pollution or overuse of water can use up clean drinking water faster than it can be replaced.

13. Think about the natural resources you need or use every day. What are some natural resources you need to live? How do you use them in your daily life? Explain your answer.

14. Complete the table to categorize the resources as renewable or nonrenewable.

Resource	Renewable	Nonrenewable
water	✓	
wind		
copper		

Renewable Resources

Renewable resources include plant and animal resources such as cotton and wool. These resources are used to make clothing, insulation, and many other products. Other renewable resources, such as wind, water, and sunlight, are used to generate electrical energy.

Solar panels absorb the energy of sunlight and transform it into electrical energy. The electrical energy then moves through a utility grid to a community. Solar panels can be found on rooftops, in fields, offshore, and even on spacecraft.

The fleece of these alpacas is similar to wool, which is sheep hair. Like wool, alpaca fleece is used to make clothing such as sweaters, hats, and mittens.

Nonrenewable Resources

Fossil fuels—coal, natural gas, and oil—formed from the remains of organisms that lived hundreds of millions of years ago. There were large swampy landscapes and seas at different times in Earth's history. In those conditions, massive amounts of organic material accumulated. Those materials were buried and slowly changed to form fossil fuels. They are nonrenewable, because we use them much faster than they form. Other resources, such as metals and minerals, are also nonrenewable.

Coal is mainly used as a fuel that is burned to generate electrical energy.

How Natural Resources Are Used

The use of technologies and natural resources varies from region to region, and depends on several factors, including resource availability, cultural traditions, and economic conditions. In general, populations of richer, industrialized nations use more natural resources than populations of less industrialized nations do. As societies become more industrialized, they tend to consume more resources. New technologies and more efficient practices can allow consumption to level off or decline.

15. **Engineer It** A developer is building an office building in a small town near the Mojave desert. The developer is deciding whether to install solar panels to generate electrical energy or to connect the building to the existing utility grid. The grid generates electrical energy from both renewable resources, such as moving water, and nonrenewable resources, such as fossil fuels. If a criterion of the plan is to reduce the use of fossil fuels, which option should the developer choose? State your claim, and support your claim with evidence and reasoning.

EVIDENCE NOTEBOOK

16. What natural resources do you think are available in northern Africa? How are these resources used? Record your evidence.

Hands-On Lab
Model Resource Use

You will model the relationship between population size and resource use.

MATERIALS
- beans
- cups, small

Procedure

STEP 1 Choose the number of people you want to have in your first model population and set out one cup for each person. Place two beans in each cup to model resource use. Record the population and the total number of beans that were used by this population. Empty the cups.

STEP 2 Increase your population by one or more people (cups). Distribute the resources so that each person is again using two beans. Record the population and the total number of beans that were used by this population.

Analysis

STEP 3 Which of your model populations used more resources?

STEP 4 Use your models to support a general statement about the relationship between population growth and resource use.

STEP 5 Suppose the beans represented a nonrenewable resource. What impact could an increasing population have on a nonrenewable resource? How could you model this using the cups and beans?

Resource Use and Population Growth

Government agencies and other organizations track resource use in populations over time. The data collected can be used to show how rates of resource use change.

Resource Use over Time

Resource use changes over time due to a variety of factors. For example, the use of oil increased as the number of gasoline-powered vehicles increased. To help compare resource use at different times, data can be measured as units used per time period. For example, the use of oil is generally measured in barrels of oil consumed per day or year. The data can be shown using models, such as graphs, which make comparisons easier.

Population Growth and Resource Use over Time

The use of natural resources commonly increases as a population increases because more people are using these resources. However, more efficient use of a resource can also have an effect on overall use of that resource. For example, the graph shows that water use in the United States increased at a rate greater than the rate of population growth for many years. But as time went on, engineering and water use practices improved, and overall water use has decreased since 1980.

The availability of resources also affects where people live. Throughout human history, higher population densities have occurred in areas with resources that humans use, including food, water, and materials used for shelter. Improved transportation and engineering have allowed resources to be available in places where they were not available before. However, human populations still tend to be higher in and near areas that have more resources available for use.

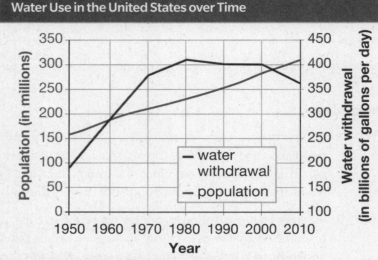

Water Use in the United States over Time

Source: USGS, "Estimated Use of Water in the United States in 2010," 2014;
Credit: Adapted from "World Population Prospects" by UN Population Division. Copyright ©2015 by United Nations. Reprinted with the permission of the United Nations.

Analyze Trends in Timber Consumption

17. Compare the data in the graph for population and lumber use. What trend or trends do you see in the population size and lumber use in the United States from 2003 to 2010?

_____

_____

_____

_____

_____

_____

18. What might these trends indicate about changes in the use of lumber during this time period?

_____

_____

_____

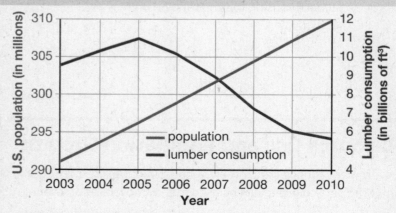

Lumber Use in the United States over Time

Wood that is used for building structures is called *lumber*. This graph shows population size and lumber use over time.

Source: U.S. Census Bureau, Statistical Abstract of the United States: 2012;
Credit: Adapted from "World Population Prospects" by UN Population Division. Copyright ©2015 by United Nations. Reprinted with the permission of the United Nations.

Analyzing Per Capita Consumption

Analyzing how populations use resources can show large-scale changes and overall trends. These overall trends can be used to predict future resource use and can help people predict future needs. Understanding the trends can also help people develop ways to reduce resource use.

Individual resource use is also important. Each individual makes an impact on the availability of natural resources. The use of a resource by individuals, when added together, results in the overall resource use of a population. Consider the group of people eating peaches in the photos. The group will use more peaches if each person eats two peaches than if each person eats only one peach.

Both individual and group uses of resources affect resource availability.

19. **Discuss** How does the way each individual in your class uses resources affect the resource use of your class population?

Model Factors in Resource Use

You will model the use of a resource by individuals to determine how changes in individual use can affect the overall use of a resource by a population. The cups represent individuals, and the beans represent the resource. You can decide what resource the beans represent and how much of that resource each bean represents.

MATERIALS
- beans (70)
- cups, small (5)

Procedure

STEP 1 Decide how many beans to use in total. Distribute the beans evenly among the people (cups). Record the results of your model in the table below.

STEP 2 Model two or three different scenarios using different populations or different amounts of the resource. Design your models so that you can draw conclusions about the factors that affect the overall use of a resource.

Model	Total Population	Total beans used	Beans used by each person	Total beans left over
A				
B				
C				
D				

Analysis

STEP 3 How can an increase in the amount of a resource each person uses affect the overall resource use if the population stays the same? What would happen if the population also increased? Use your models to support your answer.

STEP 4 Did one of your models include a scenario in which there were not enough beans to give each person the same amount? If not, model a scenario like that now and record the results. How does this model relate to situations in the real world when there may not be enough of a resource for each person to have the same amount?

Per Capita Consumption

Resource use can be reported as the overall amount of a resource used by a population during a certain period. It may also be reported as the average amount of a resource used by each individual in a population. **Per capita consumption** is the amount of a resource that one person consumes in a given amount of time. Per capita consumption is a ratio that is calculated by dividing the total amount of a resource used in a certain time period by the number of people in the population.

Per Capita Consumption of Cotton

A town of 100 people uses 1,200 kg of cotton each year. The per capita consumption of cotton in this town is 12 kg per person per year.

small town of **100** people

1 person in the town

1,200 kg of cotton each year

12 kg of cotton each year

20. How could you determine the per capita consumption of oranges in your town or city in kg per year?

   A. add up the kg of oranges that people in the population use in a year

   B. divide the total kg of oranges used in a year by the number of people in the population

   C. multiply the kg of oranges that one person uses in a year by the number of people in the population

21. Find the per capita consumption of oranges for each city in the diagram.

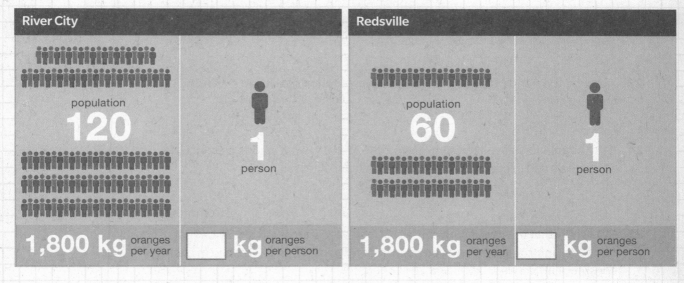

River City

population **120**

1 person

1,800 kg oranges per year

☐ **kg** oranges per person

Redsville

population **60**

1 person

1,800 kg oranges per year

☐ **kg** oranges per person

22. What factors might account for the different per capita consumptions of each of these two cities?

Trends in Per Capita Consumption

You can track per capita consumption over time by using tables and graphs. Look for trends in the per capita consumption of fish and shellfish in the table and graph.

Per Capita Consumption of Fish and Shellfish in the U.S.								
Year	2006	2007	2008	2009	2010	2011	2012	2013	2014
lbs	16.5	16.3	15.9	15.8	15.8	14.9	14.2	14.3	14.6
kgs	7.48	7.39	7.21	7.17	7.17	6.76	6.44	6.49	6.62

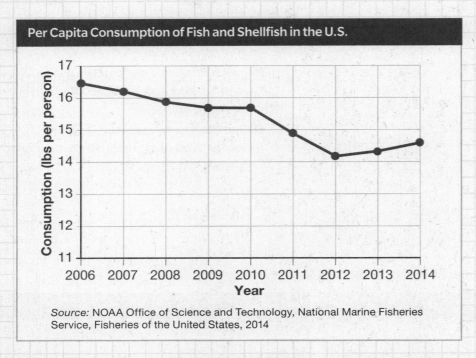

Per Capita Consumption of Fish and Shellfish in the U.S.

Source: NOAA Office of Science and Technology, National Marine Fisheries Service, Fisheries of the United States, 2014

23. Describe the trends you see in per capita consumption of fish and shellfish.

24. If the population stayed the same from 2006 to 2014, what could you conclude about the trend in overall consumption of fish and shellfish?

25. Data show that the population of the U.S. increased from 2006 to 2014. What additional information would you need in order to determine the trend in overall consumption between 2006 and 2014?

EVIDENCE NOTEBOOK

26. How might the availability of a necessary resource in a region affect the number of people who can live in that region? Record your evidence.

Do the Math
Calculate Rate of Consumption

Suppose the population of a community is 10,000 people and the per capita consumption of fish is 6.6 kg per person each year. How much fish would be consumed per year if the population grows by 2,500 people?

Fish is a popular food resource in many communities.

STEP 1 Use proportional reasoning to calculate the total fish consumption for the original population of 10,000.

$$\frac{6.6 \text{ kg}}{1 \text{ person}} \quad \begin{array}{c} \times 10,000 \\ \longrightarrow \\ \times 10,000 \end{array} \quad \frac{\boxed{} \text{ kg}}{10,000 \text{ people}}$$

STEP 2 Then use proportional reasoning to calculate the additional amount of fish that would be consumed by the additional 2,500 people.

$$\frac{6.6 \text{ kg}}{1 \text{ person}} \quad \begin{array}{c} \times 2,500 \\ \longrightarrow \\ \times 2,500 \end{array} \quad \frac{\boxed{} \text{ kg}}{2,500 \text{ people}}$$

STEP 3 Now add the two amounts together to find the total amount of fish resources expected to be consumed by the larger population. Record your answer in the table.

_____ kg of fish

27. The table below lists resources and their per capita consumption for the same community. How much will the total consumption of each resource be after the additional 2,500 people join the population?

Resource consumed	Per capita consumption	Overall resource consumption (after population increase)
fish and shellfish	6.6 kg/year	_____ kg per year
carrots	5.4 kg/year	
gasoline	1,514 L/year	

Language SmArts

Relate Resource Use to Per Capita Consumption and Population Size

Predictions about how long a nonrenewable resource will last are based on how much of the resource is available and the rate of resource use. These predictions are based on per capita consumption and trends in population growth.

In the questions below, your evidence could be an example that illustrates your claim.

28. What happens to the rate of resource use when a population stays the same, but per capita consumption increases? Make a claim, and use evidence and reasoning to support your claim.

The vegetables shown are renewable resources, but the foil, which is made from aluminum, is a nonrenewable resource.

_____

_____

_____

_____

_____

29. What happens to the rate of resource use when a population stays the same, but per capita consumption decreases? Make a claim, and use evidence and reasoning to support your claim.

_____

_____

_____

_____

_____

30. What happens to the rate of resource use when a population increases, but per capita consumption stays the same? Make a claim, and use evidence and reasoning to support your claim.

_____

_____

_____

_____

_____

Continue Your Exploration

Name: _____   Date: _____

Check out the path below or go online to choose one of the other paths shown.

Careers in Science

- **Find Your Resource Use**
- **Hands-On Labs** ✋
- **Propose Your Own Path**

Go online to choose one of these other paths.

Conservation Scientist

Thousands of scientists work all across the world as conservation scientists. They provide input and expertise on questions about how to manage natural resources. A conservation scientist could work for or with any group or individual who owns or manages land. For example, they might work with a government group, an organization, a business, or a private landowner. These scientists may conduct research about the overall health or condition of an area of land or of a particular resource. They record, report, and interpret the data they gather and often use computer modeling and mapping to make predictions and to identify trends.

Conservation scientists use a variety of equipment to help accurately gather, record, and map information about resources in an area.

Continue Your Exploration

The emerald ash borer (EAB) is an insect that can destroy ash trees. It is spreading across much of the United States. Ash trees are an important material resource because they are used for building furniture and other wooden items. Without treatment, ash trees infested with the EAB are expected to die. Treatment is possible but costly. Living, uninfested ash trees may be cut down to help prevent the spread of the EAB.

1. How does EAB affect the availability of resources? If human use remains the same, is ash wood a renewable or nonrenewable resource?

2. In what ways will treatment or removal of ash trees to prevent the spread of EAB affect overall and/or per capita use of ash trees as a resource?

3. How can human actions affect the rate at which infestations of the beetle spread? How would humans affect the rate at which ash resources could be renewed?

4. **Collaborate** The U.S. Forest Service outlined objectives for a nationwide management plan to address EAB threats. These objectives include:

   - prevent the spread of EAB and prepare for EAB infestations
   - detect, monitor, and respond to new EAB infestations
   - manage EAB infestations in forests
   - harvest ash trees—both infested and uninfested—for economic use and to prevent the spread of EAB
   - work to restore forest ecosystems that were affected by EAB

Source: U.S. Forest Service Department of Agriculture

Work with classmates to prioritize these objectives. Discuss which objectives you think are most important and should be given priority. Provide a rationale for all arguments, and order the objectives according to your decisions. Then, compare your prioritized list and the list of another group. Discuss similarities and differences.

© Houghton Mifflin Harcourt Publishing Company

Can You Explain It?

Name: _____   Date: _____

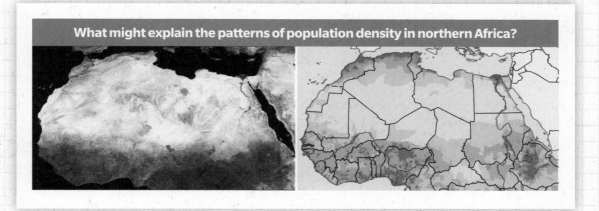

What might explain the patterns of population density in northern Africa?

EVIDENCE NOTEBOOK

Refer to the notes in your Evidence Notebook to help you construct an explanation for what might determine population density in northern Africa.

1. State your claim. Make sure your claim fully explains what might determine population density in northern Africa.

2. Summarize the evidence you have gathered to support your claim and explain your reasoning.

Checkpoints

Answer the following questions to check your understanding of the lesson.

3. Which factors contribute to population growth? Circle all that apply.

   A. increase in birth rate

   B. increase in death rate

   C. new farming technology

   D. improvements in health care

Use the table to answer Question 4.

4. Which statement is supported by the data in the table?

	Population	Consumption of rice (in kg)	Per capita consumption
Middleville	60,000	720,000	12.0 kg
Toptown	40,000	720,000	?

   A. The population of Toptown is increasing.

   B. The per capita consumption of rice is higher in Toptown than in Middleville.

   C. Per capita consumption of rice is decreasing in both Toptown and in Middleville.

   D. Individuals in Middleville and Toptown consume the same amount of rice.

Use the graph to answer Question 5.

5. Which statement about the per capita consumption of yogurt is supported by the data in the graph?

   A. In 2012, each person consumed more than twice the amount of yogurt they consumed in 2010.

   B. More people ate yogurt in 2014 than in 2013.

   C. On average, each person ate about 14.9 pounds of yogurt in 2014.

   D. The people in the United States consumed a total of 14 pounds of yogurt in 2012.

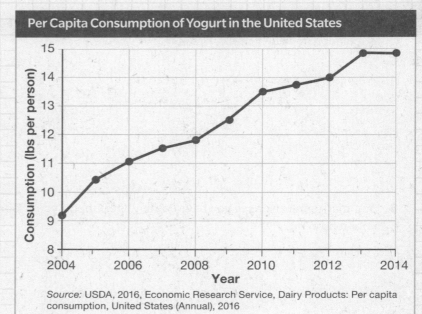

Per Capita Consumption of Yogurt in the United States

Source: USDA, 2016, Economic Research Service, Dairy Products: Per capita consumption, United States (Annual), 2016

---

6. In general, how is resource use related to population size?

   A. Resource use is usually not affected by population size.

   B. Resource use usually increases as population increases.

   C. Resource use usually decreases as population stays the same.

   D. Resource use usually increases as population decreases.

Interactive Review

Complete this section to review the main concepts of the lesson.

The rate of human population growth has increased significantly in the recent past.

A. What are some factors that contributed to the dramatic change in the rate of growth of the human population?

People rely on renewable and nonrenewable resources for food, materials, and energy.

B. Summarize how population growth can impact resource use.

Per capita resource use is an average that describes the amount of a resource that one person consumes in a given amount of time.

C. If a population's size does not change, how would a change in per capita consumption affect the overall use of a particular resource?

Human Activities Affect Biodiversity and Ecosystem Services

This coastal community in Seward, Alaska, is home to a port used by cruise ships sailing through Alaska's waterways. This community is located near important natural resources.

Explore First

Modeling Water Filtration Pour muddy water into a paper cup with a small hole in the bottom. Catch what comes out of the cup in a bowl or basin. Then fill the cup partly full of damp sand and pour the muddy water into the cup again. How does the water that comes out of the cup with sand compare to the water that came out of the cup without sand?

CAN YOU EXPLAIN IT?

Why does most of the water from the Colorado River no longer reach the ocean?

Legend	
	Upper basin
	Lower basin
＼	Dam location
★	Basin divide
•	City

km 0   200

mi 0   100 200

Source: Colorado River Commission of Nevada, "Colorado River Basin Climate Variability and Change: Background, Tools, and Activities," 2008

The Colorado River is a valuable water resource in the western United States. It winds its way over about 2,300 km from the Rocky Mountains in Colorado to the ocean. In some places, the water creates raging whitewater rapids. Yet, little water from the river reaches the ocean.

1. How do people use water resources such as the Colorado River?

2. What are some reasons that a river's water level might decrease?

EVIDENCE NOTEBOOK As you explore the lesson, gather evidence to help explain why most of the water in the Colorado River does not reach the ocean.

Relating Rates of Resource Use to Impacts on Earth's Systems

Coaches are planning a soccer tournament. They need enough water for all of the players. They will need to supply more water if more teams play. More water will also be needed during hot weather when the players drink more water. The coaches need to consider the total number of players—the size of the population. They also need to think about the average amount of water each player will drink—the per capita consumption.

The water used at a soccer tournament and the land in a rain forest have something in common. They are both natural resources that are used by humans. The impact that total population and per capita consumption have on the use of natural resources is similar to the situation in the soccer tournament. Both the size of the population and the per capita consumption affect the amount of Earth's resources that humans use.

This area of rain forest near Altamira, Brazil, was clear-cut to provide resources, including land on which grow crops.

3. Which statements are likely reasons that forests in Brazil, like the one shown in the photo, were cut down? Select all that apply.

   A. The local population increased, and more land was needed for farming.

   B. The local population decreased, and less land was needed for farming.

   C. People around the world were using more products from farming.

   D. People around the world were consuming fewer products from farming.

Earth's Systems

The Earth system can be divided into four subsystems—the atmosphere, biosphere, geosphere, and hydrosphere. The atmosphere is the mixture of gases that surrounds the planet. The biosphere is all of the living things on Earth, including humans. The geosphere is the solid part of Earth. The hydrosphere is all of the water on Earth.

Changes in one subsystem may affect the other subsystems. For example, the trees in a forest, which are part of the biosphere, are rooted into soil. The soil is part of the geosphere. The trees are also connected to the hydrosphere and atmosphere, because trees take in water from the ground and carbon dioxide from the air, and they give off water vapor to the atmosphere.

The Rate at Which We Use Resources

You are one of more than 7 billion people in the world using Earth's resources. People and societies use resources to meet their needs and desires. Needs may include food, water, shelter, clothing, and transportation. People in different places around the world may meet these needs in different ways. But, they all use Earth's resources. Everything people use, from computers to table salt, comes from Earth's natural resources.

As the world population grows, more people will use Earth's resources. The consumption of natural resources commonly increases as population increases. Per capita consumption is the average amount a person uses. If it increases, resource use also increases even if the population stays the same. The graphs below show how resource use changes as the population and per capita consumption change.

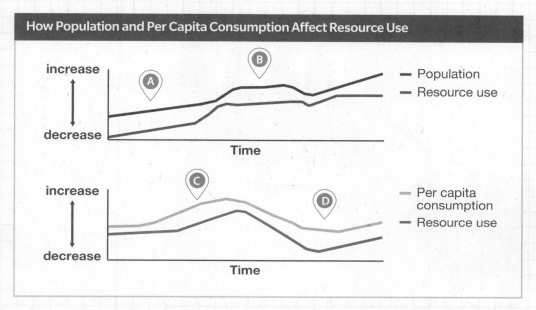

How Population and Per Capita Consumption Affect Resource Use

4. Look at the pointers on the graph. Circle the correct words to complete the statements that go with each pointer to explain why resource use is different at each point.

   Resource use is *greater / less* at point A than at point B because the population is smaller and *more / fewer* people are using resources.

   Assuming the total population did not change, resource use is *greater / less* at point C than at point D because per capita consumption is higher. That is, the same number of people are using *more / fewer* resources.

5. **Discuss** In a small group, discuss how changes in your class population and per capita consumption affect the use of objects or materials used by the class, such as tablet computers or paper. Discuss how these changes impact the use of Earth's natural resources.

EVIDENCE NOTEBOOK

6. How might the total consumption of water near the Colorado River have been changed by increases in population or changes in per capita consumption? Record your evidence.

Impacts of Resource Use on Earth's Systems

Clear-cutting is the cutting down and removal of all of the trees in an area. Think about how clear-cutting in the rain forest causes changes to both the biosphere and the geosphere. The trees are cut to obtain timber or to clear land. People may put up buildings on the land. They may also use the land to grow crops or raise animals. At first, only a few trees may be removed, causing only small changes to the environment. Removing some trees can have a positive influence as more sunlight is available to smaller, understory trees and plants. However, more trees could be cut down to provide for an increasing population or for an increasing demand by a stable population. As more trees are cut, the impact on the environment increases. An immediate effect of clear-cutting is that many living things lose their habitat. Over a longer time, water or wind may remove soil from the land.

7. The diagram shows resources obtained by cutting down trees in a forest. Complete the diagram by drawing in examples of how people might use the cleared land and timber from the trees.

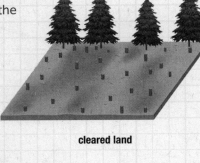

cleared land

forest

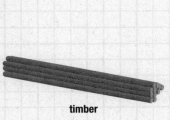

timber

8. Obtaining resources that people use may have

   positive / negative / both positive and negative effects on humans

   and positive / negative / both positive and negative

   effects on the environment. The impacts can be

   short term / long term / both short term and long term.

9. How will the environmental impact of obtaining and using resources change as the population increases and the demand for resources increases? Explain your reasoning.

Biodiversity and Ecosystem Services

Ecosystems can contain a wide variety of plant and animal life. The greater the number of species and the greater the genetic variation within each species, the higher the biodiversity of the ecosystem. An ecosystem with high biodiversity also tends to be a healthy ecosystem. Ecosystems with high biodiversity are often better able to recover from a disturbance than an ecosystem with low biodiversity. If an event affects one species negatively, another species may take over the role of the affected species, which keeps the ecosystem in balance. For example, if pine bark beetles killed many pine trees in a forest, other species of trees in the forest could still provide services. When an area has low biodiversity, there may not be another species to help stabilize the ecosystem.

Humans benefit from the ecosystem services of healthy ecosystems. An ecosystem service is a benefit that humans obtain from an ecosystem. An example of an ecosystem service is trees filtering pollutants out of the air. Plants that grow in wetland areas contribute to soil health. Healthy soils support more life, which in turn contribute to more healthy soils. These soils filter water, which benefits many different organisms that depend on clean water, including humans.

Wetlands are areas that consist of marshes or swamps. The land is saturated with water most or all year. Many wetland areas are lost to human development. This restoration project in the Don Edwards San Francisco Bay National Wildlife refuge is returning abandoned industrial salt ponds to wetlands.

10. Wetlands occur naturally in many coastal areas. These wetlands provide habitats for many species. Wetlands also provide many services, such as filtering water and preventing flooding by slowing storm surges and absorbing heavy rainfall. Humans often develop these coastal areas, by paving over them and constructing buildings.

Paving over a wetland would have a positive / negative effect on the services provided by the wetland. Biodiversity in an urban area is usually

less than / greater than / the same as biodiversity in a wetland area.

Resource Use Management

When humans use too much of a resource or use a resource too quickly, Earth's systems are often negatively affected. For example, deforestation leads to habitat loss for many species of animals. Trees cannot grow fast enough to replace the forest and provide new habitat for displaced animals. However, the negative impact can be reduced if resources are managed well. Effective management includes finding ways to reduce the per capita consumption of resources as populations grow. Negative impacts can also be reduced if the activities and technologies involved in obtaining resources are engineered in a way that reduces the environmental impact. Humans can also lessen the effects by finding ways to replenish renewable resources.

11. In order to reduce the negative impact of logging, what could be done to reduce the number of trees that are cut down?

Do the Math
Analyze Impacts to Earth's Systems

People in the town depend on the resources in the forest to build homes.

The *per capita consumption of land* is the average area of land used by one person. In one town, the per capita consumption of land is 12,000 m². The population is growing. More land is needed to build schools and housing. People in the town must decide to clear land in a nearby forest.

12. The town's current population is 4,790 people. The population is expected to increase by 7.0% over the next 5 years. Based on the current per capita consumption, how much land must be cleared to accommodate population growth?

_____

_____

_____

13. Urban planners want to reduce the impact of the town's growth on the environment. They want to reduce per capita land consumption by $\frac{1}{4}$. In this case, how much new land would need to be cleared in order to make space for the growing population? Use variables to write an expression that helps you solve this problem.

_____

_____

_____

_____

Analyzing the Impact of Human Use of Water

When you use water to brush your teeth or to drink, you are using a resource. Think about how much water your family, your community, or your state might use each day. All this human use of water impacts Earth's systems. Sometimes the impact can be immediate, such as when people use more water than can be supplied. Other times, the impact can take many years to see, such as when lakes slowly dry up. Whether an impact is even noticeable depends on how much water is available, how much is used, and how it is used.

The hydrosphere is connected to the rest of Earth's systems. For example, the water lilies and other living things in and around this lake depend on its water.

14. How is the water in the lake important to the organisms in the photo?

The Impact of Obtaining and Using Resources from the Hydrosphere

Water makes up more than half of each human body. Without water, the processes that take place in your body to keep you alive and healthy cannot take place. People need water to live. So, people need a reliable supply of water. Humans also use water to generate electrical energy, to grow crops, to raise animals, to wash things, to mine and make materials, and to enjoy recreational activities.

About 71% of Earth's surface is water. However, fresh water is not always located where people need it. People collect water and direct it to where it is needed. They build dams and make reservoirs to store water. They build canals so that water can flow where it is needed. People also drill wells to obtain water that is stored underground. These activities can affect other parts of Earth's systems and may result in habitat destruction. A *habitat* is the natural environment of an organism. *Habitat destruction* happens when land or water inhabited by an organism is destroyed or changed so much that it is no longer livable for the organism.

As population and per capita consumption rise, demand for resources increases. Negative impacts also increase unless engineering solutions are put into place. For example, habitats in several areas could be destroyed when canals are constructed, unless the canals are designed in a way that preserves as much habitat as possible.

15. What are the possible negative effects of increasing human use of a river's water?

Analyze Your Impact

You will track and analyze your daily use of water. Be sure to include all the different ways you use water.

Procedure

STEP 1 First, research the water flow rates of plumbing fixtures you use, such as sinks, showers, and toilets. On a separate sheet of paper, track and record how many liters of water you use or consume in a day.

STEP 2 Discuss with a partner the sources of the water you used. For example, does your water come from a well or a reservoir? Record your ideas.

Analysis

STEP 3 Choose one of the ways you consumed water daily. Record the source of the water and how it used.

STEP 4 Discuss how the water use chosen in Step 3 impacts the environment. In the table, record how using that water every day impacts each of Earth's systems.

System	Impact(s)
Geosphere	
Atmosphere	
Hydrosphere	
Biosphere	

STEP 5 How can you change your use of water to reduce your impact?

Case Study: The Elwha River

Humans build structures that control where water goes and how fast it flows. For example, dams are built to serve many purposes. Fresh water from rivers is stored in reservoirs behind dams so that it can be used when needed. Dams also control water flow to prevent flooding. Hydroelectric dams harness the energy of the water to generate electrical energy, which reduces the use of fossil fuels to generate electrical energy. Many dams, including the Hoover Dam, have been built along the Colorado River.

Dams do, however, have some negative effects. The Elwha River in Washington shows several of these effects. Water in the river flowed freely until the early 1900s. Then two dams were built to meet the needs of a growing population. One of the immediate impacts was that the land behind the dams flooded, forming lakes. Other changes to the environment happened over a period of years.

16. Identify whether each effect of building a dam is *positive* or *negative*.

Statement	Positive /Negative
Area upstream of the dam floods and covers trees	
Reduces pollution from using fossil fuels used to generate electrical energy	
Sediment stopped by the dam does not flow to the mouth of the river	

The Impact of the Elwha River Dam

The first Elwha River Dam was finished in 1913 to provide hydroelectric power to paper mills.

 The dam kept sediments behind it. This stopped sediments from moving downstream. Sediment is an essential part of the salmon habitat.

 The Elwha Dam was not engineered to allow fish to pass through it. So, fish such as salmon were unable to migrate up and down the river.

 Water flow below the dam decreased. This resulted in wetlands around the river drying up. A wetland is an important habitat that helps to purify water and control flooding. The slower water flow also caused temperature increases in the water. As a result, oxygen levels in the water decreased.

Salmon and Sediment on the Elwha River

Each year, salmon swim up the Elwha River from the ocean to lay eggs. The river's dams reduced salmon habitats by 90%. As a result, salmon populations declined rapidly. Before the dams changed the river, more than 400,000 salmon traveled upstream each year. After the dams were built, only about 3,000 adult salmon returned each year.

Before the dams, sediment was carried to the mouth of the river. There, it expanded the delta and formed large beaches. The dams blocked the flow of river water and prevented sediment from flowing downstream. Without the addition of sediment from upriver, the delta of the river lost land mass. This loss of land reduced the habitats for many plants and animals that live in the delta area.

Because of the dams' negative impacts, the dams were removed, starting in 2011. Efforts to restore the river and its habitats continue, and the ecosystem is recovering.

The Impact of Dam Removal on Sediment and Number of Salmon

The graph shows the amount of sediment flowing in the river and the number of salmon before and after dam removal.

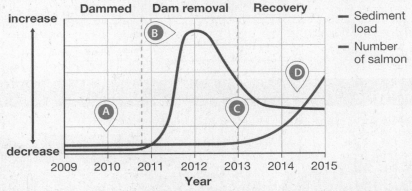

Source: USGS Washington Water Science Center, Elwha River Sediment Monitoring Maps, 2013

(A) The dam blocked most of the sediment from flowing down the river toward the ocean, which limited habitats for salmon to spawn. Few salmon swam upstream in the river.

(B) As the dam was removed, large amounts of sediment (500 mg of sediment per liter of water) flowed downstream.

(C) As habitats were reconnected, the salmon populations began increasing.

(D) In the years after the dam was taken down, the amount of sediment flowing in the river leveled off to 100 mg/L. Salmon populations continue to increase. They are expected to increase at a regular rate over the next 20 to 30 years.

17. **Write** Use the graph to compare the amount of sediment flowing down the river and the number of salmon when the dam was in place and when it was removed. On a separate sheet of paper, write an argument that includes claims, evidence, and reasoning about how the dam affected the sediment flow, the number of salmon moving through the river, and the number of salmon spawning.

18. How might the impact of the Elwha River dams on the biosphere and geosphere have influenced the decision to remove the dams?

 EVIDENCE NOTEBOOK

19. How could the use of dams affect the amount of water in the Colorado River that reaches the ocean? Record your evidence.

Analyze Water Use

20. Which statement about water consumption does the graph support?

 A. Water use steadily increased as the population increased from 1990 to 2015.

 B. Water use declined as population declined after 2008.

 C. After 2007, per capita consumption decreased.

 D. Per capita consumption was the same from 1990 to 2015.

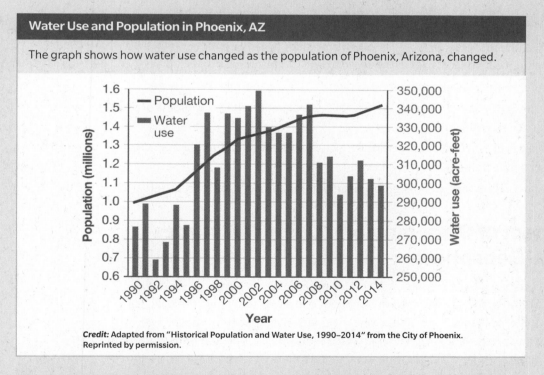

Water Use and Population in Phoenix, AZ

The graph shows how water use changed as the population of Phoenix, Arizona, changed.

Credit: Adapted from "Historical Population and Water Use, 1990–2014" from the City of Phoenix. Reprinted by permission.

21. Phoenix gets most of its water from the Salt, Verde, and Colorado Rivers. How would droughts in the areas of these rivers affect the water supply in Phoenix? Would the water use in Phoenix need to change?

_____

_____

_____

Analyzing the Impact of Human Use of Land Resources

Whether you live in a large city or a small town, you and everyone in your community depends on Earth's systems. Everyone depends on land for food and a place to live. Land is used for gardens and parks. Buildings and roads are built on land. Land also provides natural materials that are used to make products. For example, minerals, including most metals, are mined from the land. Many fuels that are used to produce electrical energy are mined from the land, including coal, petroleum, and natural gas.

Fertilizers contain chemicals that help plants grow. However, these chemicals can be harmful to the environment when they are used in large amounts, especially when they seep into streams and rivers.

22. How do the effects of one person using fertilizer differ from the effects of 100,000 people using the same fertilizer in the same town? Circle all that apply.

   A. The effects are the same when one person or 100,000 people use fertilizer.

   B. The effects of 100,000 people using fertilizer are greater than the effects of one person using fertilizer.

   C. The effects of 100,000 people using fertilizer spread to a larger area than the effects of one person using fertilizer.

   D. The effects cannot be compared because different amounts of fertilizer are used.

The Impact of Obtaining and Using Resources from the Geosphere

When resources are removed from the land and used, all of Earth's systems can be affected. For example, the geosphere can be changed in a way that limits the space or nutrients available for plants. Such a change can negatively impact the whole Earth system. The atmosphere can be affected because plants add oxygen and remove carbon dioxide and other gases from air. Plants affect the geosphere by preventing erosion. Plants provide habitats for other organisms in the biosphere. And plants help the hydrosphere by filtering water in places such as marshes.

Many people depend on one kind of fuel resource—fossil fuels. These fuels must be mined from beneath Earth's surface. Many minerals that people use, such as copper and gold, are also mined. Mining causes immediate changes to the geosphere, as tunnels or holes are dug to access the resources. The removal process can add harmful materials to the air, water, and land and can harm living things.

Resource Use during the Industrial Revolution

During the second half of the 1800s, the Industrial Revolution happened in the United States. The population grew rapidly. During this time, technology improved agricultural efficiency. Manufacturing increased and transportation systems expanded. One important invention—the steam engine—helped power the Industrial Revolution. Coal was burned to generate the steam used by the engine. Steam engines were commonly used in trains. Coal was also burned to make steel, which was in great demand for many construction projects.

Most coal is burned to generate energy that is used for making other materials or is converted into electrical energy.

As people began to consume more products and more energy, the per capita consumption of coal increased. Because most coal is mined from underground deposits using large machinery, the increased need for coal had a significant impact on Earth's systems.

23. How do you think the increased use of coal during the Industrial Revolution might have affected Earth's systems?

Resource Use and Pollution

One negative effect of the Industrial Revolution was an increase in pollution. **Pollution** is an undesired change in air, water, or soil that negatively affects the health, survival, or activities of humans or other organisms. For example, burning coal and other fossil fuels causes air pollution because gases and other substances are released into the air. The gases that are given off can cause smog. The gases from burning fossil fuels can also combine with water in the atmosphere to form acids and cause acid rain. Burning fossil fuels also increases greenhouse gases in the atmosphere. Greenhouse gases absorb and reradiate energy in the atmosphere, which raises Earth's average global temperature.

Pollution can lead to other negative impacts on the Earth system because pollution changes the chemical and physical makeup of the atmosphere and hydrosphere. For example, acid rain can result in habitat destruction and the death of organisms. These changes alter the makeup of the biosphere.

Although we know that the technologies required to use material and energy resources often cause pollution, people will not necessarily stop using those technologies and resources. The human use of technologies and resources and the limitations on that use are driven by individual and societal needs, desires, and values. Scientific knowledge can inform people about the effects of human behaviors on Earth's systems. But, this knowledge does not tell people what they should do or how to act. Society must balance needs and desires that require resources with the value of protecting the environment in order to decide how to use technologies and resources.

Case Study: Pollution in the Atmosphere

When fossil fuels are burned, carbon dioxide, a greenhouse gas, is produced. The concentration of carbon dioxide is about the same everywhere in the atmosphere. Humans add more carbon dioxide to the atmosphere than any other greenhouse gas.

Increasing amounts of greenhouse gases warm the atmosphere, leading to changes in Earth's climate. A warmer atmosphere also affects the hydrosphere. For example, the ocean becomes warmer. Increasing amounts of carbon dioxide also change the chemical makeup of the ocean, making it more acidic. These changes can have negative effects on living things.

The concentrations of greenhouse gases in the atmosphere have increased as populations around the world have increased. As populations grow, the demand for electrical energy and consumption of products produced by using fossil fuels has increased.

24. What conclusions can you draw from the data shown in these two graphs? Circle all that apply.

   A. The amount of energy used in the world is increasing as the population increases.

   B. The amount of energy used in the world has leveled off as the population increases.

   C. The amount of carbon dioxide in the atmosphere is increasing as the world energy consumption increases.

   D. The amount of carbon dioxide in the atmosphere has leveled off as the population increases.

The data show that human use of fossil fuels has increased over the past 200 years. It is known that burning fossil fuels contributes carbon dioxide to the atmosphere. However, people can engineer processes, behaviors, or technologies to reduce the use of fossil fuels or to reduce the addition of carbon dioxide to the atmosphere when burning fossil fuels.

World Energy Consumption

Since the Industrial Revolution, the use of energy resources has increased. Most of this energy is generated by burning fossil fuels and biomass, which release carbon dioxide and other greenhouse gases.

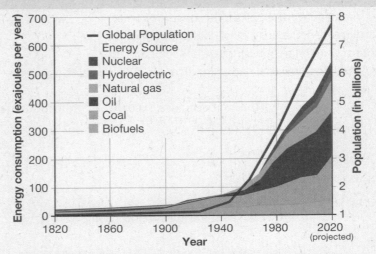

Credit: Adapted from "The World at Six Billion" by UN Population Division. Copyright ©1999 by United Nations. Reprinted with the permission of the United Nations. Adapted from "World Energy Consumption Since 1820" from Our Finite World by Gail Tverberg, March 12, 2012. Reprinted with permission by Gail Tverberg.

Atmospheric Carbon Dioxide at Mauna Loa Observatory

Scientists have taken careful daily measurements of the amount of carbon dioxide in the air.

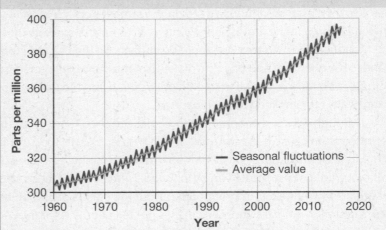

Source: Scripps Institution of Oceanography, NOAA Earth System Research Laboratory, "Atmospheric CO$_2$ at Mauna Loa Observatory," 2017

25. **Engineer It** Your individual use of fossil fuels depends largely on how much electrical energy you use in a day. What solutions could you design to reduce the amount of fossil fuels you use in a 24-hour period? On which solutions are you more likely to act, and why?

Analyze Arable Land Resources

Modern farmers use technologies that were designed to make farming more efficient. Some farmers use plants that have been engineered so that each plant produces more of the parts that humans use.

The graph shows the amount of available arable land and the world population from 1960 to 2020. The number for the 2020 world population is a prediction. Arable land is land that can be used to grow crops.

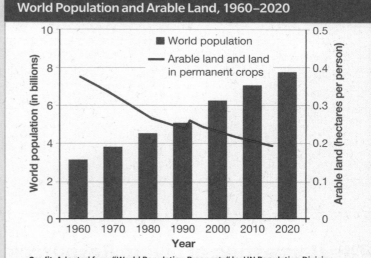

World Population and Arable Land, 1960–2020

Credit: Adapted from "World Population Prospects" by UN Population Division. Copyright ©2015 by United Nations. Reprinted with the permission of the United Nations. Adapted from Land and Irrigation dataset. Copyright ©2014 by Food and Agriculture Organization of the United Nations. Reproduced with permission.

26. Which of Earth's systems are affected by farming? Choose all that apply.

   A. atmosphere

   B. biosphere

   C. geosphere

   D. hydrosphere

27. Describe the relationship shown by the graph.

_____

_____

28. What is a possible explanation for this relationship?

_____

_____

_____

_____

Analyzing the Impact of Human Use of Plants and Animals

Changes humans make to the atmosphere, geosphere, and hydrosphere as they use resources also affect the biosphere. For example, when habitats on land or in water are damaged, many organisms can no longer live there. Pollution in the air and water can also have negative effects on organisms.

Humans also affect the biosphere by harvesting plants and animals as a resource. Harvesting is the gathering of living things for human consumption.

29. What are potential effects of harvesting fish as human population increases and humans eat more fish? Fill in the table below.

A commercial fishing boat brings in a net full of salmon. Some groups of commercial vessels catch tons of fish daily.

Influence on resource use	Number of fish harvested	Impact of change on fish harvest
Human population increases	increases	Not enough fish left to meet demand
Per capita consumption of fish increases		
Human population and per capita consumption of fish increase		

The Harvesting of Living Resources

Humans harvest plants, animals, and other organisms from the biosphere. Examples of things humans harvest include corn, birds, and mushrooms. When humans harvest living things, the land, water, and air can also be affected.

Overharvesting results when a species is used so much that the population becomes very small. Overharvesting sometimes puts the survival of a species at risk. For example, overfishing is one type of overharvesting. The beluga sturgeon is a type of fish. Its eggs are used as food that many people want. The sturgeon has been overharvested. Now, the species survives mostly because sturgeon are grown in fish hatcheries. When the sturgeon population decreases, many other living things are affected. When the population of a species changes, any Earth system the species interacts with will be affected. Species that were food for the sturgeon or for which the sturgeon was food will be directly affected. These changes may then affect other Earth systems.

Animal Resources

One type of horseshoe crab lays billions of tiny eggs in the Delaware Bay each spring. These eggs are food for many other organisms, including a bird called the red knot. Each spring, red knots migrate to the Delaware Bay just as the horseshoe crabs spawn, and the red knots feed on the crab eggs. However, overfishing of the horseshoe crab for use as bait has caused the horseshoe crab population to decrease. As a result, the red knot population in the Delaware Bay area has also decreased.

Many plants and animals that were once common for people to eat are now endangered or extinct, such as the passenger pigeon.

passenger pigeon

30. Analyze the diagram about passenger pigeons. Why did the passenger pigeon go extinct? What might have been done to prevent its extinction?

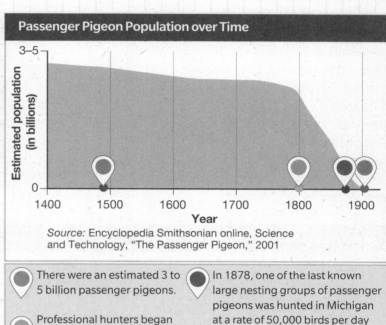

Passenger Pigeon Population over Time

Source: Encyclopedia Smithsonian online, Science and Technology, "The Passenger Pigeon," 2001

There were an estimated 3 to 5 billion passenger pigeons.

Professional hunters began hunting and trapping passenger pigeons. They sold the birds at markets for people to eat.

In 1878, one of the last known large nesting groups of passenger pigeons was hunted in Michigan at a rate of 50,000 birds per day for nearly 5 months.

The last passenger pigeon died. The passenger pigeon was officially declared extinct.

Plant Resources

Trees are plant resources that have many uses. Sometimes, trees are harvested by cutting down or burning large forest areas. These actions destroy forest habitats, and as a result, soil may be eroded, and water in nearby lakes or streams may become polluted. The atmosphere is also affected because trees take in carbon dioxide from the air and give off oxygen.

31. How might an increasing human population cause the changes shown in the satellite images of the rain forest?

1985

2000

The satellite images show changes in a rain forest in Matto Grosso, Brazil, between 1985 and 2000.

Language SmArts
Analyze Extinctions and Land Use

The loss of habitat can have a negative effect on a species. As habitat destruction occurs, there is less space for individuals or populations to occupy. There is also less room for the plants and animals that the species depends on for food.

You learned how the loss of horseshoe crab eggs as a food source affected the red knot. When human use of resources decreases an animal's food source, other species that interact with the animal are also affected. If those species cannot find another source of food or another place to live, their populations will decrease. Some species may become extinct.

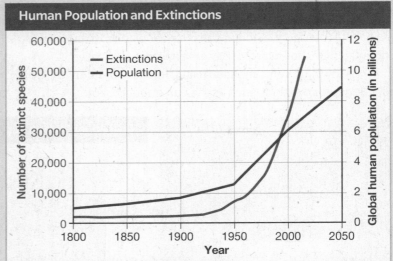

Human Population and Extinctions

Source: Scott, J.M., *Threats to Biological Diversity. Global, Continental, Local,* U.S. Geological Survey, Idaho Cooperative Fish and Wildlife, Research Unit, University of Idaho, 2008;
Credit: Adapted from "The World at Six Billion" by UN Population Division. Copyright ©1999 by United Nations. Reprinted with the permission of the United Nations.

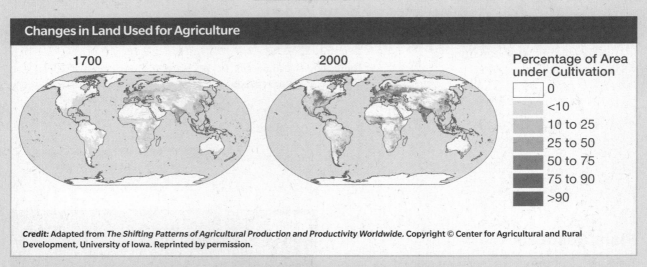

Changes in Land Used for Agriculture

Credit: Adapted from *The Shifting Patterns of Agricultural Production and Productivity Worldwide.* Copyright © Center for Agricultural and Rural Development, University of Iowa. Reprinted by permission.

32. Construct an argument about how changes in global population relate to agricultural land use and species extinctions. Use evidence from the graph, map, and lesson to support your argument.

_____

_____

_____

_____

_____

_____

_____

Continue Your Exploration

Name: _____   Date: _____

Check out the path below or go online to choose one of the other paths shown.

| The Atmosphere as a Resource | • The Need for More Resources
 • Hands-On Labs ✋
 • Propose Your Own Path | Go online to choose one of these other paths. |

Suppose someone talks about Earth's energy resources. Which of Earth's systems do you think of? Often, people do not think of the atmosphere as an energy source.

A wind turbine is a device that captures the energy of moving air. Wind turbines use the movement of air to generate electrical energy. The wind's energy is transferred to the turbine when wind turns the turbine's large blades. The blades are connected to a shaft, or long cylinder, which turns when the blades move. The spinning shaft turns a generator that transforms the kinetic energy of the spinning shaft into electrical energy.

Wind turbines are often grouped together in wind farms. These farms can generate a larger amount of electrical energy than a single turbine can. Wind farms generate the most energy in places with windy climates, such as the plains of West Texas or mountain passes in California. So, the location of wind farms is determined in part by the availability of constant or strong winds. Wind energy is a renewable source of energy that is clean. It also uses almost no water. However, wind farms take up space on land.

Wind farms can consist of hundreds of wind turbines. The turbines in these farms are often placed relatively far apart. The land between them is used for other purposes, such as farming.

Continue Your Exploration

1. What are two positive impacts of using wind turbines to generate electrical energy?

2. How might the increasing use of renewable energy technologies, such as wind turbines and solar panels, affect Earth's systems as the world population increases?

3. One of the negative impacts of wind turbines is the noise of the spinning turbine. Near the blades of the turbine, the noise level is similar to that of a lawn mower. Farther away, at around 400 meters from the turbine, the noise level is similar to that of a refrigerator. As a result, wind turbines cannot be put closer than 300 meters to the nearest house in some areas. How does this requirement affect the use of wind farms in areas where people live close together?

4. **Collaborate** Wind turbines and hydroelectric dams use the energy of motion to generate electrical energy. Brainstorm other motions in Earth's systems that could be used to generate electrical energy. Draw a simple model of how electrical energy would be generated by one of these motions.

Can You Explain It?

Name: _____   Date: _____

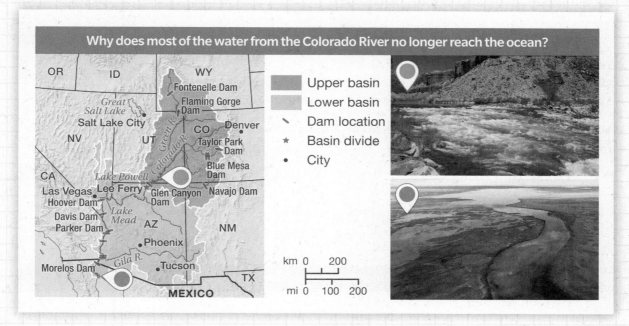

Why does most of the water from the Colorado River no longer reach the ocean?

Legend:
- Upper basin
- Lower basin
- Dam location
- ★ Basin divide
- • City

EVIDENCE NOTEBOOK

Refer to the notes in your Evidence Notebook to help you construct an explanation for the decreased flow of the Colorado River.

1. State your claim. Make sure your claim fully explains why most of the water in the Colorado River no longer reaches the ocean.

2. Summarize the evidence you have gathered to support your claim and explain your reasoning.

Checkpoints

Answer the following questions to check your understanding of the lesson.

Use the data in the table to answer Questions 3–4.

3. Circle the correct words to complete the sentences.

   The number of cars decreases / *increases* / changes randomly as the population increases. This change in resource use will likely increase / *decrease* / not affect the negative impact of obtaining and using resources.

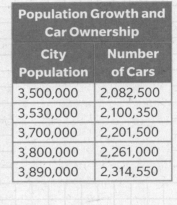

Population Growth and Car Ownership	
City Population	Number of Cars
3,500,000	2,082,500
3,530,000	2,100,350
3,700,000	2,201,500
3,800,000	2,261,000
3,890,000	2,314,550

4. How can the impacts of car use be reduced if the number of cars per person stays the same? Select all that apply.

   A. improving the bus and train system

   B. using carpools

   C. increasing the use of hybrid and electric cars, which produce less carbon dioxide

   D. finding new places to mine for the metals needed to make cars

---

Use the information in the graph to answer Questions 5–6.

5. The graph shows deforestation decreased / *increased* as the population decreased / *increased*. This trend has *a positive* / a negative / no effect on the geosphere and atmosphere.

6. How does deforestation directly affect the biosphere?

   A. It causes erosion.

   B. It causes poor water quality.

   C. It emits greenhouse gases.

   D. It reduces the population of trees.

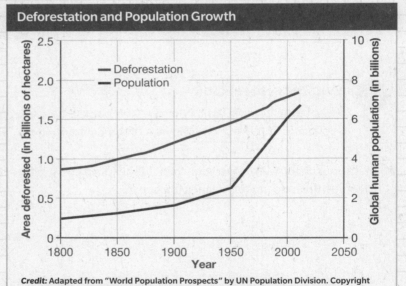

Deforestation and Population Growth

Credit: Adapted from "World Population Prospects" by UN Population Division. Copyright ©2015 by United Nations. Reprinted with the permission of the United Nations. Adapted from "State of the World's Forests". Copyright ©2012 by Food and Agriculture Organization of the United Nations. Reproduced with permission.

---

7. A town wants to build a dam across a river. Which statements are evidence that the dam would negatively affect the environment? Select all that apply.

   A. It would reduce the flow of sediments.

   B. It would provide more habitat for salmon.

   C. It would decrease the number of wetlands along the river.

   D. It would provide a lake for recreation.

8. An herb that is used as medicine is threatened with extinction. How might human activities be contributing to this threat? Select all that apply.

   A. People have planted it as a crop in places where it is not native.

   B. The herb has become more popular as medicine, leading to overharvesting.

   C. Human population has grown in regions where the herb is a popular medicine.

Interactive Review

Complete this page to review the main concepts of the lesson.

Human use of resources affects Earth systems. The environmental impact increases as resource use and consumption increase.

A. What happens to resource use as a population increases and per capita use does not change?

Human use of water resources impacts Earth systems.

B. Give at least two examples of how human use of water affects Earth systems.

Human use of land for buildings, for agriculture, and for resources such as metals and fossil fuels impacts Earth systems.

C. Give at least two examples how the human activities of obtaining and using resources from land affect Earth systems.

Human use of plants and animals for food, materials, and fuel impacts Earth's systems.

D. Give at least one example of how overharvesting a resource affects an Earth system.

Humans Use Waves to Collect and Communicate Information

Electromagnetic waves, transmitted between towers such as these, are used to communicate.

Explore First

Using a String Phone Connect two paper cups using a string between three and eight feet long. Pull the string taught and use the phone to communicate a message to a partner. Which waves are involved in this communication method? How do the waves relate to the sound you hear?

Go online to view the digital version of
the Hands-On Lab for this lesson and to
download additional lab resources.

CAN YOU EXPLAIN IT?

How can a video from the Internet appear the same every time you watch it?

Explore Online

Videos are shared on the Internet constantly. Some videos are watched billions of times on many different devices. Even though a video may have already been watched millions of times and is streaming from a server thousands of miles away, the video will still appear the same every time that you watch it.

1. What are some ways you communicate with friends or family in different cities or towns?

 EVIDENCE NOTEBOOK As you explore the lesson, gather evidence to help explain how an Internet video can appear the same every time you watch it.

Analyzing Waves in Communication

Think of the ways in which you interact with your friends and family every day. When you are together, you might speak, gesture, or use sign language to share ideas and information. These are examples of communication. Communication is the process of sending and receiving information using a signal. A **signal** is anything that can transmit information.

There are many types of communication between humans, including voice, writing and gestures. Communication is only effective when the information being sent can be understood when it is received. When someone is near it is simple to communicate, but how can people communicate over long distances? Throughout history, people have used different methods to communicate over long distances.

2. What do the historical communication technologies in these photos have in common?

Drums have often been used to communicate across long distances. Drums can produce loud sound signals that can be heard from far away.

The light from lamps and lanterns has also been used as a signal. A lantern allows for more control than a signal fire and can be used to send more complex light signals.

Encode and Decode Information

Communication involves encoding information into a signal. **Encoding** is the process by which information is represented in a signal. The signal is then sent to a receiver, where it is decoded. *Decoding* is the process of getting information out of a signal. To effectively communicate, the sender and receiver must use a set of rules to properly encode and decode the signal. When humans use speech to communicate, the signal is the sound waves that are transmitted. These sound waves are decoded into words that have the same meaning to the receiver as they did to the sender. All forms of communication use encoding and decoding.

Samuel Morse invented an electric telegraph in 1837. The telegraph sent electric signals through a wire. The telegraph could quickly send complex messages over a long distance.

Hands-On Lab
Encode a Message

You and a partner will create an encoding system and use it to encode and decode a message.

MATERIALS
- index cards
- pencils

Procedure

STEP 1 Create a visual code that allows you to encode a short message. Write a key on one index card that would allow your partner to decode a message written in your code.

STEP 2 Write a short message using your encoding system on a second index card.

STEP 3 Give both cards to your partner and allow him or her to decode the message.

STEP 4 Trade roles with your partner. Repeat Steps 1–3.

Analysis

STEP 5 **Discuss** With your partner, discuss the following questions: Was it easier to encode a message or decode a message? Did anything about this process surprise you? Record your ideas.

STEP 6 How might you revise your code to make it easier to encode and decode messages?

Morse Code

Morse code was a popular form of code developed by Samuel Morse for communicating using a telegraph. Each letter in the alphabet and the numerals 0–9 were encoded using different combinations of electric pulses. These pulses were transmitted over a wire, where they were received and decoded back into letters and numerals. Telegraph operators needed to be familiar with Morse code in order to encode and decode these messages. The telegraph became less popular when the telephone was introduced. The telephone enabled sound to be transmitted as an electric signal over wires. The receiver then transformed the electric signal back into sound. Unlike the telegraph, the telephone did not require any special training to encode and decode messages.

3. Morse code uses combinations of two pulses of different lengths to represent numbers and letters. A dash (—) is used to represent a long pulse, and a dot (•) is used to represent a short pulse. When messages are sent, the dashes and dots are turned into sounds. Each dash is a long beep and each dot is a short beep. A combination of dashes and dots can be used to represent each letter in the alphabet. Using the International Morse Code key shown, decode this three letter message: • • — •   • • —   — •

A •—	N —•	1 •————
B —•••	O ———	2 ••———
C —•—•	P •——•	3 •••——
D —••	Q ——•—	4 ••••—
E •	R •—•	5 •••••
F ••—•	S •••	6 —••••
G ——•	T —	7 ——•••
H ••••	U ••—	8 ———••
I ••	V •••—	9 ————•
J •———	W •——	0 —————
K —•—	X —••—	
L •—••	Y —•——	
M ——	Z ——••	

4. **Collaborate** Send a message to a partner using Morse code. You can hum short and long sounds to represent dots and dashes. For example, to send the letter "C" you would say, "daaah dih daaah dih." Try decoding your partner's message and then switch roles. Record any difficulties that you encountered when sending Morse code messages to one another.

Make Encoding and Decoding Easier

Most modern communication devices, such as computers and cell phones, send information using signals that are not directly understandable by humans. These devices encode and decode information automatically. These devices convert information that can be understood by a user into a signal that can be transmitted, and then convert the transmitted signal back into information that can be understood by a user. So, computers may send and receive electric signals that are converted to sound or images for users.

Waves in Communication

Nearly every form of communication is made possible by waves. *Waves* are disturbances that transfer energy from one place to another. Waves are well suited for sending information because they do not permanently move matter, and they can be varied in many ways to hold information. One common type of wave is sound, which we use to talk to each other. However, sound, like all waves, loses energy as it travels. Different types of waves lose energy at different rates. You might be able to see a light from many miles away at night, but you could not hear your friend singing from the same distance.

Lighthouses indicate the location of land to ships at sea. While other navigation technologies exist, many lighthouses are still in use today.

Explore Online

5. **Language SmArts** Choose a long-distance communication method, and explain how it uses waves to send encoded information. Use diagrams to clarify your explanation.

Electromagnetic Waves and Electric Signals

Early communication technologies such as the telegraph and telephone required wires to send electric signals over long distances. It required a lot of time and money to install the wires for worldwide communication. Advances in scientific understanding of waves and electronics technologies have led to the design of communication devices that transmit information wirelessly using electromagnetic waves. Electromagnetic waves can travel long distances through different media and can travel through the vacuum of space. These systems can be expanded more quickly than old systems that required physical wires to connect transmitters and receivers.

Electromagnetic Waves in Communication

Electromagnetic waves, such as light waves and radio waves, have characteristics that make them ideal to use for communication. Images, videos, sounds, and other types of information can be encoded into an electromagnetic wave by varying certain properties of the wave. Electromagnetic waves travel at a speed of about 300,000 km/s. This speed allows for quick communication over long distances. These waves can also travel through a vacuum, making communication through space possible.

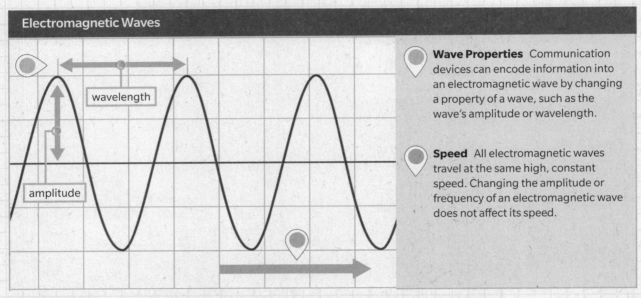

Electromagnetic Waves

wavelength

amplitude

Wave Properties Communication devices can encode information into an electromagnetic wave by changing a property of a wave, such as the wave's amplitude or wavelength.

Speed All electromagnetic waves travel at the same high, constant speed. Changing the amplitude or frequency of an electromagnetic wave does not affect its speed.

6. High-frequency electromagnetic waves usually travel along straight paths. How can these waves be used to communicate from one side of Earth to the other?

Engineer It
Compare Communication Methods

Imagine that you are exploring a forest with some friends. You all realize that you need to be able to signal one another if one of you gets lost. Each person in your group has a phone, a whistle, and a flashlight. Consider the features of each device and how useful the device would be for sending an emergency signal.

7. What are the advantages and disadvantages of each communication device?

_____

_____

_____

_____

_____

_____

Analyzing Analog and Digital Information

Not all information is the same. Some information exists as distinct values, such as the letters in a word. Some information can vary continuously, such as the sounds produced when you say a word out loud.

The thermometer on the left displays a digital signal. The thermometer on the right displays an analog signal.

Digital

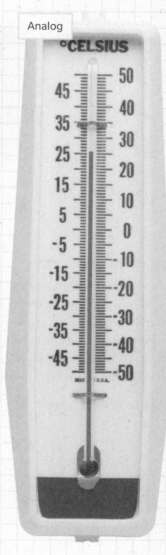

Analog

8. How many values can the digital thermometer show between 25.0 °C and 25.4 °C? What are those values?

9. How many values can the analog thermometer show between 25.0 °C and 25.4 °C? Explain your answer.

Compare these two thermometers. The digital thermometer shows values to a tenth of a degree. The analog thermometer varies continuously along its scale. It may be hard for someone reading the analog thermometer to know exactly what the temperature is to a tenth of a degree, especially if the value is between two tick marks.

Types of Information

Information can be either analog or digital. Analog information is information that varies continuously. Digital information is information that jumps between values. Sometimes analog information may be represented digitally, as in the case of the digital thermometer shown earlier. The original information, temperature, is actually analog information, but the digital thermometer can only show temperature values to the nearest tenth of a degree. This does not mean that temperature values jump from 25.0 °C to 25.1 °C. In reality, the temperature can be an infinite number of values between 25.0 °C and 25.1 °C.

10. What are some types of analog information?

The mass of water in this glass increases continuously as the glass is filled.

Analog Information

Much of the information we deal with is analog information. For instance, your height is analog information. For convenience, we typically measure ourselves in feet and inches, but your height is not limited to those values. When you grow, you do not suddenly become one inch taller. Instead, you will slowly grow taller over time. If you grow from 5 feet tall to 5 feet and 1 inch tall, you will at some point have been every height in between those two measurements.

11. What are some types of digital information?

The mass of soybeans in this bowl increases in increments equal to the mass of a soybean.

Digital Information

Digital information only exists as discrete values. For instance, if you count the number of desks in your classroom, you would never have half a desk. If you add a desk to your classroom, your classroom would suddenly just have one more desk. The number of desks in your classroom can only be certain numbers. That makes the number of desks a set of digital information.

Graphs of Analog and Digital Signals

Analog information and digital information have to be communicated in different ways. Whether information is communicated using a graph, a wave, or any other type of signal, the two types of information will be encoded differently. A signal containing analog information must be able to show all of the continuous information. A signal containing digital information must be able to clearly show the different distinct values.

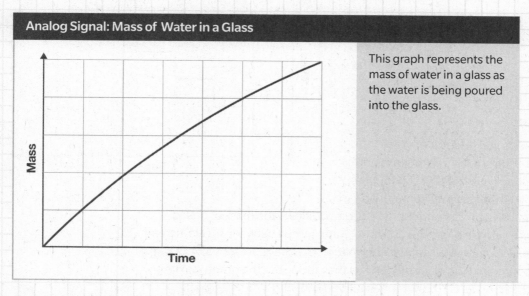

Analog Signal: Mass of Water in a Glass

This graph represents the mass of water in a glass as the water is being poured into the glass.

12. This graph contains analog information. What features of the graph indicate that it contains analog information?

Analog Signals

An **analog signal** is a signal that contains analog information. Analog information is continuous and can be any value. So, any signal that communicates analog information also must be continuous. A graph of analog information will show smooth changes in between values. Imagine zooming into the graph. The values will appear to change smoothly no matter much you zoom in. The graph showing the mass of water in a glass shows how the mass increases smoothly, with no breaks in the graph. Every single part of the line communicates some information. The line does not simply jump between data points. Instead, it moves through a range of values. A light signal, a sound signal, or an electromagnetic wave signal could all be analog signals if analog information were encoded into them.

13. What do you notice about this graph compared to the graph of analog information?

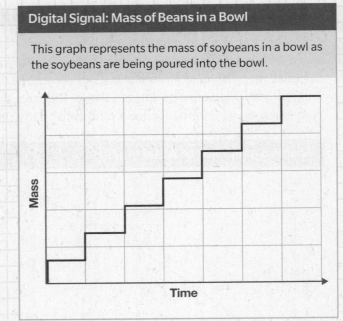

Digital Signal: Mass of Beans in a Bowl

This graph represents the mass of soybeans in a bowl as the soybeans are being poured into the bowl.

Mass (y-axis)

Time (x-axis)

Digital Signals

A signal that contains digital information is a **digital signal**. Digital information is not continuous; it jumps between distinct values without being the values in between. So any signal that communicates digital information will also be discontinuous. The graph shows the mass of beans increasing as soon as a single soybean falls in. The graph jumps between levels instead of varying continuously. Sometimes, analog information may be represented by a digital signal. Imagine graphing the height of someone as they grow, but the graph can only show values in 1-inch increments. That graph would be showing a digital signal.

Binary Digital Signals

A computer processor consists of many switches that have two states—on and off. Because each switch can be only on or off, with no value in between, computers use digital signals. Because the signals can only have two values, they are called *binary digital signals*. Binary digital signals are usually written using the numbers 0 and 1, which represent the values "on" and "off." In order to communicate complex information, these 0s and 1s are strung together in a series. Every piece of information that you see on a computer can be represented as a series of 0s and 1s. The code in the table uses a series of 8 bits, binary digits, in the code; this is 8-bit code.

14. Look at the table showing the binary codes for the numbers 0–9. Using this table, sketch a graph that represents the number 5.

Numbers in Binary	
Number	**Binary Code**
0	00000000
1	00000001
2	00000010
3	00000011
4	00000100
5	00000101
6	00000110
7	00000111
8	00001000
9	00001001

15. **Do the Math | Number of Levels in a Signal** These digital waves use different *y*-axis values (levels) to encode information. Write the number of different values shown in each graph.

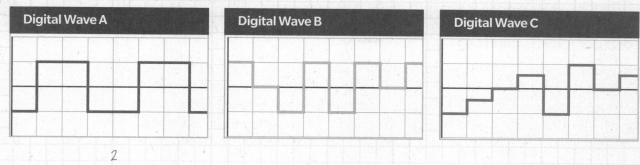

Digital Wave A

Digital Wave B

Digital Wave C

_____2_____

_____

_____

16. Digital signals have a limited number of values. How can a computer, which uses binary digital signals, represent complex information using only two levels?

 EVIDENCE NOTEBOOK

17. If you are streaming a video from a website, what type of signal is being sent to your computer from the website? Record your evidence.

Identify Signal Types

18. Think about the different types of signals presented in this lesson. Write at least two examples of analog signals and at least two examples of digital signals that can be used to send information.

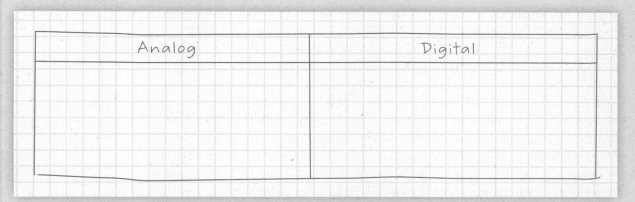

Analog	Digital

Encoding Information in Waves

Wave Modulation

Many communication devices, such as radios and phones, use electromagnetic waves as signals. These devices send and receive a carrier wave that has a constant frequency and amplitude. To encode information into the carrier wave, either the frequency or amplitude of the carrier wave is changed. Changing the frequency or amplitude of the carrier wave is called *modulation*. Both analog and digital information can be encoded into a carrier wave.

19. How might a modulated wave look different than a carrier wave? How can you determine whether the information contained by a modulated wave is analog or digital information?

A Modulated Wave

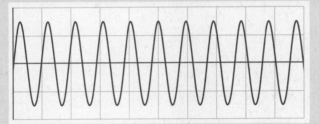

This wave has not been modulated. No information has been encoded into the wave.

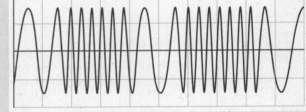

The frequency of this wave has been modulated. Information has been encoded into the wave.

Encoding Signals

The process for encoding analog and digital signals into a carrier wave is similar; however, due to the differences in the two types of signals, the resulting modulated waves are different. Analog information is continuous. When analog signals are encoded on a carrier wave, the frequency or amplitude of the modulated wave changes continuously. When a digital signal is encoded on a carrier wave, the frequency or amplitude of the signal will jump between discrete values.

For many years, radio stations transmitted analog information, which was decoded by radios. A radio would be tuned to the frequency of the carrier wave. In frequency modulated (FM) radio, the radio would transform changes in the frequency of the carrier wave into electric signals. Amplitude modulated (AM) radio transformed changes in signal amplitude into electric signals. Many radio stations now encode digital signals onto their carrier waves to reduce the noise issues that affect analog signals.

Encoding Information

Differences in analog and digital signals produce different modulated waves when they are encoded onto a carrier wave. Look at the diagrams to see how the amplitude of a carrier wave might be modulated with an analog signal and a digital signal.

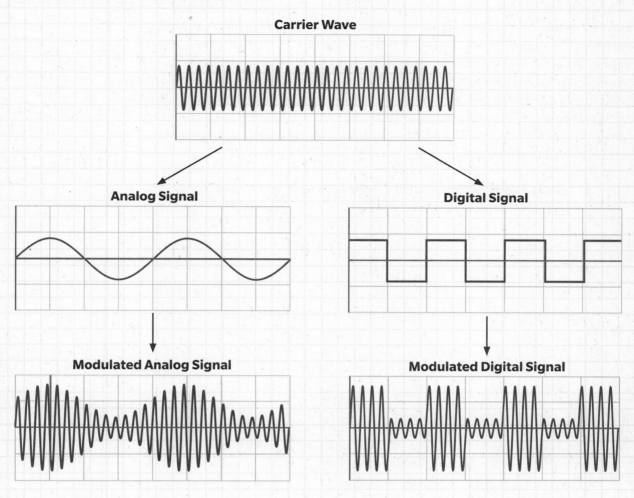

Carrier Wave

Analog Signal

Digital Signal

Modulated Analog Signal

Modulated Digital Signal

20. Compare the modulated analog signal and the modulated digital signal. How are they similar, and how are they different?

Using Digital Signals to Represent Analog Information

Much of the information we collect and communicate is analog. However, we often digitize this information, so that it can be collected, stored, and transmitted using digital technology. When analog information is encoded in a digital signal, some information is lost. The resolution of a digital signal affects how closely the digital signal can represent the original analog information. Resolution may be increased by adding more levels to a digital signal, or in the case of binary digital signals, more bits may be used to represent the analog information. Using a digital signal to represent analog information helps the signal to be more reliably stored and transmitted. This process of converting analog information to digital signals happens when music is recorded and stored on a computer, when a digital camera captures an image, and when your voice is captured and sent by a modern wireless phone.

 21. Language SmArts Explain the advantages and disadvantages of using digital signals to represent analog information.

Modulate a Radio Wave

22. The first diagram shows a carrier wave . The second diagram shows a digital signal. Draw the modulated wave that would result from encoding the digital signal into the carrier wave by modulating the amplitude of the carrier wave.

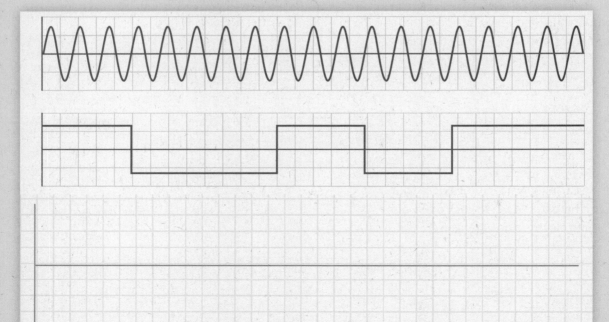

Explaining How Noise Affects Signals

When you talk to friends in a loud, busy room, it can be hard to understand what they are saying. Their voices might get drowned out by other sounds. You might hear someone else say something and think it was one of your friends. Your friends might need to speak loudly for you to understand them. The noise in the room makes it harder for you to understand what your friends are saying, because you are hearing other sounds at the same time.

23. Imagine you are in a room with a lot of noise and you are trying to tell something to a friend. What are some ways that you could improve the communication between you and your friend?

24. Could a similar phenomenon occur when using signals such as signal fires or radio waves to communicate? Explain your answer.

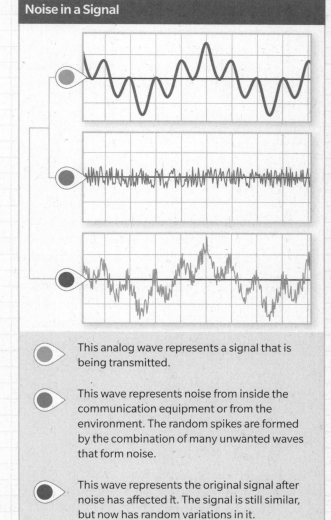

Noise in a Signal

- This analog wave represents a signal that is being transmitted.

- This wave represents noise from inside the communication equipment or from the environment. The random spikes are formed by the combination of many unwanted waves that form noise.

- This wave represents the original signal after noise has affected it. The signal is still similar, but now has random variations in it.

Noise

The concept of noise does not only apply to sound. **Noise** is any unwanted change to a signal. When you hear a lot of other sounds in addition to your friends' talking, the signals reaching you are different from the signals that your friends are sending. Sound from other activities is interfering with the sound of your friends' voices.

Noise can affect all types of signals. Sunlight can make it hard to see a fire. Electronics can interfere with electric signals. Noise can occur any time a signal is transmitted, stored, or recorded. Whenever the signal that reaches the intended receiver is different from the signal that was originally transmitted, noise has affected the signal.

Hands-On Lab
Transmit and Record a Signal

You will be examining the noise that accumulates in analog and digital signals as they are sent and received.

MATERIALS
- two recording devices (cell phones, voice recorders, or computers)

Procedure and Analysis

STEP 1 Record yourself reading a sentence from a book.

STEP 2 Play the message back and record it onto the second recording device. Do not make the recording on the second device by connecting the two devices with a cable. Instead, play the first recording on the first device and make the second recording using the microphone of the second device.

STEP 3 How do your two recordings compare?

STEP 4 What do you think might happen if you kept rerecording each new recording? Make a prediction supported by your observations and information from the text, and then test it.

STEP 5 Your original recording was an analog signal. It was a recording of a continuous sound wave. Now, record a digital signal of your reading by repeating Steps 2–4, except this time, you will use a cable to connect both devices, which transmit the signal digitally.

STEP 6 Compare the results of your analog rerecordings and your digital rerecordings. How did each type of rerecording compare to your initial recording? How did your results compare to your predictions?

Noise in Analog Signals

Because the information in analog signals varies continuously, any noise that changes the wave becomes a part of the signal. Once noise has been added to an analog signal, there is no way to completely remove it. In the final version of the message that you recorded, it is impossible to tell what parts of the signal are noise and what parts are the original signal. When an analog signal is changed due to noise, the information in the signal is also changed.

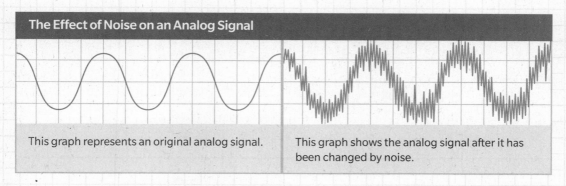

The Effect of Noise on an Analog Signal

This graph represents an original analog signal.

This graph shows the analog signal after it has been changed by noise.

Noise in Digital Signals

The information in digital signals is not continuous. Because the signal has defined levels, noise does not have as large an effect on the decoding of a digital signal as it has on the decoding of an analog signal. For instance, imagine that you recorded a signal that varied between silence and a loud clap. When there is a loud clap, you can still hear it even if there is noise. And noise would not make the silent portions loud enough to be confused with claps. Unless there is so much noise that the different levels of the digital signal cannot be told apart, the information in a digital signal can be decoded more reliably than an analog signal can be.

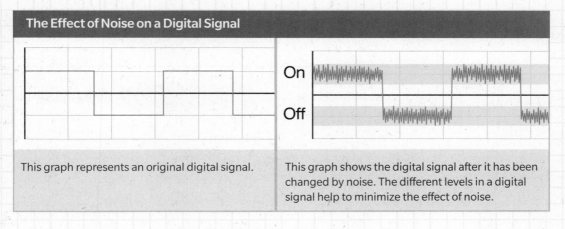

The Effect of Noise on a Digital Signal

This graph represents an original digital signal.

This graph shows the digital signal after it has been changed by noise. The different levels in a digital signal help to minimize the effect of noise.

© Houghton Mifflin Harcourt Publishing Company

EVIDENCE NOTEBOOK

25. When you are watching a video on the Internet, could there be any sources of noise that would make it hard to recognize the original signal? Record your evidence.

Engineer It
Explain Reliability in Signal Storage

Many methods have been used to store signals. Vinyl records store analog sound signals. A waveform is cut into a spiral groove in a vinyl record. To play the record, a needle is dragged through the groove, causing it to vibrate with the same waveform as was recorded. Digital signals are stored in a variety of ways. Every digital storage method, from CDs to hard drives, uses a series of 0s and 1s.

Analog Storage

These waveforms show two different playbacks of an analog vinyl record.

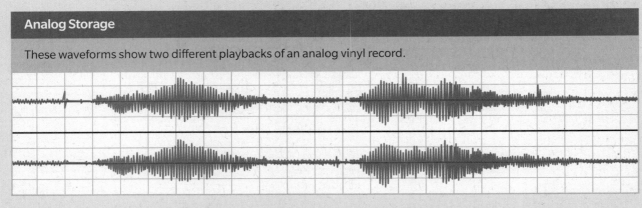

26. What might cause the slight differences between the two sound waves?

_____

_____

_____

Digital Storage

These waveforms show two playbacks of a digital sound file.

27. Can you observe any differences between the two waveforms? If you noticed differences, what were they? If not, what might that tell you about digital signals?

_____

_____

28. Digital signals have replaced analog signals in many uses. How do you think the differences in analog and digital storage might have driven this change?

_____

_____

_____

Continue Your Exploration

Name: _____   Date: _____

Check out the path below or go online to choose one of the other paths shown.

| Careers in Engineering | • Communication Devices
• Hands-On Labs ✋
• Propose Your Own Path | Go online to choose one of these other paths. |

Cell Tower Technician

The cell phone, and especially the smartphone, have changed how we communicate. Business, casual conversation, and even scientific study all use cell phones. Cell phones rely on an extensive infrastructure. Landline telephones send information using electric signals that run through wires. The wireless features of cell phones add another step to this process. Cell towers transfer information between individual cell phones and the rest of the phone system. Noise may occur in many different parts of the system, so modern mobile phones are designed to use digital signals. Cell tower technicians help to install, repair, and maintain the infrastructure that allows for cell phones to function. Equipment found on cell towers includes antennae for sending and receiving radio signals, Global Positioning System (GPS) receivers, and computerized switches that protect and monitor the cell tower equipment.

1. Cell towers receive radio wave signals from cell phones and must convert them into electric signals. These electric signals are sent over wires to other cell towers. Cell towers can also send and receive digital data from smartphones. What are some skills that might be useful for a cell tower technician? Choose all that apply.

    A. an understanding of electronics

    B. an understanding of computers

    C. an understanding of chemical engineering

    D. an understanding of how radio waves behave

Continue Your Exploration

2. Cell tower technicians often have to install and maintain transmitters and receivers that are attached to tall buildings or cell towers. What might be the advantage of having transmitters and receivers in high places?

3. Cell towers are often placed in busy areas. What might be some considerations when deciding whether an area requires more cell towers? Choose all that apply.

   A. the number of cell phones connecting to each tower

   B. the number of landline telephones in an area

   C. the reception that phones get in an area

4. Cell tower technicians often work on a large number of cell towers. These cell towers form a patchwork to cover a large area. Based on your knowledge of radio signals, why might many cell towers with smaller areas be used instead of a couple towers with much larger areas?

5. **Collaborate** With a partner, make a list of other professions that would require knowledge of communication technology. How would someone working in one of these professions use communication technology?

Can You Explain It?

Name: _____   Date: _____

How can a video from the Internet appear the same every time you watch it?

Explore Online

EVIDENCE NOTEBOOK

Refer to the notes in your Evidence Notebook to help you construct an explanation for why a video from the Internet appears the same every time you view it.

1. State your claim. Make sure your claim fully explains why a video from the Internet appears the same every time you view it.

2. Summarize the evidence you have gathered to support your claim and explain your reasoning.

Checkpoints

Answer the following questions to check your understanding of the lesson.

3. A radio tower transmits music to nearby radios. The radio tower uses radio waves, a type of electromagnetic wave, to transmit the music. Which statements accurately describe this situation? Choose all that apply.

   A. The radio tower encodes information into the radio wave signal.

   B. A listener will need a radio to decode the signal and listen to music.

   C. Information is encoded into the radio wave by modulating the radio wave.

4. What does changing the frequency do to the speed of a radio wave?

   A. It increases its speed.

   B. It decreases its speed.

   C. It does not affect the speed.

Use the illustration to answer Questions 5 and 6.

5. The signal represented in the illustration is *an analog / a digital* signal. The variations that occur within the blue bands *are / are not* noise because they are random variations in signal strength. In this type of signal, the variations usually *do / do not* have a large effect on the decoding of the signal.

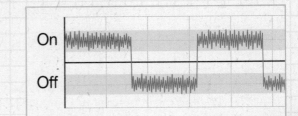

6. This signal is very noisy. Why is the signal still able to encode and transmit information reliably?

   A. Noise cannot change the information in a digital signal.

   B. The noise level is small compared to the change in the digital signal levels.

   C. The noise causes the amplitude to change too frequently to be detected.

In this illustration, the top waveform represents a transmitted signal and the bottom waveform represents the signal that was received. Use the illustration to answer Question 7.

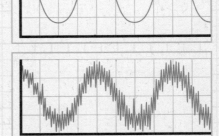

7. Why are these two signals different from one another?

   A. Analog signals are always noisy because they vary continuously.

   B. The process of converting between an analog signal and a digital signal introduced noise.

   C. Noise was introduced by random variations in the signal during the processes of transmitting and receiving the signal.

8. Why are digital signals generally better than analog signals for transmitting data over long distances? Choose all that apply.

   A. Digital signals do not use waves, so they do not pick up any noise.

   B. Noise can usually be removed from a digital signal.

   C. In a digital signal, the level of noise must be high in order for one level to be interpreted as another level.

   D. Digital signals are transmitted faster than analog signals, so there is less chance for noise to be introduced.

Interactive Review

Complete this section to review the main concepts of the lesson.

Electromagnetic waves move quickly and can be encoded with information, making them ideal for encoding signals.

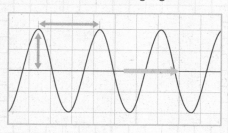

A. What are two methods that you could use to communicate with a friend? Describe two methods that each use a different type of signal.

An analog signal contains continuous information. A digital signal contains information that is represented as a number of specific values.

B. How can you identify whether a set of information is analog or digital information?

Electromagnetic waves are modulated differently depending on whether analog or digital information is being encoded into the wave.

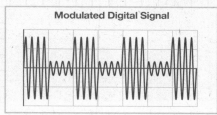

Modulated Digital Signal

C. Compare and contrast a modulated digital wave and a modulated analog wave.

Both analog and digital signals gain noise when they travel from one place to another, but the information in a digital signal is less affected by noise.

D. Explain why noise has less of an effect on the interpretation of digital signals than on the interpretation of analog signals.

Using Digital Technologies to Sustain Biodiversity

A mule deer browses in Yosemite National Park.

Explore First

Surveying Biodiversity Go outside or look at photos of an ecosystem. Write a list of all the types of plants and animals that you observe. Count how many plants and animals you saw, and discuss whether the area has high or low biodiversity. How might your observations of this area change if you viewed the area at night?

Go online to view the digital version of the Hands-On Lab for this lesson and to download additional lab resources.

CAN YOU EXPLAIN IT?

How can a motion-triggered digital camera contribute to biodiversity monitoring?

This photo of a mountain lion in Griffith Park near Los Angeles was taken by a motion-triggered digital camera. This mountain lion is also being tracked with a radio transmitter collar.

1. What kinds of data could be gathered from photos taken in an ecosystem?

2. What is one advantage and one disadvantage of a motion-triggered camera compared with a camera that is programmed to take an image every few seconds?

EVIDENCE NOTEBOOK As you explore this lesson, gather evidence to help explain the impact of using motion-triggered digital cameras to collect biodiversity data.

Monitoring Biodiversity

Ecosystems may contain any number of plant and animal species. An ecosystem with many species and large genetic variation within species is an ecosystem with high biodiversity. The biodiversity in an ecosystem can be an indicator of its health. Plants and animals in an ecosystem depend on each other. If a few species disappear, all will be affected. Humans also depend on healthy ecosystems for ecosystem services, such as climate control, disease control, and food production. Collecting data is important to understanding how human activity may be impacting biodiversity. The data can then be used to develop solutions for sustaining or improving biodiversity.

A forest has been cleared to make room for a housing development.

3. **Discuss** The image shows a new housing development being built on land that was previously wooded. How might this affect biodiversity in the area?

Challenges of Monitoring Biodiversity

Collecting and analyzing biodiversity data involves many challenges. For example, animals move and can be unevenly distributed throughout an ecosystem. Animals may also change their behavior around humans. Some plants and animals are difficult to observe from a distance because they are small. Surveys may need to be done over very large areas to accurately measure variations in plant and animal distributions. Often, the engineering design process can be used to find solutions to these monitoring problems.

After collecting the data, scientists analyze it. To get an accurate understanding of biodiversity, large amounts of data must be collected. These data can take a long time to analyze using statistical methods. Computer technology makes it possible for scientists to analyze data and models more quickly now than they could without computers.

EVIDENCE NOTEBOOK

4. What challenges of biodiversity monitoring does a motion-triggered camera address and not address? Record your evidence.

5. Digital technology and the Internet make it _easier / more difficult_ to share data reliably with others. Because large amounts of data must be collected and analyzed to accurately monitor biodiversity, it is helpful to be able to share data with many people to _reduce / increase_ the amount of time it takes to analyze the data.

Early Biodiversity Monitoring

Monitoring biodiversity has always had challenges. In the early days of monitoring, data collection was a very manual process that required people to go out into the field to collect data in person. Scientists would collect samples by hand and sometimes tag animals to help track a particular organism.

Scientists often used new technology to improve their data collection techniques. For example, in the late 1800s and early 1900s a photographer named George Shiras III was one of the first to capture nighttime photos of wildlife using automated techniques. One of his techniques was to attach bait to a trip-wire. When an animal tried to take the bait, the trip-wire caused a flash to go off and the camera would take a photo. Scientists sometimes still use bait to attract animals to a location for study. Trip-wires and film cameras have been replaced by digital technology such as motion sensors and digital cameras.

Startled deer in a photo taken by George Shiras III.

George Shiras III pioneered early wildlife photography in the early 1900s. Here he silently canoes and uses a flash to capture nighttime images of wildlife.

6. Which of the following are limitations of a single person collecting biodiversity data manually? Select all that apply.

A. amount of space covered

B. quality of data collected

C. time it takes to collect the data

D. presence of a human

Modern Biodiversity Monitoring

Advances in technology have improved our ability to monitor biodiversity. Sometimes samples still must be collected in person, and animals still have to be tagged, but technology has improved these techniques. Improved batteries and renewable energy sources enable remote devices to function for longer periods of time. Satellites may collect data, including images, over large areas in relatively short amounts of time. In the past, these data may have been collected by a person on foot or in a plane.

Digital technology has made it easier for scientists across Earth to communicate and work collaboratively. Where data were once only available written in a scientist's notebook, now the data can be digitized and stored on a computer. These data can then be quickly shared worldwide via the Internet. Communication satellites are important in transmitting data for the Internet, but they also enable high-quality phone calls worldwide. Scientists not only collaborate with other scientists, but are now taking advantage of large numbers of non-scientists to collect and analyze data using crowdsourcing. Crowdsourcing is a method where scientists put out a request for data or post data to be analyzed online and anyone can help. This helps scientists collect or analyze large amounts of data more quickly.

Tools can be powered for longer amounts of time in remote areas because of improved batteries.

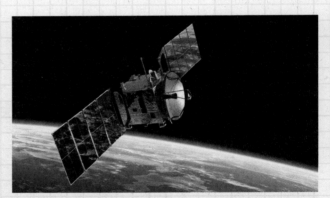

Satellites allow for worldwide communication and can collect and transmit biodiversity data across Earth.

Digital cameras provide instant feedback on photo quality and store data reliably.

Computers and the Internet enable data to be stored and accessed quickly by people all over the world.

7. Match the following digital technologies with an application related to biodiversity monitoring.

digital camera	can collect detailed images of plants and animals
GPS tracker	can collect and transmit data across long distances
satellites	can document where an animal is after it has been tagged

8. **Act** Write and perform a discussion between a modern day scientist and a scientist from the early 1900s who are studying the same problem of biodiversity. The scientists should discuss the different technologies they use in their studies.

Monitoring to Sustain Biodiversity

Monitoring biodiversity not only gives scientists information about how an ecosystem is doing currently, but also how it can be sustained. Scientists monitor the biodiversity in an ecosystem to see if it is struggling or declining. Both plants and animals should be monitored to better understand the needs of the entire ecosystem. Then, the collected data can be used to help develop a solution to sustain biodiversity if needed.

When monitoring biodiversity, a scientist cannot pay attention to just one organism because everything is connected in some way. And there could be more than one factor causing a change in an ecosystem. Consider a scientist studying a particular species of plant. The number of plants suddenly begins to decrease. To develop a sustaining solution, the scientist must know why the plant population is decreasing. This might involve identifying the introduction of pollutants or other environmental changes or the introduction of a new species in the area. Similarly, if an animal is being monitored, understanding what the animal eats, what eats the animal (if anything), and what is part of the animal's habitat is important. Changes in one or more of these factors may affect the survival of the animal and affect the sustaining solution.

Human activities in an ecosystem may also need to be monitored because human activities may affect the biodiversity of an ecosystem. For example, when previously wild areas are developed for human uses, habitats may be destroyed or fragmented. Humans may hunt species or introduce new species to an area. Humans may harvest plants or plant new species. All of these activities may affect biodiversity in an area.

9. Which of the following should be monitored in an ecosystem in order to sustain biodiversity? Select all that apply.
    A. animal populations
    B. plant populations and growth
    C. ecosystem elevation
    D. number of plant and animal species
    E. amount of rain

© Houghton Mifflin Harcourt Publishing Company

Analyze Technology to Monitor Bird Calls in Nature

Ludwig Koch was an expert at recording animal sounds. As a child in 1889, he made the first known recording of a bird call on a machine called an Edison wax cylinder. This machine recorded sound by carving a groove into a layer of wax and then played back the sound by tracing the wave.

At first, Koch was only able to record birds in captivity. But recording technology advanced throughout Koch's lifetime. By the time Koch made his final bird call recording in 1961, he was able to go out into nature to record the calls of birds in their natural habitat. He used a magnetic tape recorder to accomplish the feat. Magnetic tapes were not as sensitive as wax cylinders to environmental conditions. However, as an analog technology, these tapes were still prone to noise during playback.

Recording technology has continued to advance since Koch's last recording. Scientists are now able to make high-quality, digital recordings in the wild with improved microphones. They are then able to store and analyze the recordings on computers to study and better understand the calls.

10. Technology improvements, including digital / analog signals, have improved scientists' understanding of bird calls because the recordings are longer / more reliable.

11. Language SmArts Write an argument that explains how understanding bird calls in nature helps in monitoring and sustaining biodiversity.

_____

_____

_____

_____

_____

_____

_____

_____

_____

_____

An Edison wax cylinder, an early analog device that could record and play back sound.

Koch used a magnetic tape recorder to make his last recordings of wild birds in 1961.

A scientist uses a digital microphone to make a high-quality recording of bird calls in the wild.

Analyzing Solutions for Monitoring and Sustaining Biodiversity

The Pacific fisher is a member of the weasel family that is in danger of becoming extinct. They live in mature forests in parts of the United States and Canada. They are opportunistic carnivores, which means they will eat a variety of small animals depending on what is available. They are one of the few animals that prey on porcupines. Uncontrolled populations of porcupines may destroy areas of forest by stripping the bark off of trees. In the 1800s, the Pacific fisher was widely hunted for its fur, a practice that is now illegal. More recently, the Pacific fisher's populations have continued to decline as human development and the lumber industry destroy their natural habitats. They are also threatened by predation, disease, being hit by vehicles, and being accidentally poisoned.

The Pacific fisher is about the size of a large house cat and lives in mature forests in North America.

12. What are some of the ways the Pacific fisher population could be monitored?

Range of the Pacific Fisher

This map shows the range of the Pacific fisher around 1800 and today.

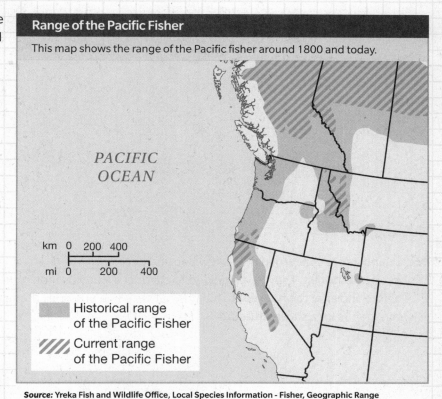

PACIFIC OCEAN

km 0   200 400
mi 0   200   400

Historical range of the Pacific Fisher

Current range of the Pacific Fisher

Source: Yreka Fish and Wildlife Office, Local Species Information - Fisher, Geographic Range

13. Why is it concerning that the Pacific fisher is in danger of going extinct? Select all that apply.

A. They live in forests.

B. They help keep a forest healthy.

C. Humans will not be able to use their fur.

D. They help control the porcupine population.

Biodiversity Monitoring Solutions

In Yosemite National Park, the Pacific fisher population is monitored in multiple ways. Some are caught and tagged so that scientists can monitor the fishers using radio telemetry. Radio telemetry uses radio waves to send location data for a tagged animal so that scientists can see where the animal spends its time. Scientists also set up motion-triggered cameras around the park to capture the behavior of the animal. These methods allow scientists to get more detailed information about the location and behavior of the remaining Pacific fishers.

The criteria and constraints for a given biodiversity monitoring solution depend on the situation and the potential impacts on the environment and on the organisms being studied. So, a solution that works for one situation may not work in another situation.

14. The red spots on the map show tracking data for a particular animal. Based on the data, mark three of the boxes to show which three locations would be the best places to put cameras to monitor the animal.

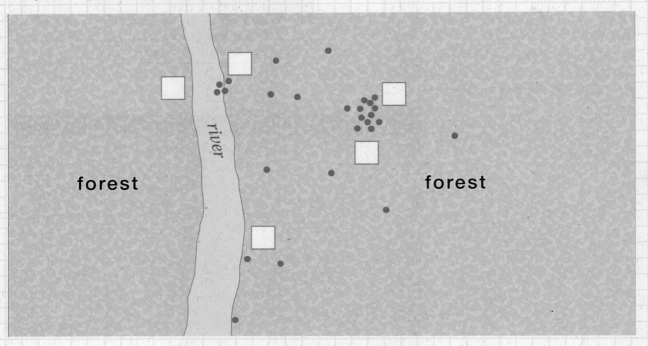

15. Scientists are concerned that a new housing development will affect the biodiversity in a nearby forest. They have decided to conduct a study by monitoring biodiversity before and after the houses are built. What are some possible criteria and constraints for a successful study?

EVIDENCE NOTEBOOK

16. What types of biodiversity data is a motion-triggered camera able to collect? Record your evidence.

Biodiversity Sustaining Solutions

Collecting and analyzing biodiversity data is part of the process of developing solutions for sustaining biodiversity. Park rangers in Yosemite National Park have observed that several of the Pacific fishers in the park have been killed by vehicles while trying to cross the road. Data showed that more of these vehicular deaths happened after heavy rains or during the spring thaw. Park rangers noticed that some of the fishers were using culverts to get to the opposite side of the road. A culvert is a tunnel built underneath a road that allows water to flow from one side to the other. Scientists set up cameras to monitor the culverts to see when the fishers used the culverts. The cameras showed that during dry times Pacific fishers and some other animals used the tunnels to cross the road. During times of high water flow, the culverts could not be used by the animals, which forced them to cross the roads. The Yosemite scientists decided to install more culverts under the roads of the park and put them in dry areas so the Pacific fishers and other animals could cross the road safely year round.

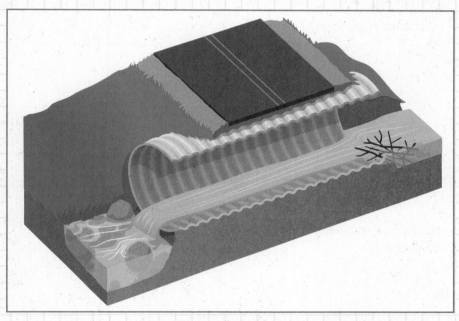

Culverts were originally designed for water to flow under roads, but it may be possible to redesign culverts to also solve biodiversity concerns.

17. How can scientists determine if building safe crossing structures benefits the biodiversity in the area? Select all that apply.

   A. set up cameras to see if animals are using them

   B. compare populations before and after

   C. use structures that are successful elsewhere

   D. measure to see if they are big enough for animals

18. Explain why you chose your answers.

Do the Math
Evaluate a Biodiversity Sustaining Solution

Suppose that scientists have been monitoring the biodiversity of a desert ecosystem. They noticed that the population of prickly pear cactus is much lower now than it was 20 years ago. Scientists determined that an acceptable sustaining solution would increase the population of prickly pear cactus by 5–10% in the next year. When the study began, the population of prickly pear cactus in an area was 100. After a year of implementing the solution and monitoring the population of prickly pear cactus, the population increased to 120.

19. Calculate the percent growth of the prickly pear cactus population and determine if it falls within the acceptable increase the scientists set.

$$\text{percent change} = \frac{(\text{current population} - \text{original population})}{(\text{original population})} \times 100$$

The percent change of the population of the prickly pear cactus was _____.

20. Did the sustaining solution to increase the population of prickly pear cactus satisfy the growth criterion the scientists set?

   A. No, it was too low.

   B. Yes, it fell in their range.

   C. No, it was too high.

   D. Yes, it was higher, but that is ok.

21. Increasing the population of an organism can be positive for the biodiversity of an ecosystem. Can too much growth in a population be bad for the biodiversity in an area? Explain.

Developing Solutions for Monitoring Biodiversity

The Engineering Design Process

The engineering design process (EDP) may be used to find solution to a wide variety of problems. Problems may be as simple as keeping a glass of water cold or as complex as monitoring the biodiversity in an area. The EDP has many steps, and the steps may be repeated or revisited as you work toward finding a solution for the problem. And while the process follows the same steps regardless of the problem, the results of the steps depend on the particular problem you are trying to solve.

A scientist collects water quality data using digital technology.

One important aspect of developing solutions for almost any problem is collecting reliable data. Digital technology has improved scientists' ability to collect, store, and analyze data reliably.

22. Why are reliable data important for the EDP to be successful?

Identify the Problem

When it comes to biodiversity, the first problem that must be solved is how to monitor biodiversity in a particular area. After a solution for monitoring biodiversity is developed and implemented, the collected data can be used to determine if biodiversity is threatened. If it is, the problem shifts from monitoring to sustaining biodiversity, with different criteria and constraints. The declining fisher populations, described previously, are an example of a problem shifting from monitoring biodiversity to sustaining biodiversity. After a solution is implemented, the problem shifts back to monitoring to see if the solution has worked.

Monitoring biodiversity is a complex issue, so a monitoring solution may only monitor a small part of an ecosystem. When identifying a problem, the problem statement should be as specific as possible. Writing a problem like "I want to monitor seals," is not helpful for designing a solution. What about the seals needs to be monitored? Do you want to monitor their health, their movement, or their breeding habits? A better, more specific problem could be written as, "I want to measure the population of harbor seals within 25 kilometers of the California Channel Islands."

After the problem is identified, research should be done to see how similar problems have been solved in the past. Research also involves gathering existing data about the problem. This research can then be used to refine the problem statement before further defining the problem by identifying criteria and constraints.

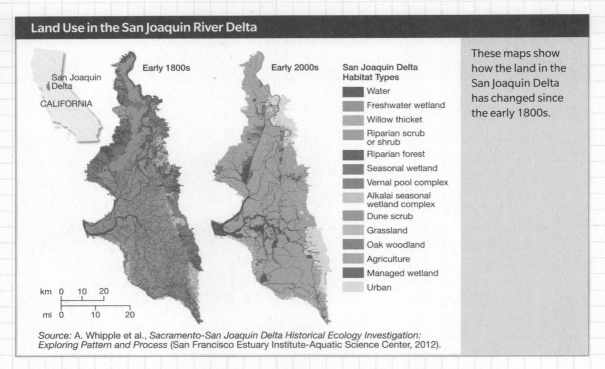

Land Use in the San Joaquin River Delta

San Joaquin Delta

CALIFORNIA

Early 1800s

Early 2000s

San Joaquin Delta Habitat Types
- Water
- Freshwater wetland
- Willow thicket
- Riparian scrub or shrub
- Riparian forest
- Seasonal wetland
- Vernal pool complex
- Alkalai seasonal wetland complex
- Dune scrub
- Grassland
- Oak woodland
- Agriculture
- Managed wetland
- Urban

km 0 10 20

mi 0 10 20

Source: A. Whipple et al., *Sacramento-San Joaquin Delta Historical Ecology Investigation: Exploring Pattern and Process* (San Francisco Estuary Institute-Aquatic Science Center, 2012).

These maps show how the land in the San Joaquin Delta has changed since the early 1800s.

23. **Discuss** Look at the maps and discuss how the changing land use might affect biodiversity in the deltas. With a group, generate as many questions as possible related to the problem of monitoring biodiversity in the deltas. Then, select the question you think best identifies the problem you would investigate.

Define the Problem

Defining a problem involves identifying the criteria and constraints specific to the problem. Remember, criteria are the desired features of the solution. Criteria might include the type of data needed. Constraints are limitations or obstacles that must be overcome to develop an acceptable solution. Constraints may involve time limits, budget concerns, and the laws of physics. The criteria and constraints should be specific. When solutions are brainstormed and tested, they are judged against the criteria and constraints of the problem.

A constraint for a study monitoring the biodiversity of this area might be that the interactions of the sea lions and the cormorants should not be affected by the study.

Identify Criteria and Constraints

Problems may have any number of criteria and constraints. Consider the problem of monitoring seals. Seals spend much of their life underwater in the ocean, but sometimes sun themselves on rocks or shorelines. The criteria for this monitoring problem should specify if the monitoring will include both underwater and above water monitoring and what other types of data the solution should provide. Constraints include making sure the chosen technology can be used in saltwater if underwater measurements are desired.

24. Which of the following constraints apply to the problem of monitoring seals? Select all that apply.

    A. transmit in saltwater

    B. waterproof

    C. withstand high pressure

    D. work at high altitudes

    E. withstand dry climate

    F. work in low amounts of light

Rank Criteria

When it is not possible to find a solution that satisfies all of a problem's criteria within the constraints, tradeoffs must be made. Sometimes multiple solutions may satisfy all of the criteria. To help choose the best design, engineers must decide the importance of each criterion relative to the other criteria. The design that better satisfies the more important criteria is the more desirable solution.

25. Which of the following two criteria related to monitoring seals is more important? Explain your reasoning. Solution A collects data about seal behavior 24 hours a day. Solution B collects data for at least three months.

Case Study: Monitor a Kelp Forest

Sea kelp forests off the coast of California provide food and shelter to many marine organisms. If scientists were to monitor the health of the sea kelp forests, what criteria would need to be met, and what constraints would they have? Some criteria might be that the solution measures the average length of a strand of kelp, the amount of pollution in the area, and the number of other plants growing in the area. Constraints for this problem could include that the technology used must work in saltwater and the amount of time and people it will take to measure the kelp along the many miles of California coastline.

Long strands of kelp form an underwater forest. Many animals rely on kelp forests for protection and food.

© Houghton Mifflin Harcourt Publishing Company • Image Credits: ©Ethan Daniels/Shutterstock

Hands-On Lab
Brainstorm and Evaluate Solutions for Monitoring Biodiversity

You will develop criteria and constraints and then brainstorm and evaluate possible solutions for monitoring marine biodiversity in a coastal area.

A city is concerned about the marine biodiversity in a nearby coastal area. Your job is to present a possible solution to the city for monitoring biodiversity.

MATERIALS
- computer for research
- paper
- pencil

Criteria	Constraints
• provides data about the types and numbers of plant life	• solution works in an ocean environment
• provides data about the types and numbers of animal life	• solution requires no more than two scientists for data collection
• data can be stored on a computer for analysis	
• collects data over a six-month time period	

Procedure and Analysis

STEP 1 Research current and past methods for monitoring biodiversity.

STEP 2 With a partner, study the criteria and constraints listed. Decide whether to add to them or change them before continuing. Consider scientific principles and impacts on the environment that might limit possible solutions.

STEP 3 Brainstorm possible solutions for monitoring biodiversity in a coastal area. Record these on a separate piece of paper.

STEP 4 Choose the three most promising solutions, based on your knowledge, to analyze in more detail. Write a short description of the three solutions.

© Houghton Mifflin Harcourt Publishing Company

STEP 5 Complete a decision matrix to compare your three most promising solutions from Step 4. Give each criterion a rating from 1-5, with 5 being the most important. Multiple criteria may have the same rating. Then give each design a score between 1 and the maximum value for each criterion. In other words, the maximum value that can be used for each score is equal to the criterion rating. Sum the scores for each design. The design with the highest total score is likely to be the most promising. If you made changes to the criteria in Step 2, make your decision matrix on a separate piece of paper.

Criterion	Criterion rating (1-5)	Design 1 score	Design 2 score	Design 3 score
Provides data about the types and numbers of plant life				
Provides data about the types and numbers of animal life				
Data can be stored on a computer for analysis				
Collects data over a six-month time period				
Total score				

STEP 6 Evaluate and choose a solution. You may choose to combine two or more solutions to create a better solution. Describe your chosen solution.

STEP 7 Present your solution for monitoring biodiversity in a coastal area to your class. Include a visual display in your presentation.

Compare Animal Tracking Requirements

Tracking devices are invaluable for biodiversity monitoring. Motion triggered cameras only capture a moment in time while GPS trackers can capture day's worth of information about an animal. When tagging an animal, the device should not interfere with the animal's daily life. For this reason, tracking devices are more commonly used with large animals, because larger animals can carry more weight without it affecting their daily life. Consider how the tracker used on a grizzly bear needs to be different from one used on a tiger shark.

The GPS trackers on a shark attaches to its dorsal fin.

Bears may wear GPS trackers on collars around their necks.

26. Which of the criteria and constraints apply to tracking devices designed for tracking a shark, bear, or both?

    A. can transmit through salt water _____

    B. can transmit over long distances _____

    C. is resistant to ultraviolet light from sunlight _____

    D. will not fall off during expected activities _____

    E. is not corroded by salt water _____

27. **Language SmArts** Tracking devices can collect not only the location, but also other data, such as temperature or pressure, from the environment around the tagged animal. Devices may transmit these data along with the tracking information, or the data may be stored locally on the device to be collected later. Storing the data locally extends the battery life, but the data must be manually retrieved later. Make an argument for which option you would choose.

_____

_____

_____

_____

_____

_____

Continue Your Exploration

Name: _____   Date: _____

Check out the path below or go online to choose one of the other paths shown.

People in Science

- **Motion Sensors**
- **Hands-On Labs** 🖐
- **Propose Your Own Path**

Go online to choose one of these other paths

Kathryn Purcell, Biologist

Kathryn Purcell shows a western pond turtle tagged with a radio transmitter.

Dr. Kathryn Purcell is a research wildlife biologist who focuses on how to maintain animal populations. She has always had an interest in biology and has a Ph.D. in Ecology, Evolution, and Conservation Biology from the University of Nevada, Reno.

The western pond turtle is a reptile that spends much of its life in water. From 2009 to 2015, Purcell and her team studied a small population of western pond turtles near a stock pond in the San Joaquin Experimental Range in Madera County, CA. The stock pond in the area is not fed by a stream or creek. During years with normal precipitation, the pond fills with enough rainfall runoff during the wet winter months to last year-round, despite losing water to evaporation during the hot, dry summers. During the years of the study, the region was hit by a long and sustained drought. The pond dried up completely early in the summer or toward the end of summer, depending on the amount of winter precipitation.

Purcell and her team tracked the turtles' locations and then gathered additional data about the turtles' behavior. All of the tagged turtles survived during years of normal precipitation. During drought years when there was very little precipitation, many of the turtles died, and those that did survive showed unusual behaviors. Some turtles traveled long distances to find new sources of water. Another turtle ended up living completely on land for almost two years, which had never been observed before for this species of turtle. This turtle ended up in a water trough for livestock.

A western pond turtle suns itself near the edge of a pond.

Continue Your Exploration

1. What effects did the drought have on the western pond turtle population?

   A. the population decreased

   B. the population increased

   C. the population did not change

Dr. Purcell and her team attached radio transmitters to the turtles, and then they used hand-held receivers to track the locations of the tagged turtles. To tag the turtles, each turtle needed to be trapped first. Each transmitter had a life span of up to two years. Sometimes the transmitters fell off or stopped working, and then the data from those transmitters could not be included in the study.

2. Compare this method of monitoring the turtles to other possible methods. What are the benefits and drawbacks of this method compared to other methods?

3. The tracking data are only part of the monitoring story. What other data are needed to know how drought affects the western pond turtle?

4. How can the turtle tracking data be used to develop a solution to help sustain similar species in future droughts?

5. **Collaborate** With a partner, discuss what solutions could be implemented to help with the populations of western pond turtles during times of drought.

Can You Explain It?

Name: _____   Date: _____

How can a motion-triggered digital camera contribute to biodiversity monitoring?

EVIDENCE NOTEBOOK

Refer to the notes in your Evidence Notebook to help you construct an explanation of how motion-triggered digital cameras contribute to biodiversity monitoring.

1. State your claim. Make sure your claim fully explains how motion-triggered digital cameras contribute to biodiversity monitoring.

2. Summarize the evidence you have gathered to support your claim and explain your reasoning.

Checkpoints

Answer the following questions to check your understanding of the lesson.

Use the photo to answer Question 3.

3. Which of the following would minimize the impact of the road on biodiversity in the area shown in the photo? Select all that apply.

   A. Add bridges or tunnels to help animals safely cross the road.

   B. Paint the road green so it blends in with the surroundings.

   C. Set a low speed limit and add speed bumps to slow traffic.

   D. Add fences to prevent animals from trying to cross the road.

Use the graph to answer Questions 4 and 5

4. When the population of species 1 increases, species 3
   increases / decreases / does not change.

5. Which of the statements are true, based on the graph?

   A. Biodiversity in the area is increasing.

   B. Biodiversity in the area is decreasing.

   C. More data are needed to describe the biodiversity in the area.

   D. An increase in species 1 is causing species 2 and species 3 to decrease.

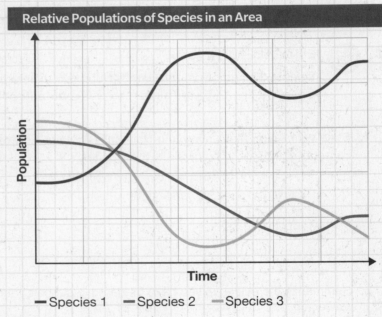

Relative Populations of Species in an Area

Population

Time

— Species 1   — Species 2   — Species 3

6. Digital technology has improved / not changed scientists' ability to monitor biodiversity. Compared to analog data, digital data is more / less reliable because it is more / less sensitive to noise when it is stored, transmitted, or accessed. Biodiversity data must be collected in nature where noise is / is not an unavoidable factor.

7. Engineers and scientists choose solutions for biodiversity problems based on their opinion / criteria and constraints. A solution is / is not influenced by society.

Interactive Review

Complete this section to review the main concepts of the lesson.

Advances in technology have helped scientists collect and analyze biodiversity data to develop solutions to sustain biodiversity.

A. Explain how digital technologies have impacted the ways that scientists collect and analyze biodiversity data.

Solutions for monitoring and sustaining biodiversity vary and must be evaluated against their own unique requirements.

B. Scientists are concerned about the biodiversity in a forested area. Can the same technologies and methods be used to monitor both plant and animal life? Explain why or why not.

The engineering design process is helpful for developing solutions to monitor and/or sustain biodiversity.

C. Scientists want to track a deer and a squirrel using a GPS tracker. How are the constraints for these monitoring problems different?

Choose one of the activities to explore how this unit connects to other topics.

☐ People in Science

Dr. Dolly Garza, Marine Advisory Agent
Traditional knowledge of ecology from her Native Alaskan community and studies of fisheries and marine resources both inform Dr. Garza's work as a Marine Advisory Agent. She uses her knowledge of sustainable practices in her work as a community educator, a policy advisor, and a spokesperson for her community.

Research fishing industry regulations. Create a presentation that explains how one or more of these regulations are intended to help preserve biodiversity in a marine or freshwater ecosystem.

☐ Technology Connection

Signal Transformation Information transfer technologies often receive one type of signal and change it into another. For example, a radio receives electromagnetic radio wave signals and transforms them into electric signals. Speakers convert the electric signals into sound waves in the air.

Conduct research to learn how an information technology you use daily converts signals from one form to another, and summarize what you learn in a well-written paragraph. Explain how engineers designed the device to minimize loss of signal clarity while performing signal transformations.

☐ Life Science Connection

Frogs and Pollution Frogs and other amphibians respire through their skins, so they are some of the most sensitive animals to pollution in the environment. Frog and toad species across the world are in danger of extinction because of pollution.

Research the effects of pollution on different species of frogs, toads, or salamanders. Explain the effects the pollution has on the amphibian and its environment. Create a poster or visual display that explains how frogs or other amphibians can be used to monitor the effects of resource use on Earth's systems.

Name: _____   Date: _____

Use the graph to answer Questions 1–4.

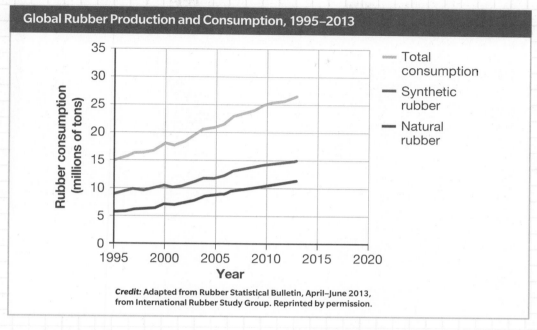

Global Rubber Production and Consumption, 1995–2013

Credit: Adapted from Rubber Statistical Bulletin, April–June 2013, from International Rubber Study Group. Reprinted by permission.

1. What trend can you see in the graph in the consumption of natural and synthetic rubber between 1995 and 2013?

2. What might account for the trend? Explain your reasoning.

3. How does an increase in rubber consumption affect Earth's systems?

4. Based on what you know about human population change, how would you expect the consumption of rubber, natural rubber, and synthetic rubber to change in the future? How might this change affect Earth's systems? Use evidence and scientific reasoning to justify your claims.

Use the compact disc diagram to answer Questions 5–8.

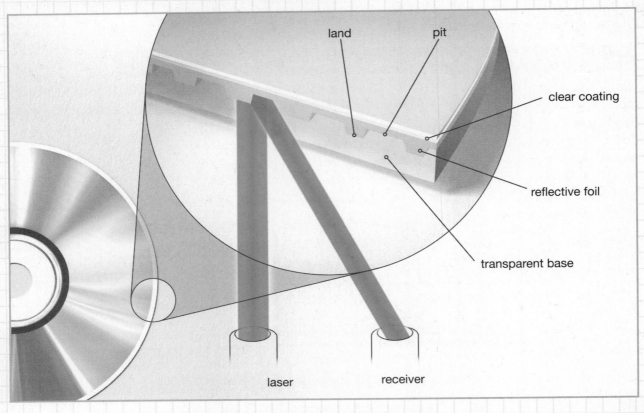

5. What evidence presented in the diagram shows that the compact disc is a form of digital storage?

6. How does the use of light to "read" the pits and lands minimize noise in comparison to a needle "reading" the groove on a vinyl record?

7. What big ideas about waves did engineers need to know to develop CD technology?

8. Music is increasingly stored digitally and accessed remotely through the Internet. How does this situation compare with storing and accessing music locally on a CD?

Name: _____   Date: _____

How does population change affect energy consumption in Japan?

Since 1990, Japan's population growth has slowed significantly, and the nation's population began to decline after 2010. However, Japan's electrical energy consumption remains high, especially in rural areas. You have been asked to explain these trends to Japanese energy officials. Research how energy is generated and used in Japan, in Japan's cities, and in rural Japan. You may need to evaluate population change and demographics, regional differences in energy use, and per capita use. Present your findings as a multimedia presentation, animation, flow chart, or series of if-then statements that explains the patterns of population change and energy use in Japan.

Population Change and Electricity Consumption in Japan and in Rural Japan

The first figure shows the changes in population and electrical energy use for all of Japan. The second figure shows the same information for rural areas of Japan.

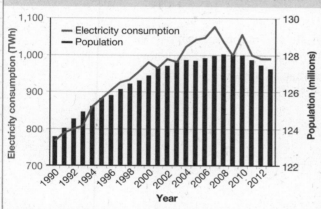
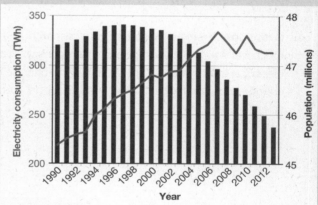

Credit: Adapted from "Population decline and electricity demand in Japan" by Akira Yanagisawa, from IEE Japan, June 2015. Reprinted by permission.

The steps below will help guide your research and help you draw conclusions.

1. **Ask a Question** Write a question that defines the problem you have been asked to solve. You may also want to list questions you have about population change and energy consumption in Japan. These questions may help guide your research.

2. **Conduct Research** How do people in Japan use energy? What type of resources do they use to generate electricity? How does the use of these resources affect Earth systems? What social or technological trends might affect how electrical energy is used in rural areas and in urban areas?

3. **Analyze the Data** Use the information you gathered to identify proportional relationships between population change, per capita use, and resource use in Japan. Describe the proportional relationships between the three variables, and identify how those patterns can be used to predict changes in electrical energy use in Japan.

4. **Draw Conclusions** Based on your research, draft a statement that explains electrical energy consumption patterns in Japan and makes predictions about how electrical energy consumption is likely to change in Japan's future and how those changes could affect Earth systems. Support your claim by using evidence and scientific reasoning.

5. **Communicate** Present your findings to the board of energy officials in Japan. Use words and images to explain to them what has caused the energy consumption in Japan to remain high despite the drop in population.

✓ **Self-Check**

	I asked a question about how energy consumption relates to population change and trends in energy use.
	I researched the per capita use rates and how energy is used in Japan.
	I identified relationships between population change, per capita use, and energy use in Japan and used this information to make a claim.
	My conclusion was clearly stated and communicated to others.

Go online to access the **Interactive Glossary**. You can use this online tool to look up definitions for all the vocabulary terms in this book.

Pronunciation Key

Sound	Symbol	Example	Respelling	Sound	Symbol	Example	Respelling
ă	a	pat	PAT	ŏ	ah	bottle	BAHT'l
ā	ay	pay	PAY	ō	oh	toe	TOH
âr	air	care	KAIR	ô	aw	caught	KAWT
ä	ah	father	FAH•ther	ôr	ohr	roar	ROHR
är	ar	argue	AR•gyoo	oi	oy	noisy	NOYZ•ee
ch	ch	chase	CHAYS	o͞o	u	book	BUK
ĕ	e	pet	PET	o͞o	oo	boot	BOOT
ĕ (at end of a syllable)	eh	settee lessee	seh•TEE leh•SEE	ou	ow	pound	POWND
ĕr	ehr	merry	MEHR•ee	s	s	center	SEN•ter
ē	ee	beach	BEECH	sh	sh	cache	CASH
g	g	gas	GAS	ŭ	uh	flood	FLUHD
ĭ	i	pit	PIT	ûr	er	bird	BERD
ĭ (at end of a syllable)	ih	guitar	gih•TAR	z	z	xylophone	ZY•luh•fohn
ī	y eye (only for a complete syllable)	pie island	PY EYE•luhnd	z	z	bags	BAGZ
îr	ir	hear	HIR	zh	zh	decision	dih•SIZH•uhn
j	j	germ	JERM	ə	uh	around broken focus	uh•ROWND BROH•kuhn FOH•kuhs
k	k	kick	KIK	ər	er	winner	WIN•er
ng	ng	thing	THING	th	th	thin they	THIN THAY
ngk	ngk	bank	BANGK	w	w	one	WUHN
				wh	hw	whether	HWETH•er

Index

A

Abell-370 galaxy cluster, 294, *291*
absolute age, 16, 320–322, 348
absolute dating, **320**, 322
absorption, **505**
absorption of wave, 505–506, 507
acanthostega, *352*
acceleration, **55**
    effect of collision during, 106
    friction effect on, 79, 84
    rate of velocity changes, 76
    in relationship to mass, 81–85
    speed's relationship to, 55
    unbalanced forces changing,
      77–80, 97, *97*
acid rain, 603
acoustic panel, 512, *512*
acquired trait, 396
Act, 9, 79, 217, 241, 246, 532, 643
action force, 86–88, 96
adaptations, **427**
    of cactus and their predator, 409,
      409
    evolution of, 398
    identifying, 428, *428*
    of manta rays, 394, *394*
    of predator, 399–403, 409, *409*
    of rafflesia flowers, *395*
    traits for organism survival,
      427–428
adenine (A), 419, *419*
adenoviruses, *464*, *464*
African elephant, 378–379, *378*
agriculture
    changes in land used for, 608, *608*
    population growth rate affected by,
      573, *573*
air, light traveling through, 518–519
airbag, 80, *80*
airplane, 478, *478*
air resistance, 193, 196
algae, 391
allele, 437, *437*, 442, *442*

allele frequency, 405
alpaca, 435, *435*, 449, *449*, 576, *576*,
    589, *589*
alphadon, 357, *357*
Altamira, Brazil, 592, *592*
Alvarez, Luis, 8, *8*, 11
Alvarez, Walter, 8, *8*, 11, 15, 23
amber, 336, *336*
ambulocetus natans, 353, *353*, 370,
    370
American badger, 308, *308*
amino acid chain, 420, *420*, 421, *421*
ammonites
    in ancient sea, 311, *311*, 325, *325*
    index fossil of, 318
amphibian, evolution of, 352, *352*
amplitude, **489**
amplitude of waves
    energy of partial reflection and, *508*
    of light wave, 522, *522*, 539
    modulating, 626, *626*
    volume relating to, 506, *506*
    as wave property, 489–492
    wave size affected by, 504–506,
      515, *515*
anacus, *379*
analog information, 622, *622*
analog signal, **623**
    analyzing, 621–625
    compared to digital signal, 565
    continuous information, 623–624,
      623, 637
    converting to digital, 628
    modulating, 626–627
    noise affecting, *629*, 631, *631*, 637,
      644
    storage of, 632, *632*
analysis
    of apparent motion of the sun, 217
    of correlation, 20
    of design process, 148
    of Earth, moon, and sun system,
      242

    of Earth's tilt, 550
    of Earth-Sun model, 549–554
    of electrical force, 127, 129, 130–131
    of electromagnet, 153
    of encoding messages, 617
    of energy, 28–31
    of energy in systems, 43–44
    of extinction and land use, 608
    of extinction data, 356
    of factors in resource use, 580
    of falling objects, 186
    of forces, 58–61, 83
    of fossil record, 358–359
    of fossil to describe Earth's past,
      314
    of gravitational forces, 188
    of growth curve data, 376, *376*
    of impact of water use, 598
    of inferences from evidence, 377
    of kinetic and potential energy,
      35–38
    of law of universal gravitation, 258
    of light transmission, 531
    of longitudinal and transverse
      waves, 487
    of magnets, 143, 144–145, 146–147
    of mechanical waves generation,
      501
    of the moon's craters, 16
    of motion of falling objects, 195
    of observations, 289
    of other galaxies, 291–296
    of packing materials, 103–104
    of parallax, 224
    of population growth and resource
      use, 577–578
    of protein folding, 422
    of rock layers, 317, 334
    of salamander species distribution,
      401–402
    of selected traits in vegetables,
      438–439
    of signal, 630
    of solar system model, 281–282

of sunlight distribution, 545

of timeline, 337

of trends in timber consumption, 578, *578*

of water use, *601*

of waves, 490

anatomical data, 378

anatomy, 371

evolutionary similarities and differences in, 371–372, 378–379

of wild cabbage, 438, *438*

andesite, *319*

Andromeda, 284, 286, 291, 296

angiosperm, 357, *357*

animal

artificial selection, 439–440

body symmetry of, 375, *375*

breeding of, 436

challenges in monitoring, 640–641

embryo development of, 373–375

first mammal, 339, *339*

fossilization of, 313, *313*

fossil record of, 6, 311, *311*, 325, *325*

human influence on traits of, 436

impact of human activities on, 606–608, 613

monitoring biodiversity in, 640–644

natural selection in, 398–403

recording sounds of, 644, *644*

tagging for monitoring, 646

timeframe of ancient animal, 311, 325

animal resource, 607

annular solar eclipse, 248, *248*

Antarctic Circle, 555–556, *556*

anthracothere, 369, *369*

antibiotic resistant bacteria, 407, 429–430

Appalachian Mountains, 330–331

applied force, as net force, 81

Aquila, 220, *220*

arable land, 605, *605*

archaeosperma **genus,** 351, *351*

Arctic Circle, 555–556, *555, 556*

argon, 320

Aristotle, 222, *222*

armadillo, 348, *348*

arrow, *32, 33, 33*

Art Connection

Art and Extinction, 472, *472*

Kinetic Sculpture, 112, *112*

arthropod, 350, *350*

artificial satellite, 266, *266*

artificial selection, 439

defined, 439–440

genetic basis for, 441–443, 451

genetic engineering compared to, 455

impact on society, 446

meeting needs and desires, 445

modeling of, 442, *442*

predicting outcomes of, 440, *440*

solving problems with, 444–446, 451

traits influenced by, 434–446

Ashfall Fossil Bed, 323–324, *323,* 380, *380*

Asian elephant, 378–379, *378*

Assessment

Lesson Self-Check, 23–25, 47–49, 67–69, 91–93, 109–111, 137–139, 161–163, 179–181, 203–204, 235–237, 253–254, 275–277, 299–301, 325–327, 343–344, 363–365, 383–385, 413–415, 431–433, 449–451, 469–471, 495–496, 513–514, 537–539, 557–559, 587–589, 611–613, 635–637, 657–659

Unit Performance Task, 115–116, 209–210, 305–306, 389–390, 475–476, 563–564, 663–664

Unit Review, 113–114, 207–208, 303–304, 387–388, 473–474, 561–562, 661–662

asteroid, *41,* **231**

collision with Earth, 6

crater size effected by size and speed of, 15

cretaceous-paleogene mass extinction, 357

effects of collision on Earth's systems, 18–19

energy transformation at impact, 41–42

evidence of impact of, 10–16, 25, *25*

gravity's effect on, 88

mass extinction hypothesis of, 9, *9,* 354, *354*

modeling impact of, 42, *42*

scale of, 230–231, *230–231*

Vesta, *232,* 262, *262*

asteroid belt, 230, 233

astronaut, 86, *86,* 185, *185,* 244

astronomer

advances of, 226–228, 230, 233–234, 237

Aristotle, 222, *222*

Brahe, 227, *227*

Copernicus, 226, *226,* 237

early theories of, 222–228, 262, 287

formation of solar system hypothesis, 262–265

Galileo Galilei, 227, *227*

Kepler, 227, *227*

measuring distances, 284

Ptolemy, 223, *223,* 226

technology advancements, 227, *227,* 229, 237

astronomical unit (AU), 281

asymmetrical body plan, 375, *375*

Atacama Large Millimeter Array (ALMA), 268, *268*

atmosphere

becoming oxygen rich, 329, *329,* 343, *343*

blocking electromagnetic radiation, 520, *520*

changes of recorded in fossils, 6

ejecta in, 18, *18*

electromagnetic waves interacting with, 542

greenhouse gases warming, 604

pollution changing, 603

pollution in, 604–605

resource of, 609–610

as subsystem of Earth, 592

atom

chemical potential energy in, 34

in magnets, 147

potential energy in, 31

aura satellites, 266, *266*

aurora, 164, *164,* 206, *206*

automotive safety engineers, 45–46, 98

average speed, 74

axis, tilt of, 549, *549*

B

bacillus thuringiensis (Bt), 463, *463*

background rate of extinction, 354

© Houghton Mifflin Harcourt Publishing Company

© Houghton Mifflin Harcourt Publishing Company

monitoring and sustaining
biodiversity in, 357, *357*, 565, 566,
566, 590–608, 638–654, 657, 659
natural selection impacted by, 398,
415
of the past, 314, *314*
enzyme, 425
eon, 321, *321*, 338, *338*, 339, *339*
epicycle, 223, *223*
epoch (in geological time scale),
321, *321*
equation. *See also* **formulas**
of acceleration, mass, and force, 85
of kinetic energy, 37
for law of universal gravitation, 189
of second law of motion, 84
for wave speed, 491
equinox, 553
era, 321, *321*, 338, *338*, 339, *339*
erosion
impact craters hidden by, *10*, 262
rate of geologic change from,
330–331, 345
in rock formation, 312
sedimentation, 315, *315*
ethics, 467
eukaryotic cell, 418, *418*
Europa, *228*
eusthernopteron **(fish),** 352
evidence
inferring from, 377
of ancient collision, 4–20
of asteroid impact, 10–16
of asteroid impact at Chicxulub, 12,
12
of change over time, 397
of dinosaurs, 5, *5*
of Earth's past, 332–335
on geologic timeline, 329, *329*, 343,
343
of gravitational fields, 168
of history of life, 348–353
of mass extinction, 6
of solar system structure, 214–232
of star system formation, 267–272
supporting claims, 23, 47, 67, 91,
109, 137, 161, 179, 188, 203, 235,
253, 272, 275, 299, 325, 343, 363,
380, 383, 413, 431, 449, 469, 495,
513, 537, 557, 587, 608, 611, 635,
657

Evidence Notebook, 5, 9, 16, 19, 23,
27, 38, 42, 47, 51, 57, 64, 67, 71,
80, 85, 91, 95, 101, 105, 109, 121,
125, 126, 129, 132, 137, 141, 142,
147, 150, 153, 154, 161, 165, 167,
172, 174, 179, 183, 186, 197, 200,
203, 215, 218, 221, 225, 227, 230,
235, 239, 240, 250, 253, 257, 266,
271, 272, 275, 279, 287, 289, 284,
299, 311, 318, 322, 325, 329, 333,
340, 343, 347, 350, 359, 363, 367,
372, 375, 379, 383, 395, 403, 406,
409, 413, 417, 422, 426, 427, 431,
435, 440, 441, 445, 453, 459, 463,
469, 481, 484, 488, 449, 495, 499,
501, 510, 513, 517, 528, 530, 537,
541, 544, 554, 557, 569, 576, 582,
587, 591, 593, 601, 611, 615, 625,
631, 635, 639, 640, 646, 657
evolution, 368, 398
biotechnology and, 391–476
by natural selection, 399–403
in populations over time, 369
requires genetic variations, 404
of shrimp, 411–412, *411*
evolutionary relationship, 369, *369*,
371–375, 376–380, 385
Exploration
Analyze Earth-Sun Model to Explain
Seasons, 549–554
Analyzing Analog and Digital
Information, 621–625
Analyzing Current and the Magnetic
Force, 149–154
Analyzing Electric Charge, 122–125
Analyzing Energy, 28–31
Analyzing Energy in Systems,
39–44
Analyzing Evidence About the
History of Life, 348–353
Analyzing How Forces Act on
Objects, 52–57
Analyzing How Waves Interact with
a Medium, 504–506
Analyzing Human Influence on the
Inheritance of Traits, 436–440
Analyzing Human Perception of
Light Waves, 525–528

Analyzing Human Population Data,
570–574
Analyzing Kinetic and Potential
Energy, 35–38
Analyzing Moon Phases, 240–244
Analyzing Newton's First Law of
Motion, 77–80
Analyzing Newton's Second Law of
Motion, 81–85
Analyzing Newton's Third Law of
Motion, 86–88
Analyzing Other Galaxies, 291–296
Analyzing Patterns in the Numbers
of Life Forms Over Time, 354–360
Analyzing Patterns in the Sky,
216–219
Analyzing Patterns of Natural
Selection, 407–410
Analyzing Per Capita Consumption,
579–584
Analyzing Solutions for Monitoring
and Sustaining Biodiversity,
645–648
Analyzing the Impact of Human Use
of Land Resources, 602–605
Analyzing the Impact of Human Use
of Plants and Animals, 606–608
Analyzing the Impact of Human Use
of Water, 597–601
Analyzing Waves in Communication,
616
Applying Artificial Selection to Solve
Problems, 444–446
Applying Newton's Law to
Collisions, 96–101
Building a Hypothesis of How the
Solar System Formed,
262–265
Comparing Longitudinal and
Transverse Waves, 485–488
Compiling Evidence of Earth's Past,
332–335
Describing Geologic Change,
330–331
Describing Magnets and the
Magnetic Force, 142–148
Describing Motion, 72–76

© Houghton Mifflin Harcourt Publishing Company

F

fall
  in Earth's revolution around sun, *552*
  equinox in, 553, *553*
  leaves changing color in, 540, *540*
  star patterns in, 220, *220*
  temperatures and weather
    conditions of, 543, *543*
family tree, constructing, 308, *308*
fault, disruption in rock layer, 317,
  317, 318, *318*
feather, 371
fern, fossilized, 314, *314*
ferrofluid, 169, *169*
ferromagnetic material, 148
fertilized egg, *373*
fertilizer, 447, 448, 602, *602*
field, 167
  areas forces act at distance, 164–176
  features of, 169
  measuring and drawing, 171–172
  modeling force lines in, 167, *167*
  modeling of, 170–176, 181
  in science, 167
  sharing common properties, 170
  types of, 170–176
field geologist, 334
film camera, 641, *641*
filters, affecting perceptions of
  color, 528, *528*
Firdousi Crater, 262, *262*
first law of motion, 70, 77–80, 98, 99
first quarter moon, 243, *243*
fish
  artificial selection, 440, *440*
  electrical energy used by, 135, *135*
  embryo development of, 373–375,
    374
  first appearance of, 329, *329*, 343,
    343, 351, *351*
  impact of dams on, 599, *599*
flagellum, 457, *457*
floodlight, 525, *525*
flowering plant
  first appearance of, *351*
  rafflesia flowers, 395, *395*, 413, *413*

food
  energy from, 34
  population growth rate affected by,
    573, *573*
foraminifera, 16
force, 52
  action and reaction forces, 86–88
  analyzing actions of, 52–57
  applications of causing movement,
    28
  applied force, 81
  balance of, 53–54, *53*, 69
  collisions, energy, and, 1–116
  combinations of, 63
  diagrams of, 56–57, *56*
  effects of, 54–57
  electric, 126–132
  examples of, 58–61
  field of, 164–176
  friction, 60, 79, *79*
  identifying, 61, *61*
  magnetic, 59
  motion of objects affected by, 50–69
  net force, 62
  newton (N) of, 53, 69
  Newton's Laws of Motion, 70–88
  noncontact, 61, 117–210
  observing, 59–60, 71, *71*
  of opposite electrical charges,
    123–125, *123*, *124*
  pairs of, 86–88, 96
  push or pull, 52, 142
  in relationship to mass, 81–85
  relationship with acceleration, mass,
    and, 85
  on roller coaster, 65–66
  strength of, 62–64
  of swimmer, 86, *86*
  unbalanced, 77–80, *78*
  of wind, 57, *57*
forest elephant, 378
forest habitat, 607, 640, *640*
Formula One racecar, 85, *85*
formulas
  acceleration, 76
  acceleration, mass, and force, 85
  average speed, 74
  balanced force, 77
  change in velocity, 100

  effects of collision during
    acceleration, 106
  frequencies, 405
  human lives in one million years,
    331
  kinetic energy, 36–37, *36*
  law of universal gravitation, 189,
    258
  net force, 63–64
  per capita consumption, 583
  percent change, 648
  scale models, 282, 283
  second law of motion, 84
fossil, 313
  in ashfall, 323–324
  increasing complexity of, 351, *351*
  of *confuciusornis*, 367, *367*, 383, *383*
  evidence in, 346–360
  evidence of earliest life forms,
    348–350
  formation of, 312–314, *313*
  modeling formation of, 310
  in Morrison Formation, *314*
  providing evidence of evolution,
    366–380
  relationship to living organisms,
    378–379
  studying age of, 315–319
  3D models of, 371, *371*
  of *tyrannosaurus rex* (t. rex), 328,
    328, 376, *376*
  transitional, 352, *352*, 361–362
  of whole animals, 314
fossil fuel
  impact of obtaining and using, 602
  increasing greenhouse gases, 603
  as nonrenewable resource, 576, *576*
  pollution from burning, 604–605
fossilized cell, 349, *349*
fossil record, 6
  absent of in rock layer, 347, *347*,
    363, *363*
  compilation of all Earth's known
    fossils, 333, 345
  defined, 318
  of early mammals, 340, *340*
  evidence of ancient animals, 311,
    311, 325, *325*

mass (continued)
gravitational force of, 173
gravity effected by, 187, 189–191, 258
impact crater based on, 262
inertia in relationship to, 80
kinetic energy dependent on, 35–37, 49
measurement of, 184–185
on the moon, 184, *184*
relationship with acceleration, force, and, 85
shape of space objects relative to, 259, *259*
of sun, 200

mass extinction
causes of, 20, *20*, 25
defined, 7–8
fossil record recording, 6, 354–355
hypothesis of, 9, 19

mastodon, *379*

mastodon tooth, 378, *378*

Math Connection
Leap Year, 302

mathematical laws, 189

mathematical models
of planets, 230
of solar system, 226, 229, 280
of sound wave, 560

matter
attracted to other matter, 189–191
interactions with light, 529–534
light refracted by, 532–534
light transmitting through, 530–531
reflecting light by, *529*
in solar system, 198
solar system formed by, 256–272
wave interacting with, 498–510
wave medium, 482, 500, *500*

Mauna Loa Observatory, 604, *604*

measurement
of current, 157
of distance using brightness, 295
of light reflection, 536
light year, 284
of work, 28

mechanical energy, defined, 30

mechanical wave, 500
absorption of, 505–506, *505*
generating, 501–502, 515
partial transmission, 509
reflection of, 508–509, *508*
sea floor maps generated by, 499, *499*, 513, *513*
spreading out of, 505
types of, 500–503, *502*

medicine, 573, *573*

medium, 482

medium ground finch, 410, *410*

medium or media (of wave), 482
behaviors of waves at boundaries of, 507–510, 515, *515*
refraction and, 533, *533*
speed of light through, 519, *519*
types of, 500, *500*
wave speed dependent on, 503, *503*

meganeura, 360, *360*

melanin, in eye color, 454, *454*

Mendel, Gregor, 437, *437*, 441

Mercury
comparing to other space objects, *232*
composition of, 260
density of, *260*
Firdousi Crater on, 262, *262*
gravity of, *258*
movement of, 221
scale model of, *280*

metal, 576

metaspriggina, 351, *351*

meteor
energy of, 30, *30*, 49, *49*

Meteor Crater, Arizona, 96, *96*

meteorite
absolute age of, 322
composition of, 271, *271*
rate of geologic change from, 330–331
rocks recording, 312
scale of, 230–231, *230–231*

metric system
gram (g), 184
kilogram (kg), 184

micrograph, of drug-resistant bacteria, 429, *429*

microscope, 148

microscopic marine life, 16

microwave, 30, 520, *520*

Milky Way
counting stars in, 285
early theories of, 287, 288
Earth's place in, 290, 299, *299*
galaxy, 287
galaxy of, 212, *212*, 278, *278*, 284–286, 301
map of, 288
model of, 279, *279*, 287–290
motion of stars in, 183, *183*, 203, *203*
shape of, 288
size of, 284–285

Mimas, Herschel Crater, 262, *262*

mineral, 602

mining, 602

mirror, 529, *529*

model
of asteroid impact, 42, *42*
of change, 394
of Earth, moon, and sun system, 241–242
of Earth-sun-model, 549–554, *549*
Earth's tilt, 550, *550*
factors in resource use, 580
of fields, 171–172, 181
of fossil formation, 310
genetic basis for artificial selection, 441–443
genetic modification of bacteria, 457–458, *457*
of light as wave, 516–534
of light wave, 522–524, 539
of longitudinal and transverse waves, 486–487
of Milky Way, 212, *212*, 279, *279*, 287–290
of natural selection, 398–403
nebular disk formation, 265–266
of noncontact forces, 166–169
of objects behaviors, 32, *32*
of properties of waves, 489–492
of protein folding, 421–422
of relationship between population and resource use, 577–578
of relative age, 316–317
of solar and lunar eclipses, 245
of solar system, 222–225

Neptune
    compared to other space objects, *232*
    composition of, 260, *260*
    exploration of, 233
    gravity on, *258*
    orbit of, 273, *273*
    scale of, 230, *230*
    visibility of, 229, *229*
nerve cell, 458, *458*
net charge, 123, *123*
net force
    applied force, 81
    calculating, 63–64
    identifying, 62, 69
neutral object, 124–125
New Horizons spacecraft, 233
new moon, 243, *243*
newton (N), 53
    of balanced force, 77
    calculating, 82–83
    measuring forces, 184
    of net force, 63
Newton, Isaac, 77, 184, 189, *189*
Newton's cradle, 101, *101*
Newton's Laws of Motion, 70–88
    applying to collisions, 96–101
    first law, 77–80, 93, 99
    second and third law combined, 88, *88*, 93
    second law, 81–85, 93
    third law, 86–88, 93, 99
nickel, magnetism of, 142, 148
nine banded armadillo, 398, *398*
noise, 629–632, **629**, 637, 644
noncontact force, 61, 117–210
    behavior of, 166
    electric force, 126–132
    fields of, 169, 181
    modeling of, 166–169
    in space, 170
    types of, 167
nonrenewable resource, 575–576
Northern Hemisphere
    seasons in, 542–548
    star patterns in, 220, *220*
northern lights, 206, *206*
north magnetic pole, 177

north pole
    on compass, 149, *149*
    of magnet field, 174, *174*
    of magnets, 142, 147
    star patterns in, 220, *220*
North Star, 219, *219*
not-to-scale model, 280
Nova Stella, 225, *225*
nuclear energy, defined, 31
nucleotides, 419
nucleus
    of cells, 418, *418*
    potential energy in, 31

O

oak tree, 368
object
    collision of objects in contact, 101
    collisions between, 94–106
    collision with different or equal mass, 99
    colors of, 527, *527*
    electrical force attracting or repulsing, 126
    electric charge of, 175, *175*
    electric forces acting on, 120–134
    energy transformation of, 72
    first law of motion, 77–80
    forces acting on, 52–57, 62–64, 69
    forces changing shape of, 54
    gravitational field of massive objects, 200
    light color affecting perception of, 528, *528*
    in motion, 78
    motion of falling objects, 194–195
    motions of in space, 198–200
    potential energy of, 72
    reference points and frame of, 73
    at rest, 78
observation, of forming star systems, 270, 272
OCA2 gene, 454, *454*
ocean
    extracting oil from, 575, *575*
    impact of pollution on, 604
    life began in, 352, *352*
    wave properties of, 480, *480*

ocelot, 428, *428*
octopus, 70, *70*
offspring
    looking like parent, 368, *368*
    parents passing traits to, 396
    receiving inherited traits from parents, 418, *418*, 427, 436–439
    of sexual reproduction, 368, *368*
oil rig, 575, *575*
Okamoto, Steve, 112, *112*
online activities
    Explore ONLINE! 27, 28, 30, 42, 47, 71, 72, 91, 121, 126, 133, 137, 141, 149, 153, 154, 155, 161, 169, 175, 183, 193, 203, 215, 235, 251, 257, 269, 275, 319, 368, 396, 456, 481, 482, 483, 495, 502, 504, 522, 541, 544, 556, 557, 615, 619, 626, 635
    Hands-On Labs, 14, 43, 59, 82, 103, 127, 143, 144, 152, 171, 186, 194, 217, 224, 241, 246, 265, 281, 286, 316, 337, 358, 377, 401, 421, 438, 457, 486, 490, 501, 531, 545, 550, 577, 580, 598, 617, 630, 652
    Take It Further, 21, 45, 65, 89, 107, 135, 159, 177, 201, 233, 251, 273, 297, 323, 341, 361, 381, 411, 429, 447, 467, 493, 511, 535, 555, 585, 609, 633, 655
    Unit Project Worksheet, 2, 118, 212, 308, 392, 478, 566
    You Solve It, 1, 117, 211, 307, 391, 477, 565
opaque material, 530
operating cost, 524
optical illusion, 529, 533, *533*
orbit, 185, 196, **219**
    of artificial satellites, 266, *266*
    of Earth, 240, 250, *250*
    Earth-sun plane, 250, *250*
    elliptical shape of, 196, 205, 227
    of moon, 240–244, 250, *250*
    of planets, 257, *257*, 271, *271*
    velocity and, 196–197
order of magnitude, 285
Oregon, rock layer in, 310, *310*

Y

yellow light, *526*

Yellowstone National Park, Wyoming, 332

Yosemite National Park, *638, 638,* 646–647

You Solve It, 1, 117, 211, 307, 391, 477, 565

Yucatan Peninsula

    asteroid impact crater on, 11, *11*

    rapid geological change on, 330–331

Z

zircon, 322